T0399505

ROUTLEDGE HANDBOOK OF NON-VIOLENT EXTREMISM

This *Handbook* provides the first in-depth analysis of non-violent extremism across different ideologies and geographic centres, a topic overshadowed until now by the political and academic focus on violent and *jihadi* extremism in the Global North.

Whilst acknowledging the potentiality of non-violent extremism as a precursor to terrorism, this *Handbook* argues that non-violent extremism ought to be considered a stand-alone area of study. Focusing on Islamist, Buddhist, Hindu, far-right, far-left, environmentalist and feminist manifestations, the *Handbook* discusses the ideological foundation of their 'war on ideas' against the prevailing socio-political and cultural systems in which they operate, and provides an empirical examination of their main claims and perspectives. This is supplemented by a truly global overview of non-violent extremist groups not only in Europe and the United States, but also in Africa, Asia, Oceania and the Middle East. The *Handbook* thus answers a call to decolonise knowledge that is especially prescient given both the complicity of non-violent extremists with authoritarian states and the dynamic of oppression towards more progressive groups in the Global South.

The *Handbook* will appeal to those studying extremism, radicalisation and terrorism. It intersects several relevant disciplines, including social movement studies, political science, criminology, Islamic studies and anthropology.

Elisa Orofino is Academic Lead for Research on Extremism and Counter-Terrorism at the Policing Institute for the Eastern Region, Anglia Ruskin University, UK. She has published extensively on extremism, vocal extremist groups, radicalisation, Muslims in the West and social movements. Her publications encompass journal articles, book chapters, edited books and monographs, including *Hizb ut-Tahrir and the Caliphate* (Routledge, 2021).

William Allchorn is Visiting Associate Professor of Politics and International Relations at Richmond, the American International University in London, and Interim Director of the Centre for the Analysis of the Radical Right. He is an expert on anti-Islamic radical right social movements in the United Kingdom and has most recently advised the UK, US and Australian governments on their approaches to radical right extremism. His first book, *Anti-Islamic Protest in the UK: Policy Responses to the Far Right*, was published by Routledge in 2018, and his second book, *Moving beyond Islamist Extremism: Assessing Counter Narrative Responses to the Global Far Right*, was published in February 2022.

ROUTLEDGE HANDBOOK OF NON-VIOLENT EXTREMISM

Groups, Perspectives and New Debates

Edited by Elisa Orofino and William Allchorn

Routledge
Taylor & Francis Group

LONDON AND NEW YORK

Designed cover image: © Getty Images

First published 2023
by Routledge
4 Park Square, Milton Park, Abingdon, Oxon OX14 4RN

and by Routledge
605 Third Avenue, New York, NY 10158

Routledge is an imprint of the Taylor & Francis Group, an informa business

British Library Cataloguing-in-Publication Data
A catalogue record for this book is available from the British Library

Library of Congress Cataloging-in-Publication Data
Names: Orofino, Elisa, editor. | Allchorn, William, editor.
Title: Routledge handbook of non-violent extremism : groups, perspectives and new debates / edited by Elisa Orofino, William Allchorn.
Description: Abingdon, Oxon ; New York, NY : Routledge, 2023. | Includes bibliographical references and index.
Identifiers: LCCN 2022037688 (print) | LCCN 2022037689 (ebook) | ISBN 9780367470081 (hardback) | ISBN 9781032419541 (paperback) | ISBN 9781003032793 (ebook)
Subjects: LCSH: Radicalism. | Nonviolence.
Classification: LCC HN49.R33 R678 2023 (print) | LCC HN49.R33 (ebook) | DDC 303.48/4–dc23/eng/20220923
LC record available at https://lccn.loc.gov/2022037688
LC ebook record available at https://lccn.loc.gov/2022037689

ISBN: 978-0-367-47008-1 (hbk)
ISBN: 978-1-032-41954-1 (pbk)
ISBN: 978-1-003-03279-3 (ebk)

DOI: 10.4324/9781003032793

Typeset in Bembo
by Newgen Publishing UK

To Stefano and Lydia for without whom none of this would be possible.

CONTENTS

Contents

ILLUSTRATIONS

Figures

Tables

CONTRIBUTORS

Heather Alberro is a lecturer in global environmental challenges and sustainable development at Nottingham Trent University, in the Department of History, Languages and Global Culture. Her background and interests span a range of disciplines including green utopianism, critical posthuman theory, environmental ethics and literary ecocriticism. Her publications include an article entitled "'Valuing Life Itself': On Radical Environmental Activists' Post-Anthropocentric Worldviews" published in 2020 in the *Journal of Environmental Values*, and 'Interspecies' in the *The Cambridge Companion to Literature and the Anthropocene* published in 2021. Heather also serves as co-convenor for the Political Studies Association's environmental politics specialist group and writes frequently for The Conversation UK. Contact: Heather. alberro@ntu.ac.uk.

Jan Ali is a religious sociologist specialising in Islam. He holds a joint appointment as Senior Lecturer in Islam and Modernity in the School of Humanities and Communication Arts and as the Community and Research Analyst in the Religion and Society Research Centre at the Western Sydney University. His main sociological focus is the study of existential Islam. In recent years, Jan has been invited by a number of non-governmental organizations and government agencies in various Australian capital cities and overseas to deliver public lectures on Islamic revivalism, *shari'a*, terrorism and various other important topics on Islam.

William Allchorn is Visiting Associate Professor of Politics and International Relations at Richmond, the American International University in London, and Interim Director of the Centre for the Analysis of the Radical Right. He is an expert on anti-Islamic radical right social movements in the United Kingdom and has most recently advised the UK, US and Australian governments on their approaches to radical right extremism. His first book, *Anti-Islamic Protest in the UK: Policy Responses to the Far Right*, was published by Routledge in 2018, and his second book, *Moving beyond Islamist Extremism – Assessing Counter Narrative Responses to the Global Far Right*, was published in February 2022.

Daniel Baldino is Discipline Head of The Politics and International Relations program at the University of Notre Dame, Fremantle, Western Australia. His current research specialises in Intelligence, Policing, Surveillance and Spycraft. His recent publications include the following: "The Australia-Israel security relationship, oversight and the paradox of intelligence sharing" (2020); "Anti-Government Rage: Understanding the Sovereign Citizen Movement in Australia" (2019); *Intelligence and the Function of Government* (2018).

Mark Balnaves is an academic in Creative Industries at Monash University Malaysia and an adjunct Research Fellow with the University of Notre Dame, Fremantle, Western Australia. His research specialises in digital ethnography, the cultural history of media research, media audiences and strategic communication. Recent publications include the following: "A Return to the Good Old Days: Populism, Fake News, Yellow Journalism, and the Unparalleled Virtue of Business People" in: *The Palgrave Handbook of Management History*; and *A New Theory of Information and the Internet: Public Sphere Meets Protocol* (2011).

Tamir Bar-On is a member of Mexico's National System for Researchers and has been a professor-researcher in the School of Social Sciences and Government, Tec de Monterrey, Mexico, since 2009. He is the author of *Fighting the Last War: An Essay On Confusion, Partisanship, and Alarmism in the Literature on the Radical Right* (2022); *The Right and Radical Right in the Americas* (2021); *Responses to the COVID-19 Pandemic by the Radical Right: Scapegoating, Conspiracy Theories, and New Narratives* (2021); *Where Have All the Fascists Gone?* (2019); and *Rethinking the French New Right: Alternatives to Modernity* (2013); paperback in 2016.

Mehmet F. Bastug is Assistant Professor in the Department of Sociology, Criminal Justice and Criminology at the University of Scranton. He received his PhD from Rutgers University. He did postdoctoral research at the University of Cincinnati and taught at Lakehead University and University of Ontario Institute of Technology. Bastug has published numerous peer-reviewed journal articles, book chapters and conference papers. His research focuses on terrorism, cyberterrorism, online radicalization, violent extremism and cybercrimes.

Valerio Alfonso Bruno is Senior Fellow and Deputy Head of the Populism Research Unit at the Centre for Analysis of the Radical Right (CARR). He is also Assistant to the Chair of International Relations at the Catholic University of Milan and cooperates with the Observatoire de la Finance in Geneva. Bruno is currently working on a monograph on the populist radical right in Italy, co-authored with James F. Downes and Alessio Scopelliti (Forthcoming in 2022) with Ibidem-Verlag/Columbia University Press.

Dustin J. Byrd is Associate Professor of Philosophy, Religion, and Arabic at Olivet College, the United States. He received his PhD in Social and Political Philosophy from Michigan State University in 2017. He is the author of numerous monographs, including *The Frankfurt School and the Dialectics of Religion: Translating Critical Faith into Critical Theory* (2020), and *Islam in a Post-Secular Society: Religion, Secularity, and the Antagonism of Recalcitrant Faith* (2016). He has also co-edited books on Malcolm X, Ali Shariati, Frantz Fanon and Syed Hussain Alatas (Brill). He is the founder and editor-in-chief of Ekpyrosis Press.

Edward Chan is Research Assistant at the Department of Politics and Public Administration at The University of Hong Kong. His research interests encompass key issues in Global Comparative Politics, ranging from authoritarianism to populist parties in Europe.

Yavuz Çobanoğlu is Associate Professor at the Department of Sociology in Munzur University. Dr. Çobanoğlu studies political culture, symbols, mentality, morality and Islamism and is the author of "Altın Nesil"in Peşinde: Fethullah Gülen'de Toplum, Devlet, Ahlak, Otorite (In Pursuit of a Golden Generation: Fethullah Gülen's Perception of Society, State, Morality, and Authority) İletişim Yayınları, 2012 and 2016.

Milo Comerford is Head of Policy & Research, Counter-Extremism; **Jacob Davey** is Head of Policy & Research, Far-Right and Hate Movements; and **Jakob Guhl** is Policy & Research Manager at the Institute for Strategic Dialogue, an international counter-extremism think tank.

Alexandra Coțofană is an anthropologist and Assistant Professor in the College of Humanities and Social Sciences at Zayed University, Abu Dhabi. Her research interests bridge historical connections between the right wing and the environment in Romania and beyond.

Melany Cruz is Lecturer in International Politics (Global South) at the University of Leicester, the United Kingdom. Her research focuses on theories of political violence, non-violence and feminism in Latin America. Her current research project on civil disobedience and the feminist movement in Chile was partially funded by the International Center on Nonviolent Conflict.

Suat Cubukcu is Professorial Lecturer in the Department of Justice, Law, and Criminology at American University in Washington, D.C. His research focuses on terrorism, extremism, disinformation and policing. Cubukcu also serves as a consultant senior researcher and analyses global and regional trends and patterns of terrorism incidents and creates innovative data visualizations for the US government. He actively publishes in reputable peer-reviewed journals, including IOS Press; *Studies in Conflict and Terrorism*; *Homicide Studies*; *Journal of Policing, Intelligence, and Counterterrorism*; *International Criminal Justice Review*; and the *International Journal of Media and Cultural Politics*.

Milad Dokhanchi, a Canadian-Iranian scholar of political Islam, received his PhD in Cultural Studies from Queen's University, Canada. He is the author of *Pasā-Islāmism, Bāznegari-e rābeteye siāsat va mazhab dar Irān* (2020) [Post-Islamism, Rethinking the Relation between Religion and Politics in Iran].

James F. Downes is Lecturer in Comparative Politics, Head of Undergraduate Admissions, and a Programme Management Member of the MSSc in Public Policy Programme in the Department of Government and Public Administration at The Chinese University of Hong Kong. He is Senior Fellow and Head of The Populism Research Unit at CARR, alongside Research Fellow in the Global Europe Centre at the University of Kent/Brussels School of International Studies.

Julian Droogan is Senior Lecturer in the Department of Security Studies and Criminology at Macquarie University in Sydney (Australia). He has undertaken research on Islamist extremist narratives, far-right extremism in Australia, and the confluence of social media and violent extremism. He is also Editor of *The Journal of Policing, Intelligence and Counter Terrorism* (Routledge).

Kate Galloway is Associate Professor at Griffith Law School. She can be contacted at the following email address: kate.galloway@griffith.edu.au. Kate's research and teaching is focused on the impact of the law on land. Her work is anchored in the theory of property, the law of land tenure and questions of justice.

Giray Gerim earned his PhD in sociology from Eötvös Loránd University with a cum laude distinction by defending his dissertation entitled "The Nationalist Discourses in Hungary and Turkey during the Right-Wing Domination: The Cases of Fidesz and AK Party" in January 2021. He is currently a lecturer at the Faculty of Political Sciences at Istanbul University. His research interests include political sociology, citizenship, nationalism, populism and ethnic conflicts.

Zana Gulmohamad is Associate Lecturer of Politics at Edge Hill University and is the author of *The Making of Foreign Policy in Iraq: Political Factions and Ruling* Elites (2021).

Ahmad Fauzi Abdul Hamid is Professor of Political Science, School of Distance Education, Universiti Sains Malaysia, Penang, Malaysia, and Visiting Professor at the Faculty of Social Science and Humanities, Universiti Malaysia Sarawak, Kota Samarahan, Sarawak, Malaysia, 1 February 2021–31 January 2022. He graduated from the universities of Oxford, Leeds and Newcastle, United Kingdom. He has published widely on political Islam in Malaysia and assists the Malaysian government as a consultant expert for the Home Ministry on terrorism cases investigated under the Security Offences (Special Measures) Act 2012. From 17 January 2021 to 20 June 2021, he was Scholar-in-Residence at the Oxford Centre for Islamic Studies, United Kingdom.

Gavin Hart is Lecturer in Criminology at Liverpool Hope University. Gavin researches the impact of immigration and diversity on politics and society more broadly, focusing especially on Northern Ireland. His research interests also include racism, hate crimes, conflict and extremism. His recent main publications include the following: "Tribunes, racism and deadlock politics in Northern Ireland"; "When bi-nationalism meets multiculturalism: Ethnic politics and minority languages in Northern Ireland" (2020); and "Why we still need multicultur-alism: A critical review of approaches to cultural accommodation" (2020).

Sarah Holmes is a PhD student in the Department of Security Studies and Criminology at Macquarie University (Australia). She has undertaken research into the evolution of Australia's counter terrorism governance, and for her current PhD she has conducted an online social media analysis to examine the mobilisation narratives used by Antifa in Australia, the United Kingdom and the United States.

Antoinette Huber is Lecturer in Criminology at Liverpool Hope University. In 2015, she was awarded an MPhil in Criminological Research from the University of Cambridge and completed her PhD at Liverpool John Moores University in 2020. Antoinette's PhD examined the impact of image-based sexual abuse on women and their experiences within the criminal justice system. Her previous research has focused upon gendered representations of offenders in the media, with a particular focus on "couples who kill". Antoinette has worked closely with domestic violence organisations and currently works with Victims of Internet Crime and the Revenge Porn Helpline. She has also worked with Crisis Skylight Merseyside providing educational support in the fight to end homelessness. Recent publications include the following: "Revenge Porn Law is Failing Victims – Here's why" (2018) [available online] and *Voices of Resistance: Subjugated Knowledge and the Challenge to the Criminal Justice System* (EG Press, 2017).

Genevieve Johnston is a PhD candidate and former SSHRC Vanier scholar at Carleton University in Ottawa, Canada. Her research interests include youth homelessness, radical social movements, intersectionality, marginalised populations and the sociology of space. Her doctoral research will explore belonging among formerly homeless young people in Canada. Her work has appeared in Contemporary Justice Review and Social Movement Studies.

Kira Jumet is Assistant Professor of Government at Hamilton College and is the author of *Contesting the Repressive State: Why Ordinary Egyptians Protested During the Arab Spring* (Oxford University Press, 2017).

Tahir Karakaş is an assistant professor of philosophy at Munzur University in Turkey. His research concerns critiques of modernity, Nietzsche, pragmatism, philosophy of ecology and degrowth thought and movement.

George Kordas is a PhD candidate in the Department of Political Science and History, Panteion University of Social and Political Sciences, Athens, Greece. His dissertation focuses on how the refugee and migration crisis has affected the European values' presentation in the European Parliament, and especially in its Southeast European member-states. His research interests are also directed on the extreme-right subcultures, in Southeastern Europe.

Elżbieta Korolczuk is Associate professor in sociology working at Södertörn University in Stockholm, and American Studies Center, Warsaw University. Her research interests involve social movements, civil society, politics of reproduction, as well as right-wing populism and mobilizations against "gender". Her recent publications include a monograph *Anti-gender Politics in the Populist Moment* written with Agnieszka Graff (2021, Routledge). She is also a commentator and a long-time women's and human rights activist.

Peter Lehr is Senior Lecturer in Terrorism Studies at the Centre for the Study of Terrorism and Political Violence at the University of St Andrews. He is a regional expert on South and Southeast Asia, with a special research interest in violent grey area phenomena such as terrorism, political violence and religious violence. His research philosophy follows Max Weber's *Verstehen*, that is, seeing and understanding an action from the actor's perspective – not to sympathise but to empathise with them and their actual beliefs, cultural values and motivations.

Mark Littler is Associate Professor of Criminology at Liverpool Hope University, where he is Subject Lead for Criminology. He is also Co-Chair for the European Society of Criminology's Working Group on Radicalization, Extremism, and Terrorism, Series Editor for Routledge's *Studies in Digital Extremism*, and Editor of the journal *Extremism*.

Chas Morrison is Assistant Professor, Centre for Trust, Peace and Social Relations, Coventry University. His main research interests are legacies of civil war, civilian protection and domestic responses to conflict and disaster. He has a background in humanitarian reconstruction.

Elisa Orofino is Academic Lead for Research on Extremism and Counter-Terrorism at the Policing Institute for the Eastern Region, Anglia Ruskin University, UK. She has published extensively on extremism, vocal extremist groups, radicalisation, Muslims in the West and social movements. Her publications encompass journal articles, book chapters, edited books and monographs, including *Hizb ut-Tahrir and the Caliphate* (Routledge, 2021).

Suleyman Ozeren is Professorial Lecturer in the Department of Justice, Law and Crimonology with the School of Public Affairs at American University, Washington D.C. and formerly Assistant Professor in the School of Sciences at Barton College, in Wilson, NC, and an adjunct professor at George Mason University. He formerly served as the Director of the International Center for Terrorism and Transnational Crime (UTSAM). His research focuses on international security, terrorism and counterterrorism, countering violent extremism conflict resolution, Turkey-US relations and Turkish domestic and foreign policy. Ozeren has worked collaboratively with the European Union; the Organization for Security and Co-operation in Europe; US Congress; George C. Marshall European Center for Security Studies; and Global Counterterrorism Forum.

Mario Peucker is Senior Research Fellow at the Institute for Sustainable Industries and Liveable Cities at Victoria University in Melbourne (Australia) and Senior Fellow at CARR). He has undertaken research and published on ethno-religious community activism, citizenship and political radicalism since 2003, both in Australia and Europe.

Che Hamdan Che Mohd Razali is Senior Lecturer, Faculty of Administrative Science and Policy Studies, Universiti Teknologi MARA, Raub, Pahang, Malaysia. He graduated from the International Islamic University Malaysia, the National University of Malaysia and Universiti Sains Malaysia. His primary research interests are civil society, Islamist movements and elections.

Dishani Senaratne is Project Director of Writing Doves, a non-profit initiative that seeks to enhance Sri Lankan young learners' intercultural understanding through a literature-based approach. She's also a published poet and an independent researcher.

Naveed S. Sheikh teaches Middle East studies, security studies and terrorism studies in the School of Social, Political and Global Studies at Keele University, United Kingdom, and is Editor-in-Chief of the journal *Politics, Religion & Ideology* (Routledge). He has published extensively on the intellectual and political history of modern Islam, and has held visiting appointments at Cambridge Muslim College, College of Europe (Warsaw), Harvard University, Hosei University (Tokyo), University of Louisville and the University of Notre Dame.

Alice Sibley is a PhD candidate and lecturer at Nottingham Trent University. Her PhD focuses on the British anti-Islam far-right and her research interests include the Populist Radical Right, the Extreme Right, Fascism and Terrorism.

George Stevenson is a lecturer in Social and Cultural Studies at INTO Newcastle University. His research interests are in second-wave feminism, class politics and the construction of political identities in modern Britain. He is the author of *The Women's Liberation Movement and the Politics of Class in Britain* (Bloomsbury, 2019) and is currently using the Mass Observation Project archive to explore vernacular models of class at the end of Thatcherism.

Paul Stott is Head of Security and Extremism at the London-based think tank Policy Exchange. He can be found on twitter @MrPaulStott.

Lorenzo Vidino is the director of the Program on Extremism at George Washington University. His latest book is *The Closed Circle: Joining and Leaving the Muslim Brotherhood in the West* (Columbia University Press, 2020).

Sabine Volk is based at the Institute for European Studies at the Jagiellonian University in Kraków and is a doctoral researcher in political science with a focus on comparative government at the University of Passau. Her work focuses on the far right, protest politics and political culture in post-socialist eastern Germany. Sabine has contributed to edited volumes and published articles in peer-reviewed journals such as *German Politics*, *Frontiers in Political Science: Comparative Politics* and *Journal of Genocide Research*.

Manès Weisskircher is a postdoctoral fellow at the Department of Sociology and Human Geography and the Center for Research on Extremism, University of Oslo. He holds a PhD from the European University Institute in Florence. His work focuses on the study of social movements, political parties and democracy. Manès is one of the authors of *Gains and Losses: How Protestors Win and Lose* (Oxford University Press). His research has been published in journals such as the *European Journal of Political Research*, *Political Studies*, *Government & Opposition*, *Social Movement Studies*, *Politics and Governance*, *The Political Quarterly*, *Sociological Perspectives*, and the *Journal of Intercultural Studies*.

FOREWORD

Matthew Feldman

In 1964 U.S. Supreme Court opinion attempting to define pornography for legal purposes, Justice Potter Stewart summed up the nebulous nature of the concept in seven now-infamous words. He couldn't offer a workable definition, he wrote, but "I know it when I see it".

More than fifty years later, we find this test applied to one of the world's most pressing problems, a rising tide of extremist movements that are destabilizing civil societies around the globe.

Thus opens J.M. Berger's (2018) study for MIT's 'Essential Knowledge Series', *Extremism*. In a way, this slim and helpful book is very much of a document of our times. For more than a century, "I know it when I see it" was good enough when it came to understandings of extremism, whether popular or academic. Nor was this helped by tautological definitions, like that still offered by the Oxford English Dictionary: an extremist is "a person who holds extreme political or religious views". Berger is one of a number of scholars taking the issue seriously over the last generation; a period which has fundamentally shaped approaches to extremism, national security and terrorism – and not always for the better.

Yet we can be confident the conception, if not the definition, of extremism dates much further back than the 19th century, when the term entered Anglophone usage. Berger's edition ranges from the sack of Carthage to the Zealots, Kharijites and Cathars – all of whom still have their defenders – to colonial extermination of dehumanised natives and institutions of slavery in the early modern period. Nor is this list exhaustive. Far from any modern vintage, a self-consciously demarcated 'in-group' advocating hostile actions against an illegitimate 'out-group' may just be "part of the human condition" (Berger, 2018, pp. 1 & 4).

Despite long suffering from definitional looseness, then, several key features of extremism have long been identified: crisis conditions; in-group appeals to the disaffected; a tension between fringe and mainstream; and the targeted designation of out-groups for actual and imagined forms of repressive action. Yet, in turn, these elements needed a crisis to be brought together and forged into a systemic object of study. The editors of this volume, Elisa Orofino and William Allchorn, are unequivocal on this point: that crisis was 9/11.

The jihadi Islamist attacks of 11 September 2001 remain the most lethal and horrifically tele-visual terrorist attack in history. Nearly 3,000 people perished after four hijacked planes struck at the arteries of American global hegemony: the World Trade Center; the Pentagon; and (although unsuccessful) the White House. In its train, moreover, 9/11 also wrought the 'Global War on Terror', and many other consequences besides – including wars in Afghanistan and Iraq and their long-lasting effects, first and foremost upon the peoples living under conditions of effective occupation. With these events also followed sizeable increases in anti-Muslim preju-dice, not just in the United States, but metastisising across Europe and into India and Myanmar. Put simply, countering terrorism became the top priority amongst many nations, including the process of radicalisation toward political or religious violence. Extremism emerged as both a response and as a subject of study in the years following 9/11.

By the end of the decade, different typologies of extremism had been variously proffered: state versus non-state extremisms; historical versus contemporary extremisms; religious versus secular extremisms; and perhaps most pertinent of all, violent versus non-violent extremisms. It is the latter that this volume's editors take up here systemically for the first time. Rightly, the intro-duction does not duck the controversies inherent in even the grainy picture sketched above. For one, the problem of non-violent extremism was formulated almost exclusively as a problem of extremism within Muslim communities. Should this prejudicial origin tar the concept of non-violent extremism, even irredeemably?

That is of course for readers to adjudge, and many will feel strongly that it ought to forever impede analysis of extremism; that is, 'extremist' is too often a label used to delegitimise or 'securitise' civil society groups, and should simply be avoided. Around the world, many have good reason to think non-violent extremism – or 'extremism' more generally – should not be a proper object of scholarly study. This volume is indispensable for them also.

That is because, paradoxically, to reject something one needs to first understand it. Just as counter-extremism must be fundamentally based upon understanding (a given manifestation of) extremism, so too must any rejection of what may soon be dubbed 'Extremism Studies' should be founded in scholarship rather than strawmen, through proper intellectual engagement rather than journalistic takes or online outrage. In short, the *Routledge Handbook of Non-Violent Extremism: Groups, Perspectives and New Debates* belongs on every scholarly and practitioner bookshelf – even, perhaps especially, for those asserting that the violent versus non-violent extremism distinction should disappear.

Arguments for both sides are faithfully rendered in the introduction and developed in the truly global selection of chapters that follow. The editors settle upon a characterisation of non-violent extremism as "opposing the enemy (mostly the establishment) with all the legal tools available (generally protests, petitions, demonstrations and online campaigns) but without using violence". Essential in the latter is a rejection of pluralism and hostility to multicultural dem-ocracy – whether by states, groups or doctrines. Drawing upon the example of Hizb ut-Tahrir, at present banned in 14 countries, the editors make the vital point that non-violent extremism is more than part of a conveyer belt toward violent extremism or terrorism. As contribution to this volume suggests, non-violent extremism can be a destination as well, not merely a way station on the way to political or religious violence.

The very diversity of subject matter suggests an area of study that is being established, rather than fleeting. Either way, this book marks an inflection in the study of non-violent extremism. Not only academics and students, but also policy-makers and practitioners will wish to have this edition close to hand. Assuming the 'it' of extremism – or at least concerns about extremism – is going no place soon, this volume shows we can do better than "I know it when I see it". In this stretching of scholarly horizons, the editors and contributors are to be heartily congratulated in providing a collection that is greater than the sum of its parts.

Reference

Berger, J.M. (2018). *Extremism*. London, Boston: MIT Press.

PREFACE

For a long-time overshadowed by violent and *jihadi* extremism, non-violent (or vocal) extremism has been the centre of inflamed conceptual and policy debates in the post-9/11 world. Different from violent organisations, who support the killing of innocents and therefore are more readily banned and persecuted by governments around the world, vocal extremists stand in a very liminal space in Western states, where the freedom of speech and association grant them the right to legally operate despite being opposed to key values and mechanisms within democratic states. Vocal extremists hold extreme ideas (mostly anti-government, anti-establishment) and seek a radical change. Still, they do not espouse violent methods and this problematic makes them quite complex non-state actors to study, hence the need for their greater consideration and research.

This volume stands as an innovative contribution within current studies on extremism, radicalisation and terrorism as it responds to the two problems characterising current literature to date as follows. Firstly, while accepting that vocal extremism precedes terrorism, this volume refuses academic assumptions on the unavoidable evolution of extremism into terrorism. This *Handbook* acknowledges the importance of non-violent extremism as a liminal space preceding terror acts but at the same time argues that non-violent extremism reserves itself as a stand-alone area of study in its own right. This volume stands as the first *Handbook* on non-violent extremism ever published before, placing this important topic on the forefront of research rather than having it relegated to the sidelines of academic debate. As a result, this volume aims to be a comprehensive source of literature touching on different kinds of vocal extremisms – traditional ones and post-modern – going beyond the almost exclusive focus on Islamism that has become typical of recent studies.

INTRODUCTION

Why Do We Need a Handbook on Non-violent Forms of Extremism?

Elisa Orofino and William Allchorn

Introduction

For a long time overshadowed by violent and *jihadi* extremism, non-violent (or vocal) extremism has been the centre of inflamed conceptual and policy debates in the post-9/11 world (Cordesman, 2017; Gilligan, 2019; Hamid, 2016; Wali, 2013; Whitespunner, 2018). Different from violent organisations, who support the killing of innocents and therefore are more readily banned and persecuted by governments around the world, vocal extremists stand in a very liminal space in Western states, where the freedom of speech and association grant them the right to legally operate despite being opposed to key values and mechanisms within democratic states (Karagiannis, 2018; Orofino, 2020a, 2020b). Vocal extremists hold extreme ideas (mostly anti-government, anti-establishment) and seek a radical change. Still, they do not espouse violent methods, and this problematic makes them quite complex non-state actors to study, hence the need for their greater consideration and research.

The complexity of vocal extremism is also exacerbated by the confusion around the terms "radicalisation", "extremism" and "terrorism". While some experts believe that all radicals will sooner or later engage in terrorism (Baran, 2005; McCauley & Moskalenko, 2008; Moghaddam, 2005), significant differences exist between these terms and the stages they represent. As definitions are not straightforward in this field, we believe that visualising the three terms into a continuum is helpful to grasp the differences.

Vocal or Non-violent Extremism: A Continuum from Radicalisation to Terrorism

As shown in Figure 0.1, for some individuals, the continuum pictured above can work as a natural path from "cognitive radicalisation" (adoption of extreme beliefs and ideology at the mere intellectual level) to "behavioural radicalisation", involving the acceptance of specific attitudes, often leading to engagement in extreme actions, which may include the use of violence and therefore terrorism (Mandel, 2009). Nevertheless, this is not always the case. Individuals can rest in the grey zone between radicalisation and extremism for a long time before moving on to terrorism, if they will ever move on in the first place. Vocal radical groups, such as Hizb ut-Tahrir, represent living evidence that individuals have moved from endorsing specific ideas

DOI: 10.4324/9781003032793-1

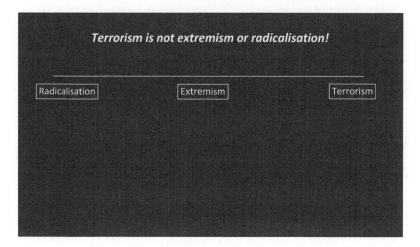

Figure 0.1   Continuum from radicalisation to terrorism.
Source: Author's own illustration.

(radicalisation) to expressing vocal opposition (extremism) without ever performing violent actions (terrorism). Although some people affiliated with the group have shifted to terrorism,[1] the organisation as a whole has steadfastly stood by a commitment to non-violence.

Radicalisation

While having in common the pursuit of specific and intertwined political, social, economic and often religious goals, important differences exist among the three stages of the continuum. At the most basic level, **radicalisation** can be defined as "the process whereby people become extremists" (Neumann, 2013, p. 874). As highlighted above, radicalisation involves the adoption of specific ideas (usually anti-establishment) that often derive from political, economic and social grievances, which in turn cause deep dissatisfaction with the current *status quo*. The individual's dissatisfaction can spring from different factors, such as experiences of discrimination, marginalisation, victimisation, an identity crisis or peer pressure (Ebner, 2017; Orofino, 2020b; Sageman, 2004; Wiktorowicz, 2005). Radicalisation has also been boldly defined as "what happens before the bomb goes off" (Neumann, 2008, p. 4), stressing that although all radicals do not naturally become terrorists, all terrorists must first be radicalised. Radicalisation differs from both extremism and terrorism, and it stands as a complex phenomenon exhibiting the following features: the acceptance of an ideology that contrasts with what is perceived as the mainstream opinion and an evident personal zeal for the newly adopted ideological views and the exclusion of more mainstream action to achieve these ideological goals. Radicalisation is a multi-pathway process, which does not automatically escalate into extremism and terrorism, but which is characterised by a specific set of ideas, often anti-government and targeting specific groups in the society (Orofino, 2020b; Sewell & Hulusi, 2016).

Extremism

Extremism stands as the second step of the continuum illustrated above and tends to happen when ideas produce strong opposition. The British Government has defined extremism as a "vocal or active opposition to fundamental British values, including democracy, the rule of law, individual liberty and mutual respect and tolerance of different faiths and beliefs" (Home Office, 2015, p. 107). Although UK-related, this definition can easily be adapted to all countries (not only Western) where extremist groups emerge as powerful non-state actors, challenging national governments by attacking their core values, mainstream lifestyle and policies, such as immigration and foreign policy. In this volume, we consider extremists as radicals who have moved to the next step, opposing the enemy (mostly the establishment) with all the legal tools available (generally protests, petitions, demonstrations and online campaigns) but without using violence.

Terrorism

When people are ready to perpetrate violence to achieve their goals, they would have reached the last and final stage of the continuum, that is **terrorism**. While there are no universally accepted definitions on terrorism, we here identify it as "politically motivated violence perpetrated against non-combatant targets by sub-national groups or clandestine agents, usually intended to influence an audience" (Ruby, 2002, p. 10). Radicalisation, extremism and terrorism all have in common specific political, economic, social and religious goals. Still, as soon as violence is used, no confusion can be made among the three stages as the individual has shifted towards the end of the continuum, reaching terrorism as a final stage.

According to the UK Terrorism Act (2000), terrorism involves serious violence against a person (and/or a group of people), inflicts serious damage to property, creates a serious risk to the health or safety of the public or section of the public or is designed seriously to interfere with or seriously to disrupt an electronic system. Again, the driving force of acts of terror is the will to influence the government and to intimidate the public for the purpose of advancing a political, religious, racial or ideological *cause* (HM Government, 2000).

Vocal or Non-violent Extremism: A New Research Agenda

The definitions explored above are useful to understand the complex theoretical space occupied by non-violent extremism and how it deeply differs from both radicalisation and terrorism. This *Handbook* starts from a dissatisfaction of the current marginal role played by research on non-violence in the study of extremism and wants to address two main problems. Firstly, the scholarly tendency to associate non-violent extremism with terrorism, assuming that sooner or later all non-violent extremists will become terrorists. Secondly, the lacuna within the current academic research in which non-violent extremism is still overshadowed by the study of a particular ideology (i.e. *jihadi* extremism).

With regard to the first problem of the literature, the most influential models (or pathways) explaining the shift from non-violent to violent extremism, such as Moghadam's (2005) "staircase" to terrorism, McCauley and Moskalenko's (2008) "pyramid" to terrorism, and Baran's (2005) "conveyor belt" to terrorism, see non-violent extremism as the beginning of a path leading to violence. But, again, this is not always the case: there are many who become radicalised and engage in extremism (opposing the system) and yet "do not become foreign fighters, engage in terrorism, or even reach the frontline" (Chassman, 2016, p. 213; see also Orofino, 2020b). The assumption that all extremists will become terrorists might prevent scholars from studying the challenge against the national governments put forth by those groups whose pressure is not exercised through violence but through the power of ideas. As seen above in the quote by Neumann (2008, p. 4), extremism is "what happens before the bomb goes off" but what happens in the moment prior to the bomb can last the whole lifetime of a group or an individual, and never evolve into terrorism in the final instance.

With regard to the second problem identified in current research, the almost exclusive focus on *jihadist* groups has left out of radar a number of organisations that continue to vocally promote a totalitarian political agenda, which creates a considerable gap in the ideologies considered as part of the research on this issue. In fact, this lack of an evidence base can further frustrate policy, with analysts fundamentally disagreeing whether to ban vocal extremists in democratic states. Those scholars supporting bans usually see vocal extremists as a conveyor belt to violent extremism able to indoctrinate people and ultimately turn them to violence (Brandis, 2017; Cordesman, 2017; Heard, 2018), when we know that is not always the case.

At the same time, the opponents to bans insist on the need for vocal extremist groups to be heard by the community to preserve freedom of speech paramount in a democracy (Berry, 2015; Espinoza, 2016; Lowe, 2017). Added to this charge, they also add that bans discourage further grievances and contribute toward a broader criminological agenda that securitises certain modes of thought. Recent research complicates this picture further, highlighting a critical disjuncture between attitudes and behaviours: individuals who hold extreme ideas (even supporting political violence) do not always engage in any violent actions (Juergensmeyer, 2018 & 2019; Smith & Talbot, 2019), and those who engage in violence are not necessarily supportive of specific political aims promoted by vocal extremist groups (Khalil, 2014; Perry, 2018).

This volume stands as an innovative contribution within current studies on extremism, radicalisation and terrorism as it responds to the two problems characterising current literature to date as follows. Firstly, while accepting that vocal extremism precedes terrorism, this volume refuses academic assumptions on the unavoidable evolution of extremism into terrorism. This *Handbook* acknowledges the importance of non-violent extremism as a liminal space preceding terror acts but at the same time argues that non-violent extremism reserves itself as a standalone area of study in its own right. This volume stands as the first *Handbook* on non-violent extremism ever published before, placing this important topic on the forefront of research rather than having it relegated to the sidelines of academic debate. As a result, this project aims to be a comprehensive source of literature touching on different kinds of vocal extremisms – traditional ones and post-modern – going beyond the almost exclusive focus on Islamism that has become typical of recent studies.

Non-violent Extremism: A Firewall or Conveyor Belt to Violent Extremism in the 21st Century?

The Conceptual Debate

Before we arrive at the question of violence, what is certain about the groups – for example Islamist, far-right, incel, far-left, environmental, feminist and religious – named in this volume is that they are all to some extent engaged in a "war of ideas" (Baran, 2005, p. 14) against the socio-political and cultural system in which they operate. This taps right at the heart of long-standing debates about what constitutes political *extremism* and political activism within a democratic state. While the former is often given a negative connotation *per se* as it is often associated with violence, radicalism is regarded as a positive element of fringe politics as it involves a critique of the democratic state (Carter, 2005, p. 22) but not necessarily an overthrow of the system itself (Eatwell, 2003, p. 14). Although violent extremism is easy to identify as an illegitimate form of political activism, non-violent forms of extremism are slightly more problematic as they still contain a kernel of extremism (i.e. anti-pluralism and a fundamental opposition to democratic governance).

While it is vital to monitor vocal extremist organisations as they represent a serious threat, it is also essential to differentiate between vocal extremism and political activism. A key aspect to distinguish the two is that while vocal extremists would strongly oppose the political, economic and cultural establishment (aiming for a radical change), even when holding vigorous opposing views activists would accept that in a democratic society change should be achieved only through popularly mandated constitutional principles and the rule of law. Scholars have insisted on the need to encourage political activism in order to discourage extremism (Lowe, 2017; Bartlett, Birdwell, & King, 2010; Karagiannis (2018): when people are free to express their dissatisfaction towards the government (activism), escalation into violent extremism is generally contained as it is often related to the denial of freedom of speech. Nevertheless, encouraging activism can also mean to encourage vocal extremism (and the shift to violence) as the boundary is not clear nor straightforward.

Besides being easily confused with activism, extremism can come in many varieties: extreme by method and not by goal, extreme by goal and not by method, or extreme by goal and method (Goodwin & Eatwell, 2010). What unifies extremists (both vocal and violent) is their rejection of pluralism, legal rules, and the economic, political, religious and social system they live within (Lowe, 2017). Nevertheless, having critical ideas of the prevailing system should not be enough to criminalise a group (or individuals) in the West where universal rights (such as the freedom of speech and association) should be granted. Criminalisation (and subsequent bans) might occur when there is evidence that a group has already worked its way along the cognitive and behavioural conveyor belt of extremism/violence. Problematically, even this has proved to be not enough to ban specific vocal extremist organisations in some Western countries, such as the United Kingdom.

To give an example to further elucidate this quandary, Omar Barki – founder of the terror group Al-Muhajiroun – is a product of British vocal extremism (Orofino, 2020b). Before creating his own terror organisation in the late 1980s, Bakri was in the leadership of the British branch of HT. HT still stands as a legal vocal extremist organisation calling for the re-establishment of the Caliphate and blaming the West and corrupted Muslims leaders for the decadence of Islam as a *din*, or "way of life". Another more recent example is Thomas Mair who shot and killed Jo Cox (a Labour Party Member of Parliament) in 2016, shouting 'Britain First' as he committed the murder. Despite current debates around the role of the group in Mair's radicalisation, Britain First (a far-right political organisation formed in 2011 by former members of the British National Party) is still legally operating in the United Kingdom (Lowe, 2017; Pearson, 2020).

Whereas the association of these two terrorists with vocal extremist organisations was crystal clear, it was not enough to trigger a ban on membership and affiliation to both organisations, whose members claim them to be "mere intellectual groups" (Badar, 2015; Doureihi, 2017). As a fact, as demonstrated by recent studies on non-violent extremist organisations, the majority of the members who join non-violent extreme organisations tend to remain non-violent (although extremist) for their whole life (Busher, 2013; Orofino, 2020b). Would it then be fair to ban a whole group for the actions of a few individuals who have crossed the line moving from extremism (i.e. opposition to democracy) to terrorism (i.e. the use of terrorist violence)? This question is still open to debate, and it is certainly not an easy one to answer.

The Policy Debate

Countries around the world have answered differently to this question, approaching the policy debate under multiple perspectives and banning vocal extremist organisations as they perceived them as conveyor belt to terrorism. Taking one more time HT as an instance, today the group is banned in at least 14 countries around the world, including many Muslim-majority countries, such as Egypt, Jordan, Saudi Arabia, Turkey and Uzbekistan (Counter Extremism Project, 2017). HT is also banned in Turkey, Russia, China and Germany where it was deemed "anti-Semitic and dangerous" (European Court of Human Rights, 2012). Other countries like Denmark and Australia have considered banning HT several times as a hub of "preachers of hate" but have not done so, apparently fearing a possible backlash of negative reactions from other Islamic revivalist groups who present themselves as mere intellectual groups.

In the United Kingdom, HT continues to legally operate, despite the fact that the Home Office has expressed its concern about HT several times. British authorities appear to agree with the ideas of the Quilliam Foundation, an anti-radicalism think tank based in the United Kingdom: "Having nasty opinions is not a good enough reason legally to ban them" (Malik, 2011). The Home Office is still convinced that unpopular ideas are not enough to proscribe an organisation, despite the potential dangers of HT propagating its anti-Semitic, homophobic and anti-Western stances (Berry, 2015).

Similar debates have circulated on the far-right, far-left and in relation to other "post-modern"[2] non-violent extremism organisations. In particular, the case of Generation Identity has come to international attention more recently due to its ties with Christchurch attack, Brenton Tarrant. Though not directly implicated in the Christchurch attack, Tarrant did donate funds to the group, and his terrorist manifesto (entitled "The Great Replacement") gave a nod to one of the core conspiracy theories propagated by the group, namely, Renaud Camus' idea that non-European demographic replacement was one of the gravest threats to European populations. This led the German domestic intelligence service (BfV) to reclassify the German chapter of the group as a far-right extremist group, joining the likes of the neo-Nazi *Nationaldemokratische Partei Deutschlands* (or NPD) on the German intelligence agency's watchlist. Whilst none of its members engaged in violent activism, its ideas of 'white genocide' or 'white marginalisation' were clearly potent enough to inspire violent action well beyond European shores.

Added to this, and coming several years ago now, there have been connections established between other far-right social movements and solo-actor terrorists. A counterpoint to the Christchurch examples is the Oslo attacker, Anders Behring Breivik. In March 2011, online records show that Breivik was reaching out online to UK anti-Islam protest street movement, the English Defence League (EDL), for "inspiration, courage and even hope that we might turn this evil trend with Islamisation" (*BBC News*, 26th July 2011). Despite some comments claiming that he wished to join one of the EDL's demonstrations, Breivik (in his terrorist screed, *2083 – A European Declaration of Independence*) went on to tellingly belittle the EDL as a radical, non-violent (though still) extremist actor – calling the group "naive fools... that still believe the democratic system can solve Britain's problems" (*BBC News*, 26th July 2011). As mentioned before, links between non-violent extremists and solo-actor terrorists therefore should also be treated with extreme caution. In fact, we know from ethnographic and polling research done among EDL activists that pro-democratic, non-violence is a key part of the group's value system (Bartlett & Littler 2011; Busher, 2013; Busher, Holbrook, & Macklin, 2019) – despite the violent picture painted by early demonstrations.

In terms of post-modern forms of non-violent extremism, radical feminism has also been at the centre of inflamed debates over the last decades. Emerging in the United States at the end of 1960s against the oppression of women, radical feminists have expanded and evolved in different organisations holding diverse stances. Liberal Feminists, Marxist and Socialist Feminists, Cultural Feminists and Eco-Feminists all want to enhance and protect women in society but with different goals and tools. While these groups are not usually regarded as a threat *per se*, others organisations – although non-violent in principle – are at the centre of policy debates for their role as alleged hate groups. This is the case of Trans-Exclusionary Radical Feminists (TERF), notably in the anti-men and anti-trans veins.

Experiencing wide expansion in the 2000s, some critics would argue that TERF ideology has become the "*de facto* face of feminism in the UK" (Burns, 2019). The reasons behind this argument are related to the narrow space devoted to gender-critical thought in the country, which has led to very strong statements from the group. A famous instance is the Australian radical feminist Sheila Jeffreys who went before the UK Parliament in March 2018 and declared that trans women are nothing but "parasites" (Gander, 2018). To add on Mrs. Jeffreys' declarations, some TERFs hold extreme beliefs about sex – arguing that "penis in the vagina is always rape" (Gander, 2018). Such strong statements can work as triggers towards violence against specific groups, in this case men and the transgender community.

Added to this gendered hatred has obviously been the emerging and metastising picture of the manosphere and particularly incel actors. Frustrated by pushes for gender equality and a perceived impotence in striking up relationships with the opposite sex, attacks in Florida, Toronto and Plymouth in recent years have shown how toxic forms of masculinity and extreme misogyny circulate in the online spaces and encourage offline actions. Creating sexual hierarchies and notions of uprisings by so-called 'Beta' males, such online subcultures have allowed for the development of such grievances and is something that Chapter 3 will concretely address.

Besides Incels and extreme feminists, extreme Buddhism is also at the centre of inflamed policy debates. Although usually associated with peace and non-violence, some Buddhist groups have used violent methods for religious and political purposes. This is the case of modern Sinhalese Buddhist nationalism, which emerged in Sri Lanka between the late 1900s and the early 2000s to counter British colonialism and Christian influence (Gregg, 2014). With this purpose in mind, monks have preached against Christian centres and churches in the country, demonising them and leading to increased attacks on the Christian community in the country (U.S. Department of State, 2004). Extremist Buddhist clergy's hate speeches led to extreme acts which include arson, acts of sacrilege, death threats, violent disruption of worship, stoning, abuse, unlawful restraint and even interference with funerals (Pew Research Centre, 2014).

Not to mention the ethnic cleansing of the Rohingya people in Buddhist-majority Myanmar, which stands as one of the most evident instances of violent extreme Buddhism (Rosenthal, 2019). Due to the escalation of violence, Ma Ba Tha (The Committee for the Protection of Race and Religion, a Nationalist Buddhist group) was formally banned in Myanmar in 2017, but apparently they rebranded and continue operating under another name, i.e. the Buddha Dhamma Philanthropy Foundation (Mandalay, 2017). Although Buddhism is the religion least associated to violence, this does not prevent extreme ideas to trigger segments of followers towards violence.

Finally, and turning away from proscription and towards other policy debates around the links between extremism and violence, environmental extremist groups have also been on the radar of security services for a while in Western democracies. Interestingly, for example, violent animal rights groups, like the Animal Liberation Front, the Animal Rights Militia, the Justice Department, and the Provisional Animal Liberation Front, have not been proscribed in the United Kingdom due to their perceived links with domestic disorder and extremism and not terrorism (Monaghan, 2013). Despite their use of extreme saboteurial tactics on animal testing and scientific laboratories as well as violent attacks on scientists involved in such activities since the early 1970s, a more tailored criminal justice and public order response has been used against such groups that has stopped short of banning membership of such organisations outright (Monaghan, 2013, p. 934). Instead, special units, intense monitoring procedures and new protections afforded to those targeted by such activism have been used to tighten the net on such groups (Monaghan, 2013, pp. 941–2). Such a case demonstrates the importance of definitions and concepts that have real-world policy effects.

The Need for a *Handbook* on Non-violent Extremism

As discussed so far, the need for a volume devoted to an exclusive study of non-violent extremisms – traditional and post-modern ones – was motivated by at least three macro-factors: the lack of analysis of non-violent extremism in relevant literature, the excessive focus on Islamist violent extremism and the confusion around certain key terms, such as radicalisation, extremism and terrorism. This volume stands as the first comprehensive source of literature to study non-violent extremist groups of different ideologies contextualised in the various countries in which they operate. This study aims to fill the gaps in relevant literature discussed above and to explore the controversial role of vocal extremists by shedding light on liminality between violence/non-violence within these organisations.

Furthermore, this project presents the following objectives: (1) to provide an up-to-date picture of the most active non-violent extremist groups in Europe, Africa, Asia, Oceania, the Americas and the Middle East; (2) to discuss the ideological foundation of their "war of ideas", their claims and their perspectives; (3) to explore the main operative methods used by these groups according to the context they operate and the related political opportunity structure within their respective locations; (4) and to identify new trends of analysis for this still under-explored category of non-state actors.

Relevant contributions included in this volume refer to the objectives mentioned above, focusing on specific groups as case studies. This *Handbook* consists of four main parts, each one exploring a different kind of non-violent extremism. Following this introduction, Part 1 is devoted to the study of *extremism across multiple ideologies* and it includes contributions approaching vocal extremism through a comparative perspective (that also includes incels). Part 2 deals with *religious extremisms* and it includes contributions on non-violent Islamist, Buddhist and Hindu movements explored in different national contexts. Part 3 deals with far-right vocal extremism and offers an overview of the main extremist groups active in various countries, analysing their actorship and pressure both on governments and on civil society. Finally, Part 4 embraces contributions on "post-modern extremisms", i.e. non-violent left-wing, feminist and environmental movements. This *Handbook* acknowledges the importance of these expressions of non-vocal extremism. Acting as pressure groups against governments and winning more and more members across the globe, post-modern extremism certainly needs more research – especially when it taps into mainstream debates on contemporary social issues and identity politics.

Notes

1 This is the case of Omar Barki, founder of the terror group Al-Muhajiroun. Before creating his own terror organisation in the late 1980s, Bakri was in the leadership of the British branch of HT.
2 Here, "post-modern" is used to identify the post-material, ideological causes of non-violent extremist groups that sit beyond the realm of traditional religious and political actors. These post-68 concerns include environmentalism, feminism and some socio-cultural aspects of left-wing activism.

References

Badar, U. (2015, November 4). The Counter-Terrorism Fiction| 2015 Conference 'Innocent Until Proven Muslim'. [YouTube video]. Retrieved from www.youtube.com/watch?v=usmupi6bjdi – action=share.

Baran, Z. (2005). Fighting the War of Ideas. *Foreign Affairs*, 84(6), 68–78. doi:10.2307/20031777.

Bartlett, J., Birdwell, J., and King M. (2010). The Edge of Violence: A Radical Approach to Extremism. Retrieved from www.demos.co.uk/files/Edge_of_Violence _web.pdf.

BBC News. (2011, 26 July). Norway massacre: Gunman 'wanted to join EDL rally' Retrieved from www.bbc.co.uk/news/uk-14292142.

Bartlett, J. and Littler, M. (2011). Inside the EDL: Populist Politics in a Digital Age'. London Demos. Retreived from: https://www.demos.co.uk/files/Inside_the_edl_WEB.pdf.

Berry, A. (2015, 19 March). Hizb ut-Tahrir: should Britain ban radical Islamist group? The Week. Retrieved from www.theweek.co.uk/63010/hizb-ut-tahrir-should-britain-ban-radical-islamist-group

Brandis, G. (2017). Petition to ban Hizb ut-Tahrir in Australia. Retrieved from www.change.org/p/attor ney-general-george-brandis-ban-hizbut-tahrir.

Burns, K. (2019, September 5). The Rise of Anti-trans 'Radical' Feminists, Explained, Vox online. Retrieved from www.vox.com/identities/2019/9/5/20840101/terfs-radical-feminists-gender-critical.

Busher, J. (2013). Grassroots Activism in the English Defence League: Discourse and Public (dis) order. In M. Taylor, P.M. Currie, & D. Holdbrook (Eds.), *Extreme Right-Wing Political Violence and Terrorism* (pp. 65–84). London: Bloomsbury.

Busher, J., Holbrook, D., & Macklin, G. (2019). The Internal Brakes on Violent Escalation: A Typology. *Behavioral Sciences of Terrorism and Political Aggression*, 11(1), 3–25.

Carter, E. (2005). *The Extreme Right in Western Europe: Success Or Failure?* Manchester: Manchester University Press.

Chassman, A. (2016). Islamic State, Identity, and the Global Jihadist Movement: How is Islamic State Successful at Recruiting 'Ordinary' People? *Journal for Deradicalization*, Winter(9), 205–259.

Cordesman, A. H. (2017). Islam and the Patterns in Terrorism and Violent Extremism. Centre for Strategic and International Studies. Retrieved from https://csis-prod.s3.amazonaws.com/s3fs-public/publication/171017_Report_Islam%20and%20the%20-War_on_Terrorism_.pdf?i14pb6Py.S_5J9D73 QmtXxX5NlXev5bv.

Counter Extremism Project. (2017). Hizb ut-Tahrir. Retrieved from www.counterextremism.com/thr eat/hizb-ut-tahrir.

Doureihi, W. (2017). Hizb ut-Tahrir Australia Conference 'Hatred Rising Living Islam in a Hostile West'. Talk 3 | Embracing and Confronting Reality [video]. Retrieved from https://madmimi.com/s/d6ce2a.

Eatwell, R. (2003). Ten theories of the extreme right. In P. Merkl & L. Weinberg (Eds.), *Right-Wing Extremism in the Twenty-first Century*, pp. 45–70. London: Routledge.

Ebner, J. (2017). *The Rage: The Vicious Circle of Islamist and Far-Right Extremism*. London, New York: I.B. Tauris.

Espinoza, J. (2016, 16 January). Extremist Groups must be allowed to preach on British Campuses, New Oxford Head says. *The Telegraph*. Retrieved from www.telegraph.co.uk/education/educationnews/12102509/Extremist-groups-must-be-allowed-to-preach-on-British-Campuses-new-Oxford-head-says.html.

European Court of Human Rights, (2012, June 12). Decision on Hizb ut-Tahrir and Others against Germany. Retrieved from http://freecases.eu/Doc/CourtAct/4581998.

Gander, K. (2018, March 15). Academic Says Trans Women Are Parasites for 'Occupying the Bodies of the Oppressed'. *Newsweek*. Retrieved from www.newsweek.com/trans-women-are-parasites-occupy ing-bodies-oppressed-says-academic-846563.

Gilligan, A. (2019, 21 February). 'The Baroness, Islamic Extremists and a Question of Free Speech.' *The Telegraph*. Retrieved from www.telegraph.co.uk/news/uknews/11488175/The-baroness-Islamic-ext remists-and-a-question-of-free-speech.html.

Goodwin, M., & Eatwell, R. (eds.) (2010). *The New Extremism in 21st Century Britain*. London: Routledge.

Gregg, H. S. (2014). *The Path to Salvation: Religious Violence from the Crusades to Jihad*. Lincoln: University of Nebraska Press, Potomac Books.

Hamid, S. (2016). *Sufis, Salafis and Islamists: The Contested Ground of British Islamic Activism*. London, New York: I.B. Tauris.

Heard, L. S. (2018). Britain is too Soft on Extremists. *Gulf News*. Retrieved from https://gulfnews.com/opinion/op-eds/britain-is-too-soft-on-extremists-1.2284992.

HM Government. (2000). Terrorism Act 2000. Retrieved from www.legislation.gov.uk/ukpga/2000/11/contents.

Home Office. (2015). Counter-Extremism Strategy. Retrieved from https://assets.publishing.service. gov.uk/government/uploads/system/uploads/attachment_data/file/470088/51859_Cm9148_Accessi ble.pdf.

Juergensmeyer, M. (2018). Thinking Sociologically about Religion and Violence: The Case of ISIS. *Sociology of Religion: A Quarterly Review*, 79(1), 20–34. doi:10.1093/socrel/srx055.

Juergensmeyer, M. (2019). Do Religious Ideas Cause Violence? *Critical Review*, 31(1), 102–112, doi: 10.1080/08913811.2019.1565737.

Karagiannis, E. (2018). *The New Political Islam: Human Rights, Democracy, and Justice*. Philadelphia: University of Pennsylvania Press.

Khalil, J. (2014). Radical Beliefs and Violent Actions Are Not Synonymous: How to Place the Key Disjuncture Between Attitudes and Behaviors at the Heart of Our Research into Political Violence. *Studies in Conflict & Terrorism*, 37(2), 198–211. doi:10.1080/1057610X.2014.862902.

Lowe, D. (2017). Prevent Strategies: The Problems Associated in Defining Extremism: The Case of the United Kingdom. *Studies in Conflict & Terrorism*, 40(11), 917–933. doi:10.1080/1057610X.2016.1253941.

Malik, S. (2011, July 18). Watchdog Recommends Tory U-Turn on Banning Hizb ut-Tahrir. *The Guardian*. Retrieved from www.theguardian.com/politics/2011/jul/18/watchdog-tory-uturn-hizb-ut-tahrir-ban.

Mandalay, J.Z. (2017, May 30). Ultra-nationalist Buddhist Monks seek to avoid Myanmar Ban. UCA News. Retrieved from www.ucanews.com/news/ultra-nationalist-buddhist-monks-seek-to-avoid-myanmar-ban/79356.

Mandel, D. R. (2009). Radicalization: What Does It Mean. In T. M. Pick, A. Speckhard, & B. Jacuch (Eds.), *Home-grown Terrorism: Understanding and Addressing the Root Causes of Radicalisation among Groups with an Immigrant Heritage in Europe* (pp. 101–113). Amsterdam, Berlin, Tokyo, Washington DC: IOS Press.

McCauley, C., & Moskalenko, S. (2008). Mechanisms of Political Radicalization: Pathways Toward Terrorism. *Terrorism and Political Violence*, 20(3), 415–433. doi:10.1080/09546550802073367.

Moghaddam, F. M. (2005). The Staircase to Terrorism: A Psychological Exploration. *American Psychologist*, 60(2), 161–169. doi:10.1037/0003–066X.60.2.161.

Monaghan, R. (2013). Not Quite Terrorism: Animal Rights Extremism in the United Kingdom. *Studies in Conflict and Terrorism*, 36(11), 933–951.

Neumann, P. R. (2008). Introduction. In Perspectives on Radicalisation and Political Violence. Paper presented at the First International Conference on Radicalisation and Political Violence. London: International Centre for the Study of Radicalisation and Political Violence. http://icsr.info/wp-content/uploads/2012/10/1234516938ICSRPerspectivesonRadicalisation.pdf.

Neumann, P. R. (2013). The Trouble with Radicalization. *International Affairs*, 89(4), 873–893. doi:10.1111/1468-2346.1204.

Orofino, E. (2020a). Framing, New Social Identity and Long-Term Loyalty. Hizb ut-Tahrir's Impact on its Members. *Social Movement Studies*, 1–18. doi:10.1080/14742837.2020.1722629.

Orofino, E. (2020b). *Hizb ut-Tahrir and the Caliphate: Why the Group is Still Appealing to Muslims in the West*. London: Routledge.

Pearson, E. (2020). Gendered Reflections? Extremism in the UK's Radical Right and al-Muhajiroun Networks. *Studies in Conflict & Terrorism*, 1–24. doi:10.1080/1057610X.2020.1759270.

Perry, D. L. (2018). *The Global Muslim Brotherhood in Britain: Non-Violent Islamist Extremism and the Battle of Ideas*. London: Routledge.

Pew Research Centre. (2014). Religious Hostilities Reach Six-Year High. Retrieved from www.pewforum.org/2014/01/14/religious-hostilities-reach-six-year-high/.

Rosenthal, R. (2019, November 1). Is Buddhism Violent? Lion's Roar. Retrieved from www.lionsroar.com/buddhism-violence/.

Ruby, C. L. (2002). The Definition of Terrorism. *Analyses of Social Issues and Public Policy*, 2(1), 9–14.

Sageman, M. (2004). *Understanding Terror Networks*. Philadelphia: University of Pennsylvania Press.

Sewell, A., & Hulusi, H. (2016). Preventing Radicalisation to Extreme Positions in Children and Young People. What does the Literature Tell us and should Educational Psychology respond? *Educational Psychology in Practice*, 32(4), 343–354. doi:10.1080/02667363.2016.1189885.

Smith, D., & Talbot S. (2019). How to make Enemies and influence People: A Social Influence Model of Violent Extremism (SIM-VE). *Journal of Policing, Intelligence and Counter Terrorism*, 14(2), 99–114. doi:10.1080/18335330.2019.1575973.

U.S. Department of State. (2004). *International Religious Freedom Report: Sri Lanka.* Retrieved from https://2009-2017.state.gov/j/drl/rls/irf/2004/35520.htm.

Wali, F. (2013). *Radicalism Unveiled.* Farnham: Ashgate.

Whitespunner, B. (2018). Islamists can't be allowed freedom of speech. *The Telegraph.*

Wiktorowicz, Q. (2005). *Radical Islam rising: Muslim Extremism in the West.* Lanham, Boulder, Toronto, Oxford: Rowman & Littlefield.

PART 1

Between Extremisms

Violence and Non-violence across Multiple Ideologies

PART I

1

STICKY IDEOLOGIES AND NON-VIOLENT HETERODOX POLITICS

Daniel Baldino and Mark Balnaves

Introduction

Extremism is not a single movement. Yet what consists of "left" or "right" has become a more indistinct and contentious task in navigating different subcultures and the undercurrents of mistrust and grievance within extremist landscapes.

In particular, it will be argued that a blurred-lined polarity is emerging that is in no way "traditional". In linking radicalisation to both non-violent antisocial and violent behaviour, the creation and transition of interpretations of conceptions such as "sovereign" citizenship will continue to be increasingly relevant in academic and political debates especially in terms of preventative and intervention measures. Such debate will need to incorporate ways to break down conspiracy theories, the nature, adaptability and depth of online transnational associations and how existing counter-terrorism policy approaches might be reformed in the context of new forms of extremism in which static political boundaries have broken down.

The spread of Sovereign Citizen movement (SCM) – solidified around a notion that individuals are not bound to obey law and that government is an illegitimate, fraudulent corporate entity – will be used as an overarching case study to illustrate the parameters of this extremist challenge and the incorporation of related ideas like "leaderless resistance" in dealing with components of non-violent anti-government extremist belief. Yet adding another level of complexity, while not only has the study of non-violent extremists repeatedly been overlooked, the liminality between violent and non-violent extremism and the mobilisation to violence remains properly understood. As such, the chapter attempts to explain the cross-border dynamics of radicalisation, the overlap among Sovereign Citizen (SC) ideologies to justify behavioural patterns and the shift to trajectories that bind members and potentially rationalise the use of violence.

Indeed, the authors aim to identify and highlight new types of reasoning and related cognitive bias associated with radicalisation within growing anti-government and anti-establishment movements. Critically, this study argues the emergence of certain "sticky" ideologies, facilitated by misinformation and conspiracy theories via social media platforms, which can shape offline identity and behaviour around extreme ideas. The term "sticky" is used to refer to a worldview that can unite often isolated members and that is perversely persistent and resistant to rationality. Such "sticky" narratives of denialism and anti-government ideology are not necessarily

DOI: 10.4324/9781003032793-3

coherent in the conventional way of thinking and can be seen as a larger part of the challenges of a "post-truth" world.

So while counter terrorism discourse has been consumed, quite rightly, by violent threats from extreme right-wing groups and religious zealots, there has been little focus on the rise of a strange mix of non-violent subcultures with fluid identities that breach common starting points for understanding the role of ideology and the spread of ideological extremism. Idiosyncratic connections can mobilise online while conspiracy theories can oscillate between "right" and "left". Additionally, the expression "sticky ideology" emphasises the fact while anti-statist narratives might be incongruous, paradoxical and fall into a variety of fallacies, if individuals are committed to self-empowerment (even if symbolic) and self-actualisation in order to deliver some perceived freedom from the jurisdiction of all laws, it does not matter if SC belief systems are inconsistent and rooted in cognitive dissonance.

Critically, SCs are not predominantly violent, they are not a rigid hierarchical group and no formal membership is required. The language and the actions of SCs, though, have become part of the lexicon and actions of individuals outside the United States where it originated. This form of radicalisation is difficult to analyse precisely because it is diffuse and can be found in a 13-year-old girl in court refusing to give her name on the grounds she is a "SC" to a retired farmer clogging the court with meaningless litigation using very specific sovereign language. As such, the authors argue that the extremist landscape in contemporary industrial societies has become much more fragmented. The authors also present a pilot investigative ethnographic approach that might assist in analysing these new styles of reasoning, in part, to better understand processes and conditions in which an individual might assume an anti-government identity.

In regard to methodology, the authors' pilot work on this phenomenon extends the work of Kreissl (2018). It proposes an investigative digital ethnography methodology that keeps close to the idiom of the subject practices, including recognition of different kinds and styles of thinking as well as the value of language register, in particular, communicative situations. In order to understand the idiom of the subject practices, that is, the actual people being studied, it is important to understand the language, or register, of a style of reasoning (both formal and informal). At the very least, the complex history and trajectory of the SCM since the 1970s does suggest a different and distinctive challenge from a policy prevention and mitigation perspective, including diverse and novel connections between conventional and unconventional politics as well as progressions of ideological fragmentation.

The first part of this chapter demonstrates that highly decentralised radical movements are emerging that are not tied to a single alliance. They cut across ideological, demographic or geographic profiles. Moreover, the belief systems of those who identify with these movements are based on adaptive and even incongruous ideas that do not necessarily result from specific personality traits or purely psychological mechanisms. The concept of styles of reasoning is raised to demonstrate that heterodox personal and political transformation can be tied to the construction of identity that is rooted in social relations and distinctive styles of reasoning (seen as organising concepts that will shape behavioural patterns).

The second part of the chapter presents the authors' pilot investigative digital ethnography, created as a counterpoint to methodological individualistic approaches to extremism. The methodology focuses on language, register and styles of reasoning (both formal and informal) at idiographic, micro and nomothetic (macro) levels. Pilot data are drawn from analysis of Facebook, Reddit and Instagram, displaying new types of innovative movements that lack an ethnic, political and cultural cohesiveness. The mapping of this ecology of the platforms exposes a sharing and co-opting of extremist language linked to a hybrid ideological anti-statist sentiment. The methodological challenge is to avoid mischaracterisation and misclassification of these heterodox groups precisely because their anti-government patterns and connections are radically different from other types of extremist behaviour and, indeed, language.

Conspiratorial Narratives and Anti-government Movements

Given a fluctuating climate of widespread mistrust in the representative mediation of politics, SCs and equivalent variations such as "constitutionalists" and "freemen" are paradigm examples of movements whose language, having emerged on the margins in the 1970s, is now moving into popular culture. SCs do not believe they are subject to federal, state or local law nor any partnered regulations, or only so far as they choose to interpret it. Most SCM activity is non-violent; many of those who act violently (as explored below) do not necessarily have an explicit "grand plan" in place (Meyer, 2017).

Notably, in March 2021 at a Senate Judiciary Committee hearing, FBI Director Christopher Wray testified that terrorism has been "metastasizing" into "blended ideologies" (Mallin and Barr, 2021). Wray explained that

> One of the things that we struggle with … is that more and more the ideologies … that are motivating some of these violent extremists are less and less coherent, less and less linear and less and less easier to pin down …. And in some cases it seems like people [are] coming up with their own sort of customized belief systems and people are maybe combined with some kind of personal grievance (Mallin and Barr, 2021).

At the very least, the complex history and trajectory of the SCM since the 1970s does suggest a different and distinctive challenge from a policy prevention and mitigation perspective, including diverse and novel connections between conventional and unconventional politics. Such breaking away from established democratic norms and the adoption of antisocial behaviour aligned with elements of multiple and even contradictory ideologies – including the production of a spider web of conspiracy theories – can feed into extremist ways of thinking about and interpreting threatening events or situations (Malkki and Sinkkonen, 2016; Wimelius et al., 2018).

The Annual Societal Security Report (Kreissl, 2018, p. 2) devised the term "heterodox (or alternative) politicisation" to describe its findings in 2018 from an analysis of online groups which shared many anti-government, anti-establishment and anti-elite features. While not forming a homogenous movement, these ad hoc groups and actors nonetheless shared a set of common ideas: all of them rejected the state and its institutions and refused any form of cooperation with government authorities, yet they appropriated often bizarre quasi-legal language to prosecute their ideas. The report found that an individual might initially align to an alt-right, left, ecological or other political or social movement but then move and mix between them, "creating a network of different and highly heterogeneous communities" (Kreissl, 2018, p. 12). Some of these alignments seem paradoxical, at best.

There are approximately 300,000 to 500,000 SC activists in the United States alone (Sarteschi, 2020, p. 2). Moreover, the SCM ideology, and changing notions of citizenship, are not limited to the United States; such belief systems are steadily gaining popularity in other democratic countries including Australia (Freemen on the Land), Germany (Reichsbürgers) and the United Kingdom (Lawful Rebellion). For instance, anti-government rage in Australia has found its expression in themes such as nationhood, taxation and legitimacy, with a core claim being that the Commonwealth of Australia was not properly federated in 1901, and hence, all of its subsequent actions are unlawful (McGowan, 2020). Analysis of digital ethnographic heterogeneous movements, such as SCs who might believe themselves to be exempt from all laws, also indicates ideologically motivated cognition as a form of information processing that can cut across established dichotomies of left and right. The contours of this dilemma were captured by a US law enforcement agency in stating that the term "SC" "… should be viewed as an umbrella under which you will find thousands of loosely organised groups or individuals that share one basic ideological principle [e.g. that laws do not apply to them] but approach it through different paths" (Finch and Flowers, 2012).

aProponents of these new forms and radical narratives of political protest and activity often exhibit a sense of disenfranchisement, disempowerment and a victim mentality (Kundnani, 2012). But while such individuals and groups might share characteristic styles of reasoning, their focus is wide and somewhat haphazard. Of course, streams of discourse can entail legitimate political questions ranging from income inequality to government corruption. But such grievances can simultaneously be fuelled by misinformation and co-exist among a spider web of conspiracy theories that rejects both traditional politics and the democratic process.

So heterodox groups like SCs will draw on a pool of unsubstantiated claims and manipulative narratives to rationalise their prescriptions that can oscillate from left-wing anti-capitalism to right-wing, radical anti-semitism to materialist economic analysis to transcendental spiritualism. In their efforts to better understand underlying human values and motivations, Gartenstein-Ross and Blackman (2019) have named as "fringe fluidity" this tendency of individuals to drift between ideologies. In other words, such a mindset, even if based on dubious or unreliable or contradictory assumptions, is related to a mistrust of authority (or experts) and can generate different goals, aims and methods among subgroups; anti-government movements that are interconnected through "articles of faith", a state of personal anxiety and recurrently dystopian type scenarios.

An example is the promotion of the "Great Reset" theory related to climate change which dismisses sustainability and renewable energy initiatives as part of a secret elite agenda for global domination and control. "The nebulousness of this conspiracy theory means it has found followers among anti-vaccine activists, anti-lockdown campaigners, new-age healers, and those on the far right and far left" (BBC News, 2021). Or as captured by George Monbiot (2021), "…this synthesis of left-alternative and right-wing cultures has been accelerated by despondency, confusion and betrayal". As mentioned, the SCM can be exposed as comprising a sticky ideology with its anti-government platforms drawing on a mixture of conspiracy theories, constitutional reinterpretations and alternative versions of history that populate the internet. The process for an SC to formulate a rebuttal to a law, for instance, has been described as follows:

> …start by looking for a combination of quotes, definitions, court cases, the Bible, Internet websites, and so on that justify how you can ignore the disliked law without any legal consequences. Be imaginative. Pull a line from the 1215 version of the Magna Carta, a definition from a 1913 legal dictionary, a quote from a founding father or two, and put it in the blender with some official-sounding Supreme Court case excerpts you found on like-minded websites. Better yet, find someone else online who disliked that same law and pay them $150 for a three-ring binder filled with their word salad research.
>
> *(MacNab, 2012)*

Certainly, disinformation, belief in conspiracy theories and susceptibility to propaganda may be bracketed with increased radicalised and extremist behaviour (van Prooijen and Acker, 2015).

And again, while the SC anti-government worldview does not overtly promote nor explicitly support political violence, a current lack of consensus does exist as to how SCM individuals might move from simply having feelings of powerlessness or resentment towards action, for example, accepting violence as a necessary mode of political struggle (see Stephens et al., 2021). At the same time, the SCM and many of its co-opted ideas do remain distinct in that they are not tied to an acknowledged central leader and they lack a robust and obvious organisational structure.

Nonetheless, the internet provides a critically important platform for SCs to share ideological resources (including by means of encrypted messaging) and access opportunities for social connections that strengthen in-group identification and help transcend the barriers presented by physical distance. In short, the internet allows previously alienated and disaffected people to find and connect with each other. It also provides a space for those looking for acceptance, recognition and a sense of approval. Problematically, as information is often unfiltered and unfounded, some of the most extreme forms of dialogue, comprising dehumanising and hateful ideas, can target biases which then become self-reinforcing and normalised in offering a target to blame for various perceived ills (see Baldino and Lucas, 2018). At the very least, the internet has clearly changed the way in which individuals interpret (and/or participate in) social life and has been a medium acting to accelerate a polarised political discourse fuelled by misinformation.

Nonetheless, how to recognise and connect different indicators as predictors of radicalisation that might lead to acts of violence – such as push, pull and personal factors – remains a contested and controversial topic within Critical Terrorism Studies (Vergani et al., 2020).

As a starting point, social media sites that encourage individuals to embrace particular styles of reasoning, biases and organising concepts which contribute to radicalisation and related fallacies are part of a highly toxic ecosystem that has proven able to bring together like-minded citizens and extremist groups, especially in backdrops of insecurity and disempowerment. This "melting pot" includes those with strong militant and "patriot" platforms (who, for example, perceive the US Constitution's Second Amendment – the right to keep and bear arms – as a safeguard against tyranny). It has also been argued that militant extremists in locations such as the United States may be gaining popular support and new recruits (including younger and older SCs) by espousing alternative realities that play on fears about the government becoming a totalitarian force (Grisham, 2021).

A number of de-radicalisation strategies are based on the underlying assumption that thought comes before action (see Stephens and Sieckelinck, 2020). Various Counter Violent Extremism (CVE) models consequently focus on education as a panacea, preventing people from developing anti-democratic views and beliefs in the usefulness of violence, or from developing a particular ideology that, for example, spreads hate and encourages harm. For instance, UNESCO (2017, p. 36) has proposed that civics and global citizenship education "is particularly relevant to foster learners' resilience to exclusionary worldviews that pit one group against another". So concepts such as "democratic resilience" have been favoured as a means of protection against radicalisation and have provided a regular basis for policy frameworks for the prevention of violence. The following is an example:

> A somewhat different strand of thought, yet still within the general orientation of building resilient individuals, is the focus on the promoting or strengthening of certain values or ideas. Rather than focusing on traits or characteristics, this strand of thinking builds on the underlying assumption that the attraction of an extremist ideology or group can be assuaged through holding to a stronger, alternative framework of values.

> Most prominently advanced in this regard is the notion of citizenship and human rights.
>
> *(Stephens et al., 2021, p. 349)*

Of course, such CVE frameworks to withstand forces of radicalisation should be carefully calibrated in order to address the problems related to reactionary violence and the rise of a strange mix of subcultures with fluid identities. But it can also be argued that anti-democracy groupings like SCs do offer a unique challenge in this CVE space. One noteworthy feature of past counter-terrorism work is that of "cultural competence", which is defined as an attitude or a willingness to understand that each individual brings his or her own explanatory model of the world to a relationship or interaction, and that this explanatory model has been shaped by the particular culture from which they come (Wimelius et al., 2018). The European Commission (2016, p. 11) stated that "combatting social exclusion and discrimination, and promoting social justice and protection are objectives of the EU in their own right. Such societies should prove to be more resilient to the threats of violent extremism".

This brand of integrative framework corresponds with efforts to foster bridging social capital within a community in order to build relationships of trust. It can incorporate the promotion of social cohesion and tolerance as well as supporting social bonding to help communities develop their capacity to resist radicalisation. Contemporary practices in resilience-building are especially influenced by notions of tension existing between traditional ideas of multiculturalism and broader social cohesion. In short, much current literature tends to frame resilience within the context of multicultural and pluralist societies, with a focus on how ethno-cultural minorities navigate their host cultures whilst retaining their cultures of origin (Ellis and Abdi, 2017; Grossman et al., 2017). Various government policies have echoed this sort of ethno-racial framing to prevent and tackle extremism with explicit and persistent references to multiculturalism, diversity and social cohesion in official policies; and clear funding focus on multiculturally oriented programming as part of wider community resilience building activities (see Australian Government, 2018).

This is perhaps an inevitable result of the fact that much work in CVE has been heavily focussed on Islamic extremism, especially post 9/11, and conceivably more recently on white Supremacy. While it is not the position of this chapter to evaluate the appropriateness of all such programming, this clear policy and discursive inclination does present a fresh issue: since current ideas of "community" and "culture" are primarily defined along racial, religious and ethnic lines, this leads to a potential blind spot as it relates to groupings like SCs. As noted, the SCM is not neatly organised along traditional racial or ethnic lines and does appear to have fundamentally different concepts of both community and culture, constructs that are at the core of resilience work in this space. In other words, if prevention of SCM violence is to become a priority for counter-extremism policy and programming, central concepts such as "community" and "culture" will need to be expanded. Policy agendas focused on the prevention of violence will therefore need to take into account the anti-statist SC vision of citizen or community as well as the creation of alternative identities that embrace self-governing practices with the crafting of alternative governments.

As a starting point, in efforts to understand (and disrupt) permissive environments and radicalisation vectors for extremists, and in express relation to the push factors for SCs (personal beliefs and societal circumstances that push individuals into extremist groups), the Anti-Defamation League (2012) has identified some broad organisational classifications. While the default structure of the SCM does remain that of a large mass of individuals or loosely aligned and informal/ad hoc groups, in efforts to map profiles and patterns, identifiable groupings have been considered and classed as follows:

1 People who are financially stressed. Whether the stress is due to unemployment, bankruptcy, creditors, spousal or child support, tax problems or something else, the desperation and anxiety that comes with financial troubles can be powerful motivators.
2 Hard-core and grievance-fuelled ideologues who are angry and hostile at government, including government regulation. This may relate to belief in a "Deep State" – that is, a supposed cabal of powerful, unelected bureaucrats secretly pursuing their own malevolent agenda.
3 Con artists and grifters who aim to exploit and monetise anti-government sentiment. The SC movement is full of theories that promise people quick riches or other seemingly miraculous benefits, from being able to eliminate a mortgage to being able to hide one's income in a series of trusts and make it immune to government scrutiny (Anti-Defamation League 2012, 6–8).

Given that SCs build identities and theories based, in part, on idiosyncratic interpretations and circumstances, behavioural patterns and methods of anti-government protest have been highly mixed. Yet a number of tracks are characteristic of the SCM. For example, SCs have a record of opposing components of procedural democracy and relying on pseudo-legal language, discredited legal arguments and esoteric legislative loopholes in order to drive conduct, as well as taking action to hound or demonise public officials, to avoid taxes and to obstruct law enforcement. It is not uncommon for SCs to initiate vexatious litigation by filing reams of paperwork and nonsensical documents directed at government bodies (Wilson, 2016). This so-called "paper terrorism"' is the use of financial instruments such as frivolous tax returns and bogus liens in retaliation against government employees and law enforcement (Challacombe and Lucas, 2019). According to Fleishman (2004, p. 9), "even a simple traffic stop can ripen into years of legal battles with parties who do not recognise the authority of local government". In prosecuting such campaigns, SCs tend to rely on warped forms of jargon, hyphens, decrees, codes and symbols – all purportedly to ensure freedom from government control as well as a sort of magic diction formula to guarantee financial or legal rescue (Sharrock, 2011).

Sovereign anti-government lore and language have proven to be both highly alluring and adaptive. This may be despite the fact that they borrow from a hodgepodge of ideological and conspiratorial narratives, or because of it. And such decentralised models and groupings tend to

> either subscribe to an elitist model, defining their body politic as comprised of the few enlightened individuals, excluding all others, or they strive for a completely new state order, emulating a full-blown blueprint of the existing institutional set-up, though with new heterodox metaphysics.
>
> *(Kreissl, 2018, pp. 15–16).*

Interestingly, such emerging forms of grassroots political activism aligned by rejecting the basic legitimacy and constitutional principles of democratic governance have found shape in both secular-based lifestyles and religious conflations – like Christian Identity adherents.

For instance, some elements of the SCM aim to meld the defence of the US Constitution with promotion of the Bible and white Christian identity, or assert that individual rights derive from God rather than government (Parker, 2014). Alternatively, newer anti-government

SCM groups have witnessed an appropriation of ideology and tactics by a wide assortment of non-white demographic groups including indigenous groups or African American Moorish movements (see Sarteschi, 2020). In addition, other mobilisations appear to be drawn from the incorporation of SC ideologies that blend with analogous "Deep State" perspectives and retain a high-frequency conspiratorial and paranoid orientation. This includes the more recent social media-inspired ideologically motivated extremist movements groups like QAnon, in which established democratic norms are seen as negotiable or even irrelevant (Cosentino, 2020). All of these groupings with changing demographics consolidate around alternative practices of self-empowerment beyond or outside the existing institutional (political and economic) structures.

As mentioned, it has been argued that SC tactics in claiming "independent" living or the creation of parallel governments have largely tended to be more litigious than violent (Meyer, 2017). However, lines can be blurred and some SC tactics do overlap with those of "citizen" militia movements, including the use of offensive forms of violence in the expectation that citizens will have to remain hyper-vigilant in order to confront government treachery and impending violence. It is of course difficult to determine the precise ideological motivations behind human conduct. Non-violent grievances, nuisance activities and low-level criminal histories might or might not represent a precursor for pre-attack violent behaviours although such individuals might all share a dislike for law enforcement and government agencies and authorities. At the same time, research reveals that disproportionately cracking down on political movements and protest, with, for instance, "hard" coercive actions, can push non-violent members into the arms of more violent extremists (see Waldman, 2016).

In linking radicalisation to violent behaviour, the creation and transition of extreme interpretations of citizenship do remain pertinent. It is clear that some SCs have gravitated to "cherry-picking" anti-government justifications to cause political or social change and justify the use of threats and force. One of the most notorious examples of a domestic terrorist attack is Terry Nichols who helped plan the Oklahoma City bombing in 1995 that killed 168 people and wounded hundreds of others (Conroy, 2017). Nicholas was affiliated with the SCM. Other similar violence incidents have been directly linked to the more paranoid conspiracists who invoke "warfighting" or apocalyptic rationalisations to validate their rage. For example, white-power groups have long promised a catastrophic race war. Such "accelerationist ideologies" "… promise a moment when the institutions of government, society and the economy will be wiped out in a wave of catastrophic violence, clearing the way for a utopia that will supposedly follow" (Taub and Bennhold, 2021).

In efforts to counteract susceptibility to violent extremist ideologies, the fact that some acts of violence by SCs have been at times portrayed as the doings of "lone actors" should not discount sources of anxiety and disempowerment as well as online (and offline) lessons about how an individual's status can become fused with an identity-based anti-government narrative (Challacombe and Lucas, 2019). Interestingly, in relation to violent and lethal incidents, a 2015 Department of Homeland Security (DHS) intelligence assessment contended that SCM motivations and tactics do in fact diverge from those of other violent extremists and militia groups in that such attacks are generally reactive, unplanned and personal, rather than strategic, political and symbolic (DHS, 2015, p. 4).

The report added that other, traditional domestic terrorists were differentiated as more capable and typically involved in premeditated attacks of opportunity in order to spread a wider political (or religious) message. Among the findings of the intelligence assessment was that SC violence "… will occur most frequently during routine law enforcement encounters at a suspect's home, during enforcement stops and at government offices" (DHS, 2015, p. 3). The report added that "law enforcement officers will remain the primary target of (SC) violence over the next year due to their role in physically enforcing laws and regulations" (DHS, 2015, p. 3). So the central concern was that an SCM adherent might resort to spontaneous, impulsive acts of violence when confronted, for example, by law enforcement during a standard engagement like a traffic stop. Based on this Homeland Security evaluation, it may be that the SCM has expanded from a nuisance or quirky irritant to a more dangerous, unconventional threat to law and order in the United States and elsewhere. In sum, the ability of CVE programs to partition between anti-statist political views and a transition to more aggressive and proactive violent anti-government behaviour does remain a highly difficult and challenging task.

Styles of Reasoning

At first glance, the diverse SCM might appear to be a problem that is straightforwardly linked to pathology. It has been argued that there are particular personality types that tend to reason in a paranoid and conspiratorial way. Lewandowsky and Cook's (2020) *The Conspiracy Theory Handbook* asserts that a person may draw on apocalyptic thinking or non-evidence-based reasoning because they have feelings of powerlessness, propose highly unlikely events to handle uncertainty, cope with threatening events by using unrelated events to give unsubstantiated cause and dispute mainstream politics to give themselves an empowering identity that plays off emotions. The goal of information gathering is to reaffirm feelings or sentiments and to create a sense of purpose, security and control to satisfy important psychological needs.

The Debunking Handbook 2020 (Lewandowsky et al., 2020) also argues that particular sequences of argument can change a person's worldview and explain a general "conspiracy mindset" that impacts on higher order belief systems and interpretations of evidence. For instance, conspiracy theories may be deployed as a rudimentary rhetorical tool to escape inconvenient conclusions or in order to preserve beliefs in the face of uncertainty. This might include a model associated with epistemic motives (Lewandowsky et al., 2020, p, 12):

> Lead with the fact if it's clear, pithy, and sticky – make it simple, concrete, and plausible. It must "fit" with the story. Warn beforehand that a myth is coming... mention it once only. Explain how the myth misleads. Finish by reinforcing the fact—multiple times if possible. Make sure it provides an alternative causal explanation.

The authors do not doubt that there is significant and valuable cognitive science research behind the proposed model. However, there are some shortcomings with this methodological individualism and an all-purpose reliance on individualist cognitivist construction – at the very least, it can be argued that there is a diversity of kinds and styles of thinking. Belief systems – and an erosion of trust in the truth – based on adaptive and even incongruous ideas can result from other factors, not simply tied to personality traits and purely psychological mechanisms.

Let us take, for example, Carl Jung, the famous psychologist and psychiatrist, and his style of reasoning on Jews:

> The Jew, who is something of a nomad, has never yet created a cultural form of his own and as far as we can see never will, since all his instincts and talents require a more or less civilized nation to act as a host for their development... The Aryan consciousness has a higher potential than the Jewish; that is both the advantage and the disadvantage of a youthfulness not yet fully weaned from barbarism.
>
> *(Jung, 1934, p. 165)*

In many cases, it can be argued that the organising concepts of a style of reasoning have nothing to do with traditional pathology. It is worthwhile looking briefly at Hesse's (1963) and Hacking's (1982) ideas on analogy to clarify how inferential relations and styles of reasoning work. For Hesse (1963, p. 65), an analogy exists between two objects because of their common properties. In the example below, the vertical relation, sculptor and statue have a causal relationship. We can observe that a sculptor can create a statue. The relation between God and the world, however, is tentative in science, a model and not a theory. There is a horizontal relationship of similarities between the idea of sculptor and God as a creator.

Inductive, deductive and abductive reasoning are established organising concepts in science.[1] In the case of God and the world, people accept that abductive reasoning – the fair guess – can apply given a person's experience. It is not unreasonable to propose the existence of God. Such styles of reasoning are held by cultures and by communities who select and accept particular standards of evidence to stimulate actions. Such organising concepts are also "essential to the very functioning of our society. We are stuck with them, which is not to say … that they are not changing as I speak" (Hacking, 1982, p. 65).

It can be argued that despite the often incomprehensible jargon in which it is expressed, the SCM does have a style of (problematic) reasoning and demonstrates an overlap of interactive and hybrid discourses, that places an emphasis on integrative styles of reasoning that can inform and reinforce radical judgements. Alternatively, cognitive scientists tend to provide ahistorical and a-cultural reductive models to distinguish between those who are thinking "normally" and those who are not (see Lewandowsky et al., 2020, p. 3).

The above illustrates a core point about abductive logic (the fair guess) – that individuals, even including scientists, can put together links in a chain of evidence that are not obvious or that are too simplistic. The cognitive science organising model is not suitable at adequately incorporating abductive logic in reasoning. Indeed, it can be argued that what counts as a "fact" or what should be seen as "plausible" is not perpetually self-evident – facts are capable of multiple interpretations and there are styles of reasoning behind language that are constantly changing and are being developed and refined and filtered over time.

Similarly, alternative explanations of anti-establishment attitudes that weaken traditional democratic bonds and norms come out in the work of Kreissl (2018). New patterns of association, social action and communicative processes are emerging in the information environment that can create hasty generalisations and adaptive and adhesive anti-government expressions in the search to categorise a well-defined enemy. For example,

> [A] closer look at the patchwork of ideological narratives circulating in the realm of heterodox discourses reveals a kind of family resemblance and one can find a number of *common themes* across our sample of groups that seem to have very little in common at first glance.
>
> *(Kreissl, 2018, p. 14).*

Methodology: "Order at All Points" in Investigative Digital Ethnography

Styles of reasoning do matter in studying monistic extremist anti-government beliefs (including ideas that the government is an illegitimate corporation exploiting its citizens as collateral for its debts) in specific contexts. These types of virtual (and physical) connections have provided an array of eclectic individuals with an opportunity to loosely coordinate activities, to share propaganda, to promote pseudo-legal tactics and to potentially harden extremist viewpoints that rationalise a refutation of the existing political and legal order.

The expression "order at all points" in social interaction comes from Harvey Sacks (1992, p. 62). It describes an important aspect of human culture – that a precise style of reasoning found in one person's account can often be generalised to a whole group or culture.[2] The reference to Carl Jung, above, is a good example. Anti-Semitic statements take a particular manner and there are direct as well as indirect implications in the creation and maintenance of a social order. Conventional thinking does not exist independent of the community in which it is nurtured and accepted. Moving people from conspiratorial thinking to conventional thinking is not simply a scientific matter but also a matter of interactional routes and the product of strategies of persuasion that will influence an individual's beliefs, attitudes, norms and values (which, as argued, have their own organising concepts).

Various types of persuasion have the ability to convince people to produce motivated judgements in distinctive ways. An argument that appeals to authority or credibility or character can play a highly suggestive role in contemporary debate that attempts to debunk non-scientific thinking. As an example, most people would not fully understand the mathematics behind climate science research; simpler explanations are given to citizens as proxies to the mathematical lines of analysis. The authority of scientists is used to confirm those proxy explanations. Such argument by authority, of course, is itself a style of reasoning – the acceptance that certain people or groups in society represent "trust" as a foundation of a stable and democratic society. Indeed, Misztal (2001) identified three critical functions performed by trust in a working of democracy: (1) it makes social life more predictable, (2) it creates a sense of community and (3) it makes it easier for people to work together.

Organising concepts and styles of reasoning in a culture can be captured ethnographically. Friedberg (2020) proposes an investigative digital ethnography to better understand the foundations and spread of disinformation campaigns, the dynamic back and forth between humans and networked communication technologies and how this discursive relationship challenges social institutions. It is an "order at all points" methodology because what is captured is intended to clearly represent a specific phenomenon of different heterodox groups marked by distinct rituals, beliefs and cultural production that can co-exist and interact within a value orientation that rejects basic principles of democratic governance.

Once more, Kreissl's (2018) study provides an important opening to, in part, study long-term sociotechnical phenomena because it gives an indication of what the new organising concepts, and modes of persuasive techniques, might entail analysing disinformation at scale. Kreissl's (2018) approach included investigating the intersect of shared contacts, likes, share and comment between the Facebook accounts in Austria of individuals belonging to a range of SC and alternative media accounts. Further, Kreissl's (2018) study highlights a divergent range of interest groups and links to a variety of political ideologies audiences that are sharing within larger ideological and political networks.

The use of clusters of overlapping likes, share and comments between different association or cause type by Kreissl (2018, p. 35) illustrates a certain range of heterodox interests and indicates the potential ideologies linked to them – which usually are not neatly aligned. In investigating the degree and quality of links between audiences in respect to the reception of and interaction with SC accounts, Kreissl's conclusion (2018) is that:

> all of these groups aspire to alternative (or heterodox) practices of self-empowerment beyond or outside the existing institutional (political and economic) structures. This

can take on the form of creating new independent "states" by declaration, claiming independent and sovereign territories, developing forms of self-sustained, rural communal living in remote areas or simply expressing discontent with the existing political system through robust and innovative forms of collective action (like not paying taxes and fines).

2018, p. 15

If a concept like self-empowerment is the organising concept, it is not surprising that an individual might join any grouping that could assist them in gaining agency in their life choices and/or that acknowledges (real or perceived) unfair and one-sided treatment. Such a scenario can create and encourage a sense of fellow-feeling, identity and unity, even if the specific areas of grievance spawn and fluctuate. Such in-group social mobilisation can take place even if behavioural choices are illegal and contest against an out-group like law enforcement or government officials. Given radicalisation is a social process, an enabling group ecosystem can provide a potent social and emotional stimulus for making distinctions between "us" and "them" and simplistically attributing blame to those responsible for wrongdoing (i.e. governments through their various functions and/or ethnic and other minority groups) while offering justifications for antisocial behaviour in the name of provocations, liberty and self-defence. "The theme of 'salvation' through 'regaining consciousness' is featured in an esoteric outlet … while sharing, an affinity with more mundane techniques of self-help/-optimization" (Kreissl, 2018, p. 37).

US Federal air marshal Paul Steward 42, is a good example of motivated reasoning and how anti-government SC ideas can "stick" to everyday practices. Stewart was caught riding his Sea-Doo watercraft on the Susquehanna River in Maryland without registration. He was given three citations. Steward did not pay the fines, with his lawyer arguing in court filings that the prosecutors were "foreign agents" and the court was a "private corporation". Stewart also claimed the rights of legal defiance in stating that the judge did not have any power of attorney over him. Despite a strong in-group SC identity and a mirroring of SC tactics, his lawyer also argued that Stewart had never associated or been affiliated with any group aligned with any "SC" movement (Devine, 2020).

Paul Steward had never had a prior criminal conviction, had no mental health issues and was a successful, well-respected air marshall. The idea that Steward would risk his career and reputation on citations in part indicates the difficulties encountered when loosely affiliated individuals and social groups set themselves apart from society by rejecting the legitimacy of the established legal system. In working from an ideological framework that supported activities opposed to the existing political and legal establishment, Steward's words epitomised SC language, including website critiques arguing that the police are not "agents of Common law". He had also cited obscure provisions of commercial law with the bulk of his court filings based on online templates. If we use Hesse's (1963) analogical models, then it is possible to see how horizontal analogies can hold at one level but not vertically:

Self-empowerment (choice)	:	Conventional thinking
I am sovereign		Obey the law and follow the rules

The Steward case is, for the purposes of this chapter, an example of "order at all points". Steward's confrontational anti-government tone, entrenched attitude, position and sense of autonomy together form a profile or persona which is becoming increasingly familiar in defining the parameters of non-violent extremist challenges. Such distrust in governance institutions is adopted by those who wish to exert control over a particular environment that can be found across a wide variety of landscapes based on an individual's own political or social context and related set of grievances.

Similarly, the COVID-19 pandemic offers an ideal case study of the cross-pollination of a wide tangle of conspiracy theories about health and medicine and related false scientific content in the overall context of widespread public uncertainty, confusion and mistrust about existing institutional and governmental mandates.

Significantly, the COVID-19 pandemic laid bare how subsets of social networks can align while also being susceptible to an assemblage of covert, deceptive and misleading online intergroup messaging. This includes conspiratorial theories advanced within self-selected social media networks that offer multilayered and nebulous interpretations of events that can be resistant to disconfirmation (see Douglas, 2021). In the midst of pandemic panic and the push to engage in informed and preventive evidence-based behaviours to limit the spread of COVID, "... increasing connectivity and reliance on information technology is a vulnerability that is being targeted by two key threats: cyber-attacks, and the subversion of our democratic institutions and social cohesion. Both are recognised challenges to ... national security" (Dowse and Bachmann, 2019). Or from another angle of analysis, rejecting evidence and opposition to official policy and health directives can arise from "... distrust towards institutions such as governments, scientists, the media and medical authorities. This distrust drives the belief in a conspiracy and is central to the identity of groups that people already associate with" (Bortolotti and Ichino, 2020).

Anti-vax and the Anti-government Rage Register

Auschwitz survivor Primo Levi once identified propaganda, misinformation and the speed and swiftness of change in the ways that people can interpret cues and data as one of the most fundamental threats to political stability and social cohesion. Reflecting on the backdrop of the Holocaust and the organised extermination of human beings, Levi (1986) observed:

> Among other precautions, in order to keep the secret, only cautious and cynical euphemisms were employed by the official language: one did not write "extermination" but "final solution," not "deportation" but "transfer," not "killing by gas" but "special treatment." Not without reason, Hitler feared that this horrendous news, if it were divulged, would compromise the blind faith that the country had in him, as well as the morale of the fighting troops.

Today, the emergence of a non-violent heterodox politics, along with anti-government identities that can act as an umbrella for multiple conspiracy theories, can encourage acceptance of an illogical reality and actions by citizens that distort moral responsibilities. As mentioned, these heterogeneous groups can encompass fluid identities and a varied demographic base, but these individuals can be brought together by a shared worldview such as the government is a corrupt and illegitimate corporate entity. Examination of SC accounts has revealed that "... the range of concerns they raise links them to both traditionally libertarian and 'left' as well as 'right' modes of critique and politics" (Kreissl, 2018, p. 30). Similarly, recent detailed research by Rozbroj et al. (2019) on Australian anti-vax supporters found that loss of trust in government was a major driver of anti-vax sentiment, with variables such as income levels and age not playing a major role.

Indeed, health-related misinformation has grown exponentially during the COVID-19 pandemic. Anti-vax supporters exemplify how self-empowerment can be deployed as a negative

Table 1.1 Investigative digital ethnography

Investigative digital ethnography	Identify styles of reasoning (idiom of the subject practices)	Idiographic mapping of online participants
Identify topic or artefact Identify media and participants Create a monitoring environment Develop monitoring strategies Audit key assumptions Archive and analyse findings	Organising concepts and analogical thinking Register (field, tenor and mode)	Software that enables retrieval of actual participant's language Simple non-contestable indicators of links between participants or groups

Source: see Kreissl (2018).

right – freedom from interference from others. In rethinking frameworks to examine the large-scale circulation of vaccine-specific misinformation, one of the main Australian anti-vax sites was used by the authors as the pilot study in language and logic that fed into a variety of other linked sites that expanded vaccine misinformation on mainstream social media. The authors' approach, using an investigative ethnography framework, used an idiom of the subject practices as opposed to an idiom of theoretical interpretation or an idiom of cause (why something happened) and effect (what happened). This allowed the authors to stay as close as possible to actual styles of reasoning and avoid translating them into a theoretical language, which Hesse (1963) would count as an error.

In order to understand the idiom of the subject practices, that is, the actual people being studied, it is important to understand the language, or register, of a style of reasoning (both formal and informal). Halliday (1978, p. 110) distinguishes between dialect – what a person says, determined by who they are, and register – what a person says, determined by what they are doing at the time. We therefore need both concepts because they deal with different but related aspects of language. Halliday included in the register the field (subject matter of a situation), its tenor (the relationship of those involved) and mode (the types of communication).

Studying the register of interactions in language that are rooted in social relations provides a precision that generalised categories cannot. Steward is deploying SC language without having the stigma of being labelled, or even self-identifying as, an SC. The authors' methodology, as an extension of Kreissl's (2018) work, is summarised in Table 1.1.

Pilot Data: Facebook, Reddit and Instagram

Facebook provided the authors with access to CrowdTangle, Facebook's research database accessible to approved researchers. The database includes all public Facebook, Reddit and Instagram data, time limited to the last 12 months. CrowdTangle tracks interactions, which is defined as reactions, comments and shares. Interactions are also known as engagement. Table 1.2 shows the overall engagement for the terms "SC", "Anti vax" and "QAnon" for Australia and for all posts. Significant conversations can be generated by only a few posts, as can be seen for SCs, 46,119 interactions – likes, dislikes, commentary, news – against 167 posts on Facebook.

These data keep close to the idiom of the subject practices, actual expressions within the dataset. For the purposes of this paper, the data, which cover those who like or dislike or report on the terms demonstrate scale, how the terms have become a part of public discourse in a very

Table 1.2 Australia and all posts – Facebook, Reddit, Instagram interactions (engagement) – June 2020 to June 2021 – number of posts in brackets

	Facebook	*Reddit*	*Instagram*
"Sovereign Citizens"			
Australia	(46,119: engagement) (167: number of posts in brackets)		
All Posts	715,079 (2,778)	67,583 (584)	218,250 (349)
"Anti-vax"			
Australia	245,541 (930)		
All Posts	4,145,955 (2,045)	2,006,019 (6,056)	4,145,955 (2,045)
"QAnon"			
Australia	611,330 (2,649)		
All Posts	52,237,825 (125,762)	9,594,271 (33,027)	31,728,280 (20,580)

Source: CrowdTangle Team (2020). CrowdTangle. Facebook, Menlo Park, California, United States. Search terms "Sovereign Citizen", "Anti Vax" and "QAnon", 23 June 2021.

short time. The CrowdTangle database allows researchers to see the relevant public posts against which interactions, or engagement, are measured.

The CrowdTangle dataset fits well with the authors' emphasis on a methodology that can go from aggregation to the individual. Table 1.2 demonstrates that:

1 SC, Anti Vax and QAnon cultural phrases have rapidly entered the Australian national conversation;
2 Whether pro or anti, these cultural terms, the language of these conversations is now well known – a part of the register;
3 Posts dealing with the topics clearly generate significant interaction – for example, 167 posts on SCs generated 46,119 interactions between June 2020 and June 2021 on the Australian Facebook.

In terms of scale, the authors have provided "all posts", which is all posts on the specific cultural term, worldwide. QAnon has clearly attracted worldwide attention across Facebook, Reddit and Instagram.

Thus, ethnographic methodology and correlated language and information-focused case studies that spotlight anti-government groups like SCs can be one worthwhile method for situating forms and processes of radicalisation that can capture the complexity of such phenomena. This might be extended to future efforts to incorporate cues for exploring methods to identify, prevent and counter extremist websites and narratives as well aid in the development of behavioural markers as a common language for identifying actions based on ideas such as government must be resisted by any means necessary. Such investigations might also be of value in exploring intra-group process of decision-making and how conceptions of crises (existential or otherwise) can promote a feeling of personal unrest and conspiratorial thinking that can directly threaten democratic institutions – as well as areas like public health. Crucially, such styles of radical citizenship will manifest itself in idiosyncratic and non-static sets of experiences, ideas and tactics – an underlying logic that rejects foundational elements of modern citizenship and has translated into both non-violent and sometimes violent actions to challenge established channels of political power in democratic societies.

Concluding Remarks

When exploring a smorgasbord of independent individual motivations, including those that might stimulate the crafting of alternative histories and pseudo-legal arguments, the process of radicalisation does remain cluttered, non-linear and multifaceted. But the larger SCM is not just an odd aberration or constrained to the United States. It is transnational. Nor should the SCM be dismissed as inconsequential or simply the result of individual pathology.

Extremism is a contentious term. But extremism is also not a single or static movement. And diverse forms of extremism have been spreading into new forms of blended or "sticky" ideology. Notably, extremist ideas today do cross-pollinate, especially online, and intermingle with other distinct and indistinct groupings that might incorporate or co-opt beliefs such as the illegitimacy of governments or hierarchies of superiority that will place individuals in conflict with government authorities. The elevation of new types of "sticky" ideologies can provide a stronger emphasis on the fact that some actors do stick to, or gravitate towards, convenient and opportune ideas suited to a particular political or personal context.

Modes of non-violent radicalisation can take numerous shifting shapes, profiles and varieties and arguably point to an epistemic crisis within modern-day democracies. Additionally, the SCM itself does not have a cohesive and entrenched shared values base: it cuts across demographic clusters and can be drawn into a wide variety of convenient ideologies to rationalise anti-government hostility or suspicion. This decentralised co-opting and melding of extremist ideas is usually underpinned by conspiracy theories about government illegitimacy that are "cherry-picked" and reinforced via easily accessible online discourses. Such interpretations of sovereign doctrine can mistakenly be pigeonholed as simply right-wing propaganda but, as the presentation in the above chapter suggests, it is far more complex and nuanced.

The term "sticky" ideology implies how anti-statist individuals and heterodox groups share rumours and misinformation and have a propensity to attach to extreme but fuzzy and shallow ideas, many of which are contradictory, inconsistent and grounded on pseudo-legal and pseudo-historical assumptions. Part of the CVE policy challenge relates to the ubiquity of misinformation online as well as the emergence of new ways of thinking in which citizens from a variety of backgrounds are becoming less democratic in their foundational thinking and less trusting of established legal and political institutions. In linking radicalisation to antisocial or violent behaviour, the creation and transition of extreme interpretations of notions such as citizenship will continue to be increasingly pertinent in blueprints for social cohesion as well as threat assessments. Emerging and evolving cases of heterodox politicisation do, at the very least, indicate a weakening of traditional political and social bonds within democratic countries and a rise in non-violent extremism ideology that transcends traditional right- and left-wing categorisation.

Acknowledgement

Thanks to Naomi Shiffman at CrowdTangle for her assistance and good sense of humour. Thanks also to the expert work of Claire Williams, professional editor, www.linkedin.com/in/claire-williams-412a632a/?originalSubdomain=au.

Notes

1 Deduction starts with a general hypothesis and examines the possibilities to reach a specific and precise conclusion. Inductive reasoning is the opposite of deductive reasoning and will make broad generalizations from specific observations such as pattern recognition. Finally, abductive reasoning is to

make an assumption from the information that is known and to "best guess" a conclusion based on the available evidence.

2 In the context of this analysis, interactions are regarded as methodical and organised. When we hear a person deploying the language of Sovereign Citizens, we do not need to do a survey or construct a statistical sample to find out what that language signifies. "I am a Sovereign Citizen. I will not pay my parking ticket because I have no contract with the government" is "order at all points". No matter where a person hears it or from whomever they hear it, they know what it means.

References

Anti-Defamation League. (2012). *The lawless ones: The resurgence of the Sovereign Citizen Movement.* 2nd Edition. New York. Retrieved from www.adl.org/sites/default/files/documents/assets/pdf/combat ing-hate/Lawless-Ones-2012-Edition-WEB-final.pdf

Australian Government. (2018). *Living safe together: Partners: Government.* Canberra, Australia. Retrieved from https://web.archive.org/web/20180313081115/https://www.livingsafetogether.gov.au/partn ers/Pages/government.aspx

Baldino, D. and Lucas, K. (2018, May 11). This isn't Helter Skelter: Why the internet alone can't be blamed for radicalisation. *The Conversation.* Retrieved from https://theconversation.com/this-isnt-hel ter-skelter-why-the-internet-alone-cant-be-blamed-for-radicalisation-94825

BBC News. (2021, June 24). What is the Great Reset – and how did it get hijacked by conspiracy theories? *BBC News.* Retrieved from www.bbc.com/news/blogs-trending-57532368

Bortolotti, L. & Ichino, A. (2020, December 9). Conspiracy theories may seem irrational – but they fulfill a basic human need. *The Conversation.* Retrieved from https://theconversation.com/conspiracy-theor ies-may-seem-irrational-but-they-fulfill-a-basic-human-need-151324

Challacombe, D. J. & Lucas, P. A. (2019). Postdicting violence with sovereign citizen actors: An exploratory test of the TRAP-18. *Journal of Threat Assessment and Management,* 6(1), 51–59. doi: 10.1037/tam0000105

Conroy, J. (2017, May 15). They hate the US government, and they're multiplying: the terrifying rise of 'sovereign citizens'. *The Guardian.* Retrieved from www.theguardian.com/world/2017/may/15/ sovereign-citizens-rightwing-terrorism-hate-us-government

Cosentino G. (2020). From Pizzagate to the Great Replacement: The globalization of conspiracy theories. In: *Social media and the post-truth world order* (pp. 58–86). Cham: Palgrave Pivot.

Department of Homeland Security. (2015, February). Sovereign citizen extremist ideology will drive violence at home, during travel, and at government facilities. *Office of Intelligence and Analysis* (Unclassified). Retrieved from https://fas.org/irp/eprint/sovereign.pdf

Devine, C. (2020, January 30). Bizarre case involves a US air marshal, his Sea-Doo and accusations of his fringe, anti-government views. *CNN News.* Retrieved from https://edition.cnn.com/2020/01/30/ politics/air-marshal-sovereign-citizen-invs/index.html

Dew, S. (2016). "Moors know the law:" Sovereign legal discourse in Moorish science religious communities and the hermeneutics of supersession. *Journal of Law and Religion,* 31(1), 70–91. doi: 10.1017/jlr.2016.3

Douglas, K. M. (2021). COVID-19 conspiracy theories. *Group Processes & Intergroup Relations,* 24(2), 270–275. doi: 10.1177/1368430220982068

Dowse, A. & Bachmann, S.-D. (2019). Explainer: What is 'hybrid warfare' and what is meant by the 'grey zone'? *The Conversation,* 17 June. Retrieved from: https://theconversation.com/explainer-what-is-hyb rid-warfare-and-what-is-meant-by-the-grey-zone-118841

Ellis, B. H. & Abdi, S. (2017). Building community resilience to violent extremism through genuine partnerships. *American Psychologist,* 72(3), 289–300. doi: 10.1037/amp0000065

European Commission. (2016). *Supporting the prevention of radicalisation leading to violent extremism.* Brussels: European Commission. Retrieved from https://eur-lex.europa.eu/legal-content/EN/ALL/ ?uri=CELEX:52016DC0379

Finch, R. & Flowers, K. (2012, September 21). Sovereign Citizens: A clear and present danger. *Police Magazine.* Retrieved from www.policemag.com/340836/sovereign-citizens-a-clear-and-present-danger

Fleishman, D. (2004, Spring). Paper terrorism: The impact of the 'sovereign citizen' on local government. *Public Law Journal,* 27(2), 7–10. Retrieved from https://perma.cc/KLF7-AFC4

Friedberg, B. (2020, October). *Investigative digital ethnography: Methods for environmental modeling*. MediaWell. Retrieved from https://mediawell.ssrc.org/2020/10/21/investigative-digital-ethnography-methods-for-environmental-modeling-media-manipulation-casebook/

Friedlander, S. (1997). *Nazi Germany and the Jews: The years of persecution 1933–1939*. London: Weidenfeld & Nicolson.

Gartenstein-Ross, D. & Blackman, M. (2019). Fluidity of the fringes: Prior extremist involvement as a radicalization pathway. *Studies in Conflict & Terrorism*, 1–24. doi: 10.1080/1057610X.2018.1531545

Grisham, K. (2021, January 23). Far-right groups move to messaging apps as tech companies crack down on extremist social media. *The Conversation*. Retrieved from https://theconversation.com/far-right-groups-move-to-messaging-apps-as-tech-companies-crack-down-on-extremist-social-media-153181.

Grossman, M., Ungar, M., Brisson, J., Gerrand, V., Hadfield, K., & Jefferies, P. (2017). Understanding youth resilience to violent extremism: A standardised research measure. *Alfred Deakin Institute for Citizenship and Globalisation*. Melbourne: Deakin University.

Gruenewald, J., Dooley, K. M. G., Suttmoeller, M. J., Chermak, S. M., & Freilich, J. D. (2016). A mixed-method analysis of fatal attacks on police by far-right extremists. *Police Quarterly*, 19(2), 216–245. doi: 10.1177/1098611115623061

Hacking, I. (1982). *Language, truth and reason*. In Hollis, M. & Lukes, S. (Eds.), *Rationality and relativism* (pp. 48–66). Oxford: Blackwell.

Halliday, M. A. K. (1978). *Language as a social semiotic: The social interpretation of language and meaning*. London: Edward Arnold.

Hanson, S. J. (2020). *Concepts and practices: A brief history of disengagement and deradicalization*. In: Hanson, S. J. & Stian, L. (Eds.), *Routledge handbook of deradicalisation and disengagement*. London: Taylor & Francis.

Hesse, M. (1963). *Models and Analogies in Science*. Indiana: University of Notre Dame Press.

Huff-Corzine, L., McCutcheon, J. C., Corzine, J., Jarvis, J. P., Tetzlaff-Bemiller, M. J., Weller, M., & Landon, M. (2014). Shooting for accuracy: Comparing data sources on mass murder. *Homicide Studies*, 18(1), 105–124. doi: 10.1177/1088767913512205

Jung, C. (1934). 'The state of psychotherapy today' ('Zur gegenwartigen Lage der Psychotherapie'). In: *Collected Works* (p. 165). New Jersey: Princeton University Press.

Kreissl, R. (2018). *Annual Societal Security Report 4*. Retrieved from https://raffaellopantucci.files.wordpress.com/2021/03/f1810-source_d3.7_assr4.pdf

Kundnani, A. (2012, June). *Blind Spot? Security Narratives and Far-Right Violence in Europe*. ICCT Research Paper. Retrieved from www.icct.nl/app/uploads/download/file/ICCT-Kundnani-Blind-Spot-June-2012.pdf

Levi, P. (1986, February 17). Primo Levi's heartbreaking, heroic answers to the most common questions he was asked about survival in Auschwitz. *The New Republic*. Retrieved from https://newrepublic.com/article/119959/interview-primo-levi-survival-auschwitz

Lewandowsky, S. & Cook, J. (2020). *The conspiracy theory handbook*. Cornell Alliance for Science. Retrieved from http://sks.to/conspiracy

Lewandowsky, S., Cook, J., Ecker, U. K. H., Albarracín, D., Amazeen, M. A., Kendeou, P., Lombardi, D., Newman, E. J., Pennycook, G., Porter, E. Rand, D. G., Rapp, D. N., Reifler, J., Roozenbeek, J., Schmid, P., Seifert, C. M., Sinatra, G. M., Swire-Thompson, B., van der Linden, S., Vraga, E. K., Wood, T. J., Zaragoza, M. S. (2020). *The Debunking Handbook 2020*. Retrieved from: https://sks.to/db2020. doi:10.17910/b7.1182

MacNab, J. J. (2012, February 13). What is a Sovereign Citizen? *Forbes*. Retrieved from www.forbes.com/sites/jjmacnab/2012/02/13/what-is-a-sovereign-citizen/#5c8c748d6012

Malkki, L. & Sinkkonen, T. (2016). Political resilience to terrorism in Europe: Introduction to the special issue. *Studies in Conflict & Terrorism*, 39(4), 281–291. doi: 10.1080/1057610X.2016.1117325

Mallin, A. & Barr, L. (2021, March 3). FBI director says Capitol assault 'domestic terrorism,' no evidence of antifa. *ABC News*. Retrieved from https://abcnews.go.com/Politics/fbi-director-testifies-time-capitol-assault/story?id=76187365

McGowan, M. (2020, August 2). The threads that don't connect: Covid gives Australian conspiracy theorists a common home. *The Guardian*. Retrieved from www.theguardian.com/australia-news/2020/aug/02/coronavirus-conspiracy-theory-covid-19-australia-agenda-australian-theorists-groups-anti-vaxxers-antivax-vaccine-face-masks

Meyer, C. (2017). 5 common crimes committed by sovereign citizens [Text]. *Police1*. Retrieved from PoliceOne website: www.policeone.com/community/articles/360819006-5-common-crimes-committed-by-sovereign-citizens/

Misztal, B. A. (2001). Trust and cooperation: The democratic public sphere. *Journal of Sociology* (Melbourne, Vic.), 37(4), 371–386. doi: 10.1177/144078301128756409

Monbiot, G. (2021, September 22). It's shocking to see so many leftwingers lured to the far right by conspiracy theories. *The Guardian*. Retrieved from www.theguardian.com/commentisfree/2021/sep/22/leftwingers-far-right-conspiracy-theories-anti-vaxxers-power

Parker, G. F. (2014). Competence to stand trial evaluations of sovereign citizens: A case series and primer of odd political and legal beliefs. *Journal of the American Academy of Psychiatry and the Law*, 42(3), 338–349. Retrieved from: https://jaapl.org/content/jaapl/42/3/338.full.pdf.

Pytyck, J. & Chaimowitz G. A. (2013). The Sovereign citizen movement and fitness to stand trial. *International Journal of Forensic Mental Health*, 12(2), 149–153. doi: 10.1080/14999013.2013.796329

Rahman, R., Meloy J. R., & Bauer R. (2019). Extreme overvalued belief and the legacy of Carl Wernicke. *The Journal of the American Academy of Psychiatry and the Law*, 47(2), 180–187. doi: 10.29158/JAAPL.003847-19

Rozbroj, T., Lyons, A., & Lucke, J. (2019). Psychosocial and demographic characteristics relating to vaccine attitudes in Australia. *Patient Education and Counseling*, 102(1), 172–179. doi: 10.1016/j.pec.2018.08.027

Sacks, H. (1992). *Lectures on conversation*, 2 vols. Cambridge, MA: Blackwell.

Sarteschi, C. M. (2020). Sovereign citizens: A narrative review with implications of violence towards law enforcement. *Aggression and Violent Behavior*, 60, 101509. doi: 10.1016/j.avb.2020.101509. Retrieved from: https://www.sciencedirect.com/science/article/pii/S1359178920302135?casa_token=XsfLqwjgBxoAAAAA:ohWxfypnwnMtRihdeGEJKOB3wBZfA52LVcAaNyTF_1uGKDYY6WQQfxKgptn-SAAIvrFOdno3jGT4

Schouten, R. & Brennan D. V. (2016). Targeted violence against law enforcement officers. *Behavioral Sciences & the Law*, 34(5), 608–621. doi: 10.1002/bsl.2256

Sharrock, J. (2011, January 11). Explained: Jared Loughner's grammar obsession. *Mother Jones*. Retrieved from www.motherjones.com/politics/2011/01/sovereign-citizens-jared-lee-loughner/

Stephens, W. & Sieckelinck, S. (2020). Being resilient to radicalisation in PVE policy: A critical examination. *Critical Studies on Terrorism*, 13(1), 142–165. doi: 10.1080/17539153.2019.1658415

Stephens, W., Sieckelinck, S., & Boutellier, H. (2021). Preventing violent extremism: A review of the literature. *Studies in Conflict and Terrorism*, 44(4), 346–361. doi: 10.1080/1057610X.2018.1543144

Taub, A. & Bennhold, K. (2021, June 7). From Doomsday Preppers to Doomsday Plotters. *The New York Times*. Retrieved from www.nytimes.com/2021/06/07/world/accelerationism-qanon-day-x.html

UNESCO. (2017). *Preventing violent extremism through education: A guide for policy-makers*. Paris: UNES.

van Prooijen, J. W. & Acker, M. (2015). The influence of control on belief in conspiracy theories: Conceptual and applied extensions. *Applied Cognitive Psychology*, 29(5), 753-761. doi: 10.1002/acp.3161

Vergani, M., Iqbal, M., Ilbahar, E., & Barton, G. (2020). The three Ps of radicalization: Push, pull and personal. A systematic scoping review of the scientific evidence about radicalization into violent extremism. *Studies in Conflict and Terrorism*, 43(10), 854–854. doi: 10.1080/1057610X.2018.1505686

Waldman, S. (2016, November). *Countering violent extremism on social media*. Defence Research and Development Canada. Retrieved from https://cradpdf.drdc-rddc.gc.ca/PDFS/unc262/p805091_A1b.pdf

Wilson, J. (2016, August 5). What you need to know about one nation's Malcolm Roberts and 'sovereign citizens'. *The Guardian*. Retrieved from www.theguardian.com/commentisfree/2016/aug/05/what-you-need-to-know-about-one-nations-malcolm-roberts-and-sovereign-citizens

Wimelius, M. E., Eriksson, M., Kinsman, J., Strandh, V., & Ghazinour, M. (2018). What is local resilience against radicalization and how can it be promoted? A multidisciplinary literature review. *Studies in Conflict & Terrorism*, 1–18. doi: 10.1080/1057610X.2018.1531532

2

"SCREW YOUR OPTICS"

The Ambivalent Role of Violence in Islamist and Far-Right Extremism

Milo Comerford, Jacob Davey and Jakob Guhl

The Policy and Research Landscape Around "Non-violent Extremism"

This chapter focuses on the evidence base around the ambivalent role of violence within extremist groups. While some researchers claim that non-violent extremist thought serves as an entry point to extremist violence (Silber & Bhatt, 2007; Baran, 2005; Vidino, 2015), others have argued that political extremism can serve as an effective bulwark against violent extremism (Githens-Mazer & Lambert, 2010; Ravndal, 2016).[1] Within this debate, we have seen the emergence of twin paradigms, with non-violent extremists described as either a "firewall" or a "conveyor belt" to violent radicalisation (El-Badawy, 2019).

Similar disagreements about how to treat extremist groups that do not openly call for political violence have manifested among policymakers. Some government officials have argued that non-violent extremism needs to be tackled to reduce the risk from terrorism and violent extremism. From this perspective, tackling non-violent extremism is crucial, as such ideologies are perceived to indirectly legitimise terrorism and violent extremism.[2] Their critics have argued that the "ideological credibility" (primarily of extremist groups genuinely opposed to violence) should be harnessed in order to dissuade individuals who are tempted by violent extremism. In addition, the focus on the security challenges posed by extremist movements has, in turn, been criticised as being too narrow, and dismissive of broader symbolic and practical harms extremism represents for a multicultural liberal democracy (Guhl, 2018).

In this chapter, we argue that the distinction between non-violent and violent extremists across the ideological spectrum is often not as clear-cut as the terminology may indicate, and suggest that the category of "non-violent extremism" has limited analytical value. Drawing on existing literature as well as previous research containing primary data on the online discourse of nominally non-violent movements, in this chapter we begin by making the case that a significant ideological overlap exists between non-violent and violent groups, and that individuals move back and forth between such groups. We analyse how non-violent extremist groups often take ambivalent stances towards violence, and outline examples of where loose online extremist networks (which have grown in the context of an increasingly "post-organisational" far-right) contain both non-violent and violent extremists. Finally, we explain how extremist ideologies may inspire acts of violence without actively calling for them.

DOI: 10.4324/9781003032793-4

In particular, this chapter will focus on the far-right ethno-nationalist group, Generation Identity and the revolutionary Islamist organisation Hizb ut-Tahrir.[3] Both groups have been labelled extremists by government authorities in the UK, but claim to eschew violence, and actively distance themselves from militant violent extremist groups. This analysis is framed within discussion of the debates around non-violent extremism, and some of the major disagreements among policy-makers and researchers as to how to view this phenomenon.

Policy Context

The UK government was among the first that focused on extremist ideology as a key component of terrorist violence. The Prevent strategy, a pillar of its 2006 CONTEST counter-terrorism strategy, emphasised the role of extremist ideology and instituted a public programme (Channel) tasked with delivering early interventions to prevent violent extremism. The idea of non-violent extremism was controversial from the outset, as some feared it would result in government overreach into radical, but still legitimate, forms of political activism.

Some Salafi groups[4] such as the American al-Maghrib Institute and the Tashih ul-Afkar al-Mutatarrifah (TAM, "rectifying extremist ideologies") or the STREET program in the UK have argued that, given a perceived theological credibility combined with genuine disapproval of terrorist violence, they could serve as a firewall against the violent extremisms (Elliot, 2011; Hitchens, 2018). This view was supported by academics such Githens-Mazer and Lambert (2010), who argued that the Salafist STREET program in Brixton, which was funded by the UK government for a period, proved effective in preventing young people from moving towards violent extremism. While equating Salafism as a whole with extremism would be controversial, as quietist Salafists abstain from direct involvement in politics, critics questioned whether the (potential) security benefits of funding such projects really outweighed the potentially negative implications for social cohesion and liberal values (Olidort, 2015). Maher and Frampton (2008) argued for applying a value-based criteria when deciding which Muslim groups the government should support and partner with.[5]

After the Conservatives won the UK general election in 2010, the Prevent strategy underwent a revision. The revised strategy stated that "preventing terrorism will mean challenging extremist (and non-violent) ideas that are also part of a terrorist ideology" (HM Government, 2011a, p. 6). The revised version of Prevent therefore stated even more clearly that non-violent extremism is viewed as a precursor of violent extremism, not a firewall against it (HM Government, 2011b). This new approach to extremist ideologies was most prominently presented by the former Prime Minister of the UK, David Cameron, at the Munich Security Conference in 2011. In the speech, Cameron identified ideology as a root cause of Islamist terrorism, arguing that

> we have got to get to the root of the problem, and we need to be absolutely clear on where the origins of where these terrorist attacks lie. That is the existence of an ideology, Islamist extremism … As evidence emerges about the backgrounds of those convicted of terrorist offences, it is clear that many of them were initially influenced by what some have called "non-violent extremists."
>
> *(Cameron, 2011)*

The 2015 UK counter-extremism strategy further emphasised the importance of tackling non-violent and violent extremism across the ideological spectrum, defining extremism as "the vocal or active opposition to our fundamental values, including democracy, the rule of law, individual liberty and the mutual respect and tolerance of different faiths and beliefs" (Home Office, 2015, p. 9). In the UK context, the threat of non-violent extremism has also increasingly been viewed by the government as extending beyond narrow security concerns. As the UK's Commission for Countering Extremism pointed out in their 2019 report, the societal harms caused by extremism include, but are not limited to, violence (Khan, 2019).

The specific term non-violent extremism is not as prominent in other Western countries, such as the US, Canada and Australia, where it lacks a legal or working definition (Lowe, 2019). Nevertheless, a similar importance is placed on challenging extremist ideologies in other European contexts. As Said and Fouad point out in a 2018 article, the aim of German approaches to preventing violent extremism and countering violent extremism is "countering extremism in all forms, be it violent or non-violent" (p. 2). This applies to the activities and annual reports by the German Federal and State Intelligence Services, which monitor anti-constitutional actors across the ideological spectrum. Instead of describing certain extremists as non-violent, a distinction is drawn between extremists "willing to use violence" and those who are not. Similarly, programmes aimed at democracy promotion and preventing extremism by the Federal Ministry for Family Affairs, Senior Citizens, Women and Youth as well as the Ministry of the Interior, Construction and Homeland are designed to tackle non-violent manifestations of left-wing, right-wing and Islamist extremism before they become a violent or a major political threat (Said & Fouad, 2018).

The understanding that Germany is a "militant democracy" (Loewenstein, 1937; Minkenberg, 2006) which needs to challenge extremism at large, not just prevent its violent expressions, is manifested in its approach to Salafism, for example. In 2011, an assessment of Salafism in Germany was presented to the conference of state Interior Ministries, which identified Salafism as they key ideological underpinning of violent Islamist radicalisation. While the grey zone between non-violent and violent forms of Salafism is acknowledged, it was argued that attitudes towards violence among political Salafists were ambivalent and that the ideology and aims of political and jihadist Salafists were ultimately the same. Following the conference, intelligence agencies declared Salafism to be an "object of observation" (Biene et al., 2016, pp. 47–48). In contrast to other geographic contexts, German government and public discourse on Salafism has broadly come to frame this form of Islamic theology as inherently "extremist", and is often implicitly or explicitly reduced to its political and violent manifestations.

Beyond the threat of violent radicalisation, Salafism is perceived as contradicting key principles of the German constitution, including parliamentary democracy, the rule of law, popular sovereignty, human dignity (conflicts with corporal punishments), freedom of religion, freedom of conscience, equality between men and women and the peaceful coexistence between peoples. Writing in an article for the Federal Agency for Civic Education, the former intelligence analyst Pfahl-Traughber (2015) stated that "For even in the constituent parts of the ideological self-understanding [of Salafism], one can note a conflict with the minimal conditions of modern democraciesand open societies."

Research Debates

The term non-violent extremism and the relationship between non-violent and violent extremism, both in terms of radicalisation pathways and the interaction between the two, have not only been controversial among policy-makers, but also been the subject of fierce debate among researchers in the field.

Terminological Criticism

The terrorism scholar Alex Schmid (2014) criticised the term non-violent extremism, and argued that it was misleading term as it failed to differentiate between the tactical and ideological refusal to use violence. Schmid (2014, p. 13) draws a distinction between "non-violent" tactics, exemplified by civil resistance movements that take a principle stand against the use of political violence, and "not-violent" extremist individuals, groups and movements that merely do not use violence at a given moment in time. For the latter, a changing political context could lead to the adoption of violent methods.

Non-violent Extremism as a Precursor of Violent Extremism?

The relationship between non-violent and violent extremism has been explained using different models and metaphors. Some of these models have suggested that non-violent extremism plays a major role as a precursor to violent extremism. They often assumed a fairly linear progression. For example, the "conveyor belt theory" (Baran, 2005) and the NYPD model (Silber & Bhatt, 2007) view radicalisation processes as passing through different stages of ideological commitment which would ultimately (though not inevitably) lead to violent extremism.

Western government data on the backgrounds of foreign fighters and people convicted for terrorism-related offences provides some support for this. A 2016 assessment by the German federal police and intelligence services, for example, stated that 96% of all German foreign fighters were associated with an Islamist group before traveling to Syria and Iraq (Bundeskriminalamt, Bundesamt für Verfassungsschutz und Hessisches Informations- und Kompetenzzentrum gegen Extremismus, 2016). Klausen (2010) similarly noted that 80% of jihadists in the UK belonged to a few well-known Islamist circles. Research by the Tony Blair Institute for Global Change also looked at the backgrounds of 200 *jihadists*, finding that 51% of the cases from the Middle East and Africa had previously been involved with non-violent Islamist movements before moving on to violent movements (Ahmed et al., 2016).

One of the main criticisms of the research on this topic that has accrued over recent years is that there is nothing inevitable about moving on to violent groups. A 2010 report by the London-based think tank Demos found that non-violent extremists do not automatically become violent extremists (Bartlett et al., 2010). The psychologist and terrorism scholar John Horgan claimed that violent extremists need not necessarily be the most ideologically radicalised, arguing that "involvement [in violent extremism] is not a sign of a state being reached but of an act being done" (Horgan, 2014, p. 84). There have even been a number of terrorism scholars who argued that extremist views are not only sufficient but also not a necessary precursor for engagement in terrorist violence (Abrahms, 2008; Vidino, 2010; Bjørgo, 2011; Borum, 2011; Horgan, 2014; Schuurman & Eijkman, 2015). One of these scholars Borum (2011) therefore suggested that the focus for researchers and security services should be on "action pathways" that actually result in involvement in violent extremism instead of processes of ideological radicalisation (pp. 8–9).

Safety Valve

In the context of increasing attention towards far-right terrorist incidents, a similar debate emerged about the role of far-right parties and movements that do not actively call for violence. This was in part caused by the growing visibility of nominally non-violent movements, such as the Identitarian movement, the "New Right" and the so-called Alt-Right (Bruns et al., 2016;

Davey & Ebner, 2017; Davey & Ebner, 2019; Zúquete, 2018; Salzborn, 2017; Hawley, 2017). This coincided with a reported rise into hate crime in several European and North American countries and a number of high-profile instances of extreme-right violence or terrorism in Christchurch, Pittsburgh, Poway, Charlottesville, London, Hesse, Halle and Hanau (ADL, 2018; SPLC, 2019; Community Security Trust, 2019; TellMAMA, 2018; UK Home Office, 2018; FBI, 2018; German Interior Ministry, 2019). These parallel debates led to debates about the potential connection between the growing visibility of nominally non-violent far-right movements and the reported rise in far-right violence.

While public commentators often make claims about non-violent far-right politics con-tributing to extreme-right violence in the aftermath of attacks, some academic researchers have been careful in drawing a direct line. For example, Ravndal (2016) claimed that such groups may even serve as a "safety valve" against recruitment into violent extremist groups in the first place, as they offer alternatives through peaceful activism (p. 11). A high level of deadly right-wing terrorism and violence was instead found in countries in electoral support for radical-right parties was low, and the level of repression of radical -right opinions was high. In conclusion, Ravndal (2018) argued that "countermeasures intended to constrain radical right politics appear to fuel extreme-right violence, while countermeasures that may constrain extreme-right violence would imply an advancement of radical right politics" (p. 845).

Islamism and "Non-violent Extremism"

The "conveyer belt"/"firewall" dichotomy outlined above has its origins in the evolving debate among policy makers in the wake of 9/11 around the role of non-violent extremist Islamist groups in either preventing or facilitating terrorist violence. In an analysis of non-violent Islamist movements in Europe, Muslim Brotherhood[6] expert and contributor to this volume Lorenzo Vidino (2010) claimed "there is substantial anecdotal evidence supporting both positions sim-ultaneously, but no systematic, comprehensive studies that can definitively prove either" (p. 11).

However, close analysis of Islamist groups and ideologies clearly reveals that drawing a hard and fast binary dichotomy between violent and non-violent is both unhelpful and unrep-resentative of the realities of these multifaceted movements. In this section, we explore the unsatisfactory distinction between non-violent and violent Islamist movements, looking at the permeability of these distinctions on an individual and group basis, exploring the ideological proximity between non-violent and violent Islamist groups, as well as providing a case study of ambivalent attitudes to violence among an archetypal "non-violent" Islamist movement, Hizb-ut-Tahrir.[7]

Islamism, here defined according to a social identity theory of extremism, is understood as the advocacy of a system of belief that promotes the creation of an exclusionary and totali-tarian Islamic state, within which those who do not subscribe to this vision are portrayed as an inferior "out-group" and are subjected to implicit, explicit or violent means of subjugation and prejudice. Islamist extremists propagate a dehumanising "othering" mindset that is anti-thetical to pluralism and the universal application of human rights. Islamist extremist groups pursue and advocate a systemic political and societal change that reflects this world view (Berger, 2018).

Crucially, this may be achieved through non-violent, gradualist means, as pursued by groups such as Jamaat-e-Islami[8] and the Muslim Brotherhood, as well as through violent and ter-roristic means, and is represented most prominently by groups such as the Islamic State of Iraq and Syria (ISIS) and al-Qaeda. Such a definition, intended to be both exhaustive and restrictive, captures the broader harms of extremism beyond just terrorist violence, isolating the key extremist "ingredients" of supremacist totalitarianism and the dehumanisation of the other, which are antithetical to human rights-based inclusive societies.

Extremist groups are not solely defined by their violence or non-violence . Significantly, even violent extremist groups feature significant "non-violent" elements within their approach and world view. ISIS, renowned for the ultraviolent methods used in service of their extremist ideology, dedicate considerable elements of their propaganda towards non-violent, utopian and idealistic narratives. Studies by noted ISIS scholar Charlie Winter have found that over half of all the group's media output at the height of the so-called "Caliphate" was geared towards painting a utopian picture of civilian life in the caliphate, from education and farming to conservation and images of a welfare state (Winter, 2017). Simply put, the distinction between violent and non-violent Islamist groups is more marbalised than black and white distinctions suggest.

Ideological Distinction Between "Violent" and "Non-violent" Islamist Extremist Groups

When considering the extent of ideological overlap between "violent" and "non-violent" Islamist extremism, a foundational question concerns whether differences in attitudes and approaches to violence are simply tactical (i.e. a calculated choice about the utility of violence vs. political engagement for achieving the same ends), or whether there are distinct worldviews underpinning these positions. This distinction between tactical and strategic deployments of non-violence is significant, telling us about the extent to which so-called "non-violent" extremist groups and individuals are rejecting violence out of principle, or as a means of knowingly staying on the right side of the law.

Some researchers have addressed this question through comparative studies of specific ideological precepts. Emily Dyer explored the overlap of ISIS and al-Qaeda views on women and gender with "non-violent" extremist groups, such as Hizb-ut-Tahrir, finding that although there are significant variations in positions regarding women's roles in society, much of this variance is due to ISIS' declaration of a Caliphate, and belief in the establishment of an idealised Islamic state by Abu Bakr al-Baghdadi in June 2014. In contrast, Hizb-ut-Tahrir believes that the Caliphate is yet to have been established, with Dyer finding that "HT's theoretical position is broadly mirrored within IS' propaganda and practice " (Dyer, 2016, p. 2).

Taking a more quantitative research approach, similar conclusions were reached in 2017 research by Milo Comerford and Rachel Bryson, using a natural language processing-based approach to establish an empirical comparison on the key ideological differences and overlap between non-violent political Islamist extremism and Salafi-jihadism. Drawing on over 3,000 texts from a range of groups – including the Muslim Brotherhood, Jemaat-i-Islami, Hizb-ut-Tahrir, ISIS and al-Qaeda – this approach analysed the respective use of ideological concepts across different types of groups, allowing for direct comparison of the arsenal of ideas deployed by violent and non-violent Islamist extremists. It found a 70% overlap in core ideological concepts between Islamist and Salafi-jihadi material. *Jihad*, an Islamic state or Caliphate, and concern with polytheism and the status of non-Muslims were found to be conceptual priorities and – crucially for this chapter – were all held in common by violent and non-violent extremists (Comerford & Bryson, 2017).

Pathways Between Violence and Non-violence

In the previously mentioned 2011 security conference speech in Munich, David Cameron noted that, "many of [those convicted of terrorist offences] were initially influenced by what some have called 'non-violent extremists', and they then took those radical beliefs to the next level by embracing violence " (Cameron, 2011).

One of the most prominent examples of such transformations from non-violent to violent milieus is the case of Omar Bakri Mohammed – a Syrian national who joined the Muslim Brotherhood as a teenager and helped establish Hizb-ut-Tahrir in Britain in the 1990s. According to Bakri, Muslims who live in non-Muslim countries that do not oppress them or prevent them from practising their faith are living in a "Covenant of Security" (Nesser, 2018, p. 43). According to this covenant, Muslims should not carry out acts of violence in exchange for their religious freedom. However, Bakri came to believe that Hizb-ut-Tahrir's rejection of violence was an ineffective method for transforming society and restoring the Caliphate, leading to his establishment of the designated terror group Al-Muhajiroun, whose ideology states that all Muslims are required to take up arms to spread the message of Islam and defend its lands.

Data find that this kind of journey is not unique among violent extremist individuals. In a Tony Blair Institute for Global Change study of the profiles of over a hundred violent Islamist extremists from the UK, 70% were found to have had prior links to non-violent Islamism, either through connections to political Islamist groups or through close relationships to non-violent Islamist ideologues, such as the hate preacher Anjem Choudary, the co-founder of Islamist organisation al-Muhajiroun (Bryson, 2017).

From a group-based perspective, this dividing line between non-violent and violent is similarly permeable. A number of Salafi-jihadi groups began life as non-violent Islamist movements. In Somalia, the Islamic Courts Union, which emerged in Mogadishu in 1994 in response to the crumbling state apparatus in the country, sought to apply an interpretation of Islamic law through non-violent methods, but its youth wing went on to form the al-Qaeda affiliate, al-Shabaab, in 2006. Meanwhile, Boko Haram started out as a non-violent movement to establish an Islamic state in northern Nigeria. Rising tensions with Abuja led to a violent insurgency which spread across the Lake Chad region, and in 2015 it pledged allegiance to ISIS. Unsurprisingly, environmental factors and conflict dynamics make a huge impact on strategic considerations around the deployment of violence by groups.

For both individuals and groups, such transformations do not point to an inevitable causal relationship – there are many Islamist groups that have remained non-violent – but they do show the potential for sublimation between political extremism and militancy, particularly in conflict zones. Notably, data are much less readily available about the counterfactual – that is, groups that have remained non-violent or indeed even desisted from violence – making claims around causality around such transformations spurious.

Case Study: Hizb-ut-Tahrir

The international Islamist group Hiz-ut-Tahrir (HT) has become an emblematic example of the "non-violent extremist" group in the public consciousness. Founded by the Palestinian Taqi al-Din al-Nabhani al-Filastyni in 1953, HT seeks to unite the global Muslim community (the *ummah*) under a theocratic Caliphate, through activism and political action.

Banned in most countries in the Middle East, UK authorities have over the years voiced serious concerns about HT, with successive British governments having explored the potential for proscribing the organisation. They have been unsuccessful because they could not establish to a sufficient legal standard that HT intended to incite or glorify violence.

Both "conveyor belt" and "firewall" paradigms have been applied to the group. While a spokesman for the Sydney-based wing of Hizb-ut-Tahrir said the organisation had a "divine" belief against violence, "where we consider it a crime against God" (Safi, 2015), Zeyno Baran of the Hudson Institute has called Hizb-ut-Tahrir a "conveyor belt" for terrorists, claiming that once inculcated into the group's ideology, HT members are vulnerable to more explicit messages of militancy. She uses the example of British citizen Omar Sharif, who attempted to blow up a bar in Tel Aviv in 2003. British intelligence officers found HT literature in Sharif's UK home. In a similar case, ISIS terrorist Mohammed Emwazi (known as " Jihadi John") reportedly also attended events with HT speakers while at university in Great Britain (Baran, 2004).

However, such approaches make a fundamental mistake in framing the group through a binary lens of violent or non-violent. For HT, violence is irrelevant to their role as a political revolutionary project. While individuals may undertake violence, and the group may have opinions about issues such as suicide bombing and jihad as military obligation, it is not the function of the party itself to undertake material actions, nor does it agitate for this. In this way, focusing on organisations in relation to violence can be a red herring, rather it is the ideas they perpetuate that have greater resonance in individuals' pathways to violence.

While HT does not call for violence, it does discuss the justification of violence, and shows an apparent willingness to make excuses for violence committed by others in the cause of Islamism. Analysing its core texts, it is clear to see HT praises a violent interpretation of *jihad* but insists that it does not use "material power to defend itself or as a weapon ..." using the example of the Prophet Mohammed's period in Mecca by "restricting itself to political actions alone and ... not exceed[ing] them by resorting to material actions against the rulers or against those who opposed its *da'wah* (call to Islam)", and stating that he "did not carry out any material actions until he had migrated to Madinah " (Hizb-ut-Tahrir, n.d.).

Whilst the group publicly disavows efforts to achieve its goals of a caliphate through violent means, the group does support the concept of violent "defensive jihad", stating

> whenever the disbelieving enemies attack an Islamic country it becomes compulsory on its Muslim citizens to repel the enemy ... Whenever there is a Muslim Amir who declares *jihad* to enhance the Word of Allah (swt) and mobilises the people to do that, the members of Hizb ut-Tahrir will respond in their capacity as Muslims in the country where the general call to arms was proclaimed.
>
> *(Hizb-ut-Tahrir, 2015)*

According to a Tony Blair Institute for Global Change report analysing the public propaganda of non-violent Islamist extremists, HT also makes several calls for "Muslim armies to rise" and liberate Muslims from oppression, as shown by this statement from 2010:

> *The Muslim Ummah knows that there is no solution except to move armies to end the blockade and liberate Palestine; and that these armies must remove the rulers who confine them to barracks and thus prevent them from fulfilling this duty.*
>
> *(Tony Blair Institute for Global Change, 2019a, p. 43)*

HT has also sought to justify acts of terrorism or violence against Western individuals or targets on a basis of such actions being a consequence of Western policies. In comments shared on one of HT's websites in 2015, a senior member commented on the knife attack on MP Stephen Timms by the student Roshnora Choudry:

> *The reality is that it is a response that comes out of the policy of the British government. That's the sad fact, that anyone, whether Muslim or not Muslim, whether British citizen or from*

> *another land, the reality is that when the policy creates this enmity, when the people see that the policy you've adopted is false, when they see it as an imposition, when they see it as an act of oppression, it creates this anger and it creates this resentment. And whatever action that comes from this is a natural response to that aggression.*
>
> *(Tony Blair Institute for Global Change, 2019a, p. 43)*

Such statements show the multifaceted nature of approaches to violence within Islamist groups, revealing a significant grey zone between violent and non-violent extremism as well as demonstrating the limitations of the latter category as a useful analytical classification when there is such marbalisation between violence and non-violence in the rhetorical foundations and practices of a group's particular form of activism.

The Far-Right and "Non-violent Extremism"

If one considers contemporary neo-Nazi, extreme right-wing terrorist organisations, such as Atomwaffen, The Base or Feuerkrieg Division, it would seem apparent that they are distinct from nominally "non-violent" extremist groups, as well as networks of reactionary ideologues and far-right political actors.

Commonly inspired by the "Siege Culture" promoted by American Neo-Nazi James Mason, these groups are unequivocal in their belief that violence against non-white people and "race traitors" is necessary and desirable (SPLC, n.d.). Violence here is framed under the theory of "accelerationism" (Beauchamp, 2019), where it is anticipated that mass killings and assassinations will hasten the destabilisation and ultimate downfall of the state, providing the conditions for a race war, after which white supremacists will be able to establish an ethnostate. The prioritisation of violence as a strategy would appear to be starkly at odds with organisations which prioritise the use of street protests, publicity stunts or political engagement to advance their agenda. Indeed, in the face of terrorist attacks inspired by different strands of far-right ideology, such as the March 2019 Christchurch terror attack, a number of far-right actors sought to distance themselves from such activity (Tony Blair Institute for Global Change 2019b). Accordingly, when considering the specific security risks posed by these organisations, drawing a line distinguishing between violent and not-violent extremism seems highly pertinent.

"Post-Organisational" Far-Right Extremism

However, a deeper analysis of the ways violent and non-violent far-right extremists organise and the directions of ideological influence underpinning the contemporary far-right extremist landscape reveals that the lines between violent and non-violent are not clear cut.

Firstly, it has been observed that contemporary right-wing extremist activism increasingly fits into a "post-organisational" paradigm (Comerford, 2020). Here communities of right-wing extremists are coordinating and organising in a looser fashion, often defined by adherence to key tactical, cultural and ideological tropes rather than membership of particular groups. Indeed, accelerationists encourage logistically autonomous and self-motivated acts of violence (Gartenstein-Ross et al., 2020), meaning that membership of a particular movement is by no means a prerequisite of committing an attack. This was highlighted by the New Zealand Government's inquiry into the Christchurch attack, which revealed that the individual who committed the attacks was not a member of any specific extreme right-wing groups, but did engage with extreme right-wing communities online (Royal Commission of Inquiry, 2019).

Accordingly, when considering whether violent or non-violent are appropriate divisions to adopt when creating policy responses to far-right extremism, it is also important to consider whether adherence to a specific group or movement remains universally useful as a lens when analysing extremist activity.

Digital Spaces: Blurring the Lines Between Non-violent and Violent Extremism on the Far Right

When considering these organisational dynamics, the role of digital fora which pay host to these loose communities is particularly important. Digital platforms provide the infrastructure for radicalisation and the formulation of shared cultural and ideological reference points (Conway et al., 2019; Crawford et al., 2020). In these digital fora, affiliation to specific groups arguably becomes less important, whilst the lines between violent and non-violent activity are blurred.

The now-defunct anonymous imageboard 8chan's/pol/board has been observed as one particularly influential platform to contemporary extreme-right mobilisation (Crawford et al., 2020). It was used by three terrorists to place manifesto documents ahead of attacks in Christchurch, New Zealand; Poway, California; and El Paso, Texas.

8chan's parent website the imageboard 4chan has also been observed as a crucial hub for contemporary extreme-right mobilisation too (Papasavva et al., 2020). An analysis of the /pol/board on the imageboard 4chan reveals that although the platform was a hotbed of hate speech and extremism, users were not however ideologically coherent (Colley & Moore, 2020). Furthermore, the heavy use of irony and cultural norms which prioritise highly egregious and vile language-use mean that even instances of specific calls for violence cannot be considered sincere (Colley & Moore, 2020). Similarly, despite the importance of 8chan in the announcement of terrorist attacks in 2019, the platform was by no means primarily used for violent activity. Indeed, a topic modelling exercise performed by Baele et al. (2020) found that the top discussion topic on the platform was current events. Accordingly, in a landscape where involvement in far-right extremism is often characterised by the anonymous and incoherent use of chaotic online spaces, focussing on adherence to specific movements, violence or non-violence has limitations.

Of course, the use of imageboards, whilst important to contemporary extreme-right mobilisation, does not represent the entirety of extreme right-wing activity online. There do remain specific platforms which are more effectively geared towards mobilisation across group lines. One such platform is the encrypted messaging application Telegram. Telegram allows for members to create publicly accessible group communication channels (Telegram, n.d.). Furthermore, until increased calls for temperance of far-right extremism online in January 2021 (Bedingfield, 2020), the platform was noted for its highly limited moderation efforts against extreme right-wing communities (Collier et al., 2021). This combination of secure, easily accessible group channels and laissez-faire approach to extremism facilitated the growth of a community of particularly violent extreme-right channels dubbed "Terrorgram" (DFR Lab, 2020). These channels are focussed on promoting accelerationism, contain instructional material on how to prepare and commit attacks and at times are expressly affiliated with terrorist organisations.

To better understand how this community is structured, and how it connects with broader extreme right groups, the Institute for Strategic Dialogue performed an analysis of 208 white supremacist channels on Telegram (Guhl & Davey, 2020). Of these channels, 49 were deemed "pro-terrorist" in that they promoted groups who endorse politically motivated violence or glorified individuals who have committed attacks. A further seven contained tactical information which might be useful in the preparation of terrorist attacks or in a broader insurgency, and the remainder were associated more broadly with the discussion of extreme right-wing ideology, or as general community groups for individuals to chat, share memes or "shitpost". Due to the way Telegram is structured, it is easy for users to share content between different platforms, and this "cross posting" dynamic is widespread. Accordingly, the report mapped a network of these different Telegram channels to examine how they were interlinked, finding that 205 of the 208 channels studied linked to one another. In many cases, channels which were not explicitly violent were still closely connected to those where endorsement of violence was prominent, including channels affiliated with specific terrorist organisations.

This densely networked right-wing extremist ecosystem again highlights the challenges of using the violent/non-violent binary to classify and understand contemporary extreme-right wing activity. Here, the fact that channels tied to violent extremist organisations bled into a looser network of non-violent hubs for extremist mobilisation demonstrates how in the digital arena the boundaries between violent and non-violent spaces are amorphous. Individuals can enter into discussion hubs associated with violent groups from largely non-violent discussion spaces easily, and can also promote content produced by violent organisations backwards. Given that contemporary extreme-right terrorists often promote self-activated (or "leaderless") violence as a key tactic, then this would suggest that at an ecosystem level, analysis and monitoring of non-violent far-right extremism is important to understand violent far-right extremism and vice-versa.

Case Study: Generation Identity

As well as examining the blurred and ambiguous boundaries between violent and non-violent communities, the ideological barriers between violent and non-violent extremists are also worthy of attention. One key case study can be found here in the "Great Replacement" theory. The theory, which originated in France under the (2011) authorship of Renaud Camus (Davey & Ebner, 2019), focusses on the perceived ethnic replacement of "native" Europeans through migration, and declining birth-rates (Eleanor, 2019), with proponents often painting this as part of a sinister plot by (often Jewish) "elites" to deliberately alter the permanent ethnic makeup of European countries (Schwartzenburg, 2019).

One of the key proponents of the theory is the pan-European group Generation Identity, which has chapters across many European countries such as Les Identitaires in France, the Identitäre Bewegung in Germany and Austria or Generation Identity UK and Ireland and is part of the wider Identitarian movement.[9] Generation Identity bill themselves as a "driving force to defend European identities and traditions against globalization and the mass migration that Europe is facing" aiming to "stop and invert the dangerous demographic trend, that will lead to the replacement of our peoples and to the end of our values and civilisation" (Generation Identity, n.d.). The group have been clear in publicly painting themselves as non-violent (Cox & Meisel, 2018; Ebner, 2019). Instead, they prioritise awareness raising through publicity stunts and activism, as well as advocacy for drastic policy change such as "remigration" – the forced repatriation of people of non-European heritage to their ancestral countries (Al-Jazeera, 2018).

This theory played a key inspirational role in the terrorist attack in the 2019 attack on Christchurch, New Zealand. The manifesto document left behind by the perpetrator of this attack was named after the theory, and the document grounds the rationale for the attack in the Great Replacement's key talking points. Additionally, to show appreciation for their activism, the attacker donated €1,500 to Martin Sellner, head of the Austrian branch of Generation Identity, and €2,200 to the French branch Generation Identitaire (Baynes, 2019; NZ Herald, 2019).

Whilst the broader Identitarian movement decried the attack, it has been observed that they (and other far-right organisations) believed the attack was an inevitable result of policies designed to foster multiculturalism and globalism (Tony Blair Institute for Global Change 2019b). This does not suggest that the Generation Identity had any hand in the planning or execution of the attack; however, it does reinforce how the deleterious and crisis-type ideas promoted by nominally non-violent extremism organisations can encourage more explicit violent activity, and also highlights how non-violent extremists recognise that their worldview can help create inspiration for violent activity.

Importantly, the concepts promoted by Generation Identity have a two-way direction of travel. As well as inspiring terrorist violence, they have also been promoted by politicians. Previous analysis by ISD into discussion around the Great Replacement identified four European politicians explicitly referencing the theory and five others using related language and conspiracy theories in their campaigns between 2016 and 2019 (Davey & Ebner, 2019).

Here, there is a clear line connecting narratives used by elected officials, and narratives used by terrorists. This should certainly not be taken to suggest that these politicians desire or call for violence, but rather demonstrates that both violent and non-violent actors draw ideational succour from the same conceptual pool.

More broadly, this points towards a commonality in extreme-right thinking where groups are united by their belief that "European" (white) culture, identity and ethnic stock are under threat, and this requires radical action to remedy, which can inspire individuals to commit attacks or seek recourse through democratic means.

Accordingly, as organisational boundaries between violent and non-violent communities become increasingly fluid, and membership of specific movements which can more easily be described as violent or non-violent becomes less important, drawing lines in the current post-organisational moment between "violent" and "non-violent" extremism seems increasingly impractical.

Conclusion

This chapter provides an analysis of the evidence base around the ambivalent role of violence within extremist groups, drawing on examples from both Islamism and the far right. It reviewed the policy and research debates around non-violent extremism, including the emergence of the twin paradigms that described non-violent extremists either as a "firewall" or as a "conveyor belt" to violent radicalisation.

We argued that the distinction between non-violent and violent extremists is often not as clear-cut as it may appear at first sight. While outfits such as the far-right ethno-nationalist group Generation Identity and the revolutionary Islamist organisation Hizb ut-Tahrir usually do not actively call for violence, their relationship with violent extremism remains ambivalent.

Not only do individuals move back and forth between non-violent and violent groups, but analysis of the key texts of these movements also reveals a significant ideological overlap between non-violent and violent groups and at times, an ambivalent stance by nominally non-violent groups towards violence. In the context of an increasingly "post-organisational" revolutionary Islamism and far-right *milieu*, loose online extremist networks provide a shared technological space for non-violent and violent extremists alike, and facilitate the overspill of acts of violence by small cells and lone-actors through more extreme interpretations of the calls to action contained within non-violent extremist ideologies.

Notes

1 Jacob Ravndal (2016 & 2018), who distinguishes between the radical and extreme right, has argued that the electoral success of the radical right is inversely correlated with extreme-right violence.
2 We define extremism as the advocacy of a system of belief that claims the superiority and dominance of one identity-based "in-group" over all "out-groups". Extremism also promotes a dehumanising "othering" mindset that is antithetical to pluralism and the universal application of h uman rights. Extremist groups pursue and advocate a systemic political and societal change that reflects their world view. While they may do so through violent means, not all extremist groups openly engage in or actively call for violence. The latter phenomenon would be referred to as "non-violent extremism".
3 Hizb ut-Tahrir's goal is to establish a totalitarian and expansionist Islamic caliphate and aim to unite Muslims worldwide and annex all other state (Ahmed & Stuart, 2009).
4 Salafism is a current within Sunni Islam which advocates a return to the practices of the first three generations of Muslims (the *salaf* or "ancestors") who lived immediately after the prophet Mohammed. Within Salafism there are different currents, which differ significantly in their interpretations of the holy scriptures of Islam and their implications for political action. While quietist Salafists reject political activism, political Salafists are actively engaged in transforming society according to their ideological ideas. Jihadist Salafists use violence to implement a Salafist interpretation of Islamic law.
5 Maher and Frampton (2008) argued that the UK government should not engage with organisations that support terrorism (whether in the UK or abroad), the destruction of UN member states, the targeting of British soldiers or UN forces, discrimination based on religion, race, sexual orientation or gender or oppose civil liberties granted in the UK.
6 The Muslim Brotherhood is an Islamist party and social movement with affiliates across the world. The Muslim Brotherhood was founded by the scholar Hassan al-Banna in British-ruled Egypt in 1928, with the key aims of establishing a political and societal order based on its understanding of Islamic values. After facing varying levels of repression under authoritarian rulers in post-independence Egypt, the Muslim Brotherhood won the 2012 presidential elections after the fall of Mubarak regime in 2011. From 2013 onwards, however, the group faced severe repression again, with president Morsi being ousted and the Brotherhood being banned as a terrorist organisation by the Egyptian military regime. (See: Hamid, Shadi. *Temptations of Power: Islamists and Illiberal Democracy in a New Middle East.* Oxford University Press, 2014; Frampton, Martyn. *The Muslim Brotherhood and the West: A History of Enmity and Engagement.* Harvard University Press, 2018.)
7 For a comprehensive study of Hizb ut-Tahrir's "non-violent" Islamist extremist ideology, and how the group seeks to proselytise to Muslim communities in Western countries, see: Elisa Orofino (2020). *Hizb ut-Tahrir and the Caliphate.* London: Routledge, https://doi.org/10.4324/9780429268892.
8 Jamaat-e-Islami is an international Islamist movement founded in 1941 in British India (now Pakistan) by the Islamic scholar Abul Ala Maududi. It is often considered Pakistan's Muslim Brotherhood analogue and one of the country's most influential Islamist organisations (Asif Luqman Qazi, "How to Islamize an Islamic Republic: Jamaat-e-Islami in its own words," *Brookings Institution*, 25 April 2017 www.brookings.edu/research/how-to-islamize-an-islamic-republic-jamaat-e-islami-in-its-own-words/)
9 Beyond the local chapters of Generation Identity who closely cooperate and use a shared visual identity, there are authors, outlets and activists not directly involved in the group who adhere to Identitarian ideas. Additionally, international groups such as Identity Evropa and the Traditionalist Workers Party in the USA or Action Zealandia could be viewed as part of the broader Identitarian movement.

References

Abrahms, M. (2008). What terrorists really want: Terrorist motives and counterterrorism strategy. *International Security, 32*(4), 78–105. doi: https://doi.org/10.1162/isec.2008.32.4.78
ADL. (2018). Audit of Anti-Semitic Incidents: Year in Review 2018. *ADL.* Retrieved from www.adl.org/audit2018
Ahmed, H., & Stuart, H. (2009). *Hizb-u t-Tahrir.* London: Centre for Social Cohesion. Retrieved from http://henryjacksonsociety.org/wp-content/uploads/2013/01/HIZB.pdf
Ahmed, M., Comerford, M., & El-Badawy, E. (2016). Milestones to militancy: What the lives of 100 Jihadis tell us about a global movement. *Tony Blair Institute for Global Change.* Retrieved from https://institute.global/policy/milestones-militancy-what-lives-100-jihadis-tell-us-about-global-movement

Al-Jazeera. (2018, December 9). Generation Hate: French far right's violence and racism exposed. *Al-Jazeera.* Retrieved from www.aljazeera.com/news/2018/12/9/generation-hate-french-far-rights-violence-and-racism-exposed

Baele, S. J., Brace, L., & Coan, T. G. (2020). The T arrant effect: What impact did far-right attacks have on the 8chan forum? *Behavioral Sciences of Terrorism and Political Aggression,* 1–23. Advanced Online Publication. doi: https://doi.org/10.1080/19434472.2020.1862274

Baran, Z. (2004, April 2). The road from Tashkent to the Taliban. *National Review.* Retrieved from https://hudson.org/research/3976-the-road-from-tashkent-to-the-taliban

Baran, Z. (2005). Fighting the war of ideas. *Foreign Affairs,* 84, 68. doi: https://doi.org/10.2307/20031777

Bartlett, J., Birdwell, J., & King, M. (2010). The edge of violence: A radical approach to extremism. *Demos,* 5–75. Retrieved from www.demos.co.uk/files/Edge_of_Violence_-_web.pdf

Baynes, C. (2019, March 27). New Zealand terror attacker had financial links with European far-right group Generation Identity, Austrian chancellor reveals. *The Independent.* Retrieved from www.independent.co.uk/news/world/europe/new-zealand-terror-attack-generation-identity-austria-kurz-a8841841.html

Beauchamp, Z. (2019, 18 November). Accelerationism: The obscure idea inspiring white supremacist killers around the world. *Vox.* Retrieved from www.vox.com/the-highlight/2019/11/11/20882005/accelerationism-white-supremacy-christchurch

Bedingfield, W. (2020, March 1). How Telegram became a safe haven for pro-terror Nazis. *Wired.* Retrieved from www.wired.co.uk/article/hope-not-hate-telegram-nazis

Berger, J. M. (2018). *Extremism.* Cambridge, MA: MIT Press.

Biene, J., Daase, C., & Junk, J. (Eds.). (2016). *Salafismus und Dschihadismus in Deutschland: Ursachen, Dynamiken, Handlungsempfehlungen.* Frankfurt am Main: Campus Verlag.

Bjørgo, T. (2011). Dreams and disillusionment: Engagement in and disengagement from militant extremist groups. *Crime, Law and Social Change,* 55(4), 277–285. doi: https://doi.org/10.1007/s10611-011-9282-9

Borum, R. (2011). Radicalization into violent extremism: A review of social science theories. *Journal of Strategic Security,* 4(4), 7–36. doi: https://doi.org/10.5038/1944-0472.4.4.1

Bruns, J., Glosel, K., & Strobl, N. (2016). *Die Identitären: Handbuch zur Jugendbewegung der Neuen Rechten in Europa.* Münster: Unrast.

Bryson, R. (2017). For Caliph and country: Exploring how British jihadis join a global movement. *Tony Blair Institute for Global Change.* Retrieved from https://institute.global/policy/caliph-and-country-exploring-how-british-jihadis-join-global-movement

Cameron, D. (2011, February 5). *PM's speech at Munich Security Conference.* GOV.UK. Retrieved from www.gov.uk/government/speeches/pms-speech-at-munich-security-conference

Colley, T., & Moore, M. (2020). The challenges of studying 4chan and the Alt-Right: 'Come on in the water's fine'. *New Media & Society.* doi: https://doi.org/10.1177/1461444820948803

Collier, K, Anna S., & Ezra K. (2021, January 14). Telegram, a recent haven for the far right, purges extremist content. *NBC News.* Retrieved from www.nbcnews.com/tech/tech-news/telegram-recent-haven-far-right-purges-extremist-content-n1254215

Comerford, M. (2020, August 19). Confronting the challenge of post-organisational extremism. Retrieved from www.orfonline.org/expert-speak/confronting-the-challenge-of-post-organisational-extremism/

Comerford, M., & Bryson, R. (2017). Struggle over scripture charting the rift between Islamist extremism and mainstream Islam. *Tony Blair Institute for Global Change.* Retrieved from https://institute.global/policy/struggle-over-scripture-charting-rift-between-islamist-extremism-and-mainstream-islam

Community Security Trust. (2019). ANTISEMITIC INCIDENTS REPORT 2019. *Community Security Trust.* Retrieved from https://cst.org.uk/news/blog/2020/02/06/antisemitic-incidents-report-2019

Conway, M., Scrivens, R., & McNair, L. (2019). Right-wing extremists persistent online presence: History and contemporary trends. *International Centre for Counter-Terrorism,* 1–24. doi: https://doi.org/10.19165/2019.3.12

Cox, S., & Meisel, A. (2018, 19 September). Martin Sellner: The new face of the far right in Europe. *BBC.* Retrieved from www.bbc.co.uk/news/stories-45572411

Crawford, B., Keen, F., & Suarez-Tangil, G. (2020). Memetic irony and the promotion of violence within Chan Cultures. *Centre for Research and Evidence on Security Threats.* Retrieved from https://crestresearch.ac.uk/resources/memetic-irony-and-the-promotion-of-violence-within-chan-cultures/

Davey, J., & Ebner, J. (2017). The fringe insurgency: Connectivity, convergence and mainstreaming of the extreme right. *Institute for Strategic Dialogue.* Retrieved from www.isdglobal.org/wp-content/uploads/2017/10/The-Fringe-Insurgency-221017.pdf

Davey, J., & Ebner, J. (2019). The great replacement: The violent consequences of mainstreamed extremism. *Institute for Strategic Dialogue.* Retrieved from www.isdglobal.org/isd-publications/the-great-replacement-the-violent-consequences-of-mainstreamed-extremism/

DFR Lab. (2020, April 20). Terrorgram: A community built on hate. *Medium.* Retrieved from https://medium.com/dfrlab/terrorgram-a-community-built-on-hate-e02fd59ee329

Dyer, E. (2016). Women and the Caliphate: Women's rights and restrictions in Islamist ideology and practice. *Centre for the Response to Radicalisation and Terror.* Retrieved from http://henryjacksonsociety.org/wp-content/uploads/2016/03/Women-and-the-Caliphate_FINAL_2.pdf

Ebner, J. (2019, April 4). Who are Europe's far-right identitarians? *Politico.* Retrieved from www.politico.eu/article/who-are-europe-far-right-identitarians-austria-generation-identity-martin-sellner/

El-Badawy, E. (2019). Evidence for the relationship between non-violent extremism and violent radicalization: Conveyor belt or firewall? In Richards, A. (Ed.), *Jihadist Terror: New Threats, New Responses* (pp. 53–66). London: IB Tauris.

Eleanor, P. (2019, August 9). The deadly myth of the Great Replacement. *New Statesman.* Retrieved from https://www.newstatesman.com/world/2019/08/deadly-myth-great-replacement

Elliott, A. (2011, March 17). Why Yasir Qadhi wants to talk about jihad. *The New York Times.* Retrieved from www.nytimes.com/2011/03/20/magazine/mag-20Salafis-t.html

FBI. (2018). *2018 Hate crime statistics.* Retrieved from https://ucr.fbi.gov/hate-crime/2018

Frampton, M. (2018). *The Muslim Brotherhood and the West.* Cambridge, MA: Harvard University Press.

Gartenstein-Ross, D., Hodgson, S., & Clarke, C. (2020). The growing threat posed by accelerationism and accelerationist groups worldwide. *Foreign Policy Research Institute.* Retrieved from www.fpri.org/article/2020/04/the-growing-threat-posed-by-accelerationism-and-accelerationist-groups-worldwide/

Generation Identity. (n.d.). Website not directly referenced for ethical reasons.

German Interior Ministry. (2019). *Politisch motivierte Kriminalität im Jahr 2019.* Retrieved from www.bmi.bund.de/SharedDocs/downloads/DE/veroeffentlichungen/2020/pmk-2019.pdf?__blob=publicationFile&v=8

Githens-Mazer, J., & Lambert, R. (2010). Why conventional wisdom on radicalization fails: The persistence of a failed discourse. *International Affairs,* 86(4), 889–901. doi: https://doi.org/10.1111/j.1468-2346.2010.00918.x

Guhl, J. (2018). Why beliefs always matter, but rarely help us predict jihadist violence. The role of cognitive extremism as a precursor for violent extremism. *Journal for Deradicalization,* (14), 192–217. Retrieved from https://journals.sfu.ca/jd/index.php/jd/article/view/139/113

Guhl, J., & Davey, J. (2020). A safe space to hate: White supremacist mobilisation on Telegram. *Institute for Strategic Dialogue.* Retrieved from www.isdglobal.org/isd-publications/a-safe-space-to-hate-white-supremacist-mobilisation-on-telegram/

Hamid, S. (2014). *Temptations of Power: Islamists and Illiberal Democracy in a New Middle East.* Oxford: Oxford University Press.

Hawley, G. (2017). *Making Sense of the Alt-right.* New York: Columbia University Press.

Hitchens, A. Y. M. (2018). Salafism in America: History, evolution, radicalization. *Program on Extremism.* Retrieved from https://extremism.gwu.edu/sites/g/files/zaxdzs2191/f/Salafism%20in%20America.pdf

Hizb-ut-Tahrir. (2015). *Press Release 20150531: Conference in Chicago.* Retrieved from https://hizb-america.org/press-release-20150531-conference-in-chicago/

Hizb-ut-Tahrir. (n.d.). *Hizb-ut-Tahrir website.* Retrieved from www.hizb-ut-tahrir.org/index.php/en/def

HM Government. (2011a). *Prevent strategy.* Retrieved from https://assets.publishing.service.gov.uk/government/uploads/system/uploads/attachment_data/file/97976/prevent-strategy-review.pdf

HM Government. (2011b). *CONTEST.* Retrieved from www.gov.uk/government/uploads/system/uploads/attachment_data/file/97995/strategy-contest.pdf

Home Office. (2015). *Counter-extremism strategy.* Retrieved from https://assets.publishing.service.gov.uk/government/uploads/system/uploads/attachment_data/file/470088/51859_Cm9148_Accessible.pdf

Home Office. (2018). Hate crime, England and Wales, 2018/19. Retrieved from https://assets.publishing.service.gov.uk/government/uploads/system/uploads/attachment_data/file/839172/hate-crime-1819-hosb2419.pdf

Horgan, J. (2004). *The Psychology of Terrorism.* London: Routledge.

Khan. (2019). *Commission for countering extremism. Challenging hateful extremism.* United Kingdom. Retrieved from https://assets.publishing.service.gov.uk/government/uploads/system/uploads/attachment_data/file/874101/200320_Challenging_Hateful_Extremism.pdf

Klausen, J. (2010). Al-Qaeda affiliated and Homegrown Jihadism in the UK: 1999-2010. *Institute for Strategic Dialogue*.

Loewenstein, K. (1937). Militant democracy and fundamental rights. *American Political Science Review,* 31(3), 417–432. doi: https://doi.org/10.2307/1948164

Lowe, D. (2019). Legislating non-violent extremism in prevent strategies: The example of the UK. *Dealing with Terrorism*, 192–210.

Maher, S., & Frampton, M. (2008). Choosing our friends wisely. *Policy Exchange*. Retrieved from https://policyexchange.org.uk/publication/choosing-our-friends-wisely-criteria-for-engagement-with-muslim-groups/

Minkenberg, M. (2006). Repression and reaction: militant democracy and the radical right in Germany and France. *Patterns of Prejudice,* 40(1), 25–44. doi: https://doi.org/10.1080/00313220500482662

Nesser, P. (2018). *Islamist Terrorism in Europe*. New York: Oxford University Press.

NZ Herald. (2019, April 5). Christchurch mosque shootings: Accused gunman donated $3650 to far-right French group Generation Identity. *NZ Herald*. Retrieved from www.nzherald.co.nz/nz/christchurch-mosque-shootings-accused-gunman-donated-3650-to-far-right-french-group-generation-identity/2WIK5AI6HWPKYEVNLYHFHB2DVY/

Olidort, J. (2015). The politics of "Quietist" Salafism. *Brookings*. Retrieved from www.brookings.edu/wp-content/uploads/2016/07/Brookings-Analysis-Paper_Jacob-Olidort-Inside_Final_Web.pdf

Orofino, E. (2020). *Hizb ut-Tahrir and the Caliphate*. London: Routledge.

Papasavva, A., Zannettou, S., De Cristofaro, E., Stringhini, G., & Blackburn, J. (2020, May). Raiders of the lost kek: 3.5 years of augmented 4chan posts from the politically incorrect board. In *Proceedings of the International AAAI Conference on Web and Social Media,* Vol. 14, pp. 885–894. Retrieved from https://ojs.aaai.org/index.php/ICWSM/article/view/7354/7208

Pfahl-Traughber, A. (2015). Salafismus – was ist das überhaupt? Definitionen – Ideologiemerkmale – Typologisierungen." *Bundeszentrale für politische Bildung*. Retrieved from www.bpb.de/politik/extremismus/radikalisierungspraevention/211830/salafismus-was-ist-das-ueberhaupt

Qazi, A. L. (2017). How to Islamize an Islamic republic: Jamaat-e-Islami in its own words. *Brookings*. Retrieved from www.brookings.edu/research/how-to-islamize-an-islamic-republic-jamaat-e-islami-in-its-own-words/

Ravndal, J. A. (2016). Right-wing terrorism and violence in Western Europe: Introducing the RTV dataset. *Perspectives on Terrorism,* 10(3), 2–15. Retrieved from www.jstor.org/stable/pdf/26297592.pdf

Ravndal, J. A. (2018). Explaining right wing terrorism and violence in Western Europe: Grievances, opportunities and polarisation. *European Journal of Political Research,* 57(4), 845–866. doi: https://doi.org/10.1111/1475-6765.12254

Royal Commision of Inquiry. (2019). *Report: Royal Commission of Inquiry into the terrorist attack on Christchurch masjidain on 15 March 2019*. Retrieved from https://christchurchattack.royalcommission.nz/

Safi, M. (2015, February 20). Hizb-ut-Tahrir insists it rejects violence following Abbott's 'desperate' accusation. *The Guardian*. Retrieved from www.theguardian.com/australia-news/2015/feb/20/hizb-ut-tahrir-insists-it-rejects-violence-following-abbotts-desperate-accusation

Said, B. T., & Fouad, H. (2018). Countering Islamist radicalisation in Germany: A guide to Germany's growing prevention infrastructure. *International Centre for Counter-Terrorism*. Retrieved from https://icct.nl/publication/countering-islamist-radicalization-in-germany-a-guide-to-germanys-growing-prevention-infrastructure/

Salzborn, S. (2017). *Angriff der Antidemokraten*. Weinheim/München: Beltz Juventa.

Schmid, A. P. (2014). Violent and non-violent extremism: Two sides of the same coin. *ICCT Research Paper*, 1–29. Retrieved from www.icct.nl/app/uploads/download/file/ICCT-Schmid-Violent-Non-Violent-Extremism-May-2014.pdf

Schuurman, B., & Eijkman, Q. (2015). Indicators of terrorist intent and capability: Tools for threat assessment. *Dynamics of Asymmetric Conflict,* 8(3), 215–231. doi: https://doi.org/10.1080/17467586.2015.1040426

Schwartzenburg, R. (2019, August 5). The 'white replacement theory' motivates alt-right killers the world over. *The Guardian*. Retrieved from www.theguardian.com/commentisfree/2019/aug/05/great-replacement-theory-alt-right-killers-el-paso

Silber, M. D., & Bhatt, A. (2007). Radicalization in the West: The homegrown. A New York City Police Department Report, NYPD Intelligence Division. Retrieved from https://seths.blog/wp-content/uploads/2007/09/NYPD_Report-Radicalization_in_the_West.pdf

SPLC. (2019). The year in hate: Rage against change. *SPLC*. Retrieved from www.splcenter.org/fighting-hate/intelligence-report/2019/year-hate-rage-against-change

SPLC. (n.d.). Extremist files: James Mason. *SPLC*. Retrieved from www.splcenter.org/fighting-hate/extremist-files/individual/james-mason

Telegram. (n.d.). Channels FAQ. *Telegram*. Retrieved from https://telegram.org/faq_channels

TellMAMA. (2018). Annual Report 2018: Normalising hatred. *TellMAMA*. Retrieved from https://tellmamauk.org/tell-mama-annual-report-2018-_-normalising-hate/

Tony Blair Institute for Global Change. (2019a). Narratives of division: The spectrum of Islamist worldviews in the UK. *Tony Blair Institute for Global Change*. Retrieved from: https://institute.global/sites/default/files/2019-01/Narratives%20of%20Division%20report.pdf

Tony Blair Institute for Global Change. (2019b). Narratives of hate: The spectrum of far-right worldviews in the UK. *Tony Blair Institute for Global Change*. Retrieved from https://institute.global/sites/default/files/2019-09/Far%20Right%20report.pdf

Verfassungsschutz. (2016). Constitutional Protection Report. Retrieved from www.verfassungsschutz.niedersachsen.de/download/119041/Verfassungsschutzbericht_2016_-_Vorabfassung.pdf

Vidino, L. (2010). The role of non-violent Islamists in Europe. *CTC Sentinel, 3*(11–12), 9–11. Retrieved from www.ctc.usma.edu/the-role-of-non-violent-islamists-in-europe/

Vidino, L. (2015). Sharia4: Fconfrontational activism to militancy. *Perspectives on Terrorism, 9*(2), 2–16. doi: www.jstor.org/stable/pdf/26297356.pdf

Winter, C. (2017, December 20). Inside the collapse of Islamic State's propaganda machine. *Wired*. Retrieved from www.wired.co.uk/article/isis-islamic-state-propaganda-content-strategy

Zúquete, J. P. (2018). *The Identitarians: The Movement against Globalism and Islam in Europe*. Notre Dame, IN: University of Notre Dame Press.

3

"BOYS WHO HATE GIRLS, WHO HATE BOYS, WHO HATE GIRLS"

A Quantitative Exploration of the Relationship Between Misogyny, Socio-Political Outlook, and Support for Violence in Europe

Gavin Hart, Antoinette Huber and Mark Littler

Introduction

While the volume of scholarship addressing both violent and non-violent extremism has grown substantially over the last 20 years, much of the contemporary research base focuses on two – highly distinctive – risks: jihadism and right-wing extremism. Despite the low number of attacks and fatalities linked to both, and the unlikelihood of terrorists effecting major change in Western societies (Mueller, 2005), the volume and febrility of news coverage around these risks ensures that we perceive them as "ubiquitous and permanent" threats that must be understood and then acted upon (Jore, 2020). As research funding (and thus, research effort) tends to track political priorities, and these generally reflect media interests (Schmid, Forest, & Lowe, 2021), the focus of academic "extremism studies" has become a foregone conclusion. Simply put, research focussing on alternate sources of risk is largely neglected, and has remained a cottage industry.

Recent developments have, however, highlighted the need to guard against such a narrow research agenda. The pandemic and post-2016 political instability have seen the number – and diversity – of extremist risks multiply, with new conspiracy theories such as QAnon (Enders et al., 2021), and COVID anti-vax paranoia (Hotez, 2020), joining anti-5G groups (Pantucci, 2021), resurgent eco and environmental organisations (Richardson, 2020), animal rights activists (McAlister & Monaghan, 2020), the far-left (Allington, McAndrew, & Hirsh, 2019), and non-Islamic religious groups (Littler, 2020) to create a complex and confusing milieu. Violence against politicians, institutions, and infrastructure has become, if not common, then less unexpected, while the corrosive power of non-violent extremist discourse has been widely recognised in the aftermath of the US Capitol attacks of January 2021.

It is against this backdrop that the rise of so-called *Involuntary Celibacy* (or Incel) extremism should be understood. While gender-based and misogynistic extremism had received comparably

DOI: 10.4324/9781003032793-5

little attention in the scholarship on extremism, recent years have seen a boom in scholarly attention, with Google scholar reporting over 1,000 papers in the last five years. While this is still a minute proportion of the overall academic output on extremism, it is a welcome change given both the relatively recent emergence of a recognisable Incel ideology and the fact that there have now been several high-profile acts of violent extremism attributed to this ideology.

Despite this, it remains the case that comparably little is known about the socio-political drivers of misogyny and Incel extremism, and there is little reliable empirical evidence to support the identification of pathways into violence for individuals associated with extreme misogyny. This chapter is an attempt to speak to these gaps and contribute to the ongoing debate about the causes of misogynistic extremism and its relationship with violence. It proceeds by first contextualising the spread and scale of extreme misogyny in online communities, before considering the evidence on the spread of misogynistic views in the broader population, the strength of the relationship between misogyny and support for political violence, and the demographics of those who hold these extreme positions. It will then present the findings of a series of analyses undertaken exploring the link between socio-political traits and misogynistic attitudes, and between misogynistic attitudes and support for political violence using quantitative data from the most recent wave of the European Values Study (EVS). The final section will present a discussion of these results in the context of existing scholarship and policy responses.

Understanding Contemporary Misogyny

Technological advancements, particularly the advent of the internet and social media, have provided new means of communication that have rapidly impacted upon the social and political landscape. This has facilitated many positive developments, but it has also increased the opportunities for abuse, victimisation, and hatred, including online misogyny (Yar, 2012). While the internet was originally expected to create a space where free speech and equality could prosper (Barlow, 2019), it has become clear that gender inequality offline has permeated online contexts (Bartlett et al., 2014). Women and girls regularly face forms of online abuse, particularly on platforms where content is largely user-generated (End Violence Against Women, 2013; Franks, 2011), with message boards, social media platforms, and blogs all being found to contain significant volumes of misogynistic content (Jane, 2017).

Bartlett et al.'s (2014) research examining misogynistic Twitter posts in the UK found that in just a three-week period, the word "rape" was used 100,000 times and that in 12% of cases it was employed in a threatening way. Terminology, which is also often used to judge, humiliate, and police women's behaviour (Dines, 2010) (such as the terms "slut" and "whore") was found to have been used 131,000 times, with 18% of posts being characterised as misogynistic. However, it is not unreasonable to assume that this is a gross underestimate given the limitations of the research and the exclusion of images (Bartlett et al., 2014). Indeed, Jane's (2017, p. 3) work goes further, suggesting that rape threats have become a:

> ... lingua franca – the "go-to" response for men who disagree with what a woman says, who dislike the way a woman looks, who are unhappy with the response to the unsolicited "dick pics" they keep sending ... Misogyny, in short, has gone viral.

This response, it is argued, reflects the historical treatment of women offline, and explains why women form the overwhelming majority of those attacked online as well as underscores why they are attacked more severely and in more violently sexualised ways (Jane, 2017, p. 10; Marganski, 2018, p. 19).

Moreover, the architecture of the internet has facilitated and amplified misogyny through the development of "echo chambers" (Powell et al., 2018) and "filter bubbles" (Rowland, 2011). The former argues that the development of spaces in which people share the same views results in those views being legitimised and reinforced, while the latter sees the filtering out of alternative or conflicting viewpoints through algorithmisation. As a result, on platforms where harmful ideologies are shared, users can rapidly become immersed in extreme narratives as they engage with an increasing number of people sharing the same views. This creates a disconnect from information that could counteract harmful views and behaviours, in this context providing spaces that allow for the development and intensification of misogynistic views (End Violence Against Women, 2013; Franks, 2011). While this is evident across a wide number of online groups, it is perhaps most notable in so-called "Incel" forums, which have proven potential for radicalisation into extremism (Hoffman et al., 2020).

A Brief History of Incels

Research identifies the origin of the term Incel as *Alana's Involuntary Celibacy Project*, an online community formed in the early 1990s to explore and discuss difficulties around establishing and maintaining sexual relationships (Kelly & Aunspach, 2020). However, while providing the terminology used to frame contemporary misogynistic extremism, this early incarnation of the Incel community bore none of the hallmarks of contemporary misogynistic extremism. Indeed, its metastasisation appears to have taken place in the following decades as online communities migrated to social platforms including 4chan and Reddit. In these more lightly regulated spaces, contributions became increasingly dominated by participants perceiving themselves as victims of an unfair society dominated by women and a small group of attractive or wealthy men (Cottee, 2020). It is against this backdrop that Incel discourse began to adopt a more overtly anti-feminist character.

Radicalisation in the Incel Community

While the extremity of the language employed in the Incel community has doubtless increased, it is worth remembering that the phenomenon remains almost exclusively non-violent, it is therefore not appropriate to speak of Incels as being a violent extremist organisation. While it is true that there have been acts of violence perpetrated by Incel figures (e.g. Alek Minassian) that explicitly referenced Incel communities online, and there has been evidence that some (e.g. Jake Davidson) expressed misogynistic views online and were active within virtual Incel communities prior to their attacks (Weaver & Morris, 2021), the vast majority of online participants appear non-violent. Moreover, there is no evidence of a specific group emerging that actively organises Incel violence, and it is difficult to speak of the dispersed group of individuals as a formal organisation (Cottee, 2020). Nevertheless, the literature on radicalisation can provide useful insight into the process by which individuals come to internalise the Incel worldview.

Discussions on radicalisation generally discuss an organisation that is specifically seeking to recruit new members through spreading extremist propaganda (Doosje et al., 2016). Moreover, theories of radicalisation tend to predict a group membership phase in the process where an individual participates in ideological learning within a structured environment (Moghaddam, 2005). In the case of Incels, there are no active groups dedicated to the promotion of a political agenda. If such groups do exist, they are yet to make a noticeable impact. It is more appropriate to think of Incels as participating in a loosely affiliated online community that can nonetheless have a radicalising effect on its members. This idea is explored in the work of Brzuszkiewicz who draws upon the concept of a *radical milieu* to frame how Incels interact on online forums, noting that they provide spaces for support and legitimisation of male grievances against women without necessarily causing radicalisation or instigating violence.

While it is difficult to capture accurately how many people are part of the Incel community, we can gather pieces of information that offer some insight. For instance, before the Incel community was banned from the Reddit forum spaces in 2017, it is estimated that around 40,000 participants were linked with Incel discussion boards (Solon, 2017). As mainstream online spaces have become more effective at tackling misogynistic discussion groups, the Incel community has largely moved underground, communicating on encrypted spaces such as Telegram, or in darker corners of the deep web (Rogers, 2020). This has made it harder to get a sense of how many people currently populate the Incel community. However, certain existing Incel forums have conducted research on their members and shared the information so that we might get a sense of the group demography.

Moderators at an Incel site named Incel.co released information about its contributors in 2020. Perhaps unsurprisingly, the vast majority of contributors were men aged 18–30 years. Within this age category, more members were towards the younger end of the spectrum with 36% of respondents aged between 20 and 22 years (Anti-Defamation League, 2020, para 9). Around 55% self-identified as Caucasian, with a wide-ranging blend of other racial or ethnic identities split across the remaining 45% (Anti-Defamation League, 2020, para, 11). Most respondents came from Europe or North America though there was a truly global blend of different nationalities within the sample. The survey also asked respondents questions about their sense of personal mental health. An overwhelming majority reported feelings of unhappiness, with 88% stating that they regularly felt unhappiness or depression (Anti-Defamation League, 2020, para 21). This is a significant issue for the Incel community with the majority of those involved seeing the community as a support network for depressed and potentially suicidal individuals (Daly et al., 2021).

Similarly, research on the Incel community highlights a strong sense of loneliness and social disconnection that is shared by its members. Cottee (2020) provides a useful insight into this particular crossover of toxic misery in his suggestion that "Incels attribute their misery to two twin-evils: sexual frustration and loneliness" (p. 97). Sugiura (2021) who has provided one of the most in-depth and comprehensive pieces of research into Incel culture describes a group of young men who are not only marked by a sense of sexual failure but have also struggled to build any meaningful attachments in life. Similarly, Menzie's (2020) research captures a sense in which Incels feel deprived of "socio-sexual capital" which pertains not just to a lack of sexual opportunity, but also to other forms of important social capital. This connects with broader literature on extremism that emphasises the importance of a perceived lack of social capital to the adoption of radical ideas (see Putnam, 2000; Schafer et al., 2014; Kaakinen et al., 2018). This is an important point because while the vast majority of Incels participate in these communities to seek support for their loneliness, once they become active in these forums they are exposed to a selection of potentially extreme ideas. The next section of this overview will draw upon existing research to enable us to highlight the broad outlines of the concepts and narratives associated with the Incel community.

Incel Ideology

A common theme among Incel discussions is based on the rejection of feminism. In this sense, the Incel community mirrors other societal groups who reject feminist ideas and yearn for what they see as a more natural patriarchal social order (Kelly et al., 2020). Similar to many other extremist groups, Incels commonly idealise a semi-mythical past in which their group was dominant or possessed a greater share of societal power (Saucier et al., 2009). Research on Incel ideas commonly highlights a tendency to depict women as inferior to men and nefarious in their intentions (Fowler, 2021). While Incels feel a sense of particular grievance toward perceptions of feminine power, they also argue that all men are emasculated by the effects of a female-dominated "sexual marketplace" (O' Malley et al., 2020). There are certain areas of crossover between Incel views and those of extreme right-wing movements. For instance, both groups reject feminism; both see the world in terms of a genetic hierarchy; both perceive themselves as victims of a prevailing culture of political correctness; both tend to inhabit unfiltered online spaces in which radical views are discussed and alternative views are removed through the banning of dissenting voices (Glace et al., 2021).

For loosely affiliated online communities such as those inhabited by Incels, it is difficult to establish a coherent ideological core that ties together its various members. Similarly, it is difficult to determine the extent to which those associated with these groups take these ideas seriously. However, there is sufficient research that has focussed upon Incel forums for us to sketch the common ideological narratives that are used by "group members" to make sense of their world and their place within it. Brzuszkiewicz (2020) identifies three core areas of discussion that serve to tie together the ideological narratives of the Incel milieu: self-perception and identity; gender relations and misogyny; and the futility of being kind to women (p. 5). This sense of self-perception can be broadly described as a state in which Incels perceive themselves as victims of an unfair social hierarchy. In this reading of the situation, they determine that their personal traits make them unsuitable for participation in sexual relationships with women. With regard to discussions of gender relationships, Incels frequently invoke anti-feminist narratives to explain their victimhood in the face of changing social trends. This leads to an idolisation of the pre-feminist era and the advocacy of measures such as arranged marriages to ensure that sexual activity is more equally distributed. Finally, Incels perceive women as inherently drawn towards promiscuity with certain types of men in a way that automatically excludes themselves from relationships regardless of how they treat women. This leads to the conclusion that treating women with respect and kindness is effectively a waste of time, as it will not lead to an outcome of sexual gratification (Chang, 2020).

Another important area of Incel discourse is their invocation of ideas such as the blue pill, the red pill, and the black pill. Incel message boards share this terminology with other online communities such as the alt-right and conspiracy theorists suggesting a potential overlap between these groupings (Kelly, 2017). To explore this particular ideological formulation in greater depth, it is useful to draw upon the work of Ging (2019). Ging notes that the concept of the 'red pill' has carried across the different parts of the 'manosphere.' Her work notes the origins of the pill narrative in the 1999 movie *The Matrix*. In this movie, human beings are being effectively farmed by an alien civilisation and are maintained in a dream-like state. Certain humans who are still conscious manage to infiltrate the dreams of the exploited in order to wake them and enable them to perceive reality as it truly is. Those in the dream are then offered the choice to take a blue pill that will allow them to continue to sleep or to take a red pill that will wake them from their slumber but they will be forced to engage with a nightmarish reality.

This idea has been translated by men's rights groups and other travellers of the manosphere to explain their perception of a reality in which men are subjugated by women. Broadly speaking, those men who are 'blue pilled' are deemed to be unaware of the dominant position that women hold in society. They are blissfully ignorant of the effects of feminist ideas upon the status and agency of men. Those who perceive themselves as being aware of this power struggle and the subjugation of men refer to themselves as being 'red pilled' or having 'taken the red pill'

(Ging, 2019). These men claim that conceptions of male dominance are a lie stemming from a feminist conspiracy to oppress men without their knowledge (Bates, 2021).

Those who adopt the red pill outlook in this context will often seek to find ways to navigate this perceived reality through strategies such as "looks maxing." This means that to be successful in a sexual marketplace dominated by females, men must adapt to meet the unfair standards that have been set by women (Tranchese & Sugiura, 2021). However, Incel forums have tended to focus upon the idea of becoming "black pilled" which is to suggest that certain men are genetically unable to participate in relationships with women due to personal characteristics that cannot be modified (Preston et al., 2021).

The black pill approach argues that there is no point in seeking to attract female attention and leads to either a defeatist positioning strategy or a fundamental societal change. Those who adopt the defeatist position will advocate coping mechanisms or possibly suicide as a response to their perceived inferior status (Baele et al., 2019). Others who advocate for societal change may put forward ideas based on potentially violent activity to tackle what they see as female domination in the sexual sphere. This is largely a response underpinned by the hatred of "normies" or non-Incels who are often labelled "Chads", "Stacys", or "Beckys". For those who have taken the black pill, "Chads" are considered to be attractive men who selfishly dominate the sexual marketplace, further reducing the chances of sexual success for Incels. "Stacys" are the most attractive women who seek out relationships with Chads, whilst "Beckys" are those women who can attract sexual partners despite the fact they are less conventionally attractive (Bates, 2021). Ultimately, this argument states that women dominate the sexual market because almost all women (regardless of attractiveness) can engage in sexual activity whilst less attractive men are not afforded the same opportunity, leading Incels to make claims of sexual oppression.

It is the black pill approach that has most often been considered as a driver of extreme belief systems within the Incel movement. While much of this terminology is new and the means by which they are spread are dependent on modern technological information sharing platforms, much of the core of Incel rhetoric ultimately derives from a rejection of feminist ideals and, in this sense, shares a common core with older varieties of misogynistic thinking. As such, it is useful for us to consider how these communities discuss feminist principles and the perceived effects of feminism on society and men.

While the views that have been discussed here represent the most extreme strata of misogynistic thinking in the Incel community, there is still a relatively limited body of research that seeks to understand the broader relationship between misogyny and extremism. Focusing upon the Incel community enables us to tease out the ideas espoused by a hard-core minority group so that we might use this information to support a deductive approach to data analysis. It is in this area that this chapter makes a novel contribution through drawing upon data collated in a mass survey exercise to investigate the connection between these schools of thought. Do those who reject the principles of female equality also tend to embrace ideas about changing society through potentially violent means? Also, what are the wider social markers that we might associate with those who hold sexist or misogynistic views? For this purpose, we will move to consider data gathered by the EVS to provide insight into these questions. The following section will outline the particular methodological approach that was taken to conduct this investigation.

Method

To test the two core research questions, the analysis employed quantitative data from the fifth wave of the EVS. Prior to analysis, an approximation of a latent construct – misogynistic attitudes – was formed for use as dependent and independent variable using eight items from the EVS exploring women's roles in society. The details of this process are outlined below. A measure of support for political violence was also formed by dichotomising a 10-point scale of support for political violence around its central point.

Analysis exploring the first research area – the relationship between social and political attitudes and the holding of misogynistic attitudes – utilised linear regression with the misogynistic attitudes factor as dependent variable, alongside independent variables measuring key social, attitudinal, and political traits identified from the existing literature. Analysis exploring the second research area – the relationship between misogynistic attitudes and support for violence – utilised logistic regression with the binary measure of support for violence as dependent variable, and the factor approximating misogynistic attitudes as independent variable alongside control covariates for age, gender, education level, and social status.

Factor Analysis

Quartimax rotated principal axis factoring was used to construct a factor approximating misogynistic attitudes. Forced extraction was utilised to ensure all components loaded onto a single factor which had an Eigenvalue of 4.314. Outputs were stored as a simple regression coefficient. The Kaiser-Meyer-Olkin test of sampling adequacy returned a result of .881, while the Bartlett test of sphericity was highly significant, suggesting that it was appropriate to use this approach with the data (χ^2 (36) = 168941.317, $p < .001$). Details of the component loadings are reproduced in Table 3.1.

The component loadings indicate that this factor adequately proxies the latent construct, misogynistic attitudes, with respondents receiving a higher score likely to hold more extreme positions than those receiving lower scores.

Results

In order to explore the first question – identifying which social and political traits predict misogynistic attitudes – a series of linear regression models were run using the factor approximating misogynistic attitude as dependent variable alongside dichotomous control measures for age, gender, marital status, and post-secondary education. The results of this analysis are presented in Table 3.2.

In a bare model including only controls, all measures were all found to be highly significant predictors of misogynistic attitudes, with older, less educated, married, and male respondents

Table 3.1 Misogynistic attitude factor component loadings

Component	Loading
The child suffers with a working mother	.620
Women really want home and children	.664
Family life suffers when woman has a full-time job	.788
A man's job is to earn money; a woman's is to look after home and family	.730
Men make better political leaders than women	.614
University education is more important for a boy than for a girl	.712
Men make better business executives than women	.653
The child suffers with a working mother	-.271

Source: Author's own analysis/tabulation.

Table 3.2 Base Linear Regression Model

	B	SE B	β
(Constant)	-.175	.015	
Age	.005	.000	.087****
Male	.205	.009	.109****
Married	.073	.009	.039****
Post-Secondary Education	-.354	.009	-.189****

*p < .1, **p < .05, ***p < .01, ****p < .001
Source: Author's Own Analysis/Tabulation.

Table 3.3 Social and political predictors of misogyny

	B	SE B	β
Happiness	-.184	.007	-.129***
Social Trust	-.427	.009	-.217***
Control	-.050	.002	-.112***
Life Satisfaction	-.084	.002	-.184***
Right-Wing Political Positioning	.056	.002	.138***
Authoritarianism	.312	.004	.348***
Membership of a Religious Organisation	-.276	.011	-.115***
Membership of a Cultural Activity Group	-.374	.013	-.130***
Membership of a Trade Union	-.453	.012	-.165***
Membership of a Political Party	-.139	.019	-.033***
Membership of an Animal Rights Group	-.432	.017	-.115***
Membership of a Professional Association	-.424	.016	-.122***
Membership of a Sports or Recreation Group	-.460	.011	-.193***
Membership of Charitable or Humanitarian Groups	-.465	.014	-.148***
Membership of a Self-help or Mutual Aid Group	-.185	.023	-.036***

*p < .05, **p < .01, ***p < .001
Source: Author's own analysis/tabulation.

significantly more likely to report high scores for misogynistic attitudes than younger, female, unmarried, and educated respondents.

In order to explore the research question, 15 social and political trait variables were iteratively added to the model, with the results reported in Table 3.3.

The results of this analysis suggest that involvement in all types of organisations considered exert a negative impact on misogynistic attitudes, with belonging to a religious organisation, membership of self-help and mutual aid groups, charitable and humanitarian groups, sports and recreation groups, professional associations, animal rights groups, political parties, trade unions, and cultural organisations all appearing to reduce the exhibition of misogyny. Both happiness and social trust also correlated with lower levels of misogynistic attitudes, as did life satisfaction and feelings of control. Conversely, holding right-wing political positions and expressing a preference for strong authoritarian leadership were indicators of a tendency towards the holding of misogynistic attitudes.

Table 3.4 Misogynistic attitudes and support for political violence

	B	SE B	OR
Age	−.008	.001	.992***
Male	.138	.048	1.147**
Married	−.246	.048	.782***
Post-Secondary Education	−.069	.049	.934
Misogynistic Attitudes	.262	.025	1.299***
(Constant)	−2.684	.080	.068***

*p < .05, **p < .01, ***p < .001

Source: Author's own analysis/tabulation.

Analysis exploring the relationship between misogyny and support for violence utilised binary logistic regression with the dichotomised measure of support for political violence as dependent variable, the factor approximating misogynistic attitudes as independent variable, and age, gender, marital status, and post-secondary education as control covariates. Nagelkerke pseudo-R2 and Hosmer-Lemeshow tests were used to assess model performance, with an increase in the former following the addition of the Misogyny factor suggestive of an improvement in predictive power (ΔR^2 = .006), while the non-significant result for the latter ($\chi^2(8)$ = 14,977, p = .060), suggests that observed data did not significantly differ from the predictions of the model. The results of this analysis are presented in Table 3.4.

All items except education (OR = .934, p = .158) were found significant, with increasing age and marriage associated with reduced support for political violence, and male respondents more likely to support political violence. Misogynistic attitudes were found to be a significant predictor of support for political violence, with those reporting higher scores for misogynistic attitudes more likely to express support for political violence than those reporting lower levels of misogyny.

Discussion

There have been several attacks linked to Incel ideology including the killing of six college students in California by Elliot Rodger in 2014 (Scaptura and Boyle, 2020) and the murder of five people by Jake Davison in Plymouth in 2021 (Casciani & De Simone, 2021). It is also estimated that around 50 lives have been lost as a result of Incel violence (Hoffman et al., 2020). Despite this, there remains comparably little academic evidence linking expressions of misogyny and political violence. In validating the existence of a relationship between the two, this paper has provided essential empirical confirmation of existing qualitative and anecdotal evidence. While further work is necessary to offer a more nuanced understanding of the pathways through which individuals come to engage in violence – notably around the other aspects and levels of causation (Bjørgo & Silke, 2018) – its results should be read as consistent with the existence of a relationship, and evidence of the seriousness with which the threat of misogynistic extremism should be understood.

Moreover, our analysis focussed on support for political violence rather than its commission, and while it is true that most Incels engaged in violence speak in support of attacks against women (O'Malley et al., 2020), a very limited number of those who publicly espouse violence are willing to engage in attacks themselves (Scaptura & Boyle, 2020). It is impossible to tell from our results what differentiates these active attackers from more passive inciters which, taken alongside the evidence on non-coordination by those who engage in Incel violence (Hoffman et al., 2020), may seem to characterise it as a fundamentally stochastic phenomenon.

While both the relationship identified in our analysis and media reports highlighting increases in the levels of support for Incel violence may be seen to reinforce demands for its categorisation as a form of terrorism (Beckett, 2021; Casciani & De Simone, 2021), policymakers should also remember that misogynistic attitudes, especially when they manifest in the growth of extremist groups, are fundamentally problematic. Regardless of our results, extreme misogyny may well play a role in, or help predict, broader forms of violence against women.

In terms of predicting misogyny, our results indicate statistically significant relationships with a number of key social, political, and attitudinal traits. Levels of happiness, control, and satisfaction predicted misogynistic attitudes in our analysis, with rising levels of misogyny characterised by less favourable outcomes on all three measures. Research examining Incel groups has indicated that feelings of depression, isolation, and limited agency are common amongst members of these communities and that online discussions often contain conversations about suicide (Baele et al., 2019; Cottee, 2020). Therefore, it is important to consider how the emotional state of Incel members might influence their perceptions of social issues and tolerance of alternative views. Literature examining the impact of emotional states has demonstrated that emotions have a significant impact on perceptions and decision making, particularly concerning politics (Capelos & Exadaktylos, 2017) and societal groups (Tenenbaum et al., 2018). For example, Tenenbaum et al.'s (2018) experiment examining prejudicial attitudes of 16–21-year-olds found that those participants who were induced with feelings of happiness showed more tolerant attitudes towards asylum seekers compared to those who had been induced with fear as well as the control group. This suggests that happiness, satisfaction, and agency may play a key role in how tolerant we may be of others and/or alternative views. With Incel members displaying feelings of unhappiness, this data, alongside the literature surrounding happiness and tolerance, suggest that the emotional state of Incel members may be a contributing factor to misogynistic attitudes. Happiness was also found to impact upon levels of trust in Dunn and Schweitzer's (2005) experiment, which found that happy participants were significantly more likely to be trusting than sad or angry participants. With Incels displaying particularly low levels of happiness, and the fact that this often manifests as anger toward women (Menzie, 2020), it seems likely that the emotional state of Incel members contributes to their lack of trust in women (Jaki et al., 2020).

The concept of trust also proved to have a significant impact on misogyny with data showing that as generalised social trust decreases, misogyny increases. Whilst Incels are particularly distrusting of women, research on these communities also highlights a lack of trust in the broader male population. Incel ideology is based upon the belief that men are marginalised and subjugated by women in society (Prażmo, 2020). Women are seen to be naturally evil, manipulative, and cruel (O'Malley et al., 2020), and there are grounds to suggest that Incel ideology reinforces positivist ideas stemming from theorists like Lombroso, Ferrero, and Pollak that women's deviancy is a result of biology (Lombroso & Ferrero, 1898; Pollack, 1950). More specifically, Pollack's (1950) explanation of female behaviour is mirrored in Incel discourse. Their sex-based theory centred on the idea that women's crime and deviance was not less common than men's but was hidden by women's biological and social ability to lie, manipulate, and deceive. The biological ability to deceive was argued to centre on the fact that, unlike men, women were able to fake orgasms. As a result of this natural ability to deceive and exploit, women were seen as able to manipulate men into doing their bidding.

Whilst these explanations of women's characteristics and behaviour are widely discredited, when examining Incel ideology it is evident that these beliefs continue to underpin misogynistic attitudes. For example, Incels believe that females are naturally evil and that women can use their sexuality to manipulate men into doing their bidding (O'Malley et al., 2020). The fact that women are seen to exploit unsuspecting men results in those men becoming untrustworthy due to corruption. This is supported by Incel beliefs that any men who have not taken the black pill are considered 'Chads' or 'Cucks.' Chads are those men who are perceived as sexually dominant and Cucks are unfortunate dupes who are betrayed by women (Menzie, 2020). These men are unaware of the manipulative powers of women and therefore become part of the problem through their adherence to women's rule (Preston et al., 2021). With Incels showing distrust of all women (around half of the population) as well as distrust in those men who are seen to be corrupted, Incels fundamentally lack trust in the vast majority of the population. Therefore, if we compare our findings with these broader themes within the literature on extreme misogyny, it seems unsurprising that there is a connection between low levels of trust and misogynistic attitudes.

Importantly, the data suggest that those who are most active in civil society are least likely to exhibit misogynistic traits. Our findings on membership of professional associations, political parties, religious groups, cultural activity groups, recreational and sporting organisations all suggested that these forms of societal participation mitigated against support for misogynistic ideas. This seems to correspond with research on Incels suggesting that group members struggle not only to establish and maintain sexual relationships but also to connect more generally with the world around them (Cottee, 2020; Menzie, 2020). This might also be explained with reference to the concept of social capital (Putnam, 2000), where low levels of social bonding are seen as a progenitor of a range of negative social outcomes (Murray et al., 2020). The literature on radicalisation highlights that a lack − or perceived lack − of social capital can serve as a catalyst in radicalisation processes (Kanniken et al., 2018) and can diminish political trust, a key determinant of support for violence (Littler, 2017). Taken together, it seems likely that just as social disconnection can facilitate extremist positioning on a range of broader political issues, misogyny is subject to similar pressures.

Finally, the results suggested a relationship between certain types of political views, activities, and the likelihood of misogynistic beliefs. For instance, there was a significant relationship between left/right partisan affiliation and misogyny. Those on the right were more likely to identify with sexist or misogynistic ideas. Other factors included membership of a trade union and the suggestion that participation in these traditionally left-wing bodies meant that respondents were less inclined towards misogyny. Finally, we noted that those who identified with misogynistic ideas were more likely to favour authoritarianism. These factors highlight a general trend suggesting a relationship between the authoritarian right and misogyny. This may not be surprising for a number of reasons. It is commonly recognised that reactionary forces on the right of the political spectrum reject feminist ideals and argue in favour of what they perceive as 'traditional' gender relationships (Kelly & Aunspach, 2020). Looking back to our review of Incel-related research, this may draw us towards the areas of linguistic crossover between the alt-right online and the Incel community, particularly with reference to the use of the 'pill' construction to describe their sense of ideological awakening. This blend between discourses related to misogyny and other forms of extremist thinking forms a deeply concerning relationship that needs to be unpacked with additional research.

Conclusion

This chapter has provided insight into an area of contemporary extremism that is largely non-violent, though deeply problematic in its ideas. Existing research in this area tells us that in unregulated online spaces views are being shared that espouse radically changing society in ways that are harmful to women. This type of misogynistic discourse has been connected with violent outbursts from lone-wolf terrorists, though the vast majority of those who communicate these views have refrained from the use of violence in pursuit of political goals. Like many of the contributions in this edited volume, we can see the broad outlines of a group of individuals who may not personally engage in violent actions, but who might serve to inspire others to participate in forms of extremist activity.

Our research has discussed the findings of empirical research into misogyny and political extremism. In particular, we have explored the social and political factors that predict misogynistic attitudes and considered whether these ideas correlate with support for political violence. The findings suggest that there is a strong connection between misogynistic views and support for political violence. Furthermore, we have identified a selection of social and political characteristics that are related to misogynistic beliefs. We have identified factors such as a lack of social trust, a tendency towards personal unhappiness, a sense of disconnectedness, and a general trend towards right-wing politics that act as markers for those that hold misogynistic views. Throughout the chapter, we have drawn upon insights from research into the Incel community to guide our analysis. While this literature focuses upon the most extreme varieties of misogyny, it has proven very instructive in helping to make sense of the findings from the EVS research and our specific modelling strategy.

It must be recognised that this contribution raises a selection of important questions that are beyond the scope of this chapter. For instance, we are unable to determine a relationship between the holding of anti-feminist beliefs and support for other forms of violence outside the specifically political sphere. Additionally, while we may observe areas of potential ideational crossover between the alt-right and the Incel community, it would be useful to carry out qualitative research in the online spaces that they inhabit to provide greater clarity on this relationship. This would make a particularly instructive research program for those interested in the spread of extremist ideas in online communities. Ultimately, this is a broad area of research that will continue to grow in the coming decades. Incels have so far had a relatively limited profile in terms of carrying out political violence. However, through cross-fertilisation with other extremist groups, this may change quickly. Furthermore, beyond questions related specifically to violent activity, we need to understand online misogyny better so that we might educate young men and prevent them from being drawn into these harmful echo chambers. Participation in these online spaces not only causes damage to the participants but also has the potential to lead to social division and a widening culture of misogynistic hatred.

References

Allington, D., McAndrew, S., & Hirsh, D. (2019). *Violent extremist tactics and the ideology of the sectarian far left*. London: Commission for Countering Extremism. Retrieved from: https://assets.publishing.serv ice.gov.uk/government/uploads/system/uploads/attachment_data/file/834429/Allington-McAnd rew-Hirsh-2019-Jul-19.pdf.

Anti-Defamation League (2020). Online Poll Results Provide New Insights into Incel Community. Retrieved from: https://www.adl.org/blog/online-poll-results-provide-new-insights-into-incel-community.

Baele, S. J., Brace, L., & Coan, T. G. (2019). From "Incel" to "Saint": Analyzing the violent worldview behind the 2018 Toronto attack. *Terrorism and Political Violence*, 33(8), 1–25.

Barlow, J.P. (2019). Selling wine without bottles: The Economy of Mind on the Global Net. *Duke Law & Technology Review*. 18, 8–31. Retrieved from: https://scholarship.law.duke.edu/dltr/vol18/iss1/3.

Bartlett, J., Norrie R., Patel, S., Rumpel ,R., & Wibberley, S. (2014). Misogyny on Twitter. London Demos. Retrieved from: https://www.demos.co.uk/files/MISOGYNY_ON_TWITTER.pdf

Bates, L. (2021). *Men Who Hate Women: From Incels to Pickup Artists: The Truth about Extreme Misogyny and How it Affects Us All*. Naperville, IL: Sourcebooks.

Beckett, L. (2021). 'The Misogynist Incel movement is spreading. Should it be classified as a terror threat?,' *The Guardian* [online]. Retrieved from: www.theguardian.com/lifeandstyle/2021/mar/03/Incel-movement-terror-threat-canada

Bjørgo, T. & Silke, A., (2018). Root causes of terrorism. In *Routledge Handbook of Terrorism and Counterterrorism* (pp. 57–65). London: Routledge.

Brzuszkiewicz, S. (November 2020). Incel Radical Milieu and External Locus of Control. *The International Centre for Counter-Terrorism – The Hague (ICCT) Evolutions in Counter-Terrorism*, 2, 1–20. doi: 10.19165/2020.5.21

Capelos, T. & Exadaktylos, T. (2017). Feeling the pulse of the Greek debt crisis: Effect on the web of blame. *National Identities*, 19(1), 73–90.

Casciani, D. & De Simone, D. (2021). Incels: A new terror threat to the UK, BBC News [online],13 August. Retrieved from: www.bbc.co.uk/news/uk-58207064

Chang, W. (2020). The monstrous-feminine in the incel imagination: Investigating the representation of women as "femoids" on/r/Braincels. *Feminist Media Studies*, 22(2), 1–17.

Cottee, S. (2020). Incel (e) motives: Resentment, shame and revenge. *Studies in Conflict & Terrorism*, 44(2), 93–114.

Daly, S. E. & Reed, S. M. (2021). "I think most of society hates us": A qualitative thematic analysis of interviews with incels. *Sex Roles*, 86, 1–20.

Dines, G. (2010). *Pornland: How Porn has Hijacked Our Sexuality*. Boston: Beacon Press.

Doosje, B., Moghaddam, F. M., Kruglanski, A. W., De Wolf, A., Mann, L., & Feddes, A. R. (2016). Terrorism, radicalization and de-radicalization. *Current Opinion in Psychology*, 11, 79–84.

Dunn, J. R., & Schweitzer, M. E. (2005). Feeling and believing: The influence of emotion on trust. *Journal of Personality and Social Psychology*, 88(5), 736–748. https://doi.org/10.1037/0022-3514.88.5.736

Enders, A., Uscinski, J. E., Klofstad, C., Wuchty, S., Seelig, M., Funchion, J., ... & Stoler, J. (2021). Who supports qanon? A case study in political extremism. *Washington Post*. Retrieved from: www.washingtonpost.com/politics/2020/08/03/who-supports-qanon-heres-what-our-new-poll-finds/

End Violence Against Women. (2013). 'New Technology: Same Old Problems: Report of a Roundtable on Social Media and Violence Against Women', [Available Online] December 2013: End Violence Against Women Coalition.

Fowler, K. (2021). From chads to blackpills, a discursive analysis of the Incel's gendered spectrum of political agency. *Deviant Behavior*, 1–14. Advanced Online Publication. doi: 10.1080/01639625.2021.1985387.

Franks, M. A. (2011). Unwilling avatars: Idealism and discrimination in cyberspace. *Columbia Journal of Gender and Law*, 20(2), 244–261.

Ging, D. (2019). Alphas, betas, and incels: Theorizing the masculinities of the manosphere. *Men and Masculinities*, 22(4), 638–657.

Glace, A. M., Dover, T. L., & Zatkin, J. G. (2021). Taking the black pill: An empirical analysis of the "Incel". *Psychology of Men & Masculinities*, 22(2), 288–297.

Hoffman, B., Ware, J., & Shapiro, E. (2020). Assessing the threat of Incel violence. *Studies in Conflict & Terrorism*, 43(7), 565–587.

Hotez, P. J. (2020). Anti-science extremism in America: Escalating and globalizing. *Microbes and Infection*, 22(10), 505–507.

Jaki, S., De Smedt, T., Gwóźdź, M., Panchal, R., Rossa, A., & De Pauw, G. (2019). Online hatred of women in the Incels.me forum: Linguistic analysis and automatic detection. *Journal of Language Aggression and Conflict*, 7(2), 240–268.

Jane, E. A. (2017). *Misogyny Online*. London: Sage.

Jore, S. H. (2020). Countering radicalisation in Norwegian terrorism policy: A welfare state approach to societal security. In *Nordic Societal Security* (pp. 179–198). London: Routledge.

Kaakinen, M., Räsänen, P., Näsi, M., Minkkinen, J., Keipi, T., & Oksanen, A. (2018). Social capital and online hate production: A four country survey. *Crime, Law and Social Change*, 69(1), 25–39.

Kelly, A. (2017). The alt-right: Reactionary rehabilitation for white masculinity. *Soundings*, 66(66), 68–78.

Kelly, C. R. & Aunspach, C. (2020). Incels, compulsory sexuality, and fascist masculinity. *Feminist Formations*, 32(3), 145–172.

Littler, M. (2017). Rethinking democracy and terrorism: A quantitative analysis of attitudes to democratic politics and support for terrorism in the UK. *Behavioral Sciences of Terrorism and Political Aggression*, 9(1), pp. 52–61.

Littler, M. (2020). 'Demonic slappers' and 'fascists'? Exploring extreme British anti-abortion activism on Facebook. In *Digital Extremisms* (pp. 157–176). Cham: Palgrave Macmillan.

Lombroso, C. & Ferrero, W. (1898). *The Female Offender*. New York: Appleton.

Marganski, A. J. (2018). Feminist Theory and Technocrime: Examining Gender Violence. In *Technocrime and Criminological Theory*. London: Routledge.

Mason-Bish, H. & Duggan, M. (2020). 'Some men deeply hate women, and express that hatred freely': Examining victims' experiences and perceptions of gendered hate crime. International Review of Victimology, 26(1), 112–134.

McAlister, R. & Monaghan, R. (2020). Animal rights extremism and the internet. In *Digital Extremisms* (pp. 133–156). Cham: Palgrave Macmillan.

Menzie, L. (2020). Stacys, Beckys, and Chads: The construction of femininity and hegemonic masculinity within Incel rhetoric. *Psychology & Sexuality*, 13(1), 1–17.

Moghaddam, F. M. (2005). The staircase to terrorism: A psychological exploration. *American Psychologist*, 60(2), 161–169.

Mueller, J. (2005). Six rather unusual propositions about terrorism. *Terrorism and Political Violence*, 17(4), 487–505.

Murray, B., Domina, T., Petts, A., Renzulli, L., & Boylan, R. (2020). "We're in this together": Bridging and bonding social capital in elementary school PTOs. *American Educational Research Journal*, 57(5), 2210–2244.

O'Malley, R. L., Holt, K., & Holt, T. J. (2020). An exploration of the involuntary celibate (Incel) sub-culture online. *Journal of Interpersonal Violence*, 37(7–8). https://doi.org/10.1177/0886260520959625

Pantucci, R. (2021). Mapping the one-year impact of COVID-19 on violent extremism. *Counter Terrorist Trends and Analyses*, 13(2), 1–9.

Pollak, O. (1950). *The Criminality of Women*. Philadelphia: University of Pennsylvania Press.

Powell, A., Stratton, G., & Cameron, R. (2018). *Digital Criminology*. London: Routledge.

Prażmo, E. (2020). Foids are worse than animals. A cognitive linguistics analysis of dehumanizing metaphors in online discourse. *Topics in Linguistics*, 21(2), 16–27.

Preston, K., Halpin, M., & Maguire, F. (2021). The black pill: New technology and the male supremacy of involuntarily celibate men. *Men and Masculinities*, 24(5), 23–841. https://doi.org/1097184X21 1017954

Putnam, R.D. (2000). *Bowling Alone: The Collapse and Revival of American Community*. New York: Simon & Schuster.

Richardson, B. J. (Ed.). (2020). *From Student Strikes to the Extinction Rebellion: New Protest Movements Shaping Our Future*. Cheltenham and Camberley: Edward Elgar.

Rogers, R. (2020). Deplatforming: Following extreme Internet celebrities to Telegram and alternative social media. *European Journal of Communication*, 35(3), 213–229.

Rowland, (2011). Review of the book The Filter Bubble: What the Internet is Hiding from You. *Libraries and the Academy*, 11(4), 1009–1011. doi:10.1353/pla.2011.0036.

Saucier, G., Akers, L. G., Shen-Miller, S., Knežević, G., & Stankov, L. (2009). Patterns of thinking in militant extremism. *Perspectives on Psychological Science*, 4(3), 256–271.

Scaptura, M. N. & Boyle, K. M. (2020). Masculinity Threat, 'Incel' Traits, and Violent Fantasies Among Heterosexual Men in the United States. *Feminist Criminology*, 15(3), 278–298.

Schafer, J. A., Mullins, C. W., & Box, S. (2014). Awakenings: The emergence of white supremacist ideologies. *Deviant Behavior*, 35(3), 173–196.

Schmid, A. P., Forest, J. J., & Lowe, T. (2021). Terrorism Studies. *Perspectives on Terrorism*, 15(3), 142–152.

Solon, O. (2017). 'Incel': Reddit bans misogynist men's group blaming women for their celibacy. Guardian online. Retrieved from: www.theguardian.com/technology/2017/nov/08/reddit-Incel-involuntary-celibate-men-ban

Sugiura, L. (2021). An introduction to incel. In *The Incel Rebellion: The Rise of the Manosphere and the Virtual War Against Women* (pp. 1–13). Bingley: Emerald Publishing.

Tenenbaum, H. R., Capelos, T., Lorimer, J., & Stocks, T. (2018). Positive thinking elevates tolerance: Experimental effects of happiness on adolescents' attitudes toward asylum seekers. *Clinical Child Psychology and Psychiatry*, 23(2), 346–357.

Tomkinson, S., Harper, T., & Attwell, K. (2020). Confronting incel: Exploring possible policy responses to misogynistic violent extremism. *Australian Journal of Political Science*, 55(2), 152–169.

Tranchese, A., & Sugiura, L. (2021). "I Don't Hate All Women, Just Those Stuck-Up Bitches": How Incels and Mainstream Pornography Speak the Same Extreme Language of Misogyny. *Violence Against Women*, 27(14), 2709–2734. Doi: https://doi.org/1077801221996453

Weaver. & Morris (2021). Plymouth gunman: a hate-filled misogynist and 'incel'. *The Guardian*. Retrieved from: www.theguardian.com/uk-news/2021/aug/13/plymouth-shooting-suspect-what-we-know-jake-davison

Yar, M. (2012). E-Crime 2.0: The criminological landscape of new social media. *Information and Communications Technology Law*, 21(3), 207–219.

PART 2

'Old' and 'New' Religious Extremisms

Non-violent Islamist, Buddhist and Hindu Movements

4

WHEN IDEOLOGY IS ALL THAT MATTERS!

Exploring Non-violent Islamism Through Fetullah Gülen and Taqiuddin An-Nabhani

Elisa Orofino and Yavuz Çobanoğlu

Introduction

Jihadi terrorism still plays a pivotal role in current scholarship on extremism, terrorism and counter-terrorism. Whether "lone wolf" or group-affiliated, terrorists are still the object of analysis of many studies (Andersson Malmros, 2021; McCann, 2021; Romaniuk, 2019). However, *jihadi* terrorism stands as the peak of an iceberg having much deeper roots, that is,. a powerful ideology daily disseminated by organisations that legally operate in Western states. Thanks to their open rejection of violence, non-violent but extreme groups[1] use the master frame of human rights (e.g. freedom of speech, freedom of opinion, freedom of association) to win more supporters to their cause (Karagiannis, 2018). Ideology is what moves people to join these organisations and remain as members for a long time (Orofino, 2020b). Espousing the core tenets of a group, developing a "group identity" and endorsing specific frames,[2] it is through ideology that reality and grievances are interpreted and keeps individuals within the organisation – even if they are confronted with terrible consequences, such as prosecutions and imprisonment (Orofino, 2020b).

Long-living non-violent Islamist groups, such as Hizb ut-Tahrir (HT) and Hizmet, stand as good examples of non-violent extreme groups who have the power to both attract new members and retain them today. HT and Hizmet also stand as forerunners of contemporary Islamist activism and were chosen as case studies for this analysis because of their current appeal to many individuals around the world. Moreover, both organisations have inspired several violent and non-violent movements and individuals.[3] As non-violent Islamists, both groups operate in a very problematic space in the West where the fundamental freedoms grant them the right to legally operate – despite their open opposition to key values of democratic states (Orofino, 2020a, 2020b).

This chapter addresses the ideological appeal of vocally extreme (but non-violent) organisations using HT and Hizmet as case studies. This chapter will focus on the founders – Taquiddin An-Nabhani (HT) and Fethullah Gülen (Hizmet) – to better explore the origin of the ideological tenets of both groups. While emerging in different countries and 13 years apart,[4] HT and Hizmet present many commonalities. Firstly, in spite of their troubled relationship with

DOI: 10.4324/9781003032793-7

national authorities and their ban in several countries,[5] both HT and Hizmet proudly define themselves as intellectually non-violent Islamist organisations, strongly condemning the use of violence.[6] Both groups champion a non-violent version of Islamism focusing instead on education, charity work, social care and media campaigns.

The power of ideology is another element HT and Hizmet have in common. While persecuted, tortured and often jailed, members of both groups are still loyal to their organisations; thanks to their strong social identity, which is closely related to the founders, the values they have conveyed and their charisma. Although the authors decided to focus on commonalities in order to serve the purpose of this research, they are fully aware that there are great differences between HT and Hizmet. These include their stance on political participation, which is not analysed in detail in this chapter due to space limitations and the specific scope of this study.

The purpose of this chapter is then to navigate the reader through the core ideological premises of both An-Nabhani and Gülen in order to grasp the elements that made those ideas so appealing to ensure wide membership and the survival of the groups over the decades. This chapter also aims to shed light on the premises that might work as a "conveyor belt" (Baran, 2005, p. 11) to violence for some individuals. To do so, this study first focuses on An-Nabhani's and Gülen's background and personalities, highlighting how charisma and religious purism worked as two major triggers for the expansion of both groups. This chapter then analyses the concept of clash of civilisations, the continuous struggle between Islam and sin and the relationship with national authorities (Hizb ut-Tahrir, 2002). The final part of this research is centred on the core role played by education in the methodology of both organisations to recruit and detain more members as well as to revive Islam around the world.

An-Nabhani and Gülen: Religious Purism and the Struggle Against Sin

An-Nabhani and Gülen stand as two charismatic Islamist thinkers of modern history. Although not as famous as the leaders of *jihadi* organisations (such as Osama Bin Laden or Abu Bakr al-Baghdadi), the ideas of An-Nabhani and Gülen have influenced thousands of people around the world. Given the numerous branches in all continents and the wide plethora of sister associations supporting both groups, questions around the secret of their success come to mind.

The answer to these questions is strongly related to the personality of the founders. An-Nabhani and Gülen were able to create the image of a trustworthy *persona* grounded on their pristine image as knowledgeable leaders driving people towards religious purism. An-Nabhani and Gülen both came from very religious families. An-Nabhani was born in 1909 in Ijzim (Palestine) and his household was well-known for their expertise in Islamic science: his parents were scholars in Islamic jurisprudence and his maternal grandfather served as judge in Islamic courts during the Ottoman Empire (Taji-Farouki, 1996; Pankhurst, 2013, 2016). An-Nabhani's wit was evident since his youth, and by the age of 19 he was simultaneously enrolled at both al-Azhar University and Dar-ul-'Ulum College in Cairo (Pankhurst, 2013).

Gülen's educational path was a bit more complicated. Gülen was born in 1941 in Erzurum's Pasinler district (Turkey) where he started primary school. He had to drop out after his father (an *imam*) was assigned to another village (Alvar), and he could not complete school education or attend university as An-Nabbani did. Nevertheless, Gülen's religious education continued, and he was strongly encouraged by his father who impacted Gülen's views on a number of topics – among them, the belief that Islam is the only source of "security and order within a state" and "the main factor guiding and disciplining individuals' behaviour" (Gülen, 2003, p. 173).

Not only did An-Nabhani and Gülen share a common religious background imprinted by their families, but they also developed their career as teachers. While An-Nabhani worked as a high school teacher back in Palestine, Gülen worked more as an *imam* in mosques around Turkey.[7] After he was recognised as a religious educator by several mosques under state control (including Edirne Üçşerefeli mosque),[8] Gülen taught courses on the *Qur'an* – mostly to children. As soon as Hizmet became popular and resourceful in the 1970s, Gülen and his group became established religious education providers to young people in Turkey (Erdoğan, 1995).

An-Nabhani and Gülen's charisma and their religious purism made them extremely influential in their communities. Both leaders strongly underlined the need for Muslims to go back to the roots of Islam, to its purity, and both of them claimed to be very knowledgeable on how to do it. However, their approach was different in some ways. An-Nabhani exhibited a quite harsh vocal stance against the West as a system of political, social, economic and religious values which he considered not compatible with Islam as a *din*, or way of life (Hizb ut-Tahrir 2002; Orofino, 2015, 2018, 2020b). An-Nabhani believed that Western states (mostly the US and European powers) had a hidden agenda aimed at annihilating Islam and the Muslims (Taji-Farouki, 1996; An-Nabhani, 1998, 2002). This everlasting battle between the oppressive greedy West and the Muslims is a pillar of Islamist ideology today but it dates back to An-Nabhani. HT founder was convinced that Western states were carrying out a double-fold attack strategy in the Middle East, which was both military and cultural (An-Nabhani, 2002).

While military invasion was evident and exacerbated by the creation of the state of Israel in 1948 and the forced Palestinian exodus, the cultural war was harder to uncover as perpetrated through secularisation. An-Nabhani believed that the Europeans were slowly importing their *haram* ("forbidden" in Islam) concepts, beliefs and lifestyle to the heart of the Muslim world (Hizb ut-Tahrir, 1996). An-Nabhani was also persuaded that even Western missionary centres and charities were a mere *façade* to destroy Muslims and subjugate them culturally:

> The cultural and missionary invasions against Islam started until the Western civilisation achieved the destruction of the Islamic State, fragmented it, and divided the community of Muslims. Nor did Western Capitalism stop at that limit; rather it worked to spread its concepts of nationalism, patriotism, democracy, freedom, man-made canons, and imaginary borders among Muslims.
>
> *(Hizb ut-Tahrir, 2002, p. 36)*

These words on Western-imported concepts mirror An-Nabhani's hatred for what he considered as being intrinsically un-Islamic. For instance, capitalism was grounded on materialism and the focus on profit, which is in contrast with the focus on spiritual matters as promoted by Islam. Not only this, but democracy (as the rule of people), personal freedom and man-made laws all to be contrasted with the very meaning of Islam, which entails submission to God. An-Nabhani had a precise idea on how to preserve purism among the members of HT: to avoid any compromise with corrupted Muslim rulers and Westerners and to keep focusing on their spiritual dimension.

An-Nabhani believed Islamic law (*shari'a*) to be the only set of rules able to give people a safe and good life (An-Nabhani, 2007). Therefore, HT founder stressed the need for the Hizbies (HT members) to abide with *shari'a* in order to do what is approved by God and therefore good (*khair*). Conversely, An-Nabhani was convinced that *kuffar* (unbelievers) who lived according to non-Islamic principles were prone to commit *sharr* (bad actions), namely, everything Allah dislikes (An-Nabhani, 2007; Orofino, 2020b).

Gülen's purism also echoes An-Nabhani's distinction between *khair* and *sharr* and emphasises the need for practising good deeds to avoid sin (Gülen, 1991, 2005a). Gülen asked his followers to live a balanced life between the two concepts and to lean towards *khair*. Nevertheless, he acknowledged that the constant tension between good and bad can cause anxiety and suffering among believers as they would live their life as a constant trial, trying to do *khair* and to avoid sin (Gülen, 1995a). To do so and focus on what is *khair*, Gülen suggested observing religious obligation closely and attentively. In his mind, what is religious is good and honourable whereas what is non-religious is often bad. As a result, Gülen was convinced that the community played an essential role to lead single individuals towards what is good: "being a beneficent *ummah* [Muslim community] and believing in Allah by bidding the good and forbidding the bad" (Gülen, 2003b, p. 319) was the panacea. Differently from An-Nabhani (who strongly rejected national authorities), Gülen placed a lot of emphasis on the role of the state. Hizmet's founder believed that individuals doing what is *khair* should support the state by working as law enforcement officers in order to ensure control on others to make sure they perform *khair* actions as well (Gülen, 2006).

Gülen tried to de-individualise the responsibility of acting good by placing it at the social level: individuals in a community should look after each other and check that they are behaving well. In Gülen's mind, this type of community control was also useful to rehabilitate sinners, people who have performed *sharr* (Gülen, 2003a, 2005a). A society where everyone looks after the other will be a devout, safe and peaceful society (Gülen, 2003a). Hizmet's founder also envisaged some obstacles to the constitution of his ideal society. As An-Nabhani, Gülen considered the West as a great problem. The Western social model might prevent Muslims from achieving the ideal society because of some concepts that he considered to be against Islam (Gülen, 1991). Among them, capitalism that he associated with materialism, impiousness, crusader mentality, egoism, impertinence, drinking, gambling, secularism, prostitution, corruption and a morality crisis.

Gülen agreed with An-Nabhani on the idea that the West was a corrupt civilisation grounded on materialism where there is no space for the spiritual dimension (Gülen, 2003a). The lack of spirituality, the rejection of religious rules has caused the decline of Western society and will cause the decline of Islam if Muslims get acculturated with *kuffar* (unbelievers) practices (Gülen, 2002, 2003a). For these reasons, Gülen stressed the role of the community as a "shelter" ensuring protection was extended to everyone. This protection was not only from sin but also from Western cultural invasion. Gülen insisted that life within the community[9] was the only effective tool to protect Muslims from sin (Gülen, 1996c). In fact, the community was able to give an amiable culture to people of faith, giving them a purpose of life and guidelines on how to live according to what pleases God (Gülen, 2005a).

In line with Gülen, An-Nabhani also considered the believers' life as a continuous struggle against sin. He was convinced that the only way to keep purism was to feed one's mind with *khair* concepts that would lead to *khair* behaviours (An-Nabhani, 2007). The only place where an individual could be cultured with *khair* concepts was within the group (HT), where study groups *(halaqaat)* and informative sessions could drive members towards the truth and what pleases God (An-Nabhani, 2002). An-Nabhani presented his organisation as the "educator of the masses", the only one able to teach the *ummah* (global community of Muslims) ideas and concepts in line with Islamic teachings (Orofino, 2020b, p. 229).

The Clash of Civilizations

The aversion towards sin and the ambition to create an organisation/community that would work as an educator of the masses are not the only common elements between An-Nabhani and

Gülen. The latter echoes An-Nabhani's ideas exposed above when insisting on the connection between sin and materialism (Gülen, 1996b). More precisely, Gülen speaks about the "enemy front" to identify Western lifestyle and culture as fully oriented towards the satisfaction of material needs and pleasure rather than spiritual needs (Gülen, 1991; Gülen, 2003d).

Gülen also refers to a "seduction network" (Gülen, 2003d, p. 84; Gülen, 2003a, pp. 74–75) made up of materialist and positivist minds who try to steer Muslims away from their religion as a *din* and encourage them to sin: "materialist thoughts in emotion, belief, philosophy and natural sciences have destroyed our belief, by destroying our customs and traditions" (Gülen, 2005a, p. 145). As highlighted by these words, Gülen was strongly persuaded (as An-Nabhani) that Western influence was destroying Islam and diverting Muslims from the right path, driving them towards un-Islamic concepts including positivism, atheism and anarchism. As the greatest evil for each Muslim is disbelief (Çobanoğlu, 2012), Gülen was committed to avoid the decadence of Muslims by removing all Western (or ideas incompatible with Islamic teaching) from society and creating a community based on faith.

This sort of incompatibility between Islam as a *din* and the West is also well explained in the book *The Inevitability of the Clash of Civilizations*, published by HT in 2002. Containing all An-Nabhani's ideas on the troubled relationship between Islam and the West, here An-Nabhani defines civilisation as "a collection of concepts about life" (Hizb ut-Tahrir, 2002, p. 5), as a result Islam and the West are clearly depicted as intrinsically divergent. This perpetual opposition relates to the Western search for profit, power and the satisfaction of personal pleasures rather than after-life and works that please God (Hizb ut-Tahrir, 2002). This book mirrors An-Nabhani's conviction on the great damage inflicted by a "soft Western invasion" (mostly cultural and missionary) to the *ummah*, as they were slowly pushed far from Islam and brought closer to the *kuffar*.

In his book *Concepts of Hizb ut-Tahrir* (2007), An-Nabhani depicts Western states as "enemies of Islam" who have cleverly introduced laws and principles incompatible with Islam:

> From the end of the eleventh century *hijri* (seventeenth century C.E.) up to the present day, the Islamic world has been subjected to cultural and missionary invasions, followed by the political invasion of the West … rules contradicting *shari'a* were laid down using the excuse that these agree more with the time, and it is necessary that Islam suit every age, time and place … this resulted in the detachment of Islam from life.
>
> *(pp. 6–7)*

According to An-Nabhani, Muslims' estrangement from their '*Aqeedah* (doctrine) was caused by a false belief – promoted by Western colonisers – that Islam should be reinterpreted to fit the cultural and historical context. An-Nabhani strongly believed that Islam should not be re-interpreted to fit modernity or human pleasures as this was *haram* (forbidden) *per se*. An-Nabhani believed that Islam is an uncompromising religion and way of life that should not be altered over the centuries. Instead, it should remain exactly that same as what was revealed to Prophet Mohammad in 610 CE (Mohammad, HT Australia, personal communication, 19 March 2016).[10]

Both An-Nabhani and Gülen believed that the only way to stop Muslims from regressing to *jahiliyyah* (or a state of ignorance characterising unbelievers) was to promote an Islamic revival. According to Gülen, "being a believer" is the only way to avoid decadence because faith is what revives the spirits (Gülen, 1995b). An-Nabhani's and Gülen's thought could resonate with most Islamist groups today (both violent and non-violent) having an extreme approach to the West as a corrupted system. The idea that Muslims have moved away from Islam as a *din* because they have been influenced by a continuous stream of *kuffar* concepts has been the starting point for Islamists to stress the need for action. Both An-Nabhani and Gülen believed that Muslims were not practicing "real Islam" (Çobanoğlu, 2018a) and they stressed the need to revive the Islamic "golden age".[11] While methods differs from group to group, the idea of pristine Islam still remains a *forte* and both An-Nabhani and Gülen emerged as knowledgeable leaders able to drive their followers to the pure/non-contaminated version of Islam.

When Purity Attracts Persecutions: Hizb ut-Tahrir

An-Nabhani's battle against sin and pursuit of purism marked his difficult relationship with national authorities. In the case of HT, the need to bring Muslims closer to the example of the Prophet Mohammed and his companions – the pious ancestors (*salaf al-salihin*) – made the group an uncompromising organisation, very bold in both actions and words. Since the early days, the Hizbies refused to support what they considered as "illegitimate authorities" (Taji-Farouki, 1996; Orofino, 2015, 2020b). Their illegitimacy mainly derived from the fact that Muslims were not living within the Caliphate (the Islamic state), that is, the only system based on *shari'a* and therefore the only system Muslims should abide by. Instead, Muslims were living abiding by man-made laws and this was *haram* (or forbidden or unlawful) in an-Nabhani's eyes.

HT's funder believed that the only way to start a revolution of ideas to restore the purity and glory of Islam was to refuse any institutional setting other than the Caliphate. The rationale behind this argument is that Muslims have the religious obligation to live according to the prescriptions of *shari'a*. As the Caliphate is the only system fully grounded on *shari'a*, all Muslims – according to the Hizbies – ought to seek the restoration of the Caliphate and to reject any other form of government based on man-made laws (An-Nabhani, 2002; Orofino, 2015). These premises marked the Hizbies' problematic relationship with contemporary Arab rulers, mainstream Muslims outside the group and Western former colonial powers. Since the foundation, HT leaders have never hesitated to define national rulers in the Arab world as *kuffar*, apostates and puppet rulers at the service of Western states (Taji-Farouki, 1996). The outspoken despise for Muslim politicians who did not espouse HT ideology triggered the conviction that HT could be a potential cause for civic strife among national governments in the Middle East since the 1950s. For this reason, HT members have frequently been arrested and many have ultimately decided to leave their homelands to escape persecutions (Pankhurst, 2016; Taji-Farouki, 1996).

The situation remains the same today: given its bold stances, HT is banned in almost all Muslim-majority countries. The Hizbies continue to be jailed and even tortured by national authorities and secret services.[12] Lebanon represents an exception in the Muslim world – together with Yemen and the United Arab Emirates – where HT still legally operates and members are not persecuted (Marcos, 2011). For this reason, HT has chosen Lebanon as the location for its Middle East headquarters and central media office. HT does not partake in electoral politics in the Middle East or in the Western world and discourages its members from voting or participating in any aspect of *kuffar* lifestyle, including fashion, popular music and other forms of popular entertainment (Hizb ut-Tahrir, 1996).

Instead, HT supports a clear separation from the *jahili* using this term to refer to non-Muslims as well as Muslims who are not part of the group.[13] The Hizbies' holistic vision of the world leaves no room for more moderate versions of Islam. Since the group is regarded by its associates as the only righteous one, all other Muslims who do not share HT's interpretation of Islam and the deriving religious duties are considered as living in a state of ignorance about their religion and their obligations to God (Hizb ut-Tahrir, 1996).

Discipline as a Social Good: Gulen's Relationship with Authorities

Although Gülen has extensively preached against sin, his purism was never intended to create any conflict with national authorities in Turkey. This is one of the main differences between the two groups. Gülen was not keen on the idea of opposing any authority in general. According to Gülen, authorities are called to apply discipline and therefore they should not be confronted or criticised; instead they should be respected (Gülen, 1995a). Gülen's respect for authorities derives from his belief that this is a *halal* (legitimate) thing as respect produces social order (Gülen, 1995a, p. 240; Çobanoğlu, 2016, pp. 266–275).

The social order envisaged by Gülen was based on a set of prohibitions and prescriptions that would prevent any sort of unrest or rebellion. In Gülen's mind, the key concept to keep stability was discipline. Gülen believed that discipline was essential to provide a good life in all realms, including especially in the family, school and other public spaces (Çobanoğlu, 2016). Gülen often referred to the *Qur'an* to support his view on discipline as he believed that the real aim of the *Qur'an* was "to discipline human and social life with a firm morality" as "everything is controlled with discipline in Islam" (Gülen, 1995a, p. 185).

The idea that discipline and order stood as two Islamic pillars shaped Gülen's vision of mosques as "heavenly training camps disciplining the believers" (Gülen, 2003a, p. 176). In his view, discipline was the core element for a good life both within the religious community and within the state where the community is based. While Islam was considered by Gülen the greatest source of discipline, the state appeared in his mind as the main guardian of discipline. Therefore, national authorities had the right/duty to curb any action aimed at undermining discipline. Standing very differently from An-Nabhani, Gülen believed that obedience to the state (even to a secular regime) was essential to ensure discipline and social order (Gülen, 2005b). Whoever was in power had to be respected for a greater purpose, that is, stability.

For these reasons, Gülen and his movement did not face authorities directly, but they aimed to change the political situation by reorganising the community and educating them on what is good and honourable (Çobanoğlu, 2016). Gülen envisioned a "golden generation"[14] that he would be able to raise through education and who would eventually become the new Turkish leadership (Hendrick, 2009). Gülen did not call for the re-establishment of the Caliphate (as An-Nabhani did), but he worked to change the *status quo* through a "controlled form of activism", refusing violence and opposition to national authorities (Özdalga, 2006, p. 238). This controlled form of activism was heavily grounded in community: collecting donations to open new educational centres, training new students, providing support to businesses, dormitories and schools were all examples of controlled activism. The majority of Hizmet work was (and still is) centred on young people so that they can become familiar with Hizmet principles from their childhood (Erdoğan, 1995). Gülen's controlled activism and his relationship with national authorities experienced a turning point when the Justice and Development Party (AKP) led by Recep Tayyip Erdoğan came to power in Turkey in 2002.

The Hizmet became an official partner of the government having members involved in the judiciary system, the police and the army. Gülen himself backed many political decisions of Erdoğan until major disagreements happened in 2013. After the emergence of corruption records against the AKP administration, the relationship between Hizmet and the AKP became quite problematic. Some Hizmet supporters (Gülenist military officers) organised the military coup on 15 July 2016 (Yavuz & Koç, 2018). The coup failed and the AKP retaliated against

Hizmet and Gülen. Members were expelled from public offices, thousands were arrested and the lucky ones managed to escape abroad. Although Gülen has always denied any participation in the coup or support for it, this event compromised Gülen's relationship with the AKP, who became his worst enemy. Gülen is today among the most wanted people in Turkey after an official arrest warrant was issued for him in 2016. Gülen was stripped of his Turkish citizenship and he is stateless since 2019. He currently lives in the United States, whose government refuses to hand him over to Turkey as they believe that AKP accusations of Gülen being a terrorist are not credible.

Ironically, events have led Gülen and Hizmet exactly to the same point of An-Nabhani and the Hizb: persecuted by national authorities. Although Gülen has always tried to avoid any kind of confrontation with political powers, the coup took place and he lost what he has long worked for: support and stability for his movement by national authorities. Gülen and the Hizmet movement have always declared that they stood by the state, regardless of who was in charge. As a fact, governments have changed over time, but the respect for authority has never changed within Hizmet. For this reason, the group has been kept in high regard until the coup attempt on 15 July 2016. Among the privileges enjoyed by Hizmet, there are generous state bids awarded, their presence in public offices and land gifted to Hizmet educational premises. However, this all came to an end in 2016. Today, five years after the coup, the debates are still inflamed. The ruling party AKP (Justice and Development Party) and the opposition parties agree that the coup was planned and organised by officers under the command of Gülen and the Hizmet, as well as their civilian extensions.

However, Gülen and the Hizmet state claim that they had nothing to do with the attempted coup. After the coup attempt, 125,000 civil servants were dismissed from their jobs in public institutions due to the assumption that they were members of Hizmet (Özgan, 2019). This figure still continues to increase with ongoing investigations. The state and its political apparatus – with whom Gülen tried to avoid conflict his whole life – now accuse him of being the mind behind the coup and seek to arrest him.

"Intellectual Islamists": A Methodology Based on Education

HT and Hizmet are often defined by their members as "mere intellectual organisations" to avoid any association with violent groups (Badar, 2015; Doureihi, 2017; Ebaugh, 2010; Özdalga, 2006). Over the years, both groups have emerged as intellectual champions, a role model for intellectual Islamists promoting the revival of Islam in different countries through a wide system of schools, mosques and education centres. Their main aim is to build strong Islamic public personalities[15] and teach the right Islamic concepts in line with their ideology (Orofino, 2018). Although HT and Hizmet present many differences in the actions and tools they use, both groups place great importance on education.

Hizb ut-Tahrir: The Educator of the Masses

Education is at the basis of HT activities. The group claims to be an "educator of the masses" (Orofino, 2018, p. 185) able to lead people towards what pleases God (*khair*) and distancing them from what is regarded as bad (*sharr*). This attitude is in line with a specific verse of the *Qur'an* adopted by HT to legitimise its actions all over the world: "And let there be [arising] from you a nation inviting to [all that is] good, enjoining what is right and forbidding what is wrong, and those will be the successful" (*Qur'an* 3:104). As a result, HT presents itself as a "blessed leader" able to guide the *ummah* to fully restore the glory of Islam. The idea of HT as an intellectual champion was instilled by the founder An-Nabhani, and it stands a central pillar of the group's ideology today (Orofino, 2015). HT's focus on education impacted both the internal dimension of the group (the members, the Hizbies) as well as the external cohort of individuals and groups HT deals with.

The Impact of Education on the Internal Dimension: The Hizbies

When looking at the Hizbies (internal dimension), it is evident that culturing is essential in all stages of membership.[16] Culturing starts, is fuelled and reiterated through the *halaqaat* (study circles). *Halaqaat* are compulsory for every member to attend, regardless of his/her position inside the organisation. *Daris* (student), junior, senior members and leaders all attend their *halaqaat* and progress according to their level of membership. Every *halaqah* is run by a *Mushrif* (instructor) who is responsible for dealing with appropriate themes fitting the intellectual maturity of the attendees (Orofino, 2020b). An-Nabhani himself conceived this system of learning (based on study circles) to lead the individual from the student status up to senior membership through the acquisition of essential notions and experience over the years (Orofino, 2020b; Pankhurst, 2016).

For this reason, *daris halaqaat* – for people who are not yet "full members" but students (new recruits) – focus on the 14 books constituting the official adopted literature of the group, most of which was written by the founder.[17] These books constitute the pillars of HT ideology, and therefore all students need to study them thoroughly for a few years before becoming full members of the organisation (Orofino, 2018, 2020b).

This meticulous learning process reveals the importance HT places on education, and this process does not end once the individual achieves full membership. After that, members need to continue to attend weekly *halaqaat* to progress in knowledge and learning, as An-Nabhani envisaged seven decades ago. Being an intellectual himself, the focus on education has always characterised An-Nabhani's vision for his group. HT founder believed that a group can be effective and long-living only if it is based on three main elements: an idea, a clear method to implement it and sincere people who espouse the idea and the method, after a process of learning and culturing to the main concepts (An-Nabhani, 2001).

While the idea and a method are clearly elucidated in the 14 books of HT official adopted literature, the continuous culturing process is something each HT branch takes responsibility for. Given the expansion of the group to over 45 countries and the survival of bans and persecutions, An-Nabhani's strategy proved to be effective as new members are attracted and retained by HT today.

> We are not about numbers, but ideas. A person becomes a member when he is fully aware of his Islam and religious obligations. Our aim is to build personalities and carry the *Dawah* (call to Islam) to the society.
>
> *(Mohammed, Hizb ut-Tahrir Australia, personal communication,*
> *19 March 2016).*

This quote from Mohammed (pseudonym used for a senior member of HT Australia) stresses again the crucial role played by education in HT's vision. Ideas are depicted as the major strength of the group to generate strong personalities and to call new members to HT vision of Islam. Ideas are also regarded by the Hizbies as their main strength against new forms of Western colonisation. In order to curb Western detrimental influence on Muslims in all fields (political, social, economic and religious one), the group needs to continue to implement a top-down culturing approach where each member, from whatever hierarchical position, has fully espoused the group ideological tenets making them as his own, transforming his priorities into the group's priorities and his vision into a group-common vision (Ali & Orofino, 2018).

Binding individuals to the core ideas of the group through education rather than binding them to a charismatic leader – who is in charge for a time and then disappears with his followers – has been the strength of HT for all these decades. The Hizbies are not attached to a specific personality but they have fully espoused the core ideology of the organisation and relentlessly continue to do so every week in the *halaqaat*, building their group identity day after day which slowly replaces their individual identity (Orofino, 2020b).

The Impact of Education on the External Dimension: Hizb ut-Tahrir's Three-Fold Strategy

After discussing how education has been vital for the survival of the group over the decades, ensuring members' loyalties to the group through a process of continuous learning (internal dimension), this section addresses the importance of education in HT activities devoted to the external audience (or what is called here the "external dimension"), with a specific focus on recruitment. In order to attract new members, HT has merged education with strategic goals and this powerful mix has generated HT's three-fold strategy for recruitment, known as "Shock, Demolish and Rebuild Strategy" (Orofino, 2015, p. 404).

The very name of the strategy suggests three different steps where individuals are taught the core ideas and goals of the group. By the end of this process, new recruits will have a positive view of the in-group (HT) and a very negative vision of the out-groups (all other people, including other Muslims who are not members of HT) as *jahili* far from the truth (Orofino, 2020a, 2020b). Going back to the phases of the strategy, everything starts by 'shocking' the audience both in virtual and in physical places. Official HT websites, blogs, YouTube channels are all characterised by striking images or stories that serve to cause individuals to question previous beliefs, which is what Wiktorowicz (2005) calls "moral shocks" (p. 95). The same happens during HT lectures, public talks, rallies where moral shocks are triggered by news concerning Muslim killings and massacres around the world – mostly by Western perpetrators – and due to the absence of the Caliphate presented as the only means to protect the *ummah*.

This kind of news is likely to shock the audience, especially young second generation Muslims living in the West willing to do something for their *ummah*. The shock provoked by such stories is what triggered the membership to HT form many HT Australia senior members (Orofino, 2015, 2020b):

> I have always had my heart broken for Palestine and I wanted to do something for my *ummah*. When my brother joined HT and he started telling me about the *Khilafah* (Caliphate) and its glorious time, I became persuaded that it was the only solution to protect Muslims.
>
> *(Amina, HT Australia, personal communication, 6 November 2015)*

Amina (pseudonym) had been a member of HT Australia for 20 years at the time of the interview

As suggested by her own words, she has always wanted to do something in favour of all Muslims, but she decided to join the group after her brother started sharing with her stories about the Caliphate and the need for Muslims around the world to be protected. Furthermore, the fact that it was her brother to introduce her to HT stresses another core point of HT's powerful methodology: keen/peer influence, also known as " the power of love" (McCauley & Moskalenko, 2008, p. 421). One of the tenets of HT is that all members should disseminate HT ideas in their families as well as among their friends (Orofino, 2020b). Proselytising is an essential aspect of the Hizbies' activities.

Individuals will be more inclined to espouse HT ideology and its radical expression of Islam as they are animated by romantic or comradely love. Moreover, as in the case of Amina's brother, the person who first becomes a member of HT is usually regarded by the others as a model in terms of religiosity, political awareness and social commitment, and therefore strongly encourages membership among the people surrounding him/her (Orofino, 2020b). The Hizbies' determination to educate the people they care about on the right (HT-sponsored) concepts and the need to raise their awareness on shocking stories are two core triggers for entering the first shock phase.

Once this is complete and the shock has taken place, HT aims at demolishing the individual's previous convictions in contrast with those of the group. For instance, HT stresses the relevance of the Caliphate in the modern world. As evidenced by the interviews with current HT members, the great majority of Muslims consider the Caliphate a mere historical relic (Orofino, 2015, 2020b):

> Before HT, I never heard about the Caliphate. I thought it was a 'historical relic', as it is usually thought even within Muslim circles. That is because Colonialism changed the school curriculum, reducing the Caliphate to a mere utopia.
> *(Mohammad, HT Australia, personal communication, 21 March 2016)*

> Even if I grew up in Turkey, I have never thought about the Caliphate as a viable system to be pursued in the modern world since Muslims rarely speak about it.
> *(Atifa, HT Britain, personal communication, 5 December 2015)*

As stressed by the words of Mohammad and Atifa, before their contacts with HT, they would never have thought about the Caliphate as a viable political system in the modern world. Nevertheless, after being "shocked" by certain truths, they entered the "demolishing phase", which most likely takes place within *halaqaat*, lectures and other educational events (such as public talks and women-only events). In these occasions, more data are presented to back up HT ideas so that individuals start questioning their previous certainties, becoming more familiar with HT's frames. Again taking the Caliphate as an instance, the Hizbies use strong intellectual and religious arguments to convince their audience of the superiority of the Caliphate as the only effective political, social and economic system is based on *shari'a*. The Caliphate is sponsored as the universal remedy for all problems of humanity. Using historical facts and narrations, the Hizbies depict the Caliphate as an ideal nation where Muslims and non-Muslims could finally enjoy a better life under the protection of a just ruler (the Caliph) within a system grounded on social justice and accountability as allegedly based on the fairest and just law in the world, that is, *shari'a* (Orofino, 2015).

Through regular meetings, peer gatherings and a large amount of HT literature material, the individual is likely to gradually shift his/her ideas to align them with HT values. Once individuals have abandoned their previous beliefs, they enter in the third phase of the strategy, that is, "rebuild". This is when the new recruit starts a process of self-identification with the group as all his/her beliefs are now being rebuilt in line with HT's ideology (Orofino, 2015, 2020a). The individual is now bound to the group, feels a deep sense of belonging to HT that has given his or her life a purpose: working to re-establish the Caliphate to build a better world (Orofino,

2020a). In the rebuild phase, the Caliphate is not a new concept anymore; it has fully been endorsed by new recruits and it has become an obligation for them (Orofino, 2020b):

> The Caliphate is an obligation for us Muslims because it is the only system able to implement *shariʻa* … Allah wants us to live our lives according to His regulations, therefore every Muslim should desire the Caliphate and work for its re-establishment.
>
> *(Farah, HT Australia, personal communication, 6 March 2016)*

As in the case of Farah – 40 at the time of the interview, a member of HT since she was 18 – members perfectly align their thoughts with HT's vision, eventually. Through a continuous process of culturing, individuals espouse HT's ideology, become committed to the group's priorities and associate loyalty to the organisation to their loyalty to God. Once the person has gone through HT's three-fold strategy, he or she will identify the group's claims as "noble" and in line with "God's will". Membership is usually a long-term one, as confirmed by the case of Farah. As a result, HT's strategy based on education is able to not only attract new members today, but also works as a powerful tool to retain these memberships over the decades.

Education and Methodology: The Hizmet's Strategy

Education plays a crucial role also within Hizmet. Gülen regarded education as a vital means to forge his "golden generation" with a specific moral code based on the right interpretation of Islam as a *din* (Hendrick, 2009). Gülen regarded education and religion as deeply intertwined: "religion is unifying and brings forth common elements that bind people together … at the same time, through education, people's minds are illuminated with knowledge and their hearts are equipped with moral values, love and respect for others and nature" (Gülen, 1999, p. 105). As stressed by this quote from Hizmet founder, education plays a sort of sacred role as it stands as the main tool to disseminate the core tenets of Islam and to equip people with the rightful concepts.

Gülen also had a positive view on sciences (such as physics, chemistry and astronomy) which he believed should be passed on to young generations together with religious tenets. Gülen was convinced that science was essential to boost progress and new important achievements but religious education was not to be neglected. Instead, it had to be well nurtured as the main conveyor of morality and righteousness (Gülen, 2002). While promoting education, Gülen was determined to fight ignorance, especially religious ignorance and lack of awareness on national problems. Education was regarded as the main tool to fight the darkness of ignorance as the means "that enables people to be in whatever position Allah wants them to be" (Ebaugh, 2010, p. 95).

According to Gülen's idea of social order, only individuals who have a strong religious education could be spiritually equipped to occupy leadership positions as they would have to create social norms and an effective social order (Gülen, 1996a). For these reasons, Gülen's educational strategy aimed at creating new leaders. To do so, the first step was to convert student accommodations into schools. More precisely, *Işık Houses* (Lodgings) were the designated spaces to start this transformation. These Houses were reserved to thousands of students with low income living in major Turkish cities, including Istanbul, İzmir and Ankara (Çelik, 2017). *Işık Houses were transformed* by Hizmet as main venues providing training to new members. The group would take care of the students providing for their needs and delivering religious education through study groups, reading materials and lectures.

Hierarchy was a core element of *Işık Houses*: senior members were called "big brothers/sisters" and their rules could not be questioned or disobeyed (Çobanoğlu, 2018a). Female students had restrictions on dressing code and private life, such as having a boyfriend. Furthermore, disobeying the elder sisters could imply immediate expulsion (Çobanoğlu, 2018a, pp. 249–251). The hierarchical system and the religious training received over the years in *Işık Houses* was essential to breed new Hizmet members and prepare them for life outside the Houses. After the training was complete, Hizmet would offer new members prestigious positions in the government, as public servants, or other business opportunities. As members settled in high offices, they would then open their doors to new members and continue the placement.

Gülen's educational strategy was not limited to *Işık Houses*: it focused on schools in general, which were considered essential to venues for the group to grow. Hizmet opened many schools in Turkey where the curriculum was characterised by both secular and religious education, based on Gülen's understanding of Islam.[18] Teachers were normally chosen among exemplary group members and taught Islamic history together with moral parables and positive sciences. Gülen considered education and learning as the best way to "enter people's hearts" (Gülen, 2003d, p. 73) and this is why he insisted on the importance of teaching religion together with sciences as they both had to be in the hearts of Hizmet members.

This process is also known as "Islamisation of secular knowledge" (Agai, 2003, pp. 157–158), and it is based on merging secular knowledge with faith. Through his educational strategy, Gülen wanted to ensure the rise of a new generation able to lead Turkey towards progress and wealth. This generation would have been loyal not only to their country but also to their *din*. Needless to say, this was the plan before the group was banned as a terror organisation in Turkey in (2016) and Gülen had to give up his dreams as he became one of the most wanted people in Turkey.

Conclusion

Shifting the focus of research on powerful ideologies rather than on terror attacks, this paper innovatively analysed two of the most influential Muslim thinkers of modern history, Taquiddin An-Nabhani and Fetullah Gülen. Their thoughts inspired people around the world to join their organisations (HT and the Hizmet) and provided them with the strength to survive ban and persecutions. This chapter explored the personality of the two founders, their idea of purism and their interpretation of clash of civilisations.

The analysis of these ideological premises shed light on the war of ideas perpetrated by these groups against sin and immorality and their will to restore the glory of Islam. While these premises work as triggers towards terrorism for some – as they are intrinsically anti-Western and aimed at restoring Islamic purity in the Muslim world – they still stand as a paramount for members of vocal Islamist groups who continue to reject the use of violence.

Through the study of HT and Hizmet, this chapter showed their powerful intellectual appeal for many people around the world who eventually hold extreme views but do not espouse violence. As discussed in the text, both groups are engaged in a battle of ideas and their main weapon is education. As envisaged by the founders, HT and Hizmet have a specific recruitment and culturing strategy based on education that is aimed at providing the members with rightful/*khair* concepts so that they will advocate for their organisations over time without waving their loyalty. Both groups stand as "educators of masses" in the countries where they operate, winning members not out of fear but through the power of their arguments.

However, this study acknowledges that some ideological premises used by HT and Hizmet can certainly resonate with *jihadi* organisations, such the vision of the West as a corrupt economic, political and social system. Therefore, it is essential to keep pushing research towards the power of ideology rather than on the act of terrorism itself. As ideology is what motivates an individual to act, it is essential to understand the basis of the ideological premises behind specific actions, their origin and how they work differently in individuals who engage in extremism in all its forms, that is, vocal and violent.

Notes

1 The terms "groups", "organisations" and "community" are used as synonyms in this study.
2 Social identity is intended as "the persons' knowledge that they belong to a certain group together with some emotional value and significance to them of this group membership" (Tajfel, 1972, p. 72). Frames are schemata of interpretation that enable individuals "to locate, perceive, identify, and label occurrences within their life space and the world at large" (Benford & Snow, 2000, p. 614).
3 This is the case of Omar Barki, founder of the terror group Al-Muhajiroun. Before creating his own terror organisation in the late 1980s, Bakri was in the leadership of the British branch of HT.
4 HT was founded in Palestine in 1953 while Hizmet emerged in Turkey in 1966.
5 HT is currently banned in at least 14 countries, including many Muslim-majority countries, such as Egypt, Jordan, Saudi Arabia, Turkey, Uzbekistan, Pakistan and Indonesia (Counter Extremism Project, 2017). Hizmet is also currently banned in Turkey, Pakistan, Northern Cyprus and Kazakhstan. Since 1 March 2020, the schools owned by Hizmet in Turkey were either closed or transformed into state property. According to the Turkish government, 38 more countries (including Pakistan) followed the Turkish example, dismantling schools and other organisations related to Hizmet (see www.mfa.gov.tr/feto.tr.mfa).
6 See Hizb ut-Tahrir (www.hizb-ut-tahrir.org/index.php/EN/def) and the Gülen movement official website (www.gulenmovement.com/).
7 In 1958, Gulen was awarded a state preacher's license after attaining excellent examination results (www.gulenmovement.com/fethullah-gulen/who-is-fethullah-gulen).
8 Edirne is a city in the northwest of Turkey. It was the capital city of the Ottoman Empire from 1369 to 1453.
9 Community (*Cemaat*) was intended as the group, Hizmet, which was able to provide guidelines on how to live a pure and rightful Islamic lifestyle (Çobanoğlu, 2016, pp. 168–169).
10 All names of the interviewees used in this chapter are pseudonyms.
11 The Islamic "golden age" (*Al-'asr al-dhahabi lil-islam*) was a period of cultural, economic and scientific flourishing which started in the 8th century and lasted until the 14th century.
12 This was the case of three Britons – Reza Punkhurst, Maajid Nawaz and Ian Nisbet – who were arrested in Egypt in 2002 over their links with HT. The group is banned in Egypt and everyone associated with it is likely to suffer severe punishments. During their four-year imprisonment in Egypt, Punkhurst and his companions were repeatedly beaten, electrocuted, forced to sleep deprivation and solitary confinement with no bed, no lights and even no toilets (Bowcott, 2006).
13 The term *jahili* derives from *jahiliyyah*, which refers to the state of ignorance characterising unbelievers (Suarez-Murias, 2013).
14 "Golden Generation" is the name of Fethullah Gülen's first book presented at a conference in Izmir on 30 April 1976. See: Gülen, F. (1976), *Altın Nesil* (Latif Erdoğan, ed.). İzmir. Akyol Matbaa İşletmesi.
15 By strong "Islamic personalities", HT members usually refer to people who fully accept HT's ideological tenets, espouse HT's goals and operative methods and have changed their personality and religiosity according to HT standards (Orofino, 2018).
16 By culturing, we here intend the "process initiated by an organisation to instruct its affiliates on specific values and meanings" (Orofino, 2018, p. 96).
17 For an overview of the books that make up HT's adopted literature, see "The books of Hizb ut-Tahrir" on the website Daily Islam (www.daily-islam.com/2016/01/the-books-of-hizb-ut-tahrir.html).
18 After the coup attempt in 2016, 1043 schools related to the Hizmet movement were closed (See: www.yenisafak.com/kapatilan-okullar-ve-ozel-okullar-listesi-aciklandi!-tikla-sorgula-h-2498435l).

References

Agai, B. (2003). "Fethullah Gülen Hareketi'nin Eğitime İslâmî Etik Kazandırma Projesi". *Küresel Barışa Doğru/Kozadan Kelebeğe -3*. (Cemal Uşak, ed.). İstanbul: Gazeteciler ve Yazarlar Vakfı Yayınları.

Ali, J. and Orofino, E. (2018). Islamic Revivalist Movements in the Modern World: An Analysis of Al-Ikhwan al-Muslimun, Tabligh Jama'at, and Hizb ut-Tahrir. *Journal for the Academic Study of Religion, 31*(1), 27–54. doi:10.1558/jasr.3505

Andersson Malmros, R. (2021). Prevention of terrorism, extremism and radicalisation in Sweden: A sociological institutional perspective on development and change. *European Security*, 1–24. doi:10.1080/09662839.2021.1974403

An-Nabhani, T. (1998). *The Islamic State*. London: Al-Khilafah Publications.

An-Nabhani, T. (2001). *Structuring of a Party*. London: Al-Khilafah Publications.

An-Nabhani, T. (2007). *The System of Islam* (Translated from the Arabic Edition). London: Al-Khilafah Publications.

Badar, U. (2015, November 4). The Counter-Terrorism Fiction | 2015 Conference 'Innocent Until Proven Muslim'. [YouTube video]. Retrieved from www.youtube.com/watch?v=usmupi6bjdi – action=share.

Baran, Z. (2005). Fighting the War of Ideas. *Foreign Affairs, 84*(6), 68–78. doi:10.2307/20031777

Benford, R. D., & Snow, D. A. (2000). Framing processes and social movements: An overview and assessment. *Annual Review of Sociology*, 26, 611–639. Retrieved from www.jstor.org/stable/223459

Bowcott, O. (11 April 2006). People were begging for mercy. *The Guardian*. Retrieved from: https://www.theguardian.com/world/2006/apr/11/egypt.owenbowcott.

Çelik, C. (2017). Örgütlü Dinî Gruplarda Hegemonik Dönüşüm Nurculuktan Post-Nurculuğa. Cemaatten Örgüte Gülenist Yapının Sosyolojik Kodları. *Journal of Humanity and Society, 5*(1), 25–68.

Çobanoğlu, Y. (2012). The Western Perception of Fethullah Gülen: A Story of 'The Good', 'The Bad' and 'The Ugly'. *Alternatif Politika, 4*(3), 262–284.

Çobanoğlu, Y. (2016). *Altın Nesil"in Peşinde/Fethullah Gülen'de Toplum. Devlet, Ahlak, Otorite*. Second Edition. İstanbul: İletişim Yayınları.

Çobanoğlu, Y. (2018a). 'Women in the Gülen Movement: Life in a Postmodern Display, Enshrined with Sacredness'. In *Turkey July 15*th *Coup: What Happened and Why* (M. Hakan Yavuz & Bayram Balci, eds.). Salt Lake City: The University of Utah Press, 2017, 237–261.

Çobanoğlu, Y. (2018b). *Yeni Türkiye ve Post-İslâmcılık/Hayalin Gerçeği İmhası*. Ankara: Gece Yayınları.

Counter Extremism Project. (2017). *Hizb ut-Tahrir*. Retrieved from www.counterextremism.com/threat/hizb-ut-tahrir

Doureihi, W. (2017). Hizb ut-Tahrir Australia Conference 'Hatred Rising Living Islam in a Hostile West'. Talk 3 | Embracing and Confronting Reality [video]. Retrieved from https://madmimi.com/s/d6ce2a

Ebaugh, H. R. (2010). *The Gülen Movement: A Sociological Analysis of a Civic Movement Rooted in Moderate Islam*. New York: Springer.

Erdoğan, L. (1995). *Fethullah Gülen Hocaefendi "Küçük Dünyam"*. İstanbul: AD Yayıncılık.

Gülen, F. (1976). *Altın Nesil*. (Latif Erdoğan, ed.). İzmir: Akyol Matbaa İşletmesi.

Gülen, F. (1991). *Asrın Getirdiği Tereddütler 3*. İzmir: T.Ö.V. Yayınları.

Gülen, F. (1995a). *Fasıldan Fasıla 1*. İzmir: Nil Yayınları.

Gülen, F. (1995b). *Yitirilmiş Cennete Doğru (Çağ ve Nesil 3)*. İzmir: T.Ö.V. Yayınları.

Gülen, F. (1996a). *Buhranlar Anaforunda İnsan*. İzmir. T.Ö.V. Yayınları.

Gülen, F. (1996b). *İnancın Gölgesinde 1*. Ankara: Nil Yayınları.

Gülen, F. (1996c). *İnancın Gölgesinde 2*. Ankara: Nil Yayınları.

Gülen, F. (1999). *Bulgar Gazetecilerin Sorularına Cevaplar, Medya Aynasında Fethullah Gülen (Kozadan Kelebeğe)* (Mustafa Armağan & Ali Ünal, eds.). İstanbul: Türkiye Gazeteciler ve Yazarlar Vakfı Yayınları.

Gülen, F. (2002). *Çekirdekten Çınara (Bir Başka Açıdan Ailede Eğitim)*. İstanbul: Nil Yayınları.

Gülen, F. (2003a). *Günler Baharı Soluklarken (Çağ ve Nesil 5)*. İzmir: Nil Yayınları.

Gülen, F. (2003b). *Kırık Testi*. İstanbul: Zaman Kitapçılık.

Gülen, F. (2003c). *Ölçü veya Yoldaki Işıklar*. İstanbul: Nil Yayınları.

Gülen, F. (2003d). *Örnekleri Kendinden Bir Hareket (Çağ ve Nesil 8)*. İstanbul: Nil Yayınları.

Gülen, F. (2005a). *Işığın Göründüğü Ufuk (Çağ ve Nesil 7)*. İzmir: Nil Yayınları.

Gülen, F. (2005b). *Ümit Burcu (Kırık Testi 4)*. İstanbul: Türkiye Gazeteciler ve Yazarlar Vakfı Yayınları.

Gülen, F. (2006). *Fikir Atlası (Fasıldan Fasıla 5)*. İstanbul: Nil Yayınları.

Hendrick, J. D. (2009). Globalization, Islamic Activism, and Passive Revolution in Turkey: The Case of Fethullah Gülen. *Journal of Power, 2*(3), 343–368. doi:10.1080/17540290903345849

Hizb ut-Tahrir. (1996). *The American Campaign to Suppress Islam*. London: Al-Khilafah Publications.

Hizb ut-Tahrir. (2002). *The Inevitability of the Clash of Civilisations*. London: Al-Khilafah Publications.

Hizb ut-Tahrir Australia. (2016, July 19). Footage of French crimes in Algeria [Facebook update]. Retrieved from www.facebook.com/hizbaust/videos/854941941305463/

Karagiannis, E. (2018). *The Activism of Hizb ut-Tahrir* (E. Karagiannis, ed.), *The New Political Islam: Human Rights, Democracy, and Justice* (pp. 53–73). Philadelphia: University of Pennsylvania Press.

Marcos, A. A. (2011). Hizb ut Tahrir in Lebanon: Its Contributions to Political Islam. *Revista CIDOB d'Afers Internacionals*, 93–94.

McCann, W. S. (2021). Islamic Extremism and CBRN Terrorism. *Terrorism and Political Violence*, 1–21. doi:10.1080/09546553.2021.1964964

McCauley, C., & Moskalenko, S. (2008). Mechanisms of Political Radicalization: Pathways Toward Terrorism. *Terrorism and Political Violence, 20*(3), 415–433. doi:10.1080/09546550802073367

Orofino, E. (2015). Intellectual Radicals Challenging the State: The Case of Hizb ut-Tahrir in the West. *Contemporary Social Science, 10*(4), 401–412. doi:10.1080/21582041.2016.1236212

Orofino, E. (2018). *Longing for the Caliphate while living in the State: An Agent-Structure Analysis of the Appeal of Hizb ut-Tahrir to Muslims in the West*. PhD Thesis, University of Melbourne.

Orofino, E. (2020a). Framing, New Social Identity and Long-Term Loyalty. Hizb ut-Tahrir's Impact on its Members. *Social Movement Studies, 20*(1), 1–18. doi:10.1080/14742837.2020.1722629

Orofino, E. (2020b). *Hizb ut-Tahrir and the Caliphate*. London: Routledge.

Özdalga, E. (2006). *İslâmcılığın Türkiye Seyri/Sosyolojik Bir Perspektif*. İstanbul: İletişim Yayınları.

Özgan, O. (2019, January, 29). En fazla ihraç Emniyet'te. *Yeni Şafak*. Retrieved from: www.yenisafak.com/gundem/en-fazla-ihrac-emniyette-3443669

Pankhurst, R. (2013). *The Inevitable Caliphate? A History of the Struggle for Global Islamic Union, 1924 to the Present*. Oxford: Oxford University Press.

Pankhurst, R. (2016). *Hizb-ut-Tahrir: The Untold History of the Liberation Party*. London: Hurst.

Romaniuk, S. N. (2019). Terror in France: The rise of Jihad in the West. *Critical Studies on Terrorism*, 1–2. doi:10.1080/17539153.2019.1589785

Suarez-Murias, A. (2013). *'Jihad is the Way and the Death for the Sake of Allah is Our Highest Aspiration': A Narrative Analysis of Sayyid Qutb's Milestones*. Master Thesis, Wake Forest University Winston-Salem, North Carolina.

Tajfel, H. (1972). Experiments in a vacuum (I. Joachim & H. Tajfel, eds.). *The Context of Social Psychology: A Critical Assessment* (Vol. 7, pp. 69–119). Oxford, England: Academic Press.

Taji-Farouki, S. (1996). *A Fundamental Quest: Hizb Al-Tahrir and the Search for the Islamic Caliphate*. London: Grey Seal.

Wiktorowicz, Q. (2005). *Radical Islam Rising: Muslim Extremism in the West*. Lanham, Boulder, Toronto, Oxford: Rowman & Littlefield.

Yavuz, M. H. & Koç, R. (2018). *The Gülen Movement vs. Erdoğan: The Failed Coup* (M. Hakan Yavuz & Bayram Balcı, eds.). In *Turkey's July 15th Coup / What Happened and Why*. Utah: The University of Utah Press. www.yenisafak.com/gundem/en-fazla-ihrac-emniyette-3443669

5

THE TABLIGH JAMA'AT AND ITS NON-VIOLENT RESOLUTENESS

Jan Ali

Introduction

Tabligh Jama'at (Conveying the Message of Islam Group) is a non-violent Islamic transnational pietist missionary and revivalist movement of self-reformation and faith renewal. It was founded in 1927 in a desolate town of Mewat, south of Delhi, by Maulana Muhammad Ilyas Kandhlawi (1885–1944) as a direct response to the competition over sacred space with the Hindu Arya Samaj sect (Sikand, 2002). Its aim was to protect Muslims from the threats to their faith and their religious identity posed by Arya Samaj and the prevailing socio-economic and political conditions (Ali, 2010b).

Since its humble beginnings and headquartered in the Delhi suburb of Nizamuddin,[1] the Tabligh Jama'at has grown gradually and has become one of the largest non-violent Islamic transnational revivalist movements today. The group has a presence in around 200 countries and its membership exceeds 80 million (Ali, 2010a). Its *modus operandi* is literalist/functionalist, meaning *Tablighi*s (members of the movement) literally visit fellow Muslims who may be religiously neglectful in their homes, oftentimes preaching and inviting them towards what the movement considers true Islam. The Tabligh Jama'at has always worked at the grassroots level reaching out to Muslims from all walks of life and from all sectarian, ideological, ethnic, and parochial backgrounds. The aim is to facilitate faith renewal and inculcation of a high ethico-moral order in individual Muslims through self- improvement so they can become reformed examples for others to emulate (Pieri, 2019).

The movement's work is given particular impetus by the conditions of the modern world. In the group's view, the modern world is in a state of *jahiliyyah* (ignorance or absence of the awareness of one unified God) and, thus, in crisis. The world needs rescuing and the movement sees itself having the solution in its non-violent Islamic faith renewal method. It seeks to avert the crisis by giving modernity Islam – a perfect and total way of life. The movement steers away from the world of excessive materialism, socio-economic manoeuvring, and politicking (until recently, see endnote 1). In light of this, how will the movement transform modernity into, what it might consider, a just and harmonious reality? According to the group, it is by working from bottom up, that is, rather than seeking structural changes and reforms in the economy, social institutions, and political structures, it is seeking to turn nominal Muslims into practicing believers. It is for this reason it is considered to be a non-violent Islamist or

DOI: 10.4324/9781003032793-8

revivalist movement. This is a fitting description of the movement because its central concern is to remove accretions introduced through modern and other foreign practices in normative and ritualistic Muslim practices and replacing them with rituals, practices, and values subscribed in Islamic scriptures – i.e. the *Qur'an* (Muslim holy book) and *Hadith*s (or the saying and traditions of Prophet Muhammad) (Ali, 2012). The movement sees inviting Muslims to the *Tablighi* (*Tablighi* is a member of the Tabligh Jama'at) path as the most effective way of achieving this and solving the problems besieging modernity and so it does this with the tool of *khuruj* (preaching tour) (Metcalf, 1996).

Islamist extremism is often described in public discourse, media reports, policy-making forums, and political rhetoric as a homogeneous phenomenon with a violent nature and equated with global terrorism (Jackson, 2007). This is critically problematic because research shows that Islamist extremism is neither a homogeneous phenomenon nor necessarily violent in nature (Alvi, 2019; Maher, 2016). This chapter is a study of non-violent Islamist extremism. It is not an empirical but a conceptual work that problematises the construction of Islamist extremism as violent and seeks to better understand why Islamist extremism has emerged in an epoch generally characterised as progressive and prosperous modernity. The chapter argues that Islamist extremism is generally a non-violent reaction to the negative consequences or "crisis" of modernity, that is, the Islamists find that there are some ill-conceived ideas about modernity that ultimately lead to a crisis and so there is, with some exceptions, a general state of existential disenchantment and anxiety such as meaninglessness, de-rootedness, hopelessness, depravity, and a constant decline of material well-being. The chapter further explains that Islamist extremism is internally a diverse reality and is not entirely driven by religious ideology or anti-modernity sentiment. Its many variants are not violent and all they seek is a global constructive and wholesome social transformation and Tabligh Jama'at is a good example of this project. Focusing on the Tabligh Jama'at, this chapter illustrates that Islamist extremism is engaged in non-violent efforts to bring about social transformation through the process of self-reformation involving making Muslims more righteous, morally and ethically engaged, and materially disinterested and aloof.

A Brief Overview of the History of the Tabligh Jama'at

The Tabligh Jama'at (Convey the Message of Islam Group) was originally founded by Muhammad Ilyas al-Kandhlawi (1885–1944), a Deoband-educated Muslim scholar in 1927 Mewat, south of Delhi, India. It emerged in a direct response to the rise of Hindu Arya Samaj sect from which had arisen two proselytising movements of Shuddhi (Purification) and Sangathan (Consolidation) (Ali, 2012). They were engaged in large-scale efforts to "win" back Hindus who had accepted Islam during Muslim political hegemony in India. The Arya Samajis who claimed to be the new defenders of Hinduism, which they alleged had become a forgotten faith and slipped into decadence in the hands of the Brahmans, concentrated primarily on 'winning back' marginal Muslims – those who, even though they had accepted Islam previously and adopted many Islamic rituals and practices, never completely gave up the quintessential practices of Hinduism and were therefore seen as Muslims in name only (Sikand, 2002).

In order to counter the Arya Samaj's proselytising amongst the Meos, the Tabligh Jama'at embarked on a non-violent mission of Islamic faith renewal and awakening among the Meos of Mewat and the broader Muslim population of India. The Tabligh Jama'at realised that the true teachings of Islam had been grossly neglected by Muslims, particularly those living in India. Ilyas realised that this needed to be countered and embarked on a mission of Islamic faith renewal and awakening among the Meo community of Mewat, and subsequently the wider

Muslim community in India with *khuruj* (preaching tour) as its non-violent instrument. It sought to do this by seeking out ordinary Muslims and inviting them to undertake missionary work, *da'wa* or *tabligh* (Metcalf, 1996, p. 114). Vahed noted that the "Tabligh aimed at the transformation of society by social actors without political mediation" (2003, p. 319). It steered away from active political activity and engagements; hence the description of the movement as apolitical remains valid even today (Gaborieau, 1999, p. 21). As a non-violent missionary religious movement, Tabligh Jama'at placed particular emphasis on personal renewal, spiritual elevation, and a revival of the prophetic tradition. Based on the missionary-preaching method, Tabligh Jama'at established itself over the years as a non-violent transnational network with a membership estimated at between 70 and 80 million (Burton and Stewart, 2008) and "has become the largest Islamic revivalist movement in the world with members present in more than 200 countries, covering all five continents" (Ali, 2010a, p. 149). Membership of Tabligh Jama'at is voluntary and those who join cover their own expenses. Participants are from varying socioeconomic and ethnic backgrounds:

> Tabligh includes many levels of participation, from those who have virtually no other activity to people engaged in household or paid employment who yet manage to meet the movement's standards for participation in gatherings and travel, to those who join on occasional missions, to those who may occasionally or regularly pray where Tablighis congregate and listen to their discussions.
>
> *(Metcalf, 1996, p. 111)*

In order to have systematicity in his work, Muhammad Ilyas devised six basic principles. First is the *Shahada* or article of faith, which is the assertion that there is no deity but God and that Muhammad is His messenger. The second principle is *Salat*, the five daily prayers. The third principle is *Ilm* and *Dhikr* (knowledge and remembrance of God), and the fourth *Ikram-i-Muslim* (respect every Muslim). The fifth principle is *Ikhlas-i-Niyat* (emendation of intention and sincerity), and the sixth *Tafrigh-i-Waqt* (to spare time). These six principles formed the basis of the movement's ideology.

Jan Ali (2012) notes that *Tablighi* ideology centres on the relationship between the faithful and God. The central claim is that nothing is more important and worth pursuing than establishing this relationship and cherishing it. According to *Tablighi* ideology, which in many respects is a reflection of orthodox Islamic belief, Islam consists of certain beliefs, (in one unique God, the existence of angels, God's revelations and His prophets, the Last Day, the next life) and the manifestation of those beliefs in forms of worship (prayer, charity, and fasting) – all of which relate to the faithful's relationship with God (Ali, 2012).

The relation between the *Tablighi* and God is embedded in a common socio-physiological basis, which is in itself social (Ali, 2012). A *Tablighi* achieves this through his introduction to the movement and training in the message of Islam (*tabligh* – preaching), routines and rituals, through which he learns about God, gets to know about His omniscience and omnipotence, and ultimately, through pure spiritual devotion, feels a constant nearness to God (Sikand, 2002). The command to convey the message of Islam could be explained as an invitation to join Tabligh Jama'at and participate in its routines and rituals to practice the faith in the omnipresence of God, who is always with the faithful (Masud, 2000).

The joining of the movement is linked to the notion of "remaking" the Muslim (Ali, 2012). This is the overall objective of the movement which by its very nature is non-violent yet transformative seeking personal change leading to social transformation in a world seen by *Tablighi*s deeply submerged in *jahiliyyah* (ignorance). The Tabligh Jama'at aims to change this *jahili* (un-Godly) state by actively opposing popular Islamic practices, purging them of foreign accretions, and infusing authentic Islamic values and practices into Muslim daily life though non-violence means of itinerant missionary preaching. It seeks to do this through the revival of Islam involving replacing culture with scripture.

To achieve its goal, Tabligh Jama'at has members working "in more than two hundred countries" (Horstmann, 2007, p. 27) that are spread all over the world. As for membership, some estimate between 70 to 80 million active members globally (Burton and Stewart, 2008). Tabligh Jama'at has become an important and highly dynamic transnational movement with a consistent exchange of personnel in all local areas, as well as overseas. It is worth noting that these established personal networks are strengthening transnational social spaces not only in local areas, but also globally. In this sense, one way of explaining what attracts Muslims to Tabligh Jama'at – making a commitment to religion, valuing the travelling cultures, and severing ties with traditions – is the satisfaction arising from the movement's self-empowerment programme. This has been the reason why many Muslims forfeit their worldly pursuits and commit themselves to the *Tablighi* path – a non-violent way of pursuing Islamic way of life and inviting others towards such a pursuit. For some, such a path is desirable and they actively seek it, but for some Muslims and non-Muslims, it may be non-violent mode of existence but yet practically and in principle extreme.

The chapter is less focused on the discussion of religious extremism than examining Tabligh Jama'at as part of Islamist extremism which in principle is non-violent. What follows in the next two sections is a discussion of the concepts of "extremism" and "non-violent extremism" to enable clearer and better understanding of the phenomenon of Islamist extremism and the part of the Tabligh Jama'at in it.

Extremism

Extremism is a multivariate term generally denoting a tendency for thought, belief, or action considered unreasonable or outside the established acceptable norms. The term "extremism" can be used in a variety of conversations or contexts with its meaning constantly fluctuating. Primarily, though it is used in political or religious conversations referring to an ideology that is considered by those participating in the conversation to be far beyond the established acceptable norms or outside the mainstream views of society, it can also be used in other contexts such as in economic discourse or socio-cultural exchange. For instance, the global financial crisis of 2007–8 triggered a social reaction producing far-right socio-cultural extremism in Europe and elsewhere and giving rise to anti-system and anti-liberal social parties and groups who talk about taking radical or extreme actions such as road blockages for their losses. The term usually has pejorative connotations. However, it may also be used in a more positive manner purely descriptively and academically and not so deleteriously.

Having extremist views are often frowned upon because they are considered to be closed, fixed, intolerant, and impervious to change and they are contrasted with moderate ideas. For example, in Western feminism, the distinction between extremist feminists and mainstream or moderate feminists is usually stressed. In politics agendas, considered to be an extremist can include those from the far-left politics or far- right politics, for example, the ultra-nationalist and Eurosceptics who see the European Union as a supranational organisation engaged in undermining nation states' power and authority as well as fundamentalism, fanaticism, and radicalism, for instance, ISIS with extreme views about the West and its Muslim supporters who it considers its enemy and the enemy of Islam.

There are different causes of extremism, and they range from personal and individual factors to socio-cultural, economic, and political factors. Sotlar (2004) notes that:

> There are many factors that influence the definition itself, such as a (non) democratic nature of the political system, the prevailing political culture, the system of values, ideology, political goals, personal characteristics and experiences, ethnocentrism, and many others.
>
> *(p. 703)*

In their work using thematic analysis and content analysis research methods, Sarah Knight et al. (2017) found a number of underlying variables or factors responsible for both violent and non-violent extremism. They were *internal factors* comprising psychological issues (such as mental illnesses) and potential traumas (such as experiencing the loss, death, or long-term separation from loved ones); *grievances* as potential underlying extremist attitudes and actions, for instance, feelings of marginalisation and experiences of racism and prejudice; *identity* as a crisis and so seeking a sense of self, searching for purpose and meaning in life, and attempting to connect with like-minded others; and *connectedness* where individuals may feel isolated and alienate in its absence and, therefore, wanting to be part of a team of some sort or seeking belongingness (Knight et al., 2017, pp. 236–37).

These complex causal factors make the meaning of the term "extremism" to constantly fluctuate and in the process assign it many different definitions or meanings. In this regard, Sarah Knight et al. (2017) assert that:

> However, within the literature there is a lack of clear definition or consensus regarding extremism: Many studies fail to define what is meant by the term, and tend to be vague regarding whether the term extremism refers to a person's opinions, actions, or both.
>
> The main issue regarding different definitions of extremism and radicalization is that some studies use either or both terms, sometimes to refer only to extremist thought processes, sometimes to infer that action (mainly violence) is an inevitable outcome of increasingly extremist viewpoints, whereas others do not clearly or overtly distinguish between extremist viewpoints and violent action.
>
> *(italics in original, p. 233)*

As a term, a concept, and a phenomenon, extremism is not easy to define and is inherently complex. This is because, for instance, for some individuals or groups, resorting to arm struggle in defence of liberty may be seen as an "extreme" behaviour, but for those actually involved in the struggle, it can be viewed as a "just cause" and "moral virtue". Another example can be that for some people a fervent pursuit for justice can be perceived as a virtuous act but for others it may be construed as excessive and unvirtuous.

Sotlar (2004) explains that:

> Extremism in terms of terrorism, racism, xenophobia, interethnic and inter-religious hatred, left- or right-wing political radicalism and religious fundamentalism is essentially a political term which determines those activities that are not morally, ideologically or politically in accordance with written (legal and constitutional) and non-written norms of the state; that are fully intolerant toward others and reject

democracy as a means of governance and the way of solving problems; and finally, that reject the existing social order.

(p. 703)

Peter Coleman and Andrea Bartoli (n.d.) observe that:

Extremism is a complex phenomenon, although its complexity is often hard to see. Most simply, it can be defined as activities (beliefs, attitudes, feelings, actions, strategies) of a character far removed from the ordinary. In conflict settings it manifests as a severe form of conflict engagement. However, the labelling of activities, people, and groups as "extremist", and the defining of what is "ordinary" in any setting is always a subjective and political matter.

(p. 2)

Thus, extremism is a double-edged sword. For one person, it is a wicked and deplorable enterprise, but for another, it is a good and acceptable endeavour depending on one's values, political stance, moral compass, and the nature of their relationship with the "extremist". Furthermore, one's sense of just or unjust nature of a given act of extremism may change with the change in conditions or set of circumstances. Accordingly, the prevailing and past context of extremist acts contribute to forming our assessment of them. Another point worth noting is that power variances also play a role in defining extremism. In a conflict situation, the activities of members of a group with little power tend to be regarded as more extreme than similar activities undertaken by members of a group supporting the existing state of affairs. Generally speaking, extreme acts are more likely to be performed by individuals or groups who feel marginalised, excluded, and rejected and find the normative forms of conflict engagement strategies out of their reach or inequitable (Justino and Litchfield, 2003; Kane, 2008).

Their poor conditions such as poverty, inadequate access to healthcare, education, and employment; the state or social denial of basic human needs such as group identity and political participation; and endless experiences of humiliation and an ever-growing divide between the powerless and the empowered potentially lead to extreme acts as the usual avenues for achieving the needs are met with obstacles and blockades. Dominant groups also can do the same, that is, employ extreme activities, for example, the extreme force used by the Australian Federal Police and the New South Wales Police Force in the Lindt Café siege in Martin Place, Sydney, in December 2014.

It is for this reason any discussion of extremism needs to consider the fact that the definitions I mentioned above and similar ones that appear in the literature but not explored here lack legal precision to be effective and also they might be philosophically, psychologically, anthropologically, sociologically, and politically imprecise (Mudde, 2000). However, definition is necessary for extremism to make any sense and for benchmarking so that something that is "mainstream" or "normal" can be compared with that which is extreme and far removed from the ordinary and, therefore, in this chapter it means: *harbouring a thought or belief, engaging in activities, and behaving in a manner generally considered irrational, morally and ethically deficient, removed from the ordinary and the mainstream, and/or external to the prevailing acceptable norms and conventions.*

Recently, extremism as a multifaceted phenomenon is being used to refer to both violent and non-violent forms of expression. In terms of violent forms extremist acts differ in levels and intensities targeting infrastructure and military destruction and civilians and children killing (Midlarsky, 2011). Disempowered individuals or groups falling in the category of extremism may employ direct or random forms of violence such as igniting explosives, whereas powerful groups with superior organisational structure and resources use more covert forms of violence, for instance, the state department sanctioning informal police brutality (Coleman and Bartoli, n.d.). Although extremism is a strategy in a game of power struggle, this doesn't mean that it is a homogeneous phenomenon and extremist individuals and groups constitute a cohesive and unitary body. Extremist individuals and groups differ from one another and also differ internally within themselves. Therefore, extremism is a multidimensional phenomenon and extremists are a heterogeneous group which need to be investigated as such.

In post 9/11 era, a significant and perturbing convergence between the terms "extremism" and "terrorism" particularly "Islamic/Muslim terrorism" has occurred in both public discourse and political discussions to the point where they are progressively being used interchangeably and reproducing the same frames of reference for both concepts. This has created, particularly in politics, the assumption that extremism has transitioned into terrorism with an increasing use of the terms "violent extremism" and "non-violent extremism" as a substitute for one another. Extremism has been increasingly framed as a conduit to terrorism raising concerns among academics and scholars (Kirkpatrick and Onursal, 2019) who claim that defining terrorism in this manner inevitably cover both violent and non-violent extremism. Thus, what was in the past exclusively deemed "terrorism" is now gradually being framed interchangeably as "extremism" resulting in the meaning of non-violent extremism progressively being reduced to solely mean terrorism. This highlights the underlying assumption that extremism always operates as a conduit to terrorism.

The problem with this is that such a framing of extremism and conflation of extremism with terrorism influences people's understanding of these phenomena and shapes how they respond to them. In other words, the way extremism and terrorism are framed in political discourse and bureaucratic and technocratic circles reflects and shapes how various state apparatus implement policy and how the public views policies and reacts to them. Treating non-violent extremism as terrorism is hugely problematic because it puts counter-terrorism energies against the individual's or group's socio-political identities instead of the actual violence. Kruglanski et al. (2017) suggest that violent extremism should be treated differently as a specific type of extremism and others focusing on behavioural differences among extremists with similar ideological outlooks, differentiating between "actions" and "words", recommend examining the roles and functions extremists perform and differentiate the types of extremists appropriately and not lumping them together (Perliger et al., 2016). Extremism and terrorism are two different phenomena and their interchangeable use should be avoided at all costs because whilst terrorism by its nature is violent and destructive, extremism, particularly non-violent extremism, as we will see in the next section, is not necessarily so.

Non-violent Extremism

Non-violent extremism is a form of *non-violence* which is an umbrella term referring to a variety of techniques for dealing with conflicts or conflict situations that share the common principle that violence against *other* (outside one's in-group) people, is not permitted and practised (Schmid, 2014; Sen, 2006). Thus, whilst violent extremism can be "violent" but not necessarily have to be so, non-violent extremism by nature is not violent and in essence is a form of resistance where an individual or a group having an agency seeks to bring about change in society by engaging in activity that can shift the power from the powerful to less powerful and pave the way for change to occur (Sookdheo, 2008). For certain individuals it is about being part of a "winning team" so to speak and it is this that motivates them towards non-violent extremism as a resistance instrument which can be much more effective than the armed struggles or violent confrontations. Contrary to violent extremism which resorts to violence as a means to affect change in society (Kirkpatrick and Onursal, 2019) non-violent extremism is a resistance mechanism which socialises individuals "to non-violent forms of participation and by providing concrete avenues to voice grievances" (Chapman, 2008, p. 516).

However, like extremism non-violent extremism has multiple meanings. Although there is a growing awareness of and debates surrounding "non-violent extremism", there is apparently a widespread confusion about what non-violent extremism really is. The confusion emanates from using terms such as "pacifism", "non-violent resistance", "non-violence", and "passive resistance" interchangeably. On the one hand, the phenomena are relatively little known, and on the other, those involved, meaning, the proponents as well as the opponents of these tactics, are often emotionally charged which leads to the hijacking of the clarity of thought about them. It may be that at first glance, all that is "not violent" may seem to be the same or one kind. However, what is "not violent" is a matter of interpretation and cannot be generalised or essentialised. Different various types of non-violence or what constitutes "not violent" shouldn't be lumped together but clearly distinguished to avoid unfavourable consequences.

"Non-violent extremism" and "non-violence" both indicate a position at some distance from "mainstream", "centralist", or "moderate" positions and closely share one common value and that is the non-use of violence on both pragmatic and principle considerations even in the face of a violent opponent. It is for this reason some scholars use the terms interchangeably and this is also the case in this paper fully acknowledging, however, the contention in the literature (Schmid, 2014) surrounding the use of the terms interchangeably.

Non-violent extremism can prove more popular and effective than violent extremism because it can appeal to a wide spectrum of individuals from a wide range of backgrounds including men and women, young and old, city-dwellers and rural-residents, professionals and laypersons, educated and uneducated, and rich and poor all being able to participate in some way in non-violent resistance (Stephan, 2009). In such a resistance is a challenge for violent extremism and for the non-violent extremism members the powerful feeling of solidarity and a sense of agency to work together at grassroots level in an attempt to bring about transformation in the society.

The discussion of non-violent extremism often takes place within the purview of political philosophy of "non-violence" where the focus usually is on the elevation of the principle of employing only peaceful means to achieve socio-economic and political goals. In a sense, "non-violence" is principled (meaning emphasis is placed on social harmony and a rejection of violence and coercion on moral grounds), absolute (complete, fixed, and unchangeable), and universal (comprehensive and all-encompassing). If we take Gandhi and his philosophy of non-violent resistance which taught avoidance of shedding blood as an example, non-violent extremism in this tradition refers to an activist and at times even radical mode of conflict resolution using all means possible, except violence or threat of violence even in the face of violence by the opponent. Non-violent extremism or non-violence as an activist strategy is not confined to passivity and peaceful resistance but can involve a collection of direct socio-political actions, both at an individual level as well as social level, for instance, hunger strikes, demonstrations, marches, rallies, and acts of civil disobedience and other combination of persuasive and coercive strategies such as industrial strikes, protests, walkouts, and blockades. However, in employing these strategies, violence against people or institutions is never prescribed or used. Non-violent extremism acts as a positive concept because adherence to the means and ends of this political philosophy is non-violent.

Non-violent extremism is non-violence as well as non-violent and so it is not only in principle opposed to violence but by its very nature is "not-violent". Hence, it is not just about avoiding violence as a form of political conduct but is about being committed to avoiding killing at all costs and also at the same time actively making every effort to create conditions in which killing doesn't occur. Based on this doctrine, it is opposite to violent extremism that embodies killing as necessary, effective, and even gallantry, with some extremists such as violent Islamists actively pursuing opportunities for violence and killing because of the doctrinal promise for those who sacrifice themselves during the "struggle" to be handsomely rewarded in the next life.

Weber and Burrowes (1991) explain non-violent extremism or nonviolence as follows:

> it is a "weapon" available to all, it is least likely to alienate opponents and third parties, it breaks the cycle of violence and counter-violence, it leaves open the possibility of conversion, it ensures that the media focus on the issue at hand rather than some tangential act of violence and it is the surest way of achieving public sympathy. Further, it is more likely to produce a constructive rather than a destructive outcome, it is a method of conflict resolution that may aim to arrive at the truth of a given situation (rather than mere victory for one side) and it is the only method of struggle that is consistent with the teachings of the major religions.
>
> *(p. 1)*

Kumar, relying on Gandhian Satyagraha – the philosophy of non-violent conflict resolution which many non-violent activists and scholars draw upon – says:

> Nonviolent action is an important technique for conducting social, economic and political conflict without the use of physical violence. It served as a tool of empowering parties in conflicts with oppressive and powerful opponents. Famous Salt Satyagraha is one of the important examples in nonviolent action. Gandhian Satyagraha is included in several form of nonviolent actions like non cooperation, boycotts, picketing, leafleting, strikes, civil disobedience, fasting, the nonviolent occupation of various government facilities, vigil and fasts, mass imprisonments, refusal to pay taxes, and a willingness at all times to be abused by the authorities and get to respond non violently, with politeness, courage and determination. It also has a positive meaning as people strive to remove causes of violent conflict, both human and environmental.
>
> *(2017, p. 2)*

Gene Sharp (1928–2018), an American political scientist, offers a more widely accepted definition of non-violent action in his Waging Nonviolent Struggle (2005) stating that it is a:

> general technique of protest, resistance, and intervention without physical violence. . . . Such action may be conducted by (a) acts of omission—that is, the participants refuse to perform acts that they usually perform, are expected by custom to perform, or are required by law or regulation to perform; (b) acts of commission—that is, the participants perform acts that they usually do not perform, are not expected by custom to perform, or are forbidden by law or regulation from performing; or (c) a combination of both.
>
> *(p. 547)*

Thus, non-violent extremism or non-violent action or non-violence are by definition actions or human engagements that are simply not violent occurring outside the context of usual social, economic, or political conduct. In this respect, what qualifies as an act of non-violent extremism or non-violent action or non-violence is to an extent context specific. For instance, carrying a dagger in the city streets may be a normal behaviour and, therefore, not considered violent, non-violent, or extreme in a particular country, say in Punjab in India; however, such a conduct may be viewed as dissension or outside normal conduct and, therefore, an act of non-violent extremism or even violent extremism in another country, say in United States in Los Angeles City where carrying weapons such as a knife in the streets is currently prohibited.

Whether or not an act of non-violent extremism is considered normal social, economic, and political behaviour in a particular country, scholars (Schock, 2005; Perry, 2019) claim that history and contemporary experiences reveal that acts of non-violent extremism have often been used to complement and enhance normal social, economic, and political behaviour. For example, in a particular country, a group may use the usual everyday methods to bring about change (such as lobbying the government or filing a lawsuit); however, it may also engage in acts of non-violent extremism (such as protests, strikes, and blockades) to make their voice being heard and intensify their efficacy.

There is a misconception about non-violent extremism as a technique that it is inherently religious or ethical in nature. Historically, non-violent extremism has been successfully practiced by individuals and groups with religious or ethical agenda and course; however, individuals and groups with other non-religious and non-ethical courses have also pursued non-violent extremism to bring about socio-economic and political transformation.

In the era of "war on terror", the politics of fear became a defining feature of political rhetoric bringing variety of issues connected to Islam and Muslims including non-violent Islamist extremism under intense scrutiny. As far as non-violent Islamist extremism is concerned, it is being viewed as a threat particularly to the Western world and the Western way of life. With the politicisation of the fear of terrorism, non-violent Islamist extremism is often equated with international terrorism. The fear of terrorism makes it hugely difficult to have an open, objective, and meaningful debate about the subject.

At first glance, the link between non-violent Islamist extremism and terrorism seems obvious because of the assumption that "Islamists" by nature are violent and that their extremism only enhances that "nature". In this conceptualisation, non-violent Islamist extremism is seen as a mode of thinking which sanctions violence in the service of God and, therefore, the extremists are only too willing to kill as their non-violence posture is seen as only a charade behind which lurks serious violent tendency. As such, they are described to have no regard for human life particularly those of their victims because they view them as enemies of God. They are understood to be always ready to give up their own lives in anticipation for great and prompt afterlife rewards in return for becoming "martyrs".

It is far too easy for analysts from both Muslim and non-Muslim backgrounds to focus on the small minority of the extremist threat that Muslim extremists pose to Muslims and non-Muslims alike or to demonise the world's second largest religion, and to drift into some form of Islamophobia and denounce a religion for patterns of violence that are driven by a very small minority of Muslims based on factors such as government corruption and incompetence, social tensions, economic discontents, and political crises. If Islam as a religion or if religion in general is the cause of non-violent religious extremism that transforms into violent religious extremism or terrorism, then why the vast majority of the terrorist organisations are not religious? (Iannaccone and Berman, 2006) or if the afterlife rewards are so important, then why so many suicide bombings are linked to non-religious groups such as Tamil Tigers? Also, why do non-violent religious extremist groups devote huge amounts of time and energy to social welfare activities (such as running health clinics and schools and providing charity to the poor)?

Thus, it is vital that any contemporary analyses take up the challenge of better understanding the nature of non-violent Islamist extremism and the driving forces behind it. Often, non-violent Islamist extremism is characterized as anti-modernity and driven by an anti-West ideology and, therefore, posing a threat to the West and its way of life. This chapter offers a rather different view that non-violent Islamist extremism is not entirely driven by religious ideology or anti-modernity. Rather, it is a response to the crisis of modernity, namely, secularism and Westernism and a variety of socio-economic – rapid urbanization and the forces of economic globalization in many Muslim countries and political – government corruptions and incompetence, authoritarianism in Arab and non-Arab countries quandaries.

To illustrate this, the structural conditions in which a non-violent Islamist extremist movement (called the Tabligh Jama'at) emerged and its ideology and activities will be explored.

Tabligh Jama'at's Ideology: A Non-violent Approach to Remaking the World

The Tabligh Jama'at finds the modern world steeped in *jahiliyyah* (ignorance or absence of the awareness of one unified God) and thus is in crisis characterised by the existence of secularism (separation of religion from politics) and Westernism (behaviour, attitudes, traditions, techniques, and practices considered characteristic of people of the Occident or the Western culture). The cause of the crisis according to them is the loss of a universal beacon of guidance, that is, an absence of a kind of a universal ideal life pattern in which God sits at its apex and in which God is the sovereign and not men and excessive individualism producing a rupture in social bond. The functional relationship and inter-relationship among the members of the community in the modern society are viewed to be weak and since human beings are self-seeking creatures as manifested in their pursuit of individual interests, there is a serious threat to social integration and social harmony.

The social problems of modern society are complex and manifold. Poverty, inequality, unemployment, discrimination, population pressure, police brutality, political corruption and incompetence, crime, xenophobia, suicide, and wars to mention but a few undermine the dynamics of relations in the family and the society broadly because of the damage inflicted on those directly and indirectly concerned. Different social conditions constitute a problem in the society because they threaten the life and future of those living in the society. Either directly or indirectly social problems impact on inter-relationships in the society based on community members' idea of what is valuable and what is useless. For instance, political corruption and incompetence destroys political stability, economic disequilibrium damages equitable distribution of wealth, and adultery ruins family stability.

The movement posits that the modern world cannot be allowed to be in such a state and continue to be so because Muslims as well as non-Muslims are constantly suffering in it and this will only end up in a tragedy and monumental disaster. The menace of social problems in modern society has to be nipped in the bud in a systematic and non-violent manner. The task, therefore, is to bring people out of the darkness created by modernity through the means of true *din* (Islam as a complete way of life). Through *tabligh* (face-to-face preaching), *Tabligh*is (members of the Tabligh Jama'at) argue that those in the darkness have to be brought out into the light; those immersed in ignorance have to be given knowledge; and those being disobedient have to be taught obedience. They say that *din* (religion) has to be revived at least minimally involving the retrieval of fundamentals of Islam (daily ritual prayers, alms, fasting, remembrance, etc.) or the return to the basics of faith and this is the purpose of *tabligh*. *Tabligh* may be interpreted within the framework of the *Qur'anic* teaching which defines the movement's mission along the following lines, "And who is better in speech than one who invites to Allah and does righteousness and says, 'Indeed, I am of the Muslims'" (Fussilat, 41, p. 33). Reviving the *din* from the movement's perspective involves members of the movement engaging in *khuruj* (preaching tour; Ali, 2012).

Changing the *jahili* (un-Godly) state of the modern world is an aim shared by all non-violent Islamist extremist movements. These movements also share the ultimate objective to restructure Muslim society in line with the *shar'iah* (Islamic law), at least at its basic level as a starting point. What distinguishes these movements is their methodology, not their goals (Ali, 2020). Hence, what sets the Tabligh Jama'at apart from other non-violent Islamist extremist movements is its methodology of preaching and missionary work, particularly the *khuruj* (preaching tour) to "remake" Muslims.

Tabligh Jama'at's "remaking" of the Muslim is thus a non-violent response to the failures of modernity and, as the movement claims, the departure of Islamic spiritualism from the lives of many Muslims. By encouraging Muslims to reinvent themselves and seek higher spirituality through preaching tours, Tabligh Jama'at makes inroads by conquering the hearts of Muslims. Seeking to penetrate the core of Muslim consciousness and making Muslims seek out God, the movement claims to restore faith in God. In seeking out God, the "self" plays a central role. There is a mutual dependency between "self" and social environment. Individuals are not separate from or independent of the social environment and vice versa (Parsons, 1949; Giddens, 1984). Therefore, Tabligh Jama'at seeks to create an interpersonal context in which the *Tablighis* can nurture the "self". The general social environment poses various behavioural challenges which, according to the Tabligh Jama'at, steers Muslims away from religious conviction and self-improvement. It, thus, seeks to remedy this by turning the interpersonal context into a social facilitator influencing individuals' performance in self-improvement, particularly in religious rituals and practices.

Social interaction, the Tabligh Jama'at argue, plays an important role and, therefore, view it as the source of meaning making. Through interpretive process, individuals indicate, define, assess, modify, and recreate meanings emerging from their interactions with others. Meanings, then, are understood as emerging not only from social interaction but also relative to their own set of personal circumstances.

The Tabligh Jama'at's non-violent Islamist extremism reveals itself not in any other form such as non-violent actions like non-cooperation, boycotts, picketing, strikes, civil disobedience, vigil, so forth and so on characteristic of many non-violent extremists movements but in the remaking of the "self". The Tabligh Jama'at engages in a total self-reformation, seeking the elimination of individual problems through a change in personal character and individual improvement. It demands personal renewal and individual reform for the betterment of self. Motivated by the *Qur'anic* promises of a blissful existence in the next life and the idea of salvation in inviting people towards good and stopping them from doing evil, the movement carves out a path to conquering the "hearts" of the people. Seeking to penetrate the core of Muslim consciousness and making Muslims seek Allah's forgiveness, a faith in Allah is evoked again. By calling others towards righteousness, one learns about "self" first. One learns about his or her own strengths and weaknesses. In material modernity, "good life" and "successful life" are measured by the possession of material wealth. The Tabligh Jama'at sees the "good life" purely in a spiritual sense which it sees is devoid of materialism. *Halal* (permissible) earning, peace of mind, contentment, pleasure in worship, love for Allah and worldly success procured by lawful means constitute "authentic success". Therefore, "authentic success" is both the success in this world and in life after death. It is described as a complete "package". Personal crisis and problems are attributed by the *Tablighis* to the weakness of personal character. A weak character leads one astray. *Tablighis* describe a weak character as one who participates in all sorts of social evil, manifesting in corruption, sexual promiscuity, and moral decay, for example. By doing away with the material pursuit of happiness and worldliness, the *Tablighi* doctrine helps members forge a new unity with Muslims and ultimately with Allah.

The *Tablighi*s reject a self-centred life and the pursuit of happiness through consumerism. *Tablighi*s stop competing for material pursuit of happiness to which others aspire. They embark on a new quest for happiness and meaning. The happiness and meaning offered by the material world are rejected because they are perceived as temporary, superficial, and devoid of value or substance. What surpasses these is the immeasurable and eternal value hidden in spiritualism and the worship of Allah. Therefore, the six principles of the movement combine to become the means of forging a bond between the *Tablighi* and Allah.

The movement itself, then is – in the words of *Tablighi* activists – the place where the constitutive parts of the Muslim identity come together without any use of force or violence but simple preaching.

To change the situation and save the world from drifting further into the state of *jahiliyah* (ignorance), the Tabligh Jama'at suggests that Islam has to be revived and re-established as a dominant global belief system through non-violent and non-political means. For the Tabligh Jama'at, this is a desirable yet practically a distant prospect. The means it de scribes is a personal journey of returning to the basics of Islam approach. The philosophy that resonates with the Tabligh Jama'at here is to save oneself before saving others. Therefore, Muslims themselves need to first and foremost enter totally into the fold of Islam, says *Tablighi*s, and base their entire life on the *Qur'an* and the *sunnah* (sayings and practices of the Prophet Muhammad). In so doing they, the *Tablighi*s, will become examples for others to emulate and become the beacon of hope for a better and just modern world. This is a bottom-up approach – starting at the "self" and rising to global socio-economic and political reordering and success through indirect means, that is, by making oneself reformed, changing from the inside involving character refinement and saturation of pattern of life with Islamic symbols, values, principles, and rituals, and becoming a righteous Muslim with correct conduct, mannerisms, and attitudes. Such a reformed Muslim in the *Tablighi* circles is seen as the ideal type, one who has transformed into the image of Prophet Muhammad is then worthy of all emulations. For the *Tablighi*s, this personal transformation leads to social transformation

Conclusion: The Tabligh Jama'at and Its Non-violent Resoluteness

The Tabligh Jama'at participates un-orthodoxically and rather distinctly in reordering crisis-ridden modernity through itinerant missionary work which by nature is non-violent. Its resolute non-violent means of Islamic faith renewal involves Islamisation of Muslim everyday living and institutionalisation of Islam. Through using *khuruj* (preaching tour) as a tool instead of normative non-violent processes or approaches, activists of the Tablighi Jama'at work internally making Muslims become "good Muslims" who dedicate their whole life to the service of Allah. The idea is to affect social change indirectly through personal transformation involving making oneself in the image of Prophet Muhammad and becoming a model for others to emulate.

For the Tabligh Jama'at, the modern world is in *jahiliyyah* (ignorance) and needs rescuing. However, it doesn't have the material, financial, and technical resources to engage in direct meaningful rescuing mission. In light of this, it has opted for an indirect approach which is to bring about social transformation through radical personal change. For some, despite the movement's non-violent activism, the whole missionary endeavour may still seem extreme since *Tablighi*s do go through radical personal transformation. This may exemplify Tabligh Jama'at as an extremist movement and its nature can be rigorously debated. The point, however, is that the movement is not violent in nature or in its activist endeavours. This is clearly evident in the movement's longevity (1927–current) and popularity (present in around 200 countries with over 80 million members). It is engaged in an itinerant approach to Islamic faith renewal with stringent and regimental rituals – detailed preaching tours – and practices such as daily prayers and remembrance of Allah. Like other non-violent Islamist movements, the Tabligh Jama'at anticipates the modern world becoming positively transformed in which justice will prevail and life will be harmonious and governed by Islam and its rules.

Note

1 It is worth noting that Tabligh Jama'at split into two factions over leadership dispute in 2016. Although old organisational structure and organisational functions at Niẓam u'd-din remain very much unchanged, it is, however, no longer the sole dispenser of instructions to all Tablighis as the breakaway faction members now receive their instructions from their headquarters mosque in Nerul near Mumbai, India.

References

Ali, J. (2010a). Tablighi Jama'at and the 'Re-Making' of the Muslim. *Australian Religion Studies Review*, 23(2), 148–172.

Ali, J. (2010b). Tablīgh Jamā'at: A Transnational Movement of Islamic Faith Regeneration. *European Journal of Economic and Political Studies*, 3, Special Issue, 103–131.

Ali, J. (2012). *Islamic Revivalism Encounters the Modern World: A Study of the Tabligh Jama'at*. New Delhi: Sterling Publishers.

Ali, J. (2021). Tabligh Jama'at as an Emulatable Model of Faith Renewal. In R. Lukens-Bull and M. Woodward (eds.), *Handbook of Contemporary Islam and Muslim Lives* (pp. 1–21). Cham: Springer.

Alvi, H. (2019). Terrorism in Africa: The Rise of Islamist Extremism and Jihadism. *Insight Turkey*, 21(1), 111–132.

Burton, F. and Stewart, S. (2008). Tablighi Jamaat: An Indirect Line to Terrorism. *Statfor Worldview*. Retrieved from https://worldview.stratfor.com/article/tablighi-jamaat-indirect-line-terrorism

Cas, M. (2000). *The Ideology of the Extreme Right*. Manchester: Manchester University Press.

Chapman, T. (2008). Unravelling the Ties Between Civic Institutions and Attitudes Towards Political Violence. *International Studies Quarterly*, 52(3), 515–553.

Coleman, P. and Bartoli, A. (n.d.). *Addressing Extremism*. New York and Fairfax City, Virginia: The International Center for Cooperation and Conflict Resolution and The Institute for Conflict Analysis and Resolution.

Gaborieau, M. (1999). Transnational Islamic Movements: Tablighi Jama'at in Politics? *ISIM Newsletter*, 3(99), 20–21.

Giddens, A. (1984). *The Constitution of Society: Outline of the Theory of Structuration*. Berkeley and Los Angeles: University of California Press.

Horstmann, A. (2007). The Tablighi Jama'at, Transnational Islam, and the Transformation of the Self between Southern Thailand and South Asia. *Comparative Studies of South Asia, Africa and the Middle East*, 27(1), 26–40.

Iannaccone, L. and Berman, E. (2006). Religious Extremism: The Good, the Bad, and the Deadly. *Public Choice*, 128(1/2), 109–129.

Jackson, R. (2007). Constructing Enemies: 'Islamic Terrorism' in Political and Academic Discourse. *Government and Opposition*, 42(3), 394–426.

Justino, P. and Litchfield, J. (2003). *Economic Exclusion and Discrimination: The Experiences of Minorities and Indigenous Peoples*. London: MRG.

Kane, I. (2008). *Protecting the Rights of Minorities in Africa: A Guide for Human Rights Activists and Civil Society Organizations*. London: MRG.

Kirkpatrick, D. and Onursal, R. (2019). Not all Types of Extremism are Terrorism – Conflating the Two is Dangerous. *The Conversation*. Retrieved from https://theconversation.com/not-all-types-of-extremism-are-terrorism-conflating-the-two-is-dangerous-116211

Knight, S. Woodward, K. and. Lancaster, G. (2017). Violent Versus Nonviolent Actors: An Empirical Study of Different Types of Extremism. *Journal of Threat Assessment and Management*, 4(4), 230–248.

Kruglanski, A. Jasko, K. Chernikova, M. Dugas, M. and Webber, D. (2017). To the Fringe and Back: Violent Extremism and the Psychology of Deviance. *American Psychologist*, 72(3), 217–230.

Kumar, M. (2017). Gandhi's Concept of Conflict Resolution", Available at Social Science Research Network. Retrieved from https://ssrn.com/abstract=2927388

Maher, S. (2016). *Salafi-Jihadism: The History of an Idea.* London: Penguin Books.

Masud, M. (2000). *Travellers in Faith: Studies of the Tablighi Jama'at as a Transnational Islamic Movement for Faith Renewal.* Leiden: Brill.

Metcalf, B. (1996). New Medinas: The Tablighi Jamaat in America and Europe. In Barbara Metcalf (ed.), *In Making Muslim Space in North America and Europe* (pp. 110–130). Berkeley: University of California Press.

Midlarsky, M. (2011). *Origins of Political Extremism: Mass Violence in the Twentieth Century and Beyond.* Cambridge: Cambridge University Press.

Mudde, C. (2000). *The Ideology of the Extreme Right.* Manchester: Manchester University Press.

Parsons, T. (1949). *The Structure of Social Action.* New York: Free Press.

Perliger, A. Koehler-Derrick, G. and Pedahzur, A. (2016). The Gap Between Participation and Violence: Why We Need to Disaggregate Terrorist 'Profiles. *International Studies Quarterly*, 60(2), 220–229.

Perry, D. (2019). *The Global Muslim Brotherhood in Britain nonviolent Islamist Extremism and the Battle of Ideas.* London: Routledge.

Pieri, Z. (2019). Daily Ritual, Mission, and the Transformation of the Self: The Case of Tablighi Jamaat. *Numen*, 66, 360–380.

Schmid, A. (2014). *Violent and nonviolent Extremism: Two Sides of the Same Coin?* The International Centre for Counter-Terrorism (ICCT) – The Hague. Hague: Government Printing Office.

Schock, K. (2005). *Unarmed Insurrections: People Power Movements in Nondemocracies* Minneapolis: University of Minnesota Press.

Sen, A. (2006). *Identity and Violence: The Illusion of Destiny.* London: Allen Lane.

Sharp, G. (2005). *Waging Nonviolent Struggle: 20th Century Practice and 21st Century Potential.* Boston: Porter Sargent.

Sikand, Y. (2002). *The Origins and Development of the Tablighi Jam'aat (1920– 2000): A Cross-Country Comparative Study.* New Delhi: Orient Longman.

Sookdheo, P. (2008). *Global Jihad: The Future in the Face of Militant Islam.* McClean: Isaac Publishing.

Sotlar, A. (2004). Some Problems with a Definition and Perception of Extremism within a Society. In G. Mesko, M. Pagon and B. Dobovsek (eds.), *Policing in Central and Eastern Europe: Dilemmas of Contemporary Criminal Justice* (pp. 703–707). Kotnikova: Faculty of Criminal Justice, University of Maribor.

Stephan, M. (2009). Introduction. In M. Stephan (ed.), *Civilian Jihad: Nonviolent Struggle, Democratization, and Governance in the Middle East* (pp. 1–14). New York: Palgrave.

Vahed, G. (2003). Contesting Orthodoxy: The Tablighi-Sunni Conflict among South Asian Muslims in the 1970s and 1980s. *Journal of Muslim Minority Affairs*, 23(2), 313–334.

Weber, T. and Burrowes R. J. (1991). Nonviolence: An Introduction. *Peace Dossier*, Series No. 2, 1–10.

6

REACTION, RESTORATION, AND THE RETURN OF ALPHA-ISLAM

Wahhabism from Premodern Ideas to Postmodern Identities

Naveed S. Sheikh

Introduction: The Vicissitudes of a Contentious Term

In the course of the recent two decades, the growth and subsequent globalization of a curious trend of Islamic puritanism, popularly known as "Wahhabism," has attracted widespread academic scrutiny. The theological entailments as well as political consequences of the Wahhabi phenomenon have elicited considerable public debate, particularly after the 9/11 attacks on the political and financial nuclei of America, which drew unprecedented attention to the vexing question of the relationship between theology and militancy in the Muslim-majority world. Capitalizing on a culturally conditioned angst of the Oriental genus, Western commentators and policymakers made Islamicate glossaries commonplace in public discourse: "jihad," of course, being the primary example, but also increasingly "Wahhabism." In the wake of the 7/7 bombings in London—Britain's smaller but equally paradigmatic calamity—the then-Prime Minister Tony Blair in a speech before the Labour Party's national conference did not prevent his lack of expertise from identifying the roots of terrorism within "extreme forms of Wahabi [sic] doctrine" (BBC, 2005).

As any exonym—applied from the outside, usually by critics or detractors—the notion of Wahhabism retains complex genealogies. In colonial history, the British overlords would, in a most problematic application of the term, refer to the Indian mutineers of the mid-nineteenth century as "Wahhabis" (Allen, 2007; Stephens, 2013). Towards the end of the twentieth century, Russian neo-conservatives both politicized and popularized the term in reference to Chechen secessionists (Knysh, 2004). The term "Wahhabism" is thus not a value-free or objectivist, but rather signifies *positionality*. As Foucault (1978) has argued, the production and application of conceptual terms are simultaneously manifestations of power and necessary precursors to orders of subjugation (cf. Said, 1994). The development of an adversarial discourse around a reified "Wahhabism" is therefore suspect both on intellectual and political grounds.

Still, the disclaimer can go too far. *Pace* Davis (2018), Wahhabism as a discursive construct was not manufactured by Western intellectual elites, for the Arabic equivalent to the term

DOI: 10.4324/9781003032793-9

Wahhabism (*al-wahhābiyya*) dates back to the founding decades of the movement.[1] Within intra-Islamic polemics, too, "Wahhabism" remained an etic, and even oppositionalist, signifier, not dissimilar to the labelling practice among Christian theologians of naming presumed heresies after their founder. Deployed mostly by theological foes, thus, the expression "Wahhabi" is shunned by adherents (for rare historical cases of followers embracing the term, see Zarabozo, 2010, pp. 158–59). Rather, subscribers to the Wahhabi credo refer to themselves with a variety of locutions, such as *al-salafiyyūn* (lit. "followers of the *salaf*," i.e. the religious forebears), *ahl al-tawḥīd* ("the people of *tawḥīd*," i.e. monotheism), *al-muwaḥḥiddūn* ("upholders of *tawḥīd*"), or more recently as the *ahl al-sunna* ("adherents to the *sunna*," i.e. the archetypal Prophetic mode of behaviour). None of these varied endonyms, however, offer clarity on inclusion criteria.

The extant scholarly literature, too, remains divided on the usage of the term "Wahhabism." Albeit used in the titles of academic works (e.g. Ayoob & Kosebalaban, 2009; Firro, 2018; Nahouza, 2018; Valentine, 2015), the general tendency has been to bypass the abrasive term, even if alternatives were not readily identifiable (cf. Knysh, 2004). Commins (2015) has argued for a temporal distinction, proffering that Wahhabism was the initial manifestation of a historical movement that, in the twentieth century, became Salafism, thus vitiating the possibility of a contemporary Wahhabism. A few authors have simply opted to hyphenate the identity of the movement as "Wahhabi-Salafism," or "Salafi/Wahhabi" (Davis, 2018; Oliveti, 2002). At least one authoritative voice has used the terms Salafism and Wahhabism interchangeably (Wiktorowicz, 2005, 2006), though, in general, the endonymous term Salafism is preferred.

Even if widespread, the (self-)appellation "Salafi" has possibly caused more confusion than clarity, not least because divergent groups in Muslim history have been associated with the label, including distinct streams of Muslim modernism, which flourished in the metropolitan centres of Cairo, Damascus, Baghdad, and beyond from the late-nineteenth century (Lauzière, 2016, 2021; Weismann, 2001, 2009). In acknowledgment of internal contradictions within the contemporary Salafi repertoire, and the resultant frailty of "Salafism" as a coherent signifier, its analytic use has increasingly been challenged. At best, Salafism remains an "umbrella term" for religious advocates who "share a family resemblance" (Poljarevic, 2016, p. 482). Given the porosity of Salafism *qua* analytic category, there may well be heuristic value in retaining the term Wahhabism—not as a blanket synonym for Salafism (which would serve only to replicate the analytic imprecisions of the latter) but rather as a designation for the discrete ideas espoused by Wahhabism's eponym, Muhammad ibn 'Abd al-Wahhab (1703–91), and his recognized theological heirs. Elsewhere I have argued for a typology of contemporary Salafism in which Wahhabism designates specifically the Saudi-led stream within the conformist school of Salafism (Sheikh, 2021). Such an approach allows for a relatively bounded coherence to the notion of Wahhabism, while not conflating it with Salafism.

To embrace, on pragmatic grounds, Wahhabism as an analytic term is not to make a statement about its empirical discernibility or social causality. In the social world, individuals carry multiple, composite, and hybrid identities that are not easily reduced down to a single signifier. Any reduction of complex social phenomena to first principles or theological meta-narratives runs the risk of reproducing the Orientalist fallacy of negating dynamic life-worlds in which material and ideational dimensions intersect (Said, 1978). On the other hand, to deny the existence of collective thought complexes—or intersubjectively shared semantic fields—would be tantamount to foregoing key epistemological elements in obtaining an understanding of the mindsets and "mentifacts" (Huxley, 1955) that, at least in part, constitute self-identity and condition preference formation.

Key book-length works on the origin and development of Wahhabism have indeed sought to navigate this difficult terrain between essentialism and anti-foundationalism, albeit not always successfully (DeLong-Bas, 2004; Commins, 2006; Crawford, 2014). Analytic approaches to the intellectual and political history of Wahhabism are divided, offering three generic tendencies to the study of the Wahhabi phenomenon. Firstly, a central tendency of the literature is predicated on the "securitization" of Wahhabism, positing it as a threat to both regional security and global order (e.g. Algar, 2002; Oliveti, 2002; Schwartz, 2002; Gold, 2003; Murawiec, 2003; Ward, 2017; Illahi, 2018). This analytic approach suggests a rectilinearity between the historic ultra-conservatism of Wahhabism and the violent extremism of militant Salafism. The opposing tendency offers an often apologetic "mainstreaming" of Wahhabism, exonerating it from the excesses of the militants (Delong-Bas, 2004; Oliver, 2004; Rentz, 2004; Zarabozo, 2010; Davis, 2018). The third scholarly tendency adopts an analytic approach that could be articulated as a "localization" of the Wahhabi–Salafi repertoire. Book-length studies have engaged Saudi Arabia (Al-Rasheed, 2007; Ayoob & Kosebalaban, 2009; Lacroix, 2011); other parts of West Asia (Bonnefoy, 2011; Wagemakers, 2016); North, West, and East Africa (Gauvain, 2012; Østebø, 2012); and European minority contexts (Olsson, 2019).

The remainder of this chapter will proceed in three main sections: The initial section will seek to interrogate pivotal precepts and preoccupations in Wahhabism with a focus on its epistemological commitments and theological constructs. The second section will turn to an analysis of Wahhabism as a form of fundamentalism, offering a critical reading of social-identity dynamics among Wahhabi believers. The third section will situate Wahhabism within the broader Salafi spectrum, identifying key schisms and debates, while ending with an assessment of hardline Wahhabism's (violent) opposition to Islamism. Finally, the conclusion will offer thoughts on the ambiguities of Wahhabism both as an analytic signifier and as a theological current.

Epistemic Commitments in Wahhabi Theology: The (R)age of the Righteous

A minority dispensation outside of Saudi Arabia (albeit only slightly shy of mainstream in neighbouring Qatar), Wahhabi religious normativity has nevertheless globalized in the course of the last six decades. Within Muslim-majority as well as Muslim-minority societies, an increasing quantity of (petrodollar-funded) material or personnel for religious instruction and proselytization continues to articulate Wahhabi preferences (Abou El Fadl, 2005; Cesari, 2005). Discursively, such preponderance of Wahhabiesque theological concepts is anchored in a claim to superior *authenticity*, guided by (and, ostensibly, towards) the Islam that antedated the development of scholastic theology (*kalām*) and the consolidation of the Sunni jurisprudence (*fiqh*). As such, Wahhabism is anchored in (an imagined conception of) the religiosity of the righteous ancestors (*al-salaf al-ṣāliḥīn*), commonly understood as the first three generations of Islam (Afsaruddin, 2007). The Wahhabi religious cosmos is thus transfixed on the period of the Prophet and his immediate Companions (*ṣaḥāba*), their Successors (*tābi'ūn*), and the Successors that followed those (*atbā al-tābi'ūn*), cumulatively covering the common-era period from approximately the beginning of the seventh until the closing decades of the ninth century.

As Muhammad ibn 'Abd al-Wahhab's movement ushered from the Central Arabian hinterland of Najd in the mid-eighteenth century, it would self-consciously style itself as a puritan reform movement, but not a new sect. It was rather a movement of "old believers"—those who were faithful to original faith praxes of the founding community 11 centuries earlier. Borrowing another term from Christian church history, it would not be amiss to describe Wahhabism as "restorationist." Christian Restorationism, as it emerged from the late-eighteenth century onwards, deplored the multiplicity of churches, sought a unitary ecclesiastic expression, believed that doctrine and rites could be unified based on the Biblical text and early Christianity, and strived for creedal and terminological unity amid theological schisms on the pattern of the primordial church (Murch, 1962; North, 1994). Similarly, Wahhabism was "restorationist" in its belief that Islam had to be the restored along the paradigm of the Prophetic or immediate post-Prophetic periods, purified of later accretions, and unified on the model of the first generations. The millennium-long break between Ibn 'Abd al-Wahhab's lived reality and the distant past that he so intensely idealized proffered him to see the evolution of Islamic intellectual history as one of regress (Crawford, 2014).

Central in Ibn 'Abd al-Wahhab's theology was the retrieval of *tawḥīd* (monotheism)—the core of the Prophet's message which had allegedly been lost in both scholastic discourse and popular devotion. His mission thus became to restore an ancient (but imagined) orthodoxy, which prevailed before the codification of Sunni creed, and similarly to reinstate an orthopraxy that eschewed the accretions of popular Islam and sought guidance only from the Texts. So wary was he of the hidden germs of polytheism embedded within popular acts of devotion, that his writing came to betray a form of theological obsessive compulsive disorder. His central work, titled *Kitāb al-Tawḥīd*, or "Treatise on Monotheism," penned around 1739, elucidated on themes that became characteristic of the Wahhabi *oeuvre*: denouncing false idols (*tawāghīt*; sing. *ṭāghūt*), and warning against the manifest and opaque forms of polytheism (*shirk;* lit. "associationism"). These included acts such as producing or wearing talismans, making portraits or sculptures, venerating tombs or relics, seeking saintly intercession, participating in magical practices, or engaging in exaggerated praise of the righteous and prophets (Bin Abdul-Wahhab, n.d.). All such aspects of folk religiosity were anathema to Ibn 'Abd al-Wahhab's reform theology.

The new Najdite mission (*al-da'wa al-najdiyya*) sought to eradicate not only culturally embedded traditions in ("low-church") folk Islam—which it discarded as superstitions and doctrinal errancy (*khurāfa*)—but also the long-held positions of ("high-church") scholastic Islam, many of which it challenged as innovations (*bidaʿ*, sing. *bid'a*) or simply invalid (*bāṭil*) inferences from the Text. Such infractions included, among other time-honoured practices, the annual commemoration of the Prophet's birth (*mawlid*), collective forms of ritual remembrance (*dhikr*), and visitations of shrines (*ziyāra*). To eradicate authoritative opposition, the Wahhabi school condemned the "blind emulation" (*taqlīd*) of scholastic opinion in matters of doctrine as well as law, thus loosening the epistemic control of those religious scholars (*ulamā*) with whom they disagreed (S. Ibn 'Abdul Wahhab, 2020; cf. DeLong-Bas, 2004, p. 106).

In Wahhabi theory, compliance was owed to the text, not human intermediaries (such as the *mujtahid* scholar among the Sunni schools of law, the sufi *shaykh* in Sufism, the infallible *imām* in the Shi'i tradition). The ascription of sacredness to saints and the veneration of graves and relics—themes that are prominent in both Sufi and Shi'i forms of Islam—were abhorrent to the Wahhabis, who regarded such practices as polytheism (*shirk*), just as they disaffirmed custom (*'āda*) or tradition (*'urf*) as bases of Islamic legal praxis. Nevertheless, as Svensson (2014) has called attention to, even as the Wahhabi school espouses (primary) deference of the text, it was never free of (secondary) deference of specific scholastic authorities, in a way that is sometimes even more pronounced that those they criticized for *taqlīd*. The Wahhabi canon thus consisted of a limited set of authorities, the writings of whom would constitute the core of an increasingly canonized didactic literature.[2]

Overall, the Wahhabi thought complex revolved around a set of fixed binaries: monotheism (*tawḥīd*) versus polytheism (*shirk*); faith (*imān*) versus disbelief (*kufr*); purity (*ṭahāra*) versus impurity (*najāsa*); the incumbent (*furūḍ*) versus the illicit (*ḥarām*); the prophetic way (*sunna*) versus the contrived way (*bid'a*); the knowledge obtained via transmission (*naql*) versus reason

(*ʿaql*). Strongly bipolar, both animus and geniality was inbuilt in the Wahhabi doctrine. From the nineteenth century, a central notion in Wahhabi thinking became expressed in the conjunction of *al-walāʾ wa-l-barāʾ*, denoting the believer's simultaneous fealty (*al-walāʾ*) to religion and co-religionists, and a repudiative disavowal (*al-barāʾ*) of non-Islam and non-Muslims, however defined (Wagemakers, 2012). The dual notion came to signify a key trope in Wahhabi thought: namely, the categorical and insurmountable difference between the righteous Self and the (ir)religious Other. While the Self was singular, as a solitary community (*jamāʿa*) of believers, the Others were multiple and often dressed with flowery epithets: there were the outright disbelievers (*kuffār;* sing. *kāfir*), but also the overt or covert polytheists (*mushrikūn;* sing. *mushrik*), the irredeemable heretics (*mulḥidūn;* sing. *mulḥid*), the heterodox (*zanādiqa;* sing. *zindīq*), the profligates (*fāsiqūn;* sing. *fāsiq*), and the hypocrites (*munāfiqun;* sing. *munāfiq*).

Hanbalism on Steroids: The Wahhabi "New Deal"

The central epistemological hallmark of Wahhabism was the self-sufficient authority of the scripture, construed not only as the Qurʾan, the celestial revelation itself, but also as the *aḥādīth* (sing. *ḥadīth*)—the reports of the Prophet's statements, actions, and demeanour, preserved in numerous compendia that were transmitted orally and in writing, often in unbroken chains (*isnād*) of transmission (*riwāya*) from the first generation (Siddiqi, 1993; Brown, 2018). This—and nothing more—was the source of true knowledge and authentic beliefs. The epistemological constriction applied not only in the principle that transmitted knowledge (*naql*) trumped inferred knowledge (*ʿaql*), but later also in the reduction of the body of *aḥādīth* that were deemed admissible by an insistence that the chains of transmission be irreproachable (*ṣaḥīḥ*), while weaker (*daʿīf*) traditions be discarded, even if they were supported by continuous practice of the community or the opinions of senior Companions (thus vitiating, in particular, established Maliki and Hanafi juristic principles).

While scripturalism is standard fare in Sunni orthodoxy, Wahhabism relied on a vigorous form of Hanbalism, historically the least subscribed to of the extant Sunni *madhāhib* (sing. *madhhab*, viz. school of law). Some early taxonomies of Islamic legal schools did not even count the eponymous founder-imam Ahmad ibn Hanbal (780–855 CE) among the initiators of a *madhhab* for his lack of explication of jurisprudential principles (*uṣūl al-fiqh*) by which legal pronouncements could be derived from the primary proof texts (Haddad, 2007, pp. 303–04; cf. Melchert, 2006, pp. 70–78). In the name of Hanbali fideism, Wahhabism probably came closer to the brazen literalism of the stauncher, but effectively defunct, Zahiri school, the most celebrated champion of which was the Andalusian ʿAli Ibn Hazm (994–1064). The latter had espoused a form of rigid constructionism and eschewed extra-textual inferential methods (*qiyās*), characteristic of the remaining three jurisprudential schools of Sunni Islam and temperate forms of Hanbalism.

Ibn ʿAbd al-Wahhab's fideism, or strict adherence to the literal purport of the text, found its clearest expression in matters of doctrine. Leapfrogging the canonical articulations of dogma within the dominant Ashʿari or Maturidi theological schools in Sunni Islam, he sought a return to the doctrinal simplicity of the primary sources, even if ostensibly anthropomorphic, insisting that, in the reading of the text, the literal meaning was invariably what was intended: *prima facie* was *sancta ratio*. The Wahhabi mission thus entailed a back-to-basics approach to scripture, allowing for no figurative elucidation (*taʾwīl*) nor for a relegation of the meaning unto the exclusive realm of divine knowledge (*tafwīḍ*) (Nahouza, 2018). Although the latter is a standard trope in the traditional Hanbali, or Athari, approach to the ambiguous texts (*mutashābihāt*), the

Wahhabi creed rejected the suspension of judgement (*irjā*) and insisted on affirmation (*ithbāt*) of those divine attributes mentioned in scripture, even if it gave rise to anthropomorphic imaginations (*tamthīl*), thus reproducing an old doctrinal heresy outside of traditional Sunni interpretation (Al-Azmeh, 1988; Commins, 2005). Strictly speaking, Ibn 'Abd al-Wahhab's re-engagement with the Text did not constitute independent interpretation (*ijtihād*) but was rather a rediscovery of the original intent. As such, his epistemological approach entailed a dual "originalism" that sought to return to both original sources and original understandings (on the variant forms of originalism, see Pushaw, 2020).

Styling his protestantism as unitarian (*muwahhid*) and shattering the historical Sunni theological *modus vivendi*, the reformer became a self-professed faith restorer (*mujaddid*). In one of his epistles to his followers, Ibn 'Abd al-Wahhab made a startling claim to originality:

> I did not know the meaning of "there is no god but God" [the Muslim testimony of faith], nor did I know the religion of Islam, before this blessing (khayr) which God vouchsafed to me. Likewise not one among my teachers knew it; if any of the scholars [...] claims that he knew the meaning of "there is no god but God," or knew the meaning of Islam, before this time, or maintains that any of his teachers know it, he lies, fabricates, leads people astray, and falsely praises himself.
>
> *(Cook, 1992, p. 202).*

Nevertheless, in his theology, Muhammad ibn 'Abd al-Wahhab was guided, albeit imperfectly, by a paradigmatic precursor in the form of the thirteenth-century Damascene *imām*, Taqi al-Din Ahmad ibn Taymiyya (1263–1328) and the latter's foremost student, Muhammad ibn Qayyim al-Jawziyya (1292–1350), both of whom had challenged what they saw as the excessively speculative theology of the established mainstream. Their ascendant neo-orthodoxy would berate the dominant Sunni schools of theology for their interpretative license (*tāʾwīl*), conflating the traditional orthodoxy of the Ash'ari–Maturidi condominium with the defunct rationalist heterodoxy of the Mu'tazili school (Abou El Fadl, 2005; Hoover, 2019; Rahman, 2000, pp. 132–44).

A central area of disputation pertained to the multiple forms of polytheism that nominally Muslim believers could be guilty of, owing to their incomplete comprehension of *tawhīd* (Crawford, 2014, p. 37). It was no longer sufficient to declare, with the Islamic testimony of faith, "There is no god but God," rather the Muslim had to persistently negate any subservience to non-deities (Commins, 2006, p. 14). To Ibn Taymiyya—and Ibn 'Abd al-Wahhab who, with minor semantic changes, followed him in this—a genuinely Islamic monotheism consisted of a triune understanding of God's unicity, namely, in relation to His sovereign Lordship (*tawhīd al-rubūbiyya*), His unicity in relation to all adoration being directed to Him alone (*tawhīd al-'ulūhiyya,* or *tawhīd al-'ibāda*), and His unicity in relation to the splendid uniqueness of His names and attributes (*tawhīd al-asmāʾ wa-l-ṣifāt*). To be a Muslim, it no longer sufficed to proclaim God's transcendence; one continuously had to patrol the boundaries of the three forms of monotheism (Haykel, 2009). Wahhabi theory and practice, thence, became mutually divergent: its expanded monotheism was far from simple (incongruously, it relied on *kalām* schemata otherwise abhorred); yet the subscription to this particular creedal formulation became necessary for those who aspired to salvation (or, in times of Wahhabi military assaults, survival).

In the hands of the Wahhabi "renewal," Ibn Taymiyya's ideas became not only a mission but also a movement that would in 1744 ally with the political power of the Saudi chieftains. The religio-political pact between Ibn 'Abd al-Wahhab and what was to become the House of

Sa'ud became the basis of successive iterations of the Saudi state, which continued to expand in all directions—east and west, north and south—from its homeland on the Arabian plateau.[3] In the process, Realpolitik merged with Idealpolitik. The dictum of "prescribing virtue and proscribing vice" (*al-amr bi-l-ma'rūf wa-l-nahī 'an al-munkar*) became a clarion call for the forceful elimination of practices that were deemed antithetical to pristine Islam, while also clearing the way for the ascent of Saudi power. Even as it came to demand war and bloodshed, to the Wahhabi partisans, the new orthodoxy was decontaminating and purifying the faith from accretions (DeLong-Bas, 2004; Commins, 2006). Characteristic of their approach was the indiscriminate use of anathematization or excommunication (*takfīr*) for both theological and political infractions in a way that had not seen antecedents since the days of the Abbasid inquisition, the *miḥna* (833–47 CE). In the process, the historic pluralism of theological and juristic approaches in Sunni Islam was suspended and a uniform code of belief and practice imposed.

A Form of Fundamentalism: Surveillance Theology and the Psychosocial Dynamics of Wahhabism

Religious devotion, *qua* the production of meaning, entails both ideational and identity commitments (Hood, Hill & Williamson, 2005). By extension, fundamentalism—as a form of *strong* religious devotion—is not merely a way of positioning oneself in regard to the divine but is equally a way of positioning oneself in relation to the world (Bartoszuk & Deal, 2016, p. 150). Even as the term "fundamentalism" is no longer intellectually on trend—partially in response to a creeping acknowledgement of its ethnocentric origins in Anglo-American reactions to late-nineteenth-century liberal Biblical hermeneutics in Europe (Sandeen, 1970; Marsden, 1980)—the concept remains meaningful when carefully demarcated. Altemeyer and Hunsberger's (1992) classic definition of fundamentalism is useful:

> By "fundamentalism" we mean the belief that there is one set of religious teachings that clearly contains the fundamental, basic, intrinsic, essential, inerrant truth about humanity and deity; that this essential truth is fundamentally opposed by forces of evil [or, in the Islamicate context, misguidance] which much be vigorously fought [or, opposed]; that this truth must be followed today according to the fundamental, unchangeable practices of the past; and that those who believe and follow these fundamental teachings have a special relationship with the deity.
>
> *(Altemeyer & Hunsberger, 1992, p. 118)*

Since the Iranian revolution, academic inquiry and even more so public discourse have unhelpfully conflated two distinct analytic concepts, viz. fundamentalism and radicalism. On the one hand, fundamentalism entails an exclusionary *theological* intemperance, often wedded to the primacy of scripture, whereas, on the other, radicalism signifies *ideological* immoderation, predicated on discourses of virulent political opposition and possibly (but not necessarily) a legitimization of violence. Important analytic distinctions must therefore be drawn between, firstly, the insular religiosity of the fundamentalist strain; secondly, the ideologization and politicization of religion enacted by (potentially radical) theo-political activists; and, finally, the militarization enacted by religious revolutionaries. That the construction "Islamic fundamentalism" has been used interchangeably with "Islamism" (e.g. Sidahmed & Ehteshami, 1996; Jansen, 1997; Choueiri, 2010) is unfortunate and not congruent with rigorous usage under which ideological or partisan mobilization by Islamists is pitted against the fundamentalist cult of doctrinal purity (Gauvain, 2012). *Contra* Almond, Appleby, and Sivan (2003), then, fundamentalism is not about "strong" religion but rather about the amalgamation of "true" religion and "strong" (viz. exteriorized) religiosity.

Fundamentalists often see themselves as islands of fidelity amid oceans of depravity, seeking redemption by regimented lifestyles and exclusionary (often exteriorized) faith praxes. Positioned within abnegating "enclave cultures," fundamentalists remain distrustful towards outsiders and resist the dominant culture in order to prevent "pollution by the malevolent outside" (Almond, Appleby & Sivan, 2003, p. 32). When understood in this way, Wahhabism is Muslim fundamentalism proper, as opposed to both the ideological appeal within Islamist movements (such as the Muslim Brotherhood, the Jama'at-e Islami, Hizb al-Tahrir, etc.) and the "terrorology" of militant Salafis (as manifest e.g. in al-Qa'ida or the *soi-disant* Islamic State group). Zarabozo's (2010) self-definition is both succinct and revealing:

> When one hears the word "Wahhabi" today, one knows that it refers to someone who is calling to a true following of the Quran and Sunnah, the following of [scriptural] evidence, the ordering of good and eradicating of evil, the elimination of heresies and superstitions and an adherence to the way of the righteous predecessors.
>
> *(p. 159)*

As other fundamentalists, adherents to Wahhabi Islam take pride in being "strangers" (*ghurabā*) to a modern social ecology, and instead position themselves as the embattled true believers in a world both hostile and fallen. Even as the inerrancy of doctrine remains at the forefront of the fundamentalist prototype, ancillary moral judgements, often pertaining to quotidian practices, ultimately erect social distinctions (Haidt, 2012; Lakoff, 2002). The theological safe haven—a sacred habitus of fidelity—is surrounded by multiple, or tiered, sets of securitized identity. In the process of continuous boundary defence, the faithful not only cognitively remake the world around them as continuously threatening and encroaching but also cultivate a distinctive social identity.

The demarcation line between the inside and the outside consists of the new catechism—orthodoxy redefined—which must be policed and therefore takes the form of a "surveillance theology." By the neology surveillance theology, I mean to impart the meaning of a theology that is strictly patrolled by an epistemic community (here: the Wahhabi elites and the social hierarchy of their followers), demarcating the boundaries between the inside and the outside, the rightly guided and the astray, thus demanding and legitimizing persistent scrutiny of subjects as a means of continual boundary protection (but therefore also boundary production). It is the functional extension of the principle of protection and repudiation (*al-walā wa-l-barā*).

What, then, explains the appeal of such zealotry? A central characteristic of fundamentalism is that it is, in one way or another, reactionary (Herriot, 2009, p. 9). According to Olivier Roy (2004), precipitating structural conditions of late-modernity favoured the globalization of "neo-fundamentalism." Among such macro-conditions are the availability of new modes of non-hierarchical communication, the facility of cost-efficient travel, and the possibility of trans-continental religio-cultural export, predicated on (largely Gulf-originated) capital infusion and missionary enterprise. Cesari (2005) adds the ideational structures to the material, noting, "A puritan and separatist version of Islam is appealing to many young people, and in certain cases can even be a response to cultural and social ghettoization" (p. 45). Similarly, Winter (2009) points to the "centrifugal forces" of the postmodern condition which "allow nothing to remain constant" and makes "human beings very insecure," forcing them to "look around for something to hold onto, something that will give them an identity" (p. 305).

That something is, potentially, not only Islam, but also alpha-Islam. By the expression "alpha-Islam," one does not mean to engage in psychometrical profiling of adherents but rather to offer an argument about the social psychology of the in-group. Alpha-Islam is easily recognizable, exhibitionistically religious, socially dominant, and hostile to challenge. Its outlook is puritan, and the demeanour which follows is often impositionist. Above all, it is "pure" from the doctrinal and cultural deviancies that has historically dwindled the virility of Islam. Olivier Roy (2004, p. 270) has referred to the processes of purifying Islam from perceived extraneous influences as "deculturation" in which the objective becomes to jettison local customs and detach Islam from cultural context. In the process, multiple Islams are distilled into one pristine (alpha-)Islam.

Social Identities, "Retrotopian" Socialization,
and the Construction of Counterculture

Because the fundamentalist mindset does not take shape in a vacuum but is intersubjectively constituted within groups, normatively members are "jointly committed to believe as a body" (Gilbert & Pilchman, 2014, p. 198). The social identity approach—both as social identity theory and the parallel strand of self-categorization theory—aids our understanding of the processes of social categorization, identification, and differentiation, which take place within fundamentalist ideational milieus. Henri Tajfel (1978) initially demonstrated the phenomenon of in-group prototyping (predicated on in-group preferentiality) and out-group stereotyping (predicated on out-group bias), establishing how prototyping is a way of not only establishing difference but also superiority in reference to an out-group. Of course, the social Self is not simply pitted against a binary Other, which acts as a negative mirror image, but requires the Other as existential precondition (Czarniawska, 2008). Without the insincere, thus, there can be no "true believers."

The way Wahhabi adherents negotiate their identity entails the creation of hierarchies and bounded oppositionalities (cf. Gschwandtner, 2016). When, using terms from the *ḥadīth* corpus, the Wahhabi dispensation self-ascribes as the "saved sect" (*al-firqa al-nājiya*) or the "triumphant faction" (*al-ṭāʾifa al-mansūra*), this should be viewed in terms of valence: When the social group to which one belongs is victorious, the individual member too gains self-esteem, because "it is the self that is victorious by proxy" (Herriot, 2007, p. 99). For the individual adherent, group membership in the imagined community of "true believers" resolves uncertainty and imbues the group with positive valence predicated on both a newly recovered self-esteem and social attraction to fellow group members. As Meijer (2009) has insisted, membership in a puritan group "transforms the humiliated, the downtrodden, disgruntled young people, the discriminated migrant, or the politically repressed into a chosen sect […] that immediately grant privileged access to the Truth" (p. 13).

Paul Ricoeur (1991) has usefully suggested that identities emerge in a continual struggle between concordance and discordance, navigating aspired and lived realities. In fundamentalist psychology, thus, the dialectic between how things are and how they should be is continuously at play. Yet perhaps the term utopia (from the Greek *eu-topos*, lit. "no place")—signifying disembodied unrealizability according to Mannheim (2015 [1929], p. 177)—is less apt for Wahhabi schema than Bauman's (2017) term "retrotopia" (lit. "past place"). From such a "retrotopian" perspective, the original seventh-century faith community in Medina can be idealized as moral epitomes, and the return to the way of the ancients can be posited as panacea for both theological errors and lived depravities. In their values and actions, the Wahhabi faithful are concerned with re(dis)covering the past. What is progress to the secularists is regress to the believers, and the entropy entailed in the contemporary beliefscape may appear rather dim, indeed dystopic, to the committed Wahhabi.

As a form of subjectivity, Wahhabism "transcends the Muslim minority–majority context dichotomy" (Poljarevic, 2016, p. 478), for the "true believers" constitute a perpetual minority. They also act accordingly in the production of a religious counterculture, which stands in opposition to both secular modernity and, notably, traditional modes of religiosity. It is possible, therefore, to conceive of dual dissonance in the Wahhabi standpoint: the (secular) world has to be eschewed and the (religious) order remade. Neither can be embraced. Poljarevic (2016) correctly distinguishes between traditional Sunni orthopraxy and the Wahhabi mission, for where the former seeks to "preserve the historically contingent order of religious institutions," the latter seeks to "change, purify, or even abolish those same institutions and erect their own" (Poljarevic, 2016, p. 489).

As a counterculture, Wahhabism is simultaneously (externally) dissident and (internally) conformist. Self-inculcated prototyping in the Wahhabi counterculture emphasizes the importance of internal conformity by means of "extensive socialisation into a tightly-knit and mutually reaffirming group" (Herriot, 2007, p. 47). When, however, the out-group becomes exceedingly heterogeneous or inclusive, as is increasingly the case in social geographies dominated by Western liberalism, only an extreme prototype will differentiate the in-group from out-group members (cf. Herriot, 2007, pp. 34–38). Consider, thus, how as the female head covering (*hijāb*) has become increasingly commonplace in European and North American metropolises, the Wahhabi faithful have ferociously argued that it doesn't quite pass religious muster and, in a display of religious one-upmanship, the female face veil (*niqāb*) is insisted upon as mandatory.

Self-categorization as strong believers is intimately associated with such impression management; hence the conspicuousness of sartorial and other social-identity markers in Wahhabi social networks—from face veils and voluminous beards, to distinctive vocabulary and behaviour patterns, to manners of greeting and even hand gestures (Duderija, 2014, p. 127; Svensson, 2012). In encountering this exteriorization of religiosity, observers can be forgiven for viewing Wahhabi puritanism as a form of "exhibitionism" (Roy, 2004, p. 267), but within the mental frame of the Wahhabi believer, such primordialization of daily life is a form of virtue signalling: it shows adherence to alpha-Islam. The faithful emulation (*ittiba'*) of the Prophet and the predecessors in quotidian practices comes to constitute the ultimate measure of devotion and authenticity (Olsson, 2012, p. 73). Yet, as in other forms of puritanism, the social symbols remain selective: for instance, the turban (*'amāma*) is eschewed, although it is the quintessential Islamic headgear (indeed, the *sunna*), often opting instead for the bareheaded look or the Gulf-style kerchief (*ghutra* or *shumāgh*), just as the prophetic dress of the loincloth (*'izār*) is not seen as emblematic, whereas relevant *ahadīth* proscribing covering the ankles (*isbāl*) are applied to trousers and pyjamas, too.

Conformity flows from strong socialization. Religious knowledge (*'ilm*) is transmitted via testimonial chains from reverential leaders. In subservience to Wahhabism's stress on the authentic religious understanding, the dedicated adherent is, whether enrolled in a formal programme of learning or autodidact, a "seeker of knowledge" (*tālib al-'ilm*). The term bestows legitimacy to the individual as a serious aspirant to religious leadership. For those below the level of seekers (*tullāb*), but engaged in proselytization or public outreach (*da'wa*), the term *dā'ī* (roughly meaning lay missionary) is used as a (self-)designation, possibly as a way to circumvent critique of lacking credentials (Olsson, 2012, p. 87). At the top of the hierarchies are the *shuyūkh* (sing. *shaykh*), and above them the indisputable beacons of knowledge, often styled with the honorific title *imām* (denoting leadership of the *umma*, the worldwide Muslim community, at large).

Despite this religious hierarchy, Wahhabism denounces the traditional modes of investiture and accreditation of Sunni clergy (*'ulamā*). Originally, the Arab resentment against the Turks coalesced with Wahhabi antipathy toward the Ottoman religious hierarchy (Cook, 1992; Firro, 2013). Wahhabi antisacerdotalism and animus to establishment clergy thus predated the French Revolution by more than half a century. Though an ersatz clerical estate later emerged—mostly as the progeny of Ibn 'Abd al-Wahhab and consecutive generations of close students and confidants—the theological hallmark of Wahhabism was its *populism*. Wahhabism not only subverted the age-old method of accreditation (*ijāza*) and scholarship by chains of transmission (*isnād*), but it also loosened the epistemic control of the past schools of learning so much so that the layman could accuse the traditional leaders of heresy.

Even as the traditional procedure of anathematization (*takfīr*) entails an elaborate judicial process by the learned authorities, among Wahhabi adherents *takfīr* became everybody's prerogative, requiring no special qualification or designation. Ibn 'Abd al-Wahhab's own treatise on the "nullifiers of Islam" (*nawāqiḍ al-islam*), listing ten actions by which faith was vitiated, offered the argument for such universalization of *takfīr*. The third action was, ominously, an inaction: "Whoever does not hold the polytheists to be disbelievers or entertains doubts about them being disbelievers or considers their ways and beliefs to be correct has committed disbelief" (M. Ibn Abdul Wahhab, 2014, p. 47). *Takfīr*, accordingly, was not a privilege; it was an obligation or, at least, a precautionary obligation—those who refused it or hesitated could render themselves disbelievers on account of their unwillingness to pronounce others disbelievers. The ever-expanding circle of *takfīr* was thus born.

Ideational Contestations Between Wahhabism and Rival Forms of Salafism: The Recurrent Trichotomy

Although Wahhabism was never a coherent dispensation, it was always closely constrained by the political and epistemic control of its Saudi patrons. Wahhabism's exposure to other international currents—from the anti-madhhabism of the Yemeni reformers Muhammad ibn Ismail al-Amir al-San'ani (1688–1769) and Muhammad ibn 'Ali al-Shawkani (1759–1839) to the neo-orthodoxy of the Indian Ahl-i Hadith, led by Sayyid Ahmad Barelwi (1786–1831) in Raebareli, Sayyid Nadhir Hussayn (1805–1902) in Delhi, and Siddiq Hasan Khan in Bhopal (1832–90); to the activism of the Egyptian Muslim Brethren, originated by Hassan al-Banna (1906–49)—led to a more assertive belief system (Sheikh, 2021). In the 1950s and 1960s, the mass arrival of Egyptian and Syrian *Ikhwanista* into the Kingdom of Saudi Arabia, seeking refuge from the persecution of Nasserite and Ba'athist regimes, respectively, produced a shift in both the reach and tenor of Wahhabism. The new synthesis first transmogrified beyond the confines of the Saudi state and, ultimately, challenged the Saudi—Wahhabi *modus vivendi*, wherein the clergy would have control of certain domestic institutions—primarily education, religion, and the courts—and the royalty be left with uncontested power in the other domains (Lacroix, 2011; Ménoret, 2005; Niblock, 2006). The resultant hybrids in all of their global variegations are commonly, but not accurately, referred to as Salafism.

Far from unitary, contemporary Salafism is characterized by fierce intergroup rivalries and remains a heterogeneous discourse, rather than a homogenous social identity. The classic typology of Salafi currents was initially articulated by Wiktorowicz (2006), who usefully posited the differences between Salafi groups as a tri-partite division, distinguishing between the "purists" (for those driven by a primacy of theology, enacted through polemics, propagation, and education), the "politicos" (for those driven by a primacy of politics, enacted through social mobilization or partisan activism), and, finally, the "jihadists" (for those driven by a primacy, or at least legitimacy, of militancy enacted in pursuit of revolutionary or anti-systemic goals). Though all groups within Salafism could be viewed as "extremists"—with respect to either *values* or *actions* (cf. Eatwell & Goodwin, 2010)—their extremism can be differentiated: the "purists" are extremist in their sectarianism, the "politicos" in their political rejectionism, and the "jihadis" in their resort to militarism.

Though the three ideal types within Salafism largely share creedal standpoints (*ʿaqīda*), based on the writings of Ibn Taymiyya and Ibn ʿAbd al-Wahhab, they differ on the question of what constitutes primary threats, and hence what ought to be the primary modality of engagement with the world. The splits among self-declared Salafis thus relate to *manhaj*, which could be translated as method, *modus operandi*, or "mobilization strategy" (Poljarevic, 2016). These range from religious proselytization and study circles on the one end of the spectrum, to political activism and agitation, to non-state military combat at the other end (Wiktorowicz, 2006). Alternatively, the division could be differentiated *qua* levels of engagement (Poljarevic, 2016): Purists are concerned with the micro-level (individual adherence to the correct creed), as opposed to the meso-level engagement of activists (concerned with statecraft and the Islamicity or otherwise of political systems), which in turn is pitted against the macro-level of the militants (geopolitical and armed resistance against a West-centric world order). Furthermore, their understanding of the Islamic body-politic differs. To adopt terms from German sociology, the idea of faith praxis among purist Salafis revolves around the construction of a *Gemeinschafft* (or community) of true believers. The political Salafis, however, tend to focus on both *Gesellschafft* (society) and *Staatsordnung* (system of government). Militant Salafis, finally, are concerned with *Macht* (power) as a way of remaking the world in their own theo-political image.

Across hundreds of research outputs, the fundamental trichotomy of the Salafi spectrum has withstood scholarly scrutiny, even as individual analysts have taken issue with the term "purists" (e.g. Wagemakers, 2016). Elsewhere I have, based on applicable Arabic terms, suggested a taxonomy based on the distinction between politically conformist Salafism (*al-salafiyya al-taqlīdiyya*), activist Salafism (*al-salafiyya al-ḥarakiyya*), and militant Salafism (*al-salafiyya al-jihādiyya*), offering thus slight modifications of existing terminology (Sheikh, 2021).

Critically, the politically conformist Salafis can be subdivided into three broad streams that differ primarily in ethos and leadership, rather than in core principles: Firstly, there is "epistemic Salafism" (*al-salafiyya al-ʿilmiyya*), concerned with purification (*taṣfiya*) of the faith tradition, education (*tarbiya*) of adherents, and propagation (*daʿwa*) to non-adherents (Al-Albani, 2004). Politically, they stay aloof of politics, and accordingly are referred to as "aloofists" by Wagemakers (2016, pp. 16–17), though they could equally be referred to as *strategic quietists*. The iconic protagonist of this stream was the preeminent *ḥadīth* scholar of the Salafi movement, the Albanian-born, Syrian-reared scholar Muhammad Nasir al-Din al-Albani (1914–99), and his international circle of students, particularly from his period in Jordan, such as Muhammad Musa Nasr (1954–2017), ʿAli al-Halabi (1960–2020), Salim al-Hilali (b. 1957), and Mashhur Hasan Mahmud Salman (b. 1960). Occasionally, thus, the stream is referred to as "Albani Salafism" (Brachman, 2009, pp. 31–34).

The second stream is constituted by "establishment Wahhabism," controlling key positions in Saudi and Saudi-funded endowments for religious instruction, research, and publication. Although occasionally referred to as "apolitical," this would appear naïve, for loyalism and status-quoism invariably remain political positions. The leading scholars of "establishment Wahhabism" include ʿAbd al-ʿAziz bin Baz (1912–99), Muhammad bin Salih al-ʿUthaymin (1929–2001), ʿAbdullah al-Ghudayyan (1926–2010), Ahmad al-Najmi (1928–2008), Salih Muhammad al-Luhaydan (1932–2022), ʿAbd al-Muhsin al-ʿAbbad (b. 1933), and Saleh bin Fawzan al-Fawzan (b. 1933). Thirdly, adjacent to establishment Wahhabism is a newer trend, now eponymically known as "Madkhalism" after the Medina University professor Rabi' bin Hadi al-Madkhali (b. 1933), though the Ethiopian professor in Medina, Muhammad Aman al-Jami (1927–96) was his teacher and immediate intellectual precursor. Their Wahhabism is ultra-loyalist and politically reactionary, ferociously agitating against political activism, public criticism, or opposition to any established regime. If "agitational quietism" were not an oxymoron, it would be apt for this group, as they condemn political engagement, both peaceful and violent, and whether through political parties, social movements, or militant organizations.

Where, then, does "Wahhabism" fit in? Though it would be allowable to use the Wahhabi epithet as a shorthand for all streams of purist/politically conformist Salafism, I have above differentiated further for reasons of analytic precision, using the term for only two of the three streams, namely, for "establishment Wahhabism" and "Madkhalism." In the context of the present chapter, then, Wahhabism is that branch of the global Salafi movement which espouses loyalty to the founding pact between Muhammad ibn 'Abd al-Wahhab and the Saudi rulers. They hold firm to the Saudi religious establishment, from whence they draw guidance, even if they are themselves non-Saudi. They further remain affiliated to late Hanbalism, as rearticulated by Ibn Taymiyya, unlike the broader Salafi dispensation which is more eclectic and offers a greater latitude for *de novo* interpretation (*ijtihād*) based on the primary textual sources (*naṣṣ*), particularly the *ḥadīth*. Indeed, the foremost *ḥadīth* scholar of the Salafis, Nasir al-Din al-Albani, critiqued the Saudi establishment Wahhabis precisely for being too wedded to the Hanbali school over the breadth of the *ḥadīth* corpus and twice—in 1963 and 1978—faced repercussions for this legal non-conformism while teaching in Saudi Arabia (Olidort, 2015).

Wahhabis Versus Salafis: Seven Differentiators

Eschewing attempts of relating an exonym to an endonym, the extant literature has not sought to clearly delineate the Wahhabis from the broader group of Salafis. Although learned observers have used the terms Salafi and Wahhabi interchangeably, today Wahhabism is best identified as a sub-school within the purist/politically conformist tendency of Salafism, deferent to (all) political authority and (particularly) Saudi religious authority. In Saudi history, such deference is a product of the historical Saudi–Wahhabi founding pact whereby the House of Sa'ud (*āl sa'ūd*) and the progeny of Ibn 'Abd al-Wahhab (*āl al-shaykh*) agreed on a division of power (Al-Rasheed, 2002, 2007). For the citizens, in turn, their social contract consisted in pure obedience (*ṭā'a*) in relation to Palace and Mosque, a contract that was underwritten by the rentier economy of an oil-producing state (Gause, 1994; Niblock, 2006; Aarts & Roelants, 2016; Rich, 2017).

Far from semantic, the difference between Wahhabism and Salafism thus extends to affiliation, positioning, and scope. With regard to affiliation, just as Wahhabism has its origin in the heartland of what is today Saudi Arabia, it has remained closely allied to its religious establishment, in the process benefitting from Saudi patronage and largesse (Varagur, 2020). Wahhabis are thus direct beneficiaries of the Saudi state, both in the form of domestic clientelism and global partnerships within a tiered epistemic community. The religious domain is tightly regulated in Saudi Arabia by institutions such as the Council of Senior Clergy (*Hay'at kibār al-'ulamā'*), the judicial *fatwa* council (*Dār al-ifta*), lower-ranked associations, research institutes, universities, seminaries, government-funded publishing houses, and government-appointed *imāms* and *qāḍīs* (religious judges; Mouline, 2014). Internationally, too, the Wahhabi networks are monitored and controlled by Saudi-trained functionaries, often in coordination with Saudi organizations or diplomatic representatives (Oliveti, 2002; Varagur, 2020). Salafis, while sharing major theologico-epistemological foundations with Wahhabis, have been more independent (financially as well as intellectually), and some have altogether turned against the Saudi establishment on matters of principle or policy (Meijer, 2009).

Secondly, and relatedly, Wahhabism entails a theo-cultural isomorphism, reflected in anything from architectural to sartorial styles (for men white ankle-length robes and Gulf-style headgear, and for women black overcoats with face veil and gloves). For Wahhabi preachers, accreditations from Saudi institutions or endorsements (*tazkiyāt*) from Saudi-trained scholars are a *sine qua non*. Socialization is thus strong and legitimacy is bestowed by way of affiliation, as a direct student or a student of a student of one of the clerical "greats" (*kibār*). Salafis, on the other hand, have broader lineages. For instance, the South Asian Salafis, the *Ahl-i Ḥadīth*, have their own scholarly authorities and institutions that sometimes predate the global influence of Wahhabism (Amin & Majothi, 2022). They also retain local dress codes, self-published religious literature, and indigenous architectural styles.

Thirdly, Wahhabism is overtly focused on the rectification of doctrine, the restitution of orthodoxy, and the retrieval of an orthopraxy that is undergirded by theological first principles. Wahhabis often berate activist, political, or militant forms of Salafis for being insufficiently committed to the ideas of doctrinal and praxiological purity, thus losing sight of the centrality of both 'aqīda and manhaj. Even tactical alignments with other Salafi groups are seen as anathematic to the purity of faith, and, as such, Wahhabis are simultaneously isolationist and puritan.

Fourthly, epistemologically, both Wahhabis and Salafis espouse the primacy of the text (in practice, the central focus remains on the *aḥādīth* rather than the Qur'an), but Wahhabi textualism evolves through the prism of its Hanbali heritage and the proof texts therefore are more partial. Salafis are more principled in their blanket opposition to adherence to schools of Islamic law (*taqlīd*), and often seek to transcend the Hanbali genealogy, seeking a *de-novo* engagement with the text and comparative legal opinions. At times, Salafi scholars arrive at different legal rulings to the Wahhabis—in matters such as the required length of the beard, the obligation of face-covering, the correct postures in the prayer, and, more consequentially, in matters of politics. Overall, Salafi writings are characterized by being more exploratory and less reliant on the dogmatic regurgitation of past opinion.

Fifthly, the social dynamics differ: Wahhabis are exclusivists, taking pride in being the select group. Even if privately uncompromising, Salafis often aspire to have mass appeal. This has implications for gender roles, too. Where Wahhabi seek to exorcise women from the public square, insisting on face veils and strict gender segregation (Olsson, 2020), Salafis may seek to organize women as an important constituency to spread the movement (Mahmood, 2005). To be certain, though, the Salafis remain conservative in their attitude to gender (for instance, in much of the Middle East, avoiding using the personal names of their female relatives in public). In contrast, the Wahhabi faithful could be considered ultraconservative (avoiding having their female relatives out in public).

Sixthly, in contrast to Wahhabi social insularity, part of the Salafi repertoire is politically engaged and oftentimes more overtly confrontational. Some Salafis deploy *takfīr* in matters beyond theology, including in matters that could be characterized as ideological, following Sayyid Qutb (1906–66), the Muslim brotherhood theoretician, who formulated a quasi-anarchist doctrine of militant resistance to Muslim regimes which did not rule by the Shari'a (Calvert, 2010). While inter-Salafi heterogeneity is exposed in dramatically different political stances, the Wahhabi position is unswervingly one of support for incumbent regimes and the preservation of the *status quo*. While Wahhabism is not necessarily monarchist, it is invariably loyalist. Wahhabi religious leaders can be called upon to defend a regime and condemn state-challengers, often giving the fealty-and-abnegation principle (*al-walā' wa-l-barā'*) political form (Sheikh, 2003; Wagemakers, 2012; Weismann, 2017). Indeed, the Madkhali trend is, as we shall see, overtly counter-revolutionary.

Finally, Salafis and Wahhabis differ on questions of political authority, for Wahhabis are content to acknowledge a separation between religion and the political. Still, they are not secularists, insofar as they require that governance accord with the Shari'a, but, in general, they do not see the ruler's infringements of the Shari'a to constitute major disbelief (*kufr akbar*), on the ground that they can be excused, for instance, on the basis of their ignorance of religious law (*al-'udhr bi-l-jahl*) or on the basis of executive difficulties or other contingencies. Rather than encroaching on the ruling classes, the same operative principle is applied vis-à-vis them and the general public, namely, sincere advice (*naṣīḥa*) and propagation (*da'wa*). The Salafi spectrum is wider, and while one stream—that led by al-Albani—remains detached from the political, others vigorously contest the norms of modern statecraft, and some, following Sayyid Qutb, anathematize on the basis of "ruling by other than what Allah has decreed" (*al-ḥukm bi ghayr mā anzal Allāh*).

Madkhalis and Their Enemies: Contending Extremisms

Contemporary Salafism is increasingly fragmented between, on the one axis, activist versus loyalist currents and, on the other axis, between non-violent versus militant expressions. In theory, thus, four combinations, or quadrants, exist in the Salafi repertoire: militant activists, non-violent activists, non-violent loyalists, and militant loyalists. According to this schema, which could be viewed as an alternative to Wiktorowicz's (2006) model and its later iterations, the Wahhabis are in general non-violent loyalists, but, where situations demand, they can slip into militant loyalists. In the following, I shall explore how.

Though not from the official clerical elite in Saudi Arabia, one religious leader has in recent decades seen much prominence as head of a particular hardline Wahhabi faction. Rabi' bin Hadi al-Madkhali, a former student of both 'Abd al-'Aziz bin Baz and Nasir al-Din al-Albani who rose to become the Head of Sunna Studies at the University of Medina—the most important Wahhabi seat of learning (Farquhar, 2016)—has consistently warned against the Islamism of Muslim Brotherhood activists. Their penetration of Saudi society was embodied in Muhammad Qutb (1919–2014), the younger brother of Sayyid Qutb, and Muhammad Surur Zayn al-'Abideen (1938–2016), a former Syrian Brotherhood activist (Lacroix, 2011). From the 1980s, the emerging current of Saudi Islamism took shape in the form of the Saudi *ṣaḥwa* (revival) movement—led, *inter alia*, by Safar al-Hawali (b. 1950) and Salman al-'Awda (b. 1956)—against which Madkhalism mobilized. The Madhkhali dominance of the Islamic University of Medina (hence sometimes known as "Medina Salafism") facilitated the dissemination of this trend internationally, including into Western metropolises, via graduates, iterant scholars, and cyberspace.

Al-Madkhali's discourse against ideological enemies—whom he considers theological enemies, too, on the premise that errors in *manhaj* relate to errors in '*aqīda*—is repeated across multiple English-language websites (such as www.themadkhalis.com, www.salafitalk.net, and www.troid.com). The prose is angry, aggressive, and *ad hominen*. Curiously, the Madkhalis seek to delegitimize rival opinions within the Salafi movement by recourse to an expanded application of the classical science of examining the moral soundness of hadith narrators (*ruwāt*, sing. *rāwī*). Rather than engaging with intellectual arguments, thus, they seek disparagement (*jarḥ*) of the uprightness of out-group scholars, thus negating the latter's views by a strategy of character defamation. In an effort to render credence to their opinions, in-group scholars are, at the same time, given high praise (*ta'dīl*), often in terms so reverential that the group appears cultic (Meijer, 2011).

Just as a sizeable section of "ultra-orthodox" Haredim in Judaism are virulently opposed to political Zionism—on the grounds that the latter constitutes a heretical movement which is not Torah-true (Mor, 2016)—many Wahhabis remain bitterly hostile to Islamism (*mutatis mutandis*, the Muslim parallel to Zionism), on the grounds that the latter is not *manhaj*-compliant. Madkhalism goes further, though: all political activism (*ḥarakiyya*) is seen as dissent, because it creates partisan identities (*ḥizbiyya*), whereas Wahhabi identity construction is founded on creedal, not political, attachment. To the Madkhalis, monotheism is centripetal but ideological politics discordant and thus centrifugal. In addition, similar to other political conformists, the Madkhali current eschews political mobilization for a variety of reasons: because politics is contingent, whereas religion is absolute; because politics is governed by whim and desires, not truth; because politics is the prerogative of the rulers, not the masses; because politics is a distraction from propagation and worship; and because politics is characterized by alignments or alliances that would compromise one's (puritan) religion (cf. Wagemakers, 2016). Madhkhalis see political agitation and public demonstrations as forms of rebellion (*khurūj*) against the ruler, and thus religiously proscribed. Rather, obedience (*'iṭā'a*) is owed to political authority (*walī al-amr*), even if it be wayward (*fāsiq*), nefarious (*fājir*), or disbelieving (*kāfir*).

As such, the Madkhalis denounce political action, whether pacific and militant, even by those who profess Ibn 'Abd al-Wahhab's theology. Militant Salafis are described as betrayers of the Salafi way or as *khārijiyya* (using the name for an anti-caliphal secessionist group from early Islamic history, infamous for killing the fourth caliph, 'Ali ibn Abu Talib, and regarding their Muslim adversaries to be infidel; Brachman, 2009, pp. 30–31). Political Salafists and Islamists broadly are deemed "people of whims" (*ahl al-hawā'*), whereas particular ire is directed at the Qutbist worldview. Though Sayyid Qutb shared vocabulary with Ibn 'Abd al-Wahhab in notions such as false gods (*ṭawāghīt*), heathenism (*jāhiliyya*), polytheism (*shirk*), doctrine (*'aqīda*), and excommunication (*takfīr*), his *oeuvre* was not theological but political, and he deployed the terms accordingly. He also extended the Taymiyyan understanding of monotheism with a fourth category: unicity of sovereignty (*tawḥīd al-ḥākimiyya*), which demanded that all positive law had to align with God's law, as revealed in Scripture (Khatab, 2006). To Madkhalis, his theological thinking was absurd, his political constructs inauthentic, and his programme pure sedition (*fitna*). Where Qutb and his followers had anathematized on political grounds, al-Madkhali condemned Qutb on both his politics and his theology (Al-Madkhalee, 1997).

Though they forbid voting, as an act of doing politics, living in authoritarian states poses no conceptual difficulty for Madkhali celebrants, whose ethos is reactionary and counterrevolutionary. For this reason, Madkhali propagandists have been welcomed to bolster besieged regimes from Saudi Arabia to Yemen to Jordan to Egypt to Sudan to Libya to Algeria and beyond as a counterbalance to Islamist movements. As the Arab Spring posed a threat to the status quo in the Middle East and North Africa, Madkhali sensibilities were challenged. Fiercely anti-radical, the Madkhalis witnessed the unsettling deterioration of the rectitude of their erstwhile allies in conformist circles, which at times embraced the new openings for political engagement. For instance, the *Aḥrār*, or Freemen, Movement in Egypt, launched in October 2012, became the very kind of agitational Salafism that took to the streets with populist messages of social justice, revolution, and anti-Americanism while avoiding formal political processes (Tadros, 2014). Albeit virulently opposed to the Morsi regime, the Ahrar drew inspiration precisely from Sayyid Qutb's writings on *jāhiliyya* and *ḥākimiyya*, even as they eschewed political *takfīr* (Awad, 2016, April 29). For Madhkhalis, this politicization of Salafism made for a corruption of the faith, and they insisted that both *manhaj* and *'aqīda* had to be correct in order to qualify for the lofty epithet of Salafism. If the *manhaj* was tainted with *bid'a*, it indicated a corruption of *'aqīda*, because *manhaj* followed from *'aqīda* (Moosa, 2020, June 1).

Another instance of troubling slippage came in the form of the so-called "Costa Salafis," after their preference for meeting in Costa coffee houses. Their Salafism became emblematic of new discourses on citizenship, civil rights, and social reform, over doctrinal matters. While the coffee shop propagation method was known from the early preaching of the founder of the Muslim Brotherhood, Hassan al-Banna, it was alien to the Wahhabi ethos of staunchness. To them, coffee shops and shisha bars were dens of depravity from whence no good could come. The gradual relaxation of the focus on *'aqīda*, too, rendered the *Zeitgeist* unbearable. In Libya, finally, the Madkhalis would take up arms and form militias to prevent an Islamist–Jihadist takeover and, in conformity with Saudi foreign policy, supported the Libyan-American General Khalifa Haftar (b. 1943), who in turn gave them control over mosques, foundations, and religious affairs (Ali, 2017, June 6). Madkhalism, thus, had come full circle: its insistence on opposing all forms of political Islam forced it into a military alignment with those who espoused no ideology beyond power.

Concluding Thoughts: Wither Wahhabism?

When Muhammad ibn 'Abd al-Wahhab first declared the rediscovery of monotheism in his mid-eighteenth century theological tracts, he could hardly have anticipated either the world-wide spread of his mission or the persistent permutations of the movement into feuding and mutually excommunicating factions a quarter of a millennium later. Embracing bigotry, his reform theology set in motion contending claims of being the "saved group" (*al-firqa al-nājiya*). Anti-pluralist, Wahhabism negated the historical *modus vivendi* in Sunni Islam, centred on the historical pluralism of schools of jurisprudence and the effective duopoly of schools of theology. The circle of believers were shrunk to those who professed an expanded notion of monotheism (*tawḥid*), but later also to those who professed a particular "method" (*manhaj*) of engaging with the text and the world. In time, the restorationist impulse was both strengthened and subverted by Saudi patronage, as the initial pact between the royalty (*āl sa'ūd*) and clergy (*āl al-shaykh*) legitimized the new "alpha-Islam" but also made religion subservient to power.

Globally, the syncretism between Wahhabism and the associated retrotopian dispensation of Salafism rested on both ideational affinities and strategic interests, and successive waves entailed both a "Salafization" of Wahhabism—courtesy of human and intellectual resources beyond Saudi Arabia—and a "Wahhabization" of Salafism—courtesy of the global reach of Saudi financial resources (cf. Commins, 2015). The Wahhabi–Salafi interactions continued to redefine both traditions as they would reinterpret concepts and rearticulate ideas in response to both external stimuli and internal synthesis. Modernity and heteronomous subjectification augmented the Wahhabi mission: the colonial onslaught on not only Muslim polities but the scholastic estate within had also weakened traditional modes of Islamic education and saw the rise of revivalist discourses and demands for cultural autarky amid angst, alienation, and anomie. The late-modern development of new modes of printed and electronic dissemination across countries and continents conditioned a mainstreaming of dogmatism. Periods and areas which saw protracted cultural or political conflicts were particularly hospitable to the absolutism of the Wahhabi credo.

Today, Wahhabism, as much as a theological critique, is a social(ized) identity based on segregation, supremacism, and social enclavism vis-à-vis a perpetually encroaching and hostile world. Surrounded by a host of threatening Others, the Wahhabi subject is driven deeper into (anti-social) distancing, reinforcing oft-rehearsed notions surrounding out-group abnegation (*barā'*) and in-group fealty (*walā'*). Yet the Wahhabi consortium is fragmenting as the in-group itself is unstable. Persistent tropes, but evolving practices, signify the increased complexity of the Wahhabi appellation. The political content in Wahhabism was always entailed in polit-ical consent, i.e. in "religious interpretations that require subservience to political authority" (al-Rasheed, 2007, p. 26). While the doctrinaire Wahhabi streams thus eschewed political activism, it was from the outset embedded in a socio-cultural (micro-)politics of identity, or a "politics of lifestyles" (de Koning, 2012). Moreover, a politics of positioning applied, too, as anathematization (*takfīr*) of non-Wahhabi Others was extended to other Muslims, including erstwhile Salafist associates whose mobilization strategies could include politicking or militant enterprise, thus entailing a violation of the neo-orthodox *manhaj* of teaching, preaching, and purifying the faith tradition.

Yet, to analysts, the question remains whether the diversity in the Wahhabi–Salafi repertoire amounts to distinct ideational-cum-operational categories or instead constitute a linear, thus connected, spectrum, where theological extremism is a mere precursor to politicization and violentization. While Western literature often depicts Wahhabi puritanism as a "conveyor-belt" (Schmid, 2014) to Salafi jihadism, the Wahhabi establishment posits itself as a firewall against the latter. Arrogating to themselves doctrinal purity, and thus salvific exclusivity, they continue to default into a standard "surveillance theology" mode, as guardians of orthodoxy, discur-sively policing the boundaries between themselves and militant dogmatics. Still, the boundaries between theological extremism and political extremism remain permeable. That the Madkhali anti-jihadists would not shy away from taking up arms, thus militarize, under the guise of obedience to political power in Libya, showed the precariousness of the Wahhabi condition. As with all grand signifiers, Wahhabism could not remain static. It continues to evolve and transform.

Notes

1 Sulayman ibn 'Abd al-Wahhab's (1699–1793) speedy yet scathing critique of his brother's mission was posthumously retitled *al-Ṣawā'iq al-ilāhiyya fī al-radd 'alā al-wahhābiyya* ("Divine Lightening in the Refutation of Wahhabism"). Some authors appear to misapprehend this as its original title (Ménoret, 2005, p. 55; Firro, 2018, p. 81), while Redissi (2008, p. 162, fn. 14) appears cognizant of the uncertainty surrounding the original title. The work has recently been translated into English under its original 35-word title which translates, in part, to "Divine Lightening: The Decisive Speech [...] in answer to Muhammad ibn 'Abd a-Wahhab" (S. Ibn 'Abdul Wahhab, 2020).
2 The six most oft-rehearsed tracts of Muhammad ibn 'Abd al-Wahhab all relate to *tawhid* and the ever-present dangers of *shirk*. They are *Kitāb al-tawḥīd* (Treatise on Monotheism); *al-Uṣūl al-thalātha* (The Three Principles); *al-Qawā'id al-arba'a* (The Four Maxims); *Nawāqid al-islām* (The Nullifiers of Islam); *Shurūṭ lā ilāha illallāh* (The Conditions of [the Declaration] There is No God But Allah); and *Kashf al-shubuhāt* (The Removal of Doubts). Interestingly, his *Kitāb al-kabā'ir* (The Book of Major Sins) has far less circulation, which may illustrate how Wahhabism is a puritanical, but not necessarily pietist, movement.
3 The first Saudi state lasted from 1744 until an Ottoman-Egyptian invasion toppled the Saudi patriarch in 1818. The second Saudi state resumed power in 1824 and lasted until 1891. Saudi conquests begin-ning in 1902 saw their culmination in 1932 with the establishment of the current Kingdom of Saudi Arabia.

References

Aarts, P. & Roelants, C. (2016). *Saudi Arabia: A kingdom in peril* (2nd ed.). London: Hurst& Co.

Abou El Fadl, K. (2005). *The great theft: Wrestling Islam from the extremists.* New York, NY: Harper.

Afsaruddin, A. (2007). *The first Muslims: History and memory.* Oxford: Oneworld.

Al-Albani, M.N.A.-D. (2004). *Tasfiya & tarbiya: Purification and cultivation and the need the Muslims have for them.* (S. Al-Kashmeeree, Trans.).London: Ar-Risala. Retrieved from: www.islamicbooks.webs ite/Books/Tasfiya%20&%20Tarbiya%20(2004)%20by%20Muhammad%20Nasiruddin%20al-Alb ani.pdf

Al-Azmeh, A. (1988). Orthodoxy and Ḥanbalite Fideism. *Arabica*, 35(3), 253–66. doi: 10.1163/157005888X00026

Algar, H. (2002). *Wahhabism: A critical essay.* Oneonta, NY: Islamic Publications International.

Ali, A.S. (2017, June 6). Haftar and Salafism: A dangerous game. Atlantic Council. Retrieved from: www.atlanticcouncil.org/blogs/menasource/haftar-and-salafism-a-dangerous-game/

Allen, C. (2007). *God's terrorists: The Wahhabi cult and the hidden roots of modern jihad* (2nd ed.). London: Abacus.

Al-Madkhalee, R.I.H. (1997). *The methodology of the prophets in calling to Allaah: That is the way of wisdom and intelligence.* (D. Burbank, Trans.). Birmingham: Al-Hidaayah Publishing.

Almond, G., Appleby, S. & Sivan, E. (2003). *Strong religion: The rise of fundamentalisms around the world.* Chicago, IL: University of Chicago Press.

Al-Rasheed, M. (2002). *A history of Saudi Arabia.* Cambridge: Cambridge University Press.

Al-Rasheed, M. (2007). *Contesting the Saudi state: Islamic voices from a new generation.* Cambridge: Cambridge University Press.

Altemeyer, B. & Hunsberger, B. (1992). Authoritarianism, religious fundamentalism, quest, and prejudice. *International Journal for the Psychology of Religion*, 2(2), 113–33. doi: 10.1207/s15327582ijpr0202_5

Amin, H. & Majothi, A. (2022). The Ahl-e-Hadith: From British India to Britain. *Modern Asian Studies*, 56(1), 176–206. doi: 10.1017/S0026749X210000931207/s15327582ijpr0202_5

Awad, M. (2016, April 29). Revolutionary Salafism: The case of Ahrar movement. Current trends in Islamic ideology. Retrieved from: www.hudson.org/research/12310-revolutionary-salafism-the-case-of-ahrar-movement

Ayoob, M. & Kosebalaban, H. (Eds.). (2009). *Religion and politics in Saudi Arabia: Wahhabism and the state.* Boulder, CO: Lynne Rienner.

Bartoszuk, K. & Deal, J.E. (2016). Personality, identity styles, and fundamentalism during emerging adulthood. *Identity*, 16(3), 142–53. doi: 10.1080/15283488.2016.1190725

Bauman, Z. (2017). *Retrotopia.* New York, NY: John Wiley.

BBC. (2005, July 16). Full text: Blair speech on terror. *BBC News.* Retrieved from: http://news.bbc.co.uk/1/hi/uk/4689363.stm

Bin Abdul-Wahhab, M. (n.d.). *Kitab at-tauhid.* Riyadh: Dar-us-Salaam.

Bonnefoy, L. (2011). *Salafism in Yemen: Transnationalism and religious identity.* London: Hurst & Co.

Brachman, J.M. (2009). *Global jihadism: Theory and practice.* Abingdon: Routledge.

Brown, J.C. (2018). *Hadith: Muhammad's legacy in the medieval and modern world* (2nd ed.). Oxford: Oneworld.

Calvert, J. (2010). *Sayyid Qutb and the origins of radical Islamism.* London: Hurst & Co.

Cesari, J. (2005). Ethnicity, Islam and les banlieues: Confusing the issues. Retrieved from: https://items.ssrc.org/riots-in-france/ethnicity-islam-and-les-banlieues-confusing-the-issues/

Choueiri, Y.M. (2010). *Islamic fundamentalism: The story of Islamist movements* (3rd ed.). London: Continuum Books.

Commins, D. (2005). Traditional anti-Wahhabi Hanbalism in nineteenth-century Arabia. In I. Weismann & F. Zachs (Eds.), *Ottoman reform and Muslim regeneration: Studies in honour of Butrus Abu-Manneh* (pp. 81–96). London: I.B. Tauris.

Commins, D. (2006). *The Wahhabi mission and Saudi Arabia.* London: I.B. Tauris.

Commins, D. (2015). From Wahhabi to Salafi. In B. Haykel, T. Hegghammer & S. Lacroix (Eds.), *Saudi Arabia in transition: Insights on social, political, economic, and religious change* (pp. 151–66). Cambridge: Cambridge University Press.

Cook, M. (1992). On the origins of Wahhābism. *Journal of the Royal Asiatic Society*, 2(2), 191–202. doi: 10.1017/S1356186300002376

Crawford, M. (2014). *Ibn ʿAbd al-Wahhab.* London: Oneworld.

Czarniawska, B. (2008). Alterity/identity interplay in image construction. In D. Barry & H. Hansen (Eds.), *The SAGE handbook of new approaches in management and organization* (pp. 49–62). London: Sage Publications. doi: 10.4135/9781849200394.n8

Davis, R. (2018). *Western imaginings: The intellectual contest to define Wahhabism.* Cairo, Egypt: The American University in Cairo Press.

de Koning, M. (2012). The "other" political Islam: Understanding Salafi politics. In A. Boubekeur & O. Roy (Eds.), *Whatever happened to the Islamists? Salafis, heavy metal Muslims and the lure of consumerist Islam* (pp.153–78). London: Hurst & Co.

de Koning, M. (2013). The moral maze: Dutch Salafis and the construction of a moral community of the faithful. *Contemporary Islam,* 7(1), 71–83. doi: 10.1007/s11562-013-0247-x

DeLong-Bas, N. (2004). *Wahhabi Islam: From revival and reform to global jihad.* Oxford: Oxford University Press.

Duderija, A. (2014). Neo-traditional Salafis in the West: Agents of (self)-exclusion. In S. Yasmeen & N. Marcović (Eds.), *Muslims citizens in the West: Spaces and agents of inclusion and exclusion* (pp. 125–42). Abingdon: Routledge.

Eatwell, R. & Goodwin, M.J. (Eds.). (2010). *The new extremism in 21st century Britain.* Abingdon: Routledge.

Farquhar, M. (2016). *Circuits of faith: Migration, education, and the Wahhabi mission.* Stanford, CA: Stanford University Press.

Firro, T.K. (2013). The political context of early Wahhabi discourse of Takfir. *Middle Eastern Studies,* 49(5), 770–89. doi: 10.1080/00263206.2013.811648

Firro, T.K. (2018). *Wahhabism and the rise of the House of Saud.* Brighton: Sussex Academic Press.

Foucault, M. (1978). *The history of sexuality,* vol. I. (R. Hurley, Trans.). New York, NY: Pantheon Books.

Gause, G.F. (1994). *Oil monarchies: Domestic and security challenges in the Arab Gulf states.* New York, NY: Council on Foreign Relations.

Gauvain, R. (2012). *Salafi ritual purity: In the presence of God.* Abingdon: Routledge.

Gilbert, M. & Pilchman, D. (2014). Belief, acceptance and what happens in groups: Some methodological considerations. In J. Lackey (Ed.), *Essays in collective epistemology* (pp. 189–212). Oxford: Oxford University Press.

Gold, D. (2003). *Hatred's kingdom: How Saudi Arabia supports the new global terrorism.* Washington, DC: Regnery.

Gschwandtner, C.M. (2016). Philosophical reflections on the shaping of identity in fundamentalist religious communities. *International Journal of Philosophical Studies,* 24(5), 704–24. doi: 10.1080/09672559.2016.1242642

Haddad, G.F. (2007). *The four imams and their schools.* London: Muslim Academic Trust.

Haidt, J. (2012). *The righteous mind: Why good people are divided by politics and religion.* New York, NY: Pantheon Books.

Haykel, B. (2009). On the nature of Salafi thought and action. In R. Meijer (Ed.), *Global Salafism: Islam's new religious movement* (pp. 33–57). London: Hurst & Co.

Herriot, P. (2007). *Religious fundamentalism and social identity.* London: Routledge.

Herriot, P. (2009). *Religious fundamentalism: Global, local and personal.* London: Routledge.

Hood, R., Hill, P. & Williamson, W. (2005). *The psychology of religious fundamentalism.* New York, NY: Guilford.

Hoover, J. (2019). *Ibn Taymiyya.* Oxford: Oneworld.

Huxley, J.S. (1955). Guest editorial: Evolution, cultural and biological. *Yearbook of Anthropology,* 2–25. doi: 10.1086/yearanth.0.3031134

Ibn Abdul Wahhab, M. (2014). *The Ten Nullifiers Of Islam.* (S. Sirajudin, Trans.). London: Darussalam.

Ibn 'Abdul Wahhab, S. (2020). *The divine lightning: The decisive speech of lord of lords, the words of messenger of the King, the bestower, the statements of the people of wisdom in answer to Muhammad ibn 'Abdul Wahhab.* (A.J. Hanbali, Trans). S.l.: HTS Publications.

Illahi, M. (2018). *Doctrine of terror: Saudi Salafi religion.* Victoria, BC: Friesen Press.

Jansen, J.J.G. (1997). *The dual nature of Islamic fundamentalism.* London: Hurst & Co.

Khatab, S. (2006). *The political thought of Sayyid Qutb: The theory of jahiliyyah.* Abingdon: Routledge.

Knysh, A. (2004). A clear and present danger: Wahhabism as rhetorical foil. *Die Welt Des Islams,* 44(1), 3–26.

Lacroix, S. (2011). *Awakening Islam: The politics of religious dissent in contemporary Saudi Arabia.* (G. Holoch, Trans.). Cambridge, MA: Harvard University Press.

Lakoff, G. (2002). *Moral politics: How liberals and conservatives think.* Chicago, IL: University of Chicago Press.

Lauzière, H. (2016). *The making of Salafism: Islamic reform in the twentieth century.* New York, NY: Columbia University Press.

Lauzière, H. (2021). Salafism against hadith literature: The curious beginnings of a new category in 1920s Algeria. *Journal of the American Oriental Society,* 141(2), 403–26. doi: 10.7817/jameroriesoci.141.2.0403

Mahmood, S. (2005). *Politics of piety: The Islamic revival and the feminist subject.* Princeton, NJ: Princeton University Press.

Mannheim, K. (2015). *Ideology and utopia: An introduction to the sociology of knowledge* (L. Wirth & E. Shills, Trans.). Eastford, CT: Martino. (Original work published 1929)

Marsden, G.M. (1980). *Fundamentalism and American culture: The shaping of twentieth century evangelism 1870-1925.* Oxford: Oxford University Press.

Meijer, R. (2009). Introduction. In R. Meijer (Ed.), *Global Salafism: Islam's new religious movement* (pp. 1–32). London: Hurst & Co.

Meijer, R. (2011). Politicising al-jarḥ wa-l-taʿdīl: Rabīʿ b. Hādī al-Madkhalī and the transnational battle for religious authority. In N. Boekhoff-van der Voort, K. Versteegh & J. Wagemakers (Eds.), *Essays in honour of Harald Motzki* (pp. 375–99). Leiden: Brill.

Melchert, C. (2006). *Ahmad ibn Hanbal.* London: Oneworld.

Ménoret, P. (2005). *The Saudi enigma: A history.* (P. Camiller, Trans.). London: Zed Books.

Moosa, A. (2020, June 1). Difference between aqeedah and manhaj. Retrieved from: https://istiqaamah. net/difference-between-aqeedah-and-manhaj-2/

Mor, S. (2016). On Three Anti-Zionisms. *Israel Studies,* 24(2), 206–16. doi: 10.2979/israelstudies.24.2.16

Mouline, N. (2014). *The clerics of Islam: Religious authority and political power in Saudi Arabia.* (E.S. Rundell, Trans.). New Haven, CT: Yale University Press.

Murawiec, L. (2003). *Princes of darkness: The Saudi assault on the West.* (G. Holoch, Trans.). Lanham, MD: Rowman & Littlefield.

Murch, J.D. (1962). *Christians only.* Cincinnati, OH: The Standard.

Nahouza, N. (2018). *Wahhabism and the rise of the new Salafists: Theology, power, and Sunni Islam.* London: I.B. Tauris.

Niblock, T. (2006). *Saudi Arabia: Power, legitimacy and survival.* Abingdon: Routledge.

North, J.B. (1994). *Union in truth: An interpretive history of the restoration movement.* Cincinnati, OH: The Standard.

Olidort, J. (2015). The politics of "quietist" Salafism. Analysis paper, no. 18. Brookings Project on U.S. relations with the Islamic world. Retrieved from: www.brookings.edu/wp-content/uploads/2016/06/Olidort-Final-Web-Version.pdf

Oliver, H.J. (2004). *The "Wahhabi" myth: Dispelling prevalent fallacies and the fictitious link with Bin Laden* (2nd ed.). Toronto: TROID Publications.

Oliveti, V. (2002). *Terror's source: The ideology of Wahhabi-Salafism and its consequences.* Birmingham: Amadeus Books.

Olsson, S. (2012). Swedish puritan Salafism: A hijra within. *Comparative Islamic Studies,* 8(1–2), 71–92. doi: 10.1558/cis.v8i1-2.71

Olsson, S. (2019). *Contemporary puritan Salafism: A Swedish Case Study.* Sheffield: Equinox Publishing.

Olsson, S. (2020). "True, masculine men are not like women!" Salafism between extremism and democracy. *Religions,* 11(3), 118–33. doi: 10.3390/rel11030118

Østebø, T. (2012). *Localising Salafism: Religious change among Oromo Muslims in Bale, Ethiopia.* Leiden: Brill.

Poljarevic, E. (2016). The power of elective affinities in contemporary Salafism. *The Muslim World,* 106(3), 474–500. doi: 10.1111/muwo.12159

Pushaw, R.J. (2020). Comparing literary and biblical hermeneutics to constitutional and statutory interpretation. *Pepperdine Law Review,* 47(2), 463–91. Retrieved from: https://digitalcommons.pepperdine.edu/cgi/viewcontent.cgi?article=2524&context=plr

Rahman, F. (2000). *Revival and reform in Islam: A study of Islamic fundamentalism.* (E. Moosa, Ed.). Oxford: Oneworld.

Redissi, H. (2008). The refutation of Wahhabism in Arabic sources, 1745-1932. In M. Al-Rasheed (Ed.), *Kingdom without borders: Saudi Arabia's political, religious and media frontiers* (pp. 157–81). London: Hurst.

Rentz, G.S. (2004). *The birth of the Islamic reform movement in Saudi Arabia: Muhammad ibn Abd al-Wahhab (1703/04-1792) and the beginnings of the unitarian empire in Arabia.* London: Arabian Publishing.

Rich, B. (2017). *Securitising identity: The case of the Saudi state.* Carlton, Victoria: Melbourne University Press.

Ricoeur, P. (1991). Life in quest of a narrative. In D. Wood (Ed.), *On Paul Ricoeur: Narrative and interpretation* (pp. 20–33). Abingdon: Routledge.

Roy, O. (2004). *Globalized Islam: The search for a new Ummah.* London: Hurst & Co.

Said, E. (1978). *Orientalism.* New York, NY: Pantheon Books.

Said, E. (1994). *Culture and imperialism.* New York, NY: Vintage.

Sandeen, E.R. (1970). *The roots of fundamentalism: British and American millenarianism, 1800-1930*. Chicago, IL: University of Chicago Press.

Schmid, A.P. (2014). Violent and non-violent extremism: Two sides of the same coin? ICCT Research Paper. The Hague: International Centre for Counter-Terrorism. Retrieved from: www.icct.nl/app/uploads/download/file/ICCT-Schmid-Violent-Non-Violent-Extremism-May-2014.pdf

Schwartz, S. (2002). *Two faces of Islam: The house of Sa'ud from tradition to terror*. New York, NY: Random House.

Sheikh, N.S. (2003). *The new politics of Islam: Pan-Islamic foreign policy in a world of states*. Abingdon: Routledge.

Sheikh, N.S. (2021). Making sense of Salafism: Theological foundations, ideological iterations, and political manifestations. In J. Haynes (Ed.), *The Routledge handbook of religion, politics and ideology* (pp. 177–96). Abingdon: Routledge. doi: 10.4324/9780367816230

Sidahmed, A.S. & Ehteshami, A. (Eds.). (1996). *Islamic fundamentalism*. Boulder, CO: Westview Press.

Siddiqi, M.Z. (1993). *Ḥadīth literature: Its origin, development and special features*. In A.H. Murad (Ed.), Cambridge: Islamic Texts Society.

Stephens, J. (2013). The phantom Wahhabi: Liberalism and the Muslim fanatic in mid-Victorian India. *Modern Asian Studies*, 47(1), 22–52. doi: 10.1017/S0026749X12000649

Svensson, J. (2012). Mind the beard! Deference, purity and Islamization of everyday life as micro-factors in a Salafi cultural epidemiology. *Comparative Islamic Studies*, 8(1–2), 185–209.

Tadros, S. (2014). *Mapping Egyptian Islamism*. Washington, DC: Hudson Institute. Retrieved from: www.hudson.org/content/researchattachments/attachment/1444/mapping_egyptian_islamism.pdf

Tajfel, H. (Ed.). (1978). *Differentiation between social groups: Studies in the social psychology of intergroup relations*. New York, NY: Academic Press.

Valentine, S.R. (2015). *Force and fanaticism: Wahhabism in Saudi Arabia and beyond*. London: Hurst & Co.

Varagur, K. (2020). *The call: Inside the global Saudi religious project*. New York, NY: Columbia Global Reports.

Wagemakers, J. (2012). The enduring legacy of the second Saudi state: Quietist and radical Wahhabi contestations of al-walā wa al-barā. *International Journal of Middle Eastern Studies*, 44(1), 93–110. doi: 10.1017/S0020743811001267

Wagemakers, J. (2016). Revisiting Wiktorowicz: Categorising and defining the branches of Salafism. In F. Cavatorta & F. Merone (Eds.), *Salafism after the Arab awakening: Contending with people's power* (pp. 7–24). London: Hurst & Co.

Ward, T. (2017). *The Wahhabi code: How the Saudis spread extremism globally*. New York, NY: Arcade Publishing.

Weismann, I. (2001). *Taste of modernity: Sufism and Salafiyya in late Ottoman Damascus*. Leiden: Brill.

Weismann, I. (2009). Genealogies of fundamentalism: Salafi discourse in nineteenth-century Baghdad. *British Journal of Middle Eastern Studies*, 36(2), 267–80. doi: 10.1080/13530190903007301

Weismann, I. (2017). A perverted balance: Modern Salafism between reform and jihād. *Die Welt des Islams*, 57(1), 33–66. doi: 10.1163/15700607-00571p04

Wiktorowicz, Q. (2005). A genealogy of radical Islam. *Studies in Conflict & Terrorism*, 28(1), pp. 207–40. doi: 10.1080/10576100590905057

Wiktorowicz, Q. (2006). Anatomy of the Salafi movement. *Studies in Conflict & Terrorism*, 29(2), pp. 75–97. doi: 10.1080/10576100500497004

Winter, T. (2009). The poverty of fanaticism. In J.E.B. Lumbard (Ed.), *Islam, fundamentalism, and the betrayal of tradition: Essays by Western Muslim scholars* (2nd ed., pp. 301–13). Bloomington, IN: World Wisdom Books.

Zarabozo, J.A.-D.M. (2010). *The life, teachings and influence of Muhammad Ibn Abdul-Wahhab*. Riyadh: International Islamic Publishing House.

7

THE NEW LANDSCAPE OF EXTREMISM AND ITS INTERSECTION WITH POLITICAL ISLAMISTS IN TURKEY

Suleyman Ozeren, Mehmet F. Bastug and Suat Cubukcu

Introduction

On several accounts, Turkey stands as a unique country in terms of political Islamism and extremism. Its "distinctiveness" (Rabasa & Larrabee, 2008, p. 25) stems from a unique combination of historical, social, and ethnic factors and its geopolitical position. Besides being a bridge between religions and cultures, Turkey has been a landscape for ideological quests and a transition route for people destined to conflict zones in two bordering countries—Syria and Iraq—and throughout the Greater Middle East, including Afghanistan and Chechnya. Such a geographical position has made Turkey even more susceptible to the grassroots activities of non-violent and violent extremist groups that have historical roots in Turkey. Islamist groups that remained passive for many years have started to resurface and pursue more assertive agendas. The recent conflicts in Iraq and, particularly in Syria, have turned Turkey into a transit route, a support base, and a destination country for foreign terrorist fighters and one of the largest recruitment sources for Islamic State in Iraq and Syria (ISIS) and al-Qaeda-affiliated groups (Ozeren, Cubukcu, & Bastug, 2021). In addition to regional and geopolitical factors, Turkey's ruling party, the AKP (Adalet ve Kalkınma Partisi – Justice and Development Party), has acted as a catalyst for violent and non-violent extremism with its Islamist ideology and expansionist pan-Islamist policies.

Because of the fluid nature of the boundaries between non-violent and violent groups, it is not an easy task to differentiate these groups from each other. While there is no consensus on the definition of "extremism," the definition is even more confusing in terms of Islamist extremism. For the purposes of this chapter, extremism refers to "a rejection of 'balance,' and an application of a single ideological perspective to all elements of an individual's life with, importantly, a fervent disdain for alternative ideological perspectives" (Winter & Hasan, 2016, p. 669). Extremism does not necessarily refer to religion nor does it necessitate violence (Winter & Hasan, 2016). To identify Islamist groups, the authors adopted Yilmaz's (2009, p. 72) definition of Islamism for the purpose of this chapter: "the term generally refers to political Islam,

DOI: 10.4324/9781003032793-10

ideologisation of religion and instrumental use of Islam in politics, especially with an anti-West rhetoric." Hence, the term does not refer to Islam as a religion; rather, it refers to a "totalitarian political ideology driven by a strong anti-Western and anti-democratic sentiment" (Borum, 2011, p. 10).

There is a continuous transition and fluidity within and between violent and non-violent extremist groups in Turkey. Non-violent extremism can potentially be transformed into violent extremism, as both types of extremism are rooted in an extreme interpretation of a worldview that can envision a similar endgame or utopia. Over time, for example, some non-violent groups have become violent while some violent groups have abstained from violence. The latter groups usually continue to glorify violence but do not use violence for pragmatic or tactical considerations. Their non-violent stance is only a temporary strategy that can change when circumstances change. This chapter focuses on transformation within and transition between non-violent and violent extremist groups in Turkey by providing a historical and sociological review of these groups and their ideological construction.

In addition to *Islamist* groups, there are many *Islamic* groups in Turkey that value spirituality, piety, and being a good Muslim and a good community member rather than political goals (Esposito, 2002). Most Muslims and members of Islamic groups are against extremism and appalled by the use of violence in the name of Islam (Esposito, 2002). Islam, as a religion, holds individuals and societies responsible for their beliefs and actions and inspires the establishment of state rules based on a social agreement and common ground (Yilmaz, 2005). Islam and universal values—such as justice, freedom, rule of law, human rights, and democracy—are not to be viewed as opposites. The major Islamic religious groups in Turkey—Nurcular, Nakşibendiler, and the Gülen movement—and other moderate Sufi orders embrace peaceful coexistence, tolerance, and dialogue. Thus, these groups cannot be considered as Islamist extremist groups and will not be the focus of this chapter.

The aim of this chapter is to focus on Islamist extremist groups that have "over-politicized" (Winter & Hasan, 2016) Islam and rejected liberal-democratic values and principles (such as diversity, pluralism, and universal human rights) and exhibit fanaticism and intolerance towards others (Schmid, 2014). The chapter analyses non-violent and violent-extremist case studies, provides detailed background information on some of these groups, and discusses the symbiotic relationships between Islamist extremist groups and the AKP.

Context: The Rise of Extremism in Turkey

The Republic of Turkey was established in 1923 as a staunchly secularist nation state and successor to the Ottoman Empire, an Islamic empire and caliphate that had survived more than six centuries. Turkey, however, is not a continuation of the Ottoman Empire. The founders of Turkey abandoned the empire's Islamic and dynastic state structure and formed a secular, pro-Western republic led by Mustafa Kemal Atatürk. Atatürk acted quickly and imposed several radical reforms. For example, he abolished the caliphate, outlawed religious schools and *shari'a* courts, replaced the Arabic alphabet with a Latin-derived alphabet, and, with the intent of establishing state control over religion, created the Directorate of Religious Affairs (Başkan, 2010).

Turkey was ruled by a single-party regime until 1946 when it adopted a multiparty system with democratic elections; however, it never emerged as a full democracy. Turkey's difficult journey to democracy was interrupted several times in the 1960s, 1970s, and 1980s by military *coups*. The Turkish military assumed the role of protector of the constitution and the secular state structure. Although it was not intended by the founding fathers, Turkey evolved into a military tutelary regime after the 1950s. The regime marginalized, humiliated, and repressed religious people throughout Turkey. Aggrieved and alienated groups emerged. They resented the system and felt oppressed by it. Some of these groups formed political Islamist movements and political parties to compete with the secular system. The government's response of increased aggression towards these groups created an atmosphere conducive to the emergence of Islamist extremist groups.

As Rabasa and Larrabee (2008, p. 10) have argued, "ethnicity, regionalism, and religious politics interact in several ways in contemporary Turkey." Reactionary Islamist extremism was not the only by-product of the oppressive and nationalist state system. Exclusivist and discriminatory state policies also targeted ethnic groups such as Kurds and Armenians and sectarian groups such as Alevis. The outcome was the rise of ethno-nationalist extremist groups. Two types of extremist groups were formed within Turkey's Kurdish population: separatist groups that adhered to a Marxist ideology and reactionary Islamist groups. The former group prompted nationalist reactions that gave rise to ultranationalist extremist groups. Reactionary Islamist groups in Turkey are both violent and non-violent. The most notable non-violent group with a political Islamist ideology was the Milli Görüş (National Outlook) movement, which was represented by successive political parties, such as the Refah Partisi (Welfare Party) and the Saadet Partisi (Felicity Party).

Violent extremist groups in Turkey either adhere to a Salafist ideology[1] or are influenced by the Iranian revolution, as in the example of Hizbullah in Turkey. Salafist groups usually are affiliated with al-Qaeda or ISIS. They became more active in the last decade during AKP rule.

Revival of Islamist Extremism in Turkey

Turkey has been ruled for almost two decades by the AKP, a populist Islamist party that has become more authoritarian and fundamentalist in recent years. For the first eight years of AKP rule, a combination of democracy, modernism, and an Islamic lifestyle flourished. The situation changed abruptly when the AKP won almost 50% of the votes cast in the June 2011 national election and its third consecutive victory, making the AKP one of the most powerful political parties in the history of Turkey. Confident of its grip on power, the government started down the road to an Islamist authoritarian system with policies that embraced a political Islamist ideology (San & Akca, 2020).

This about-face is perhaps not surprising, given that the AKP was an outgrowth of the National Outlook movement, which pursued "the goal of establishing an Islamic society and government in Turkey" (Ozeren, Cubukcu, & Bastug, 2020, p. 7). President Recep Tayyip Erdogan, as he had done in previous elections, claimed in 2011 that the AKP embraces democratic values and that it had abandoned the worldview of the National Outlook movement. The country's secular establishment, however, doubted the sincerity of those claims—and rightly so. The AKP now was one of the most powerful political parties in the history of Turkey with the ability to implement an authoritarian regime.

After rounds of subsequent election victories, Islamist extremists were emboldened to become more active and visible. The country became a transit route for foreign fighters travelling to Iraq and Syria. Thousands of foreign fighters have used Turkey as a transit country on their way to join groups such as ISIS. The AKP government has turned a blind eye to the flow and acted as an enabler for al-Qaeda affiliates and ISIS in Syria since the beginning of the Syrian civil war. To carry out its neo-Ottoman policies, Turkey developed proxies in the region and engaged in mutual relationships with insurgent and extremist groups in Syria (Ozeren, Cubukcu, & Bastug, 2021).

Turkey also became a hub for extremist recruitment and a logistics base for extremist groups (Ozeren, Cubukcu, & Bastug, 2021). The increased visibility and activity of ISIS affiliated groups in the country, the return of foreign fighters, and the AKP's enabling of Islamist extremism have led to elevated levels of extremist activity in the country. The number of violent and non-violent extremist groups that are active in Turkey also continues to grow. These groups have helped the AKP to disseminate its political Islamist ideology within Turkish society, and they have established a give-and-take relationship with the AKP.

Several Islamist groups have enjoyed either direct or indirect support from the AKP government on the domestic and international fronts. These groups, however, come from diverse backgrounds in terms of how they pursue their cause. For example, some groups prefer a political Islamist revolution along the lines of the Iran revolution, while other groups prefer a violent jihadist interpretation of Islam and an ideology that overlaps with al-Qaeda's. Due to similarities in ideology and mind-set, transitivity may exist between and within these groups. These groups, however, differ primarily in terms of their methods. The groups are pragmatic, and each group's approach to the use of violence may differ.

Transition Within Violent and Non-violent Groups

Violent extremist groups that exploit Islam in Turkey could be categorized under two main groups: those that are affiliated with the Salafist-Wahhabi (also referred to as "Salafist-Jihadist") ideology and those that are affiliated with or inspired by the Islamic revolution in Iran. Turkey has witnessed several terrorist attacks by violent extremist groups representing both the Salafist-Wahhabi ideology and the pro-Iranian revolutionary ideology. The groups that are affiliated with or inspired by the Iran's Islamic revolution have a dual leadership structure consisting of a spiritual leader and a political leader. An example is Hizbullah in Lebanon, a group that was established in 1982 with the support of Iran and has been sponsored by Iran since then. In Turkey, such groups include Hizbullah-Ilim (Kurdish Hizbullah), İslami Hareket (Islamic Movement Organization), Vasat, Tevhid Selam/Kudüs Ordusu (Tawhid Salam/Quds Force), and Malatyalılar Grubu Şafak-Değişim (Malatyalılar Group-Dawn/Change). Some of these groups have been affiliated with or inspired by the Islamic revolution in Iran. On the other hand, groups such as Ceyşullah (Army of God), al-Qaeda, and ISIS follow the Salafist-Jihadist violent extremist ideology.

Other extremist groups exist that have embraced either the Salafist-jihadist ideology or the pro-Iranian Islamic revolution ideology but have not engaged in violence. These non-violent extremist groups include Rahmet (Grace), Vahdet (Unity), Yeryüzü (Earth), Yöneliş (Flow), Akabe (al Aqaba), Sahabe (Companions of Prophet Mohammed), Ekin (Crop), Burç (Tower), Tohum (Seed), Yıldız (Star), Fecr (Dawn), Tevhid-i Çekirdek (Tawhid Core), and Mücahede (Struggle) (Taşdemir, 2016). "Islamic brotherhood" and *ummah* (global community of Muslims) are the common themes shared by the non-violent and violent extremist groups. During times of crisis or conflict, individuals who are members of non-violent extremist groups are vulnerable to recruitment by violent extremist groups for indirect assistance. These individuals, for example, may agree to help by providing funds, logistical support, and safe houses while at the same time declining direct involvement in the struggle through violent means. In other words, non-violent extremists could support the violent struggle even though they are not a part of it.

Turkey is a unique case in that it has more examples for the transitioning of groups from violent extremism to non-violent extremism and relatively fewer examples for the more common path of transitioning from non-violent extremism to violent extremism. Non-violent extremist groups in Turkey either have not been involved in violence so far or they have been involved in violence in the past but, as a tactical choice, do not engage in violence now. Three groups—the Islamist Kurdish Free Cause Party (Hüda-Par), which is the successor to Hizbullah; the Islamic Great Eastern Raiders Front (İBDA-C); and the Malatyalılar Group—were chosen by the authors of this chapter to shed light on the following: transition of extremist groups from violent to non-violent; transition of a predecessor group to a successor group; and transitivity between groups with like-minded ideologies and political goals. The authors also examined a fourth group, the Humanitarian Relief Foundation (İHH), because of its unique role in providing violent groups with logistical support in the form of propaganda, funding, and recruitment even though the group does not engage in violence. Finally, we included Hizb ut-Tahrir in our analysis. This group has not engaged in violence so far in Turkey, but has an extremist ideology and agenda. The next sections provide details about each group's ideology and current modus operandi along with an analysis of their activities.

Ideology and Organizational Structures

Hizbullah and Hüda-Par

Hizbullah, also known as Kurdish Hizbullah, was composed of Kurdish members who lived predominantly in the southeastern part of Turkey. As with similar like-minded violent extremist groups, Hizbullah aimed to overthrow the secular government in Turkey and establish *shari'a* law (Ozeren & Van de Voorde, 2006). According to classified police records from the Turkish National Police, "Hezbullah sermons indicate that the group utilized teachings of anti-Western figures such as Ayatollah Ruhollah Khomeini, Sayyid Qutb, Ali Shariati, and Abul Ala Maududi" (Uslu, 2007).

The Vahdet Bookstore is the site where Hizbullah was formed in late 1979 by like-minded individuals. Hizbullah later divided into two groups—Hizbullah Ilimciler (Scientists) and Hizbullah Menzilciler (Rangers)—when disputes arose over tactics and leadership. Hizbullah Ilimciler, led by Hüseyin Velioğlu, supported a strategy of armed struggle, while Hizbullah Menzilciler, led by Fidan Güngör, opposed that strategy. Güngör eventually was assassinated by the members of Hizbullah Ilimciler, and Velioğlu became the sole leader and dominated both groups (Ozeren & Van de Voorde, 2006). On January 17, 2000, Velioğlu was killed, and his deputies, Edip Gümüş and Cemal Tutar, were arrested during a police operation in Istanbul (Sarigil & Fazlioglu, 2013) while he and some other militants were hiding in a house. During that crackdown and follow-up operations, the police seized Hizbullah's archive. The seized materials—including video recordings the group made while torturing and killing its rivals, all of whom they considered to be enemies and *kafirs* (or non believers)—revealed the gruesome tactics and brutality of Hizbullah. The bodies had been buried under houses that belonged to Hizbullah members. The violence and gruesome pictures shocked the entire nation in Turkey. By the fall of 2000, nearly 1,000 alleged members of the group were taken into custody (Ozeren, Sözer, & Demirci, 2010). About 20,000 pages of documents subsequently were recovered from computer archives (Ozeren & Van de Voorde, 2006; Demir, Basibuyuk, & Karakus, 2011). As a result of these operations, Hizbullah's activities came to a halt—until 2006, when some of the group's members established Mustazaf-Der.

Hizbullah's new leader, Isa Altsoy (also known as I. Bagasi), wrote a book in 2004 titled *Hizbullah in Its Own Words: Selections from the History of the Struggle*, which was published and distributed underground (Uslu, 2007). The aim of the book was to clarify the group's objectives and current strategies. As stated in the book, "Hizbollah seeks to establish an Islamic system on earth that will demolish tyranny, injustice, segregation and exploitationvidyHizbollah is an Islamic movement, centered in Kurdistan, dedicated to defend[ing] the Muslim Kurds . . . ." (Bagasi as cited in Uslu, 2007, pp. 131–132). After Hizbullah members were released from prison, they established Mustazaf-Der (the Association of Solidarity with the Oppressed) in Diyarbakir, Turkey (Gürbüz, 2016). Hizbullah members, meanwhile, established non-governmental organizations (NGOs), associations, and media companies and opened bookstores. Mustazaf-Der, however, was shut down by the Turkish government because of the group's affiliation with Hizbullah. In response to that action, some of the members of Mustazaf-Der established Hüda-Par (the Free Cause Party) in late 2012, claiming that they were not violent and had cut their ties with the violent past of the Hizbullah movement (Esen, 2012).

The Islamic Great Eastern Raiders Front (IBDA-C)

The IBDA-C, a Salafist jihadist group, is a terrorist organization that has been fighting for Islamic rule in Turkey. The group had emerged in 1970s and advocates the revival of pure Islam. According to the group, its "primary goal is the establishment of the Federative Islamic State" (Fighel, 2003, p. 1). The group has targeted civilians, charities, minority-affiliated targets, churches, and other groups and institutions. The group's leader, Salih İzzet Erdiş Mirzabeyoğlu, was released from prison on July 22, 2014, and immediately afterward, Erdogan called Mirzabeyoğlu and met with him later that year ("Cumhurbaşkanı Erdoğan," 2014). According to documents obtained by the Stockholm Center for Freedom, AKP officials had vouched for Mirzabeyoğlu's good character to secure the IBDA-C leader's release from prison ("Erdoğan confidant Metin Külünk," 2019).

The group does not have a strict hierarchical structure. Members who are united with the shared ideology organize independently in small groups and conduct activities without taking commands from a central authority. The organization spread its ideology and indoctrinate people through its propaganda magazines and websites (Fighel, 2003).

The Malatyalılar Group

In Turkey, radical groups sometimes are named after the group's leader, the location where the group emerged, a bookstore around which the members gathered, or the ideology of an affiliated group. The Malatyalılar Group, for example, was named after Malatya province in the eastern part of Turkey because the core leadership of the group lived in Malatya. The group officially established itself in 1989 around the Şafak (Dawn) Bookstore. Violent and non-violent extremist groups often organized around bookstores to provide a cover for their activities, including gatherings, communication, recruitment, propaganda, and fundraising. In 1992, the Malatyalılar Group reorganized as Türkiye İslam Hareketi – TİH (Turkey Islamic Movement) under the spiritual leadership of Zekeriya Şengöz (Bozkurt, 2019). Under Şengöz's leadership, TİH was involved in stockpiling weapons and explosives for a battle the group expected to wage in the future. The leader of the group's military wing was Fahri Memur. The two men met in the early 1980s and have been active in efforts to establish Sharia law and an Iranian-like regime in Turkey since then. Şengöz was imprisoned in 2007 and released in 2014. Immediately afterward, Şengöz received a phone call from Erdogan congratulating him for his release (Bozkurt, 2019).

Humanitarian Relief Foundation (İnsani Yardım Vakfı – İHH)

İnsan Hak ve Hürriyetleri ve İnsani Yardım Vakfı (Foundation for Human Rights and Freedoms and Humanitarian Relief İHH) is a Turkish NGO which was founded in 1992 with a goal to provide humanitarian relief to the victims of the Bosnian war. The organization has a Muslim brotherhood approach and extended its reach out later to other Muslims in different parts of the world as well (Tusiray & Werz, 2010). The group hit the headlines and came under scrutiny when Israeli commandos attacked a flotilla organized by the group that was headed for Gaza. Israel accused the organization of bringing supplies to support Hamas (Tusiray & Werz, 2010). The organization is considered by some to be a non-violent extremist organization (Taşdemir, 2016) with radical Islamist ideology. Yayla (2019) sees the group as a nonprofit face of jihadism. Although IHH represents itself as a humanitarian organization, many countries view it as an organization with close ties to AKP and that has political motivations (Tusiray & Werz, 2010). There has been a mutual relationship between the group and AKP. IHH provided support to AKP and Erdogan in the elections (Bilefsky & Arsu, 2010). There are AKP members of Turkish parliament who serve at the organization's board. Some argue that AKP uses the group to extend its influence into the Middle East (Yayla, 2019).

Hizb ut-Tahrir

Another group that has become more active in Turkey during the AKP rule is Hizb ut-Tahrir. The group originated in Jerusalem in the 1950s to re-establish the Caliphate (Orofino, 2020). The group has an anti-Western attitude and openly rejects freedom, democracy, and any government system other than an Islamic Caliphate (Orofino, 2015). According to the group's official website:

> Hizb ut-Tahrir is a political party whose ideology is Islam, so politics is its work, and Islam is its ideology. It works within the Umma and together with her, so that she adopts Islam as her cause and is led to restore the Khilafah [Caliphate] and the ruling by what Allah revealed.
>
> *(as cited in Bulut, 2017, p. 2)*

The group was designated as a terrorist organization in Turkey in 2004. Some members of the group were indicted with charges of disseminating terrorist propaganda. Police found illegal weapons during the operations against the terrorist cells. Although the group did not carry out a terrorist attack, their activities furthered the radical and extremist views in the society and created a fertile ground for militant recruitment and violent fanaticism. In 2018, the Constitutional Court of Turkey, which is under the control of the Erdogan regime, released previously arrested Hizb ut-Tahrir members from prisons by ruling that they had been wrongly prosecuted. The group is protected from criminal prosecutions under the Erdogan rule (Bozkurt, 2018).

A police report revealed that the organization has a secret leadership committee and organized hierarchically. It operates neighbourhood organizations at the local level which report activities to the leadership committee. The group issues a propaganda magazine called Köklü Değişim—that can be translated as Radical Change—to disseminate its ideology among the Turkish society (Bozkurt, 2018).

Methods and Use of Violence in Turkish Islamist Extremist Groups
Hizbullah and Hüda-Par

Mustazaf-Der and Hüda-Par share a similar ideology that is identical to the one espoused by their predecessor organization, Hizbullah. Indeed, Hüda-Par affiliated websites and news agencies praise Velioğlu, the former leader of Hizbullah Ilimciler; depict Velioğlu's life and his struggle as an ideal; and promote the Hizbullah ideology along with the writings of Altsoy, the current Hizbullah leader ("Hüseyin Velioğlu'nun Hayatı," n.d.). The website HuseyniSevda.biz (which can be translated as "Love to Hüseyin"), for example, depicts Velioğlu as a martyr and displays his pictures. On the tenth anniversary of Velioğlu's death, Velioğlu's followers organized a religious gathering at a mosque in Diyarbakir where they showed a recording that belonged to the late Hizbullah leader (Ipek, 2010). Hüda-Par and other NGOs claim that they are not connected to Hizbullah and that they are non-violent groups; however, the problem is that although Hüda-Par and these other NGOs seem to be pursuing their goals by engaging in politics rather than violence, their ideological foundation and source of inspiration is Hüda-Par's violent past and its leaders who engaged in the greatest terrorist attacks in the history of Turkey. For some Hüda-Par followers and NGOs, "Hizbullah is alive" and has made "a comeback with Huda-Par" ("Huda-Par's emergence," 2013).

To the AKP, Hizbullah supporters and Hüda-Par are strategic partners in the AKP's effort to divide the Kurdish vote in favour of the AKP and against its rival, the pro-Kurdish Demokratik Toplum Partisi (HDP – Democratic Peoples' Party). This "partnership" is another example of the symbiotic relationship between the AKP and extremist groups.

The Islamic Great Eastern Raiders Front (IBDA-C)

IBDA-C is a loosely organized group which does not have a rigid hierarchy. Its publications play an important role in communicating the leadership's vision and objectives. The leadership announced the targets and type of action through the group's magazines and websites, and group members then acted independently to carry out the activities (Fighel, 2003). Such venues are also used to spread the group's ideology and to recruit and indoctrinate people.

The group members have been involved in many violent terrorist attacks in the past. Although the IBDA-C was a violent extremist group in the past, it now presents itself as a non-violent group. The IBDA-C is an interesting example of how political ideology can affect the designation the AKP government gives to a particular group. To the AKP and Erdogan, the IBDA-C is not a terrorist organization because its leadership considers Erdogan to be a hero for having secured the release of the group's leader. It is true that IBDA-C has not engaged in violence in recent years; however, the group continues to recruit jihadists for violent extremist groups such as al-Qaeda and ISIS ("Erdoğan confidant Metin Külünk," 2019). In addition, the United States has listed the IBDA-C as a terrorist organization (U.S. Department of State, 2004). The IBDA-C, therefore, should be considered a violent extremist group rather than a non-violent one. It is possible, however, that political ideology could prompt government leaders (such as those in the AKP) to alter the designation of such groups from violent to non-violent even though the groups continue to support violent extremist agendas and like-minded violent groups. In other words, what appears to be the transition of a violent group to a non-violent group could be misleading because regardless of how the government defines a particular group that has a history of violent terrorist attacks, the group's ideology—including support for political change through violence—may continue to guide its future actions.

The Malatyalılar Group

With a model similar to that of Hizbullah's, the Malatyalılar Group created front organizations to collect donations, established NGOs, and published magazines, journals, books, and other materials. The Malatyalılar Group also is known as the Değişim (Change) Group, after the name of a magazine the group published. The Malatyalılar Group also engaged in youth activities under the signature name of Müslüman Gençlik which can be translated as Muslim Youth (Bozkurt, 2019). Before AKP came to power, the group was subject to many police investigations and raids. Hundreds of group members were arrested with the accusation of attempting to overthrow the constitutional regime and establishing a sharia state ("Malatyalılar Grubu'na operasyon", 2000).

The group adopted a three-phase plan to achieve their objectives: spreading its ideology and indoctrinating vulnerable people, building a large community with supporters, and engaging in jihadist activity. The group is prone to armed jihadist activity as many weapons were seized in their secret hideout (Bozkurt, 2019). However, the group has suspended its violent activity and currently pursues a non-violent extremist ideology because it has no disagreement with the current government in Turkey.

Humanitarian Relief Foundation (İnsani Yardım Vakfı – İHH)

In May 2010, the İHH organized a flotilla headed for Gaza. That decision led to the infamous Mavi Marmara flotilla incident in which several people were killed by Israeli armed forces in their attempt to stop the convoy. According to Tusiray and Werz (2010), the İHH "owned two of the six ships involved, including the Mavi Marmara, which was the scene of the violent confrontation between Israeli commandos and flotilla members." Several of the organization's board members, it should be noted, also are members of the ruling AKP. The İHH has been a cause for concern in the United States because of its relationship with Hamas. Germany, however, banned the İHH's activities in 2010 because of the organization's direct link to Hamas (Tusiray & Werz, 2010). A Center for American Progress report from 2010 (Tusiray & Werz, 2010) cites a German Interior Ministry press release that details Germany's concerns:

> Under the guise of humanitarian aid, İHH has long been providing considerable financial support to the so-called social clubs in the Gaza Strip, which are under the control of Hamas ... donations to the social clubs of Hamas, which the İHH has made in the millions, in reality supports the terrorist organization of Hamas as a whole.

The İHH also supports extremists affiliated with al-Qaeda, al-Nusra, and ISIS (Schanzer, 2014). Turkish anti-terror officers therefore launched a crackdown on the groups in 2014 for alleged weaponry support for jihadists in Syria (Schanzer, 2014). The AKP government later arrested the police officers who launched the operation against the İHH and exonerated the İHH members.

Hizb ut-Tahrir

Hizb ut-Tahrir is "quite active in Turkey" (Bulut, 2017, p. 1) today and has been since the 1960s (Hamsici, 2021). The group spends much of its time organizing conferences, meetings, and similar events as it attempts to build a global enterprise. In 1997, it named "Turkey as one of its provinces" (Bozkurt, 2018, para. 5). Restoration of the Caliphate is the group's main narrative and promotes it at every event they organize. At the same time, Hizb ut-Tahrir contends that the presidential system in Turkey is equivalent to the Caliphate system the group wants to implement. For example, when Hizb ut-Tahrir held an event titled "The Democratic Presidency Model or the Rashidun Caliphate?" at the AKP-governed Uskudar Municipality building in Istanbul, members of the group used the upcoming presidential referendum to call for reinstatement of the Caliphate. The group claims that it denounces the use of violence and seeks a non-violent revolution through the dissemination of its ideology among the public (Hamsici, 2021). However, cases have been documented where individuals who were influenced by the group's ideology had engaged in violent acts (Orofino, 2020).

The organization is active at the grassroot level through its neighbourhood clubs. Such small groups aim at creating solidarity among the group members, and recruit new members at the local level. The organization indoctrinates vulnerable people with its ideology which centres around the re-establishment of the caliphate. They organize events, demonstrations, and protests to further advance their goals (Bozkurt, 2018). There is a strong hierarchical relationship between the local organizations and the central leadership. The group is active in many countries including Western countries and calls for establishment of the caliphate at the global level. The group recruits people in many different countries, organizes large gatherings, and is considered as one of the most prominent groups in Islamist activism (Hamsici, 2021).

The Rise of a New Generation Ultra-Nationalist Islamist Groups

The AKP government has contributed to non-violent extremism in Turkey with its blend of authoritarianism and Islamist ideology. The AKP has pursued a top-down transformation from a democratic country to a security regime that uses coercion against political dissidents and suppression against political opponents. Through its embrace of authoritarian methods, the AKP has distanced itself from democratic values, outraged the Western world, sewn anti-American and anti-Western sentiment among the Turkish population, and hopped onto the nationalist and right-wing bandwagon to maintain its grip on power (Taş, 2020). Through a transactional coalition with the Nationalist Movement Party (MHP – Milliyetçi Hareket Partisi), the AKP has shifted its diplomatic language to one that is more militaristic. .

Paramilitary activities have surged dramatically during the Erdogan presidency. Erdogan's paramilitary forces are structured in three layers (Cubukcu, 2018). The first layer is composed of pseudo-military groups that function formally as security contractors (e.g. SADAT A.S. International Defense Consulting). The second layer includes gangs and mafia groups (e.g. convicted mafia leaders, such as Alaaddin Çakıcı and Sedat Peker and the Ottoman Germania, a Turkish nationalist boxing gang in Germany; Winter, 2016). The third layer includes youth clubs and hearths (e.g. the Ottoman Hearths, a pro-Erdogan youth organization, and the People's Special Operations Squad, an association founded by a former special-forces soldier) from which Erdogan's AKP recruits adolescents and young adults with the intention of ensuring their loyalty to Erdogan and his regime (Dogan, 2018).

To maintain his regime and consolidate his power, Erdogan has supported the emergence and growth of these paramilitary groups and has encouraged them to sow fear among the Turkish people and oppress political dissidents. Because non-violent groups are the focus of this chapter, the authors focus only on the AKP's mobilized youth clubs and hearths (i.e. the third layer). Pseudo-military groups (i.e. the first level) and gangs and mafia groups (i.e. the second level) are omitted because these groups actively use violence as a tactic.

Youth Clubs and Hearths

Youth clubs and hearths historically had been more common among right-wing and Islamist political parties than they were among the parties on the other end of the political spectrum. To encourage grassroots activities and recruit supporters at a young age, the AKP formed youth organizations based on the Islamist National Youth Foundation (Mili Gençlik Vakfı) and Turkey's Welfare Party, both of which were founded by Necmettin Erbakan, Turkey's first Islamist prime minister. Erdogan adopted the structure of right-wing youth clubs (e.g. Ülkücü Ocakları) with a tradition and design that could align easily with the AKP and its Islamist ideology. These clubs have become recruitment sites to turn youths into loyal supporters of Erdogan and his party, the AKP.

The Ottoman Hearths (Osmanli Ocaklari), founded in 2009, adopted the youth-club structure of the ultranationalist Grey Wolves (i.e. Ülkücü Ocakları) and then combined that structure with the organizational structure of the Welfare Party and the National Youth Foundation. The founder and chairman of the Ottoman Hearths, Kadir Canpolat, was involved in the National Outlook movement ("Osmanlı Ocakları Kurucu," 2014). The reach of the Ottoman Hearths spread rapidly to each province in Turkey and now has more than 2 million members across the country. The organization also has established itself in other countries, including the United States and Germany, that host large numbers of ethnic-Turkish people ("Osmanlı Ocakları ABD'de," 2015). While these organizations do not hold a publicly stated violent modus operandi, the groups have been under scrutiny for their activities, including violently targeting opposition party and media offices and journalists (Sharma, 2017).

Canpolat, for example, was convicted on charges of causing bodily injury, possessing and bearing a weapon without a license, and kidnapping. The actions for which Canpolat was convicted befit the organization's mission and declaration of responsibility to intervene in "social and domestic disturbances" and defend Erdogan and his regime against any kind of vigilante or insurgency. In an interview with the online news portal Middle East Eye, Ottoman Hearths Deputy Chairman Yilmaz Babaoglu said the following about the organization's actions:

> It was our way of showing our leader how much we appreciated his efforts to make our great country again under the aegis of a "New" Turkey. We love our nation's leader Erdogan and his AKP. We also believe the AKP's enemies are the nation's enemies.
>
> *(Sharma, 2017, p. 1)*

The organization's members appeared at AKP rallies and protests wearing white burial shrouds, which means that they are "ready to die" for their leaders. The Ottoman Hearths have made their presence known at anti-Erdogan protests and rallies, working diligently to crush political dissidents. The organization responded, for example, when Erdogan threatened to use the AKP base during the Gezi Park protests in 2013 and unleashed a million of his people against the demonstrators. Members of the Ottoman Hearths also serve as street vigilantes dedicated to thwarting any action they perceive as threatening Erdogan and the AKP. In the role of vigilante, the organization's members have targeted several Kurdish activists and members of the Gülen movement. For example, the head of the Ottoman Hearths' Istanbul branch, Furkan Gök, expressed on Twitter his appreciation for a suicide bomber who killed 30 civilians in Suruc on July 20, 2015, during a meeting of young Kurdish activists. Law enforcement and the AKP government, however, have ignored all these threats ("AKP'li Osmanlı," 2015). The Ottoman Hearths also successfully mobilized AKP supporters against protesters in Turkey's intensely polarized political environment. Members rallied for Erdogan and monitored protests that erupted during the 2014 presidential election and the 2017 constitutional referendum.

During the July 15, 2016, coup attempt, several media outlets and eyewitnesses reported that the Ottoman Hearths and other pro-AKP paramilitary groups (e.g. the People's Special Operations Squad and employees of the private Turkish security contractor SADAT) were present at the event and were responsible for killings and violence, including the brutal murder of cadets and conscripts who already had surrendered to the police. Two cadets, Murat Tekin and Ragıp Enes Katran from the Turkish Air Force Academy, and four military personnel surrendered on the Bosphorus bridge; however, they were stabbed to death, and their throats were brutally slit, as ISIS does to its victims. Despite the brutality and the loss of many lives, the AKP government did not initiate a criminal investigation of these lynching, killings, and beheadings.

Along with paramilitary groups, these extremist and loyalist groups will continue to exist and even thrive for as long as the AKP remains in power. The support of pro-government paramilitary groups appears to be a rational strategy for Erdogan and the AKP in the short run; however, these groups represent a significant threat to both the country and democracy as they undermine democratic institutions. Although these groups introduce themselves as non-violent groups, they can resort to violence when they believe it is necessary to do so.

Conclusion

At the crossroads of the Middle East, Asia, and Europe, Turkey has turned into a gateway and a hot spot for violent and non-violent extremism. The U.S. invasion of Afghanistan and Iraq, the Arab Spring, and the civil war in Syria all have given rise to violent extremist groups in the region. Such dynamics have dramatically affected the prevalence and nature of violent and non-violent extremism in Turkey. Another consequential dynamic—the ruling AKP's populist and pragmatist Islamist policies—has further mobilized extremist movements and facilitated transformation and transition between violent extremist groups and non-violent extremist groups. During almost two decades in power, the AKP has used public resentment against the strict secular establishment to galvanize its constituencies to rally around the Islamist cause. The symbiotic and transactional relationship between the AKP and Salafi-jihadist and pro-Iranian extremist groups has gained momentum and created an atmosphere conducive to the emergence and spread of extremist groups. It is this atmosphere that has encouraged such groups to expand and deepen their engagements within Turkish society and abroad. The give-and-take relationship between the AKP and these extremist groups has facilitated movement between and within these groups.

The authors' analysis of five extremist groups—Hüda-Par, the Malatyalılar Group, the IBDA-C, the İHH, and Hizb ut-Tahrir—has uncovered examples of the transition and movement within and between groups and highlighted the role of the populist Islamist AKP government in the transformation of violent extremist groups and non-violent extremist groups. As the successors of violent extremist groups (e.g. Hizbullah, which was involved in terrorist attacks in the past), Hüda-Par and other similar groups have become political allies and constituencies of the AKP, a development that raises a serious question about what these groups could transform into. It is important to underscore that these groups, although they are not violent now, adamantly adhere to the same ideology that violent extremist groups follow and could revert quickly to their legacy of violence when deemed necessary. On the other hand, loyalist youth clubs (e.g. the Ottoman Hearths) and violent paramilitary groups (e.g. SADAT, Esedullah Timleri [Asadullah Teams]) have emerged as part of a new generation, or 2.0 version, of extremist groups in Turkey. Although such groups are not the immediate focus of this chapter, they represent the unique characteristic of AKP-era violent extremism that could be used to sow fear among dissidents at the behest of the AKP for as long as the party deems necessary (Onat & Cubukcu, 2019). AKP support for extremist groups could be a pragmatic or a politically rational strategy aimed at using these groups as enforcers of the regime's efforts to oppress and target its opponents; however, these groups pose an existential threat to the well-being of the society at large.

Note

1 Salafism can be defined as "the idea that the most authentic and true Islam is found in the lived example of the early, righteous generations of Muslims, known as the *Salaf*, who were closest in both time and proximity to the Prophet Muhammad. Salafis—often described as "ultra-conservatives"—believe not just in the "spirit" but in the "letter" of the law, which is what sets them apart from their mainstream counterparts" (Hamid & Dar, 2016).

References

AKP'li Osmanlı Ocakları'nın Gençlik Kolları Başkanı, Suruç bombacısına rahmet diledi. (2015, July 23). *T24*. Retrieved from https://t24.com.tr/haber/akp-adayi-suruc-bombacisina-rahmet-diledi,303777

Başkan, B. (2010). What made Ataturk's reforms possible? *Islam and Christian-Muslim Relations, 21*(2), 143–156. https://doi.org/10.1080/09596411003619798

Bilefsky, D., & Arsu, S. (2010, July 15). Sponsor of Flotilla Tied to Elite of Turkey. The *New York Times*. Retrieved from www.nytimes.com/2010/07/16/world/middleeast/16turkey.html

Borum, R. (2011). Radicalization into violent extremism I: A review of social science theories. *Journal of Strategic Security, 4*(4), 7–36. https://doi.org/10.5038/1944-0472.4.4.1

Bozkurt, A. (2018). *Erdoğan shields Hizb ut-Tahrir from criminal prosecution in Turkey*. Turkish Minute. Retrieved from www.turkishminute.com/2018/11/07/opinion-erdogan-shields-hizb-ut-tahrir-from-criminal-prosecution-in-turkey/

Bozkurt, A. (2019). *Radical Malatyalılar group wields considerable influence in Turkey's governance*. Nordic Monitor. Retrieved from www.nordicmonitor.com/2019/01/radical-stealthy-group-the-malatyalilar-wields-influence-in-turkeys-governance/

Bulut, U. (2017). Hizb ut-Tahrir in Turkey Calls for Restoring the Caliphate. BESA Center Perspectives Paper No. 435. Retrieved from www.jstor.org/stable/pdf/resrep04400.pdf?refreqid=excelsior%3Ab8cfb2d5535f735b74e5fc4c14e1ff2e

Bulut, U. (n.d.). *Kurds and Israel: A real love story? The unknown truth*. Israel Nation News. Retrieved from www.israelnationalnews.com/Articles/Article.aspx/25322

Cubukcu, S. (2018. March 3). The Rise of Paramilitary Groups in Turkey. *Small Wars Journal*. Retrieved from https://smallwarsjournal.com/jrnl/art/rise-paramilitary-groups-turkey

Cumhurbaşkanı Erdoğan, Salih Mirzabeyoğlu ile görüştü [President Erdoğan meets with Salih Mirzabeyoğlu]. (2014, December 12). CNN Türk. Retrieved from www.cnnturk.com/haber/turkiye/cumhurbaskani-erdogan-salih-mirzabeyoglu-ile-gorustu

Demir, O. O., Basibuyuk, O., & Karakus, O. (2011). Social environment, individual characteristics, religion, and radicalization: The case of Turkish Hizbullah. In I. Bal, S. Ozeren, and M. A. Sozer. *Multi-faceted approach to radicalization in terrorist organizations* (pp. 42–60). Amsterdam, The Netherlands: IOS Press.

Dogan, Z. (2018, January 17). *Turkish civilians arm themselves ahead of crucial 2019 polls*. Al-Monitor. Retrieved from www.al-monitor.com/pulse/originals/2018/01/turkey-civilians-arm-themselves-ahead-crucial-2019-polls.html

Erdoğan confidant Metin Külünk investigated for al-Qaeda aligned IBDA-C terror group. (2019, October 20). Stockholm Center for Freedom. Retrieved from https://stockholmcf.org/erdogan-confidant-metin-kulunk-investigated-for-al-qaeda-aligned-ibda-c-terror-group/

Esen, E. (2012, December 17). *"Hizbullah'ın parti kurması ne anlama geliyor?"* BBC Türkçe. Retrieved from www.bbc.com/turkce/haberler/2012/12/121217_huda_party_turkey

Esposito, J. L. (2002). *What everyone needs to know about Islam*. New York, NY: Oxford University Press.

Fighel, J. (2003). *Great East Islamic Raiders Front (IBDA-C): A profile*. International Institute for Counter-Terrorism (ICT). Retrieved from www.ict.org.il/Article.aspx?ID=892#gsc.tab=0

Gürbüz, M. (2016). *Rival Kurdish movements in Turkey: Transforming ethnic conflict*. Amsterdam, The Netherlands: Amsterdam University Press.

Hamid, S. & Dar, R. (2016, July 15). Islamism, Salafism, and jihadism: A primer. Brookings. Retrieved from www.brookings.edu/blog/markaz/2016/07/15/islamism-salafism-and-jihadism-a-primer/

Hamsici, M. (2021, January 22). "Hizb-ut Tahrir: Bazı ülkelerde yasaklanan örgütün Türkiye'deki konumu ne?" *BBC Türkçe*. Retrieved from www.bbc.com/turkce/haberler-turkiye-55752612

Huda-Par's emergence. (2013, November 23). *The Economist*. Retrieved from www.economist.com/eur ope/2013/11/23/huda-pars-emergence

Hüseyin Velioğlu'nun Hayatı Ve Mücadelesi-14 [*Hüseyin Velioğlu's Life and Struggle-14*]. (n.d.). Retrieved from https://hurseda.net/Huseyin-Velioglunun-Hayati-Ve-Mucadelesi-14-21

Ipek, V. (2010, January 18). Eski Hizbullah liderinin görüntüleri internette [Images of the former Hezbollah leader on the Internet]. *Haberturk*. Retrieved from www.haberturk.com/gundem/haber/ 201433-eski-hizbullah-liderinin-goruntuleri-internette

Malatyalılar Grubu'na operasyon. (2000, October 2). *NTV*. Retrieved from http://arsiv.ntv.com.tr/news/ 34154.asp

Onat, I., & Cubukcu, S. (2019). Unresolved conflict, urban insurgency and devastating consequences in Turkey between 2015 and 2016. *Journal of Policing, Intelligence and Counter Terrorism, 14*(2), 164–182. https://doi.org/10.1080/18335330.2019.1617431

Orofino, E. (2015). Intellectual radicals challenging the state: The case of Hizb ut-Tahrir in the West. *Contemporary Social Science, 10*(4), 401–412. https://doi.org/10.1080/21582041.2016.1236212

Orofino, E. (2020). *Hizb ut-Tahrir and the Caliphate*. London: Routledge.

Osmanlı Ocakları ABD'de Ülke Başkanlığına Musaf Kızılkaya Atadı. [*Ottoman Hearths Appointed Musaf Kızılkaya as country president in the USA*]. (2015, February 14). Retrieved from http://osmanliocaklari. org.tr/osmanli-ocaklari-abdde-ulke-baskanligina-musaf-kizilkaya-atadi

Osmanlı Ocakları Kurucu Genel Başkanı "Kadir Canpolat" Kimdir? [*Who is the founding chairman of the Ottoman Hearths "Kadir Canpolat"?*]. (2014, November 9). Retrieved from http://osmanliocaklari.org.tr/osma nli-ocaklari-genel-baskani

Ozeren, S., Cubukcu, S., & Bastug, M. F. (2020). From political Islam to religious autocracy: Where will Erdogan's regime stop? *Current Trends in Islamist Ideology, 25*, 5–48. Retrieved from www.hudson.org/ research/15682-where-will-erdogan-s-revolution-stop

Ozeren, S., Cubukcu, S., & Bastug, M. F. (2021). Lessons learned from ISIS recruitment in Turkey: A paradigm shift in counterterrorism is needed. In J. A. Goldstone, E. Alimi, S. Ozeren, & S. Cubukcu (Eds.), *From territorial defeat to global ISIS: Lessons learned* (pp. 77–93). Amsterdam, The Netherlands: IOS Press.

Ozeren, S., Sözer, M. A., & Demirci, S. (2010). Militant identity in terrorist organizations: Hizbullah case in Turkey. In M. Sever, H. Cinoglu, & O. Başıbuyuk (Eds.), *Socio-psychology of terrorism* (pp. 145–174). Ankara, Turkey: Polis Akademisi Yayınları.

Ozeren, S., & Van de Voorde, C. (2006). Turkish Hizballah: A case study of radical terrorism, *International Journal of Comparative and Applied Criminal Justice, 30*(1), 75–93. https://doi.org/10.1080/01924 036.2006.9678747

Rabasa, A., & Larrabee, F. S. (2008). *The rise of political Islam in Turkey*. Rand Corporation. Retrieved from www.rand.org/content/dam/rand/pubs/monographs/2008/RAND_MG726.pdf

San, S., & Akca, D. (2020). How Turkey's democratic backsliding compromises the international dimension of democratization. *Digest of Middle East Studies*. Retrieved from https://doi.org/10.1111/ dome.12223

Sarigil, Z., & Fazlioglu, O. (2013). Religion and ethno-nationalism: Turkey's Kurdish issue. *Nations and Nationalism, 19*(3), 551–571. https://doi.org/10.1111/nana.12011

Schanzer, J. (2014, January 23). *Turkish flotilla charity tied to terrorism again*. Foundation for Defense for Democracies. Retrieved from www.fdd.org/analysis/2014/01/23/turkish-flotilla-charity-tied-to-terrorism-again/

Schmid, A. P. (2014). *Violent and non-violent extremism: Two sides of the same coin*. The Hague, Netherlands: ICCT. Retrieved from www.icct.nl/app/uploads/download/file/ICCT-Schmid-Viol ent-Non-Violent-Extremism-May-2014.pdf

Sharma, S. (2017). *Turkey's Ottoman Hearths: Menacing or benign*. Middle East Eye. Retrieved from www. middleeasteye.net/news/turkeys-ottoman-hearths-menacing-or-benign

Taş, H. (2020). *The new Turkey and its nascent security regime*. Retrieved from www.giga-hamburg.de/en/publications/22059246-new-turkey-nascent-security-regime/

Taşdemir, D. (2016). *The Salafi movement and religious radicalism in Turkey* (Unpublished master's thesis). Uludağ Üniversitesi, Bursa, Turkey). Retrieved from https://acikerisim.uludag.edu.tr/bitstream/11452/1918/1/459881.pdf

Tusiray, M., & Werz, M. (2010). *What is IHH?* Center for American Progress. Retrieved from www.americanprogress.org/issues/security/reports/2010/07/26/8129/what-is-the-ihh/

U.S. Department of State. (2004). *Appendix C: Background information on other terrorist groups*. Retrieved from https://2009-2017.state.gov/j/ct/rls/crt/2003/31759.htm

Uslu, E. (2007). From local Hizbollah to global terror: Militant Islam in Turkey. *Middle East Policy*, *14*(1), 124–141. https://doi.org/10.1111/j.1475-4967.2007.00290.x

Winter, C. (2016, November 10). *Massive German police operation targets Turkish nationalist boxing gang*. DW. Retrieved from www.dw.com/en/massive-german-police-operation-targets-turkish-nationalist-boxing-gang/a-36331416

Winter, C., & Hasan, U. (2016). The balanced nation: Islam and the challenges of extremism, fundamentalism, Islamism, and jihadism. *Philosophia*, *44*(3), 667–688. https://doi.org/10.1007/s11406-015-9634-2

Yayla, A. S. (2019). IHH: The Nonprofit Face of Jihadism. An In-Depth Review. *International Institute for Counter-Terrorism*. Retrieved from www.ict.org.il/Article/2397/IHH#gsc.tab=0

Yilmaz, I. (2005). State, law, civil society, and Islam in contemporary Turkey. *The Muslim World*, *95*(3), 385–411. https://doi.org/10.2139/ssrn.1777222

Yilmaz, I. (2009). Was Rumi the chief architect of Islamism? A deconstruction attempt of the current (mis)use of the term "Islamism." *European Journal of Economic and Political Studies*, *2*, 71–84. Retrieved from https://ssrn.com/abstract=1777206

8

THE MUSLIM BROTHERHOOD IN THE WEST

Firewall or Conveyor Belt? Insights from the British Debate

Lorenzo Vidino

What is the Muslim Brotherhood in the West?

The first active presence of Brothers in the West can be dated back to the late 1950s and the early 1960s, when small, scattered groups of militants left various Middle Eastern countries to settle in cities throughout Europe and North America. They initially represented a diffuse contingent of militants whose move reflected not a centralized plan, but rather personal decisions that fortuitously brought some Brotherhood figures to spend years or the rest of their lives in the West. Yet the small organizations they formed soon developed beyond their most optimistic expectations. Following Hassan al Banna's complex organizational model, they established youth and women branches, schools, banks, charities, and think tanks. The ample funds they received from wealthy public and private donors in the Arab Gulf allowed the Brothers to operate well beyond what their small numbers would have otherwise provided for.

By the late 1970s, while still supporting in words and deeds their counterparts' efforts to establish Islamic states in the Muslim world, they increasingly focused their attention on their new reality in the West. Over the last 50 years, in fact, the Western Brothers have tried to find ways to contextualize the teachings of their ideological forefathers to their reality as a movement operating in non-Muslim societies.

Following this logic, they have formulated goals that are somewhat different from those of the Brotherhood branches that operate in the Muslim-majority countries of the Middle East and North Africa. Foremost is the preservation of an Islamic identity among Western Muslims. As any religious conservative movement, Islamists worldwide are concerned with maintaining the morality and piousness within their communities. Such defensive attitude becomes even more important when dealing with Muslim minorities, as they incur the risk of being culturally absorbed by the host society. On this topic, Yussuf Al-Qaradawi (2000), the undisputed spiritual leader of the global and Western Brotherhood, wrote, "It is the duty of the Islamic Movement not to leave these expatriates to be swept by the whirlpool of the materialistic trend that prevails in the West" (p. 7).

Yet unlike Salafists and other Islamic trends that seek to strengthen the Islamic identity of Western Muslims, the Brothers do not advocate isolation from mainstream society. To the

DOI: 10.4324/9781003032793-11

contrary, they urge Muslims to actively participate in it, but only insofar as such engagement is necessary to change it in an Islamic fashion. According to Al-Qaradawi (2000), Muslims in the West should adopt "a conservatism without isolation, and an openness without melting" (p. 7). Finding the balance between cultural impermeability and active socio-political interaction is not easy, but the Brothers see themselves as capable of defining how Muslims can be both loyal to their faith and active citizens of European secular democracies.

Another goal, though related to the first, for the Western Brothers is, as Qaradawi defines it, "play[ing] the role of the missing leadership of the Muslim nation with all its trends and groups " (Al-Qaradawi, 2000, p. 7). Becoming the preferred – if not the exclusive – partners of Western governments and elites serves various purposes. By leveraging such a relationship, the Brothers aim to be entrusted by Western governments with administering all aspects of Muslim life in each country. They would ideally become those whom governments task with preparing the curricula and selecting the teachers for Islamic education in public schools, appointing imams in public institutions, and receiving subsidies to administer various social services. This position would also allow them to be the *de facto* official Muslim voice in public debates and in the media, overshadowing competing forces. The powers and legitimacy bestowed by Western governments would allow them to exert significantly increased influence over the Muslim community. Making a clever political calculation, the Western Brothers attempt to turn their leadership bid into a self-fulfilling prophecy, seeking to be recognized as representatives of the Muslim community in order to actually become it (Vidino, 2010).

Assessments of the Western Brothers closely resemble those of the global Islamist movement, with opinions split between optimists and pessimists. More specifically, optimists argue that the Western Brothers are simply a socially conservative force that, unlike other movements with which they are often mistakenly grouped, encourages the integration of Western Muslim communities and offers a model in which Muslims can live their faith fully and maintain a strong Islamic identity while becoming actively engaged citizens (Leiken & Brooke, 2007). Governments argue the optimists should harness the Western Brothers' grassroots activities and cooperate with them on common issues, such as unemployment, crime, drugs, and radicalization (Esposito, 1999; Peter, 2006).

Pessimists see a much more sinister nature of the Western Brotherhood. Thanks to their resources and the naiveté of most Westerners, they argue, the Western Brothers are engaged in a slow but steady social engineering program, aimed at Islamizing Western Muslim populations and, ultimately, at competing with Western governments for their allegiance. The pessimists accuse the Brothers of being modern-day Trojan horses, engaged in a sort of stealth subversion designed to weaken Western society from within, patiently laying the foundations for its replacement with an Islamic order. The fact that the Western Brothers do not use violence but participate with enthusiasm in the democratic process is seen simply as a cold calculation on their part. Realizing they are still a relatively weak force, the Brothers have opted for a different tactic: befriending the establishment.[1]

No Western country has adopted a cohesive assessment followed by all branches of its government. There is no centrally issued white paper or set of internal guidelines sent to all government officials detailing how Western Brotherhood organizations should be identified, assessed, and eventually engaged. This leads to huge inconsistencies in policies, not only from one country to another but also within each country, where positions diverge from ministry to ministry, and even from office to office of the same body. This chapter examines the debate on the role of the Muslim Brotherhood in Western countries in recent years from a counter-terrorism perspective. On this topic, policymakers and commentators have been irremediably split on whether the Western Brothers play a role in the process of violent radicalization or whether they can be seen as partners. In substance, the core dilemma is to assess if the Brothers are part of the problem or part of the solution when dealing with terrorism of jihadist inspiration. The chapter will mostly focus on the British debate, as the United Kingdom is the country where these dynamics related to the role of non-violent Islamists were first debated and where most of the thinking on it has historically been done.

The Western Muslim Brotherhood and Radicalization

While it can be argued that other perspectives are equally if not more important, the debate on the Western Brotherhood is often framed in security terms, focusing on whether the group is a terrorist organization and poses a security threat. The Brotherhood has been designated as a terrorist organization in Egypt, the United Arab Emirates, and a handful of other Middle Eastern countries. But the United States, the European Union, and all individual European countries have not designated the Brotherhood as a terrorist organization. Hamas, the Palestinian branch of the Brotherhood, has long been designated by the European Union, and individuals who have raised funds for the group have been prosecuted (albeit with scant success) throughout the continent. Concerns about the terrorist nature of individual Brotherhood outfits (e.g. in Libya, where the Brotherhood has regularly cooperated with jihadist groups, or in Egypt, where a Brotherhood offshoot has been designated by the US government) exist not just in the Middle East and the United States but also in Europe.

But, overall, there is a general consensus throughout Europe that the Muslim Brotherhood as a whole is not a terrorist organization. There is widespread agreement that the Brotherhood has never planned attacks in Europe and does not pose a direct security threat to Europe. It is argued by many that, despite some overlaps in ideology with Salafist and jihadist milieus, it would be an analytical mistake to lump the Brotherhood's ideology together with these groups (Lynch, 2016).

This differentiation between the Brotherhood and, more broadly, participationists on the one hand, and jihadists on the other, has an impact on a debate that has shaped the contemporary domestic counter-terrorism policy debate in many European countries. Over the last 15–20 years, in fact, authorities have started thinking about comprehensive counterterrorism policies. While still devoting large and much needed resources to repression, authorities consider contrasting and preventing radicalization among Muslim communities necessary components of a security strategy aimed at providing results in the long term. Many European governments have therefore enacted various counter-radicalization programs, whose characteristics and complexity vary significantly from country to country. However, all of them consider the active participation of Muslim leaders and organizations a crucial element, necessary to provide legitimacy and appeal to their initiatives.

The policy question that naturally stems from this debate is whether Islamists can be seen as partners against violent radicalization. As they do not directly engage in violence (at least in the West), could they actually be used by Western governments against violent radicalization? Can they contrast the appeal of jihadists? In substance, are they part of the problem or the solution?

The Brotherhood as Firewall

Many scholars and policymakers, even among those who do not embrace the optimist point of view on them, believe that the Brothers could play a crucial role in undermining the legitimacy and appeal of violent Islamist groups among young Muslims both in the Muslim world and the West. Supporters of this position build their argument on the premise that political Islam is a reality whose widespread popularity should be acknowledged (Zakaria, 2009). Islamism is today a global ideology that, in its very diverse forms, attracts millions of Muslims. A sensitive analysis, argue supporters of engagement, should distinguish between Islamist groups that engage in violence and those that do not, harnessing the appeal of the latter against the former. While European policymakers might disagree with many of the non-violent Islamists' positions, they should acknowledge that they do not pose a threat to Europe. Rather, they should take advantage of non-violent Islamists' condemnation of groups like the Islamic State and al-Qaeda, establishing various forms of cooperation with them against what is a common enemy.

These scholars and analysts believe, in substance, that the movement can serve as a firewall against jihadist-style radicalization. Hypothetically envisioning radicalization as a continuum whose terminal point is defined by the embracement of a jihadist worldview and violent tactics, they identify the Brothers as a force that can stop the process halfway. The Brotherhood "works to dissuade Muslims from violence, instead channeling them into politics and charitable activities" (Leiken & Brooke, 2007, p. 112). The Brothers adopt positions that are, in certain cases, extremely antagonistic towards the West and could be labelled as "radical." But they do not advocate violence against the West and actively condemn those who do. Western policymakers should be pragmatic and try to exploit this common ground in order to defeat violent Islamists. The fact that jihadist groups frequently criticize and even accuse the Brothers of apostasy because of their abandonment of *jihad* and support of democracy is seen by supporters of engagement as additional proof of the common ground that the West can find with the movement.

The Brothers' role as firewall is, according to some scholars, particularly effective because of the legitimacy the movement enjoys at the grassroots level and among the most conservative fringes of the Muslim world (Leiken & Brooke, 2007). Only the Brothers, in fact, are in a position to intellectually engage angry young men on the path towards radicalization and sway them away from violence. "Muslim 'moderates' can't defeat bin Ladenism since they don't speak to the same audience with the same language and passions," argues former CIA official *Reuel* Marc *Gerecht* (American Enterprise Institute, 2004).

Moreover, European Brotherhood organizations have consistently issued public statements denouncing the actions of jihadist groups, urging Muslims to reject its violent tactics and calling for calm during the many domestic and international crises that have taken place over the last few years. In many cases, European policymakers have publicly praised these positions, considering them extremely important in de-escalating tensions. The fact that organizations that can reach large segments of European Muslim communities and possess high levels of legitimacy among some of their most conservative fringes take these positions is something that no European government can ignore. Irrespective of a positive or negative assessment of the overall nature and aims of the movement, its public position on the use of violence in the West does make it a useful ally of any government seeking to address pressing security needs.

The idea of forging some form of cooperation with partcipationists has long appealed to several European policymakers and counter-terrorism practitioners. The country where this debate historically started and, most importantly, where the approach was first implemented, is the United Kingdom. While never developing into a formalized policy, the formation of various forms of partnership with non-violent Islamists in order to stem violent radicalization was advocated by various branches of the British government during the years immediately following the September 11, 2001, attacks.

Following this approach that saw "soft Islamists" as the antidote to violent ones, shortly after 9/11 Scotland Yard created the Muslim Contact Unit (MCU), a small, specialized unity devoted to establishing relations with the Muslim community but in particular with its Islamist-leaning cross-sections (Lambert, 2011). The MCU sought to bridge the trust gap the police suffered within the most conservative cross-sections of the Muslim community by partnering with entities that, according to the unit, enjoyed a prominent standing and had first-hand experience in tackling radicalization at the local level.

Guided by this philosophy, the MCU formed the "London partnerships" (Lambert, 2011). In one, the MCU began working with Muslim Brotherhood-linked activists from the Muslim Welfare House and the Muslim Association of Britain to counter the appeal of notorious jihadist cleric Abu Hamza in the Finsbury Park neighborhood. The partnership became particularly intense when Abu Hamza's supporters were forcefully evicted from the local mosque they had long occupied and the Brotherhood activists started running it. Since that moment, the mosque no longer harbored jihadists but, rather, rejected those who harbored such views and engaged in various joint activities with local authorities.

The MCU's unorthodox philosophy came to be known among practitioners as Lambertism, from the name of its head, Bob Lambert. An experienced policeman, Lambert argued that the "ideal yes-saying" Muslim leaders lack credibility in their communities and have no knowledge of radicalism (Robert Lambert, personal communication, December 2008). He also believed that only Islamists have the street credibility to challenge the narrative of al-Qaeda and influence young Muslims and therefore advocated "police negotiation leading to partnership with Muslim groups conventionally deemed to be subversive to democracy" (Lambert, 2008a). "Salafis and Islamists," he stated, "often have the best antidotes to al-Qaida propaganda once it has taken hold" (Lambert, 2008b, p. 23).

During those years, British authorities frequently partnered with and funded a broad array of Islamist organizations. In some cases, as exemplified by the MCU, this approach was driven by a careful assessment of the Islamist nature of their partners and the deeply held belief that they constituted the best suited partners. In other cases, for example, in instances of funding by some local councils, partnerships were constructed without much knowledge of the partners' nature. The British debate on the matter of partnering with Islamists on counter-terrorism matters has evolved over time, as the following section will explain. But the idea of partnering with non-violent Islamists to counter the appeal of the violent ones has been debated also throughout continental Europe over the last 15 years – and with particular vigor during the height of the Islamic State-related mobilization.

In recent years the debate has taken place with particular vigor in Germany ("Man kann Salafisten nicht mit Islamisten bekämpfen," 2019). Some German officials have argued that Brotherhood organizations can serve a role if not in the immediate de-radicalization of jihadists at least in re-inserting them into society.[2] Berlin Interior Senator Andreas Geisel, for example, ignited a spirited debate when he advocated partnering with non-violent Islamists to re-integrate foreign fighters returning from Syria and Iraq:

"These are not friends of the liberal-democratic basic order," he said "I am aware of that. But it is people who clearly state that they are not ready for violence, that they reject violence, and that is why, according to the experts who presented this in the Committee on the Protection of the Constitution, it is a sensible step to use these structures to at least first transfer people who were previously ready for violence into the non-violent spectrum – as a phase in de-radicalization."

(Kopietz, 2019)

The Brotherhood as Conveyor Belt

The evolution of the British debate – as said, the most sophisticated in the whole continent – on the issue of partnering with Islamists to counter the appeal of jihadists is extremely illuminating for counter-terrorism officials throughout Europe. It is therefore noteworthy that, by the end of the 2000 decade, Lambertism became widely discredited throughout the British government. The British government's revision in attitudes towards non-violent Islamists dramatically accelerated in 2010, when the Conservatives rose to power. In a landmark speech delivered a few months after becoming prime minister, David Cameron (2011) clearly outlined his views on the subject:

> Governments must also be shrewder in dealing with those that, while not violent, are in some cases part of the problem. We need to think much harder about who it's in the public interest to work with. Some organisations that seek to present themselves as a gateway to the Muslim community are showered with public money despite doing little to combat extremism. As others have observed, this is like turning to a right-wing fascist party to fight a violent white supremacist movement. So we should properly judge these organisations: do they believe in universal human rights – including for women and people of other faiths? Do they believe in equality of all before the law? Do they believe in democracy and the right of people to elect their own government? Do they encourage integration or separation? These are the sorts of questions we need to ask.

The reasons that led British authorities to a change in policy are several and overlapping. Some have argued that they were mostly political, with the Tories wanting to break from a policy that had originally been conceived under a Labour government (Vidino, 2010). This thesis does not take into consideration the fact that, by the second half of the 2000s, the Labour government had already dramatically abandoned most positive views of non-violent Islamists, including any role they could play in countering radicalization. Two consecutive Labour secretaries of State for Communities and Local Government, Ruth Kelly (2006-07) and Hazel Blears (2007-09), had opted to de-platform and de-fund Islamist actors, fully convinced of their negative impact and unacceptable views. Blears, a prominent Labour leader from a blue-collar district, was particularly vocal about this change, writing in 2009:

> The left, in particular, must be vigilant. The liberal-left is historically concerned for the underdog, for oppressed peoples, for taking a stand against racism and imperialism. It is part of our political DNA. The problem today is that these valid concerns can be mutated into support for causes and organisations that are fiercely anti-liberal and populated by people whose hearts are filled with misogyny, homophobia and Jew-hatred. Liberals' pathological fear of being branded "racist" or "Islamophobic" can lead to ideological contortions: condoning or even forming alliances with groups that are socially conservative, homophobic, antisemitic and violent towards women.

The change in the perception of Islamists was therefore not a Tory-Labour dynamic. But there was indeed a political element that was unquestionably one of the reasons why British politicians decided to end their support for Islamists. In the second half of the decade, in fact, British media routinely uncovered instances in which Islamist actors who had received public funding or had been touted by politicians as moderate allies were caught espousing wild conspiracy theories and extremist views or, in some cases, having ties to violence. This created severe embarrassments for British politicians, whose wisdom in choosing partners was publicly scrutinized.

While political embarrassments were one factor, also extremely important in making British policymakers change course was another element: limited proof of effectiveness. Unquestionably the "London partnerships" had yielded some successes. But British authorities, analyzing the overall impact of years of partnerships and substantial funding of Islamist actors, concluded that the positive impact was negligible (Charles Farr, personal communication, June 2014). The matter is obviously very complex, as it is extremely difficult to empirically determine certain dynamics, such as assessing when an individual is de-radicalized, or who and what exactly de-radicalized him/her. Despite these difficulties, it became fairly common opinion among British counter-terrorism practitioners that Islamists were hardly capable of systematically delivering tangible results in radicalization prevention and de-radicalization. While they did obtain some successes, they fell in the realm of the anecdotal and occasional (British officials, personal communication, 2019–2020).

Moreover, an additional critique of Lambertism comes from an additional perspective. Even assuming, argue critics of the approach, that non-violent Islamists can indeed sway some young Muslims from committing acts of terrorism, such short-term gains in the security field are offset by the long-term implications of such a partnership. Critics maintain that, while opposing acts of terror in the West, non-violent Islamists have views and goals that are incompatible with those of the secular and multi-faith societies of modern Europe. Seeing them as part of the problem rather than the solution, critics argue that governments should not legitimize and empower them with any form of partnership. The long-term repercussions on social cohesion and integration of such engagement, they add, would be much greater than the yet-to-be-proven short-term gains that can be achieved in preventing acts of terrorism.

In the United Kingdom, some of the sharpest proponents of this critique were Shiraz Maher and Martyn Frampton, authors of an influential 2009 report fittingly titled *Choosing our friends wisely: Criteria for engagement with Muslim groups*. "Some of the government's chosen collaborators in 'addressing grievances' of angry young Muslims," wrote Maher and Frampton, "are themselves at the forefront of stoking those grievances against British foreign policy; western social values; and alleged state-sanctioned 'Islamophobia'"(2009, p. 5). The report argued that the British government, by partnering with Islamists, was "underwriting the very Islamist ideology which spawns an illiberal, intolerant and anti-western world view. Political and theological extremists, acting with the authority conferred by official recognition, are indoctrinating young people with an ideology of hostility to Western values " (Maher & Frampton, 2009, p. 5). The government, it was argued, would never think of endorsing and funding the extremist right wing British National Party to seek its help to stem neo-Nazi radicalization. The idea would be seen as ineffective and politically inopportune. Partnering with Islamists to defeat jihadists was seen by Maher, Frampton, and several other critics as an identically ill-conceived decision.

In substance, critics suggest that the Brothers seek to benefit from what in social movement theory is known as "positive radical flank effect" – the improvement in bargaining position enjoyed by more moderate wings of a political movement when a more radical fringe emerges (McAdam, 1992; Haines, 1997, p. 440–41). According to this view, political Islam, like any other totalitarian movement, has two wings: one, represented by groups like al-Qaeda and the Islamic State, more impatient and action-prone that seeks to use violence to achieve their goals; and another, constituted by many other non-violent Islamist groups, including the Brothers, which, while not completely ruling out the use of violence, aims at employing the appropriate strategy at the right time and place. Disagreements between the two wings do exist, often taking visceral undertones. But they should be considered as dissent among fellow travelers who, while sharing similar worldviews and aims, disagree on which tactics to employ.

According to critics, since 9/11 non-violent Islamists have attempted to benefit from this dynamic, presenting themselves as sworn enemies of the jihadists, loyal partners of the state in stemming violent extremism. But according to critics like Akkari and many others, the Brothers' real aim is to use the financial support and political legitimacy obtained by convincing Western governments that they are the moderate alternative simply to further their own agenda. The emergence of a severe and prolonged terrorist threat, argue critics, has led some Western governments to lower the threshold of what is acceptable and to endorse extremist organizations as long as they oppose violence in the West. "Al Qaeda was the best thing that happened to these groups," argues Ian Johnson (2006). "Nowadays, our bar is so low that if groups aren't al Qaeda, we're happy. If they're not overtly supporting terrorism, we think they're okay. We don't stop to think where the terrorism comes from, where the fish swim."

Critics warn that Islamists could unduly benefit from the support received from the state to counter jihadism and expand its reach well beyond where it would have been able on its own, spreading its views to the larger Muslim community. They argue that the largest problem is the social engineering program envisioned by the Brothers, which entails a rejection of many core Western values. Many senior security officials in various Western countries, in fact, embrace the view that identifying the problem only in violent groups is a self-deceiving act. Alain Grignard, deputy head of Belgian police's anti-terrorism unit and a professor of Islamic studies at Brussels Free University, calls al-Qaeda an "epiphenomenon," the most visible aspect of a much larger threat that is political Islam (Gringnard, as cited in S. Besson, 2005, p. 40). Alain Chouet, the former head of DGSE, the now dissolved French external intelligence agency, agrees with Grignard and believes that:

> Al-Qaeda is only a brief episode and an expedient instrument in the century-old existence of the Muslim Brotherhood. The true danger is in the expansion of the Brotherhood, an increase in its audience. The wolf knows how to disguise itself as a sheep.
>
> *(Chouet, as cited in C. Fourest, 2008, p. 103).*

German security services have repeatedly made these views public. Already in 2005 the *Bundesverfassungschutz* was stating that non-violent Islamist organizations:

> do not carry out recruitment activities for the purpose of the violent 'Holy War' (Jihad). They might rather claim to immunise young Muslims against Jihadist indoctrination by presenting to them an alternative offer of identification. However, one has to critically ask whether their activities that are strongly directed at preserving an 'Islamic identity' intensify disintegration and contribute to the development of Islamist parallel societies.
>
> *(Integration as a Means to Prevent Extremism and Terrorism, 2007, p. 5)*

Moreover, they argued, there "is the risk that such milieus could also form the breeding ground for further radicalization," laying the ideological groundwork for violent groups (Bundesverfassungsschutz, 2005, p. 190).

A 2018 report (Verfassungsschutzbericht of Nordrhein-Westfalen, 2018) addresses this dynamic even more at length:

"In recent years," argued the report, "local Muslim Brotherhood supporters have been able to use the public focus on jihadism and the spectacular rise and fall of the Islamic State to present themselves as a supposedly unproblematic alternative to violence-oriented Islamists and as a point of contact for government agencies and civil society actors." The security services warned about this dynamic, arguing that "[t]he Muslim Brotherhood could thus become the representative of Muslim interests in the state and society, and elevate their understanding of religion within the Muslim community in Germany and North Rhine-Westphalia," clearly stating that. "such a development would be unacceptable to society as a whole and our democracy."

"In the long run," concluded the report, "the threat posed by legalistic Islamism to the liberal democratic system is greater than that of jihadism, which will always outnumber numerically .... They aspire to an Islamist order, but are prepared to allow certain democratic elements within that framework. For this reason, their extremism is often barely recognizable at first glance."[3]

The "Mood Music" Argument

As said, the Brothers and similar Islamist movements are not engaged in violence in Europe. And indeed, in some cases they have played a useful role in countering the appeal of jihadist groups, irrespective of what their motives for doing so were. But if Islamists are occasional short-term firefighters, fighting the flames of radicalization in specific cases, it is also arguable that they are, at the same time, long-term arsonists. What this means is that vocal Islamists spread a narrative that, while not directly violent, can be conducive to violence. Two aspects that are central to the narratives of Islamist groups are particularly relevant here.

Victimhood

Islamist entities consistently spread a narrative that argues that Muslims and Islam itself are the subjects of a giant, global conspiracy to undermine and subjugate them. From geopolitical conflicts such as the Israeli-Palestinian conflict and the war in Iraq to domestic issues such as anti-*niqab* laws or incidents of anti-Muslim prejudice, Islamist organizations foster a siege mentality within local Muslim communities, arguing that Western governments and societies are hostile to them and to Islam in general. The belief that the perception of a prolonged Western attack against Islam is a key factor in the radicalization process is embraced by a large number of intelligence agencies and analysts (Canadian Security Intelligence Service, 2006, p. 1; General Intelligence and Security Service of the Netherlands [AIVD], 2002, p. 29; Neumann, 2008, p. 46)

Justification of Violence

Islamist organizations consistently argue in their literature and in speeches to their internal audiences that violence is legitimate in cases in which Muslims are under attack or occupation. They therefore consistently argue that acts of violence (including against civilians) perpetrated by various groups in places like Palestine, Kashmir, or Syria are not just acceptable in Islam, but also praiseworthy acts of religiously sanctioned heroism. The presence of texts extolling the virtues of military jihad in their book stores and websites is widespread.

It is easy to see how the combination of the two elements, constantly propagated in Brotherhood-leaning networks, can be dangerous if taken to one of its most logical conclusions.

If Muslims are justified, even lionized, for carrying out acts of violence in places where they are "attacked," why not also in the West, where the very same Brotherhood narrative also says Muslims are under attack? The Brotherhood does not argue this – rather it fairly consistently condemns acts of violence in the West perpetrated by jihadist groups like al-Qaeda or the Islamic State. But it is not difficult to see how some individuals who are exposed to this logic make the leap from the Brotherhood's worldview to the jihadists', which makes an identical diagnosis of the alleged conspiracy plaguing Muslims but, unlike the Brothers, argues that violence in the West is the solution.

In substance, proponents of this theory argue that non-violent Islamists create an anti-chamber to violent extremism, a fertile environment for jihadists, who only have to convince potential recruits about the righteousness of their tactics. According to language made popular at the height of the British debate on the matter by the anti-extremism think tank Quilliam Foundation, non-violent Islamists "advocate separatist, confrontational ideas that, followed to their logical conclusion, lead to violence". "At the very least," stated the foundation, their rhetoric "provides the mood music to which suicide bombers dance" (Quilliam Foundation, 2008).[4]

Conclusion

The debate on whether non-violent Islamist groups constitute conveyor belts towards or, rather firewall against violent radicalization is one that divides scholars and practitioners, as do most other aspects of the radicalization process. The concept of "mood music" is supported by many but challenged by many others, and definitive empirical data on the matter is hard to come by (Egger & Magni-Berton, 2019).

It is interesting to note, though, that Bob Lambert – as seen, the architect of the British approach of partnering with Islamists against jihadists – seems to embrace the notion that non-violent Islamists provide a fertile environment for violent groups to operate. "From an al Qaeda perspective," writes Lambert (2011) in his book, "however, the ground to be covered in recruiting a young British Muslim from salafi and Islamist communities is generally likely to be less than in recruiting a young British Muslim from Barelvi or sufi communities" (p. 66). Lambert seems to confirm the analysis that sees the narrative of non-violent Islamists as having laid down the intellectual groundwork for jihadists and having, in substance, primed individuals to be more receptive to the recruitment efforts of jihadists. Where Lambert differs from critics of Islamists is on how to consider this proximity. "Salafis and Islamists," for the very reason of their proximity to jihadists, he argues, "are often best at spotting them and generally have the best counter-narratives to al-Qaeda propaganda once it has begun to have a telling influence upon individuals and communities" (Lambert, 2011, p. 67). But it is clear that Lambert himself sees a direct correlation between adopting the Islamist mindset and potentially making the leap into jihadism.

Various studies of the European Islamic State-related mobilization of the last decade seem to confirm the "mood music" argument. Analyses of key hubs of jihadist radicalization like Toulouse and the Brussels neighborhood of Molenbeek, both of which provided a disproportionally large number of foreign fighters and perpetrators of attacks in recent years, clearly highlight these dynamics (Micheron, 2020, p. 225–51; Rougier, Mansour, & Almakir, 2020, pp. 253–81). In both Toulouse and Molenbeek, the phenomenon of large-scale jihadist radicalization can be clearly traced, both from an ideological and social network point of view, to the growth of Brotherhood and Salafist milieus some 10–15 years prior to the Islamic State mobilization. Many of those who played a key role in recruiting others to travel to Syria or carried out attacks, in fact, had first been attracted to Islamism by an extensive network of mosques, cultural associations, and study circles (what Bernard Rougier (2020) calls "écosystèmes islamistes"). Over the years, some – not all, probably not even the majority, but definitely a substantial and, from a security perspective, a disturbingly high number – of those individuals who had gravitated around non-violent Islamist milieus made the leap into jihadism.

The topic of the Western Brotherhoods' relationship towards violence is one that unquestionably deserves additional research, considering its significant policy implications. Yet preliminary indications, which are increasingly driving the attitude of security services and governments, seem to point to, at best, an ambiguous relationship towards violence and a limited impact on preventing it.

Notes

1 These views are expressed by several scholars and commentators but, interestingly, also by the security services of most Western European countries. For example, Belgian security services have stated that

> The Internationalist Muslim Brothers have possessed a clandestine structure in Belgium for more than 20 years. The identity of the members is secret; they operate in the greatest discretion. They seek to spread their ideology within Belgium's Muslim community and they aim in particular at young, second and third generation immigrants. In Belgium as in other European countries, they seek to take control of sport, religious and social associations, and they seek to establish themselves as privileged interlocutors of national and even European authorities in order to manage Islamic affairs. The Muslim Brothers estimate that national authorities will increasingly rely on the representatives of the Islamic community for the management of Islam. Within this framework, they try to impose the designation of people influenced by their ideology in representative bodies. In order to do so they were very active in the electoral process for the members of the body for the management of Islam [in Belgium]. Another aspect of this strategy is to cause or maintain tensions in which they consider that a Muslim or a Muslim organization is victim of Western values, hence the affair over the Muslim headscarf in public schools.
>
> *(Sénat et Chambre des Représentants de Belgique, Rapport d'activité 2001*
> *du Comité permanent de contrôle des services de renseignements*
> *et de sécurité (Comité R), Session of July 19, 2002).*

Austrian security services have argued that

> [t]he political system aimed for [by the Muslim Brotherhood] is reminiscent of a totalitarian system, which guarantees neither the sovereignty of people nor the principles of freedom and equality. Such a fundamental position is incompatible with the legal and social norms of the Republic of Austria.
>
> *(Landesverwaltungsgericht Steiermark, cases LVwG 70.8-3597/2015-34,*
> *LVwG 41.8-37/2016-34 and LVwG 41.8-39/2016-34,*
> *Graz, September 9, 2016)*

Dutch security services have stated that

> not all Muslim Brothers or their sympathisers are recognisable as such. They do not always reveal their religious loyalties and ultra-orthodox agenda to outsiders. Apparently co-operative and moderate in their attitude to Western society, they certainly have no violent intent. But they are trying to pave the way for ultra-orthodox Islam to play a greater role in the Western world by exercising religious influence over Muslim immigrant communities and by forging good relations with relevant opinion leaders: politicians, civil servants, mainstream social organisations, non-Islamic clerics, academics, journalists and so on. This policy of engagement has been more noticeable in recent years, and might possibly herald a certain liberalisation of the movement's ideas. It presents itself as a widely supported advocate and legitimate representative of the Islamic community. But the ultimate aim – although never stated openly – is to create, then implant and expand, an ultra-orthodox Muslim bloc inside Western Europe.
>
> *(The radical dawa in transition, 2007, AIVD)*

2 Voices favouring some form of engagement with the Brothers include prominent Berlin Interior Senator Andreas Geisel (SPD). See Andreas Kopietz, "Radikale Islamisten sollen sich um Ex-Radikale kümmern," *Berliner Zeitung*, May 6, 2019; Frank Jansen, "Die riskante Strategie des Berliner Innensenators," *Tagesspiegel*, May 7, 2019; Frank Jansen, "Salafisten und Muslimbrüder nähern sich gefährlich an," *Tagesspiegel*, April 11, 2019.
3 See www.im.nrw/system/files/media/document/file/VS_Bericht_2018.pdf
4 See Quilliam Foundation's launch publication, April 2008.

References

Al-Qaradawi, Y. (2000). *Priorities of the Islamic movement in the coming phase*. Swansea, UK: Awakening Publications.

American Enterprise Institute. (Presenter). (2004, December 16). An Interview with Reuel Marc Gerecht. [Online Interview]. Washington, D.C. Retrieved from: www.aei.org/press/an-interview-with-reuel-marc-gerecht/

Besson, S. (2005). *La Conquête de l'Occident*. Paris, France: Le Seuil.

Bundesverfassungsschutz. (2005). *Verfassungsschutzbericht*. Berlin, Germany.

Cameron, D. (2011, February 5). PM's speech at Munich Security Conference, Munich, Germany. Retrieved from www.newstatesman.com/blogs/the-staggers/2011/02/terrorism-islam-ideology

Canadian Security Intelligence Service. (2006, June). *Radicalization and Jihad in the West*. Government Report.

Egger, C. & Magni-Berton, R. (2019, February). The role of Islamist ideology in shaping Muslim believers' attitudes toward terrorism: Evidence from Europe. *Studies in Conflict and Terrorism*, pp. 581–604. DOI: 10.1080/1057610X.2019.1571696

Esposito, J. (1999). *The Islamic threat: Myth or reality?* New York and Oxford: Oxford University Press.

Fourest, C. (2008). *Brother Tariq: The doublespeak of Tariq Ramadan*. New York City, NY: Encounter.

General Intelligence and Security Service of the Netherlands [AIVD]. (2002, December). *Recruitment for the Jihad in the Netherlands: From incident to trend*. Zoetermeer, Netherlands. Retrieved from: https://english.aivd.nl/publications/publications/2002/12/09/recruitment-for-the-jihad-in-the-netherlands

Haines, H. (1997). Black radicalization and the funding of civil rights: 1957–1970. In D. McAdam & D. A. Snow (Eds.), *Social Movements* (pp. 440–41). Los Angeles, CA: Roxbury.

Jansen, F. (April 11, 2019). Salafisten und Muslimbrüder nähern sich gefährlich an. *Tagesspiegel*. Retrieved from: https://www.tagesspiegel.de/politik/salafisten-und-muslimbruder-nahern-sich-gefahrlich-an-4056772.html.

Jansen, F. (May 7, 2019). Die riskante Strategie des Berliner Innensenators. Tagesspiegel. Retrieved from: https://www.tagesspiegel.de/politik/die-riskante-strategie-des-berliner-innensenators-5327734.html.

Johnson, I. (2006). The Muslim Brotherhood in Europe. Briefing before the Congressional Human Relations Caucus, US House of Representatives, Washington, DC, 10.

Köln: Federal Office for the Protection of the Constitution. (2007, January). *Integration as a Means to Prevent Extremism and Terrorism: Typology of Islamist Radicalisation and Recruitment*. Köln, Germany.

Kopietz, A. (2019, May 6). *Berliner-Zeitung*. Retrieved from www.berliner-zeitung.de/mensch-metropole/islamisten-in-berlin-senat-radikale-sollen-sich-um-radikale-kuemmern-li.11217

Lambert, R. (2008a). Empowering Salafis and Islamists against Al-Qaeda: A London counterterrorism case study. *PS: Political Science and Politics*, 41(1), 31–35. DOI: 10.1017/S1049096508080049

Lambert, R. (2008b). Ignoring the lessons of the past. *Criminal Justice Matters*, 73, 22–23. DOI: 10.1080/09627250802276910

Lambert, R. (2011). *Countering al-Qaeda in London: Police and Muslims in partnership*. London, UK: C. Hurst & Company.

Leiken, R., & Brooke, S. (2007, March/April). The Moderate Muslim Brotherhood. *Foreign Affairs*. Retrieved from www.foreignaffairs.com/articles/2007-03-01/moderate-muslim-brotherhood

Lynch, M. (2016, March 7). *The Washington Post*. Retrieved from www.washingtonpost.com/news/monkey-cage/wp/2016/03/07/is-the-muslim-brotherhood-a-terrorist-organization-or-a-firewall-against-violent-extremism/

Maher, S., & Frampton, M. (2009). Choosing our friends wisely. Policy Exchange. Retrieved from: www.almendron.com/tribuna/wp-content/uploads/2016/09/choosing-our-friends-wisely-mar-09.pdf

Man kann Salafisten nicht mit Islamisten bekämpfen. (2019, December 17). *Berlin Monitor*. Retrieved from www.bz-berlin.de/deutschland/man-kann-salafisten-nicht-mit-islamisten-bekaempfen

McAdam, D. (1992). Studying Social Movements: A Conceptual Tour of the Field. In *Program on Nonviolent Sanctions and Cultural Survival*. Weatherhead Center for International Affairs, Harvard University.

Micheron, H. (2020). Toulouse: la machine de prédication ou la fabrication sociale du jihadisme. In B. Rougier (Ed.), *Les territoires conquis de l'islamisme* (pp.225–51). Paris: PUF.

Neumann, P.R. (2008). Joining Al-Qaeda: Jihadist Recruitment in Europe. *Adelphi Paper 339, International Institute for Strategic Studies*, 46.

Nordrhein-Westfälische Verfassungsschutz. (2018). *Verfassungsschutzbericht des Landes Nordrhein-Westfalen*. Dusseldorf, Germany.

Peter, F. (2006). Leading the community of the middle way: A study of the Muslim field in France. *The Muslim World*, 96(4) 707–36. DOI: 10.1111/j.1478-1913.2006.00154.x

Quilliam Foundation (April 2008). *Pulling together to defeat terror*. London: Quilliam Foundation. Retrieved from: http://www. quilliamfoundation.org/images/stories/pdfs/pulling-together-to-defeat-terror.pdf.

Rougier, B. (2020). *Les territoires conquis de l'islamisme*. Paris: Presses Universitaires de France.

Rougier, B., Mansour, P.F., & Almakir, A. (2020). Molenbeek et la predication islamiste à Bruxelles. In B. Rougier, *Les territoires conquis de l'islamisme*, 253–81.

Vidino, L. (2010). *The new Muslim Brotherhood in the West*. New York: Columbia University Press

Zakaria, F. (2009, February 27). Radical Islam is a fact of life; How to live with it. *Newsweek*. Retrieved from www.newsweek.com/zakaria-learning-live-radical-islam-82353

9

NATIVIST EXPRESSIONS OF NON-VIOLENT EXTREMISM IN MALAYSIA

The Case of *Ikatan Muslimin Malaysia* (ISMA: Muslim Solidarity Front of Malaysia)[1]

Ahmad Fauzi Abdul Hamid and Che Hamdan Che Mohd Razali

Introduction

Contemporary disputes about Malay claims to indigeneity in contemporary Malaysia have given rise to a host of nativist responses which seek to defend Malay identity, seen as currently under threat of being overwhelmed by globalising forces that more often than not collaborate with local non-Malay segments of the population. The basis of what the Malay nationalists view as their inherent rights as Malaysia's definitive communal group lies in an implied social contract between Malaya's dominant races on the eve of independence in 1957. The social contract purportedly recognises the position of Malays as original inhabitants of Malaya in exchange for the granting of citizenship to non-Malays, the latter whom owe their presence to British colonial demand for cheap labour. In addition to citizenship rights, non-Malays were bestowed freedoms to use the English language for official purposes for up to ten years, to employ their mother tongue languages in primary-level vernacular schools and to subscribe to religions other than Islam – the faith of the majority Malay population. Religious liberties also extended to the construction of non-Muslim houses of worship, subject to local government regulations.

To the Malays, all of whom are automatically Muslims as provided for by Article 160 of the Federal Constitution, acknowledgements of their indigeneity are given via constitutional provisions guaranteeing the position of Malay as the national language, of Islam as the religion of the federation, of the Malay sultans as constitutional monarchs of their respective states and as the Yang diPertuan Agong – King of the Malaysian federation on a five-yearly rotational basis, and of limited socio-economic privileges with respect to services, permits and licences in order to offset their economic decline that prevailed during the early years of nation-building (Malaysia, 2010). Whenever challenges to their perceived primacy are made, commensurate responses will emerge from nativist Malay movements. Enmeshing with global trends of Islamic revival in the Muslim world from the 1980s onwards, these counter-current, reactive movements take on religious colouring to a significant degree. But owing to Malaysia's

DOI: 10.4324/9781003032793-12

coterminous boundaries dividing race and religion, stirrings in the Malay case could more accurately be termed as ethno-religious, with "Islam" and "Malay ethnicity" occupying complementary positions in mutually reinforcing one another's discursive strength in political and socio-economic mobilisation (Hussin, 1990).

Since the onset of a reformist brand of politics in 1998, challenges to notions of a Malay-dominant identity for Malaysia have arguably accelerated. Arguing along the lines of path dependency, we postulate the year 2018 to have been a type of peak in emplacing the politics of reform as an indispensable factor in Malay-Muslim politics in Malaysia (Saravanamuttu, 2020). However, the reformists' forward march has not gone unchallenged. Whilst the reform-oriented trajectory has to a significant extent assumed Islamist[2] characteristics along progressive lines of thinking, Islamist conservative groups have been spawned in Malaysia, offering alternative interpretations of Islamist politics that are akin to right-wing extremism (Ahmad Fauzi & Muhamad Takiyuddin, 2014). Both wings of Islamism, while separately claiming the Islamist mantle, proffer different versions of a mature Malaysian polity that straddle between the ethnic-genealogical and civic-nationalist visions of nationhood (Loh, 2017). The uniqueness of the Malaysian models lies in the fact that none of these groups actually advocates a distinctly secular nation state, insofar as the term "secular" carries non-religious or even irreligious connotations. The main contesting visions incorporate aspects of political Islam to varying degrees and of different types (Ahmad Fauzi, 2018).

This chapter draws heavily from the present authors' participant observation exercise conducted among the rank-and-file of a Malay-Muslim nativist group, the Muslim Solidarity Front (ISMA: *Ikatan Muslimin Malaysia*) spanning the years 2010–2018. The length of the research produced familiarity and camaraderie between the researchers and research subjects. Data were qualitatively gathered via such techniques as informal interviews and dialogues, face to face discussions, interlocution sessions, personal home visits and presence at ISMA functions and meetings. Such empirical data is weaved with information obtained from public statements by ISMA figures, ISMA documents, materials downloaded from ISMA's website and press reports.

The chapter begins with a brief background of ISMA, before proceeding to discuss its place within the global, regional and Malaysian contexts of non-violent extremism. The authors then discuss how ISMA's discourse underwent radicalisation at the hands of Middle Eastern-oriented religious leaders. While ISMA members have themselves refrained from overt violence, the authors pose the question of whether ISMA's pretensions to non-violence can be trusted on account of its extremist tendencies, which may goad other ethno-religious zealots into violent action, as has intermittently occurred. As will be shown in ISMA's case, a grey area exists separating non-violent extremist discourse from violent outcomes, even if the perpetrators of violence may not have been directly involved in the network within which the extremism originated. Herein lies the liminality between non-violent and violent extremism in the real world.

ISMA: A Brief Background

This chapter investigates the challenge of non-violent Islamist extremism in Malaysia, as represented by ISMA. Fitting the "conservative Islamist" doctrinal category, ISMA was originally founded in 1997 as a student movement, the Muslim Student Solidarity Front (*Ikatan Siswazah Muslim Malaysia*), to house returning Malay-Muslim students from overseas, principally the United Kingdom (UK) and Egypt. According to ISMA's inaugural Secretary General, the formation of ISMA was triggered by the urge to acculturate Islam in the quotidian lives of upwardly mobile young Muslims of fast expanding conurbations during an era of rapid economic growth (Radhi, 2017).

A comparatively late entrant to Malaysia's Islamist scene, ISMA nevertheless benefitted from the periodic fragmentation and re-alignments that beset Malaysia's Islamists, many of whom, it alleges, have over the years deviated from pristine Islamist objectives as they re-adjusted to the uncomfortable truths of Malaysia's plural society. ISMA claims to recapture the original thoughts of the pioneers of Islamism, as exemplified especially in the teachings of Muslim Brotherhood (MB) founder, Hassan al-Banna (1906–1949), particularly his idea of benign nationalism (*nasionalisme yang terpuji*). While paying tribute to its Middle Eastern ideological roots, ISMA tries its best to adapt its worldview and actions to Malaysia's socio-political realities (Ahmad Fauzi & Hamdan, 2016).

Global Underpinnings of Non-Violent Islamist Extremism in Southeast Asia

Using mainly examples of Islamists in Western countries, a growing number of scholars, such as Bartlett and Miller (2011) and Schmid (2014), have cautioned against the practice of some Western governments of lending too much legitimacy to the notion of non-violent Islamism. Some countries like Britain had even sought cooperation with non-violent Islamists as a strategy in combating violent Islamists. In fact, in his outline of 20 indicators for monitoring extremism, Schmid (2014, pp. 20–21) frankly proposes that the degree of extremism be measured vis-à-vis values of "constitutional liberal-democratic societies." Investigating the careers of numerous militant Islamists, research highlights the radicalisation process they underwent, showing that they ended up becoming violent extremists despite beginning on an Islamist path many would describe as non-violent, whether of the Salafi[3] or MB variety. Applying Schmid's framework to Southeast Asia, Ramakrishna (2017) raises the question of the blurred lines that separate non-violent extremists who are "not yet violent" out of expediency and other pragmatic considerations, from non-violent extremists who disavow violence as a matter of principle. The crux of the terrorist problem in the region, as far as Ramakrishna (2017, p. 11) is concerned, is with the "Islamist ideology" itself, and "not just its violent expressions."

Many of the uncompromising Islamist beliefs espoused by both "not yet violent" and violent extremists are defined by the doctrinal rigidities of Wahhabi-Salafism,[4] the revolutionary views of Egyptian Muslim Brotherhood (MB: *Ikhwan al-Muslimun*) ideologue Sayyid Qutb (1906–1966) and the dogmas of Pakistani Islamist thinker, Abul A'la Maududi (1903–1979), to whom Qutb owed an intellectual debt. The ideological marriage between Qutbism and Wahhabi-Salafism generated the violence-permitting strand of Salafi-jihadism, which found its embodiment in the anti-Soviet Union *jihad* (holy war) campaign of Abdullah Azzam (1941–1989), who effectively founded Al-Qaeda as a means to mobilise the constant stream of Arab-Afghan fighters (Wiktorowicz, 2005). For many Islamists, Abdullah Azzam's legendary heroics during the Afghan liberation war earned him a well-deserved place in the Muslim halls of fame (McGregor, 2003). In Malaysia, Azzam's treatise, *Tarbiyah Jihadiyah* (Jihadist Education), has become Islamist extremists' favourite manual in guiding their convictions and driving them into action.[5]

From Global to Local: Malaysia's Islamist Setting

On the global stage, relatively speaking, Islamists of the 1980s had focused on three main agendas, consisting of changing corrupt government regimes, maintaining fairly conservative socio-cultural norms and cultivating strong nationalist sentiments (Roy, 2004). First generation Islamists, however, suffered from their own utopian worldviews and lack of clarity on the Islamic forms of statehood they wished to implement (Roy, 1994). Second generation Islamists no longer hold to the juridical Islamic state, that is, a state in which the Shari'a is applied in totality, as their ultimate goal. They prefer instead to re-conceptualise the Shari'a based on a holistic reading of the law called *Maqasid Shari'a* (higher objectives of Shari'a). In addition, they endorse "Muslim democracy" and disavow all pretensions to violence. A recent example of such a shift is found in the transformative ideas of the Tunisian thinker, Rached Ghannouchi (1941–Present), whose conversion from Islamism to Muslim democracy epitomises his progressive thoughts that have influenced generations of Malaysian Islamists (Maszlee, 2017a).

In Malaysia, dissonance between the first and subsequent generations of Islamists are reflected in the tensions characterising the relations between their *de facto* electoral proxies. The major streams of Malaysian Islamism have come to terms with the benefits and need of upholding democracy as a means of attaining power. Mainstream Islamism in Malaysia is electorally represented by the Islamic Party of Malaysia (PAS: *Parti Islam SeMalaysia*), which has run for power in all general elections since independence, and its splinter party the National Trust Party (AMANAH: *Parti Amanah Negara*), formed out of a breakaway and supposedly more moderate faction of PAS leaders out-voted en masse during PAS's General Assembly of June 2015. While PAS activists remain essentially first-generation Islamists, AMANAH members are for all intents and purposes, second-generation Islamists, by which we mean Islamists who have generally accepted the compatibility of Islam with modern notions of statehood, such as democracy, justice and good governance.

The other pioneers of Islamism in Malaysia have been non-governmental organisations (NGOs) which specifically profess Islam to be their *raison d'etre*. These include so-called *dakwah* (missionary) movements that characterised Malaysia's Islamist revival of the 1970s–1980s, such as the Muslim Youth Movement of Malaysia (ABIM: *Angkatan Belia Islam Malaysia*), the mystically oriented Darul Arqam and the overseas-based Islamic Representative Council (IRC) (cf. Nagata, 1984; Jomo & Ahmad Shabery, 1992). Except for the now-banned Darul Arqam, many Malaysian Islamists have over the years continued to derive inspiration from the Egyptian MB, even as the movement in later times somewhat strayed from its founding objectives and precepts as laid out by its progenitor Hassan al-Banna. Mainstream Islamists generally have a non-violent orientation, with only a tiny portion of Malaysian Muslims being involved in Islamist-related violence on domestic soil, in spite of the consistently high levels of radicalisation registered by surveys and polls (Chan, 2018). In 2015 for instance, a Pew Research poll recorded a relatively high 11% of Malaysian Muslims expressing a favourable view of the Islamic State of Iraq and Syria (ISIS), putting Malaysia in joint fourth-highest position with Senegal and behind only Syria, Nigeria and Tunisia among the 20 Muslim-majority countries surveyed (Poushter, 2015).

The possibility of rogue elements within mainstream Islamism committing violence cannot be dismissed. Lone wolf aggressors, acting on a pre-meditated basis or spontaneously in reaction to the authorities, constitute a lurking but deadly threat once they come out in the open. While admittedly rare, Islamist violence in Malaysia has resulted in loss of lives, as happened in bloody confrontations between the security forces and PAS-linked Muslim extremists in Memali, Kedah in November 1985, and with the Al-Ma'unah rebels in Grik, Perak in July 2000 (Ahmad Fauzi, 2020). With the number of youths gravitating towards the version of Islamism propagated by violent outfits, such as Al Qaeda, its Southeast Asian proxy Jemaah Islamiyah (JI) and ISIS consistently increasing since the dramatic ascendancy and equally sudden fall of ISIS in the mid-2010s (Samuel, 2018, pp. 97–131), it is far from surprising that Malaysia has taken a guarded stance against radicalisation, given its potential to spill over into violent extremist outbursts in the right atmosphere. Buoyed by the election in May 2018 of a new Pact of Hope (PH: *Pakatan Harapan*) government, which is widely accused by right-wing Malay extremists to be anti-Muslim, disoriented youth could more easily become triggered into lone wolf violence against non-Muslims.

In September 2019, in Penang, for instance, police shot dead a young Malay-Muslim employee who had run amok, violently slashing his cleaver against two of his non-Muslim factory supervisors. One of the wounded victims, who was accused by the aggressor of verbally insulting the Prophet Muhammad, later died from serious injuries. Police later discovered ISIS-related videos and images of Syrian Muslim fighters in action in the perpetrator's mobile phone. However, even this episode proved insufficient in deterring a growing feeling among younger Malay-Muslims, including those connected to the former ruling United Malays National Organisation (UMNO) party, that the deceased's violent exploits had earned him a blessed martyrdom (Faisal, 2019; Ghazali, 2019). With such instances of violence in mind, the danger of under-estimating the extent to which non-violent extremists could degenerate into violent extremists becomes evident.

While PAS itself disavows violence in a manner resembling MB, which many national PAS leaders during its formative stages drew upon as its organisational exemplar (Zakaria, 2007), violent extremists in Malaysia have at one time or another nonetheless been associated with PAS. There is therefore reason to trace a slippery-slope between non-violent, first-generation Islamism and violent Islamism, which is not surprising given both streams are united by similar totalising beliefs regarding the immutability of the *sharia*, and the necessity of implementing it *in toto* as the way to gain God's pleasure in the world and hereafter (Arosoaie & Nawab 2017). A riveting debate has evolved between analysts who see such seemingly non-violent Islamists, such as MB, as either a firewall against more radical organisations or a menacing conveyor belt that supplies future foot soldiers for violent Islamist groups (Lynch, 2010, pp. 480–482).

Non-Violent Islamist Extremism in a Multi-Cultural Nation State: The Case of Contemporary Malaysia

Islam has been a core feature of Malay identity since gaining a foothold in Southeast Asia as the religion of the Malays since the 15th century, as established by court documents and contemporaneous accounts that testify to the many Islamic-based ceremonies, rituals and regulations that conditioned the lives of denizens of the early Malay sultanates. So important was the place of Islam in the Malaccan sultanate (1400–1511), for instance, that the first colonial conquest of Malayan soil in Malacca – then a pivot for intercontinental Muslim trade, was undertaken by the Portuguese as much for religious as for economic reasons (Majul, 1964, pp. 389–391). The British were the most circumspect colonial power when it came to dealing with Islam in the context of Malay society. Through treaties struck with Malay rulers, the British gave a token respect to Islam and Malay custom – the two areas in which the sultans formally retained autonomy, although, in practice, some cases of interferences were in fact recorded (Ahmad Fauzi, 2004).

Islamic elements featured prominently in Malay-led anti-colonial agitations (Ahmad Fauzi, 2007), and although independence was handed down to Malay nationalists, which many would categorise as "secular" and "Western" in orientation, Islam was nevertheless etched permanently into Malaysia's nation-building programme. For example, constitutional provisions exist to confirm Islam as the "religion of the federation" and guarantee state support for state-level Islamic institutions, such as a Council of the Islamic Religion (*Majlis Agama Islam*) to aid and advise a particular Malay Ruler in their capacity as head of the Islamic religion in their state. Likewise, a Department of Islamic Religious Affairs (*Jabatan Agama Islam*) also exists to handle Muslims' daily affairs, while Shari'a courts adjudicate in intra-Muslim disputes (Malaysia, 2010; Ahmad Fauzi, 2018).

The institutional context above is important in comprehending the Malaysian government's Islamisation initiatives since the 1980s, during Dr Mahathir Mohamad's first prime ministerial tenure (1981–2003).[6] While many Islamists co-operated with Dr Mahathir's Islamisation programme, regarding it as part of their crusade in turning Malaysia into a full-fledged Islamic state, measured by the extent to which the sharia is successfully imposed as state law, ruling Malay-Muslim politicians openly capitalised on Malay-Muslim religious sentiments for political purposes, not only drawing support from the newly emerging Islamist civil society but also skillfully playing off one group against another. To the Malay ruling elites, Islam was taken for granted as a proxy for Malay political enthusiasm; distinction hardly existed between state patronage over Islam and Malay political interests.

Islamists have thus always been targeted for co-optation by a Malay-Muslim-dominated state. In time, however, it was the Islamists who captured the state and moulded it in the shape of a mini-Islamic state (Norshahril, 2018). Malay nationalists in UMNO did not resist the transformation of their party, from one championing Malay Supremacy (*Ketuanan Melayu*), to one espousing Islamic Supremacy (*Ketuanan Islam*) (Chin, 2016). Having had their agenda hijacked by the state, many Islamists took the easy way out by joining in, or at least collaborating with, state agencies. Even the long-time opposition party, PAS, having tasted power intermittently at a state level in Kelantan (1990–Present), Terengganu (1999–2003, 2018–Present) and Kedah (2008–2013, 2020–Present), and since March 2020 at a federal level as part of the National Alliance (PN: *Perikatan Nasional*) government, settled into the idea that state power offered the best alternative for implementing Islamic governance. Islam hence became the touchstone of Malay-Muslim political identity; the defence of Islam, which politically morphed into Islamism during Najib Razak's Premiership (2009–2018) by virtue of creeping Salafisation of Malay-Muslim society, in tandem with Najib's Islamic policies (Ahmad Fauzi, 2016), was treated as synonymous with Malay political power.

ISMA: Malay-Muslim Activism in a Multi-Cultural Nation State

Overwhelmingly ethnocentric in character, ISMA has courted controversy in Malaysia by openly disavowing multi-cultural power-sharing arrangements, dismissing non-Malays as ungrateful "trespassers" and seeking to restore the hegemony of Malay-Muslims in a country ISMA argues as rightfully theirs as its indigenous community. Premising its struggle on the nativist tagline, Malay Consensus, Islam Sovereign (*Melayu Sepakat, Islam Berdaulat*), ISMA takes advantage of Malay-Muslims' beleaguered mindset, cultivated among them through long-standing hegemonic rhetoric espoused by UMNO-linked organs of the state. From the perspective of ISMA President from 2005 to 2018, the Al-Azhar-educated, Abdullah Zaik Abdul Rahman, who now styles himself as *Amir* (Commander) in a manner akin to MB's *Murshid al-'Am* (General Guide), PAS and the People's Justice Party (PKR: *Parti Keadilan Rakyat*) – product of a merger between his National Justice Party (KEADILAN: *Parti Keadilan Nasional*) and the Malay-led Malaysian People's Party (PRM: *Parti Rakyat Malaysia*) in 2003, had then colluded with subversive forces bent on undermining Malaysia's Malay-Islamic character in favour of a liberal democratic state that did not prioritise any race and religion (Abdullah Zaik, 2019). Abdullah Zaik (2012, p. 26) claims that ISMA, by contrast, aims to be a "free, non-partisan NGO, not involved in politics and not favouring any axis of power."

ISMA is essentially a Malay-Muslim nativist reaction against what it perceives as a series of piecemeal losses of Malay dominance arising from the centrifugal dispersal of political power away from a Malay-defined axis. This was epitomised, for instance, in the apparent warming of non-Malays to Dr Mahathir's "Malaysian nation" (*Bangsa Malaysia*) rhetoric advanced in his Vision 2020 scheme (Ooi, 2006). Even among opposition parties and civil society, in which non-Malays played leading roles, there was increasing recognition that multi-racial and multi-religious alliances presented better options towards accomplishing their objectives than ethnically segmented movements. The single event that prompted calls for a revamp of state–society relations in the areas of civil liberties, personal freedoms, social justice and democratic rights was Dr Mahathir's personally engineered ouster of Anwar Ibrahim from the lofty heights of national and UMNO politics in September 1998, amidst highly contestable allegations of corruption and sexual misdemeanour made against him (Weiss, 2003a). Human rights organisations such as the Voice of Malaysians (SUARAM: *Suara Rakyat Malaysia*), the National Human Rights Society (HAKAM: *Persatuan Kebangsaan Hak Asasi Manusia*), the National Consciousness Movement (ALIRAN: *Aliran Kesedaran Negara*), ABIM and the Society for Islamic Reform (JIM: *Jamaah Islah Malaysia*) spearheaded this fledgling spirit of inter-ethnic unity, which saw the beginnings of cooperation between the Islamist and non-Muslim-led wings of civil society (Weiss, 2003b).

ISMA, as stewarded initially by early-career Malay-Muslim graduates of British universities, was originally involved in the PAS-helmed, multi-ethnic initiative called the Malaysian People's Movement for Justice (GERAK: *Gerakan Keadilan Rakyat Malaysia*) (Radhi, 2017). Formed in September 1998 as an immediate response to Anwar Ibrahim's unceremonious dismissals and humiliating treatment at the hands of Mahathir-controlled powers that be, GERAK was led by PAS President, Fadzil Noor (1937–2002), who had been Anwar Ibrahim's deputy in ABIM from 1974 to 1978. A broad-minded Islamist with abundant experience in civil society activism before turning to politics, Fadzil's appeal cut across racial, inter and intra-religious boundaries (Farish, 2003), and managed to gather together organisations of motley interests in mobilising opposition against the Internal Security Act (ISA), under which Anwar was detained and mishandled by police during custody.

Apart from PAS and ISMA, other well-known groups that participated in GERAK included the Chinese-dominated Democratic Action Party (DAP), PRM, as well as civil society organisations, such as ABIM, JIM, SUARAM, the Malaysian Islamic Scholars Association (PUM: *Persatuan Ulama Malaysia*), and the Vanguard of Malay Empowerment (TERAS: *Teras Pengupayaan Melayu*). Struggling to survive the premature death of its pioneer, Fadzil Noor, in 2002, GERAK effectively served as the precursor of the also multi-racial Abolish ISA Movement (GMI: *Gerakan Mansuhkan ISA*), which endured intense state pressure until Najib Razak's government, severely weakened by the electoral setbacks that befell UMNO and the ruling National Front (BN: *Barisan Nasional*) coalition in the 2008 general elections, agreed to annul the ISA in 2012 (Maszlee, 2014). It was only in 2018 that the UMNO-led government fell, but in March 2020, UMNO leaders were able to sneak back into governmental positions following an internal coup by defecting component ruling coalition members against the short-lived PH government (Chin, 2020). More multi-racial in its composition and spirit, PH's ascendancy, albeit short in term, challenged the enduring legitimacy of the "Malay Supremacy" (*Ketuanan Melayu*) doctrine upon which Malay-centric outfits such as UMNO and ISMA thrived.

ISMA's ideology can be described as one of Islamist nationalism. The gist of ISMA's struggle is summarised in its other catchword, "Developing an *Ummah*-based Agenda" (*Membangun Umat Beragenda*). ISMA's philosophy is couched in a succinct vision: "to become a strong and influential Islamic movement," and similar mission: "to lead the (*ummah*) global community of Muslims and restore Malay-Islamic dominance" (ISMA, n.d.). Multi-racial political alignments were considered by ISMA to be a betrayal of the Malay race, of which both PAS and PKR were allegedly guilty. That conspiracy theories pervade ISMA's worldview is evident from Abdullah Zaik's attribution of Malay-Muslim backwardness to "colonial mentality," "the shrewdness of certain non-Malay leaders" and "a stealthy Jewish conspiracy," which in turn manipulates the alien ideologies of liberalism, pluralism and humanism in attempting to eradicate Malaysia's long-held national identity (Dina, 2014).

During its formative phase, ISMA's recruitment drive relied heavily on segments of Malay-Muslim civil society who were disaffected by mainstream Malay-Muslim politicians, who were seen as overly compromising towards their non-Muslim partners. Its outreach programmes overwhelmingly target Malay-Muslims. ISMA's grassroots activities had a ready audience in heavily Malay-populated areas, but as nationwide internet connectivity improved, online recruitment became more fashionable, with new members being invited from time to time to scheduled gatherings at the regional, state and national levels. Today, one can instantly register as an ISMA member upon surfing its website (ISMA, n.d.).

Radicalisation of ISMA's Discourse in the Post-Millennial Age

From 2000–2001, ISMA started to receive returning Malay-Muslim alumni from Middle Eastern universities (Radhi, 2017). In a matter of a few years, Islamic studies graduates would make up the majority of its core decision-making team. Those who flocked to ISMA upon arriving back in Malaysia shared similar IRC backgrounds with Malay-Muslim graduates of British universities, many of whom opted for JIM and later the HONOUR Association of Malaysia (IKRAM: *Pertubuhan IKRAM Malaysia*). These IRC offshoots were all Salafi-based organisations; however, while its British chapter was trained by UK-based MB diasporic members, its Middle Eastern branch, known as "Alami" in Egypt, undertook *haraki* (movement)-based training at the hands of Egyptian-based MB stalwarts. A core feature of IRC thinking was the belief that becoming a carbon copy of MB was the most effective choice in pursuing the Islamist struggle in Malaysia (Hazmi, 2016). Several failed attempts at *indimaj* (merger without sacrificing core membership of parent organisations) between rival factions ended up in ISMA and IKRAM splitting ways.[7] IKRAM-linked activists made up a disproportionate number of top guns of AMANAH, which was born out of the womb of PAS's progressive faction, which for many years had promoted the inclusive slogans of "PAS for All" and "The Benevolent State" (*Negara Berkebajikan*) on PAS's behalf (Maszlee, 2017b). ISMA, by contrast, turned inward in spectacular ethnocentric fashion.

The turning point for ISMA occurred in the aftermath of the 2008 general elections. The historic polls saw BN's two-thirds parliamentary majority overturned and the People's Pact (PR: *Pakatan Rakyat*) coalition, crafted shortly after the elections in order to unite the assorted opposition forces, forming state governments in Penang, Selangor, Kedah, Perak, and Kelantan; the latter ruled by PAS since 1990. PR was then a largely untested experiment at multi-racial political cooperation, its then-latest endeavour, the Alternative Front (BA: *Barisan Alternatif*), having crumbled in 2001 due to PAS and DAP being unable to see eye to eye on the issue of the Islamic state. Premising its Islamic struggle on MB founder, Hassan al-Banna's, notion of benign nationalism (Zulkifly, 2011, pp. 72–73),[8] ISMA does not conceal the fact that its public advocacy foregrounds the intellectual and cultural transformation of the Malay-Muslims as the primary method of inculcating in them praiseworthy character and Islamic identity, both of which would in turn engender holistic religio-nationalistic unity as reflected in its slogan, "Malay Consensus, Islam Sovereign." Seeing no contradiction between Malay nation-alism and Islam, ISMA regards Malay unity as a pre-requisite for the successful implementation of an Islamic polity in Malaysia. ISMA's professed agendas are outlined on its official website. They are: forming a distinctive Malay-Muslim mind, strengthening the consensus agenda, defending Islam as national identity, developing family and society, building a new generation, strengthening the economy and entrepreneurship, harnessing civil society, and carrying out of social and welfare activities via its *Ikhlas* (Sincere) Foundation (ISMA, n.d.).

ISMA emphasises a Salafi-centric authenticity of Islamic teachings. This is apparent from the opening verses of its official anthem, "Based on Al-Quran and Sunnah, we unite and foster brotherhood in ISMA ... In the service of the nation,[9] in order to gain God's Pleasure" (ISMA, n.d.). Allegiance to the nation, which in the Malaysian context is taken for granted to refer to the Malay rather than the Malaysian nation, acquires a leading position in the hierarchy of Islamic values that ISMA aims to cultivate in its character-building project towards recovering an *ummatic* identity for the Malays (Abdullah Zaik, 2009). Banking on efficiently distributed social services as its main community outreach programme, in the 2010s, ISMA expanded rapidly in Malay residential neighbourhoods and among Malay student populations at home and abroad, and by 2014 was claiming a membership base of around 20.000 (Shazwan, 2014). In comparison with its more senior Islamist partners, ISMA's appeal is to be found in its wide grassroots network and more down-to-earth image vis-a-vis the intellectually oriented ABIM and elitist-inclined IKRAM.

Under Abdullah Zaik's leadership, ISMA's discourse drifted decidedly towards Malay nativism under the guise of Islamic authenticity and simplicity (Abdullah Zaik, 2012). It was not easy at first for grassroots activists, many of whom are well-educated urbanites and comfortably positioned in middle class professional careers, to be convinced by Abdullah Zaik's insular message.[10] But Abdullah Zaik and his leadership team capitalised on their expansive MB-linked network and continual association with senior MB figures, drawing on high-profile visits to enhance their legitimacy among Islamic-oriented Malay-Muslims. Notwithstanding its international exposure, discursive developments in ISMA were dangerously sliding in the direction of ethnocentrism – a far cry from the great strides made in inter-ethnic relations by the more seasoned Islamists in the larger Muslim civil society. Abdullah Zaik's appeal to the Malays combines issues of purity: "historically, Malay blood has been enmeshed with Islam, their soul mixed with the spirit of Islam" (Abdullah Zaik, 2012, p. 5), and a siege mentality – the belief that Malays must reclaim their dominance that has whittled away due to unfortunate historical accidents and scheming by sinister forces who act in collusion with ungrateful Malay collaborators (Abdullah Zaik, 2012).

According to such a line of thinking, Malay-Muslims have too often been easily swayed by arguments that have effectively compromised what is rightfully theirs as owners of *Tanah Melayu* (Malay land), the original name of Peninsular Malaysia. As far as Abdullah Zaik is concerned, despite the Federal Constitution granting safeguarded citizenship rights to non-Malays upon Malayan independence from the British on 31 August 1957, Malaysia is not only autochthonously but also nomocratically Malay-Muslim for eternity (Abdullah Zaik, 2019). In other words, as the argument goes, it is Malay-Muslims who should determine Malaysia's leadership and future. With such a jaundiced intellectual outlook, it was hardly surprising when Abdullah Zaik stirred controversy in 2014 when he provocatively labelled Malaysian citizens of Chinese and Indian descent not only immigrants (*pendatang*),[11] but also trespassers (*penceroboh*), even though the bulk of them now are second and third generation Malaysians whose citizenships were automatically conferred following independence by virtue of having been born in Malaya (ISMA, 2014a). Abdullah Zaik's incendiary remarks elicited protests from not just non-Muslim Chinese and Indian groups, but even from individual non-Malay Muslims (Ooi, 2014).

As a zealous adherent to the social contract that purportedly regulates the relationship between Malay-Muslims and non-Malays, ISMA was nonetheless unrepentant. From its nation-wide campaign to galvanise Malay-Muslims into realising the importance of the social contract (ISMA, 2014b) to ISMA's constant exposes of the PH government's allegedly misleading *Rahmatan Lil-'Alamin* (Mercy to the Worlds) scheme to project Islam as a religion of unity, ISMA was fairly consistent in claiming that it is the non-Malays' gradual and calculated departure from the social contract that is primarily responsible for the deteriorating state of ethno-religious relations (Farhan, 2019). Chin and Tanasaldy (2019, pp. 969, 974) note UMNO's organic linkages with right-wing Malay-Muslim groups, among them ISMA and the Organisation for the Empowerment of the Indigenous Peoples of Malaysia (PERKASA: *Pertubuhan Pribumi Perkasa Malaysia*), led by Ibrahim Ali, a former UMNO Deputy Minister in the Prime Minister's Department. Reports have also emerged of ISMA financially benefiting from NGO funding initiatives of the BN government under Najib Razak (2009–2018), particularly during the period when son of former top religious bureaucrat, Asyraf Wajdi Dusuki, was Deputy Minister in the Prime Minister's Department (Lim, 2016).

A particularly crucial episode that cemented relations between ISMA and other Malay-centric groups, including UMNO and PAS, was their joint, mammoth rally in Kuala Lumpur against the PH government's plans, as pledged in PH's 2018 general elections manifesto, of ratifying United Nations' International Convention on the Elimination of All Forms of Racial Discrimination (ICERD). Nativist slogans, such as "Malay Rights: Jihad is our Way" (*Hak Melayu: Jihad Jalan Kami*) and "Islam and Malays Owners of This Land" (*Islam dan Melayu Tuan Tanah Ini*), enveloped banners waved during the protest (Hew, 2018). ICERD, the Malay supremacists claim, would end privileges accorded to Malays and indigenous groups as enshrined in Article 153 of the Federal Constitution. The anti-ICERD protest proved to be a forerunner to formal cooperation sealed in September 2019 between two hitherto bitter enemies of Malay politics, UMNO and PAS, which would ultimately lead to the unravelling of PH's fragile coalition at the end of February 2020 (Chin, 2020, pp. 290–291). The various anti-ICERD gatherings also occasionally raised the spectre of violence, as occurred when UMNO President Ahmad Zahid Hamidi issued veiled threats of Malays "run[ning] amok" if Malaysia ended up acceding to ICERD (Bunyan, 2018).

Can ISMA's Non-Violence Be Trusted?

In its public statements, ISMA denies being an "extremist" and "violent" organisation. Such an unrepentant attitude has brought ISMA and other nativist movements into sharp confrontation with such liberal Malay entities as the Group of 25 (G25), a group of former Malay civil servants who have voiced worries over increasing undue interference of Islam in the public realm (Group of 25, 2019). Such allegations reached a pinnacle during PH's 22 months in power (May 2018–February 2020). When ISMA launched a campaign in December 2018 to collect 1 million signatures to petition the Yang diPertuan Agong to have Malaysia declared as "an Islamic state based on its history, culture, constitution and Islamic principles" (Nadirah, 2018), G25 openly opposed it, and was later supported by the ex-servicemen body, National Patriot Association (PATRIOT) (The Sun Daily, 2019).

On the one hand, ISMA has shown its commitment to democratic procedures by contesting seven parliamentary and two state seats in the general elections of 2013. ISMA candidates ran on the ticket of the Pan-Malaysian Islamic Front (BERJASA: *Barisan Jemaah Islamiah SeMalaysia*), a moribund splinter party from PAS which briefly led an UMNO-backed Kelantan state government in the late 1970s, against PAS's wishes. While all ISMA candidates predictably lost, the margins of victories in some constituencies were far from indicating that ISMA was a spent force (Ahmad Fauzi & Hamdan, 2017, pp. 243–247). Such commitment, however, reflected more a strategic adoption of democratic methods than an unyielding devotion to democracy as an ideal. If there were any espousal of democracy on the part of ISMA, it was strictly strategic and conditional.

While it would be too presumptuous to ascribe PH's downfall solely to ISMA's grassroots work with the country's Malay-Muslim base, that ISMA's discourse aligned with that of the Malay extremists plotting a premature end to the PH government is difficult to deny. Uncompromisingly Islamist but conditionally democratic, ISMA has been critical about not only PH's alleged yielding to non-Malay interests but also about PN's sluggishness in implementing whatever Islamist reforms it had pledged to carry out at the beginning of its administration (March 2020–Present) (Ainulilia, 2021). ISMA's presence in civil society, so long as it is able to steadfastly uphold its non-violent disposition, serves the purpose of underscoring Malaysia's democratic credentials under PN. Extremist as it may be, it is precisely ISMA's disavowal of violence that deprives the state of reasons to ban it.

As a matter of praxis, ISMA distances itself from the MB it idolises, insomuch as the latter has seen its non-violent pretensions consistently crumbling through organic linkages with ISIS and Al-Qaeda (Counter Extremism Project, 2019), and its consequent designation as a terrorist organisation by the governments of Egypt, Saudi Arabia and the United Arab Emirates (Nasralla, 2013; Ajbaili, 2014; Reuters Staff, 2014). The decisive moves against MB by various governments have been given religious credence by the leading *ulama* councils of both Sunni-oriented Egypt and politically quietist Wahhabi-Salafi-inclined Saudi Arabia (Abueish, 2020; Zaid, 2020).

Concluding Remarks

Drawing from both documentary and fieldwork evidence, this chapter has analysed the extremist discourse and practice espoused by ISMA, an increasingly influential nativist Malay-Muslim organisation in contemporary Malaysia. Although ISMA itself disowns violence, the extremism foregrounded in ISMA's public presence may result in violence among the disgruntled elements of the Malay-Muslim society within which they operate. It certainly does not help that ISMA continuously refers and defers to authors and movements whom violent Islamists similarly invoke, out of respect or for guidance. In relation to the larger theme of the present volume, the boundaries separating violent and non-violent extremism can easily be blurred when the difference between the two appear to be only a matter of degree and strategy.

ISMA's greatest disservice to Islam is its racialisation of the religion, which historically has been a source of pride as evidence of its Universalist credentials. While ISMA locates its discourse in what it claims is Islam's benign accommodation of nationalism, Islam's coterminous relationship with Malay identity, as uniquely obtains in Malaysia, has led ISMA into espousing ethnocentric discourse, with little regard to the fact that such concepts of racial supremacy could be in contradiction to their avowedly Islamist pretensions. Similarly, ISMA claims that any ethno-religious bias apparent in its struggle merely indicates its steadfast upholding of the Federal Constitution, disregarding the fact that the Federal Constitution is not a *de jure* racialist document. Even Article 153, perennially quoted by Malay supremacists as ultimate proof of the Constitution's safeguarding of the inalienable "special position of the Malays and natives of any of the States of Sabah and Sarawak," actually protects as well "the legitimate interests of other communities in accordance with the provisions of this Article" (Malaysia, 2010, p. 145).

The Constitution is thus not exclusive either in text or spirit, as is often depicted by the nativist extremists. Whereas they see their special privileges as inalienable, racial extremists do not apply the same principle to the non-Malays' citizenship rights, which they perceive as liable to revocation. Such asymmetry being against constitutional norms, ISMA's disposition is deserving of the extremist tag. And while there is no reason to disbelieve ISMA's anti-violence protestations, its desire to emulate and continually be in close association with MB, gives the authorities enough justification to keep close tabs on it. In terms of future research, it will be useful to next investigate how and to what extent ISMA's nativist discourse has penetrated the thinking of mainstream Malay-Muslim society, in particular of the long-time ruling party, UMNO, which, in August 2021, managed to re-capture the position of Prime Minister through its Vice President, Ismail Sabri Yaakob.

Notes

1 The authors would like to acknowledge the *Islam Keseimbangan Acuan Malaysia* (Balanced Islam in the Malaysian Mould) research project under the auspices of the Institute of Ethnic Studies (KITA), Universiti Kebangsaan Malaysia (UKM), Bangi, Selangor, for providing funds (grant no: DCP-2017-012/3) for research leading to this chapter; and the Southeast Asia Regional Centre for Counter-Terrorism (SEARCCT), Ministry of Foreign Affairs, Kuala Lumpur, for hosting the first author as a visiting research fellow (1 October 2020–31 December 2020), during which an early draft of this chapter was written.

2 "Islamist" as used in this chapter is adjectival to Islamism – a political ideology that demands the establishment of a juridical Islamic state governed by the *Shari'a* (Islamic law) in order for practicing Muslims to be able to realize the ideals of Islam as a comprehensive way of life (*din al-hayah*) rather than to Islam as religious faith *per se*, to which the adjective "Islamic" applies. For the application of the two terms in the Malaysian context, see Liow (2009, p. 6).

3 Pertaining to the political ideology of "Salafism", see the next endnote.

4 Salafism refers the puritanical school of thought that insists that Muslims as a matter of principle return to the ways and norms of the *salaf al-salih*, that is, "pious predecessors" who lived within 300 years of the death of the Prophet Muhammad. The origins of Salafi thought is conventionally traced to the unorthodox teachings of the controversial theologian Ibn Taimiyyah (1263–1328), whose paradigm in turn influenced the Nejd-based revivalist Muhammad ibn Abd Al-Wahhab (1703–1792), from whose name we derive his eponymous puritanical stream that collaborated with tribal leader Muhammad ibn Saud (1710–1765) in founding three Saudi states run on Wahhabi religious principles. Marrying both currents as Wahhabi-Salafism differentiates it from other Salafi strains such as the Egyptian-based Al-Manar reformist circle pioneered by Jamal Al-Din Al-Afghani (1838–1897), Muhammad Abduh (1849–1905) and Rashid Rida (1865–1935).

5 First author's experience as consultant expert to advise Malaysia's Home Ministry on terrorism cases investigated under the Security Offences (Special Measures) Act (SOSMA) 2012.

6 Mahathir Mohamad (1925–present day), was Prime Minister of Malaysia twice. First, as chairman of the National Front (BN: *Barisan Nasional*) coalition and President of the United Malays National Organisation (UMNO), he was Malaysia's fourth Prime Minister from 1981 until 2003. In May 2018, as chairman of the Pact of Hope (PH: *Pakatan Harapan*) coalition that beat BN in the 14th General Elections, Mahathir became Malaysia's seventh Prime Minister. His second stint lasted until February 2020, when he resigned after losing support from his Malaysian United Indigenous Party (PPBM: *Parti Pribumi Bersatu Malaysia*) that subsequently left PH.

7 Telephone interview with Selangor state assemblyman for Hulu Kelang representing AMANAH, Saari Sungib (1957–Present), on 6 June 2021. A veteran IRC activist during his student days in the UK, Saari led JIM since its inception (1990–1999), during which he was catapulted to the forefront of Malaysia's human rights and anti-ISA struggle. Detained twice under the ISA, Saari then became a full-time politician, losing in the 2004 general elections but faring better in 2008 as the victorious PAS candidate for Hulu Kelang, a seat which he has held since.

8 As elaborated by Abdullah Zaik in his keynote address at the Convention on Hasan al-Banna's Thought in Drawing the National Agenda [KOBANNA: *Konvensyen Pemikiran Hasan Al-Banna dalam Melakar Agenda Bangsa*], Sarjana Hall, Universiti Tenaga Nasional (UNITEN), Putrajaya, 30 January 2010, attended in person by the present second author.

9 The Malay word used in the song for "nation," "bangsa," is too often conflated as the meaning of "race," which in the Malaysian context refers to one's ethnic identity, that is, Malay, Chinese, Indian, Iban, Kadazandusun, Eurasian, etc. Hence, when rendered in Malay, the song automatically carries more racially exclusive connotations.

10 Observations gathered by the authors during ethnographic fieldwork conducted among ISMA rank-and-file members.

11 Among Malay supremacists, condescendingly ridiculing non-Malays as *pendatang* or *orang asing*, that is, foreigners in the same mold as illegal migrant workers (PATI: *pendatang asing tanpa izin*) have become common parlance in daily conversations and over social media – a practice sanctioned by even some UMNO politicians. In September 2008, for instance, UMNO Bukit Bendera division chief, Ahmad Ismail, warned against the *pendatang* Chinese wanting political control in addition to their already dominant economic clout, causing a furore and resulting in his party membership being suspended for three years. See Agence France-Presse (2008).

References

Abdullah Zaik, A.R. (2009, August 13). Perutusan Hari Kemerdekaan ke-52 [The 52nd Independence Day Message]. *Perjalananku* [My Journey]. Retrieved from: https://ustabdullahzaik.wordpress.com/2009/08/13/perutusan-hari-kemerdekaan-ke-52/

Abdullah Zaik, A.R. (2010, January 30). Keynote address at the Convention on Hasan al-Banna's Thought in Drawing the National Agenda [KOBANNA: *Konvensyen Pemikiran Hasan Al-Banna dalam Melakar Agenda Bangsa*]. Putrajaya, Malaysia: Universiti Tenaga Nasional (UNITEN).

Abdullah Zaik, A.R. (2012). *30 soal jawab Melayu sepakat Islam berdaulat* [30 questions and answers on Malay Consensus, Islam Sovereign]. Bangi: Media Isma.

Abdullah Zaik, A.R. (2019, August 18). Melayu, Islam dan Politik: Wawancara Bersama Abdullah Zaik [Malays, Islam and Politics: Interview with Abdullah Zaik]. *Naratif Malaysia*. Retrieved from: https://naratifmalaysia.com/2019/08/18/melayu-islam-dan-politik-wawancara-bersama-abdullah-zaik/

Abueish, T. (2020, November 11). Muslim Brotherhood is a terrorist group: Saudi Arabia's Council of Senior Scholars. *Al Arabiya English*. Retrieved from: https://english.alarabiya.net/en/News/gulf/2020/11/11/Muslim-Brotherhood-is-a-terrorist-group-Saudi-Arabia-s-Council-of-Senior-Scholars

Agence France-Presse (2008, September 9). Malaysia faces race row over 'anti-Chinese' comments. *MSN News*. Retrieved from: https://web.archive.org/web/20080917012749/http://news.my.msn.com/regional/article.aspx?cp-documentid=1667156

Ahmad Fauzi, A.H. (2004). The Impact of British Colonialism on Malaysian Islam: An Interpretive Account. *Islam and the Modern Age*, XXXV(2), 21–46.

Ahmad Fauzi, A.H. (2007). Malay Anti-Colonialism in British Malaya: A Re-appraisal of Independence Fighters of Peninsular Malaysia. *Journal of Asian and African Studies*, 42(5), 371–398. doi:10.1177/0021909607081115

Ahmad Fauzi, A.H. (2016). *The Extensive Salafization of Malaysian Islam*. Trends in Southeast Asia monograph series, No. 9. Singapore: ISEAS. doi:10.1355/9789814762526

Ahmad Fauzi, A.H. (2018). The Islamist Factor in Malaysia's Fourteenth General Elections. *The Round Table: The Commonwealth Journal of International Affairs*, 107(6), 683–701. doi:10.1080/00358533.2018.1545937

Ahmad Fauzi, A.H. (2018). Shariaization of Malay-Muslim Identity in Contemporary Malaysia. *Journal of the Malaysian Branch of the Royal Asiatic Society*, 91/2 (315), 49–78. doi: 10.1353/ras.2018.0017

Ahmad Fauzi, A.H. (2020). Islamist Violence in Malaysia: Reflections from the Pre-GWOT Era with Special Reference to the Memali and Al-Mau'nah Cases. In T.B. Chuah (Ed.), *SEARCCT's Selection of Articles 2020* (pp. 5–24). Kuala Lumpur: SEARCCT.

Ahmad Fauzi, A.H. & Muhamad Takiyuddin, I. (2014). Islamist Conservatism and the Demise of Islam Hadhari in Malaysia. *Islam and Christian-Muslim Relations*, 25(2), 159–180. doi:10.1080/09596410.2014.880549

Ahmad Fauzi, A.H. & Hamdan, C.C.M.R. (2015). The Changing Face of Political Islam in Malaysia in the Era of Najib Razak, 2009–2013. *Sojourn: Journal of Social Issues in Southeast Asia*, 30(2), 301–337. doi:10.1355/sj30-2a

Ahmad Fauzi, A.H. & Hamdan, C.C.M.R. (2016). *Middle Eastern Influences on Islamist Organizations in Malaysia: The Cases of ISMA, IRF and HTM*. Trends in Southeast Asia monograph series, No. 2, Singapore: ISEAS. doi:10.1355/9789814695923

Ahmad Fauzi, A.H. & Hamdan, C.C.M.R. (2017). Political Islamists in Electoral Politics. In M.A.M. Sani & U.A.A. Zakuan (Eds.), *Democracy at Work in Malaysia* (pp. 227–255). Sintok: UUM Press.

Ahmad Fauzi, A.H. & Hamdan, C.C.M.R. (2020). Islam and Its Racial Dynamics in Malaysia's 14th General Election. In M.L. Weiss & F.S. Hazis (Eds.), *Towards a New Malaysia? The 2018 Election and its Aftermath* (pp. 149–169). Singapore: NUS Press.

Ainulilia. (2021, June 5). PAS gagal perjuang Islam walau dah jadi kerajaan [PAS fails to stand up for Islam although it has become the government]. *Ismaweb*. Retrieved from: https://ismaweb.net/2021/06/05/1pas-gagal-perjuang-islam-walau-dah-jadi-kerajaan/

Ajbaili, M. (2014, March 7). Saudi: Muslim Brotherhood a terrorist group. *Al Arabiya News*. Retrieved from: https://english.alarabiya.net/en/News/middle-east/2014/03/07/Saudi-Arabia-declares-Muslim-Brotherhood-terrorist-group

Arosoaie, A. & Nawab, M.O. (2017). The Violent Trajectory of Islamisation in Malaysia. In S. Lemiere (Ed.), *Illusions of Democracy: Malaysian Politics and People Volume II* (pp. 161–180). Petaling Jaya: Strategic Information and Research Development Centre.

Azzam, A.A.A. (2013), *Tarbiyah Jihadiyah* [Jihadist Education] (translated by Abdurrahman Al-Qudsi). Solo: Jazera.

Bartlett, J. & Miller, C. (2011). The Edge of Violence: Towards Telling the Difference Between Violent and Non-Violent Radicalization. *Terrorism and Political Violence*, 24(1), 1–21. doi:10.1080/09546553.2011.594923

Bunyan, J. (2018, November 18). Malay-Muslims will 'run amok' if ICERD ratified, Zahid warns. *Malay Mail Online*. Retrieved from: www.malaymail.com/news/malaysia/2018/11/18/malay-muslims-will-run-amok-if-icerd-ratified-zahid-warns/1694534

Chan, N. (2018). The Malaysian "Islamic" State versus the Islamic State (IS): evolving definitions of "terror" in an "Islamising" nation-state. *Critical Studies on Terrorism*, 11(3), 415–437. doi:10.1080/17539153.2018.1447217

Chin, J. (2016). From *Ketuanan Melayu* to *Ketuanan Islam*: UMNO and the Malaysian Chinese. In B. Welsh (Ed.), *The End of UMNO? Essays on Malaysia's Dominant Party* (pp. 171–212). Petaling Jaya: Strategic Information and Research Development Centre.

Chin, J. (2020). Malaysia: the 2020 putsch for Malay Islam Supremacy. *The Round Table*, 109(3), 288–297. doi:10.1080/00358533.2020.1760495

Chin, J. & Tanasaldy, T. (2019). The Ethnic Chinese in Indonesia and Malaysia. *Asian Survey*, 59(6), 959–977. doi:10.1525/as.2019.59.6.959

Counter Extremism Project (2019). *The Muslim Brotherhood's Ties to ISIS and al-Qaeda*, May. New York, London & Berlin: CEP. Retrieved from: www.counterextremism.com/sites/default/files/Muslim%20Brotherhood%20Ties%20to%20ISIS%20and%20AQ_050119.pdf

Dina, M. (2014, May 22). Abdullah Zaik: The man behind Isma. *The Star Online*. Retrieved from: www.thestar.com.my/news/nation/2014/05/22/abdullah-zaik-man-behind-isma/

Faisal, A. (2019, September 25). Polis: Penyerang berparang terpengaruh video dari Timur Tengah [Police: Attacker with cleaver influenced by Middle Eastern videos]. *Malaysiakini*. Retrieved from: www.malaysiakini.com/news/493256

Farhan, U.M.M.F. (2019, September 27). Perpaduan Islam tonggak perpaduan rakyat Malaysia [Islamic Unity the pillar of Malaysians' unity]. *Isma*. Retrieved from: https://isma.org.my/perpaduan-islam-tonggak-perpaduan-rakyat-malaysia/

Farish, N. (2003). Blood, Sweat and Jihad: The Radicalization of the Political Discourse of the Pan-Malaysian Islamic Party (PAS) from 1982 Onwards. *Contemporary Southeast Asia*, 25(2), 200–232. doi:10.1355/CS25-2B

Ghazali, N.F. (2019, September 26). Puteri Umno dakwa penyerang ditembak polis mati syahid [Puteri UMNO claims attacker shot by police died a martyr]. *Malaysiakini*. Retrieved from: www.malaysiakini.com/news/493358

Group of 25 (2019, January 2). ISMA's Campaign to declare Malaysia an Islamic state. *G25 Malaysia*. Retrieved from: www.g25malaysia.org/single-post/2019/01/02/isma-e2-80-99s-campaign-to-declare-malaysia-an-islamic-state

Hazmi, U.D. (2016, June 13). Siapakah ISMA dan IKRAM? [Who are ISMA and IKRAM?]. [Facebook update]. Retrieved from: www.facebook.com/437866903005944/posts/siapakah-isma-dan-ikram-mereka-lahir-daripada-jim-ikuti-sejarah-jim-atau-dikenal/884320248360605/

Hew. W.W. (2018, December 18). Himpunan 812 and a new rivalry in Malay politics. *New Mandala*. Retrieved from www.newmandala.org/himpunan-812-and-a-new-rivalry-in-malay-politics/

Hussin, M. (1990). *Islam and Ethnicity in Malay Politics*. Singapore: Oxford University Press.

ISMA (n.d.). Barisan Jawatan Kuasa Pusat Ikatan Muslimin Malaysia 2019-2023 [ISMA Central Committee Line-Up 2019-2023]. Retrieved from: https://isma.org.my/tentang-isma/

ISMA (2014a, May 6). Kedatangan pendatang Cina bersama penjajah British satu bentuk pencerobohan [Arrivals of Chinese immigrants with the British was a form of trespassing]. [Facebook update]. Retrieved from: www.facebook.com/isma.malaysia/posts/berita-kedatangan-pendatang-cina-bers ama-penjajah-british-satu-bentuk-penceroboh/670421552995590/

ISMA (2014b, December 1). Kepentingan kontrak sosial – Tajuk pertama kempen pendidikan politik ISMA [Importance of the social contract – First topic of ISMA's political education campaign]. [Facebook update]. Retrieved from: www.facebook.com/isma.malaysia/posts/kepentingan-kontrak-sosial-tajuk-pertama-kempen-pendidikan-politik-ismabangi-1-d/765542326816845/

Jomo, K.S. & Ahmad Shabery, C. (1992). Malaysia's Islamic Movements. In J.S. Kahn & F.K.W. Loh (Eds.), *Fragmented Vision: Culture and Politics in Contemporary Malaysia* (pp. 79–106). NSW: Allen & Unwin.

KiniTV (2015, January 7). NGO Melayu: Kami bukan pelampau tapi pejuang Islam [Malay NGOs: We are not extremists but are Islamic strivers] [Video file]. Retrieved from: www.youtube.com/watch?v= -iKP_f8mjc4

Lim, I. (2016, February 13). Deputy minister admits Putrajaya funds Islamic groups, including Isma. *Malay Mail Online*. Retrieved from: www.malaymail.com/news/malaysia/2016/02/13/deputy-minis ter-admits-putrajaya-funds-islamic-groups-including-isma/1060021

Liow, J.C. (2009). *Piety and Politics: Islamism in Contemporary Malaysia*. New York: Oxford University Press.

Loh, F.K.W. (2017). Ethnic diversity and the nation state: from centralization in the age of nationalism to decentralization amidst globalization. *Inter-Asia Cultural Studies*, 18(3), 414–432. doi:10.1080/ 14649373.2017.1346165

Lynch, M. (2010). Islam Divided Between *Salafi-jihad* and the *Ikhwan*. *Studies in Conflict & Terrorism*, 3(6), 467–487. doi:10.1080/10576101003752622

Majul, C.A. (1964). Theories on the Introduction and Expansion of Islam in Malaysia. *Silliman Journal*, XI(4), 335–398.

Malaysia. (2010). *Federal Constitution: Reprint. As at 1 November 2010*. Retrieved from: www.agc.gov.my/ agcportal/uploads/files/Publications/FC/Federal%20Consti%20%28BI%20text%29.pdf

Maszlee, M. (2014). Islamic movement and human rights: Pertubuhan Jamaah Islah Malaysia's involvement in the "Abolish Internal Security Act Movement," 2000–2012. *Intellectual Discourse*, 22(2), 139–165. Retrieved from: https://journals.iium.edu.my/intdiscourse/index.php/id/article/view/609

Maszlee, M. (2017a). From political Islam to democrat Muslim: A case study of Rashid Ghannouchi's influence on ABIM, IKRAM, AMANAH and DAP. *Intellectual Discourse*, 25(1), 21–55. Retrieved from: https://journals.iium.edu.my/intdiscourse/index.php/id/article/view/991

Maszlee, M. (2017b). Rethinking the Role of Islam in Malaysian Politics: A Case Study of Parti Amanah Negara (AMANAH). *Islam and Civilisational Renewal*, 8(4), 457–472. doi: 10.12816/0045694

McGregor, A. (2003). "Jihad and the Rifle Alone": 'Abdullah 'Azzam and the Islamist Revolution. *Journal of Conflict Studies*, 23(2), 92–113. Retrieved from: https://journals.lib.unb.ca/index.php/jcs/article/ view/219/377

Nadirah, H.R. (2018, December 29). Malay group Ikatan Muslimin Malaysia wants Malaysia declared an 'Islamic state.' *The Straits Times*. Retrieved from: www.straitstimes.com/asia/se-asia/malay-group-wants-malaysia-declared-an-islamic-state

Nagata, J.A. (1984). *The Reflowering of Malaysian Islam: Modern Religious Radicals and their Roots*. Vancouver: University of British Columbia Press.

Nasralla, S. (2013, December 26). Egypt designates Muslim Brotherhood as terrorist group. *Reuters*. Retrieved from: www.reuters.com/article/us-egypt-explosion-brotherhood/egypt-designates-mus lim-brotherhood-as-terrorist-group-idUSBRE9BO08H20131225

Norshahril, S. (2018). *The State, Ulama and Islam in Malaysia and Indonesia*. Amsterdam: Amsterdam University Press.

Ooi, K.B. (2006). Bangsa Malaysia: Vision or Spin? In S-H. Saw & K. Kesavapany (Eds.), *Malaysia: Recent Trends and Challenges* (pp. 47–72). Singapore: ISEAS.

Ooi, M. (2014, May 6). Respon kepada Abdullah Zaik – ISMA [Response to Abdullah Zaik – ISMA] [Video file]. Retrieved from: www.youtube.com/watch?v=UrDW-r4tmW0

Poushter, J. (2015, November 17). In nations with significant Muslim populations, much disdain for ISIS. *Pew Research Center*. Retrieved from: www.pewresearch.org/fact-tank/2015/11/17/in-nations-with-significant-muslim-populations-much-disdain-for-isis/

Radhi, S.S.S.M. (2017, July 3). SELAMAT MENYAMBUT ULANGTAHUN KE 20 'ANAK'KU YG DITINGGALKAN [HAPPY 20TH BIRTHDAY ANNIVERSARY MY LOST 'CHILD']. [Facebook update]. Retrieved from: www.facebook.com/syed.m.radhi/posts/10209718143254292

Ramakrishna, K. (2017). The Growth of ISIS Extremism in Southeast Asia: Its Ideological and Cognitive Features—and Possible Policy Responses. *New England Journal of Public Policy*, 29(1), Article 6, 1–22. Retrieved from: https://scholarworks.umb.edu/nejpp/vol29/iss1/6/

Reuters Staff (2014, November 16). UAE lists Muslim Brotherhood as terrorist group. *Reuters*. Retrieved from: www.reuters.com/article/us-emirates-politics-brotherhood/uae-lists-muslim-brotherhood-as-terrorist-group-idUSKCN0IZ0OM20141115

Roy, O. (1994). *The Failure of Political Islam*. Cambridge: Harvard University Press.

Roy, O. (2004). *Globalized Islam: The Search for a New Ummah*. New York: Columbia University Press.

Samuel, T.K. (2018). *Undergraduate Radicalisation in Selected Countries in Southeast Asia: A Comparative Quantitative Analysis on the Perception of Terrorism and Counter-Terrorism among Undergraduates in Indonesia, Malaysia, the Philippines, Singapore and Thailand*, Kuala Lumpur: SEARCCT.

Saravanamuttu, J. (2020). Politics of Reform and the Triumph of Pakatan Harapan: Continuity in Change. In M.L. Weiss & F.S. Hazis (Eds.), *Towards a New Malaysia? The 2018 Election and its Aftermath* (pp. 82–108). Singapore: NUS Press.

Schmid, A. (2014). Violent and Non-Violent Extremism: Two Sides of the Same Coin. *ICCT Research Paper*, The Hague: International Centre for Counter-Terrorism.

Shazwan, M.K. (2014, May 16). In Isma, a portrait of political Islam driven by urban middle-class professionals. *Malay Mail Online*. Retrieved from: www.malaymail.com/news/malaysia/2014/05/16/in-isma-a-portrait-of-political-islam-driven-by-urban-middle-class-professi/669709

The Sun Daily (2019, January 3). Patriot supports G25 against Isma's petition for Islamic state. Retrieved from: www.thesundaily.my/local/patriot-supports-g25-against-isma-s-petition-for-islamic-state-NF337285

Wan Saiful, W.J. (2018). Islamism in Malaysian Politics: The Splintering of the Islamic Party of Malaysia (PAS) and the Spread of Progressive Ideas. *Islam and Civilisational Renewal*, 9(4), 128–153. doi:10.52282/icr.v9i4.98

Weiss, M.L. (2003a). Malaysian NGOs: History, legal framework and characteristics. In M.L. Weiss & S. Hassan (Eds.), *Social Movements in Malaysia: From moral communities to NGOs* (pp. 17–44). London & New York: Routledge Curzon.

Weiss, M.L. (2003b). The Malaysian human rights movement. In Meredith L. Weiss & Saliha Hassan (Eds.), *Social Movements in Malaysia: From moral communities to NGOs* (pp. 140–164), London & New York: Routledge Curzon.

Wiktorowicz, Q. (2005). A Genealogy of Radical Islam. *Studies in Conflict & Terrorism*, 28(2), 75–97. doi:10.1080/10576100590905057

Zaid, A.M. (2020, December 20). Al Azhar decrees prohibition of joining Muslim Brotherhood. *Arab News*. Retrieved from: www.arabnews.com/node/1780221/middle-east

Zakaria, M.F. (2007). *Pengaruh Pemikiran Sayyid Qutb Terhadap Gerakan Islam di Malaysia* [The Influence of Sayyid Qutb's Thoughts on Islamic Movements in Malaysia]. Kuala Lumpur: Jundi Resources.

Zulkifly, A.M. (2011). *From Cairo to Kuala Lumpur: The Influence of the Egyptian Muslim Brotherhood on the Muslim Youth Movement of Malaysia (ABIM)*. Unpublished M.A. (Arab Studies) thesis. Washington, DC: Georgetown University.

10

NON-VIOLENT SALAFIST POLITICAL ENGAGEMENT

Comparing Egypt's Al-Nour Party with Kuwait's Islamic Salafi Alliance

Zana Gulmohamad and Kira Jumet

Introduction

Since the September 11, 2001, terror attacks in the United States (U.S.), scholars have intensified their focus on the relationship between Salafism and violence. Works using labels such as "Salafist-Jihadism" and "militant Salafism" describe violent Islamist extremists (i.e., al-Qaeda; Islamic State) inspired by Salafism or employing Salafist rhetoric to justify their violent approach to achieving their objective of establishing an Islamic state (Bhatt, 2014). It is rare to see Salafists seeking this objective by participating in politics, as participation may signal affirmation of political systems that many Salafists reject based on their opposition to rule by the people rather than rule by their version of God's law (*shari'a*-Islamic law). Many Salafists seek to overthrow the political system or shun politics altogether (McTighe, 2014).

This chapter compares the cases of al-Nour Party in Egypt and the Islamic Salafi Alliance (ISA) in Kuwait to understand why some ideologically extreme Islamist groups have deviated from the norm by supporting existing political processes and participating in government. Given the large number of Salafists who object to political participation, the primary questions posed in this chapter are: (1) Why did ISA and al-Nour choose to participate in the formal political process and (2) What were the effects of political participation on the groups? In order to address these questions, the chapter relies on primary and secondary sources, including interviews and publications in Arabic and English. By examining the groups' doctrines and the political and historical contexts from which they emerged, we identify how and why the two movements adopted non-violent approaches to political participation within the systems of their respective countries.

This study finds that both al-Nour and ISA emerged from Islamic youth movements aiming to reform their societies spiritually through proselytizing, but both groups became political pragmatists, participating in the electoral process and fielding parliamentary candidates in order to maintain the place of Islam in society and the legal system. Al-Nour was established in 2011 as the political branch of the movement *al-Dawa al-Salafiya* (The Salafi Call) despite the latter's history of opposing formal political participation, owing to the group's competition with the Muslim Brotherhood (MB) and its desire to have a say in the post-Uprising political arena.

DOI: 10.4324/9781003032793-13

Al-Nour's subsequent participation in the 2013 coup d'état against Mohamed Morsi and its continued support of the Abdel Fattah el-Sisi government were founded on its ongoing antagonistic relationship with the MB and aim to promote Islam's status in the political system, as well as the need for political survival, given that most other Islamist groups had been outlawed or targeted by the state. However, the alliance with Sisi has made al-Nour unpopular with Islamists of all stripes, as well as with secularists, and eroded its support.

In Kuwait, ISA has had a presence since 1981 and was reorganized and formally established in 1991 (al-Daboli, 2018). It engaged in politics as an unofficial political wing of *Jamaiat Ihya at-Turath al-Islami* (the Society for the Revival of the Islamic Heritage – RIHS) to promote its ultra-conservative, purist Salafist agenda, demonstrate its support for the ruling family, and act as a competitor to the Kuwaiti MB. Similar to al-Nour's situation in Egypt, ISA's affiliation with the regime has led to the group's decline. This study argues that Kuwait's ISA and Egypt's al-Nour Party have chosen a similar route to promote their approach to Islam within the government and legal system and to counter their MB competitors. Both the Egyptian and Kuwaiti regimes have used the Salafist groups as counterweights to the MB in their respective countries; at the same time, al-Nour and ISA use their ties with the regimes in order to pursue their interests and agendas.

There is a dearth of comparative research on non-violent Salafists and their involvement in politics. The chapter contributes to the literature by: comparing the political and electoral participation of two non-violent Salafist groups, in Egypt and Kuwait; explaining how the understudied Salafist groups al-Nour and ISA adapted their purist approach to the political realities of Egyptian and Kuwaiti politics in order to gain a political platform from which to spread their religious messages; identifying the effect of al-Nour and ISA's relationships with their respective regimes on the groups' survival and popularity; and assessing how the Arab Spring impacted the political trajectory of non-violent Salafists in Egypt and Kuwait.

Approaches to Salafism

Salafism may be defined as "a branch of Sunni Islam whose modern-day adherents claim to emulate "the pious predecessors" (*al-salaf al-ṣāliḥ*; often equated with the first three generations of Muslims) as closely and in as many spheres of life as possible" (Wagemakers, 2020, p. 1). Some scholars propose that Salafism is divided into three branches: quietist Salafists, who shun political activism and focus on teaching "pure" Islam; political Salafists, who establish political parties and participate in legislative bodies; and Jihadi-Salafists, who believe in using violence to oust regimes they perceive as apostate (Wagemakers, 2020, p. 1). However, others argue that the line between quietism and political activism is blurred and that many quietists contribute to political discourse, even if they do not engage in political activities (Olidort, 2015, p. 4).

Modern-day Egyptian Salafism can be traced to the groups *Gam'iyya al-Shar'iyya* (Islamic Law Association) and *Ansar al-Sunnah al-Muhammadiyya* (Supporters of Muhammed's Sunnah) (est. 1926); both emphasized the writings of the theologian Ibn Taymiyyah and warned against Muslims' engagement in politics (Gauvain, 2010, p. 810). Egyptian Salafism has also been influenced by the Saudi Arabian approach, based on close ties between Ansar al-Sunnah and the Saudi regime and the import of the ideology by Egyptian guest workers returning from Saudi Arabia in the 1970s and 1980s (Gauvin, 2010, p. 810). Contemporary Egyptian Salafists represent all approaches, from quietists to the politically active al-Nour Party and the Jihadi-Salafist group *Wilayat Sinai* (Islamic State-Sinai Province) (Jumet & Gulmohamad, 2020).

Salafism's emergence in Kuwait at the beginning of the twentieth century was a result of two factors: kinships between Saudi and Kuwaiti tribes and interactions between some Kuwaiti *ulama* (religious scholars) and religious figures within the Saudi ruling family (A'id, 2012; Pall, 2017, p. 172). Influenced by Saudi Salafism and later even more so by Egyptian sheikh Abd al-Rahman Abd al-Khaliq (one of the founders of the activist current), the subsequent growth of Kuwaiti Salafism in the late 1960s and 1970s may be attributed to the decline of Arab nationalism, resulting in a regional Islamic revival; the 1979 Iranian Revolution that emboldened the Kuwaiti MB, leading the ruling family to support the Salafists as a counterweight to the MB; and the movement's financing by influential merchant families who became followers (Pall, 2014, pp. 4–6).

Evolution and Characteristics

There are many parallels between the evolution of Egypt's al-Nour and Kuwait's ISA. Both groups emerged from established Salafist movements (Dawa and RIHS) with the purpose of participating in formal politics. In both countries, Salafism as a non-monolithic movement has been formed through activism, and in both cases the activist approach to Salafism was inspired by Egyptian Salafi, Sheikh Abd al-Khaliq. The ISA and Dawa (prior to al-Nour) were viewed by their respective regimes as safer alternatives to the MB and were thus given greater freedom to operate and expand than their domestic Islamist counterparts. In addition, both Dawa/al-Nour and RIHS have external ties to Gulf States, namely Saudi Arabia. While Dawa and RIHS, along with their political extensions, remain non-violent, critics argue that Dawa's sectarian rhetoric may inspire violence, and RIHS has been accused of funding Islamist violent extremists abroad.

Hizb al-Nour (Party of Light) was established in 2011 as the political party of al-Dawa al-Salafiya, an Egyptian Salafist group founded by Mohamed Ismail el-Moqadem in Alexandria in the 1970s. Dawa emerged out of the 1970s student movement that was dissatisfied with established Islamist groups, such as the MB and *Ansar al-Sunnah* (the group from which el-Moqadem initially gained exposure to Salafism) (Awad, 2014). Students aimed to replace the MB message with a Salafist one while borrowing MB organizational tactics, and their "activist" approach to Salafism was sanctioned by *fatwas* (legal opinions) issued by Egyptian Salafi Sheikh Abd al-Khaliq (Lacroix, 2016, pp. 4–5). Dawa was originally founded under the name "Salafi School" in 1977 by students with ties to *Gama'a al-Islamiyya* (Islamic Group-IG) but in 1982 renamed itself al-Dawa al-Salafiya (Olidort, 2015c).

From its inception, Dawa discouraged political participation and labelled democracy "an apostate form of government" (Awad, 2014). However, the group's position was not a rejection of pursuing governing or organized political work; rather, "the Dawa's core objection was to the balance of power in Egypt, which it believed will never yield success for Islamists in open competition against the secular state" (Awad, 2014). Regarding its relationship with the regime, Dawa was careful not to criticize it publicly. The group's lack of interest in formal politics allowed it to persist with little interference from the state, which viewed Dawa as a benign group that could be used as a counterbalance to the MB and jihadists (Lacroix, 2016, pp. 4–5). Initially, Dawa aimed to spread its Salafi conception of society, not strive for political change. Some early members established themselves as *sheikhs* (preachers) and preached in Alexandrian mosques, with sermons focusing on gender segregation and against the "beliefs and practices of Sufis, Shia, Christians, and liberal Muslims" (Lacroix, 2016, pp. 4–5). The group's mission was to teach "the true word of God" and to prepare "Egypt for its predestined reversion to an Islamic state implementing all of God's laws and punishments" (Awad, 2014).

Setting aside violent clashes in the 1980s between Dawa and MB supporters over the groups' differences (Boehmer & Murphy, 2012, p. 15), Dawa has remained peaceful. Despite Dawa's total rejection of violence, "its sectarian rhetoric and regressive views on basic freedoms—stances the movement refuses to abandon as a principle of faith—has allowed many to make the case that the Dawa foments a polarizing environment that encourages violence against minorities" (Awad, 2014). Dawa and al-Nour have primarily maintained a domestic focus in terms of politics and spreading their version of Islam to the Egyptian public. In 2011, some liberal political parties accused al-Nour of obtaining financing from Gulf countries, allegations the Salafists denied (Shehata, 2011). However, since Sisi's 2013 coup against Morsi, partially sponsored by Gulf states (Werr, 2013), there have been more consistent reports that al-Nour is backed by Saudi Arabia and receives funding from Qatar and Kuwait (McTighe, 2014).

Similar to the case in Egypt, the Kuwaiti Salafist movement was also driven by purist, non-violent youth who aspired to awaken their society to the Salafist approach to Islam (Freer, 2015, p. 6). In January 1981, Salafists further organized under the RIHS, which enjoyed the support of the Kuwaiti state and urbanized elites, in particular the merchant class (Pall, 2017, p. 173). Egyptian Sheikh Abd al-Khaliq, one of RIHS's founders, advocated for Salafists engagement in parliamentary politics as a "necessary evil" to secure their rights and influence the government (McCants, 2012, p. 2). The RIHS eventually evolved into an umbrella organization for other Salafist groups. In particular, *al-Tajammu al-Salafi al-Islami* (Islamic Salafi Alliance/Gathering-ISA), a group that became dominated by *hadar* (urban dwellers of Kuwait City) (Utivk, 2014, p. 19) and advocating purist participation in parliamentary politics, has been closely connected to RIHS since its inception.

The Iraqi invasion of Kuwait in 1991 was a seminal event in the evolution of Kuwaiti Salafism. Differing positions within the movement towards the Kuwaiti government's acceptance of U.S. military support caused a split between purists, who accepted the U.S. intervention, and activists, who rejected the U.S. involvement. The two key figures leading the divide in RIHS were the activist Sheikh Abd al-Khaliq, who opposed the Gulf authorities' close ties with the West and purist Abdullah al-Sabt, who approved of the Kuwaiti government's policies. Al-Sabt accused Abd al-Khaliq of revolting against the ruler and causing disorder (Pall, 2017, p. 176). Ideological and political divides led to the creation of new movements that separated themselves from RIHS and ISA, such as *al-Haraka al-Salafiya* (the Salafi movement-SM) (est. 1996). The Salafi movement founders not only disapproved of government ties to the United States They also perceived RIHS and ISA as being co-opted by the state, exemplified by government appointments for RIHS and ISA leaders in exchange for their support (Freer, 2018, p. 3).

Since the divide in 1991, RIHS has been dominated by purists. The closely linked ISA is principally concerned with advocating the Islamization of society and laws, viewing *shari'a* as the sole legitimate approach to legislation. It also supports gender segregation, mandatory headscarves for women in public, and prohibition of music concerts and alcohol (Freer, 2015, p. 1). There is a pronounced sectarian tendency across Kuwaiti Salafist movements, including ISA, with both purists and activists viewing Shi'a as *Rawafdh* or *Rafidah* (rejectors) (S. al-Fadhli, phone interview, November 28, 2020). The ISA's agenda also includes loyalty to the government and obedience to the Emir, as well as strengthening the power of parliament to ISA's own benefit (Monroe, 2012, p. 413; Pall, 2014, p. 76).

The chief element making up the divide within Kuwaiti Salafism is the position vis-a-vis the state and ruler. The Kuwaiti monarchy's initial support for Salafists stemmed from the threat posed by the 1979 Iranian Revolution. The Revolution was a danger to Kuwait because Ayatollah Ruhollah Khomeini aimed to spread his Islamic Revolution to Shi'a populations in other Gulf states and because it had the potential to embolden other Islamists, even Sunnis such as the Kuwaiti MB, to take power and establish an Islamic regime based on *shari'a* (Pall, 2014, p. 5). In Kuwait, the MB was one of the first Islamist movements to enter politics, mobilizing in the early 1950s and forming the Islamic Guidance Society in 1952 (Brown, 2007, p. 5). In order to minimize the MB's influence in Kuwait, the monarchy first co-opted RIHS in the 1980s and, soon after, supported ISA based on ISA's unthreatening stance toward the monarchies of the Arabian Gulf (Pall, 2014, p.3; A'id, 2012). Since its inception, ISA has had close ties to the ruling family and has used its connections with powerful elites to have a role in the government. Both ISA's previous leader, prominent Salafi figure Khaled al-Sultan Bin Essa, and its current head, Dr. Ali al-A'mir, have held government positions. Whereas ISA views this relationship as a means to secure its nonpolitical goals, activist Salafist groups recognize it as a tactic to sideline the threatening opposition.

Although ISA's activities are principally domestically focused, RIHS has more transnational connections. In addition to raising funds from the Saudi religious establishment, RIHS also has ties to Salafists in North Lebanon and South Asia. The main slogan of RIHS, *Da'wa w Waa'the w Irshad* (call, preach and guidance), articulates its agenda; according to its public program, these three principles are pursued not only in Kuwaiti domestic affairs but also across the Muslim world (Medad Center, 2020). Traditionally, RIHS has been viewed as a charitable nongovernmental organization with a transnational presence and finance networks that promote Salafism globally. However, its ties with violent Salafist entities in Afghanistan and Pakistan have been scrutinized by western governments (Gartensein-Ross and Zelin, 2013), and in 2008 the U.S. Department of the Treasury placed all branches of RIHS on its Terrorism and Illicit Finance list for funding al-Qaeda (U.S. Department of the Treasury, 2021). Despite ISA's affiliation with RIHS, ISA has not been designated as a financer of terrorism.

The "Arab Spring" and its Aftermath

The 2011 so-called Arab Spring was a big turning point for Dawa/al-Nour and ISA. Al-Nour and ISA's choice to align with their regimes placed the groups at odds with secularists and reformists, while reducing their appeal to other Islamists. Both groups had histories of competition with the MB in their countries, and those rivalries came to a head because of conflicting approaches to evolving political events in Egypt and Kuwait. Al-Nour and ISA have been weakened due to their close ties with their respective regimes and, in the case of ISA, the rise of the MB as an alternative Islamist actor to the purist and quietest Salafists. In Egypt, while al-Nour was initially able to eliminate its MB rival, its turn against the MB resulted in a reduction of its own Islamist support.

In January 2011, Egyptian citizens, angered by corruption, police brutality, and the poor state of the economy, took to the streets. The January 25th protests lasted 18 days, resulting in the ouster of President Hosni Mubarak and a government takeover by the military's Supreme Council of the Armed Forces (SCAF), which ruled the country from February 2011 through June 2012. Following the initial 18 days of protest, Dawa established its political wing, al-Nour.

al-Nour's foray into politics eventually led to conflict with the MB that escalated to its participation in a coup against President Morsi, led by then head of SCAF Sisi. Both Sisi and al-Nour benefited from the Salafist party's role in the coup, Sisi using the group to demonstrate Islamist support for Morsi's removal and the coup presenting al-Nour with an opportunity to eliminate its rival. Following the coup, al-Nour continued to cite the need to protect the role of Islam in the constitution to justify its participation in politics and also altered its message to include Sisi's counterterror and stability platform. al-Nour's affiliation with the Sisi regime caused its popularity to decline with fellow Islamists, including other Salafists, and by supporting a regime that outlawed the MB and targeted other Islamists, al-Nour became beholden to Sisi for its survival.

Although Kuwait's first protests in February 2011 related to the citizenship status of Bidun (stateless people, primarily Bedouin) (Al Jazeera, 2011), similar to the Egyptian case the primary focus of demonstrations that year was corruption. Prime Minister Sheikh Nasser al-Mohamed al-Sabah and some members of parliament had been plagued with accusations of corruption for years, between 2010 and 2011 an opposition that included secular blocs, members of the Kuwaiti MB, and some Salafist groups called for an investigation of the Prime Minister based on accusations of "inappropriate use of public funds" (Freer, 2018, p. 1). On March 8, 2011, 700 people participated in a sit-in calling for the Prime Minister's resignation (Kareem, 2011). The weekly sit-ins near the National Assembly that began in the spring grew in the fall, when banks leaked information on a new bribery scandal (Ghabra, 2014). On November 16, 2011, demonstrators stormed the National Assembly and again called for the Prime Minister's resignation because of corruption (Baker, 2011). The protests comprised a wide political spectrum, including Salafists, and resulted in the resignation of the prime minister and his government as well as multiple dissolutions of parliament between 2011 and 2012 (BBC, 2012).

When anti-corruption protests persisted, prominent figures within RIHS and ISA, along with their followers, divided on the basis of support or opposition to the demonstrations, leading to ISA's domination by conservative loyalists who opposed the protests and the departure of reformists who backed them. Popular support for the ongoing protests and their demands turned Kuwaitis away from ISA and its loyalist agenda, leading to electoral gains by the opposition, ISA's eventual disappearance from the National Assembly, and the strengthening of the Islamic Constitutional Movement (ICM), a political arm of the Kuwaiti MB.

Dawa/al-Nour's Experiment with Politics and Decline

When Egypt's 25th January Uprising began, Dawa's leadership described the protests as *fitna* (chaos/sedition) and discouraged its members from participation, consistent with its policy of political quietism (Lacroix, 2016, p. 6). However, Dawa finally gave its support to the anti-Mubarak movement a few days after the president's ouster, responding to internal dissent and, in particular, pressure from Imad Abd al-Ghaffour, a doctor who had played a key role in the establishment of Dawa in the 1970s and who had been an early advocate of the anti-Mubarak demonstrations. In the wake of the Uprising, Abd al-Ghaffour founded al-Nour as the political arm of Dawa (Lacroix, 2016, p. 6), and by June 2011 al-Nour was the largest officially licensed Salafist party in Egypt (TIMEP, 2015). After over three decades during which Dawa rejected formal politics, al-Ghaffour's explanation for political participation was the group's wish to have a say in the political transition in order to protect Egypt's Islamic identity and uphold Article 2 of the constitution that claimed the principles of *shari'a* as the primary source for legislation. There was also a history of hostility between Dawa and the MB and, according to Awad, "While the rest of Egypt's non-Dawa Salafis looked up to the Brotherhood as more experienced in the realm of politics, the Dawa's suspicions of the group actually motivated it to participate in politics to serve as a counterweight" (Awad, 2014).

Al-Nour's first experiment with political coalition-building evidenced historical animosity between the group and MB and portended future conflicts between them. During the time when SCAF led Egypt's political transition, it decided to hold parliamentary elections before presidential ones (Jumet, 2017, p. 137). In June 2011, 28 political parties, ranging from Islamists to left-wing Nasserists, formed the "Democratic Alliance for Egypt." By late October only 11 parties remained in the alliance. Al-Nour was one of the parties that abandoned the Alliance, citing the strong influence of non-Islamists. However, al-Nour's departure has also been attributed to its realization that it would not top the joint electoral list of the coalition, which was dominated by the Freedom and Justice Party (FJP-the political wing of the MB) (Ahram Online, 2011). In the November 2011–January 2012 parliamentary elections, al-Nour instead partnered with the Building and Development Party (the political wing of IG) and the Salafist *al-Asala* (Authenticity Party) to form the Alliance for Egypt/Islamist Bloc (Ahram Online, 2011). Al-Nour won 111 out of 498 parliamentary seats, placing second to the FJP (TIMEP, 2015). Although Islamists prevailed in the election, al-Nour's objective was to safeguard its particular Salafist interpretation of *shari'a*, not that of the MB. Thus, tensions between al-Nour and the MB persisted in the 2012 presidential elections.

In the first round of the May/June 2012 presidential elections, al-Nour's opposition to the MB led it to endorse former MB Guidance Bureau member and "liberal Islamist" Abdel Moneim Aboul Fotouh (Al-Masry Al-Youm, 2012). Aboul Fotouh had left the MB and been rejected by the FJP, which eventually violated its commitment not to field a candidate when it supported MB Deputy Supreme Guide Khairat el-Shater, and later Morsi, FJP's president, following the disqualification of el-Shater (Fadel, 2012). When the choice in the final round became Morsi vs. Ahmed Shafiq, al-Nour reluctantly backed Morsi, the Islamist candidate (Lacroix, 2016, p. 9). While animosity between al-Nour and the FJP simmered somewhat behind the scenes, the firing of presidential adviser Khaled Alameddine on February 13, 2013 ignited open conflict between the two groups (Mekkawi, 2013). By March 2013, it became evident that the history of antagonism between the Islamist parties could not be overcome (Bayoumi, 2013), and on July 3, 2013, during a televised address by Sisi announcing the removal of Morsi, a representative of al-Nour stood beside him to show support for the coup (Jumet, 2017, p. 196).

Dancing with the Devil

There were positive and negative aspects to al-Nour's involvement in the coup: while the group was able to silence the MB and was the sole Islamist voice in the new political transition, it lost support from its Islamist base and was rejected by secularists. As Sisi strengthened his position over time, it became apparent that al-Nour had made a miscalculation. Although the group was saved from the repression faced by other Islamists, its electoral popularity tanked and it became beholden to Sisi for its survival.

Initially, al-Nour's participation in the coup provided coup leaders protection from accusations that they were anti-Islamist, and the coup leaders rewarded al-Nour for its support with a say in the transitional political process. Al-Nour played a role in selecting the interim prime minister, and Interim President Adly Mansour accorded its membership in the committee responsible for revising the constitution (Bayoumi, 2014). While some Morsi supporters believed al-Nour's presence at Sisi's televised announcement signaled that the coup was not an attack on Islam, many of the party's previous allies denounced its members as traitors, and some secular organizers of the anti-Morsi protests were angered by al-Nour's influence in the choice of interim prime minister (Kirkpatrick, 2013). Despite being caught between a rock and a hard place, al-Nour's participation in the coup was an "opportunity to capitalize on the Brotherhood's loss of support," since al-Nour was the only Islamist group in formal politics still standing (Kirkpatrick, 2013).

Although al-Nour maintained its stance that it aimed to "protect the incorporation of Islamic law in the constitution" (Kirkpatrick, 2013), allying with Sisi entailed aligning its message accordingly. Thus, al-Nour adopted Sisi's security and stability rhetoric, as well as other aspects of his platform; it campaigned for a "yes" vote in the January 2014 constitutional referendum and then supported Sisi in the May 2014 presidential elections. While the party's leaders backed

Sisi, its rank and file demonstrated little enthusiasm for a non-Islamist candidate and turned out in small numbers (Cunnningham, 2014). Despite low turnout in 2014, in 2018, amid a political climate of fear and distrust where al-Nour was struggling to prove its loyalty, the group again backed Sisi's presidential bid. Responding to the regime's concern about turnout, al-Nour bused voters from poor areas to the polls to ensure that its members were seen (Awadalla, 2018).

While al-Nour was able to escape the MB's fate of being outlawed and was able to disassociate itself from violent Jihadi-Salafists through its endorsement of Sisi's counterterrorism program (Olidort, 2015a), its affiliation with the repressive regime caused its popularity to wane. Although al-Nour survived as a political party, the beginning of its decline was evident in its poor performance in the 2015 parliamentary elections, when it won only 12 seats compared to 111 in 2011 (Wilson Center, 2015). In the August 2020 senate elections, al-Nour failed to win any seats (Emam, 2020).

Popular dissatisfaction with Morsi and Islamists contributed to the 2013 coup, and secularists distrusted the Salafist al-Nour Party – despite its participation in Morsi's overthrow. Al-Nour's alliance with the increasingly repressive Sisi regime then caused Islamist supporters to abandon the group. Al-Nour's leadership, essentially standing alone, was left at the mercy of the regime for survival. In 2020, a total of 100 members of the 300-member senate were appointed by Sisi, and al-Nour was forced to rely on Sisi's appointment of two of its members to maintain a presence in the "governing" body (Mikhail, 2020). The benefit to Sisi of appointing al-Nour representatives was that al-Nour's presence in the governing body continued to provide him cover against accusations that he was anti-Islamist or anti-Salafist, but he ensured that no more than two of its members were installed so they could not form a parliamentary bloc (Mikhail, 2020). Even though al-Nour's relationship with the regime has turned out to be more beneficial to Sisi than to the Salafist political party, at this point, al-Nour has "no choice but to support Sisi if it wants to survive in a country where Islamists of other stripes are a political and military target for the army-backed authorities" (Awadalla, 2018).

ISA's Response to Kuwaiti Protests and its Decline

When protests commenced in Kuwait in early 2011, purist Salafists, including those within RIHS and ISA, opposed the uprising, labelling it *fitna* and *Khuruj ala al-hakim* (rebelling against the legitimate ruler) (Mohamadi and Salihi, 2019; Pall, 2017, p. 183). However, as the demonstrations continued a division emerged within the leadership of RIHS and ISA between Salafi conservatives and reformists. The reformists were led by ISA's former leader Bin Essa, who was in favor of the protests, while the conservatives were led by the new leader of ISA, Dr. Ali al-Amir, who opposed the demonstrations (al-Fadhli, phone interview, November 28, 2020). The conservative position won out, and since 2012 Bin Essa has distanced himself from ISA as he uses his position in parliament to advocate for democratic reforms (Dickinson, 2012).

After demonstrators stormed the National Assembly in November 2011, Emir Sheikh Sabah al-Ahmed al-Sabah dissolved parliament in December of that year and scheduled new elections for February 2012 (BBC, 2011). An Islamist-dominated parliament was the outcome of the February election, with the reformists winning the majority of seats in a loose coalition, while ISA captured four seats (Dickinson, 2012; Monroe, p. 410). According to Tavana, "The intensity of the Majority Bloc's criticism of the government prompted the emir to dissolve the National Assembly in June 2012 after only four months in session" (Tavana, 2018, p. 2). The Constitutional Court then reinstated the previous parliament (Das, 2017, p. 199).

The Emir dissolved the Assembly again on October 3, 2012, meaning that a new election would need to be held in December, but still in October he decreed a change to the election law to benefit loyalist tribal groups over ideological political blocs, causing the fragmented opposition to create the *Etilaf al-Mu'ratha* (Opposition Coalition) and boycott the elections (Tavana, 2018, p. 2). Many purist Salafist groups, including the majority of ISA, did not join the coalition or the boycott. The effect of the boycott on the election held on December 1, 2012, was a parliament with 30 independent pro-government members out of the 50 elected (Freer, 2018, p. 2). The ISA and other pro-government groups aimed to assert influence on the state (Al-Atiqi, 2013), or at least have a presence in the political arena. Thus, when a new election was set for July 27, 2013, after the Constitutional Court invalidated the December election based on technicalities in the Emir's election decree, ISA participated in the election. Some members of the opposition continued the December boycott during the July election (Zaccara, 2019, p. 87); the result was an opposition that was fractured and weakened (Al-Atiqi, 2013).

The 2012–2013 opposition boycott contributed to ISA's ability to briefly extend its survival in the National Assembly. However, Kuwaiti citizens' support for reform was evident when an opposition parliament was elected in February 2012, portending ISA's electoral fate later in the decade. On October 16, 2016, the Emir dissolved the National Assembly because of a dispute between parliament and the government over unpopular austerity measures and "delicate regional circumstances and … security challenges" (Al Jazeera, 2016). The elections for a new parliament were held on November 26, 2016 (Al Jazeera, 2016). After years of ISA success in maintaining a presence in the National Assembly, in 2016 it failed to secure seats due to its close ties to the government, as well as accusations that it had abandoned religious purity and was only concerned with its own political interests. In contrast, independent Salafists, led by Waleed Al-Tabtabaie and Mohammad Haif al-Matt'ari, gained four seats in the election (Al-Khalidi, 2016). Independent Kuwaiti Salafists have more ambitious political programs in comparison to ISA, including aims to increase the power of the National Assembly and make the al-Sabah ruling family accountable to parliament (Bokhari and Senzai, 2013, p. 870).

In the 2016 and 2020 National Assembly elections ISA fielded several candidates but failed to secure any seats (BBC Arabic, 2020). Since 2016 there have been several governments, but ISA members have not held positions in any of them. This absence may be partly attributed to ISA's poor performance in the 2016 and 2020 elections. However, ISA still exists and continues to hold regular political bureau meetings at its headquarters. It also aims to return to politics (Hadeeth Al-Balad, 2020). As ISA's relevance has declined, the ICM has maintained its parliamentary success (Al-Qabas, 2016). While Salafists lost ground in the 2020 general election, the ICM won three seats, and MB-leaning factions, in particular *Jama'iat al-Eslah* (The Reform Society), also posted modest gains (Al-Qbra, 2020). The ISA's loss of popularity and absence from government can be ascribed to its loyalist approach, including avoidance of meaningful criticism of the government and ruling family, along with its consistent support for the ruling family amid protests in Kuwait; its pursuance of its own interests while failing to offer a fundamental reform plan in regard to governance; its refusal to join the opposition groups' 2013 boycott that demanded reform; and its ultraconservative sectarian ideology in a heterogeneous society that includes Sunni and Shi'a (al-Fadhli, phone interview, November 28, 2020).

Conclusion

The doctrines of both Dawa/al-Nour and ISA have been shaped by key religious figures in Saudi Arabia. Both groups also began as proselytizing quietist Salafist movements and only later entered politics to promote their version of Islam beyond the social sphere to within the legal system and government. Their ability to flourish was made possible by regimes that viewed them as benign in comparison to their Islamist competitors, and both groups were used by their regimes as counterweights to the MB. At the same time, al-Nour and ISA were able to leverage their affiliations with the Egyptian and Kuwaiti regimes to further their own agendas. As the events of the Arab Spring unfolded, al-Nour and ISA found themselves in opposition to reformists and other Islamists. They remained non-violent because of their purist approach to Salafism and because they allied with the regime rather than opposed it. However, in both cases, the Salafists' relationship with the state led to their downfall, as voters sought alternatives.

While there exists literature that explores various Salafist doctrines and trends (Meijer, 2014; Seidnejad, 2010), more research is needed to investigate engagement in electoral politics and government by non-violent Salafist groups and individuals. Future research might investigate conditions under which Islamists have aligned with their regimes but have not been abandoned by their supporters. Another avenue of inquiry could be the relationship between extremist rhetoric and violence, addressing the academic debate on whether "non-violent" extremists, particularly Islamist extremists, can truly be characterized as non-violent (Vermeulen and Bovenkerk, 2012; Schmid, 2014). The two groups discussed in this chapter are extremist in their religious views but chose non-violent, conciliatory tactics for their political involvement. The question is whether this position is sustainable in terms of long-term relevance or whether such groups are destined to be superseded by more polarized political parties that can generate a higher level of enthusiasm.

References

A'id, B. (2012, May 29). Salafi flight in the state of Kuwait: the real and the future. *Aljazeera Center Studies.*

Ahram Online. (2011, November 18). Democratic Alliance (Freedom and Justice).

Al Jazeera. (2011, February 18). Kuwait's stateless rally for rights. *Al Jazeera.* Retrieved from: https://www.aljazeera.com/news/2011/2/18/kuwaits-stateless-rally-for-rights.

Al Jazeera. (2016, November 27). Kuwait poll: Opposition wins nearly half of parliament. *Al Jazeera.* Retrieved from: https://www.aljazeera.com/news/2016/11/27/kuwait-poll-opposition-wins-nearly-half-of-parliament.

Al-Atiqi, S. (2013, September 12). One Man, One Vote. Washington, D.C.: *Carnegie Endowment for International Peace.* Retrieved from: https://carnegieendowment.org/sada/?fa=52947.

Al-Daboli, M. (2018, May 19). "The Kuwaiti Salafist Gathering" … Between Rise and Decline. *Al-Marjie.* Retrieved from: https://www.almarjie-paris.com/1025.

Al-Khalidi, K. (2016, November 27). Surprises in the Kuwaiti elections: the "Brotherhood" and the youth at the expense of the Salafists and the tribes. *Al-Arabi al-Jadeed.* Retrieved from: https://www.alaraby.co.uk/%D9%85%D9%81%D8%A7%D8%AC%D8%A2%D8%AA-%D8%A7%D9%86%D8%AA%D8%AE%D8%A7%D8%A8%D8%A7%D8%AA-%D8%A7%D9%84%D9%83%D9%88%D9%8A%D8%AA-%22%D8%A7%D9%84%D8%A5%D8%AE%D9%88%D8%A7%D9%86%22-%D9%88%D8%A7%D9%84%D8%B4%D8%A8%D8%A7%D8%A8-%D8%B9%D9%84%D9%89-%D8%AD%D8%B3%D8%A7%D8%A8-%D8%A7%D9%84%D8%B3%D9%84%D9%81%D9%8A%D9%8A%D9%86-%D9%88%D8%A7%D9%84%D9%82%D8%A8%D8%A7%D8%A6%D9%84-0

Al-Masry Al-Youm. (2012, April 28). Nour Party endorses Abouel Fotouh for president. *Egypt Independent.* Retrieved from: https://www.egyptindependent.com/nour-party-endorses-fotouh-president/.

Al-Qabas (2016, December 15). Why did the "Salafist Gathering" fail in the 2016 elections? *Al-Qabas.* Retrieved from: https://www.alqabas.com/article/333960-%D9%84%D9%85%D8%A7%D8%B0%D8%A7-%D9%81%D8%B4%D9%84-%D8%A7%D9%84%D8%AA%D8%AC%D9%85%D8%B9-%D8%A7%D9%84%D8%B3%D9%84%D9%81%D9%8A-%D9%81%D9%8A-%D8%A7%D9%86%D8%AA%D8%AE%D8%A7%D8%A8%D8%A7%D8%AA-20

Al-Qbra, N.S. (2020, December 9). Kuwait and parliamentary elections. *Al-Quds al-Arabi.* Retrieved from: https://www.alquds.co.uk/%D8%A7%D9%84%D9%83%D9%88%D9%8A%D8%AA-%D9%88%D8%A7%D9%84%D8%A7%D9%86%D8%AA%D8%AE%D8%A7%D8%A8%D8%A7%D8%AA-%D8%A7%D9%84%D8%A8%D8%B1%D9%84%D9%85%D8%A7%D9%86%D9%8A%D8%A9/

Awad, M. (2014, August 14). The Salafi Dawa of Alexandria: The Politics of a Religious Movement. Washington, D.C.: *Hudson Institute*. Retrieved from: https://www.hudson.org/research/10463-the-sal afi-dawa-of-alexandria-the-politics-of-a-religious-movement.

Awadalla, N. (2018, March 28). In survival mode, Egypt's last permitted Islamists back Sisi. *Reuters*. Retrieved from: https://www.reuters.com/article/uk-egypt-election-islamists-idUKKBN1H426G.

Baker, A. (2011, November 17). Storming Kuwait's Parliament: What's behind the latest Arab Revolt. *Time*. Retrieved from: https://world.time.com/2011/11/17/storming-kuwaits-parliament-whats-beh ind-the-latest-arab-revolt/.

Bayoumi, A. (2013, March 11). Egypt's Islamists spar as elections loom. *Al Jazeera*. Retrieved from: https://www.aljazeera.com/features/2013/3/11/egypts-islamists-spar-as-elections-loom.

Bayoumi, A. (2014, May 18). Egypt's Salafi party faces growing isolation. *Al Jazeera*. Retrieved from: https://www.aljazeera.com/news/2014/5/18/egypts-salafi-party-faces-growing-isolation.

BBC Arabic (2020, December 6). Safaa Al-Hashem: A discrepancy after the loss of the only female member of the Kuwaiti National Assembly. *BBC Arabic*. Retrieved from: https://www.bbc.com/ara bic/trending-55209359.

BBC. (2011, December 6). Emir of Kuwait dissolves parliament. *BBC*. Retrieved from: https://www.bbc. co.uk/news/world-16053422.

BBC. (2012, December 5). Kuwait Prime Minister Sheikh Jaber al-Sabah reappointed. *BBC*. Retrieved from: https://www.bbc.co.uk/news/world-middle-east-20614987.

Bhatt, C. (2014). The Virtues of Violence: The Salafi-Jihadi Political Universe. *Theory, Culture & Society*, 31(1), 25–48.

Boehmer, D. A., & Murphy, J. P. (2012). *The Politicization of the Egyptian Salafiyya: Principled Participation and Islamist Competition in the Post-Mubarak Era*. Washington, DC: The Elliott School of International Affairs at the George Washington University.

Bokhari, K., Senzai, F. (2013). *Political Islam in the Age of Democratization*. New York: Palgrave Macmillan.

Brown, N. (2007). Pushing toward Party Politics? Kuwait's Islamic constitutional Movement. *Carnegie Endowment for International Peace* (Middle East Center, Democracy and Rule of Law Program-Number 79), 2–20.

Cunnningham, E. (2014, June 1). Egypt's Salafist Nour party in tenuous political alliance with president-elect Sissi. *The Washington Post*. Retrieved from: https://www.washingtonpost.com/world/middle_e ast/egypts-salafist-nour-party-in-tenuous-political-alliance-with-president-elect-sissi/2014/06/01/ aff3a400-e826-11e3-8f90-73e071f3d637_story.html.

Das, H. J. (2017). National Assembly Elections in Kuwait, 2016. *Contemporary Review of the Middle East*, 4(2), 193–210.

Dickinson, E. (2012, July 29). Elections in Kuwait raise real prospect of reforms. *The National*. Retrieved from: https://www.thenationalnews.com/world/mena/elections-in-kuwait-raise-real-prospect-of-reforms-1.438435.

DW Arabic (2013, March 4). The establishment of the "coalition of the opposition" in Kuwait. *DW Arabic*. Retrieved from: https://www.dw.com/ar/%D8%AA%D8%A3%D8%B3%D9%8A%D8%B3-%D8%A7%D8%A6%D8%AA%D9%84%D8%A7%D9%81-%D8%A7%D9%84%D9%85%D8%B9%D8%A7%D8%B1%D8%B6%D8%A9-%D9%81%D9%8A-%D8%A7%D9%84%D9%83%D9%88%D9%8A%D8%AA/a-16645890

Emam, A. (2020, September 27). Uncertain future for Egypt's Salafists following Senate election defeat. *Al-Monitor*. Retrieved from: https://www.al-monitor.com/originals/2020/09/egypt-salafist-political-parties-lost-senate-elections.html.

Fadel, L. (2012, April 18). Disqualified Egyptian candidate says military rulers don't intend to cede power. *The Washington Post*. Retrieved from: https://www.washingtonpost.com/world/middle_east/egy pts-disqualified-presidential-candidate-says-military-rulers-have-no-intention-of-handing-over-rule/ 2012/04/18/gIQAt95UQT_story.html.

Faramarzi, S. (2012, April 18). Kuwait's Muslim Brotherhood. *Jadaliyya*. Retrieved from: https://www. jadaliyya.com/Details/25656.

Freer, C. (2015). *The Rise of Pragmatic Islamism in Kuwait's Post-Arab Spring Opposition Movement*. Washington, DC: Project on U.S. Relations with the Islamic World at Brookings.

Freer, C.—. (2018, August 8). Kuwait's Post-Arab Spring Islamist Landscape: The End of Ideology? Houston, Texas: *Baker Institute for Public Policy*. Retrived from: https://hdl.handle.net/1911/102789.

Gauvain, R. (2010). Salafism in Modern Egypt: Panacea or Pest? *Political Theology*, 11(6), 802–825.

Ghabra, S. (2014, May 20). Kuwait: At the Crossroads of Change or Political Stagnation. Washington, D.C: *Middle East Institute*. Retrieved from: https://www.mei.edu/publications/kuwait-crossroads-change-or-political-stagnation.

Hadeeth Al-Balad (2020, July 14). Dr. Ali Al-Omair: The position of the Salafi Islamic Gathering is clear from the leaks of Gaddafi's tent, and our approach is to stick to the book and the Sunnah. *YouTube*. Retrieved from: https://www.youtube.com/watch?v=te25ojhWYiA

Herb, M. (2016). The origins of Kuwait's National Assembly. Washington, D.C: *Middle East Center* (Kuwait Program Paper Series 39). 4–26.

Jumet, K. D. (2017). *Contesting the Repressive State: Why Ordinary Egyptians Protested During the Arab Spring*. New York: Oxford University Press.

Jumet, K., & Gulmohamad, Z. (2020). Reframing the Campaign: From Egypt's Ansar Bayt al-Maqdis to Wilayat Sinai, Islamic State's Sinai Province. *Studies in Conflict & Terrorism*. Doi: 10.1080/1057610X.2020.1862737

Kabid, A. (2013, March 3). A coalition of the Kuwaiti opposition calls for reform. *Al Jazeera*. Retrieved from: https://www.aljazeera.net/news/arabic/2013/3/4/%D8%A7%D8%A6%D8%AA%D9%84 %D8%A7%D9%81-%D9%84%D9%85%D8%B9%D8%A7%D8%B1%D8%B6%D8%A9- %D8%A7%D9%84%D9%83%D9%88%D9%8A%D8%AA%D9%8A%D8%A9-%D9%8A%D8%B7 %D8%A7%D9%84%D8%A8

Kareem, M. (2011, June 22). Kuwait's Prime Ministerial Dilemma and the Prospects for Constitutional Monarchy. Washington, D.C.: *Carnegie Endowment for International Peace*. Retreived from: https://carnegieendowment.org/sada/44775.

Kirkpatrick, D. D. (2012, June 14). Blow to Transition as Court Dissolves Egypt's Parliament. *The New York Times*. Retrieved from: https://www.nytimes.com/2012/06/15/world/middleeast/new-political-showdown-in-egypt-as-court-invalidates-parliament.html.

Kirkpatrick, D. D.—. (2013, July 8). Islamist Party Backs Out of Negotiations. *The New York Times*. Retrieved from: https://www.nytimes.com/2013/07/09/world/middleeast/al-nour-party-egypt.html.

Lacroix, S. (2016, November 1). Egypt's Pragmatic Salafists: The Politics of Hizb al-Nour. Washington, D.C.: *Carnegie Endowment for International Peace*.

McTighe, K. (2014, March 26). The Salafi Nour Party In Egypt. Doha, Qatar: *Al Jazeera Centre for Studies*. Retrieved from: https://studies.aljazeera.net/en/reports/2014/03/20143261283362726.html.

Medad Center (2020, October 1). *Guidelines on charities: Society for the Revival of the Islamic Heritage*. International Center For Research Studies. Jeddah, Saudi Arabia: Medad Center. Retrieved from: https://medadcenter.org/#ad-image-6.

Meijer, R. (2014). *Global Salafism: Islam's New Religious Movement*. New York: Oxford University Press.

Mekkawi, N. (2013, August 22). A love, hate relationship: Al-Nour and Egypt's Muslim Brotherhood. *Al Arabiya*. Retrieved from: https://english.alarabiya.net/features/2013/08/22/A-love-hate-relationship-Al-Nour-and-Egypt-s-Muslim-Brotherhood.

Mikhail, G. (2020, October 27). Sisi appoints Salafist party members to Egyptian Senate. *Al-Monitor*. Retrieved from: https://www.al-monitor.com/originals/2020/10/egypt-senate-elections-salafist-nour-party-sisi-appoint.html.

Monroe, S. L. (2012, Summer). Salafis in Parliament: Democratic Attitudes and Party Politics in the Gulf. *The Middle East Journal*, 66(3), 409–424.

Nosova, A. (2015) Kuwaiti Arab spring? In Gerges. F (Eds.), *Contentious Politics in the Middle East: Popular Resistance and Marginalized Activism beyond the Arab Uprisings* (pp. 75–96). New York: Palgrave Macmillan.

Olidort, J. (2015, March 13a). The al-Nour Party: A Salafi Partner in the Fight against Terrorism? Washington, D.C.: *The Washington Institute*. Retrieved from: https://www.washingtoninstitute.org/policy-analysis/al-nour-party-salafi-partner-fight-against-terrorism.

Olidort, J.—. (2015, November 12b). Why are Salafi Islamists contesting Egypt's election? *The Washington Post*. Retrieved from: https://www.washingtonpost.com/news/monkey-cage/wp/2015/11/12/why-are-salafi-islamists-contesting-egypts-election/.

Olidort, J.—. (2015c). *The Politics of "Quietist" Salafism*. Washington, DC: Center for Middle East Policy at Brookings.

Pall, Z. (2014). *Kuwaiti Salafism and its Growing Influence in the Levant*. Washington, DC: Carnegie Endowment for International Peace.

Pall, Z.—. (2017) Salafi dynamics in Kuwait. In Cavatorta F. and Merone F. (Eds.), *Salafism after the Arab Awakening: Contending with People's Power* (pp. 170–188). Oxford: Oxford University Press.

Pall, Z.—. (2020, Spring). The Development and Fragmentation of Kuwait's al-Jama'a al-Salafiyya: Purity over Pragmatism. *The Middle East Journal*, 74(1), 9–29.

Pierret, T. (2018, May 18). *Brothers in Alms: Salafi Financiers and the Syrian Insurgency*. Washington D.C.: Carnegie Endowment for International Peace. Retrieved from: https://carnegieendowment. org/2018/05/18/brothers-in-alms-salafi-financiers-and-syrian-insurgency-pub-76390.

Schmid, Alex P. (2014). *Violent and Non-Violent Extremism: Two Sides of the Same Coin? ICCT Research Paper*. The Hague: International Centre for Counter Terrorism – The Hague. Retrieved from: https:// icct.nl/publication/violent-and-non-violent-extremism-two-sides-of-the-same-coin/.

Seidnejad, S.B. (2010). Salafism in Iraq and Its Impact on the Islamic Republic of Iran. *Strategic Studies Quarterly*, 13 (47), 95–122.

Shehata, S. (2011, November 25). Profile: Egypt's Salafist al-Nour Party. *BBC*. Retrieved from: https:// www.bbc.co.uk/news/world-middle-east-15899539.

Tavana, D. L. (2018, August 7). The Evolution of the Kuwaiti 'Opposition': Electoral Politics after the Arab Spring. Houston, Texas: *Baker Institute for Public Policy*. Retrieved from: https://www.bakerinstit ute.org/research/evolution-kuwaiti-opposition-electoral-politics-after-arab-spring.

TIMEP. (2015, October 16). Nour Party (Hizb al-Nour). Retrieved from: https://timep.org/parliament ary-elections-monitor/al-nour/.

Ulrichsen, K. C. (2013, July 25). Kuwait votes, again. Foreign Policy. Retrieved from: https://foreignpol icy.com/2013/07/25/kuwait-votes-again/.

U.S. Department of the Treasury. (2021, January 10). Key Issues – Protecting Charitable Organizations. Washington, D.C.: U.S. Department of the Treasury. Retrieved from:www.treasury.gov/resou rce-center/terrorist-illicit-finance/Terrorist-Finance-Tracking/Pages/charities_execorder_13224- p.aspx#:~:text=June%2013%2C%202008-,Background%3A%20The%20Revival%20of%20Isla mic%20Heritage%20Society%20(RIHS)%20is,Al%2DItihaad%

Utivk, B. O. (2014). The Ikhwanization of the Salafis: Piety in the Politics of Egypt and Kuwait. *Middle East Critique*, 23(1), 5–27.

Vermeulen, Floris, and Frank Bovenkerk. 2012. *Engaging with Violent Islamic Extremism: Local Policies in Western European Cities*. The Hague: Eleven International Publishing.

Wagemakers, J. (2020). Salafism. In Barton, J (ed). *Oxford Research Encyclopedia of Religion*. Oxford: Oxford University Press. Retrieved from: https://doi.org/10.1093/acrefore/9780199340378.013.255

Werr, P. (2013, July 9). UAE offers Egypt $3 billion support, Saudis $5 billion. *Reuters*.Retrieved from: https://www.reuters.com/article/us-egypt-protests-loan-idUSBRE9680H020130709.

Wilson Center. (2015, December 6). Egypt's Islamists: Weak Presence in Elections. Washington D.C.: *Wilson Center*. Retrieved from: https://www.wilsoncenter.org/article/egypts-islamists-weak- presence-elections.

Zaccara, L. (2019). Kuwait Islamists: From Institutionalized to Informal Opposition. *International Studies Journal*, 15(4), 75–98.

Zelin, A and Daveed G. (2013, February 26). Uncharitable Organization. The Washington Institute for Near East Policy. Washington D.C.: *The Washington Institute*. Retreived from: https://www.washingt oninstitute.org/policy-analysis/uncharitable-organizations.

11

DEBATING ISLAMISM AS AN EXPRESSION OF POLITICAL ISLAM

Milad Dokhanchi

Introduction

The term "Islamism" suffers from lack of clarity particularly in its academic use. There is barely any consensus among scholars on how to define Islamism. This lack of clarity has not only led to certain ambiguity concerning the meaning of Islamism but has also made unclear the differences between various modernist versions of political Islam. For instance, the literature often refers to what took place in the Islamic Revolution in Iran and more puritanical religious oriented movements like the Taliban's and ISIS's as "Islamist"—even though these are unique movements with their own particular histories, ideologies, and ideologues. Hence, the way in which the term Islamism is deployed in academia is problematic, and such deployments fail to encompass the actual differences that exist between various ways in which Islam has activated political actors in the Middle East over the past two centuries.

Employing Michel Foucault's genealogical approach that aims at searching the line of descents but also "the subtle, singular, and sub-individual marks that might possibly intersect" (Foucault, 1984, p. 81) when studying seemingly distinct phenomena, the aim of this chapter is to account for different versions of political Islam, their areas of overlap, and also their distinct histories and theologies. Adopting the genealogical method indicates that Islamism is only *one* among four expressions of political Islam (Dokhanchi, 2021, p. 71). Besides Islamism, there are three other Islamic political orientations: *Salafism*, *Usūlism*, and *neo-Islamism*; the literature, however, often treats them as synonymous, branding them all as "Islamist" and consequently ignoring their areas of divergences, difference of political imaginations, and diversity of activisms. These four different expressions of political Islam may be succinctly defined as in Table 11.1.

This categorization and particularly differentiating Islamism from other expressions of political Islam not only helps resolving the ambiguity concerning Islamism but also clarifies what exactly Islamism refers to and how Islamism varies from movements that seem similar from the outside. Such differentiation by no means, however, indicates absolute isolation of these movements; in fact, as the case of Shariat Sanglaji (1892–1943), an Iranian religious scholar, demonstrates there are areas of overlap, intermingling, and dialectic exchange between these movements. Shariat Sanglaji was a Shi'i scholar who was heavily influenced by Salafi ideology; yet he employed Salafi critique towards folk Shi'ism as a way to modernize Shi'ism. The case of Shariat Sanglaji reveals that despite internal hostilities, unique expressions of political Islam

DOI: 10.4324/9781003032793-14

Table 11.1 Different Islamic political orientations

Salafism: Influenced by Ibn Abdul Wahhāb, Salafism is that expression of political Islam with a more puritanical and fundamentalist reading of the religious texts. Salafism has often emerged in non-modern rural and village settings and has tended to have global aspirations.

Usūlism: As post-Safavid Shi'i clerical authorities, Usūli clerics make scholastic claims for representing the twelfth Imam in the era of occultation, and exercise political power through their influence over a religious population.

Islamism: Influenced by Sayyid Jamāl al-Afghāni, Islamists have tended to emerge in modern metropolitan settings as oppositional movements to both the state and to clerics, and their project consists of making Islam and modernity compatible.

Neo-Islamism: Refers to a situation in which former Islamists have been able to take over the modern state. Neo-Islamists share the ideology of Islamists, yet they believe that through state control it is possible to create a society based on Islamic principles.

Source: Author.

never remained completely apart and they influenced each other both theologically and politically. This chapter will first focus on the debates concerning Islamism; we will demonstrate the ambiguity that exists in the literature concerning the definition of the concept Islamism. In the following step we will account for the way Islamism may be defined once differentiated from *Salafism* and *Usūlism*.

After discussing a brief history of Islamism, *Salafism* and *Usūlism*, I will comment on each expression of political Islam and ways in which every movement is different from the other. In the following step, I will make a case for the intermingle of these movements at the discursive and political level through the case of Shariat Sanglaji. This chapter concludes by outlining the differences between Islamism as a movement and Islamism as s state ideology hence further commenting on the concept: neo-Islamism. Iran will be the major area of focus not only because Iran proved to be a crossroads for various expression of political Islam but also because Iran produced the most significant expression of political Islam, namely the Islamic Revolution/Republic. The Islamic Revolution in Iran (1979) was a prominent political movement not only because it adopted Islam as a political force but also because it came to challenge western powers both as discursive and as geopolitical levels. Furthermore, Iran targeted both Al-Qaeda and ISIS as its main antagonists indicating that there are in fact differences in the political interpretation of Islam among members of Al-Qaeda and those supporting the Iranian Revolution, for instance. By appreciating these differences, one can acknowledge how and why Islam manifests itself differently in modernity and invites scholars to avoid making generalizations about various expressions of Islamic political resurgences.

The Debate on Islamism

Although Islamism is a popular concept in both the academia and the media, there is no common agreement on the definition of the concept. Scholars such as Nikki Keddi and Ali Mirsepassi use the term "Islamism" without seeing the need to provide a definition (Keddie, 1994; Mirsepassi, 2011).[1] In their accounts not only it is assumed that the reader has a clear understanding of the concept but also Islamism is treated as a static phenomenon, or to use Michel Foucault's words, a "ready-made object" (Foucault, 2007, p. 188) without its own history and evolution.[2] In these accounts, the long period between the 19th century and the present time, during which various historical events impacted the nature of Islamism, is often ignored and a single concept is expected to cover and explain the diversity of modern Islamic movements.

Asef Bayat, the theorist of liberal account of post-Islamism, provides a narrow definition of the concept and stresses that in the case of Iran, for instance, central to "Islamism was the establishment of an Islamic state based on *wilayat al-faqih*, or the "supreme rule of jurists" (Bayat, 2013, p. 38).[3] With this state-centred approach, Bayat chooses not to characterize movements such as Fadā'iyān-e Islam—which emerged long before the text *Wilāyat al-Faqih* was compiled—or Marxist-inspired Muslim movements—such as Mojahedin-e Khalq Organization, which never fully complied with Ayatollah Khomeini's doctrine of *wilāyat al-faqih*—as Islamists. In simple terms, Bayat chooses to ignore the long history of political Islam in Iran before the Iranian Revolution and that limits his definition to the moments in which Islamism has adopted state qualities.

Farhang Rajaee, author of *Islamism and Modernism: The Changing Discourse in Iran*, reserves the term for Iranian state violence that occurred between 1989 and 1997, and views Islamism and state radicalism as synonymous (Rajaee, 2007, p. 3). Ali Mirsepassi (2011) echoes Rajaee in his predominantly pejorative deployment of the concept but goes one step further and views Islamism as a phenomenon that has nothing to do with Islam. Instead, he views Islamism as a Third-World nativist intellectual aspiration influenced by Counter Enlightenment Western philosophy (pp. 5–16). To the list one may add Mehdi Mozaffari's widely cited article: "What is Islamism? History and Definition of a Concept," in which the author offers a very broad definition of Islamism and frames Shi'i Ayatollah Khomeini next to Sunni Al-Qaeda members (Mozaffari, 2007, pp. 17–33). There is no need for an exhaustive account of various invocations of the concept in order to illustrate the lack of coherency and consensus as to what exactly defines Islamism. This disparity of opinion, however, is not specific to Islamic studies. In the broader literature, specifically in political science, history, and religion, where political Islam is studied in a global context, one is able to identify the lack of consistency in the way the concept is deployed. This lack of coherency has even encouraged scholars to debate the very utility of the concept.

For instance, in the edited collection *Islamism: Contested Perspectives on Political Islam*, Donald K. Emmerson and Daniel Varisco offer arguments in favour and against using "Islamism" when discussing political Islam. While both scholars take the association, popularized in Western culture, between Islamism and violence for granted, Emmerson highlights the non-violent expressions of Islamism, and Varisco holds that negative connotations associated with Islamism make any attempt to employ the concept in a positive light futile (Emmerson, 2010). Emmerson writes in favour of using Islamism, and Varisco takes the opposite perspective. Varisco insists that Islamism still refers to those "conservative Muslims who reject Western values," and since "the underlying assumption in contemporary use of the term *Islamism* is that the violent behaviour of certain Muslims is directed against Western targets," scholars must abandon the concept all together (Varisco, 2010, pp. 40–46). Scholarly debates such as these further indicate the absence of consensus not only in the way Islamism should be defined but also on the desirability for its deployment. One must note this debate had taken place in the political atmosphere created by Western media in the post-9/11 period. It was after the attack to the Twin Towers in New York that media outlets such as Fox and CNN began to call Al-Qaeda terrorists Islamists, a term that is still loosely used in reference to ISIS or its supporters, or members of the Taliban or Al-Qaeda who reside in the West (Mozaffari, 2007, p.18).

Despite the disagreements, as reflected in Emmerson and Varisco exchange, there is a common theme in these debates and that is the expectation that a single concept, namely Islamism, should be able to address all versions of political Islam as well as satisfy scholarly and popular linguistic expectations. To provide an example for the problematic nature of such broad theorizations of Islamism, Mehdi Bāzargān (1907–1995), an Iranian engineer educated in the West with a national democratic outlook, and Abu Bakr al-Baghdādi, the self-identified leader of ISIS with a Salafi outlook, are both categorized as "Islamists." Hence, not only is the term Islamism ambiguous in terms of meaning, it is expected to signify all Muslim political movements that are not in fact similar once examined closely and interrogatively.

But how should this problem be resolved? Can the term Islamism remain reserved only for a particular expression of political Islam and not be expected to carry such heavy connotative weight? Can the ambiguity concerning Islamism be resolved? One may state that the unresolved ambiguities concerning the employment of the term "Islamism" in academia largely result from lack of differentiation of various expressions of political Islam. Both Emmerson and Varisco take political Islam and Islamism as synonymous hence failing to acknowledge various expressions of political Islam produced in diverse temporal and local situations. In other words, the attempt to employ a singular concept in reference to all expressions of political Islam has proved very problematic and has prevented scholars from engaging with political Islam with the caution and specificity it deserves. But what are the various manifestations of political Islam that if accounted for and appreciated could lessen the ambiguity concerning Islamism?

Perspectives on Islamism

Oliver Roy, the author of the seminal *The Failure of Political Islam*, has provided clues that may address the problem of confusion concerning the signifier Islamism. He published the book in 1992, hence many violent expressions of political Islam that emerged after 9/11 are not studied in his book. Yet he has provided general outlines that allow one to trace at least three different expressions of political Islam. He understands the politics of the *ulamā* (traditional religious scholars), the Salafists, and Islamists as distinct and these categorizations allow for differentiation of phenomena that may look very similar from the outside (Roy, 1992, p. 46). But what are the differences? Roy stresses that while Islamism aims to bring Islam and modernity together, for the Salafists, modernity remains a "purely external phenomenon" (p. 21). With this outlook, Roy views Islamism as a modernist and yet latently anti-clerical movement; he goes one step further and differentiates between Islamism and Salafism/Wahhābism (p. 87).

Despite his various uses of the word fundamentalism to include oppositional movements, in most contexts Roy reserves fundamentalism to either refer to the *ulamā* or refer to those traditionalists who object to women's participation in public life such as Salafists. Hence, Roy begins by listing various expressions of political Islam and uses the concept of Islamism to describe only *one* of these expressions. For Roy, unlike the *ulamā* and those with Salafi-Wahhābi leanings, Islamists are not fundamentalists, and in their position on women, for instance, Islamists "see women as people, and no longer as mere instruments of pleasure or reproduction" (p. 58). He continues: "Observers have all noted the presence and activism of women in the Islamist movement: recall the demonstrations of armed and veiled women in Iran" (p. 59). With Roy, therefore, one is presented with a rather distinct definition of Islamism from that outlined in the post-9/11 literature. Given the importance of his definition/description, it is worth quoting Roy at length:

> [Islamism] is the product of the modern world. The militants are rarely mullahs; they are young products of modern educational systems and those who are university educated tend to be more scientific than literary… They receive their political education not in religious schools but on college and university campuses where they

rubbed shoulders with militant Marxists, whose concepts they often borrowed... For them taking over the state will allow for the spread of Islam in a society corrupted by Western values and for a simultaneous appropriation of science and technology. They do not advocate a return to what existed before, as do fundamentalists in the strict sense of the word, but a re-appropriation of society and modern technology based on politics. The masses who follow the Islamists are not traditional or traditionalists either; they live with the values of the modern city—consumerism and upward social mobility... they live in a world of movie theaters, café, jeans, video, and sports... [Indeed] the guerrillas of the contemporary Muslim world are city dwellers.

(pp. 3–5)

With this sociological framework, Roy paints a particular picture of Islamism that matches political movements in Iran, Turkey, and Egypt, a picture that hardly has any relevance for movements such as Al-Qāeda or the Taliban, where the platforms of emergence have been in rural and village areas, and where invocations of religion follow puritanical and fundamentalist inclinations (Mandaville, 2014, pp. 307–313). What is common about *jihadi* movements such as Al-Qaeda, the Taliban, and ISIS is the fact that they are followers of Salafi-Wahhābi ideology, while Islamists, in Roy's definition, to a large extent find themselves at odds with proponents of this ideology. To follow Roy and Mandaville, one may refer to this Salafi-Wahhābi strand of political Islam, with its very intense literal interpretation of the faith and which takes root in less-developed areas, as *Salafism* (p. 48). Islamism and Salafism, then, are two different expressions of political Islam with rather distinct origins, but the literature on political Islam often treats the two as synonymous. In fact, Salafism and Islamism emerged as two different responses to modernity.

Islamism vs. Salafism: The Origin

In order to better understand the difference between Islamism and Salafism, one must pay attention to their origins and the two major early reform movements in the Muslim world, Islamic revival (*tajdid*) and Islamic reform (*islāh*), initiated by Mohammad Ibn Abdul-Wahhāb (1703–1792) and Sayyid Jamāl al-Dīn al-Afghānī (1839–1897), respectively (Esposito, 1998, pp. 33–61; Mandaville, 2014, pp. 56–63). Two centuries ago, pondering the predicaments facing Muslim societies, Abdul-Wahhāb preached the necessity of reviving the tradition of the Prophet Mohammad and his close companions (Mandaville, 2014, p. 46). He argued that contemporary Islam had veered off the correct path by means of various innovations (*bid'a*) throughout history (p. 47). He thus concluded that Muslims should purge all non-Islamic influences, particularly mystical, Sufi, and Shi'i practices, from Islam (p. 58).

He also argued for an intense literal reading of the *Qur'an* and maintained that reviving the example of righteous individuals and companions of the Prophet (*salaf*) would rescue Muslim societies from decline (p. 47). Later on, Abdul-Wahhāb formed an alliance with Mohammad Ibn Saud (1710–1765) and with his military support prepared to make Wahhabism the state religion of Arabia (p. 58). Wahhabism was initially a religious doctrine but later turned political and proved inspiring to adherents of a version of political Islam that sought a very puritanical and fundamentalist reading of the religion (p. 58). Similar to Ibn Abdul-Wahhāb, Jamāl al-Afghāni advocated reviving the example of the early companions of the Prophet or the *salaf.* The difference, however, was that Al-Afghānī wanted the *salaf* to be at the service of the present. Al-Afghānī is known as the father of Islamic reformism (*islāh*). It was his desire to reform Islam so that the faith would be compatible with modern civilization (p. 60). A political activist and reformer, Al-Afghāni travelled across the Muslim world and Europe and preached a pan-Islamist, anti-imperialist, and reformist understanding of Islam (Keddi, 1983). Unlike the inclinations of Abdul-Wahhāb, he did not reject modernity as a whole. Instead, he identified certain flaws in modernity, such as a lack of spirituality, and it is here that, according to Abdul-Wahhāb, Islam could enter the scene and ameliorate European modernity (Esposito, 1998, p. 49).

Unlike Ibn Abdul-Wahhāb, strict religious observation was not his primary concern. In fact, there were disputes about the strength of his religious convictions. Al-Afghāni vigorously defended the revival of Islamic philosophy and rationalist deduction of religious teachings known as *ijtihad* (Mandaville, 2014, p. 61). In this respect, Al-Afghāni offered a radically different version and vision of Islam from that of Ibn Abdul-Wahhāb. The contrast between their respective doctrines had major political ramifications and led to distinct expressions of political Islam in the 20th century. The Egyptian heir to Al-Afghani's reformist Islam was Mohammad Abdu (1849–1905), whose ideas went on to inspire Rashid Rida (1865–1935), Ali Abd al-Rāziq (1888–1966), Hassan al-Bannā (1906–1949), and Sayyid Qutb (1906–1966), and gave rise to the movement known as the Muslim Brotherhood in Egypt (Esposito, 1998, p. 50). In Iran, Al-Afghāni proved very influential in orchestrating the Constitutional Revolution (1905–1911). His ideas inspired later intellectuals and activists that sought to bring together modernity, anti-imperialism, and Muslim unity (Keddie, 1983, p. 3). Inspired by Mohammad Abdu, Turkey's Said Nursi (1877–1960) advocated the compatibility of Islam and science, an attempt that paved the way for the rise of a reformist-minded generation that founded the Justice and Development (AKP) party (Mandaville, 2014, p. 164).

In Pakistan, Al-Mawdūdī (1904–1979), the founder of Jama'at-i Islami, embarked on an intellectual project that echoed that of Al-Afghāni and contemplated issues pertaining to Muslim unity, reform, and the social and political relevance of Islam (pp. 80–81). The common feature of all the movements inspired by Al-Afghāni is that their support emerged not from the *ulamā* in traditional religious centres but in major modern metropolitan hubs in the Muslim world. Having in mind Roy's description of Islamism, one may characterize Al-Afghāni as the godfather of Islamism and Ibn Abdul-Wahhāb as the godfather of Salafism. These two figures operated on distinct grounds mainly because their medieval points of reference were different. Ibn Abdul-Wahhāb followed the works of Muslim theologian Ibn-Taymiyya (1263–1328), who was a Hanbali jurist with a staunch anti-Sufi and anti-Shi'i stance, and who advocated traditionalism or hadithism (reliance on *hadith*) (p. 46). Ibn-Taymiyya was a zealous scholar with activist tendencies who issued fatwa (religious ruling) of *jihad* against the infidel Mongols. He also sought to find a *shar'i* base for the state, the aim of which, according to Ann K. S. Lambton, was "the triumph of the word of God and establishment of a society devoted to the service of God" (Lambton, 1981, p. 146).

Sayyid Jamāl al-Dīn al-Afghānī, on the other hand, had training in Islamic philosophy and mysticism, and was influenced by the radical members of the Babi movement in the 19th century (Keddi, 1983, pp. 10–11). Babism was a heretical "Shi'i millenarian movement whose theological ideas and political aspirations can be traced back to the political philosophy of Sheikh Ahmad ... al-Ahsā'i (1703–1791) and even further back to the transcendental philosophy of Mullā Sadrā ... (1571–1640)" (Dabashi, 2008, p.40). Sheikh Ahamd Al-Ahsā'I, almost a century before Al-Afghani, had broken off from the scholastic Shi'i establishment known as *Usūli* Shi'sm and blended *Akhbāri* Shi'ism with Islamic mysticism (Amanat, 1989, p. 48). Therefore, the medieval godfather of Islamism may be identified to be Mullā Sadrā and his transcendental philosophy, particularly since al-Afghānī himself was a reader of Mullā Sadrā's philosophy, while the medieval godfather of Salafism is Ibn-Taymiyya. In his work,

Mullā Sadrā attempted to bring classic western philosophy, eastern mysticism, and Islamic theology under one banner, while Ibn-Taymiyya sought to do exactly the opposite and "purify" Islamic theology from alien influences. It was Mullā Sadrā's intellectual heritage that Al-Afghani as an advocate of his philosophy could rely on in order to bring the intellectual achievements of modernity and Islamic theology together. Such heritage was utterly absent in the case of Salafism hence leading Salafists of various generations to show little interest in reading Islam in resonance with modernity.

Usūlism

Usūlism is a certain expression of political Islam specific to the Shi'i clericalism. In fact, Usūlism is the name of a certain theological methodology that opposes *Akhbārism* for its mere reliance on traditions and for failing to take into account rationalist methodologies. The *Akhbāri-Usūli* rift had a long history in Shi'ism and it once again gained momentum in the18th century upon the victory of *Usūlis* over *Akhbāris* (p. 35). Usūlism was characterized by rationalist tendencies within Shi'ism and framed the Shi'i scholars or the *ulamā* as representatives of the hidden Imam and hence leaders of the Shi'i community (p. 34).

The *Akhbāri* trend questioned Usuli political ambitions and held that the stated traditions or *akhbār* from the Imams would be sufficient for directing religious affairs and hence there was no need for an intermediary between the Imam and the community (p. 35). Al-Ahsā'i's *Akhbāri* inclinations, along with his unconventional invocation of Mullā Sadrāa's philosophy, "invited the troubling wrath of the Usūli clerics, who sensed in him a deeply dangerous threat to their powerful status, cozy arrangements with the Qajars, and vested interest in the status quo," and that eventually led to his excommunication (Dabashi, 2011, p. 178). The followers of Al-Ahsā'i formed the *Shaykhiah* movement, from which emerged the figure of Sayyid Ali Mohammad Shirāzi (1819–1850)—known as the Bab—the founder of the radical Babi movement which questioned both the authority of the Usūli ulamā and the authority of the Qajar kings (Amanat, 1989, p, 48). The radical Babis were close associates of Al-Afghāni, and they did not hesitate to assist Al-Afghāni in his pan-Islamist agenda (Razavi, 2014, p. 11). These associations make Islamism the heir to a blend of Shi'i *Akhbāri* and Shi'i mysticism and philosophy and prove Salafism to be an offspring of Sunni traditionalism.[4]

The third expression of political Islam that Roy implicitly makes reference to is the political role of *ulamā* or the traditional clergy hence: Usūlism. It must be noted, however, that the politicization of the religious clergy in the modern period is a Shi'i phenomenon, and that the kind of clerical activism that one sees in modern Shi'ism did not have a counterpart in the Sunni world (Enayat, 1982, p. 51). Shi'i clerical authority was forged during the Safavid Empire in Iran. While its main task was to help the new dynasty solidify its authority, over time, and specifically in the post-Safavid era, the clergy was able to gain some autonomy from the state. "Financial and geographic independence…; the right to interpretation, even to innovation, on all questions; delegitimization of the state (this was new since the time of Safavids); strong hierarchy and structures: all operated to make the clergy a political force" in the post-Safavid era and into the 19th century (Roy, 1992, p. 171).

The Shi'i clergy that was predominantly part of an Usūli movement in the 19th century became a strong force of protest, the most important example of which was Ayatollah Shirāzi's (1814–1895) fatwa in 1891 that forbade the use of tobacco for as long as the British maintained a monopoly on the commodity. The Usūlis played an active role in the Constitutional Revolution, and since then they have asserted themselves as a powerful force in the Iranian political scene (Dabashi, 2011, p. 264). As early as the beginning of the 20th century, one begins to see debates on discussion of *wilāyat al-faqih*, which speaks to the fact that the Usūli claim for political power was present in public intellectual discourse (Jafariyan, 2012, p. 51). Ayatollah Na'ini (1860–1936) wrote the first treatise on the compatibility of Islam and Constitutionalism, and reasserted Usūli claims for political power in the 20th century (Dabashi, 2011, p. 265).

The main theological drive behind Usūli longing for political power is the claim for representation of the hidden 12th Imam of Shi'ism. Usūlis argue that, in the absence of the hidden Imam, managing the affairs of the Muslim community, including political rule, has been handed over to Shi'i jurist or the *faqih*. Hence, it is incumbent on the part of the Usūli jurist to enforce political rule on behalf of the hidden Imam (Dokhanchi, 2020). One must note, however, that the Islamic Revolution in Iran was "not the revolution of [*Usūli*] ayatollahs, but of … young Islamists of secular origin, who saw in [Ayatollah Khomeini] the synthesis they were seeking between political radicalism and religious conviction," something they were not able to find, for instance, in a figure like Ayatollah Khoei (1899–1992) (Roy, 1992, p. 174). The fact that Usūlis were not the leading influence in the making of the Islamic Revolution must not downplay the political role that the Usūli apparatus played in modern Iranian politics. Ayatollah Hassan Modarres (1870–1937), Abu'l-Qāsem Kāshāni (1882–1962), Sayyid Hossein Boroujerdi (1875–1961), and Mohammad Kāzem Shariatmadāri (1906–1986) are only four examples of religious scholars whose careers took them beyond religious circles.

Emphasizing the political influence of Shi'i Usūli clergy and the fact that their socio-economic background and agenda is distinct from Islamists allows one to recognize Usūlism as the third expression of modern political Islam. One must note that, despite the Usūli reliance on rationalist methodologies particularly in the field of jurisprudence, when it comes to revering traditional readings of Islam, Usūlism tends to have more in common with Salafism than Islamism. Usūli political figures, such as Ayatollah Golpaygāni (1899–1993), often advocated political interventions within modernity but not so much as a way to embrace modern political rule; Islamists such as Ali Shariati (1933–1977), on the other hand, while critiquing capitalist economy and authoritarian states, appreciated the values of freedom and justice advocated in Western school of thoughts such as existentialism and Marxism.

Synergies between Islamism, Salafism, and Usūlism

Differentiating between *Islamism*, *Salafism*, and *Usūlism* does not necessarily mean that these discourses have always remained apart. In fact, it was the fusion of Islamism and Salafism that led to the political expression of the latter's ideology. For instance, as the Egyptian Islamist Sayyid Qutb became more radicalized after enduring brutal torture by Nasser's regime, he distanced himself from social justice issues and began to see the world in the dichotomy of *jāhiliyya* (ignorance) order and a society governed by the *shari'a* (Mandaville, 2014, p. 102).

Peter Mandaville stresses that Sayyid Qutb's radicalization led him to see no middle ground between the two worlds. It was here that the concept of *jihad* was invoked to put an end to a world filled with *jāhiliyya*. In the 1960s, when followers of Qutb went to Saudi Arabia to teach at universities, they produced a fusion of Salafi–Islamist discourse, combining the activist Islam of Al-Afghani with the ideology of Ibn Abdul-Wahhāb (p. 50). In this context, whenever Salafism had the upper hand, the burgeoning of groups like Al-Qaeda and ISIS became inevitable. Meanwhile, whenever Islamism had an upper hand, one sees the rise of recent political parties such as Hizb al-Benna, w'al Tanmia, Hizb Al-Asala, and Hizb al-Watan—all Egyptian parties that became visible in the wake of the 2011 Egypt Revolution (p. 50).

A similar situation applies to the fusion of Islamism and Usūlism, exemplified in the case of Ayatollah Khomeini. He was an *Usūli* by training, yet he was a mystic and had acknowledged the importance of Sayyid Jamāl al-Afghānī's activism (Khomeini, 2000, p. 286). He was also influenced by Ali Shariati, Jalāleddin Farsi, and Jalāl-e Ale-Ahmad (1923–1969), all influential Islamist figures during the course of the Iranian Revolution (Jafariyan, 2012, p. 738). Hence, Khomeini's thought may be viewed as an expression of Islamist-Usūlism. In fact, behind most Usūli figures' political interventions operated a layer of Islamists support, the great example being the tobacco fatwa of Ayatollah Shirazi that came into effect at the invitation of Al-Afghāni.

Salafism and Islamism: The Case of Shariat Sanglaji of Iran

In Sunni Egypt, Mohammad Abdu adopted Al-Afghani's legacy and initiated the Salafiyya movement—not to be confused with Salafism—and paved the path for the rise of Egyptian Islamism (Mandaville, 2014, p. 48). As mentioned previously, the difference between the Salafiyya movement and Salafism was that Abdul Al-Wahhab's Salafism prescribed a return to the *salaf* while rejecting modernity, whereas Mohammad Abdu invoked the *salaf* such that Islam would be "relevant to contemporary social challenges thorough the creative and judicious exercise of reason and human ingenuity" (p. 62). In other words, the Salafiyya movement was Islamist and not a Salafi movement, to follow Roy's distinctions between various expressions of political Islam. Despite this major difference, however, the two movements had one agenda in common, and that was purifying Islam from corruptions, superstitions, and cultural innovations. Islamism advocated cleansing Islam from popular and superstitious elements with a bias towards modern rationality, whereas Salafism advocated the same project with a bias towards strict traditionalism.

This common agenda, albeit motivated by, and implemented in, two entirely different paradigms, at times brought the two projects together, which either made them appear very similar from the outside—hence the confusion of Western scholars about the actual differences between the two—or led the two projects to merge together. An example of this "merger" is Rashid Rida (1865–1935), an Islamic modernist and a devout student of Abdu, who started his intellectual career by attempting to bring modern and Islamic sciences together, but later, after attacks from Egyptian secular forces, Rida adopted a more conservative and literalist approach. "Where Abdu had advocated a general spirit of intellectual rejuvenation inspired by the model of the Prophet's early companions, Rida … [chose] a more constrained normativity based on the Quran and the traditions of the Prophets and his companions." (p. 67). Rida's transition from Islamism to Salafism took place because the impulse of the return to the *salaf* had already taken place in the Sunni world, but Shi'ism was hostile to Salafism due to the fact that one of Salafism's main targets was Shi'i doctrinal beliefs and practices (Mozaffari, 2007, p. 26).

Salafism had framed Shi'i rituals, doctrines, and beliefs as examples of innovations imbued with superstitions that must be eradicated in the process of returning to the model of the *salaf* (Mandaville, 2014, p. 48). This Salafi stance was a direct challenge to Shi'i Usūlis, as they were the main guardians and beneficiaries of popular Shi'ism and it was natural for them not to welcome the Salafi position with open arms. This, however, does not mean that Salafism did not make inroads into Shi'i Iran. With the advent of Islamism and the adoption of rationalist tendencies on the part of Muslim activists in the early 20th century, Iranian Muslim reformists found themselves at odds with Shi'i folk rituals and beliefs perceived as superstition, such as the divine status of the Imams, their intercession, and the return of the soul (Rahnema, 2015, p. 100). Hence, they launched a campaign against *ghuluww*, or exaggerated/extremist Shi'i views, and made an effort at rationalizing Shi'ism (p. 100).

In this process they did not deprive themselves of the work already undertaken by Sunni reformists. An example of a Shi'i reformist scholar who adopted the Sunni Salafi critique of Shi'ism was Shariat Sanglaji (1892–1943), an anti-*ghuluww* preacher who discouraged reliance on hadith attributed to Shi'i Imams and called for sole reliance on the Quran for understanding Islam. He was a champion of fighting supposedly superstitious Shi'i beliefs, and the content of his book, *Tawhid*, evidenced strong similarities with Abdul-Wahhāb's thinking. Sanglaji (1984) wrote:

> One must abandon imitation and close-mindedness and ensure that we do not come to understand the Quran from those interpreters who each followed the agenda of their own sect. These sects all appeared in the second century and each sect interpreted the religion according to their own sectarian doctrine and if we were to follow them, we will sure be led astray. We must adopt the religion not from our ancestors (khalaf) and instead from the salaf; those who existed before the rise of philosophy, Sufism, Ash'ari and Mu'tazili sects, we must learn the religion from them.
>
> *(p. 169).*[5]

Although cast in Salafi terms, the context in which Sanglaji spread his ideas was the modern city, and his followers were among "military and government mid-rank position holders, poets, writers, managers of the press and the educated youth" (p. 174). Salafism was therefore decontextualized in the Iranian context, and its literal anti-superstitious impulse came to serve a modernist agenda and found support among the religious middle class dissatisfied with the traditional clerical readings of Islam. Hence the import of Salafi thought neither served the conservative agenda of Sunni Salafism nor did it enhance the authority of the Shi'i clergy, rather Salafism appeared to serve Islamism. It was, therefore, natural for clerics to condemn Sanglaji, which they did, but as an observer in the 1960s stated, Sanglaji's "endeavor was a timely, socially responsible and conscious Islamic reaction against the danger of European civilization and its thoughts" (Saheboz Zamani, 1966, p. 137). Sanglaji thus offered a middle ground between the secularity of the emerging Iranian intelligentsia and the scholastic tendencies of the Usūli clerics, and this intellectual middle ground formulated the discursive stance of Iranian Islamism for decades to come. Mahmoud Taleghani (1911–1979), Mehdi Bāzargān (1907–1995), Ezatollah Sahābi (1930–2011), and Heidar Ali Qalamdārān (1913–1989), all important figures in the making of Islamist thought and practice, were influenced by Shariat Sanglaji, a fact that not only connects Islamism with Salafism but also shows the process through which Salafi critique of Shi'i folk culture strengthened the Islamists' position when encountering Usuli dogma.

One must mention that Sanglaji was not an Islamist per se, but his reliance on the Quran as the sole authority for deriving knowledge and his independence from the clerical apparatus have encouraged scholars to identify similarities between his reform project and the early Protestant reformism of Martin Luther and Jean Calvin in Europe (Rahnema, 2015, p. 7). Relying on Salafi doctrine, Sanglaji paved the path for the rise of future Islamists who shared little with Salafists when encountering modernity, yet who found common ground with the Salafi stance that some aspects of Shi'i folk culture must be abandoned (Richard, 1988, pp. 159–178). An example of an indirect heir to Shariat's reformist project was the famous Ali Shariati who spoke of Islamic Protestantism two decades later (Rahnema, 2018).

Thus far, we have differentiated between the three expressions of political Islam namely Islamism, Salafism, and Usūlism that were already implicit in Roy's work and only needed further elucidation. We also showed their mode of contact, and the way they challenged and helped each other. There remains a fourth expression of political Islam that proves to be Roy's main blind spot when studying "the failure of political Islam." This expression that may be called *neo-Islamism* helps to differentiate between Islamism as a movement and Islamism as an ideology ruling the modern state.

Neo-Islamism

What remains problematic about Roy's narrative of political Islam is its state-centred approach, and the fact that he assesses the success/failure of Islamism solely based on Islamists' performance in the state apparatus. Roy (1992) charges Islamists with an obsession with the state and adds that the states they have taken over "reflect first and foremost the failure of the Western-style state model, which was imported and commandeered by single parties and patronage networks" (pp. xi, 195).

Roy attentively notices Islamists' performance in charge of the state, but he does not acknowledge the difference between Islamism before and after the state takeover. Clearly there is a distinction between the two assemblages: Islamism as a movement and Islamism as a state apparatus. Islamism as a protest movement/ideology and Islamism as a state/ideology operate as two distinct phenomena, but this fact is barely noticed not only in Roy's work but also in the current literature on Islamism. In the case of Iran, neither Mirsepassi, Rajaee, nor Bayat acknowledge this dichotomy, and they neglect to take the state factor into account when considering Islamism. Even Iranian scholars writing on political Islam share the same blind spot.[6]

French theorists Gilles Deleuze and Felix Guattari believe that once a movement turns into an institution, the institutional logic will prevail and the discourse of the movement will be "appropriated" for institutional objectives (Deleuze & Guattari, 1987, p. 418). Institutions, they argue, are not neutral carriers of ideologies; they embody their own discourse and techniques of governance, and they require the ideology of the movement to conform to the ideology of the institution. To put it simply, Deleuze and Guattari believe that it is not the movement that uses the state as a tool, quite the contrary—it is the state that appropriates the movement for its survival (p. 466).

Having the case of Iran in mind, Sami Zubaida asks, "Is Iran an Islamic State?"; in answering his own question, Zubaida reveals state co-optation of the Islamist movement. He concludes that "the basic process of modernity in socioeconomic and cultural fields, as well as in government, subverts and subordinate Islamization" in Iran (1997, p. 105). In other words, Zubaida realizes that in the post-revolutionary condition, Islamism was appropriated by the modern state. Other than the rhetorical gestures of the state, "the form of organization of the state and its institutions have no particularly Islamic features," and Muslim authorities are "often forced to adapt their policies and discourses to practical considerations" of the modern state (pp. 118, 105).

Adopting Deleuze and Guattari's observation of state capture of social movements may guide researchers to realize that scholars of political Islam have often focused on the "Islam" factor of Muslim states at the expense of completely downplaying the state itself as an "apparatus of capture" (Deleuze and Guattari, 1987, p. 424). In other words, it may very well be that it is not the Islamic aspect of state that makes the Islamic state worthy of attention; rather, the state that has claimed Islam as its ideology must be under scrutiny. As Foucault writes: "Concerning the expression Islamic government, why cast immediate suspicion on the adjective 'Islamic'? The word 'government' suffices in itself to awaken vigilance. No adjective—whether democratic, socialist, liberal or people's—frees it from its obligations" (Foucault, 2005, p. 260). In a series of speeches at the Collège de France, partly informed by the Iranian experience, Foucault pondered the question of the modern state and showed how the implications of biopolitics eventually superseded the modern state regardless of its ideological claims.[7]

Assessing Roy's stance on the "failure" of Islamism against Foucault's outlook, one may state that Islamism was bound to "fail" upon the takeover of the state, even if it did have an alternative vision for the state. In other words, following the Iranian Revolution, Islamism had to conform to the realities of modern governance. What Roy and other scholars such as Mozaffari and Bayat do not take into account is that by framing Islamism as an inherently statist movement, they tend to exclude those Islamist currents with a social and cultural outlook that either resist state take-over or they became the main victim of Islamic state due to their different interpretation of Islam from those ruling the state. For instance, movements such as *Nihzat Azadi* (Freedom Movement) are considered Islamist, yet they were first to be removed from state power in the post-revolutionary Iran. Therefore, before being seized as state ideology, Islamism proved to be a strong cultural force attracting followers from university campuses, encouraging intellectual dialogues, and engaging a variety of actors in non-statist social welfare, but this image of Islamism is often ignored at the expense of highlighting the "horrors" caused by the post-revolutionary state.

This is not, however, to dismiss Roy's position entirely. To be sure, one must acknowledge that there were/are Muslim currents that have shown an "obsession" with the modern state and they continue to view the state as a mere vehicle for social and political change. Further, when critiquing those who have overlooked the modern state's impact on Islamism, one should not disregard the agency of Islam as a discourse for changing the behaviour of the state. Islamist attempts to Islamicize the nation-state may have failed in the long run, but in the short run, a Muslim outlook has left its mark on the way that Muslim nation states have behaved both locally and internationally.[8] The expression of political Islam that explains the search for a Muslim political agenda through the official apparatus of the modern state may be called *Muslim statism* or *neo-Islamism*. The term *neo-Islamism* helps to differentiate between Islamism as a movement and Islamism as the supporting discourse of the modern state.

Neo-Islamists are statist Islamists that find themselves not in opposition to, but in charge of, the modern state. *Neo-Islamists* believe that through Muslim control of the modern state, Islamist ideals will be realized. In other words, neo-Islamism explains the condition in which the biopolitics of the modern state have appropriated Islamism as its ruling ideology. The concept helps explain the politics of post-revolutionary Iran, the AKP in Turkey, and those factions of the Muslim Brotherhood that have taken the statist route.[9] The question that may arise here is whether a similar approach may be adopted regarding Salafism and differentiating between Salafism as a movement and neo-Salafism as an ideology of those Salafists in charge of the modern state. The response is that while Salafists have been able to have relative success in claiming state power, as has been recently the case with the Taliban, Salafism has barely been able to form a sovereign modern state with relative stability and long durability such as the case of Iran. Also, given the theological hostility between Salafi outlook and the core of modern political values such as freedom and pluralism, it is unlikely that Salafist would be able to have much success in forming a modern state, hence, neo-Salafism as the fifth expression of political Islam is unlikely to ever be formed.

It is true that Salafists such as Taliban and ISIS have been able to overcome their political rivals and claim power sporadically, but they have always been in the state of "war" and not being able to create a stable modern state. Therefore, to account for neo-Salafism as another expression of political Islam is nullified given the fact that Salafism as a movement has yet to be turned to a fully functional institution at the state level. One must note that differentiating the four expressions of political Islam by no means indicates that there is only one kind of Islamism or one brand of Salafism. In fact there are Islamisms as there are Salafisms. Similarly, there is not a single Usūlism nor neo-Islamism. Egyptian Islamism has differences with Iranian Islamism and Salafi Talibanism has differences between Salafism of ISIS, for instance. Neo-Islamists too are different in their approach as to how much they must adopt and endorse modern political values and institutions and Usūli rationalists are different in their methods particularly concerning political jurisprudence. Hence, to categorize various expression of political Islam under four main banners does not undermine the plurality and of course the intermingle that exist between these expressions. The categorization outlined in this chapter helps identifying the main borders that exists between various expressions of political Islam yet insisting that each of these expressions is diverse within themselves and they also do not remain completely apart.

Conclusion

Islamism, Salafism, and Usūlism had different points of origins, particularly in their medieval stages of initiation and they continue their antagonism and distinct identities in the modern period. They are also different in their political imaginations; Islamism seeks to complement modern political formations, while Salafism and, to some degree, Usūlism find themselves antithetical to modernity. Theologically speaking, Salafists tend to denounce modernity altogether viewing it as a negative human innovation. Usūlis tend to engage in a very conservative conversation with modernity through reliance on Shi'i rationalist jurisprudential methodologies, yet since their mode of engagement is merely juridical and not philosophical, Usūlism often tends to produce fatwas or political imaginations similar to that of Salafists unless Usūlis forge a merger of some kind with Islamists. The concept of neo-Islamism helps to differentiate between Islamism as an oppositional movement and Islamism as an official state discourse.

This discourse is in fact the discourse of the realities of the modern state that has adopted an Islamic and religious texture. Neo-Islamists are not committed to the Islamists ideals, in fact their main commitments are directed towards apparatuses of security and domination within the modern state and capitalist paradigm. Neo-Islamists may share the ideology of Islamists in their slogans, but ultimately their main concern is managing the biopolitics of the modern state. Therefore, there are four major expressions of political Islam: *Islamism, Salafism, Usūlism,* and *neo-Islamism.* The merit of such categorization is that it helps resolve the ambiguity concerning Islamism; it also makes evident the differences between movements that may appear very similar on the outset but when interrogated internally, divergences make themselves apparent. With these distinctions one may see the difference between Ali Shariati and Al-Baghdādi, Mehdi Bāzargān (1907–1995) and strict Usūli figures such as Ayatollah Golpaygāni and Ayatollah Khomeini before and after the Islamic Revolution. To state it once again, Islamism is not a signifier pointing to all expressions of political Islam; rather it is only *one* among others. Usūlism and neo-Islamism to the side, the mentioned distinctions also make the difference between Islamism and Salafism coherent and help scholars appreciate the ways in which the two movements parted ways not only historically and theologically, though they served each other when viewing Shi'i folk culture as their antagonism.

All expressions of political Islam have operated dialectically with each other; they have maintained distance from each other, yet they have not remained completely apart and have contributed to the development of each other whether through material antagonism or through theological exchange. Hence, when investigating political Islam, one must appreciate the differences that exist between seemingly similar movements and concurrently account for the ways these movements influenced each other through direct and indirect means.

Notes

1 Mirsepassi uses the term Islamism without defining it. He also treats Islamism and political Islam as synonymous. He generally has post-revolutionary Iran in mind when using the concept.

2 Here Foucault expands on his method of historical inquiry. He explains that throughout his work he has refused to take historical objects as given. He instead sets out to search for the origins and the evolution

of objects. Having Foucault's method in mind, one may state that in most academic use of "Islamism" the concept is treated as a given.

3 *Wilāyat al-Faqih* is a political doctrine developed by Shi'i Ayatollah Khomeini that ordains a jurist to take over as the sovereign of the modern state.

4 This is, of course, not to deny the presence of other theological influences on these movements. But there is a case to be made as to how Shi'i and Sunni traditionalist strands were behind two distinct political movements in the Muslim world.

5 Ash'ari and Mu'tazili are two opposing theological schools that flourished between the eighth and tenth centuries.

6 See Hosseinizadeh (2006). Hosseinizadeh expresses no regard for the difference between Islamism as a liberation theology and Islamism as a discourse of state control.

7 See Foucault (2008, p. 118). Here Foucault makes reference to socialism and argues that governing a state involves a series of techniques, and even the socialist state is bound to respect those techniques.

8 In the case of Iran, one identifies the obligation of women to wear a headscarf in public or the exercise of power in presidential and parliamentary elections by the Guardian Council as examples of the ways in which the "Islamic" factor of the state has manifested itself.

9 To be sure, this chapter has reserved the term Islamism for Islamic movements that have yet to become a ruling ideology even though they may aspire to capture state power. The prefix "neo" denotes recentness and similarity with Islamism yet making its difference with Islamism intelligible.

References

Amanat, A. (1989). Resurrection and Renewal, The Making of the Babi Movement in Iran, 1844-1850. London: Cornell University Press.

Bayat, A. (2013). Post-Islamism: The Changing Faces of Political Islam. New York: Oxford University Press.

Dabashi, H. (2008). Islamic Liberation Theology: Resisting the Empire. New York: Routledge.

Dabashi, H. (2011). Shi'ism, A Religion of Protest. London: The Belknap Press of Harvard University Press.

Deleuze, G. & Guattari, F. (1987). A Thousand Plateaus, trans. Brian Massumi. Minneapolis: University of Minnesota Press.

Dokhanchi, M. (2020). "A Genealogy of Velayat-e Faqih." Manchester Journal of Transnational Islamic Law & Practice, 16, 3–34. Retrieved from: www.electronicpublications.org/stuff/781

Dokhanchi, M. (2021). " What Is Iranian Islamism?" Islamic Perspective: Journal of the Islamic Studies and Humanities, 25, 69–109. Retrieved from: https://iranianstudies.org/2021/07/20/islamic-perspective-journal-volume-25-spring-2021-has-been-published-by-lais/

Emmerson, D. (2010). "Inclusive Islamism: The Utility of Diversity." In Richard C. Martin and Abbas Barzegar (Eds.) Islamism: Contested Perspectives on Political Islam (pp. 17–33). Stanford: Stanford University Press. Retrieved from: https://doi.org/10.1515/9780804773355-004

Enayat, H. (1982). Modern Islamic Political Thought. Austin: University of Texas Press.

Esposito, J. (1998). Islam and Politics. Syracuse: Syracuse University Press.

Foucault, M. (1984). "Nietzsche, Genealogy, History." In Paul Rabinow (Ed.) The Foucault Reader (pp.76–100). New York: Pantheon Books. Retrieved from: https://doi.org/10.1515/9781501741913-008

Foucault, M. (2005). "Open Letter to Prime Minister Mehdi Bāzargān." In Janet Afary and Kevin Anderson (Eds.). Foucault and the Iranian Revolution, Gender and the Seduction of Islamism (pp. 259–262). Chicago: University of Chicago Press.

Foucault, M. (2007). Security, Territory, Population. New York: Palgrave Macmillan.

Foucault, M. (2008). Birth of Biopolitics. London: Palgrave Macmillan.

Hosseinizadeh, M. (2006). Islam-e Siyāsi dar Iran [Political Islam in Iran]. Qom: Mofid Publication.

Jafariyan, R. (2012). Jaryānha va Sazmānhāye Mazhabi-Siyasi-e Iran [Religio-Political Currents and Organizationsin Iran]. Tehran: Khāne Ketāb.

Keddie, N. (1983). An Islamic Response to Imperialism: Political and Religious Writings of Sayyid Jamāl al-Dīn al-Afghānī. Oakland: University of California Press.

Keddie, N. (1994). "The Revolt of Islam, 1700 to 1993: Comparative Considerations and Relations to Imperialism." Comparative Studies in Society and History. 36(3), 463–487. Retrieved from:https://doi.org/10.1017/s0010417500019204

Khomeini, R. (2000). Sahifeh-ye Imam [Leaves of illumination: Collection of Imam Khomeini's Writings], 1981–89, Vol. V. Tehran: The Center for Publication of Imam Khomeini's Works.

Lambton, A. (1981). State and Government in Medieval Islam. London: Oxford University Press.

Mandaville, P. (2014). Islam and Politics. London: Routledge.

Mirsepassi, A. (2011). Political Islam, Iran and the Enlightenment. Cambridge: Cambridge University Press.

Mozaffari, M. (2007). "What Is Islamism? History and Definition of a Concept." Totalitarian Movements and Political Religions, 8(1), 17–33. Retrieved from: https://doi.org/10.1080/14690760601121622

Rahnema, A. (2015). Shi'i Reformation in Iran: The Life and Theology of Shari'at Sanglaji. Farnham: Ashgate.

Rahnema, A. (2018). Elahiat va Siasat-e Roshanfekri-e Irani [Theology and Politics of Iranian Enlightenment]. Tehran: Andishe Pouya. Retrieved from: http://akharinkhabar.com/Pages/News.aspx?id=174454

Rajaee, F. (2007). Islamism and Modernism: The Metamorphosis of the Islamic Discourse in Iran. Austin: The University of Texas Press.

Razavi, M. (2014). Tarikh-e Maktum [Hidden History]. Tehran: Pardise Danesh.

Richard, Y. (1988). "Shari'at Sanglagi: A Reformist Theologian of the Rida Shah Period." In Sa'id Amir Arjomand (Ed.), Authority and Political Culture in Shi'ism (pp.159–178). New York: State University of New York Press. Retrieved from: https://doi.org/10.4000/cemoti.455

Roy, O. (1992). The Failure of Political Islam. New York: Columbia University Press.

Saheboz Zamani, M. (1966). Dībācheyi bar Rahbari [An Introduction to Leadership]. Tehran: Atāi Press.

Sanglaji, S. (1984). "Tawhid (date unknown)." In N Chehardehi (Ed.), Wahabbiat va Rish-e-hay-e Aān [Wahhabism and its Roots] (pp.55–86). Tehran: Fathi.

Varisco, D. (2010). "Inventing Islamism: The Violence of Rhetoric," In Richard C. Martin and Abbas Barzegar (Eds.), Islamism: Contested Perspectives on Political Islam (pp. 33–50). Stanford: Stanford University Press. Retrieved from: https://doi.org/10.1515/9780804773355-005

Zubaida, S. (1997). "Is Iran an Islamic State?" In Joel Beinin and Joe Stork (Eds.), Political Islam (pp. 103–109). Los Angeles: University of California Press. Retrieved from: https://doi.org/10.1525/978052 0917583-010

12

ENRAGED BUDDHISM

Violent, Non-violent and "Not-violent" Extremism in Myanmar

Peter Lehr

A Violent Buddhist Mob – is This a Thing?

"A violent Buddhist mob – is this a thing?"[1] For all those who associate Buddhism[2] with peaceful meditation, social-engaged activism and, most importantly, with non-violence, this certainly is a valid question. Indeed, in the case of Burma,[3] if one thinks of the monks taking to the streets during the 2007 Saffron Revolution (explained and discussed below) and again during the current uprising against the Burmese military in Spring 2021, armed only with their alms bowls and chanting the *Metta Sutta* which is about loving kindness,[4] the idea of a violent Buddhist mob seems to be farfetched, or just borderline ludicrous. And yet, a "Buddhist mob", both non-violent and violent, is "a thing" indeed: all one needs to do is to shift attention from the non-violent anti-government protests to the violent anti-Muslim demonstrations in which monks also play a leading role. In this case, however, the *Metta Sutta* has given way to the preaching of hate – a phenomenon better known from religious figures within the three Abrahamic faiths: Judaism, Christianity and Islam.

Using the non-violent Saffron Revolution of 2007 and the violent anti-Muslim protests ongoing since 2012 as case studies, this chapter explores the liminal zone between non-violence and violence in Burmese Buddhism, exploring several interlinked research questions: Why, where and how does non-violence start to give way to violence? How does this grey zone between the "white" of non-violence and the "black" of violence look like? Is there actually a valid distinction between non-violent extremism and violent extremism? To answer these questions, the first part of this chapter will discuss the key terms used, followed by an introduction of Schmid's category of "not-violence" as a liminal zone between non-violence and violence. The second and third parts contain the case studies, that is, the 2007 Saffron Revolution as an example for a non-violent uprising, and the current campaign against the Muslim Rohingya as an example for a violent one. Both case studies focus on the liminal space between violence and non-violence. The role of monks in this liminal space will be of particular interest, to be further explored in the fourth part of the chapter where some general observations will be made. A short outlook will conclude this chapter.

As regards methodology, this chapter should be seen as a case of explanatory research. Although there is a growing body on non-violent extremism on the one hand, and violent extremism on the other, not much research has so far been carried out to illuminate the liminal

DOI: 10.4324/9781003032793-15

spaces between both phenomena: the question of how does one lead to the other still remains unanswered, and the mechanisms behind the relatively new concept of stochastic violence (to be discussed below) remain largely unexplored. By drawing on Schmid's suggestion of an in-between category of not-violent extremism situated between the two much better understood manifestations of violence, this chapter intends to make a small step forward in this regard.

Violence, Non-violence and "Not-violence": Some Definitions

To prepare the grounds for a discussion of non-violent and violent extremism within Theravāda Buddhism,[5] some clarifications are in order regarding the key terms used here. The term *violence* at first glance seems to be a straightforward one. At a second glance, this is not necessarily the case: violence can range from "structural violence" (Galtung, 1969), that is violence woven into the fabric of societies, to physical violence, and even to psychological violence and symbolic violence. Here, Jackman's definition of violence will be applied: "actions that inflict, threaten or cause injury", while pointing out that injuries can be "psychological, sociological, or symbolic, as in the case of religious desecration" (as quoted in Selengut, 2003, p. 9). Including symbolic violence, therefore, allows the inclusion of acts such as the burning of holy books, or the wholesale destruction of religious sites (such as mosques or temples). The category of psychological violence on the other hand can cover incidents in which Buddhist monks refused to accept alms offered by lay people, thus depriving them of an opportunity to make merit – which for devout Buddhists amounts to the same as an excommunication for Catholics.

In the case of *non-violence*, it would be wrong to assume that this "is simply the absence of violence," as Schmid (2014, p. 13) warns. In his view, this is not a satisfactory distinction as there is "a multitude of nuances and meanings, especially in combination with adjectives like physical, psychological, structural, cultural, direct or indirect, criminal, political, non-lethal and lethal". Schmid suggests a third category, situated between violence and non-violence, which he calls *not-violence*. The difference between both is that non-violence is principled and absolute, while not-violence is pragmatic, opportunistic and context-specific. Schmid refers to Mahatma Gandhi's campaign against the British colonial administration as an example, explaining that

> [s]uch non-violence as an activist strategy goes beyond passive, peaceful resistance: it involves an array of direct political actions […] such as hunger-strikes, demonstrations, sit-ins, blockades, acts of civil disobedience and other persuasive and even coercive tactics (such as non-cooperation in the form of strikes) – but all falling short of the use of violence against persons or objects.
>
> *Schmid, 2014, p. 13*

Compared to non-violence, not-violence is neither principled nor absolute, but just a pragmatic and tactical choice "in the sense of 'not-now-violent'" (Schmid, 2014, p. 14).

The term *extremism* is even more problematic: its meaning is contested, and many definitions have been suggested. However, for a discussion of non-violent and violent Buddhist extremism, a detailed definitional essay is not necessary – it is enough to refer to the Latin roots of the term for a working definition. Since "extreme" stems from Latin *extremus* or "utmost", it can be argued that extremists strive to reach their ultimate goals, whatever they are, with utmost zeal and an uncompromising attitude, usually violating "the norms regulating disputes, protest and dissent" (Wilkinson, 2001, p. 14) while doing so. The crucial difference is that while some of them resort to physical violence to achieve their goals, others do not. Thus, those who resort to physical violence can be defined as violent extremists, and those who do not as non-violent extremists. Schmid's additional category of not-violent extremists falls between these two opposites, albeit playing an important role.

Finally, the term *liminality* needs to be defined as well. Liminality, from the Latin term *limen* meaning "threshold", can be seen as "a period and area of ambiguity, a sort of social limbo" (Turner, 1974, p. 57), or as a phase "betwixt and between" when one phase ends and the next has not yet been reached. In this chapter, the liminal space to be explored is the one between non-violent extremism on the one hand, and violent extremism on the other – the not-violent space, as will be argued. All these deliberations beg the question of what this has to do with Buddhism. After all, Buddhism and its philosophy[6] of *ahimsa* or non-violence (lit.: "do no harm") seems to be perfectly geared towards peaceful demonstrations without even a hint of violence, however defined. But whether this is the case or not depends on the nature of *ahimsa*: is it "principled and absolute" and thus intrinsically Gandhian whenever it is used to shore up protests? Or is this *ahimsa* of a more pragmatic and tactical nature, and thus context-specific? Tessa Bartholomeusz explored this question by analysing canonical Buddhist scripture. She comes to an interesting verdict:

> [While] it is clear in the canonical texts that non-violence has priority over violence, the military presence in the texts might suggest that the obligation to be non-violent is not absolute, contrary to the argument of some scholars of Buddhism.
>
> *Bartholomeusz, 2002, p. 47*

She is not alone in arguing that non-violence is not an absolute value within Theravāda Buddhism. Hallisey (1996, pp. 39–42) for example sees non-violence as a *prima facie* duty, that is a duty which is obligatory unless it is overridden by another and more pressing duty. The protection of Buddhism as such, and of a Buddhist society, could qualify as such an overriding duty. As one Burmese Buddhist lay follower quipped: "Buddhism is not a suicidal utopianism" (Lehr, 2019, p. 212). Not only in Burma, but also in the two other leading Theravāda Buddhist countries, Thailand and Sri Lanka,[7] there is near unanimous consensus that although offensive violence is forbidden, Buddhists are allowed to defend themselves either individually or as a society, in particular if and when faced with an implacable enemy bent to destroy Buddhism and take over Buddhist countries (Lehr, 2019). Typical for such views is a comment of Ashin Wirathu, one of the leading militant monks of Burma: "In Buddhism, we are not allowed to go on the offensive […] But we have every right to protect and defend our community" (as quoted in Beech, 2013). In such cases, the duty to observe *ahimsa* is overridden by the duty to protect Buddhism and Buddhists,[8] giving way to the conviction that the end justifies the means – any means, actually.[9]

There is however an important exception to this *prima facie* aspect of violence – and this is violence committed by monks themselves. When it comes to intentional killing of human beings committed by monks themselves, or encouraged by monks, there is no ambiguity at all: the Code of Monastic Discipline (*Bhikkhu Pātimokkha*) for (male)[10] monks lists this as one of the four disrobing offences or *Pārājikas* ("Defeat", lit. "making the doer defeated").[11] These are extreme violations of the monastic code which result in an automatic expulsion from the *sangha* (lit. "company" or "community", here referring to the monastic community) without the chance to "simply re-ordain after a period of grace" (Brahmavamso, 1996). The rule reads as follows:

> Should any *bhikkhu* [monk; PL] intentionally deprive a human being of life, or search for an assassin for him, or praise the advantages of death, or incite him to die (saying,):

"My good man, what use is this evil, miserable life to you? Death would be better for you than life", or with such an idea in mind, such a purpose in mind, should in various ways praise the advantages of death or incite him to die, he also is defeated and no longer in affiliation.

Pārājika 3, Bhikkhu Pātimokkha, translated by Thanissaro Bhikkhu, 2007

Although such transgressions occasionally happen, they are very rare for monks.[12] None of the Burmese monks participating in the demonstrations discussed below so far considered this drastic course of action – not even the most belligerent ones.

If a monk deprives any non-human living being of its life, this is seen as a lesser offence: "Should any *bhikkhu* intentionally deprive an animal of life, this is to be confessed" (Pācittiya 61, Bhikkhu Pātimokkha, translated by Thanissaro Bhikkhu, 2007). Physical violence between monks is covered as well and also seen as a lesser offence: "Should any *bhikkhu*, angered and displeased, give a blow to (another) *bhikkhu*, it is to be confessed" (Pācittiya 74, translated by Thanissaro Bhikkhu, 2007), and "[should] any *bhikkhu*, angered and displeased, raise the palm of his hand against (another) *bhikkhu*, it is to be confessed" (Pācittiya 75, translated by Thanissaro Bhikkhu, 2007). As will be shown, the distinction between human and non-human lives has consequences that the Buddha could not possibly foresee. And with that, it is time now to turn to the two selected Burmese case studies: the Saffron Revolution 2007 and the current campaign against Rohingya Muslims.

Non-violence: Monks and the 2007 Saffron Revolution

The Saffron Revolution[13] commenced on 15 August 2007 as a response to a government decision: without prior warning, the long-running subsidies for fuel had been terminated, resulting in a sudden doubling of the costs for diesel, and a five-fold increase in the price of gas. As Jonathan Head of the BBC reported, "[the] impact was immediate. People could not afford to go to work, and the increased cost of transport started pushing food prices even higher" (Head, 2007). Angered by this ill-advised government decision, thousands of Burmese citizens including took to the streets. When the police moved in to arrest them, something unexpected happened: "the monks – who can accurately measure economic distress by the food put into their begging bowls every morning – took their place" (Head, 2007). In the early stage of the anti-government demonstrations, only few monks were to be seen:

> [A] small network of politically educated monks decided that it was incumbent on them to keep the demonstrations going. They and ordinary monks were acutely aware of the suffering of the people because monks go out daily to receive offerings of food from the laity. More and more people could not properly feed themselves or the monks. This was also upsetting because offering food to monks is the primary form of merit-making in Theravada Buddhism.
>
> *Fink, 2009, p. 355*

When several monks were injured during an attempt of the army to disperse protesters in the town of Pakokku on 5 September by force, the situation rapidly escalated: more and more monks joined the demonstrations, first in their hundreds, then in their thousands (between 30,000 and 50,000, according to Human Rights Watch, 2007, p. 8). At least three reasons prompted them to do so. Arguably, for a substantial number of the monks who joined the protest in its early stages, the government's refusal to apologise for the unwarranted violence against the three Pakokku monks was the main reason. But as the BBC (2007) opines, "for others, it went far beyond that". A comment of U Pannacara, a monk who participated in the protests, supports this.[14] After readily admitting that "monks are not supposed to be politically active", he nevertheless argues that because the military government obviously only cared for itself, somebody had to do something about the swiftly deteriorating situation: "That's us, the monks" (as quoted in Lintner, 2009). After all, the monkhood is one of the three powerful groups in Burma – the other two being the military and the students.

U Pannacara's oblique comment on the swiftly deteriorating situation points at yet another motive, and thus a third reason, behind the monks' decision to join the protests in force: protecting civilians against the military and, in particular, against pro-government vigilantes roaming the streets at night.

Although in September 2007, the *8888 Uprising* against the military take-over starting on 8 August 1988 (hence the name) already was 19 years in the past, it had not been forgotten that thugs in the pay of the government had been unleashed on the population to create chaos and fear, and to provoke citizens into over-reaction, for example by beating to death captured or suspected arsonists and rapists. This was then taken as a pretext by the military to crack down hard, ostentatiously to restore law and order and to prevent Burma from descending into anarchy. Their presence on the streets on behalf of the civilian population, the monks hoped, would prevent a repeat of this brutal crackdown, while also subtly reminding the more hot-blooded demonstrators of the Buddha's message of non-violence. The monks participating in these protests probably assumed that a moderating influence would be possible because monks are greatly respected, or even revered, in the Burmese Buddhist society – hence, nobody would dare to raise their hands against them, not even the military or pro-government thugs.

That monks all over Burma joined the demonstrations was not necessarily a spontaneous occurrence. Rather, it was facilitated by a movement named *All Burma Monks' Alliance* (ABMA), founded on 9 September 2007 as an umbrella organisation of several smaller monastic organisations by a network of politically active monks including charismatic U Gambira[15] (aka U Sandawbartha), arguably one of the "most visible and outspoken young monks leading the demonstrations" (Lintner, 2009, p. 82). ABMA also published some explicitly political demands: firstly, an apology by the state to the monks injured in the Pakokku demonstration; secondly, a reduction of fuel, fuel oil and gas prices; thirdly, the unconditional release of Aung San Suu Kyi as well as any other political prisoners; and fourthly, holding a political dialogue with opposition parties with the aim of starting a national reconciliation process (U Gambira, 2007; U Pyinya Zawta, 2009; Lintner, 2009, p. 64). In their attempt to force the military government to back off, the monks employed a coercive tactic they had already used in the *8888 Uprising*: they "overturned their alms bowls" (*pattam nikujjana kamma*), refusing alms offered to them by anyone associated with the government – quite a powerful weapon, as Matthews points out: "In a society where merit-making is a central responsibility, not being able to give alms to the *sangha* or receive religious instruction and blessing (*dhamma sambawga*) is a serious matter" (Matthews, 1999, p. 39). Indeed, it amounts to an excommunication, and ABMA even published a declaration defending their resort to this powerful coercive instrument in strong terms which concluded as follows:

> The clergy boycotts the evil, sadistic, pitiless, and immensely thieving [i.e. corrupt] military rulers! Excommunication together with rejection of their donations of four material things [rice, medicine, shelter and robes] and abstaining of preaching to them has come into effect!
>
> *as quoted in Human Rights Watch, 2007, p. 35*

Ultimately, their assumptions regarding the reaction of the Burmese military were proved wrong, and the Saffron Revolution was violently crushed (Human Rights Watch, 2007, pp. 43–80), aided by the state-appointed *Sangha Maha Nayaka* committee (a committee of senior monks that regulates the affairs of the Burmese monkhood) which banned monks from taking part in the protests on the one hand, and by pro-government militias, in particular the Union Solidarity Development Association (USDA) and the Swan Arr Shin ("Masters of Force") on the other. Dozens of monasteries were searched,[16] hundreds of monks were forcibly disrobed and sentenced to long prison terms ranging up to 35 years (or even 68 years in U Gambira's case), while substantial numbers fled into Thailand or India (Lintner, 2009, pp. 81–83).

Furthermore, a smear campaign via government-controlled mass media targeted the leading monks with trumped-up charges, for example accusing them of "immoral living" (such as gambling, taking drugs, watching pornography or having sexual intercourse). Activist monks in general were denounced as "political agitators in the yellow robes" (Aung Zaw, 2013), as "pseudo monks" or "bogus monks" who could hence be beaten, imprisoned and even killed without any moral qualms (Gravers, 2012, p. 15). There is indeed some evidence for bogus monks participating in the demonstrations – but these were either soldiers or criminals disguised as monks and employed by the government "to infiltrate demonstrations in order to spark violence, with soldiers ordered to shave their heads and dress as monks" (Burma Campaign UK, 2007).

In the context of this chapter's focus on non-violent extremism, violent extremism and the liminal spaces in between, four observations linking back to the definitions provided above can be made about the Saffron Revolution. Firstly, as regards physical violence, the monks who participated in the demonstrations observed an absolute and principled non-violence; secondly, as regards political demands, the monks demonstrated utmost zeal and uncompromising attitude; and thirdly, as regards their participation in political protests, they certainly violated boundaries regarding political dispute and dissent valid in Myanmar, mainly due to the fact that "monks are not supposed to be politically active", as U Pannacara (cited above) acknowledged. Fourthly and finally, as regards psychological violence, the monks' protests included at least one clearly coercive element that can be seen as such: the overturning of the alms bowls, as a powerful signal that the monks involved would deny military personnel and state officials the chance to make merit. It does not really matter whether the individuals affected by this denial were all pious Buddhists or not: the denial in itself is a stark symbolic act that is meant to ostracise, and thus to "other", those targeted. Following Schmid's argumentation introduced above, it can thus be argued that the Saffron Revolution was more than just a peaceful protest and less than violent extremism. It was a clear-cut case of non-violent extremism in the substantive Gandhian tradition, no less.

Violence and Not-violence: Monks and the Campaign against the Rohingya

Violence against the Rohingya, a Muslim minority mainly living in Myanmar's Rakhine state, is nothing new: its origins can be traced back to the late 18th century when the region (then known as *Arakan*) was conquered by the troops of Burmese king Bodawpaya (Ahmed, 2017; Wade, 2017; Ibrahim, 2018). After the conquest of Burma by British forces in the 19th century, the conflict lay dormant but flared up again immediately after independence in 1948. While the first campaign suppressed Rohingya separatism, the campaigns of 1978 and 1991/1992 simply aimed at driving the Rohingya minority out of Burma because they were seen as illegal Bengali immigrants and not as legal Burmese citizens (Amnesty International, 2004, p. 5). Why the

Rohingya are perceived as illegal immigrants can be traced back to an oversight of the British colonial administration which, in the census of 1911, mistakenly listed them not as an indigenous Arakanese group but as an Indian ethnicity (Ahmed, 2017). For the governments of independent Burma ever since 1948, this was reason enough to take the same position. In the Burma Citizen Law of 1982, for example, the Rohingya are not mentioned as one of the ethnic groups which are native to Burma.[17]

Being denied citizenship is not the only problem that the Rohingya have to face, both as a group and as individuals. The second one is distrust and suspicion: the Rohingya form a sizeable Muslim minority of 35% in the otherwise mostly Buddhist Rakhine state where they live. Compared to the 63% Buddhists among the 3.2 million inhabitants of Rakhine (the remaining 2% are Christians, Hindus and Animists), this does not appear to be a problem. In Burma, however, where the motto still is "to be Burmese means to be Buddhist", this is cause for alarm – due to the fact that the Rakhine state borders Bangladesh. With a population of 160 million, this Muslim-majority country dwarfs Buddhist-majority Burma with a population of only 53 million. As a consequence, the Rohingya are watched with deep suspicion. They are frequently accused not only to be illegal immigrants but a Bengali–Muslim "fifth column", preparing the ground for a gradual Islamisation of Burma. Hence, seen from a Burmese–Buddhist perspective, not only the survival of the Burmese state is at stake, but the survival of Buddhism itself. Seen from this Burmese–Buddhist perspective, the argument is frequently made that the *prima facie* duty of non-violence has to give way to the now far more important duty of self-defence – "Buddhism is not a suicidal utopianism", after all.

In the context of framing the Rohingya Muslims as an existential threat to both the Burmese state and Buddhism, it is important to note that the current round of anti-Rohingya violence that started in June 2012 is no longer restricted to state authorities plus pro-state militias such as the notorious USDA or the Swan Arr Shin. Rather, in the wake of the military forces' (temporary, as it now appears) withdrawal from political power, the anti-Rohingya violence was privatised. In the words of Wade (2017, p. 16), "the military, in its retreat from power, seemed to have passed a torch onto the masses of people who had spent so many years opposing its mercurial rule". It is also important to note that framing not only Rohingya Muslims but Burmese Muslims in general as the enemy, that is "othering" them in an "us versus them" sense, is nothing new as well: anti-Muslim riots can be traced back at least to the British colonial rule over Burma. The anti-Muslim riots of 1938 are an excellent example in this context, in particular since the justifications for these riots then and now are very similar: "they" (that is the Muslims) are stealing "our" (that is Buddhist-Burmese) jobs, "they" take over "our" land, "they" marry "our" women and convert them to Islam – hence, "they" must be stopped before it is too late. Even the patterns of violence are similar: Burmese–Buddhist mobs rampaging through the streets, beating up or lynching Muslims, and burning down Muslim-owned shops, houses and places of worship. In contrast to then, lurid stories about anti-Buddhist atrocities allegedly committed by Muslims plus the accompanying anti-Muslim rhetoric now are far more easily and rapidly disseminated via social media all over the country – as well as making it easier to organise mass anti-Muslim protests.

These masses also include monks, again coming to support the people, just like in the cases of the 8888 Uprising and the Saffron Revolution. And again, just as before, organisations were launched to facilitate and organise the participation of monks: the *969 Movement* and the Patriotic Association of Myanmar[18] (usually referred to as *Ma Ba Tha* according to the Burmese acronym). The 969 Movement was founded as a nationalist grassroots movement in October 2012, with Ashin Wirathu as its most prominent member and de-facto leader. Its name comes from Burmese–Buddhist numerology: as Bookbinder (2013) explains, "[t]he number 969

[…] represents the 'three jewels:' the nine attributes of the Buddha, the six attributes of his teachings, and the nine attributes of the *sangha*, or monastic order". The movement enjoys the tacit support from high-ranking government officials as well as members of the National League for Democracy and generally "has broad support, both in high places and at the grass roots" (Marshall, 2013).

Its appeal to the grassroots however also resulted in its gradual change into a somewhat broad church, with members ranging from the moderate to the stridently nationalistic and anti-Muslim. These more militant monks eventually formed a second movement, *Ma Ba Tha*. Although its origins can be traced back to mid-2012, *Ma Ba Tha* was officially launched on 15 January 2014 during a conference of Buddhist monks in Mandalay where Ashin Wirathu has his power base. Compared to the 969 Movement, *Ma Ba Tha* explicitly aimed at defending Buddhism from the very start, thus mainly appealing to the more militant among the monkhood. When *Ma Ba Tha* was ordered to disband in 2017 by the *Sangha Maha Nayaka* committee because its openly ultra-nationalist and anti-Muslim rhetoric interfered with the upholding of law and order (Radio Free Asia, 2017), it simply changed its name to Buddha Dhamma Charity Organisation and carried on as before – some of its chapters even keeping the *Ma Ba Tha* acronym (Moe Moe, 2018).

So far, the reaction of this new set of politically active monks is similar to those who participated in the Saffron Revolution: an issue emerges, and organisations are formed to address it and to facilitate participation of monks in the ensuing protests. But the role these monks now play is a substantially different one, due to a different target group (Muslims) and a different threat (perceived Islamisation of Burma). Since both target group and threat are different, it follows that the monks involved in these anti-Muslim activities had to choose a different tactic to respond to the perceived threat: since this time, their target group is not Buddhist as well (as in the case of the Saffron Revolution) but Muslim, the coercive act of overturning the alms bowls would have no effect. Even as a merely performative act aimed at a Buddhist audience witnessing this symbolic "othering" of the Rohingya would not really work, except maybe as a silent and tacit invitation to the monks' lay followers to "other" their Muslim neighbours by boycotting them. There is however a more formidable and far less subtle weapon in the array of tactics the monks can use: they can make the Muslims, in particular the Rohingya Muslims, the object of their sermons, framing them as enemies of Buddhism, determined to destroy it and to take over the country.

A telling example for this framing are the speeches of Ashin Wirathu, one of the most prominent preachers in this regard, well known in the West for his vitriolic rhetorical attacks on Muslims, and for being a "Burmese Usama bin Laden", a sobriquet bestowed to him by *Time* magazine after an interview. The content of this interview that gained him notoriety speaks for itself. In particular, he told the *Time* magazine interviewer, Hannah Beech, that "[Muslims] are breeding so fast, and they are stealing our women, raping them […]. They would like to occupy our country, but I won't let them. We must keep Myanmar Buddhist" (as quoted in Beech, 2013). He was even more explicit in an interview with the British newspaper *The Guardian*, bluntly stating that "[we] are being raped in every town, being sexually harassed in every town, ganged up and bullied in every town. […] In every town, there is a crude and savage Muslim majority" (as quoted in Hodal, 2013). Ashin Wirathu even went as far as linking the practice of halal slaughter to this alleged Muslim penchant for violence, claiming that this "allows familiarity with blood and could escalate to the level where it threatens world peace" (as quoted in Hodal, 2013). Not surprisingly, the messages to his Burmese followers are even more explicit, also revolving around the themes of Muslims being savages and of Muslims raping Burmese women while highlighting the defensive nature of his and his followers' actions. The 2019 film

Mantras of Rage contains some telling passages in this regard (Journeyman.tv, 2019). Of particular interest in this short film are the parts of his sermons where he interacts with his audience, asking largely rhetorical questions and getting the expected answers, thus reinforcing his message. An example is the following question and answer sequence:

> "ASHIN WIRATHU (Translation): They target women every day and rape them. Starting from today, do we need to protect the religion or not?"
>
> "CROWD (Translation): Yes, your Reverence".
>
> *Journeyman.tv, 2019*

As regards the call for action contained in his sermons and those of like-minded monks, it is, however, important to note that even the most militant among these monks stop short of openly calling for and condoning violent action – specifically, violent action that costs human lives: as discussed above, this would be a so-called *parajika* ("defeat") offence resulting in an expulsion from the monkhood for life. For this reason, Ashin Wirathu and his fellow monks usually do not go beyond exhorting their followers to boycott Muslim businesses and to avoid any interactions with Muslims in general. Also, and for precisely the same reason, acts of violence committed by monks themselves are comparatively rare, although not exactly unheard of.[19]

The emphasis above on human lives lost is quite an important one in this context: as discussed in the section on definitions, causing the loss of non-human lives is a lesser sin that only requires confession but does not lead to an expulsion from the monkhood. It is a well-known practice amongst the militaries of the world to dehumanise one's enemies in order to render the killing of them easier on their soldiers' consciousness. Precisely the same practice is applied within Theravāda Buddhism ever since the first justification of such practice emerged in a chapter of the Sinhalese Mahāvamsa (Great Chronicle), written at some time in the 5th century CE: "The Victory of King Dutthagamani". This chapter revolves around the aftermath of a battle when the victorious Buddhist King Dutthagamani expressed remorse for the manifold deaths he had brought about. The monks he asked for advice however respond as follows:

> That deed presents no obstacle on your path to heaven. You caused the deaths of just one and a half people, O king. One had taken the Refuges, the other the Five Precepts as well. The rest were wicked men of wrong views who died like (or: are considered as) beasts. You will in many ways illuminate the Buddha's Teaching, so stop worrying.
>
> *Mahāvamsa XXV, 108-11, as quoted in Gombrich, 2006, p. 141*

What these monks were saying was that the king and his troops mainly killed "beasts" not humans, implying that killing was excusable as long as its intention was to defend the religion and the victims were not Buddhists. In the context of Burma and the anti-Muslim protests, this reasoning was most recently used by the Sitagu Sayadaw,[20] Ashin Nyanissara, on 30 October 2017 in a sermon for an audience of Burmese army officers to tell them "that the killing of those who are not Buddhist could be justified on the grounds that they were not complete humans, or indeed humans at all" (Fuller, 2017). Here, the *Sayadaw* basically framed the current anti-Muslim violence in terms of defence of Buddhism against enemies "not completely human", probably to assuage any residual moral qualms on the side of the officers.

Nevertheless, and despite such casuistry, compared with preachers of hate from other religions such as the three Abrahamic ones (Judaism, Christianity, Islam), extremist monks need to perform a tightrope walk: on the one hand, they need to be clear enough in their messaging and, on the other, they have to steer clear from being too open. They seem to be quite successful though: as intended, their sermons are interpreted by their audience in a way that allows for a translation into violent extremism.

In the language of Terrorism and Political Violence studies, this process can be called "stochastic terrorism" or "stochastic violence", defined as "the use of mass communications to stir up random lone wolves to carry out violent or terrorist acts that are 'statistically predictable but individually unpredictable'" (Daily Kos, 2011).[21] Since those who incite such acts of violence thus cannot possibly be directly linked to them, stochastic violence comes with some sense of plausible deniability, keeping the hands of otherwise entirely respectable leaders clean (Biondi & Curtis, 2019, p. 48). Hence, it is arguably the anti-Muslim rhetoric of the extremist monks' sermons that forms a "not-violent" (as defined above), or at least "not-us-violent", bridge between the expected principled non-violence of monks on the one hand, and the manifest blatant violence of their lay followers on the other. As the militant monks see it, the theme of "Buddhism under threat" serves as the ultimate justification for the certainly unfortunate but entirely necessary replacement of principled non-violence by pragmatic violence as the new *prima facie* duty under (perceived) duress and for the purpose of (equally perceived) self-defence – again, "Buddhism is not a suicidal Utopianism".

Liminal Spaces: Monks as Fire Starters

It is time to pull together the main arguments and suggestions made in the two case studies. In the case of the Saffron Revolution, the absolute, principled non-violent and dignified behaviour of the monks certainly fulfils the expectations one usually has regarding the Buddhist philosophy of *ahimsa*: the monks protected civilians from being harassed by government forces and pro-government militias, while also having a moderating influence on the behaviour of the protesters (i.e. on no occasion did they try to instigate acts of anti-government violence via sermons with a vitriolic anti-government message). Even when they came under attack themselves, the monks refrained from retaliating with physical violence as well. They only ever went as far as applying psychological violence in the shape of coercion by overturning their alms bowls. Combined with the political demands mentioned above, it can thus be argued that the monks' role in the protests qualifies as an example of non-violent extremism.

In the case of the ongoing anti-Rohingya demonstrations, however, the monks taking part in these protests do not attempt to have a moderating influence on the blatantly violent behaviour of their followers, which includes arson, looting, rape and murder. Rather, many of these monks routinely whip their followers into a frenzy by way of hate-filled sermons with a stridently anti-Muslim and Buddhist-nationalist tone. Although the monks involved rarely actively participate in acts of violence themselves apart maybe from egging on their followers, they arguably act as inciters to violent action or "fire-starters": via the public demonisation of Muslims in general and the Rohingya Muslims in particular, they raise the statistical probability of anti-Muslim violence in one way or another, in a plausibly deniable way. Hence, it can be argued that their ostentatious reluctance to resort to, or encourage, physical violence, left alone lethal violence, is not based on an absolute and principled interpretation of *ahimsa* but on a pragmatic and tactical one – as explained above, the act of intentional killing, or encouraging others to intentionally kill, is a *Pārājika* offence that would lead to an expulsion from the monkhood. Thus, this ostentatious non-violence should rather be seen as not-violence as defined by Schmid (2014): although they themselves are not violent, their lay followers are on their behalf. In the terms of terrorism studies, these lay followers are involved in a process known as stochastic violence whereby they act on the inspiration of a notable other.

To understand the monks'[22] shift from principled and absolute non-violence in the case of the Saffron Revolution towards opportunistic "not-violence" in the case of the anti-Rohingya protests, one has to also understand the different nature of the threat: during the Saffron Revolution, it was not the survival of Buddhism that was at stake – it was all about domestic politics and the future of the Burmese political system, with the role of Buddhism unaffected. Hence, the protest constellation was civilian demonstrators (Buddhists and non-Buddhists, including Muslims, alike) plus demonstrating monks against the government. At the time of writing (September 2021), it appears that the same constellation is at work again to face down the military and its renewed bid for power. As concerns the anti-Rohingya protests, it is the very survival of Buddhism perceived to be at stake, the narrative being, "if we don't take decisive action now, 'they', i.e. the Muslims, will take over our country and wipe out Buddhism as they have done before". The targets now are Muslim Rohingya as perceived illegal immigrants from Bengal. Hence, the conflict constellation this time is government forces plus Buddhist civilians plus demonstrating monks against Muslim Rohingya (and occasionally also other Muslims in Burma). As Artinger and Rowandt comment regarding the nationalist monks' support of the renewed army take-over in May 2021

> The relationship between Buddhist nationalists and Myanmar's military is thereby symbiotic: The military advances the goals of Buddhist nationalists by protecting Buddhism against the Muslim threat, and Buddhist nationalists provide the military with religious and cultural permission for their atrocities.
>
> *Artinger and Rowand, 2021*

It would however be far too simplistic to argue that those monks supporting the military regime are mere opportunists, convenient "handmaidens of power" in the service of others. The truth is, as usual, much more complicated. Interestingly, even Ashin Wirathu as one of the most outspoken monks when it comes to anti-Rohingya and anti-Muslim agitation spent several years in jail between 2003 and 2012 for the crime of inciting religious conflict. It is thus obvious that he is not just an opportunist doing the government's bidding: he stands by his conviction that Buddhism is under threat come what may, even if and when expressing such views is against official Burmese domestic politics. Indeed, as Walton (2013) states, Ashin Wirathu "is a complex figure, having helped to organize recent [2012–2013] citizen protests against police violence but also traveling the country giving sermons in which he demonizes Muslims and urges Buddhists to join the 969 boycott campaign".

The argument that Ashin Wirathu, presumably just like other politically active monks no matter what they fight for, is "a complex figure", leads back to Schmid's (2014, p. 2) pertinent question mentioned in the introduction: "Are non-violent extremists really different from violent extremists?" The examples discussed in this chapter suggest that the answer should be an ambivalent: "it depends". If the issue at hand is a socio-economic one like the ill-advised government policy leading to the Saffron Revolution, the politically active monks are inclined to uphold and defend non-violence as an absolute value. Should the issue at hand, however, be the defence of Buddhism, then they are inclined to pragmatically dismiss non-violence for the time being in favour of a "not-violent" stance in the sense of "not-us-violent". Again, and as demonstrated in the other chapters in this volume, "Buddhism is not a suicidal utopianism"; unfortunately, it accretes worldly malevolence like any other human organisation.

Conclusion

This chapter explored the liminal space between non-violent and violent forms of (Buddhist) extremism, using Schmid's concept of *not-violence* as a bridge. It was argued that in the case of Burmese militant monks, *ahimsa* defined as principled non-violence should be seen not as an absolute value but as a *prima facie* duty that can give way to a more pragmatic position that allows for, and justifies, the use of violence by others (albeit not the monks themselves) whenever the survival of Buddhism is seen as endangered. It was also argued that this "not-violent" liminal space between non-violence and violence could be labelled as *stochastic terrorism* or *stochastic violence* in the terminology of Terrorism and Political Violence studies. In the broader context of this handbook, the chapter explored the claims and perspectives of the militant monks as actors standing between non-violence and violence, thus shedding some light on a so far under-explored aspect of extremism. However, and as the somewhat trite saying has it, "more research" certainly is required to understand this liminal space, and to get a theoretical grip on the phenomenon of stochastic terrorism or violence. This chapter is only a first step in this regard.

Notes

1 This is a question the current author was asked when talking about his research on militant Buddhism. See Lehr (2019) in the references section.
2 This chapter only discusses Theravāda Buddhism as this is the branch of Buddhism prevalent in Burma (Myanmar).
3 Since June 1989, the official name of the country is the *Republic of the Union of Myanmar*. However, the present author usually prefers the traditional name *Burma* – not out of political considerations, but to better differentiate between *Burmans* as the majority ethnic group and *Burmese* as the citizens of the state, irrespective of their ethnic origin.
4 *Metta* can be translated to "loving kindness", and *sutta* to "discourse". Strictly speaking, there are two *Metta suttas*: the *Karaṇīyamettā Sutta* (Suttanipāta Sn 1.8, see for example: Piyadassi Thera, 1999) and the *Mettānisamsa Sutta* (Anguttara Nikaya AN 11.15, see for example: Piyadassi Thera, 2005). Both *suttas* extolled the virtues of loving kindness and of *ahimsa*, and are thus frequently chanted by Theravāda monks.
5 There are three strands within Buddhism: *Theravāda* (lit. "Teaching of the Elders"), *Mahāyāna* (lit. "Great Vehicle") and *Vajrayāna* (lit. "Thunderbolt Way"; Tibetan Buddhism). *Theravāda* as the oldest and most conservative strand can be traced back to the Third Buddhist Council, held in Pataliputra (modern Patna/India) around 250 BCE under the guidance of proto-Theravādin scholar monk Moggaliputta Tissa and the (probable) patronage of Indian Emperor Ashoka Maurya. Mahāyāna emerged about 100/200 years later, while Vajrayāna can be traced back to the 4th century CE. Currently, there are an estimated 535 million Buddhists worldwide: 150 million Theravāda Buddhists, 350 million Mahāyāna Buddhists and 18 million Vajrayāna/Tibetan Buddhists (Harvey, 2013, p. 5).
6 Whether Buddhism is seen as a religion or as a philosophy is not relevant in our context. The present author would see it at least as a soteriology – which puts it more on par with religion than with philosophy.
7 Cambodia and Laos also are Theravāda-Buddhist countries, but due to their particular historical trajectories, there are different dynamics at play.
8 Interestingly, even the Dalai Lama (the leader of Tibetan Vajrayāna Buddhism) shares this view:

> [I]f the situation was such that there was only one learned lama or genuine practitioner alive, a person whose death would cause the whole of Tibet to lose all hope of keeping its Buddhist way of life, then it is conceivable that in order to protect that one person it might be justified for 10 enemies to be eliminated – if there was no other way. I could justify violence only in this extreme case, to save the last living knowledge of Buddhism itself.

He cautioned that "nevertheless once you commit violence, then counter-violence will be returned", this illustrates how widely spread the assumption is that ahimsa is not an absolute value (both quotes from Thurman, 1997).

9 The conviction that the end justifies the means is one of the five criteria for religious extremism as identified by Kimball (2002) – the others being the belief in an absolute truth; belief in the existence of an "ideal past"; belief in being part of a holy war; and blind obedience of the followers.

10 There is also a code of monastic discipline for female monks, the *Bhikkhunī Pātimokkha*, but since in the Theravādin tradition, female monkhood is no longer recognised (nuns are not on the same level as monks), it is not relevant in the context of this research – although it should be noted that nuns also participated in the 8888 Uprising, in the Saffron Revolution, in the anti-Rohingya demonstrations and again in the uprising in February–March 2021.

11 The other Pārājika offences are sexual intercourse, theft and claiming to have achieved a superior human state.

12 One well-known example is that of Sinhalese monk Talduwe Somarama Thero who shot dead the Sri Lankan Prime Minister, Solomon Bandaranaike, on 26 September 1959 because Bandaranaike, a Buddhist himself, had allegedly given in to the political demands of Hindu Tamils, thus endangering Buddhism. Hence, Talduwe Somarama Thero felt justified to resort to lethal violence in order to protect Buddhism. Interestingly, Somarama appeared at court dressed not in the saffron robes of a monk but in the white of a lay follower, and later, a couple of weeks before his execution, he even converted to Anglicanism (Jeyaraj, 2014) – allegedly in order to not besmirch Buddhism.

13 The Saffron Revolution got its name in the West because of to the colour of the monks' robes – which, however, are more of a reddish-brown or red than saffron.

14 "U" is an honorific for males in senior positions or for monks; *ashin* is an honorific just for monks.

15 U Gambira's life is narrated in Siochana and Watson (2020).

16 The military already did so in the aftermath of the 8888 Uprising. British colonial police did likewise when they quelled the riots of 1938, but profusely apologised to the Sangha later on (Braund, 1939, pp. 278–280).

17 Pyithu Hluttaw Law No. 4 of 1982. See for example at http://eudo-citizenship.eu/NationalDB/docs/1982%20Myanmar%20Citizenship%20Law%20[ENGLISH].pdf

18 Also known as Organization for the Protection of Race, Religion, and Belief.

19 It needs to be understood that all Myanmar males are supposed to be either novices or monks at least once in their lives. Hence, the monkhood has a high number of temporary members (in particular during the rainy season) who are wearing the robes only for a couple of months, or even just a couple of weeks – with the effect that their discipline and adherence to non-violence may be superficial only.

20 Sayadaw means "royal teacher" and originally was reserved for senior monks teaching the Burmese kings. Nowadays, it is a title conferred to senior monks or abbots of major monasteries. It is usual to refer to such senior monks with this combination of title and name of monastery. In this case, Sitagu Sayadaw can be rendered as Abbott of the Sitagu International Buddhist Academy in Sagaing, Burma.

21 This definition by the anonymous blogger *Daily Kos* is the first, and still the best, attempt to explain how public hate speech can incite acts of politically motivated violence.

However, since it cannot possibly be predicted whether these acts fulfil the usual criteria for acts of terrorism (which depend on the chosen definition), it would be better to define the phenomenon more broadly as "stochastic violence".

22 Anecdotal evidence shows that the monks participating in the Saffron Revolution and now in the anti-Rohingya protests do not form two different and easily distinguishable cohorts but partly overlap as it is entirely probable to be pro-democracy and anti-Muslim at the same time (Lehr, 2019, pp. 245–246).

References

Ahmed, I. (2017). The Historical Roots of the Rohingya Conflict. *IAPS Dialogue*, 4 October. Retrieved from: https://theasiadialogue.com/2017/10/04/the-historical-roots-of-the-rohingya-crisis/

Amnesty International (2004). *Myanmar: The Rohingya Minority: Fundamental Rights Denied*. 18 May. Index number: ASA16/005/2004. Retrieved from: https://www.amnesty.org/en/documents/asa16/005/2004/en/#:~:text=This%20document%20reports%20on%20the,of%20extortion%20and%20arbitrary%20taxation.

Artinger, B., & Rowand, M. (2021). When Buddhists Back the Army. *Foreign Policy*, 16 February. https://foreignpolicy.com/2021/02/16/myanmar-rohingya-coup-buddhists-protest/

Aung Zaw (2013). The Power Behind the Robe. *The Irrawaddy*, 20 September (first published in October 2007 in the print version of *The Irrawaddy*). Retrieved from: www.irrawaddy.com/from-the-archive/power-behind-robe.html

Bartholomeusz, T. (2002). *In Defense of Dharma: Just-War Ideology in Buddhist Sri Lanka*. London and New York: Routledge.

BBC (2007). Q&A: Protests in Burma. *BBC News Asia-Pacific*, 2 October. Retrieved from: http://news.bbc.co.uk/1/hi/world/asia-pacific/7010202.stm

Beech, H. (2013). The Face of Buddhist Terror. *Time*, July 1. Retrieved from: http://content.time.com/time/magazine/article/0,9171,2146000,00.html

Biondi, K., & Curtis, J. (2019). From Structural to Stochastic Violence. In K. Biondi & J. Curtis (Eds.), *Authoritarianism and Confinement in the Americas. Speaking Justice to Power III: Confinement, Cauterization, and Antipolitics in the Americas* (pp. 46–53). São Luís: Editora UEMA.

Bookbinder, A. (2013). 969: The Strange Numerological Basis for Burma's Religious Violence. *Eleven Myanmar Media*, 17 January.

Brahmavamso, A. (1996). Vinaya: The Four Disrobing Offences. *Newsletter*, April–June. Perth, Australia: The Buddhist Society of Western Australia. Retrieved from: www.budsas.org/ebud/ebsut019.htm

Braund, H. B. L. (1939). *Final Report of the Riot Inquiry Committee*. Rangoon: Superintendent, Government Printing and Stationery. Retrieved from: https://ia801609.us.archive.org/22/items/in.ernet.dli.2015.206317/2015.206317.Final-Report.pdf

Burma Campaign UK (2007). 2007 Uprising in Burma. The Crackdown. *Burma Campaign UK*. Retrieved from: https://burmacampaign.org.uk/about-burma/2007-uprising-in-burma/

Daily Kos (2011). *Stochastic Terrorism: Triggering the Shooters*. Retrieved from: www.dailykos.com/stories/2011/1/10/934890/-Stochastic-Terrorism:-Triggering-the-shooters

Fink, C. (2009). The Moment of the Monks: Burma, 2007. In A. Roberts & T. G. Ash (Eds.), *Civil Resistance and Power Politics* (pp. 354–370). Oxford: Oxford University Press (e-book).

Fuller, P. (2017). Sitagu Sayadaw and Justifiable Evils in Buddhism. *New Mandala*, 13 November. Retrieved from: www.newmandala.org/sitagu-sayadaw-justifiable-evils-buddhism/

Galtung, J. (1969). Violence, Peace, and Peace Research. *Journal of Peace Research*, Vol. 6, No. 3, 167–191.

Gombrich, R. F. (2006). *Theravāda Buddhism: A Social History from Ancient Benares to Modern Colombo*. Abingdon and New York: Routledge (2nd ed.).

Gravers, M. (2012). Monks, Morality and Military. The Struggle for Moral Power in Burma – and Buddhism's Uneasy Relation with Lay Power. *Contemporary Buddhism: An Interdisciplinary Journal*, Vol. 13, No. 1, 1–33. Retrieved from: www.tandfonline.com/doi/full/10.1080/14639947.2012.669278?src=recsys

Hallisey, C. (1996). Ethical Particularism in Theravāda Buddhism. *Journal of Buddhist Ethics*, Vol. 3, 32–43.

Harvey, P. (2013). *An Introduction to Buddhism: Teachings, History and Practices*. Cambridge: Cambridge University Press (2nd ed.).

Head, J. (2007). The Hardship that Sparked Burma's Unrest. *BBC News*, 2 October. Retrieved from: http://news.bbc.co.uk/1/hi/world/asia-pacific/7023548.stm

Hodal, K. (2013). Buddhist Monk Uses Racism and Rumours to Spread Hatred in Burma. *The Guardian*, 18 April. Retrieved from: www.theguardian.com/world/2013/apr/18/buddhist-monk-spreads-hatred-burma

Human Rights Watch (2007). Crackdown. Repression of the 2007 Popular Protests in Burma. *Human Rights Watch*, Vol. 19, No. 18 (C), December. Retrieved from: www.hrw.org/report/2007/12/06/crackdown/repression-2007-popular-protests-burma

Ibrahim, A. (2018). *The Rohingyas. Inside Myanmar's Genocide*. London: Hurst & Company.

Jeyaraj, D. B. S. (2014). *The Assassination of Prime Minister S. W. R. D. Bandaranaike 55 Years Ago*. Retrieved from: http://dbsjeyaraj.com/dbsj/archives/33515

Journeyman.tv (2019). *Film: Mantra of Rage* (Film 5956). Retrieved from: www.journeyman.tv/film_documents/5956/transcript/

Kimball, C. (2002). *When Religion Becomes Evil: Five Warning Signs*. New York: Harper.

Lehr, P. (2019). *Militant Buddhism. The Rise of Religious Violence in Sri Lanka, Myanmar and Thailand*. Cham: Palgrave Macmillan.

Lintner, B. (2009). The Resistance of the Monks. Buddhism and Activism in Burma. *Human Rights Watch*, 22 September. Retrieved from: www.hrw.org/report/2009/09/22/resistance-monks/buddhism-and-activism-burma

Marshall, A. R. C. (2013). Special Report: Myanmar Gives Official Blessing to Anti-Muslim Monks. *Reuters*, 27 June. Retrieved from: www.reuters.com/article/us-myanmar-969-specialreport-idUSBRE95Q04720130627

Matthews, B. (1999). The Legacy of Tradition and Authority: Buddhism and the Nation in Myanmar. In I. Harris (Ed.), *Buddhism and Politics in Twentieth-century Asia* (pp. 26–53). London: Continuum.

Moe Moe (2018). Ma Ba Tha Changes Name, Still Officially Illegal. *The Irrawaddy,* 3 September. Retrieved from: www.irrawaddy.com/news/ma-ba-tha-changes-name-still-officially-illegal.html

Piyadassi Thera (1999). Karaniya Metta Sutta: The Discourse on Loving-kindness (Suttanipata Sn 1.8). *Access to Insight. Readings in Theravāda Buddhism.* Retrieved from: www.accesstoinsight.org/tipitaka/kn/snp/snp.1.08.piya.html

Piyadassi Thera (2005). Metta (Mettanisamsa) Sutta: Discourse on Advantages of Loving-kindness (Anguttara Nikaya, AN 11.16). *Access to Insight. Readings in Theravāda Buddhism.* Retrieved from: www.accesstoinsight.org/tipitaka/an/an11/an11.016.piya.html

Radio Free Asia (2017). Buddhist Authorities Ban Myanmar's Ultranationalist Ma Ba Tha Group. *Radio Free Asia,* 23 May. Retrieved from: www.rfa.org/english/news/myanmar/ban-05232017152958.html

Schmid, A. P. (2014). Violent and Non-Violent Extremism: Two Sides of the Same Coin? *ICCT Research Paper,* May.

Selengut, C. (2003). *Sacred Fury. Understanding Religious Violence.* Washington, D.C.: Rowman and Littlefield.

Siochana, M., & Watson, R. (2020). *Naraka: The U Gambira Story.* Self-Published.

Thanissaro Bhikkhu (2007). Bhikkhu Pātimokkha: The Bhikkhus' Code of Discipline (Vinaya Pitaka: The Basket of the Discipline). *Access to Insight: Readings in Theravāda Buddhism.* Retrieved from: www.accesstoinsight.org/tipitaka/vin/sv/bhikkhu-pati.html#pr

Thurman, R. (1997). *Essential Tibetan Buddhism.* New Jersey: Castle Books.

Turner, V. (1974). Liminal to Liminoid, in Play, Flow, and Ritual: An Essay in Comparative Symbology. *Rice University Studies,* Vol. 60, No. 3, 53–92.

U Gambira (2007). What Burma's Junta Must Fear. *Washington Post,* 4 November. Retrieved from: www.washingtonpost.com/wp-dyn/content/article/2007/11/02/AR2007110201783.html

U Pyinya Zawta (2009). Leading saffron monk's memoir. *Mizzima News,* 2 January. Retrieved from: http://allburmamonksalliance.org/feature-articles-statements/

Wade, F. (2017). *Myanmar's Enemy Within: Buddhist Violence and the Making of a Muslim 'Other'.* London: Zed Books.

Walton, M. J. (2013). Buddhism Turns Violent in Myanmar. *Asia Times,* 2 April. Retrieved from: http://atimes.com/atimes/Southeast_Asia/SEA-01-020413.html

Wilkinson, P. (2001). *Terrorism Versus Democracy: The Liberal State Response.* London: Frank Cass (1st ed.).

13

BUDDHIST CONSTRUCTIONS AS A TOOL OF NON-VIOLENT EXTREMISM IN POST-CONFLICT SRI LANKA

Dishani Senaratne

Introduction

Sri Lanka is a multiethnic, multireligious and multilingual country where Buddhism is practised by 70.1% of the total population (Department of Census and Statistics, 2012), with followers of Hinduism, Islam and Christianity. Comprising nearly 75% of the total population, the Sinhalese who primarily speak the Sinhala language are the largest ethnic group in the country (Department of Census and Statistics, 2012). The Tamil community who speaks the Tamil language is the second largest ethnic group while other minorities include the Moors, Malays and Burghers. The vast majority of Sinhalese are Buddhists whereas most Tamils practise Hinduism. The Christian population includes members of both Sinhalese and Tamil ethnic groups. The Moors who follow Islam are mostly native speakers of Tamil but some of them speak Sinhala as their first language. According to the contested ancient chronicle *Mahavamsa*, Buddhism was introduced to Sri Lanka by Mahinda Thero (the son of the Indian Emperor, Ashoka), during the reign of King Devanampiyatissa against the backdrop of the absence of an established religion.[1]

Consequently, the Mahavihara was founded with state patronage, the first Buddhist monastery that flourished as the dominant seat of ancient Theravada Buddhism (the school of Buddhism that draws its scriptural inspiration from the Tipitaka or the Pali canon). Having been placed at the apex of the social hierarchy, the *sangha* (the Buddhist monastic order) continued to play the role of political advisors to successive monarchs who worked for the progress and the spread of Buddhism amid sporadic foreign invasions. In the 4th century AD, the left canine tooth relic of the Lord Buddha was sent from India to Sri Lanka to protect from invaders which ultimately became a powerful symbolic claim for the throne. The practice of appointing senior Buddhist monks to the Mahanayake (Chief Prelate) positions who are regarded as heads of the *sangha* originated in 1753 during the reign of King Kirthi Sri Rajasinghe with the restoration of *upasampada* (the rite of ordination by which one undertakes the Buddhist monastic life) on the initiatives taken by Weliwita Sri Saranankara Thero (1698–1778).

This watershed event also led to the establishment of three caste-based *Nikayas* (sects) among the local Buddhist monastic groups: Siam, Amarapura and Ramanna. To this date, the Buddhist

DOI: 10.4324/9781003032793-16

monks who hold the position of Mahanayake Theros continue to intervene in state matters at crucial moments. Historically, Buddhism shaped Sri Lanka's socio-economic and political fabric and sustained its pre-eminence in terms of number of followers accompanied by the state's role as patron and protector of Buddhism. However, different religious groups have coexisted with each other for centuries in Sri Lanka. This chapter is divided into five parts. First, it brings into focus the emergence of violent extremism in Sri Lanka, followed by an analysis of the conspicuous rise of non-violent extremism in the post-conflict context. Drawing from the narratives and experiences of a Northern Tamil community, this chapter next explores how Buddhist constructions perpetuate spatio-dominance in former conflict-ridden areas in Sri Lanka, serving as tools of non-violent extremism. Finally, the role played by *sangha* and military as primary agents of non-violent extremism is brought into focus, exacerbating the already tense relations between the Sinhalese and Tamils.

Eruption of Violent Extremism in Post-Independent Sri Lanka

The socio-historical and political roots of Sinhalese Buddhist nationalism can be traced back to the British colonial period. Marking a departure from their historic role of serving as political advisors to the monarchy, the *sangha* provided the leadership to mobilise people against colonial oppression. In response to continued marginalisation of and discrimination against the Tamil community in post-independent Sri Lanka, the Northern Tamil youth took up arms against the state, perhaps taking a cue from the Sinhalese-led insurrections during the 1970s. The *sangha* was instrumental in rallying public support for military action against the Liberation Tigers of Tamil Eelam (LTTE) which was indicative of their disposition towards violent extremism despite not being agents of violence against the wider Tamil community.

The Colonial Legacy of Sinhalese Buddhist Nationalism

In 1505, the Portuguese arrived in Sri Lanka and eventually took control of the maritime provinces. Although the Dutch overthrew the Portuguese in 1658, they were confined to coastal areas in the country. Following the 1815 British takeover of the Kandyan Kingdom, many locals converted to Christianity to secure government employment. The Christian missionaries established fee-levying English-medium private schools in major cities where the students were steered towards the coveted Ceylon Civil Service (CCS). On the contrary, the less privileged who attended vernacular schools had limited access to English, depriving them of good employment prospects. Sowing seeds of enmity between the Sinhalese and Tamils, the former perceived that the latter gained more socio-economic benefits under the British rule due to their higher proficiency of English.

Having discerned that the British had no interest in respecting the clause of the 1815 Kandyan Convention relating to protection of Buddhism, the *sangha* began to mobilise the masses against the British rulers. Migettuwatte Gunananda Thero (1823–1890) was a well-known Buddhist orator and a pioneer figure of the Buddhist Renaissance movement, the major driving force behind promotion of Buddhism during British rule. Anagarika Dharmapala (1864–1933), who was later known as the founder of modern Sinhalese Buddhist nationalism, propagated the idea that the Sinhalese Buddhists were the "true owners" of Sri Lanka's ancient civilisation which had been destroyed by "barbaric vandals," such as Tamils, Muslims and Europeans (Dharmapala, 1902, p. 302). Dharmapala's prejudice against ethnic and religious minority groups showed early signs of Sinhalese Buddhist supremacy in the pre-independence era. Intent on protecting

Buddhism, the *sangha* rallied against colonial oppression in the independence movement, marking a departure from their historic role of serving as political advisors to kings.

Aligning with the rapid socio-political changes under the British rule, the scholar-monk Walpola Rahula Thero's 1946 seminal text *Bhiksuvakage Urumaya* (The Heritage of the Bhikkhu) emphasised on the political role of Buddhist monks (DeVotta, 2004). As a response, Henpitagedara Gnanavasa Thero's 1948 monograph *Bhiksuvage Urumaya Kumakda?* (What is the Heritage of the Bhikkhu?) argued that Rahula Thero's assertions were outside Lord Buddha's teachings (Seneviratne, 1999). Echoing Rahula Thero's views on the role of political monks in the aftermath of the civil war to justify anti-minority propaganda, General Secretary of Buddhist Power Force (BBS) Galagoda Aththe Gnanasara Thero claimed that the *sangha* has a "sacred right to step in rather than meditate at temples, if politicians are seen to be going in the wrong direction."[2]

Youth Discontent as a Driver of Violent Extremism against State

A string of *ad hoc* constitutional changes – implemented by successive political dispensations ousting the Tamil language – cemented the institutionalisation of Sinhalese Buddhist majoritarianism in post-independent Sri Lanka. The 1956 election was characterised by "linguistic nationalism," (DeVotta, 2004) partly due to the euphoria of independence in 1948. After centuries of colonial rule, the pursuit for a revival of Sinhalese Buddhist nationalist ideologies came to the forefront at the expense of minority identities. Underpinned by the ideology of Pancha Maha Balavegaya or Five Great Forces [*sangha* (Buddhist clergy), *veda* (Ayurvedic doctors), *guru* (teachers), *govi* (peasants), *kamkaru* (workers)] with the backing of *bhikkhu*-led Eksath Bhikshu Peramuna (United Bhikkhu Front), the victorious S. W. R. D. Bandaranaike administration swiftly passed the 1956 Sinhala Only Act, replacing English as the sole official language with Sinhala.

In spite of later attempts to rectify this discriminatory legislation, dethroning the position of the Tamil language while giving exclusive recognition for Sinhala went beyond mere deepening a rift between the Sinhalese and the Tamils, ushering in the emergence of a Sinhalese Buddhist hegemonic state. This would later go on to drive Tamil nationalism as a violent reactionary movement to state marginalisation. Ironically, Prime Minister Bandaranaike was assassinated by a Buddhist monk in 1959, a major figure of the previously mentioned Five Great Forces that he himself endorsed, for allegedly betraying the Sinhalese Buddhists. Embedding Sinhalese Buddhist nationalist ideology in state policy, Sri Lanka adopted its first republican constitution in 1972 during the Sirimavo Bandaranaike administration (wife of slain Prime Minister Bandaranaike), declaring Sinhala as the sole official language while rendering Buddhism a priority position. Its predecessor, the Soulbury constitution, introduced by the British in 1947, had adopted a secular approach with the inclusion of a provision in place to safeguard the interests of different ethnic and religious groups.

Leveraging the landslide victory at the 1977 parliamentary election, the J. R. Jayewardene government enacted a new constitution in 1978, according to Buddhism a principal position and the duty of the state to protect and foster *Buddha Sasana* (the teaching of the Buddha) while providing other religions equal rights. In addition, Sinhala was declared as the official language albeit both Sinhala and Tamil were declared national languages. Later, the 13th amendment to the constitution, an offshoot of the 1987 Indo-Sri Lanka Peace Accord, stated Sinhala and Tamil as both national and official languages whereas English was given the status of a link language.

Against the backdrop of continued marginalisation of and discrimination against the Tamil community, especially in the spheres of education and legislation, the LTTE led the struggle for an independent state for Tamils (Tamil *Eelam*) in the North and East, having suppressed several rival armed groups. The political driving force of the LTTE was Tamil nationalism and its every move was justified in terms of "Tamil national aspirations" (Keerawella, 2013). Triggering the decades-long civil war, the brutality inflicted on the Tamil community during the infamous 1983 riots gave legitimacy to the LTTE cause of ideologically motivated violence.[3]

In Sri Lanka, not only the Tamil youth but also the Sinhalese youth have expressed their utmost dissatisfaction with systematic oppression by means of armed struggles (Venugopal, 2010). In the late 1960s, the leftist Janatha Vimukthi Peramuna (JVP or the People's Liberation Front) arose in Sinhalese-majority areas from frustration of graduate employment and other social injustices like the caste system. The JVP-led, 1971 and 1987–1989 youth insurrections unleashed violence against the state, providing a catalyst to redefine the role of the *sangha* to suit the concurrent socio-economic upheavals. In other words, political involvement of Buddhist monks was espoused even at the risk of their own lives to protect Buddhism from the threat of terrorism (Abeysekara, 2001). On the other hand, it is contended that the Sinhalese-led 1971 JVP insurrection provided a stimulus for Tamil youth to resort to violence against the state (Samaranayake, 2008). The state, in turn, quelled both the Sinhalese-led JVP in the late 1980s and more recently the Tamil-led LTTE. However, the JVP later entered the democratic path and is today viewed as a third party in the country's political arena. Conversely, the participation of and access to democratic and political processes for Tamil youth who were former LTTE combatants remains unthinkable, even 12 years after the LTTE annihilation by government forces.[4]

Sangha as Enablers of Violent Extremism

Following the 1985 attack on the Sri Maha Bodhiya (a major Buddhist sacred site), the LTTE violence invoked by religious hatred reached a tipping point when other religious groups and places of worship were sporadically targeted over the following years. Even though the LTTE's killing sprees continued to receive public and media attention, state violence in the form of military attacks on unarmed civilians and public places in conflict-ridden areas were rarely in the limelight. Amid escalation of fighting, President Chandrika Bandaranaike Kumaratunga (daughter of former Prime Ministers – S. W. R. D. and Sirimavo Bandaranaike) put forward a political package of devolution which culminated with the 2000 draft of a new constitution. The *sangha* played a crucial role in mobilising the masses against this negotiated political solution under the pretext of patriotism, perhaps continuing the momentum of the *bhikkhu*-led resistance sparked off in the late 1980s to the previously mentioned Indo-Sri Lanka Peace Accord.

In 2002, a ceasefire agreement was signed between the government of Prime Minister Ranil Wickremesinghe and the LTTE with Norwegian assistance. At this juncture, a number of Sinhalese Buddhist nationalist movements – like Mawubima Surakeeme Vyaparaya (Movement for the Protection of the Motherland) and Sihala Urumaya (Sinhala Heritage) – vehemently protested against Western intervention to address Tamil grievances which was deemed as sympathetic to the LTTE. The government exclusion of Buddhist monks from peacemaking efforts undermined their historic power and influence over political dynamics, paving the way for mobilisation of public support for an armed intervention to defeat the LTTE. Commenting on sermons conducted by Buddhist monks, Kent (2015) observed that these preachers employed an ethical imagination more dependent upon eschatological factors than upon individual obligations when advising the soldiers to protect the *dharma* (Buddhist teaching) that remained in the country.

The sudden death of Gangodawila Soma Thero in 2003, a champion of Sinhalese Buddhist nationalist rhetoric, triggered anti-Christian attacks across certain Sinhalese-majority areas, calling to enact anti-conversion laws. Capitalising on growing anti-Christian sentiments, a group of Buddhist monks of the Jathika Hela Urumaya (JHU or the National Heritage Party) were elected to the Sri Lankan parliament in the following year claiming to establish a *dharma raajya* (a nation based on Buddhist principles), despite debates over their suitability to engage in parliamentary politics. Even though the *sangha* was rarely seen acting as agents of violence against the wider Tamil community during the civil war, mobilisation of public support for military action against the LTTE attested to the *sangha* community's disposition towards violent extremism.

The Inconspicuous Rise of Non-violent Extremism in the Post-Conflict Context

With strong Sinhalese Buddhist nationalist support, Mahinda Rajapaksa assumed office in 2005 (Dewasiri, 2016). The already fragile ceasefire fell apart in the following year and fighting ensued that ended with the military defeat of the LTTE in 2009. In popular Sinhalese war discourse, Rajapaksa was subsequently seen as a modern-day monarch for having been able to unite Sri Lanka through his effective leadership. Resonating with the *Mahavamsa* depiction of Mahinda Thero's Buddhist mission in ancient Sri Lanka, Rajapaksa presidency was given the epithet *mahindagamanaya* (the arrival of Mahinda), for bringing about a renaissance of Sinhalese Buddhist values and priorities that had resulted as a consequence of the LTTE annihilation.

Against the backdrop of the absence of the LTTE, a number of *bhikkhu*-led movements rallied against the "new Muslim enemy" around which Sinhalese Buddhist nationalism could define and explain itself and popular ethnic sentiment might be mobilised (Haniffa, 2016). Similar to Sri Lanka, Buddhist-driven anti-Muslim sentiment is widespread in both Thailand and Myanmar in the Asian region. In 2013, *Bodu Bala Sena* (BBS), the Buddhist Power force, gained spotlight with their vociferous objections to the halal certification system. At their rallies, General Secretary of BBS Galagoda Aththe Gnanasara Thero continued to make explicit derogatory remarks about the Muslim community that had the potential to incite violence. In keeping with the new waves of Sinhalese Buddhism supremacy emanating from war victory, similar hardline Buddhist groups, such as *Ravana Balaya* (Power of Ravana), *Sinhala Ravaya* (Sound of Sinhalese) and *Sinhe Le* (Lion Blood), also emerged during this period.

With the advent of social media, propagation of Islamophobia took on a new dimension. Unlike during the fighting between the security personnel and the LTTE that largely engaged in physical warfare, online hate campaigns against the Muslim community surged exponentially with recurrent appeals for boycotting Muslim-owned businesses as a seemingly non-violent means of hindering their economic progress. According to Kadirgamar (2013), such anti-Muslim propaganda served as a distraction for the Sinhalese population from their economic woes while maintaining the Mahinda Rajapaksa regime's electoral base. The recurrent "*vanda pethi*" (infertility pills) myth exemplifies how the Muslim community is viewed with scepticism as an existential threat to the majority status of the Sinhalese, notwithstanding official figures suggest otherwise. Despite being Tamil speakers, the Muslim community rarely sided with the LTTE during the decades-long civil war partly because they were forcibly expelled *en masse* from the North in 1990, preceded by the Kattankudy mosque massacre committed by the LTTE that killed over 147 males.

Manifesting fragility of peace in a post-conflict setting, violence was perpetrated against the Muslim community in 2017 and 2018. Sadly, social hostility towards the Muslim community is not a new phenomenon and recorded anti-Muslim violence dates back to the British colonial period. Triggered by a conflict about a religious procession held in Kandy, the 1915 anti-Muslim riots spread across the country which was eventually brutally crushed by the British. The political role of the *sangha* in post-conflict Sri Lanka's ethnonationalist politics became overtly aggressive towards the Muslims, marking a departure from the *sangha's* ambivalent role as enablers of violent extremism but not acting as agents of violence during the civil war. The 2014 anti-Muslim riots in Aluthgama and Beruwela pointed to the fact that BBS' strings of racist slurs on the Muslim community were an eerie precursor to the brutal rise of militant Buddhism.

Instigated by certain Buddhist monks affiliated with hardline Buddhist groups like BBS, attacks against the Muslim community reached unprecedented heights over the following years, ostensibly under government support. Taking a step further, the *sangha*, at times, acted as agents of violence against the Muslim community as evidenced in numerous videos intermittently going viral on social networks. The *sangha* commands respect not only from the Buddhist community but also other religious groups partly because they represent the majority religion. Despite holding an esteemed position in society, the *sangha* is characterised by communalism that is evident in their role as actors of violent and non-violent extremism against the ethnic and religious minorities.

With the 2019 Easter bombings, Sri Lanka experienced Muslim-on-Christian violence for the first time in its history while anti-Christian attacks were already on the rise following the civil war's end. The apparent reprisal attacks that occurred two weeks after the Easter Sunday bombings in Minuwangoda and Kuliyapitiya were far from being isolated occurrences and highlighted successive government complacency to address recent legacies of violence against the Muslim community. However, M. H. A. Haleem's, the then Muslim Religious Affairs Minister, controversial statement about caches of swords found from a number of mosques downplayed signs of incipient Islamist extremism as a potential reactionary phenomenon.

Contrary to perceived political will to tackle Islamist extremism, successive (predominantly Sinhalese Buddhist) administrations in the post-2009 era have shied away from addressing Buddhist extremism for concerns over losing electoral foothold of the majority Sinhalese. Arguably, the wider Sinhalese Buddhist population may not necessarily concur with the violent approach of the hardline groups yet remains largely reticent about such matters, manifesting how the former sympathises with the latter's ideologies. This year, almost two years after the Easter bombings, a ban on face coverings in public was imposed on the grounds of national security, which speaks volumes about increasing government suppression of symbols of Muslim identity sans addressing systematic issues of bias and discrimination against the Muslims community.

Underpinned by Sinhalese Buddhist ethnocratic ideologies, post-conflict Sri Lanka witnessed not only eruption of violent extremism against the Muslim community but also the concomitant rise in manifestations of non-violent extremism against the Tamil population. Unlike violent extremism, the impact of non-violent extremism is less visible, making it a disincentive to promote long-term peace in conflict-fraught contexts. Framed within dominant Sinhalese Buddhist historical narratives which justify reclaiming supposed ancient sites destroyed by war, the Buddhist constructions in predominantly Tamil areas perpetuate spatio-dominance, serving as tools of non-violent extremism.

Writing about post-conflict contexts, including the recent developments in Sri Lanka, Lewis et al. (2018) advanced the term "authoritarian conflict management," to explain how both military and civilian modes of controlling spaces are embodied in spatial politics. Unarguably, the mushrooming of Buddhist constructions doesn't happen in a political vacuum. Interwoven with cultural, economic, political/military and geopolitical factors, the expansion of "Sinhala Buddhism" into the Tamil region can be termed as "war by other means," consolidating the power of the state and its ideology (Fernando, 2013, p. 201).

Drawing from the narratives and experiences of a Northern Tamil community, the case study of Sri Mathota Raja Maha Viharaya epitomises how spatially embodied non-violent extremism is perpetuated through Buddhist constructions deemed historic in Tamil-majority areas. In addition, this chapter also examines the military-*sangha* relations as joint agents of non-violent extremism in post-LTTE era.

Reinforcement of Singular Sinhalese Buddhist Historical Narratives

Situated in the Tamil-majority Northern Province's Mannar district, Manthai has the presence of Roman Catholics as well as Hindus. Located near the Palavi tank, Sri Mathota Raja Maha Viharaya (Ancient Buddhist Temple) lies within close proximity to Thiruketheeswaram *kovil* (Hindu temple) and Our Lady of Lourdes Church. The former is regarded as one of the *Pancha Ishwarams* (the five Hindu *kovils* in Sri Lanka dedicated to Lord Siva) while the latter is revered as the earliest seat of Our Lady of Madhu. With the escalation of fighting between the government forces and the LTTE in the early 1990s, an army camp was stationed on private land owned by a Tamil individual in Manthai.[5] In order to engage in religious activities, a Buddhist temple was built inside the camp by the army where there was already a makeshift *devalaya* (a shrine) worshipped by the local community.

Even though the army camp was removed during the post-2009 phase, a facelift to this temple was given by the military and a Buddhist monk came to reside there despite repeated protests by the community. Consequently, the Ministry of Buddha Sasana, the government body responsible for oversight and maintenance of the welfare of the Buddhist clergy and places of worship, cancelled the registration of the temple in 2012 (according to the respondents). However, construction restarted soon and the temple was renamed as Sri Mathota Raja Maha Viharaya, making allusions to the temple as a location steeped in history. In 2017, the community relaunched their objection against the alleged government approval for construction of the new *dharma shalawa* (preaching hall) and the installation of the Buddha statue at the temple. Today, this temple serves as a stopover destination for Sinhalese tourists *en route* to Jaffna whilst also providing budget accommodation facilities.

The historical background of Sri Mathota Raja Maha Viharaya dates back to the period when Mahinda Thero first brought Buddhism to Sri Lanka, as referred in ancient texts like *Vihara Asna*, according to the current Chief Incumbent (chief priest) of the temple. Bearing testimony to its perceived historical significance, the temple is recognised by the Ministry of Buddha Sasana as a Raja Maha Viharaya (ancient temple), the Chief Incumbent mentioned to the author (personal communication, December 14, 2018).[6] On the contrary, the community itself in Manthai stresses that the temple was developed by the army in the aftermath of the civil war.

Giving precedence to Sinhalese Buddhist historical narratives, Sri Mathota Raja Maha Viharaya has been declared an archaeological reservation. The Department of Archaeology would soon commence excavation at the temple, the Chief Incumbent revealed to the author in an interview. In contrast, neither Thiruketheeswaram *kovil* nor Our Lady of Lourdes Church has come to the attention of the Department of Archaeology, albeit having long histories.[7] This is a textbook case of how state actors play a role in reinforcing singular Sinhalese Buddhist historical narratives sans recognising inclusive histories. Observing the archaeological site of Kandarodai on the Jaffna peninsula at the northernmost tip of Sri Lanka, Harris (2019) noted, similarly, how the privileging of Sinhalese Buddhist representations of history has failed to affirm multiplicity at Kandarodai. The recent appointment of the Defence Ministry-led Presidential Task Force for Archaeological Management in the East with neither Tamil nor Muslim representation despite constituting the majority of the province's population is another example for blatant disregard of inclusive histories.

The much-believed Sinhalese claim of primordial ownership over Sri Lanka is underpinned by the unauthenticated chronological sequence of events pertaining to the arrival of Prince Vijaya in the *Mahavamsa*. The orchestration of a perceived Sinhalese Buddhist identity through institutionalised mythical *Mahavamsa* narratives asserts Sinhalese dominance, elbowing aside the identities of the minority ethnic and religious groups (Deegalle, 2013). The *Mahavamsa* records have been long projected as historical evidence in order to feed into the task of Sinhalese Buddhist nation building. To date, parallels are made in popular Sinhalese war discourse between the concluded civil war and the *Mahavamsa* narrative of Dutugemunu–Elara war for justification of waging the war against a so-called "Tamil enemy."[8] Intent on advancing religio-political interests, the dissemination of dominant Sinhalese Buddhist historical narratives through elements of popular culture gained momentum during the civil war and continues to this day. The popular TV programme *Maha Sinhale Wansa Kathawa* (The Saga of the Sinhalese) aired during the height of the war is a case in point.

According to Tambiah's (1992) sociological critique, the Sinhalese are a majority with a minority complex. Appadurai (2006) has similarly suggested that the "fear of small numbers" has historically motivated violence across the globe. Following the consolidation of the LTTE subsequent to the infamous 1983 riots, an undercurrent of fear sparked among the wider Sinhalese populace that their majority status would be lost and the LTTE would take over the country in the long run. While the civil war was ongoing, the Tamil diaspora and the politicians from the Southern Indian state of Tamil Nadu continued to stand up for the LTTE cause, fuelling a sense of insecurity and foreign interference among the Sinhalese.[9] More recently, the Muslim Council of Britain (MCB) mulled over launching a legal challenge to the Sri Lankan government policy (later reversed) that those who succumb to COVID-19 must be cremated, exposing how the minority ethnic groups are compelled to garner support of an international network in order to challenge human rights violations. The ever-rising transnational support for the minorities has been a bitter pill for the Sinhalese to swallow.

Buddhist Temples as Sites of Dominance

Encircled by six *parivara* (accompanying) Bo trees, the *bodhiya* (Bo tree) is one of the main attractions at Sri Mathota Raja Maha Viharaya. This rare presence of six *parivara* Bo trees contributes to the historical significance of the temple, the Chief Incumbent mentioned to the author. Conversely, the community in Manthai stated the Bo trees were planted by the military during the initial construction stage of the temple.

The Bo tree is perceived as a sacred symbol of enlightenment of the Buddha. The practice of cutting down Bo trees in public spaces under the pretext of development became prevalent during the British colonial period, notwithstanding the belief of Buddhists that felling Bo trees is a sacrilegious act. The move to cut down the Bo tree at Pettah (the quintessential commercial hub of Colombo) had to be suspended, in the face of a public protest led by the ethnically diverse local business community. Spearheaded by the Tamil trader S. T. Sinnadurai (commonly known as the proprietor of Leela Stores), the 1958 establishment of Eksath Bodhi Raja

Samithiya (United Bodhi Society) in Pettah is a good example of community mobilisation for protection of Bo trees in the post-independence era.

More recently, felling Bo trees has become a hotly debated topic against a larger backdrop of heightened tensions between the communities in post-conflict afterlife. A dispute over the cutting of a Bo tree prompted an attack on Grandpass mosque in 2013, in an eerie precursor to the large-scale eruption of violence against the Muslim community in Aluthgama and Beruwela in the following year.

On the other hand, the Bo tree serves as a pathway to the advent of a roadside temple, not only in predominantly Tamil areas but also across the country. Anecdotal evidence suggests that at strategic locations like junctions where there is a presence of a Bo tree (in most cases naturally grown trees), a *sivura* (a saffron robe worn by Buddhist monks) is wrapped around the tree to indicate that it has been blessed. Following the construction of multiple makeshift Buddhist constructions, a Buddhist monk (perhaps of dubious repute) would usually arrive to reside at the premises, if space permits. A loudspeaker tied to a Bo tree to broadcast *pirith* (the words of the Buddha) in the early morning and evening is another ubiquitous sight in wayside shrines as well as at established temples.

Aligning with the views of Ellawala Medhananda Thero (2003) on the calls to reclaim lost Buddhist heritage in the North and East, the Chief Incumbent has adopted a proactive approach in the expansion of the physical development of the temple.[10] The name lists on the plaques of new constructions are indicative of how high-profile Sinhalese benefactors who are based elsewhere in the country extend their financial support to the temple. In all likelihood, the temple will build more and more constructions to ensure its strong presence in Manthai despite being located in a predominantly Tamil region. Predictably, such acts of non-violent extremism could provide the initial spark to trigger violence, albeit not immediately.

Written only in Sinhala, the signboard on the main road immediately grabs the attention of the Sinhalese tourists. Moreover, the inclusion of the ancient Sinhalese name of Mannar (Mathota) to the name of temple, alongside the reference to it as an ancient site (Raja Maha Viharaya), are bound to act as drivers to incite Sinhalese passers-by to visit the temple. More importantly, the change of town names from Tamil to Sinhala adds to the wider project of expansion of Sinhalisation of the North-East Tamil areas. Predictably, the villagers' concerns are mounting that the imminent arrival of an influx of Sinhalese tourists would pave the way for further development of Sri Mathota Raja Maha Viharaya, causing disruption to the local lifestyle. The community in Manthai, however, is not without their intra-ethnic divisions. Apart from caste-based divisions, land dispute between Thiruketheeswaram *kovil* and Our Lady of Lourdes Church has led to increasing tensions between the Hindu and Catholic communities.

Similar to the proliferation of Buddhist constructions, a wave of state-sponsored monuments emerged in former conflict-ridden areas to pay homage to "war heroes" (*ranaviruwo*) in the aftermath of the civil war. Perhaps serving as implicit warnings about the future, the presence of such visible reminders of Sinhalese Buddhist hegemony dotting the landscape compound the local Tamil community's sense of victimhood (McCargo and Senaratne, 2020). While the Tamil community was constantly under pressure from the government to abstain from remembering their war experiences, the Rajapaksa administration focused heavily on carrying out large infrastructure projects in former war zones, such as 'Resurrection of the North' (*Uthuru Wasanthaya*) and 'Reawakening of the East' (*Nagenahira Navodaya*).

Combining battlefield and leisure tourism practices (Pieris, 2014), the former conflict-affected areas also saw the arrival of an inundation of Sinhalese tourists who were eager to visit war monuments, among other tourist attractions, in an act of triumphalism. Intent on catering to the needs of the booming tourism in the North, the army expanded its presence in the leisure sector by building hotels and eateries, on lands allegedly owned by Tamil individuals in some cases.

The Nexus between the *Sangha* and Military

The Sri Lankan constitution states that Buddhism is accorded the foremost position and the state should protect and foster it while other religions also enjoy equal rights. In reality, the pre-eminent position of Buddhism has been exploited for the sectarian purpose of wielding authority over the minority religions. In such context, the *sangha's* exercise of authority, power and agency permeates the country's socio-economic and political fabric, especially in the spheres of polity and politics. Armed with *pirikara* (offerings to the *sangha*), the high-profile political leaders of the country are often seen in the media paying homage to eminent Buddhist monks, in an attempt to display their affiliations to Buddhism.

During the decades-long civil war, the *sangha* rallied to hold *bodhi poojas* (a merit work) in temples across the country to invoke blessings to the armed forces to show solidarity with the "holy war" against the LTTE. Taking a step further, *pirith* strings (a piece of thread energised by the chanting of Lord Buddha's words) were tied on the hands of the military personnel for protection against the "Tamil enemy" by the *sangha*, as a mark of justification of unleashing of violence for the sake of the country and Buddhism.

Subsequent to the military defeat of the LTTE, the military–*sangha* relations reached new heights, particularly in former conflict zones. As in the case of most newly constructed Buddhist temples in the region, Sri Mathota Raja Maha Viharaya is patronised by the military. In turn, the temple serves the dual purpose of ensuring omnipresent military gaze, as evidenced by the unofficial military sentry point set up at the premises. The villagers in Manthai expressed to the author their preference to live in a demilitarised setting, similar to the Sinhalese-majority South of Sri Lanka. Even 12 years after the LTTE annihilation by government forces, withdrawal of the military from the North and East remains a pipe dream for the Tamil community.

Reflecting on the Buddha statues scattered across the country, DeVotta (2007) argued that Buddha statues are erected knowing the military will thereafter step in and prevent them being demolished. Likewise, in Manthai, stationing military personnel at Sri Mathota Raja Maha Viharaya is meant to protect the temple from potential intruders. Carrying the responsibility to protect and foster Buddhism, the *sangha* is historically viewed as *jaathiye mura detuwo* (guardians of the nation), whereas the military is seen as "war heroes" for the role played in defeating the LTTE. Exploiting such populist discourses, a culture of impunity for both groups has been established. Exposing the incumbent government's trajectory towards nurturing a culture of impunity on military abuse to retain partisan Sinhalese Buddhist support base, a presidential pardon was granted this year to a former Army Sergeant who was on death row for the murder of eight civilians in 2000.

Prior to that, a presidential pardon was granted, in the run-up to the 2019 presidential election, to General Secretary of BBS, Galagoda Aththe Gnanasara Thero, who was found guilty of contempt of court. The immunity enjoyed by both the *sangha* and military has nurtured a symbiotic relationship, enabling both groups to make a concerted effort to ensure Sinhalese Buddhist footprint in the North and East. In other words, the *sangha* and the military act as joint agents of non-violent extremism, exacerbating the already tense relations between the Sinhalese and Tamils.

Concluding Remarks

Framed within exclusivist Sinhalese Buddhist narratives which justify reclaiming supposed ancient sites destroyed by war, the ubiquitous Buddhist constructions in former conflict-affected areas maintain spatio-dominance, serving as tools of non-violent extremism. As agents of non-violent extremism, both the *sangha* and the military continue to advance the spatio-dominance project through such hegemonic Buddhist sites and constructions. As De Silva (1998) noted the Tamil are a minority with a majority complex and the mushrooming Buddhist structures – noted in this chapter – are a major deterrent to assert their identity in the Tamil traditional homeland.[11] The perpetuation of military influence that takes the guise of government development initiatives and military-run tourist hotels is likely to disrupt established ethnic and religious composition in Tamil-majority areas in the long run.

Despite having seemingly equal constitutional recognition, minority religions have always been superseded by Buddhism. In such a scenario, the *sangha's* exercise of authority, power and agency pervades through the country's socio-economic and political fabric, particularly in the spheres of polity and politics. Even though the *sangha* was rarely seen acting as agents of violence against the wider Tamil community during the civil war, mobilisation of public support for military action against the LTTE attested to the *sangha* community's role as enablers of violent extremism. Marking a departure from this ambivalent role and subsequently embracing an ethnicity-based dualistic role, the *sangha* resorted to violent extremism against the Muslim community, against the larger backdrop of post-conflict Sinhalese Buddhist ethnocratic ideologies. On the other hand, spatially embodied non-violent extremism against the Tamil community began to emerge across former war zones, in parallel with this resurgence of anti-Muslim rhetoric. Inevitably, such acts of non-violent extremism could provide the initial spark to trigger violence, albeit not immediately.

Notes

1 An exegetical explanation of the *Mahavamsa* is found in the section on the reinforcement of Sinhalese Buddhist historical narratives.
2 A detailed analysis of the contemporary hardline Buddhist groups like BBS is discussed in the section on the rise of non-violent extremism in the post-conflict context.
3 As a counter reaction to a LTTE attack on a group of army soldiers in Jaffna, Northern Sri Lanka, the Tamils in Sinhalese-majority South were systematically attacked during the 1983 riots.
4 A group of former LTTE combatants who contested under the party of Crusaders for Democracy failed to gain any seat at the 2015 parliamentary polls.
5 The fieldwork on which this section draws from two trips to Manthai during the period 2018-2020. The respective interlocutors were explained the nature of the study by the author and they did not wish to be recorded.
6 The temple is included in the national directory of ancient temples which is compiled by the Ministry of Buddha Sasana. See (http://info13.info/mbs/generalcat/rajamaha/rajamahaviharabydistrict.php).
7 The government of India has extended financial support to the ongoing renovation of Thiruketheeswaram kovil.
8 In the Mahavamsa, the Sinhalese king Dutugemunu is glorified for defending Buddhism by defeating the South Indian king Elara who is depicted as the quintessential foreign ogre.
9 The term Tamil diaspora refers to Tamil immigrants of Sri Lankan origin living overseas who had left the country under varied circumstances during the decades-long civil war.
10 Ellawala Medhananda Thero is also a former leader of the Sinhalese Buddhist nationalist party Jathika Hela Urumaya (JHU).
11 According to the Tamil community, the Northern and Eastern Provinces where the Tamil population has lived long are their traditional homelands – the Tamil *Eelam*. The Sinhalese nationalists, however, have strongly opposed this viewpoint.

References

Abeysekara, A. (2001). The Saffron Army, Violence, Terror(ism): Buddhism, Identity, and Difference in Sri Lanka. *Numen, 48*(1), 1–46. doi:1163/156852701300052339

Appadurai, A. (2006). *Fear of Small Numbers: An Essay on the Geography of Anger.* Durham and London: Duke University Press.

Deegalle, M. (2013). Foremost among Religions: Theravada Buddhism's Affairs with the Modern Sri Lankan State. In P. Kitiarsa & J. Whalen-Bridge (Eds.), *Buddhism, Modernity and the States in Asia* (pp. 41–61). New York: Palgrave Macmillan.

Department of Census and Statistics (2012). *Census of Population and Housing.* Retrieved from www.statist ics.gov.lk/PopHouSat/CPH2011/Pages/Activities/Reports/

De Silva, K. M. (1998). *Reaping the Whirlwind: Ethnic Conflict, Ethnic Politics in Sri Lanka.* New Delhi: Penguin India.

DeVotta, N. (2004). *Blowback: Linguistic Nationalism, International Decay, and Ethnic Conflict in Sri Lanka.* Stanford, CA: Stanford University Press.

DeVotta, N. (2007). *Sinhalese Buddhist Nationalist Ideology: Implications for Politics and Conflict Resolution in Sri Lanka.* Washington, DC: East-West Center.

Dewasiri, N. R. (2016). *New Buddhist Extremism and Challenges to Ethno-Religious Coexistence in Sri Lanka.* Colombo: International Centre for Ethnic Studies (ICES).

Dharmapala, A. (1902). *History of an Ancient Civilization: Ceylon under British Rule.* Los Angeles: International Buddhist League.

Fernando, J. L. (2013). War by Other Means: Expansion of Sinhala Buddhism into the Tamil Region in "Post-War" Īlam. In P. Schalk (Ed.), *Buddhism among Tamils in Tamilakam and Īlam, Part 3: Extension and Conclusions* (pp. 175–239). Uppsala, Sweden: Uppsala University.

Haniffa, F. F. (2016). Stories in the Aftermath of Aluthgama: Religious Conflict in Contemporary Sri Lanka. In J. Holt (Ed.), *Buddhist Extremists and Muslim Minorities: Religious Conflict in Contemporary Sri Lanka* (pp. 164–193). Oxford: Oxford University Press.

Harris, E. J. (2019). Contested Histories, Multi-Religious Space and Conflict: A Case Study of Kantarodai in Northern Sri Lanka. *Religions, 10*(9), 537. doi:10.3390/rel10090537

Kadirgamar, A. (2013). *Second Wave of Neoliberalism: Financialisation and Crisis in Post-War Sri Lanka.* Retrieved from www.colombotelegraph.com/index.php/second-wave-of-neoliberalism-financialisat ion-and-crisis-in-post-war-sri-lanka/

Keerawella, G. (2013). *Post-War Sri Lanka: Is Peace a Hostage of the Military Victory? Dilemmas of Reconciliation, Ethnic Cohesion and Peacebuilding.* Colombo: International Centre for Ethnic Studies (ICES).

Kent, D. W. (2015). Preaching in a Time of Declining Dharma: History, Ethics and Protection in Sermons to the Sri Lankan Army. *Contemporary Buddhism, 16*(2), 188–223. doi:10.1080/14639947.2015.1008122

Lewis, D. G., Heathershaw, J., & Megoran, N. (2018). Illiberal Peace? Authoritarian Modes of Conflict Management. *Cooperation and Conflict, 53*, 486–506. doi:10.1177/0010836718765902

McCargo, D., & Senaratne, D. (2020). Victor's Memory: Sri Lanka's Post-war Memoryscape in Comparative Perspective. *Conflict, Security & Development, 20*(1), 97–113. doi:10.1080/14678802.2019.1705070

Medhananda Thero, E. (2003). *Nagenahira Palatha ha Uthuru Palathe Sinhala Baudhdha Urumaya* [*The Sinhala Buddhist Heritage in the North and East of Sri Lanka*]. Colombo: Dayawansha Jayakody Publishers.

Pieris, A. (2014). Southern Invasions: Post-War Tourism in Sri Lanka. *Postcolonial Studies, 17*(3), 266–285. doi:10.1080/13688790.2014.987899

Samaranayake, G. (2008). Political Violence in Sri Lanka: A Diagnostic Approach. *Terrorism and Political Violence, 9*(2), 99–119. doi:10.1080/09546559708427405

Seneviratne, H. L. (1999). *The Work of Kings.* Chicago: University of Chicago Press.

Tambiah, S. J. (1992). *Buddhism Betrayed? Religion, Politics and Violence in Sri Lanka.* Chicago: University of Chicago Press.

Venugopal, R. (2010). Corporate Social Responsibility; Comparative Critiques. In K.R. Raman & R. Lipschutz (Eds.), *Business for Peace, or Peace for Business? The Role of Corporate Peace Activism in the Rise and Fall of Sri Lanka's Peace Process* (pp. 111–131). London: Palgrave.

14

CURRENT TRENDS IN BUDDHIST EXTREMISM AND ANTI-MUSLIM IDEOLOGY

A Study of Sri Lanka

Chas Morrison

Introduction

Since the end of the civil war in 2009, Buddhism in Sri Lanka has been implicated in a series of violent acts: ethnic riots and attacks on houses, places of worship and businesses. Many of these are owned by Muslims. Concurrently, there has been a rise in divisive and accusatory public discourse that scapegoats Muslims, by some politicians and Buddhist monks. This rhetoric is widely shared in the mainstream media (newspapers and television), social networks, and even political pamphlets, accusing Muslims of a variety of perceived crimes and insinuating that they are not "true" Sri Lankans. Moreover, there are claims that Muslims seek to overthrow Buddhists, that they carry out forcible religious conversions, and that they are rapidly outnumbering other ethnic groups due to high birth rates. Such hate speech has become widespread in the mass media and more recently across social media where claims, accusations and provocative images are extensive (Stewart, 2014).

Buddhism does not enjoy a worldwide presence, and extremist acts committed in its name generally have national and regional impacts rather than global. Sri Lanka is in many ways a microcosm of ethno-religious tensions experienced globally, with implications for the governing of highly heterogeneous societies, managing post-war tensions and managing societal divisions based on seemingly intractable and incompatible identity contestations. The extent and impact of Buddhist nationalist extremism was put into sharp contrast in Easter 2019, when a carefully coordinated series of bomb blasts carried out by Sri Lankan *jihadis* killed 259 and injured at least 500. This was violence on a vastly different scale from the ethnic riots of recent years, and was the most violent act since the war. These bombings selected Christian and international targets rather than Sinhalese or Buddhist symbols, despite Muslim communities having suffered so much during the war, mostly at the hands of the rebel group Liberations Tigers of Tamil Eelam (LTTE), and in the post-war years at the hands of Buddhist extremists. Sri Lankan politicians and faith leaders successfully appealed for public calm after the atrocities of 2019 which helped prevent widespread reprisal attacks. This begs the question why this was not done following previous instances of mass violence, such as ethnic riots, or attacks on mosques and businesses.

DOI: 10.4324/9781003032793-17

Buddhist extremist activity in Sri Lanka targets the country's Muslim minority and Sri Lankan Christians to a lesser extent, but the violence is not on the same scale as the systematic ethnic cleansing of Rohingya Muslims in Myanmar or China's systematic mistreatment of Uighurs. Although there are many similarities between anti-Muslim and anti-Christian activities and discourse, this chapter focusses on the former mainly due to the differing levels of violence being employed, and the range of accusations that go far beyond the issue of forced conversions seen in anti-Christian actions. Following this introduction, the chapter provides a contextual overview of Buddhist extremism in Sri Lanka, and then a section on the contested position of Islam. Subsequently, the chapter explores manifestations of violence and non-violence within Buddhism extremism. The discussion section unpacks some causal factors of extremism and situates this within exclusionary practices found in both Buddhism and Islam in Sri Lanka. The conclusion draws parallels between extremism and nationalism, and argues that the distinction between violence and non-violence loses its meaning if they are employed for exclusive and divisive purposes.

Contextualising Buddhist Extremism in Sri Lanka

The main drivers and causal factors of Buddhist extremism in Sri Lanka have much in common with religious chauvinism globally. It is the philosophy that Sri Lanka was originally, and should return to, a state of religious, linguistic and ethnic homogeneity, centred around Sinhalese culture and identity. Sri Lanka's Constitution allocates Buddhism the foremost place and specifies it is the duty of the State to protect and foster it (DeVotta, 2018), but also permits the celebration of holy days of all four principal faiths. The presence of other faiths and ethnicities may be tolerated, but they are denied an equal position in the nationhood. This fundamentalist position holds that these out-groups should accept their subservient social position and accept that they are more interlopers than integral members of society. A *relational conception of religion* (Johnson, 2016) emphasises the grounded nature of faith as it relates to concrete actions and relationships embedded within wider social and political structures. That is, religion should be analysed more by the actions of its followers, rather than what they claim or what is declared in scripture. Extremism is of course a politically loaded term. Individuals and groups labelled "extremist" tend to see themselves as defenders of the nation, freedom fighters or protectors (for instance of the nation, or women's virtue).

Religious believers often adopt protectionist and defensive attitudes towards perceived threats when they feel their status or ideals are under threat (Mahadev, 2014). Although Islam is a minority faith in Sri Lanka, the demographically dominant Sinhalese Buddhists can feel like a minority group themselves when compared to global demographics. They refer to the huge numerical dominance of Muslims across the globe, and highlight that Sri Lankan Buddhism is confined to one small island which it shares with several other faiths. Such fears of being overwhelmed need to be contextualised; Islam has its own sacred land in Saudi Arabia where followers of other faiths are legally forbidden to build houses of worship or proselytise, but no parallel protection exists for Buddhists in Sri Lanka. Muslims in Sri Lanka are free to practice their religion in ways that have no equivalent in Saudi Arabia for other faiths.

Buddhism does not emphasise proselytising and converting non-believers; Buddhists may convert to Islam, but Muslims rarely become Buddhists. Thus a fundamental tenet in Sri Lankan Buddhism is not the spread of the faith *per se*, but the protection of its homeland and exclusivity: "The idea that the ends may justify the means, and the further idea that the preservation of Buddhism is a supremely worthwhile end, are both quite widely found in the Buddhist tradition" (Gombrich, 2006, p. 31). This argument has produced a fascination with "righteous belonging"; the philosophy that certain social groups have primary claim to the island, the presence of other groups is only to be tolerated, and that they should be sensitive and simultaneously grateful for it. Buddhist extremist discourse claims that Buddhists belong in Sri Lanka, unlike Muslims or Christians whose sacred places and origin myths are thousands of miles away. Other religions all have sacred places in distant lands, but Sri Lankan Buddhists have nowhere else to go (DeVotta, 2018). This position has the broader implication of denying non-Buddhists their true place in the country, and queries their nationalist loyalties.

Sri Lanka's majority national identity perceives itself as under threat from external and international forces that seek to undermine Sinhalese Buddhism and the Sri Lankan nation; two similar but not identical entities. The post-war environment has also seen a tangible transition from ethnic to religious based identities. Faced with overwhelming demographic dominance from its neighbour India to the North, and vastly outnumbered by Muslims at a global level, some of Sri Lanka's Buddhists fear for their future. What Ali (2013, p.310) labels "religiously manufactured fear" can be contextualised with regard to claims of foreign interference during and after the war which mirrors the accusations that Sinhalese Buddhism is being undermined and corrupted by foreign religions and influences.

There are several organisations who claim to protect the nation or agitate for the rights of Buddhists, but whose ideologies and agendas can be categorised as extremist, such as the *Sinhala Ravaya* (Sinhalese Roar). Some of these groups are faith-based and others are overtly political. Sri Lanka's religious and political positions are very connected; there are large numbers of monks involved in politics, even forming their own party, the National Heritage Party (JHU – *Jathika Hela Urumaya*). All the political candidates were ordained monks, and the party's policy platform emphasised controversial nationalist and protectionist policies. Despite its core members being ordained clergy, the JHU strongly advocated using military force to defeat the LTTE. The most infamous organisation associated with Buddhist extremism is the Buddhist Power Force (BBS – *Bodu Bala Sena*), which was originally a break-away group from the *Jathika Hela Urumaya*.

The apparent tautology of a militant monkhood does have historical examples from other countries: the *dob-dob* fighting monks in Tibetan *Gelugpa* monasteries, or Japanese *Sōhei* warrior monks. The theological position of violence in Buddhism, particularly as a problem-solving mechanism, have been downplayed by both scholars and Buddhist practitioners and the peaceful teachings have been emphasised, resulting in a somewhat revisionist view of the religion. In Sri Lanka, many instances of street violence have featured robed monks, exhorting others to commit violent acts and even taking part in the fighting themselves. According to *Theravada* Buddhist scriptures, monks are completely forbidden from involvement in political affairs, and definitely any acts of violence, including violent speech. Despite this, Buddhist clergy had a practice of blessing government soldiers and their weapons during the Sri Lankan civil war (DeVotta, 2018); some monks threatened to disrobe and fight the LTTE themselves if the state persisted with its then efforts to seek a negotiated settlement to the war.

Peace activists and human rights organisations suggest that such organisations, their supporters and extremist Buddhist monks enjoy immunity from prosecution and are free to organise mass rallies and disseminate hate speech in public discourse without being censored (see Stewart, 2014 and respondents' claims cited in Morrison, 2019). Allegations by lawyers, civil society and journalists that the *Bodu Bala Sena* could operate with impunity led to further targeted attacks, including against human rights-based NGOs, peacebuilding organisations and Muslim advocacy groups. Much of the criticism of Buddhist extremists centres around their operating with government approval or at least acceptance as well as their contribution to divisive political agendas (Aliff, 2015; UK Home Office, 2018). As of 2021, the *Bodu Bala Sena* no longer enjoys the same level of government support, but the normalisation of hate speech and accusations against Muslims (and Christians) and the impunity of key leaders and perpetrators are legacies that remain.

The Contested Position of Islam in Sri Lanka

Buddhist extremists vilify Muslims in particular for a variety of perceived crimes and behaviours: excessively high birth rate, promoting Halal food consumption, encouraging Buddhists to eat beef, using loudspeakers in public places for calls to prayer (which was stopped in 2007), forced conversions of non-Muslim women, increasing "Arabification", obsession with economic gain, and refusing to integrate or follow national dress and culture (Imtiyaz & Mohamed-Saleem, 2015). In 2013, the *Bodu Bala Sena* and some associated organisations started a campaign to combat the practice of *Halal* certification, which featured abusive and insulting language. Moreover, there are repeated calls to boycott Muslim restaurants and businesses. The *Bodu Bala Sena* has had success as they were able to tap into and heighten existing local grievances, both social and economic in primarily Sinhalese majority and Muslim minority regions. Opposition to cattle slaughter and the selling and consumption of beef, has been associated with Islamification and, much as in India, reflects an anti-Muslim bias more than any concern for animal welfare (Imam, n.d). There is also the separate (but compounding) highly emotive issue of Sri Lankan women moving to the Middle East to work as domestic maids and suffering abuse and sexual harassment (Jones, 2015).

The state's victory in the civil war in 2009 helped to promote the idea that belligerence and simple messages were more effective and impactful than dialogue and peace negotiations, which are lengthy, complex and iterative. "The LTTE's military defeat emboldened nationalists" (DeVotta, 2021, p.97) and there are strong linkages between social and political changes in the post-war period and ethno-religious tensions and identities. The state and armed forces definitively tried to show that complex social conflicts could be solved by force, and investigations of root causes or conditions for armed conflict were dismissed. Dialogue, negotiations, reconciliation and national healing efforts after the war were all brushed aside and the government instead adopted a triumphalist and celebratory rhetoric that paraded the military victory over the LTTE. The victorious state and armed forces were instrumental in hindering reconciliation efforts, perceived this as further capitulation and weakness. All this assisted in constructing a narrative of Buddhist grievance, both historic and current.

Subsequently, the state, the army and the Sinhalese majority, made little effort to integrate Muslims in post-war policies or acknowledge their history of suffering and victimisation particularly during the civil war (Uyangoda, 2007). Muslims have suffered social and political exclusion, and their interests continue to be neglected (Yusoff, Hussin & Sarjoon, 2014). Much as the country has seen the development of exclusionary politics and discourse against Islam, there has also been growing influence from wealthy Gulf countries that seek to attract Sri Lankan Muslims' allegiances and loyalty. Islamic scholars in Sri Lanka admit that these cultural and economic influences are problematic for the development of an indigenous Sri Lankan Islam that is not an extension of Wahhabi philosophies and Gulf Arab cultural norms (Mayilvaganan, 2008; MacGilvray, 2011; Morrison, 2019). As Ali (2013, p.308) notes: "This new identity… promoted the growth of religious consciousness within the community and made *ummah Islamiyya* or Islamic community and not the nation of Sri Lanka the primary entity of allegiance".

Such a distinctly separate religious identity also has the additional effect of holding the country's Muslims part of a "universal *umma* whose rights and obligations are religiously determined and lie outside the dictates of a politically constructed Buddhist entity" (Ali, 2013, p.312). The anti-minority rhetoric and public discourse operates in conjunction with the shrinking of political space and the delegitimisation of Muslim concerns and grievances. Imtiyaz and Mohamed-Saleem (2015) examine the legacy of concessions by the Sinhalese political elites to co-opt Muslims into broader anti-Tamil legislation and incorporate them as allies against the LTTE given their shared histories of suffering due to Tamil separatist violence. This legacy of state concessions to enhance the alliance of anti-LTTE stakeholders had the additional impact of deepening Muslims' isolationist and separatist socio-political tendencies, which ultimately may have contributed to the 2019 Easter attacks (Imtiyaz, 2019). In other words, the ethno-religious hegemony promoted by the state is itself a likely causal factor in the 2019 *jihadi* bombings.

The influence from overseas also leads to changes in dress, education and diet, among other factors, that can feed into the accusation that Muslims reject mainstream Sri Lankan culture and seek to subvert the existing socio-religious order. Diet, dress and behaviour constitute highly visible external markers of religious identity. These symbols of Islamic piety are often now labelled in Sri Lanka as foreign, Arabic and are held to undermine the integrity of nationhood and identity. However, "there are no anti-Muslim 'historical memories' recorded in the collective Sinhala psyche that can be tapped into and exploited" (Sarjoon, Yusoff & Hussin, 2016, p.124). Therefore, "Why has the Sri Lankan state (predominantly led by its Sinhala-Buddhist constituents) now turned its back on the Muslim minority given their close historical relationship?" (Imtiyaz & Mohamed-Saleem, 2015, p.186).

At the same time there exist tensions and dissent within Sri Lankan Muslim communities, particularly around Wahhabi influences from Saudi Arabia. This argument posits, if Muslims revel in their differentiation and celebrate homelands and religious origins elsewhere, how can they also claim to be inherently "real" Sri Lankans? This development of exclusivity within Muslim communities (Ali, 2013) may have contributed to the factionalism and competing allegiances that prevented the emergence of a coherent group identity that allowed Muslims to collectively challenge enemies (Klem, 2011). Sri Lanka has not produced any specific indigenous Islamic reformist movements (McGilvray, 2011), which has parallels with the lack of a specific Sri Lankan Buddhist non-violent ideology. The lack of a Muslim ethno-religious identity distinct and belonging to Sri Lanka may have contributed to opening the way for "ultra-religious orthodoxy" spread by Christian evangelical movements and Saudi-backed Wahhabism (Ali, 2013, p.299). The waves of "ultra-Islamic orthodoxy" (Ali, 2013) in recent decades have been increasingly visible in the public arena and feed into Buddhist extremist accusations that Muslims do not belong there. There are thus parallels in the rise of both Islamic and Buddhist orthodoxies in Sri Lanka. Along with economic competition, these intractable orthodoxies among both Buddhists and Muslims are the main causes of the current conflict (Ali, 2013).

Overview of Buddhist Extremist Violence and Non-violence in Sri Lanka

The label "Buddhist extremism" is contested, and long before current events, Bartholomeusz and de Silva (1998) suggested that Buddhist fundamentalism is a more accurate term than Buddhist extremism for the Sri Lankan religious context. Their view is based on the positioning of faith as the dominant identity marker, strong in-group and out-group boundaries, and the categorical demonisation of enemies. These factors are not found to the same extent in other schools of Buddhism. Bartholomeusz and de Silva (1998, p.3) claim that "Sinhala-Buddhist fundamentalism is thus inextricably linked to ethnic chauvinism": the conflation of religious and ethnic identities. The linkages between Buddhist nationalism, ethnic hegemony and the ruling state have been well documented (Devotta & Ganguly, 2019). This follows the further positioning and debates around Sri Lankan Buddhism as inimical to Western concepts of pluralism and secularism, and to other faiths' presence on the island.

Coupled with the exclusivism that Ali (2013) highlights, this is another factor in Sri Lanka's post-war challenges to comprehensive reconciliation and forging of an inclusive national identity. Sri Lankan Buddhist hardliners and their tensions with Islam in particular, do not form part of the "clash of civilisations" as conceptualised in Western scholarship. The country's Buddhists do not perceive the West and its promotion of secular democracy as an ally against Islamic fundamentalism. Political Buddhism in Sri Lanka has much in common with political Islam in many Muslim-majority countries, with its concepts of racial purity, hegemonic religious identity for the nation and strict demarcations of in-group and out-group belonging (Ali, 2013), whose impacts increase the sharp divisions between ethnic boundaries and identities, becoming more concrete in fomenting in-group and out-group thinking. The hardening of monolithic religious identities among both Muslims and Buddhists pose severe challenges for peaceful communal living.

The rise of the global Islamic identity, and with it the promotion of religious conservatism and emphasis of doctrinal differences between Muslims and any other faith, has fed into accusations by Sinhalese Buddhist nationalists that Muslims do not truly "belong" on the island. And furthermore, that their faith is incompatible with Buddhism; in this, both Buddhists and Muslims traditionalists agree. Similarly, both faiths profess a nostalgic belief of imagined historical purity, before degeneration, race mixing and lack of true faith. Additionally, there is a lack of secular education for ordained Buddhist clergy or sufficient exposure to other cultures, ideologies and economic realities (Morrison, 2019). They lack context-specific knowledge of pressing and polarising issues such as social relations, birth control, factors driving alcohol abuse, domestic violence, suicide or premarital sex. This produces a narrow and rigid perception of modern Sri Lanka among the monks, yet they retain significant socio-cultural influence. This influence remains a powerful force shaping public opinion and political priorities, and the voices of moderate Buddhist monks and those calling for peace and reconciliation have been devalued, mocked, or even threatened (Morrison, 2019).

Mobilisation of anti-Muslim sentiment has increased since the war's end, despite the fact that the main belligerents were Tamils not Muslims. Buddhist extremist organisations – such as the *Bodu Bala Sena* – have raised their public profile and have had a close, if complex, relationship with the state. The state plays a significant role in permitting politically-motivated ethnic riots to occur, and this holds true for both democratic and authoritarian states (Wilkinson, 2009). Sri Lanka has a history of ethnic rioting, most prominently in 2014 and 2018 that featured mob violence against mostly Muslim targets, including homes, businesses and mosques. There were several deaths and many injuries, but only a small number of arrests and people charged with incitement or other crimes. However, the violence during riots is opportunistic, emotive, and retains spontaneous elements, and is a very different type of violence to pre-meditated actions by a suicide bomber or *Jihadi* who mows pedestrians down in the street.

Sri Lanka's history featured close relations and a general lack of conflict between Sinhalese and Muslims, until the events of recent years (Ali, 2013). This positive view of the past is contested by Aliff (2015, p.111) who discusses the anti-Muslim riots perpetrated by Sinhalese in 1915 and claims: "Muslim communities… have been the target of discrimination, political violence, massacres and ethnic cleansing since 1915". The issue of what constitutes non-violence is similarly contested. Galtung's position is that any impingement of civil liberties or human rights, or any type of social injustice, can be considered structural violence (Galtung, 1969).

Many Muslims now feel inadequately represented in Sri Lanka's heterogeneous environment, but conversely many Buddhist nationalists feel the same; that the country no longer belongs to them, and yet they are the rightful owners. Sri Lanka is an example of religious extremism more bound up with non-violent actions than overtly violent, although Buddhist monks' attitudes, speech and behaviour can influence other groups who employ violent methods. Within the framework of what we label religious "extremism", there is a continuum of negative behaviours that move from ostensibly non-violence to overt violence.

There is a lack of solidarity across Buddhists in different countries, and there is no pattern of the global consciousness of a collective *ummah* (global community of Muslims) as found in Islam, for example. Islam has a holy land and more than a billion followers, whereas *Theravada* Buddhism is confined to South East Asia. Buddhist monks' practice of suicide in public places to call attention to injustice have been used in Tibetan communities and in Vietnam, Japan, Korea and China, but have not occurred in Sri Lanka. One remarkable aspect of Buddhism in Sri Lanka is the absence of home-grown non-violent ideologies (DeVotta, 2018), unlike Buddhism in other countries such as Tibet, Japan or China. Buddhist monks were very visible during the war years, agitating for military solutions and attacking peaceful protests, advocates for negotiations, and other non-violent efforts to stop the conflict (Gravers, 2015). Buddhist temples were even used during the conflict to store weapons and hide armed fighters (Johnson, 2016). Despite the rhetoric of Buddhism that promotes itself as inherently peaceful, a religion whose principal tenets include non-violence as an ideal for humanity, it has not in Sri Lanka produced a coherent framework for practicing this (Bartholomeusz, 2002; Uyangoda, 1996). On the contrary, Sri Lanka's complex history of ethno-religious tensions and nationalism has helped create the conditions for a Buddhism whose followers perceive it to be under threat and hence justify violent means to protect it (Bartholomeusz, 2002).

Discussion

Religious extremism in Sri Lanka calls into question the distance between extremist actors, non-extremist believers, and the ruling state. Extremists, whether motivated by religion or nationalism or a combination, are not necessarily "engaged in a 'war of ideas'" (Baran, 2005, p.14) against the socio-political and cultural system in which they operate; there is a more nuanced relationship with state power and the security apparatus. Extremists in the Sri Lankan context often benefit from government propaganda and feed into other avenues of ethno-nationalist discourse. The state may perceive extremist actors more as allies than as threats; a tool to promote nationalist discourse, further political gains and mobilise voters. The distinction between violent and nonviolent types of extremism may exist more in theory than in practice, and symbolic, structural and latent aspects of violence must be considered as well. For example, political discourse may in itself be non-violent, yet is directly implicated in fomenting violent acts further down the line.

To label a religious phenomenon as "extremist" may also be misleading. The emergence of groups or ideologies designated extremist occurs in specific contexts and circumstances, often either where the state ignores ethno-religious grievances or conversely where the state facilitates and encourages the expression of extremist narratives and actions. Bartholomeusz and de Silva (1998) point to the close relation between Buddhism, politicians and power that emerged in the late 19th century during British occupation. What is categorised as Buddhist extremism, may therefore be more accurately understood as a positioning of exclusive nationalist positions as politically expedient for the ruling class (DeVotta, 2021). Ethno-politics and narrow inter-pretations of religion are intimately connected, and this dynamic hinders the construction of national identities that transcend socio-religious positions and prevents the formulation of a fully cohesive national identity that all ethnicities and faiths can legitimately lay claim to.

Ethnic grievances and religious extremism are closely connected. The religious syncretism that existed previously in Sri Lanka, and social identities based on ethnicity rather than religion, have largely changed, leaving the post-war social environment characterised by multiple and competing sets of grievances. The majority of Buddhists, laypeople as well as ordained monks, do not follow any extremist practices and some actively campaign against extremism and violence despite the risks that this might pose for their reputation and safety (Morrison, 2019). The silencing and undermining of religious voices calling for peace and reconciliation illustrate the extent to which Buddhist teachings of forgiveness and harmony have been subsumed under a nationalist and ethnically hegemonic narrative within the context of the Sri Lankan state.

Much like religious fundamentalists anywhere, Sri Lanka's Buddhist extremists reject the implications of a multi-racial and multi-communal society as an unwanted and foreign capitulation. The argument is that if the national identity and the land itself are not to be shared with *outsiders*, then political power should not be either. In the eyes of extremists, Sri Lankan Buddhism is merely asserting its dominant and natural position in society, after historical humiliations and weaknesses (such as those associated with British colonial subjugation), just as the state and the ethnic majority are re-establishing their rightful position, as they perceive it, after the humiliations and grievances of the war. This rationalisation permits acts and discourse that transgress Buddhism's basic tenets.

Within Sri Lankan Islam, there are elements that resist wider social integration and practice a type of self-imposed cultural isolation. This phenomenon has been remarked on Muslims themselves, by Buddhist monks and by Catholic priests (Morrison, 2020). Muslims have been able to increase their interests and representation, with more Islamic education, more *madrasat* (Islamic schools), more access to public broadcasting, more intrusion of *shari'a* law into issues like marriage, divorce and inheritance; albeit whilst Sinhalese and Tamils were fighting a lengthy civil war (Ali, 2013). There is a related charge of anti-Muslim sentiment, that they form parallel societies; that they are not loyal to their own country but always look to the Middle East for teachings and guidance. In this, the hardline Islamic fundamentalists and the nationalist Buddhists share the same view; that they are Muslims firstly, and Sri Lankans secondly. The national identity is subservient to the religious identity, whereas for the Buddhist hardliners, these two issues are the same thing.

The narrowing formulation of religious and national identities has the effect of forcing out non-members; the exclusivity itself breeds more exclusion and insularity. For these reasons, Sri Lanka's other two religious minorities, Christians and Hindus, do not experience the same tensions around belonging and identity as the island's Muslim communities. Their contestations around insularity and belonging are not subject to the same external pull factors and internal exclusionary factors.

Conclusion

To return to the research questions, the causal factors relating to the growth of fundamentalist and extremist philosophies and activity in Sri Lankan Buddhism can be viewed in parallel to the growth of factors influencing the hardening of rigid and incompatible social identities based around religious belonging that have impacted Islam significantly as well. In a complex and crowded public sphere, violent and non-violent activities can be situated on a continuum within a structural violence framework. The ramifications of ostensibly non-violent public discourse and activities may have more severe impacts on social relations than violence like riots or attacks on properties. Beyond examining religious scripture and teachings for explanations of extremism, the exogenous political, social and cultural factors should be analysed. The dangers associated with any faith group promoting the idea that their religious teachings take precedence over political and secular law are visible and manifest, but we can also see how an exclusive form of nationhood can too perpetuate structurally violent outcomes.

This has led to the current divisive political environment in the country: a legacy of the war, capture of government centred around ethnic hegemony, and the positioning of national identities through a narrow lens of religious belonging based entirely on in-group and out-group framings. Social diversity itself has become a threat to nationalist hegemony, as the concept of a national identity that transcends ethno-religious identities is anathema to fundamentalists. From a structural violence viewpoint, denying a person's agency, decision-making power and adequate collective representation all constitute aspects of violence, even if they are not physically attacked. Boycotting businesses and shops, combined with repeated hate speech and accusations, severely infringe on a group's ability to establish and protect their own security. Moreover, denying people a collective identity encourages individuals to seek identities elsewhere, which creates further cycles of exclusion.

Sri Lanka experiences multiple and competing claims of resentment and victimhood. Moving beyond tolerance, the country's minorities need to be actively integrated as full members of a rich and diverse society. Sinhalese Buddhists are demographically far more numerous than any other ethno-religious group on the island, yet some feel threatened and aggrieved. Sri Lanka has succeeded in combining democratic norms and high voter turnout with the consolidation of religious national identities in a multi-faith, multi-ethnic country. These are challenged by the factor of majoritarianism, which promotes the importance of national belonging for certain groups (*and not belonging for other groups*) over concepts like equal citizenship. This entails a move away from pluralism, towards the denial of public, political and cultural space for minorities, and encroachment of Buddhist nationalist policies onto previously secular or multi-faith policies. This denial of standard civil liberties for Muslims, or any out-group, are outward aspects of this regressive conservatism and illiberalism. Events occurring in Sri Lanka bear multiple similarities with religious extremism elsewhere.

Religious fundamentalism or extremism is a cover for political power grabs, ethnic prejudice and denial of social pluralism, and thus Buddhist extremism may be a misnomer. Nationalism may be a more accurate term than religious extremism, and has led to parallel societies existing in the same country but sharing little else. Under these conditions, the distinction between violent and non-violent extremism loses its meaning. Rather than being different categories, in certain contexts, they become different sides of the same exclusivist coin.

Bibliography

Ali, A. (2013). Political Buddhism, Islamic Orthodoxy and Open Economy: The Toxic Triad in Sinhalese–Muslim Relations in Sri Lanka. *Journal of Asian and African Studies, 49*(3), 298–314. DOI:10.1177/0021909613485708

Aliff, S. M. (2015). Post-War Conflict in Sri Lanka: Violence against Sri Lankan Muslims and Buddhist Hegemony. *International Letters of Social and Humanistic Sciences, 59*, 9–125. DOI:10.18052/www.scipress.com/ILSHS.59.

Baran, Z. (2005). Fighting the War of Ideas. *Foreign Affairs, 84*(6), 68–78 https://doi.org/10.2307/20031777

Bartholomeusz, T. J. & de Silva, C. R. (1998). Buddhist Fundamentalism and Identity in Sri Lanka. In Buddhist Fundamentalism and Minority Identities in Sri Lanka, edited by T. J. Bartholomeusz and C. R. de Silva, Chandra R. (pp. 1–30). Albany, NY: State University of New York Press.

DeVotta, N. (2018). Religious Intolerance in Post-Civil War Sri Lanka. *Asian Affairs, 49*(2), 278–300. DOI: 10.1080/03068374.2018.1467660

DeVotta, N. (2020). Promoting Covenantal Pluralism amidst Embedded Majoritarianism in Sri Lanka, *The Review of Faith & International Affairs, 18*(4), 49–62, https://doi.org/10.1080/15570 274.2020.1834980

DeVotta, N. (2021). Sri Lanka: The Return to Ethnocracy. *Journal of Democracy, 32*(1), 96–110. DOI: 10.1353/jod.2021.0003

Devotta, N. & Ganguly, S. (2019). "Sri Lanka's Post–Civil War Problems", *Current History, 118* (807). DOI:10.1525/curh.2019.118.807.137

Galtung, J. (1969). Violence, Peace, and Peace Research. *Journal of Peace Research, 6*(3), 167–191. DOI:10.1177/002234336900600301

Gombrich, R. (2006). Is the Sri Lankan War a Buddhist Fundamentalism? In Buddhism, Conflict and Violence in Modern Sri Lanka, edited by M. Deegalle, 22–37.Oxon and New York: Routledge.

Gravers, M. (2015). Anti-Muslim Buddhist Nationalism in Burma and Sri Lanka: Religious Violence and Globalized Imaginaries of Endangered Identities. *Contemporary Buddhism, 16*(1), 1–27. DOI:10.1080/ 14639947.2015.1008090

Imam, S. (no date). Are Cow-Related Hate Crimes against Muslims Only a 'New India' Phenomenon? Retrieved from https://thewire.in/communalism/cow-lynching-muslim-internet-state-sanction

Imtiyaz, A. R. M. (2019). The Easter Sunday Bombings and the Crisis Facing Sri Lanka's Muslims. *Journal of Asian and African Studies, 55*(5), 14, DOI:10.1177/0021909619868244

Imtiyaz, A. R. M. & Amjad, M.-S. (2015). Muslims in Post-War Sri Lanka; Understanding Sinhala-Buddhist Mobilization against Them. *Asian Ethnicity, 16*(2), 186–202. DOI:10.1080/ 14631369.2015.1003691

Johnson, D. (2016). Taking Liberties and Making Liberty: Religious Bounding and Political Violence in Sri Lanka. *Religion,. 46*(3), 309–330. DOI: 10.1080/0048721X.2016.1139012

Jones, R. N. B. (2015). Sinhala Buddhist Nationalism and Islamophobia in Contemporary Sri Lanka. Published Honors Thesis. Retrieved from: http://scarab.bates.edu/honorstheses/126

Klem, B. (2011). Islam, Politics and Violence in Eastern Sri Lanka. *The Journal of Asian Studies 70*(3), 730–753. DOI:10.1017/S002191181100088X

Mahadev, N. (2014). Conversion and Anti-Conversion in Contemporary Sri Lanka: Pentecostal Christian Evangelism and Theravada Buddhist Views on the Ethics of Religious Attraction. In Proselytizing and the Limits of Religious Pluralism in Contemporary Asia, edited by J. Finucane and M. Feener, pp. 211–236. New York, NY: Springer.

Mayilvaganan, M. (2008). The Muslim Factor in the Sri Lankan Ethnic Conflict. *Strategic Analysis, 32*(5), 833–853, DOI:10.1080/09700160802309217

McGilvray, D. (2011). Sri Lankan Muslims: Between Ethno-Nationalism and the Global Ummah. *Nations and Nationalism, 17*(1), 45–64. DOI:10.1111/j.1469-8129.2010.00460.x

Morrison, C. (2019). Buddhist Extremism, Anti-Muslim Violence and Civil War Legacies in Sri Lanka. *Asian Ethnicity, 21*(1), 137–159, DOI:10.1080/14631369.2019.1610937

Morrison, C. (2020). Post-Conflict Interfaith Activities, Combating Religious Extremism and Mass Atrocity in Sri Lanka. *The Journal of Peace & Conflict, 13*(1), 99–124. Retrieved from: https://revistas eug.ugr.es/index.php/revpaz/article/view/13901/13433

Sarjoon, A., Yusoff, M. A. & Hussin, N. (2016). Anti-Muslim Sentiments and Violence: A Major Threat to Ethnic Reconciliation and Ethnic Harmony in Post-War Sri Lanka. *Religions, 7*(125). DOI:10.3390/ rel7100125

Stewart, J. J. (2014). Muslim–Buddhist Conflict in Contemporary Sri Lanka. *South Asia Research, 34*(3), 241–260. DOI:10.1177/0262728014549134

United Kingdom Home Office (2018). Country Policy and Information Note Sri Lanka: Minority Religious Groups. Retrieved from: https://assets.publishing.service.gov.uk/government/uploads/ system/uploads/attachment_data/file/835663/sri-lanka-country-policy-info-note-religious-minorit ies.pdf

Uyangoda, J. (1996). Militarization, Violent State, Violent Society: Sri Lanka. In Internal Conflicts in South Asia, edited by K. Rupesinghe and M. Khawar, Vol. 11; pp. 118–130. Oslo (PRIO): International Peace Research Institute.

Uyangoda, J. (2007). Ethnic Conflict in Sri Lanka: Changing Dynamics. *Policy Studies, 32*, East-West Center Washington. Retrieved from www.eastwestcenter.org/system/tdf/private/PS032.pdf?file= 1&type=node&id=32178

Wilkinson, S. I. (2009). Riots. *Annual Review of Political Science, 12*(1), 329–343. DOI:10.1146/annurev. polisci.12.041307.075517

Yusoff, M. A., Hussin, N. & Sarjoon, A. (2014). Positioning Muslims in Ethnic Relations, Ethnic Conflict and Peace Process in Sri Lanka. *Asian Social Science, 10*(10), 199–211. DOI:10.5539/ass. v10n10p199

PART 3

Far-Right Extremism

Non-violence Among Movements on the Exclusionary Right

15

BARRIERS TO VIOLENCE ACTIVISM ON THE UK FAR RIGHT

The Case of the (Democratic) Football Lads Alliance

William Allchorn

Introduction

The UK far right has experienced a marked transition in the past decade from parliamentary to more extra-parliamentary forms of activism. Initially expressed in the form of street protest movements in the late 2000s and early 2010s, signs of vigilantism and terror groupuscules[1] have now been added to the picture mix as the UK far right transforms into a more fractured, post-organisational phase of movement development (Mulhall, 2019). Predominantly focused on anti-Muslim forms of mobilisation since the early 2000s, the UK far right experienced a shift back to more biologically racist themes in the summer of 2020 as a result of Black Lives Matter (BLM) protests in June. A large-scale protest attended by Britain First, the UK National Front and Democratic Football Lads Alliance activists as well as other anti-minority protestors in June demonstrated the exploitation of anti-BLM narratives by the organised far right (Heren, 2020), and the possibility of a unifying mobilisation theme for the fractured movement, which has struggled to retain relevance after the implosion of the neo-fascist British National Party (BNP) and UK Independence party.

In parallel with the developments at the party political level has seen the rise of culturally nationalist[2] street movements and neo-Nazi terror cells in the UK – especially in the period after the BNP's collapse. In June 2009, the anti-Islam English Defence League (EDL) street movement emerged as a strident voice against what it saw as the "creeping effects" of "Islamisation" in UK public life (EDL Website, 2013). Able to mobilise thousands of loyal foot soldiers for its events and emerging as the result of Islamist extremists demonstrating at the homecoming of UK troops in the Bedfordshire town of Luton, it hosted over fifty major demonstrations up and down the UK – under the banner of " not racist, not violent, just no longer silent" – until the exit of its founder, Tommy Robinson, in October 2013 (Goodwin, 2013). The EDL continues to be active – hosting 13 major demonstrations in 2017, 3 in 2018 and 1 in 2019 – but the scale of its demonstrations has dropped significantly – with its best turnout in the past several years being some 200 activists (Hope not Hate, 2018, p. 19).

DOI: 10.4324/9781003032793-19

Yet the EDL is not the only street-based movement to emerge in the wake of the BNP's collapse. In May 2011, another anti-Islam protest movement and political party, Britain First, emerged on the UK culturally nationalist scene. Led by a former BNP Councillor, Paul Golding, Britain First has gained notoriety for its "Mosque Invasions", "Christian Patrol", and demonstrations held in areas with sizeable Muslim populations in the UK that are explicitly designed to provoke minority communities. Despite garnering a significant online following (nearly 2.3 million Facebook followers), it was in fact offline actions by the group caught up with the movement in 2017 – with both leaders facing time in prison for conducting a Cardiff " Mosque Invasion" in November 2016 (Pasha-Robinson, 2016) and an aggressive leafleting campaign against an Asian-owned takeaway restaurants in May 2017 (Doherty, 2018). As of spring 2018, the movement and its leaders have been banned from Facebook and Twitter and its operations have largely been relegated to Northern Ireland (Cellan-Jones, 2018). The litany of criminal charges – including terrorism – lodged against its leaders has fractured and limited the group's largely confrontational form of activism, which never quite spilled over into violence (despite no explicit commitment to non-violence in its founding statements) (Britain First, 2021a–c).[3]

In addition to Britain First, the third far-right group to emerge during the UK far right's switch from the ballot box to the streets has been the Football Lads Alliance (FLA). Formed in June 2017 by property manager and Tottenham Hotspur fan, John Meighan, the movement successfully hosted several high-level demonstrations attracting tens of thousands of followers. "Uniting against extremism & violence" and lobbying for a harder line against Islamist terrorists (Chaplain, 2017), the group however became more extreme and fratitious as time went on – with the emergence of a splinter group, the Democratic Football Lads Alliance (DFLA), in March 2018 (BBC News, March 2018). Many have drawn parallels between the DFLA and the EDL – with a similar commitment to non-violence and racism being at the core of the group's outward framing (Allen, 2018; Allchorn & Feldman, 2019).

The counterfactual of what act as barriers to violence in extremist organisations has weighed heavily on the minds of extremism scholars recently. Even if only strategic, a commitment to non-violence is often held to by these far-right movements in order to steer away from being tarred with the brush of extremism. Using Busher, Holbrook and Macklin (2019) conceptualisation of barriers to violent extremism, this chapter analyses the contents of posts from the DFLA's website and its official Facebook page in order to assess how violence and non-violence is presented within the group's everyday communications. The chapter will uncover what discursive, strategic and symbolic brakes that have led both groups away from moving further up the conveyor belt of extremism to violent action and what this means for scholars and practitioners thinking about barriers to violent extremism more broadly. Moreover, it will add to the scant literature examining the (Democratic) Football Lads Alliance at the time of writing. The chapter will proceed with a literature review of students in the UK's contemporary far right before providing a concise overview of the developmental trajectory of the DFLA case study and finally providing a content analysis of the groups communiqué s and core documents in order to assess the groups' commitment to non-violence.

Purely Strategic? Frames of Non-violence within the Contemporary UK Far Right

The study of non-violence among street-based activists in contemporary UK far right is a marginal literature that has revolved around cultural nationalist[4] groups as part of this scene. The first text to outline such a commitment was Busher's (2014) chapter on anti-Muslim populism – focused specifically on the EDL – in an edited volume looking at the changing face of populism in Europe and US. Here, Busher noted that at key instances – where violence became too much or where divergence from peaceful protest was called for among a minority of activists – that the EDL generally eschew violence for more peaceful means of demonstrating against what it perceived as the " creeping effects" of " Islamisation" in UK. For example, when demonstrations in 2011 and 2012 were marked with violence, activists conducted lengthy discussions about how to quell such excesses – with some activists suggesting that they would either step back or step away from the movement if no safeguards were put in place (Busher, 2014, p.222). Moreover, when retaliatory violence was inveighed against Mosques and other Islamic centres in 2013 as a consequence of the Islamist Woolwich attack, the leadership issued a statement saying that they did not condone the spate of attacks perpetrated against mosques, and much of the activist community soon moved back towards organising more socially accepted modes of protest such as memorial marches and charity fundraisers (Busher, 2014, p.223).

Such findings and observations were also reported by Busher in an earlier volume (2013) on the use of non-violence as a performative and organisational act among the EDL. Noting five key themes as part of the EDL's group discourse, Busher noted that activists were very keen to stress that violence was the exception and not the norm at their demonstrations and that if it did occur that in came from a drunken unruly minority who didn't respect the instructions of the group's stewards (Busher, 2013, p.69). Though certain demonstrations and solo flash-type actions by EDL activists had resulted in violence, Busher's initial field work observations of 7 out of 9 EDL demonstrations found that flashpoints usually came out of confrontation with organised counter-protestors and that activists liaised well and acted courteously towards police officers as parts of " impression management" (Goffman, 1969) in order to stress that it wasn't a traditional far-right movement (Busher, 2013, pp.67–68).

One final text to again deal with commitments to non-violence as part of the contemporary UK far right is a co-authored piece by Busher, Macklin and Holbrook (2019). This used – among other Islamist and animal rights extremist groups – the neo-fascist BNP in the 1990s as an example of a group that as it strove to achieve electoral legitimacy whilst simultaneously struggling to contain the actions and growing influence of its own radical flank – Combat 18 (Busher, Macklin and Holbrook 2019, p. 6). Developing from this experience, they developed a five-fold typology to delineate the internal brakes on violent escalation expressed by the BNP.

These included: 1) Strategic identification with non- or less violent strategies as being more effective than violence, 2) Moral norms that prohibit violence, 3) Group self-identification as using limited formed of violence, 4) boundary softening in terms of out-groups or perceived " enemies" or 5) any organisational developments that aid the above (Busher, Macklin and Holbrook, 2019, p.9). For example, while part of the reason for the BNP's innovation away from violence was the realisation that they were unable to " out-violence" their antifascist opponents, the ability of " modernisers" to build support within the movement was enhanced by the identification of the potential of interventions such as their " Rights for Whites" campaign to exploit perceived political opportunities (Busher, Macklin and Holbrook, 2019, p. 9). In conclusion, Busher et al (2019) found that in the extreme right case, brakes operating on strategic logics (Brake 1) were more evident than those that work on moral logics (Brake 2) when promoting non-violent activism (Busher, Macklin and Holbrook, 2019, p.20).

In terms of the Democratic Football Lads Alliance (DFLA) itself, there has been relatively scant attention given to the group – despite the size of its demonstrations and merger with more established UK far right actors. At the time of writing, only three research reports had touched upon the group's significance, its *modus operandi* and collective identity (Allchorn & Feldman, 2019; Allen, 2019; McGlashan, 2020). Two of these articles touch upon violence explicitly, with one addressing the violent turn observed under the March 2018 DFLA splinter and the other the association of the Islamic 'other' as violent within FLA online discourse (Allchorn & Feldman, 2019; McGlashan, 2020). Contributing to this fledgling literature on the group, this chapter will test discursive and real-world commitments to non-violence in a new and understudied case of far-right street activism in the UK, the DFLA – comparing front stage social media discourses and website posts, as well as articles recording the nature of the group's demonstrations to unpick tensions between rhetoric and praxis in non-violence when it comes to the UK's far right.

Rhetorical Commitments to Non-violence: DFLA's Founding Statement, Public Facebook Page and Early Demonstrations

A prototype to the DFLA, the Football Lads Alliance was formed on 4 June 2017 by property manager and Tottenham Hotspur supporter, John Meighan. The movement successfully hosted its first " Unite Against Extremism" demonstration on 24 June 2017 in central London – rallying some 10,000 supporters at St. Paul's Cathedral before marching to London Bridge (Smith & Shifrin, 2017). Chanting " FLA, here to stay", marchers left wreaths in football club colours among the flowers and candles marking the spot where, three weeks prior, five people had been killed as a van careered into pedestrians (Smith & Shifrin, 2017). Before the march, speeches were given in Hyde Park by former EDL activist, Mohan Singh, and founder of the anti-Muslim campaign organisation, Mothers Against Radical Islam and *shari'a*, Toni Bugle, highlighting "concern" about recent terror attacks in London and Manchester, but nothing further in terms of a specific social, political or cultural agenda.

The immediate stimulus for the formation of the FLA – a group that at its core claimed to be against all forms of extremism and terrorism from its foundations – clearly emerged in reaction to several Islamist extremist-inspired terror attacks that occurred from March to June 2017. The first of these took place in March 2017 when a 52-year-old man, Khalid Masood, drove through crowds of tourists on Westminster Bridge before entering the grounds of the Palace of Westminster and fatally wounding a police officer (Allen and Henderson, 2017). The second of these came at the end of May when a young, twenty-two-year-old man of Libyan extraction, Salman Abedi, detonated an explosive vest at the end of an Arianna Grande pop concert at a large stadium in Manchester – killing twenty-two people and injuring one hundred and twenty (Evans et al, 2017). Continuing the horrific, "do-it-yourself" nature of terrorist attacks around this period, the third came at the start of June when a van yet again mounted the pavement, this time near London Bridge – after which the attackers ran to a nearby restaurants and pubs in Borough Market to continue their rampage of destruction (BBC News, 2017).

As expected, these appalling, frightening incidents gained significant pushback and reaction from both established and fringe figures on the UK far right. This is in no small measure due to the way far-right activists and groups seek to use such outrages to further a political agenda; in this case, the scapegoating of more than 3.5 million Muslims living in Britain. For example, far-right ideologue and former EDL leader, Tommy Robinson (aka Stephen Yaxley-Lennon) happened to be in London at the time of the Westminster attack – using it as a chance to claim that Britain was at "war" with "Islamic fundamentalists" (Oppenheim, 2017). Moreover, the end of June 2017 witnessed a devastating instance of "tit-for-tat extremism" when Darren Osborne responded to the London and Manchester terror attacks by ploughing into a group of Muslim worshippers at Finsbury Park Mosque (Dearden, 2018). Finally, and returning focus upon the FLA, such attacks had a cumulative effect – or "turning point" – for the otherwise obscure leader of the FLA, John Meighan who, as he stated in an interview at the time, "really felt strongly that something needed to be done." His initial aim for the group was first "bringing different [football] fans together" and second to put pressure on political elites to look again at "terror laws and preachers of hate" with an heavy emphasis on non-violence and peacefulness as part of its repertoire of action at its early demonstrations (Smith & Shifrin, 2017). Indeed, and taking conscious learnings from media coverage of early EDL protest, the FLA made efforts early on to combat accusations of racism and violence – with demonstrators instructed to not carry flags, banners or engage in racist chants (Smith & Shifrin, 2017).

Organisationally separate from the established UK far right – while at the same time owing much to click-and-march organisation of earlier groups like the EDL and Pegida – the FLA therefore started as a non-violent, non-politically aligned nationalistic and anti-establishment protest movement of working-class football casuals in the UK. Indeed, the FLA was first set up to encourage rival football firms to put aside their infighting and unite against extremism and the perceived threat it poses to "Britain and its way of life" (Allen, 2018). An example of this came at the group's second major demonstration on 7 October 2017. Demonstrating the scale of this new far right street movement, more than 20,000 demonstrators gathered on Park Lane in London to hear John Meighan rail against Diane Abbott's signing a petition tying the group to other far right outfits. Meighan also called for foreign-born terror suspects to be deported during any ongoing police investigations (Chaplain, 2017). Speaking to a mixture of football supporters and members of the Veterans Against Terrorism protest group, Meighan insisted the crowd was made of "normal people" who wanted to show concern at a "recent upsurge" in UK terrorist attacks (Murphy-Bates, 2019). Such commitments to non-violent non-politically aligned nationalistic and anti-establishment protesters seemed to be more the case than did the EDL before it, with reports from early demonstrations suggesting that on the whole demonstrators had a "small-c conservative law-n-order agenda, mostly made up of middle-aged 'common sense' dads, with a few racists hanging around fringes" (Poulter & Childs, 2018).

Testing Commitments to Non-violence: The DFLA Schism, Brushes with the Established UK Far Right and Later Demonstrations

When launched in mid-2017, the FLA's main aims revolved around the benign proposals of building a "safer community, inclusivity and acceptance of everyone, and holding politicians to account to change anti-terrorist legislation" (Football Lads Alliance, n.d.). Since the FLA–DFLA splinter in April 2018, the rhetoric and group of actors within this new protest movement have seen the group move onto issues more customarily associated with the UK far right. A key example of this has been the championing of the issue of child grooming and taking an ultra-patriotic stance on veteran's rights. This suggests that, months after their emergence the DFLA became an anti-Islamic protest movement – with more established UK far-right themes – that split from a more apolitical agenda with the FLA towards one more overtly mimicking the demands of "anti-Islamisation" championed by the EDL and Britain First.

As 2018 wore on, so it became apparent that – while the FLA had entered permanent decline – the DFLA's identity had become less differentiated from the ideology and tactics of more established UK far-right actors. At the DFLA's October 2018 demonstration in London, for example, organisers stated before the demonstration that they were protesting against " AWOL (i.e. Absent Without Leave) migrants", Asian " rape gangs and groomers" and "veterans treated like traitors" (Gayle, 2018). Moreover, at the DFLA's September 2018 protest in Sunderland, a flashpoint between DFLA demonstrators and anti-fascists saw violent clashes that ended in three arrests (Sunderland Echo, 2018). Finally, at the same demonstration, the

DFLA invited UKIP leader Gerrard Batten to speak to 700 of its supporters. As 2018 finished, therefore, some reporters started to question whether the DFLA had stuck to its original aims of anti-racism and anti-violence or was simply a reboot of the EDL (Hughes, 2018). With the same activist base, propensity towards violent behaviour and opposition to Islamist extremism, the DFLA was emerging as a new sanitised version of the EDL.

Content Analysis: Rhetorical Constructions of Non-violence in the DFLA

At the time of writing, most websites and social media pages of the FLA were unavailable. Ideally, the author would have liked to compare the changes in commitments to non-violence between the groups; however, only an archived version of the DFLA's website and the DFLA's official Facebook page could be accessed. Despite these difficulties, the DFLA's statements cast an interesting light on the leadership's use of non-violence – both as a way of othering their enemies (e.g. Islamist extremists, leftists and even the IRA) and distancing themselves from the toxicity of perceived violence that has embroiled other UK far-right street protest movements (e.g. National Front, EDL and Britain First). This positive self-negative other dichotomy is emblematic of extremist discourse more generally (Allchorn, 2018; Cabrejas-Peñuelas & Díez-Prados, 2014) and can be an important part in constructing in-group identity (Busher, 2013; Pilkington, 2016). Here, we analyse the text of 15 posts (of which 5 substantively discussed violence and non-violence) of the DFLA's (now defunct) website between August and November 2018 and a selection of relevant posts from the DFLA's official Facebook page in order to analyse positive self-negative other dichotomy when it comes to non-violence.[5] Posts were selected due to their explicit mention of violence and non-violence, their connection to official instructions and those that engaged in commentary around the group's protest events.[6] Qualitative content analysis was chosen in order to provide an in-depth analysis of how violence and non-violence are constructed by the group in text in a thorough and systematic manner.

In particular, the DFLA's mission statement is fairly similar in scope when it comes to the themes of extremism, terrorism, racism and violence. Placing the blame for "faking working class interests" at the feet of other extreme left and far-right groups, the DFLA maintain that they are an "anti-racist and anti-violence with no intention of seeking a political position" (About DFLA, August 2018). This anti-political defence is peppered through the mission statement – with a keen focus on law breakers and enemies of an imagined English working class – and is in contrast the increasingly political nature of the FLA's objective and aims towards the end of its existence (FLA About Us, 2022).

Moving on to other posts on the DFLA website, a more sustained trend emerges of singling out their opponents (so-called "Antifa", "leftists" and "radical Islamists") as being inherently violence when compared to the DFLA itself. In a post commenting on a DFLA vigilante action at Speakers Corner on 21 October 2018, for example, the writer speculates about collusion and appeasement between the police and "radical Islamists", stating that: "Obviously there was the possibility of confrontation or violence from the radical Islamist's" (DFLA Webpage a, October 2018). In contrast, the lack of disorder perpetrated by the 15 or so DFLA "patriot" there on the day is reified as an attempt to foster a positive in-group identity.

In another group of website posts by the DFLA's leadership, on a separate October 2018 demonstration, the writer of the post again counterpoised the non-violence of the DFLA versus their opponents. Describing counter protestors as "Antifa's violent masked terrorists", the writer speculates "No doubt the end game [of 'Antifa'/'leftists'] is to stop peaceful working class citizens from joining our media blanked demonstrations" (DFLA Webpage b, October

2018). Adding an even more conspiratorial, anti–state edge to their claims, the author suggests that any violence stoked by their left–wing opponents were used to ruin their relationship with the "bully boys in blue" (i.e. the UK's Police Service) and was an attempt to stoke up "state sponsored violence" against the DFLA (DFLA Webpage b, October 2018). Of course, in the end, the DFLA's discourse settles on a positive affirmation of in-group identity, with the author suggesting that the DFLA were "Trying to stop people who are provoked into violence by those who feel superior is not an easy task, but we held the line supporting the police whilst your mob laughed and jeered" (DFLA Webpage b, October 2018).

Turning to the DFLA's Official Facebook page, we can see such assurances of non-violence and speculation about violence perpetrated from the DFLA's opponents emulated in this more interactive media environment. Administrators and moderators of the page frequently remind contributors – when faced with hostility on the page and at demonstrations – not to "condone violence" and "act within the parameters of the Law" (DFLA Official Facebook page, post a). Similar to the Code of Conduct instituted by similar contemporary far-right street movements in the UK (e.g. the EDL in 2011 (Jackson, 2011, p. 22 and PEGIDA UK in early 2016)), such insistences against violence seem more a way of lending the group outward legitimacy rather than actual commitments to anti-violence per se. Adding a new enemy in order reinforce positive in-group identity when it comes to violence, posts of the DFLA's official Facebook page point out the violence perpetrated by anti-racist counter demonstrators, Stand up to racism (SUTR) and the Irish Republican Army (IRA) (DFLA Official Facebook page). In particular, and when searching for keywords and collocates of violence mentioned on the official DFLA Facebook page, both groups are represented in posts on the subject of violence – with one post, for instance, stating that "SUTR violently demonstrated [at a DFLA demonstration] in central London" and another vilifying a UK-based politician for refusing "to condemn IRA violence" (DFLA Official Facebook page, post b).

Conclusions and Recommendations

In conclusion, this chapter has explored the do-say gap in the commitment to non-violence of a relatively new actor on the UK's contemporary far right, the Democratic Football Lads Alliance. Initially committed to non-violence as part of its core identity in relation to ideations of "violent Islam" that reared their head in the UK in early 2017, the group's March 2018 FLA-DFLA splinter was both key to its organisational development as a group but also as a radicalising factor in the group's leadership, ideology and propensity to violence at its demonstrations. It was in reality, however, unsuccessfully able to police such outbursts. Demonstrations quickly descended into disorder and its ideology veered from its previously apolitical platform – with individuals from the UK's established far right and the incorporation of a nebulous of issues traditionally associated with other parts of the UK's culturally nationalist scene (Allchorn & Feldman, 2019). In conclusion, and as suggested by Busher et al (2019, p. 20) in relation to other far right groups, brakes to violence only operated at the strategic level in the DFLA (Brake 1) – rather than moral or symbolic logics (Brake 2) – when promoting non-violent activism. Moreover, and as we can see from the content analysis above, it was subsequently only used for fostering a positive collective in-group and limiting reputational damage at the elite level. To be clear, when the strategic direction of the DFLA changed after its March 2018 split with the FLA, then, so did its commitment to non-violence.

As this trajectory suggests, the DFLA has proven to be another incubator group for the far right, like the defence leagues and other anti-Muslim groups before it. Events of the summer of 2020 around anti-BLM protests in London suggest that its consciously apolitical public facing persona and ability to draw in non-aligned, small-"c" conservative football supporters could have the potential to unify and bolster the UK far right for the first time in over a decade (Heren, 2020). For this reason alone, and many others besides, simply branding the DFLA "Nazis" or "fascists" both misses the point and does little to bring non-aligned supporters back from the brink of joining the UK far right. While it is understandable that impassioned counter-protestors – whether by community locals, SUTR or Unite Against Fascism – may wish to physically contest their presence, the effects may be counterproductive and – as shown in the earlier analysis – actually foster positive in-group identity among activists. Moreover, and as other previous analyses have shown, disorder and misbranding are likely to only add to a sense of victimhood by protesters (Oaten, 2014). Such confrontations also run the risk of "tit-for-tat" escalation of abuse and even violence, and are therefore best avoided from a public order perspective.

Notes

1 Here, "Groupuscules" are defined as tiny, often neo-Nazi, bands of radical right extremists that establish a milieu with reference points that stretch out internationally as well as into the past as well (Jackson, 2021, p. 101).
2 Here, I use Bjørgo and Ravndal's (2019) distinction of culturally nationalist groups that abut the mainstream. They often have distinct, culturally racist concerns about Islam that are separate from more extreme ethno-nationalist or racially nationalist actors that observe forms of misogynist and anti-Semitic prejudice.
3 See: Britain First, "Britain First Official Policies", retrieved from: www.britainfirst.org/policies; Britain First, "Britain First Ideology", retrieved from: www.britainfirst.org/policies; and Britain First, "Principles of the Britain First Movement", retrieved from: www.britainfirst.org/principles
4 Here again, I use Bjørgo and Ravndal's (2019) distinction of culturally nationalist groups that are abut the mainstream. They often have distinct, culturally racist concerns about Islam that are separate from more extreme ethno-nationalist or racially nationalist actors that observe forms of misogynist and anti-Semitic prejudice.
5 Access to the author's database of DFLA website and Facebook page posts can be sent on request.
6 Obviously, the veracity of these accounts are limited as a given version of events by the DFLA's leadership themselves but does help paint a picture of how a movement struggling with protest event violence tries to manage this rhetorically.

Bibliography

Allchorn, W. (2019). Beyond Islamophobia? The role of Englishness and English national identity within English Defence League discourse and politics. National Identities, 21(5), 527–539, DOI: 10.1080/14608944.2018.1531840

Allchorn, W., and Feldman, M. (2019). The (Democratic) Football Lads Alliance: A Far Right Antechamber? London: Faith Matters. Retrieved from: www.faith-matters.org/wp-content/uploads/2019/04/dfla.pdf

Allen, C. (2018, 13 April). The Football Lads Alliance: The Latest Far Right Street Movement? London: Centre for the Analysis of the Radical Right. Retrieved from: www.radicalrightanalysis.com/2018/04/13/the-football-lads-alliance-the-latest-far-right-street-movement/

Allen, C. (2019). The Football Lads Alliance and Democratic Football Lad's Alliance: An insight into the dynamism and diversification of Britain's counter-jihad movement. Social Movement Studies, 18(5), 639–646. DOI: 10.1080/14742837.2019.1590694

Allen, E., and Henderson, B. (2017, 26 March). Westminster attack: Everything we know so far about the events in London. The Daily Telegraph. Retrieved from: www.telegraph.co.uk/news/2017/03/22/westminster-terror-attack-everything-know-far/

BBC News. (2017, 12 June). London attack: What we know so far. Retrieved from: www.bbc.co.uk/news/uk-england-london-40147164

BBC News. (2018, 24 March). Birmingham Football Lads Alliance demo: Thousands march in city. Retrieved from: www.bbc.co.uk/news/uk-england-birmingham-43527109

Bjørgo, T., and Ravndal, J. (2019). Extreme-Right Violence and Terrorism: Concepts, Patterns, and Responses. The Hague: ICCT. Retrieved from: https://icct.nl/publication/extreme-right-violence-and-terrorism-concepts-patterns-and-responses/

Britain First. (2021a). Britain First official policies. Retrieved from: www.britainfirst.org/policies

Britain First. (2021b). Britain First ideology. Retrieved from: www.britainfirst.org/policies

Britain First. (2021c). Principles of the Britain First Movement. Retrieved from: www.britainfirst.org/principles

Bryant, B., and Frymorgen, T. (2018a, 1 May). Football Lads Alliance: 'We could have a civil war in this country'. BBC Three. Retrieved from: www.bbc.co.uk/bbcthree/article/e5ee9e0a-18d7-49a4-a3c2-80b6b4222058

Bryant, B., and Frymorgen, T. (2018b, 20 April). Leader of Football Lads Alliance resigns amid charitable donations row. BBC News. Retrieved from: www.bbc.co.uk/bbcthree/article/e5ee9e0a-18d7-49a4-a3c2-80b6b4222058

Busher, J. (2013). Grassroots activism in the English Defence League: Discourse and public (dis)order. In: Taylor, M., Currie, P.M., & Holbrook, D. (eds.) Extreme Right Wing Political Violence and Terrorism. London: Bloomsbury. PP.65–84.

Busher, J. (2014). Anti-Muslim populism in the UK: The development of the English Defence League. In: Giusto, H., Kitching, D., & Rizzo, S. The Changing Faces of Populism: Systemic Challengers in Europe and the U.S. Lexington Books. PP.207–226.

Busher, J., Holbrook, D., and Macklin, G. (2019). The internal brakes on violent escalation: A typology. Behavioral Sciences of Terrorism and Political Aggression, 11(1), 3–25. DOI: 10.1080/19434472.2018.1551918

Cabrejas-Peñuelas, A.B., and Díez-Prados, M. (2014). Positive self-evaluation versus negative other-evaluation in the political genre of pre-election debates. Discourse & Society, 25(2), 159–185. DOI:10.1177/0957926513515601

Campbell, L. (2020, 13 June). UK protests: Far-right demonstrators clash with London police – as it happened. The Guardian. Retrieved from: www.theguardian.com/world/live/2020/jun/13/uk-news-live-patel-warns-of-health-and-legal-risks-at-blm-protests-coronavirus

Cellan-Jones, R. (2018, 14 March). Facebook bans Britain First pages. BBC News. Retrieved from: www.bbc.co.uk/news/technology-43398417

Chaplain, C. (2017, 7 October). Football Lads Association march: Thousands gather in central London in anti-extremism protest. The Evening Standard. Retrieved from: www.standard.co.uk/news/london/football-lads-association-march-thousands-gather-in-central-london-in-antiextremism-protest-a3652981.html

Daily Star (2018, 2 June). Tommy Robinson protests carry on for second day as more than 1,000 march in Manchester. Retrieved from: www.dailystar.co.uk/news/latest-news/706934/tommy-robinson-march-manchester-arena-hull-prison-football-lads-edl-castlefield

Dearden, L. (2018, 2 February). Darren Osborne: How Finsbury Park terror attacker became 'obsessed' with Muslims in less than a month. The Independent. Retrieved from: www.independent.co.uk/news/uk/crime/darren-osborne-finsbury-park-attack-who-is-tommy-robinson-muslim-internet-britain-first-a8190316.html

Doherty, S. (2018, 31 January). Britain First's leaders 'shouting and banging' outside a Ramsgate home 'left a toddler traumatised'. Kent Live. Retrieved from: www.kentlive.news/news/kent-news/britain-firsts-leaders-shouting-banging-1141962

EDL Website. (2013). 'Mission statement'. Retrieved from: www.englishdefenceleague.org.uk/mission-statement/

Evans et al (2017, 26 May). Everything we know about Manchester suicide bomber Salman Abedi. The Daily Telegraph. Retrieved from: www.telegraph.co.uk/news/2017/05/26/everything-know-manchester-suicide-bomber-salman-abedi/

Football Lads Alliance.(2022). 'About Us' page. Retrieved from: http://footballladsalliance.co.uk/ABOUT%20US.html

Gayle, D. (2018, 13 October). Anti-fascists block route of Democratic Football Lads Alliance London march. The Guardian. Retrieved from: www.theguardian.com/world/2018/oct/13/anti-fascists-block-route-of-democratic-football-lads-alliance-london-march

Goffman, E. (1969). Strategic Interaction. Philadelphia, PA: University of Pennsylvania Press.

Goodwin, M.J. (March 2013). The Roots of Extremism: The English Defence Leagues and the Counter-Jihad Challenge. London: Chatham House. Retrieved from: www.chathamhouse.org/publications/papers/view/189767

Heren, K. (2020, 13 June). Police pelted with bottles as hundreds including far-right activists gather to 'guard' London monuments. Evening Standard. Retrieved from: www.standard.co.uk/news/uk/right-wing-protesters-parliament-square-statues-a4468171.html

Hope not Hate. (2018, January–February). State of hate: Far right terrorism on the rise. . Retrieved from: www.hopenothate.org.uk/wp-content/uploads/2018/03/State-of-Hate-2018.pdf

Hughes, A. (2018, 17 September). Menace and aggression during 'new EDL' demo. Sky News. Retrieved from: https://news.sky.com/story/menace-and-aggression-dfla-is-new-edl-11500806

ITV News (2018a, 19 May). Hundreds of protesters and counter protesters gather in Manchester. Retrieved from: www.itv.com/news/granada/update/2018-05-19/hundreds-of-protesters-and-coun ter-protesters-gather-in-manchester/

ITV News (2018b, 27 September). Tommy Robinson contempt of court case adjourned. Retrieved from: www.itv.com/news/2018-09-27/tommy-robinson-quietly-confident-ahead-of-conte mpt-of-court-case/

Jackson, P. (2011). The EDL: Britain's 'New Far Right' Social Movement. Northampton: University of Northampton. Retrieved from: http://nectar.northampton.ac.uk/6015/7/Jackson20116015.pdf

Jackson, P. (2021). #hitlerwasright: National action and national socialism for the 21st century. La Revue Populism, 1(1), 109–127. https://populisme.be/articles_sc/hitlerwasrightnational-action-and-natio nal-socialism-for-the-21st-century/

McGlashan, M. (2020). Collective identity and discourse practice in the followership of the Football Lads Alliance on Twitter. Discourse & Society, 31(3), 307–328. doi:10.1177/0957926519889128

Mulhall, J. (2019). A post-organisational far right? In: State of Hate 2018 Report. London: Hope Not Hate. Retrieved from: www.hopenothate.org.uk/research/state-of-hate-2018/online-radicalisation/post-organisational-far-right/

Murphy-Bates, S. (2019, 8 October). Thousands of football supporters march against extremism in London to oppose 'recent upsurge' of UK terror attacks. The Daily Mail. Retrieved from: www.dailymail.co.uk/news/article-4958848/Thousands-football-fans-march-against-ter ror-London.html

Oaten, A. (2014). The cult of the victim: An analysis of the collective identity of the English Defence League. Patterns of Prejudice, 48(4), 331–349. DOI: 10.1080/0031322X.2014.950454

Oppenheim, M. (2017, 22 March). Tommy Robinson condemned for ranting about Islamic extremism at scene of London terror attack. The Independent. Retrieved from: www.independent.co.uk/news/uk/home-news/tommy-robinson-london-terror-attack-islamic-extremism-westminster-bridge-a7644 676.html

Pasha-Robinson, L. (2016, 15 December). Paul Golding: Former Britain First leader jailed for eight weeks. The Independent. Retrieved from: www.independent.co.uk/news/uk/crime/paul-golding-jai led-britain-first-leader-8-weeks-high-court-injunction-mosque-a7477046.html

Pilkington, H. (2016). Loud and Proud: Passion and Politics in the English Defence League. Manchester: Manchester University Press.

Poulter, J. (2018, 26 March). Two different Football Lads Alliances held Islamophobic demos in Birmingham. Vice News. Retrieved from: www.vice.com/en_uk/article/xw7d43/two-different-footb all-lads-alliances-held-islamophobic-demos-in-birmingham/

Poulter, J., and Childs, S. (2018, 23 March). Are the Football Lads Alliance another far-right street movement? Vice News. Retrieved from: www.vice.com/en_uk/article/kzx8jw/are-the-football-lads-alliance-another-far-right-street-movement

Raymond, M. (2018, 21 May). Manchester spent the weekend telling the FLA to fuck off. Vice News. Retrieved from: www.vice.com/en_uk/article/8xege3/manchester-spent-the-weekend-tell ing-the-fla-to-fuck-off

Richards, H. (2018, 18 March). Pub bombings campaigner to speak at huge football supporter demo in Birmingham. Birmingham Mail. Retrieved from: www.birminghammail.co.uk/news/pub-bombings-campaigner-speak-huge-14427361

Smith, M. and Shifrin, T. (2017, 24 June). Eyewitness report from first FLA demo: Football Lads Alliance puts thousands on the streets. Dream Deferred. Retrieved from: www.dreamdeferred.org.uk/2017/06/a-second-warning-thousands-on-the-streets-of-london-as-far-right-reorganises/

Socialist Worker (2018, 24 March). Update – The FLA shows its true colours in Birmingham – racist and bigoted. Retrieved from: https://socialistworker.co.uk/art/46333/Update+++The+FLA+shows+its+true+colours+in+Birmingham+++racist+and+bigoted

Sunderland Echo (2018, 15 September). Three arrested after demonstrations take place in Sunderland city centre. Retrieved from: www.sunderlandecho.com/our-region/sunderland/three-arrested-after-demonstrations-take-place-in-sunderland-city-centre-1-9351213

Wall, T. (2018, 17 March). Secret Facebook page reveals violence at heart of forum for 'football fans'. The Observer. Retrieved from: www.theguardian.com/world/2018/mar/17/football-lads-alliance-secret-facebook-page-racism-violence-sexism

16

THE APPEAL OF THE NEW FAR RIGHT IN THE UNITED KINGDOM

A Look Inside the New Far-Right Recruitment Pool

Alice Sibley

Fascism and the New Far Right

Research suggests that there has been a recent increase in far-right extremism within Western liberal democracies.[1] However, this phenomenon is not a unique or recent manifestation (Ravndal & Bjørgo, 2018; Shekhovtsov, 2017). After World War Two (WW2), across the world, Fascism split into three main strands (Shekhovtsov, 2017). The first strand, created by fascistic political groups, reduced their extremist rhetoric in an attempt to make themselves more compatible with emerging liberal democratic ideals (Griffin, 2003). This led to the creation of some modern right-wing political parties, such as France's National Front (Shekhovtsov, 2017). The second strand remained rooted in the core foundations of Fascism. Supporters are called revolutionary ultranationalists but are often referred to as either neo-fascist/fascist or neo-Nazi/Nazi (Shekhovtsov, 2017). The third strand is a meta-political movement network developed in the 1960s with the formation of the French New Right, which later spread across Europe. This strand began to focus on the cultural differences between peoples when biological racism was discredited after WW2 (Taguieff, 1993). After WW2, although the second strand remained overtly fascistic, the other two strands adopted a more liberal, democratic, and co-operative approach. For these two post-fascistic strands, the term New Far Right is appropriate (Traverso, 2019).

The present research focuses on three New Far-Right groups in the UK: For Britain movement, Democratic Football Lads Alliance (DFLA), and PEGIDA UK. Although some academic research on DFLA has focused on the origins, links, and the organizational structure of this group, little is known about the demographics of the supporters (Allen, 2019; Allchorn & Feldman, 2019; McGlashan, 2020). There has also been some academic research on PEGIDA UK focusing on the characteristics of the group and the news sources used by PEGIDA UK supporters (Allchorn, 2016; Puschmann et al, 2016). However, no study to date has used Facebook to gather data on the demographics of these supporters. Finally, to the researcher's knowledge, no academic research has been conducted on the For Britain movement. Therefore,

DOI: 10.4324/9781003032793-20

no academic research has identified the recruitment pool for any of these three groups, nor linked their demographics to violence. These three groups were chosen as they have a significant Facebook support network with over 15,000 followers or supporters each, and they have continued to remain active online despite Facebook's ban on many far-right groups in 2018 (Hern, 2019).

This chapter will first introduce the three New Far-Right groups followed by an outline of the methodology used in the quantitative demographic analysis. Next, this study will outline the findings based on three main variables, i.e., gender, education level and sexuality. Lastly, the chapter discusses whether and to what extent any of these findings can be linked to violence.

Origins, Ideologies, and Methodologies of Three New Far-Right Groups

For Britain Movement

For Britain movement was created in 2018 and is led by Anne-Marie Waters, a previous United Kingdom Independence Party (UKIP) candidate (Prentice, 2018). Ideologically, previous and current candidates of For Britain have expressed white supremacist and neo-Nazi views, and some For Britain candidates have connections with the banned neo-Nazi terrorist group, National Action. In 2018, Sam Mella, an ex-member of National Action, stood as a candidate in Leeds for the For Britain movement (Russia Today, 2018). However, despite these fascistic connections, the party is primarily an anti-Islam party (Prentice, 2018): Waters believes that Islam is an inherently violent religion which is eroding British democracy through its abuse of human rights, women's rights, and animal rights.

In addition to its Islamophobic stance, the group also claims to advocate for women's and LGBTQ rights (Waters, 2018). This attempt to liberalize the party positions it in the New Far Right.[2] At the organizational level, the For Britain movement is a fringe political party whose candidates can often be found running in local elections (Prentice, 2018).

The DFLA

The DFLA claims to be an anti-Islamist extremist, football-based group (Allen, 2019). The Football Lads Alliance (FLA) was created in response to the 2017 London Islamist terrorist attacks (Allchorn & Feldman, 2019). After the creator and leader, John Meighan, resigned from the group in 2018, a new leader was not appointed. This signalled the end of the FLA. Meighan's resignation acted as a catalyst for the DFLA, which had been a smaller, more committed group of supporters within the FLA (Allen, 2019). Ideologically, the DFLA, like the For Britain movement, is also driven by a predominantly anti-Islam rhetoric, despite attempting to veil this Islamophobia by stating that they oppose all forms of extremism. However, the DFLA is also concerned with Irish Republican Army terrorism, homelessness, and Catholic child abuse, making it more than just an anti-Islam group and also part of the New Far Right. At the organizational level, the DFLA is a direct-action, street-based group that has organized protests and silent marches around the UK. They largely organize themselves online through both Facebook and press releases (Allchorn & Feldman, 2019).

PEGIDA UK

PEGIDA UK is a counter-jihad, pan-European group. Tommy Robinson's counter-jihad group, the English Defence League (EDL), inspired the creation of Germany's PEGIDA, the acronym of which (translated from the original German) stands for "Patriotic Europeans Against the Islamisation of the West" (Waters, 2018, p. 59). This inspired Robinson and Waters (the For Britain movement leader) to create an off-shoot version of Germany's PEGIDA, PEGIDA UK (Ebner, 2017). Like the other two groups, PEGIDA UK is primarily driven by anti-Muslim ideology, but it also claims to defend women, sexual minorities, and the Jewish community; as such it can be classified as a New Far-Right group. At the organizational level, PEGIDA UK is primarily interested in street-based organization, such as protests, rallies, and demonstrations (Lee, 2016).

Methodology

This study aims to address the question: what does the New Far-Right recruitment pool look like in the UK and how do these demographics link to violence? In order to do this, an online quantitative demographic analysis was conducted. The internet is an important recruiting tool for extremists (Koehler, 2014) as it provides an element of anonymity, a cheap and efficient way for extremists to communicate, arrange meetings, and disseminate their propaganda materials (Poole, 2018). This allows researchers to access groups that are often difficult to reach (Wilson et al, 2012). Facebook is the most popular global social media networking platform, with 2.7 billion active monthly users worldwide as of September 2019 (Clement, 2020). Due to the popularity of Facebook and the use of Facebook as a platform by New Far-Right groups such as Germany PEGIDA, Facebook was used to manually gather quantitative data on the three case study groups (Stier et al, 2017).

This study is a Facebook quantitative demographic analysis conducted between July and November 2020. Quantitative demographic data was collected from a total of 9,000 supporters (3,000 supporters in each of the three groups), who had reacted (using Facebook's reaction buttons) to a link or picture posted on the public For Britain movement, the DFLA or PEGIDA UK Facebook pages. A criterion sample wherein only popular posts with the largest number of reactions was used to ensure a large enough sample size. Data were then collected from each individual who had reacted to these posts. Using SPSS, a simple frequency analysis was conducted on three demographic variables: gender, education level, and sexuality[3]. These three variables were chosen as they are all correlated with far-right extremism (Arzheimer, 2012; Freude & Bosch, 2019).

Although there are benefits to using online demographic data, there are also some limitations. For example, fake profiles may be an issue in online New Far-Right research. Within the EDL Facebook page, it is estimated that around 10% of the EDL supporters "could be trolls", individuals who spread disinformation (Bartlett & Littler, 2011, p. 35). Therefore, this may mean that ten percent of the profiles collected (9,000 in total) in this study were also fake. However, due to the sample size, fake profiles are unlikely to have skewed the data significantly.

Comparative Analysis of Demographics: The For Britain Movement, the DFLA, and PEGIDA UK

This section will analyse the three variables this study focuses on: gender, education level, and sexuality. Previous research has suggested that these three variables are important when outlining who is vulnerable to New Far-Right recruitment as gender, education level, and

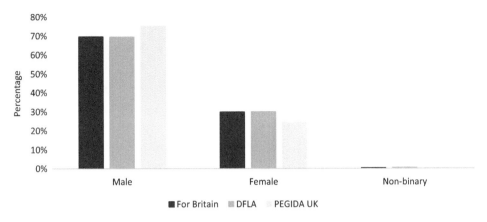

Figure 16.1   The gender difference in the For Britain movement, the DFLA, and PEGIDA UK.

sexuality are all correlated with far-right extremist activity (Arzheimer, 2012; Freude & Bosch, 2019).

Gender

Data suggest that far-right supporters are overwhelmingly male (Allen, 2011). In this study men made up 70% of the For Britain movement, 70% of the DFLA, and 75% of PEGIDA UK (Figure 16.1). In comparison to mainstream UK political parties, in 2019, 71% of the Conservative membership, 53% of the Labour membership, and 75% of the UKIP membership were men (Audickas et al, 2019). This research suggests that although still predominantly male, the For Britain movement and the DFLA may attract a greater proportion of female supporters than the Conservative Party and UKIP. However, the difference is small.

Education Level

The majority of supporters in all three groups reported that secondary school was their highest level of education (Figure 16.2). However, there are differences in relation to how many people have attended university across the three groups. The DFLA supporters are the least educated, with only 9% of supporters attending university. This is followed by PEGIDA UK, with 16% of supporters attending university. For Britain supporters are the highest educated out of the three groups, with 18% attending university. In comparison, in the UK, between 26% and 28% of 18-year-olds in the general population attend university (UCAS, 2018). This suggests that all three New Far-Right groups are undereducated compared to the general population, which supports previous findings on the New Far-Right education level (Bartlett & Littler, 2011).

Sexuality

Table 16.1 demonstrates the figures for the sexuality variable. PEGIDA UK has the highest number of bisexual supporters (5%) and the For Britain movement has the highest number of gay supporters (4%). In comparison, in 2018, 2.2% of the general population of the UK identified as part of the LGBTQ community (Office of National Statistics, 2020).

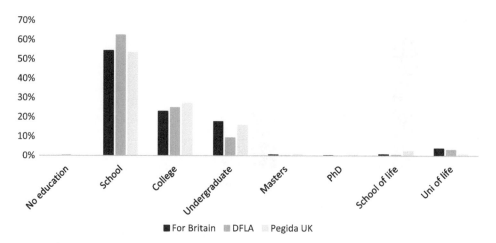

Figure 16.2   The highest education level achieved by the supporters in For Britain, the DFLA, and PEGIDA UK.

Table 16.1 Aggregated sexuality data from all three groups

	PEGIDA UK (n = 414)	The For Britain movement (n = 298)	The DFLA (n = 284)
Straight	93%	92%	95%
Gay	2%	4%	2%
Bisexual	5%	4%	3%

Source: Author's own fieldwork.

Is There a Link between These Demographics and Violence?

This study found that the majority of the supporters in the three groups, the For Britain movement, the DFLA, and PEGIDA UK are low-educated, heterosexual men. This is in line with previous research, which found that supporters of New Far-Right groups are mostly heterosexual men with low levels of education (Pilkington, 2016; Bartlett & Littler, 2011; Bitzan, 2017; Allen, 2011). Previous research suggests that the far right is often associated with violence (Taylor et al, 2013). However, as outlined earlier, no research has discussed whether there are any connections between the demographics of these three New Far-Right groups and violence. The following sections, therefore, will discuss whether there is a link between these demographics and violence.

The Path towards Violence and the Role of Conspiracy Theories

Not all far-right groups or parties are violent. However, conspiracy theories can work as a powerful conveyor belt towards violence. Previous research suggests that men are more likely to believe in conspiracy theories than women (Galliford & Furnham, 2017). In addition, research suggests that education level is highly correlated with a belief in conspiracy theories. Individuals with low levels of formal education are more likely to believe in conspiracy theories in comparison to those with higher levels of education (van Prooijen, 2017). Therefore, low-educated men tend to be more likely to believe in conspiracy theories. One way to understand the link between conspiracy theories and violence is through the "delegitimisation theoretical framework", which explains how the endorsement of conspiracy theories can encourage a group to transition to violence (Sprinzak, 1995). It argues that if there is a perceived threat from a non-ruling group (e.g. Muslims), single-targeting acts of terrorism towards the perceived threat may occur.

In addition, if there is an anticipated outsider threat and there is a perceived lack of government protection from these outsiders, this may result in acts of split terrorism where both the outsider groups and the government may be targeted. Conspiracy theories, when combined with racist and extremist ideals, can act as a radicalization multiplier by demonizing the out-group and increasing intergroup polarization. This polarization can increase feelings of alienation within, or antipathy towards, society and can increase the likelihood of violence (Emberland, 2020). As a belief in conspiracy theories can increase the likelihood of violence, it is important to discuss which conspiracy theories are common within the New Far Right. The most prevalent conspiracy theories in the three case study groups are the Eurabia conspiracy, the Great Replacement conspiracy, and the Kalergi Plan (Carr, 2006; Camus, 2018; Prentice, 2018).

Each conspiracy propagates a different narrative as demonstrated in Table 16.2. The Eurabia and Great Replacement conspiracies position Muslims as a threat, whereas the Kalergi plan positions Jewish people as the threat. Only the Great Replacement conspiracy promotes the idea that the government is in collaboration with the perceived threat, but both Eurabia and the Kalergi plan promote the idea that the European Union (EU) is in collaboration with the group identified as a threat (Carr, 2006; Camus, 2018; Prentice, 2018). The Eurabia and the Great Replacement conspiracies also encourage the use of force to prevent immigrants from staying in Europe (Davey & Ebner, 2019; Carr, 2006). There are three specific aspects of these theories that may encourage violence: the identification of an outsider threat (Muslims or Jewish people), the belief that the Government or the EU are collaborating with the outsider threat and are therefore not to be trusted, and the explicit or implicit endorsement of violence as a solution to the perceived problem. As discussed earlier, this identification of an outsider threat and the lack of trust in the Government or political institution may lead to acts of split violence and terrorism.

Although each conspiracy has a different narrative, they all share the idea that "white" Europe and America are being invaded by either Muslims or Jewish people. The Eurabia conspiracy is the theory that Europe is being deliberately Islamized, leading to European cultural extinction. One solution to stop this perceived cultural extinction is to use force to prevent people from staying in Europe. This force could include forced deportations or military force

Table 16.2 New far-right conspiracy theories: Comparison of narratives

	Muslim invasion	Government collaboration	Jewish invasion	Encourages force	Eradication of Christianity	EU collaboration
Eurabia	x			x	x	x
The Great Replacement	x	x		x		
The Kalergi plan			x			x

Sources: Carr (2006), Camus (2018), and Prentice (2018).

(Carr, 2006). Although PEGIDA UK has not explicitly supported the Eurabia conspiracy, it has previously endorsed the Eurabia narrative (Lee, 2016). The Great Replacement conspiracy states that white people are being replaced through migration, violence, and high birth rates by people from "Africa, and very often Muslims" (Camus, 2018, p. 21). Renaud Camus, the French philosopher who coined the phrase the Great Replacement, argues that this replacement constitutes genocide through substitution (Camus, 2018). A solution offered to the Great Replacement is "remigration", the forced deportation of immigrants out of White European countries (Davey & Ebner, 2019, p. 5). This, like the Eurabia conspiracy, endorses the use of violence as a solution to force immigrants out of Europe. The DFLA has previously endorsed the narratives of both Eurabia and the Great Replacement (Allchorn & Feldman, 2019). Finally, the Kalergi Plan states that Kalgeri, an EU politician, introduced an EU plan to undermine the white race through mass immigration. The conspiracy states that through the mass movement of people into Europe (immigrants and refugees), the EU will destroy the different European identities and replace them with a new mixed people. It also states that these new people would have no roots or religion.

Because of this lack of compass and support, it is believed that these people will be easy to control (Mohorita, 2017). Believers in this conspiracy argue that the elites devising the Kalergi Plan are Jewish and therefore, Jewish people are perceived to be the threatening group in this conspiracy. This is the most prevalent conspiracy theory in the For Britain movement (Hope not Hate, 2019). These conspiracies all argue that White Europeans are under threat and that either Muslims or Jewish people are the enemy. As men are more likely to believe in conspiracy theories than women, and lower educated individuals are also more likely to believe in conspiracy theories than those with higher levels of education, it is likely that some supporters of the New Far-Right groups focused on in this study believe in one or more of the three conspiracy theories outlined above. As PEGIDA UK has the highest number of male supporters and DFLA supporters are the least educated out of the three case study groups, members of both PEGIDA UK and the DFLA may be more susceptible to a belief in conspiracy theories. This belief in conspiracy theories may then act as a radicalizing multiplier and inspire acts of violence towards either Muslims or Jewish people.

The Link between Hypermasculinity, Homophobia, and Violence

A belief in conspiracy theories is not the only connection between the demographics focused on in this study and violence. This section will discuss how the gender and sexuality variables can be linked to violence through the concept of hypermasculinity. Men are much more likely to be involved in far-right crime and violence than women. Previous research highlights that although women and men have similar potential for far-right attitudes (50% of both women and men), women are less likely to be involved in organized far-right groups (making up only 10%–33% of supporters), and they are even less likely to participate in far-right crimes (5%–10%) (Bitzan, 2017, p. 70). Men, therefore, make up 90%–95% of far-right crime perpetrators (Bitzan, 2017). This overrepresentation of men within far-right groups suggests that there may be something inherently masculine about becoming involved in far-right extremism, especially in relation to far-right crime (Bitzan, 2017).

Out of the three New Far-Right groups in this study, PEGIDA UK is the group with the highest number of male supporters. Therefore, it could be assumed that supporters of PEGIDA UK are the most likely to use acts of violence. However, leaders of PEGIDA UK have actively tried to position themselves as a peaceful movement that does not tolerate either alcohol or violence at demonstrations (Allchorn, 2016). This was perceived to be a major downfall for previous New Far-Right groups such as the EDL. As alcohol is not permitted at PEGIDA UK demonstrations, which can encourage aggression and lead to violence, it may be less likely that supporters of PEGIDA UK will engage in acts of violence (Galvani, 2004). In contrast, alcohol has been seen at DFLA demonstrations (Lott-Lavigna, 2020).

The DFLA is a football-based street group with a history of football hooliganism, a scene that is dominated by men. Although the DFLA have fewer male supporters than PEGIDA UK, due to the DFLA's connection with football hooliganism and alcohol, some supporters may engage in acts of violence. Research suggests that there is a close connection between football hooliganism, hypermasculinity or hard masculinity, and violence. Groups that have high levels of hypermasculinity and are rooted in football hooliganism are more likely to be violent (Spaaij, 2008. It is therefore likely that some supporters of the DFLA engage in violence. This link is supported by previous demonstrations attended by the DFLA. For example, at one anti-Black Lives Matter demonstration in London in 2020, over 100 DFLA supporters were arrested for violent unrest (Lawrie, 2020; Wood, 2020).

The gender findings in this study suggest that men make up the majority of support in these three New Far-Right groups. The overrepresentation of men in far-right political participation is called the "gender gap" and this is a current research focus within the field of radicalization studies (Ralph-Morrow, 2020). However, this gender gap may be changing. In the 1980s more than 80% of the Front National Party membership were men. By 2012, due in part to the new female leadership from Marine Le Pen and the adoption of "femonationalist" rhetoric, the female membership level had increased from 20% to 45% (Perrineau, 2014). Femonationalism can be defined as "the exploitation of feminist themes by nationalists and neoliberals in anti-Islam (anti-immigration) campaigns" (Farris, 2017, p. 4). It also involves "the participation of certain feminists and femocrats in the stigmatization of Muslim men under the banner of gender inequality" (Farris, 2017, p. 4). Femonationalism, therefore, can be adopted by such groups in their attempts to appear more liberal and gender inclusive. For example, The Front National Party has framed the immigration debate where Front National are the protectors of democracy in a fight with Islam to uphold the rights of women, the LGBTQ community and minority groups (Mayer & Tiberj, 2015). Therefore, the adoption of femonationalist ideology may be encouraging some women to join New Far-Right groups (Farris, 2017). This increase in female participation within New Far-Right groups may reduce levels of hypermasculinity and this, in turn, may reduce the likelihood of violence.

In addition to the gender variable and hypermasculinity, the sexuality variable can also be linked to hypermasculinity. As discussed, the DFLA is a male-dominated football hooligan group. It is, therefore, unsurprising that the DFLA has the smallest number of gay and bisexual supporters. Previous research shows that a hypermasculine environment may not encourage people that do not fit into gender norms to join a group. Hypermasculinity is directly linked with homophobia, transphobia, and violence (Warriner et al, 2013; Spaaij, 2008). For example, National Action, a neo-Nazi group rooted in fascistic ideology, glorified the anti-LGBTQI[4] terrorist attack at the gay nightclub, Pulse (Macklin, 2018; Vernalls, 2018). Therefore, groups that are hypermasculine are unlikely to attract many supporters from the LGBTQ community. The DFLA is a hypermasculine group that has not attracted many members of the LBGTQ community (in comparison to the other two New Far-Right groups in this study). Therefore, because of the link between hypermasculinity, homophobia and violence, supporters of the DFLA are more likely to use violence than the other two groups.

However, with the movement away from Fascism, pro-LGBTQ narratives have become an increasing trend among Britain's New Far Right. For example, the EDL advocated

LGBTQ rights and had their own LGBTQ division (Pilkington, 2016). This is known as homonationalism which – like femonationalism – is the combination of tolerant views towards members of the Lesbian, Gay and Bisexual community, nationalism, and racism (Freude & Bosch, 2019). These are factors that would not have been tolerated together in the past. Research suggests that there are more people in the UK that hold homonationalistic beliefs in comparison to other European countries, potentially partly explaining why these UK-based New Far-Right groups are recruiting gay and bisexual supporters (Freude & Bosch, 2019). This adoption of homonationalism may also increase the number of women and members of the LGBTQ community that join New Far-Right groups, and this increase could influence the use of violence within New Far-Right groups by decreasing levels of hypermasculinity.

Conclusion

The role of violence within the New Far Right is complicated. The old fascistic far-right and neo-Nazi groups rooted their ideology in Fascism and Nazism, which are directly linked to violence. However, groups that are considered New Far Right may use violence in a different way or may not use violence at all. This shift away from violence is likely to be due to the adoption of more liberal, cooperative ideologies, such as femonationalism and homonationalism, which attract different types of New Far-Right supporters, such as women and members of the LGBTQ community. The demographics, therefore, of the New Far Right are different compared to the fascistic right. This means that not all New Far-Right groups are violent. However, some New Far-Right groups can become violent if they endorse conspiracy theories, have high levels of hypermasculinity, are linked to football hooliganism or endorse homophobia. Based on the demographics of the three groups in this study, supporters of the DFLA are the most likely to use violence. The DFLA are the least educated and have the lowest number of supporters that self-identified as lesbian, gay, or bisexual. They also have connections with football hooliganism and hypermasculinity. Therefore, based on the demographics found in this study, out of the three groups, supporters of the DFLA are the most likely to use violence.

Although demographics may help to understand who is attracted to these New Far-Right groups, demographics alone do not explain why some people choose to support them. In order to understand the motivations of New Far-Right supporters, it is recommended that future research focuses on what concerns or grievances motivate individuals to join New Far-Right groups. New Far-Right discourse could be analysed to identify the main grievance-based themes in each group. This would help identify which themes are specific to a New Far-Right group and which grievances are shared by the general population. This information could then help to identify and understand the link between grievances and acts of violence.

Future research on the New Far Right could analyse new, encrypted social media platforms such as Discord, Gab.ia, Voat, and VK. These platforms are specifically designed to uphold freedom of speech and are therefore attractive to people who wish to express more extreme views (Muis et al, 2020). The narratives of this discourse need to be analysed to understand the more extreme fringes of the New Far Right. This understanding could, in turn, become the foundation for reducing societal divisions and thereby reducing the likelihood of violence within communities.

Notes

1 While acknowledging that the word extremism has many different definitions, this chapter will use the British government's definition of extremism as "vocal or active opposition to fundamental British values, including democracy, the rule of law, individual liberty and mutual respect and tolerance of different faiths and beliefs" (Home Office, 2019, p. 1). In addition, because of the complexity of definitions within the field of extremism, the terms "right-wing" and "far-right" extremism will be used synonymously in this chapter.

2 The New Far-Right are groups that have adopted a more liberal and democratic approach in comparison to more traditional far-right groups that are rooted in fascism. These New Far-Right groups do not protest elections like fascistic groups, instead they are direct action political groups that often mobilize through new media such as Facebook.

3 Indications on sexuality were taken from the individuals' Facebook profile page where they had self-defined as straight, gay or bisexual.

4 LGBTQI stands for "Lesbian, Gay, Bisexual, Transexual, Queer (or Questioning) and Intersex."

References

Allchorn, W. (2016, January 15). *Cut from the same cloth? Pegida UK looks like a sanitised version of the EDL* [Blog post]. Retrieved from https://blogs.lse.ac.uk/politicsandpolicy/pegida-uk-relaunched/

Allchorn, W., & Feldman, M. (2019). The (Democratic) Football Lads Alliance: A far right antechamber. London: Faith Matters. Retrieved from: https://www.faith-matters.org/wp-content/uploads/2019/04/dfla.pdf.

Allen, C. (2011). Opposing Islamification or promoting Islamophobia? Understanding the English defence league. *Patterns of Prejudice*, *45*(4), 279–294. https://doi.org/10.1080/0031322X.2011.585014

Allen, C. (2019). The Football Lads Alliance and Democratic Football Lad's Alliance: An insight into the dynamism and diversification of Britain's counter-jihad movement. *Social Movement Studies*, *18*(5), 639–646. https://doi.org/10.1080/14742837.2019.1590694

Arzheimer, K. (2012). Electoral sociology – Who votes for the extreme right and why – and when? In U. Backes & P. Moreau (Eds.), *The Extreme Right in Europe: Currents, Trends and Perspectives* (pp. 35–50). Göttingen, Germany: Vandenhoeck & Ruprecht.

Audickas, L. Dempsey, N., & Loft, P. (2019). Membership of UK political parties. *Briefing Paper, Number SN05125*. Retrieved from https://commonslibrary.parliament.uk/research-briefings/sn05125/

Bartlett, J., & Littler, M. (2011). *Inside the edl populist politics in a digital age*. Retrieved from Demos: www.demos.co.uk/files/Inside_the_edl_WEB.pdf

Bitzan, R. (2017). Research on gender and the far right in Germany since 1990: Developments, findings, and future prospects. In M. Köttig, R. Bitzan, & A. Petö (Ed.), *Gender and Far Right Politics in Europe* (pp. 65–78). London, U.K: Palgrave Macmillan.

Camus, R. (2018). *You Will Not Replace Us!*. Plieux, France: Chez l'auteur.

Carr, M. (2006). You are now entering Eurabia. *Race & Class*, *48*(1), 1–22. http://doi.org/10.1177/0306396806066636

Clement, J. (2020). *Number of monthly active Facebook users worldwide as of 2nd Quarter 2020*. Retrieved from www.statista.com/statistics/264810/number-of-monthly-active-facebook-users-worldwide/

Davey, J., & Ebner, J. (2019). 'The Great Replacement': The violent consequences of mainstreamed extremism. London, UK: Institute for Strategic Dialogue. Retrieved from: https://www.isdglobal.org/wp-content/uploads/2019/07/The-Great-Replacement-The-Violent-Consequences-of-Mainstreamed-Extremism-by-ISD.pdf.

Ebner, J. (2017). *The Rage: The Vicious Circle of Islamist and Far-Right Extremism*. London: I.B. TAURIS.

Emberland, T. (2020, Feb 24). Why conspiracy theories can act as radicalization multipliers of far-right ideals. *RightNow!* Retrieved from www.sv.uio.no/c-rex/english/news-and-events/right-now/2020/conspiracy-theories-radicalization-multipliers.html

Farris, S. R. (2017). *In the Name of Women's Rights: The Rise of Femonationalism*. London: Duke University Press.

Freude, L., & Bosch, N. V. (2019). Homonationalism in Europe? A quantitative comparison of the values of Europeans. *Sexuality & Culture*, *24*, 1292–1314. https://doi.org/10.1007/s12119-019-09683-7

Galliford, N., & Furnham, A. (2017). Individual difference factors and beliefs in medical and political conspiracy theories. *Scandinavian Journal of Psychology, 58*(5), 422–428. doi:10.1111/sjop.12382

Galvani, S. (2004). Responsible disinhibition: Alcohol, men and violence to women. *Addiction Research & Theory, 12*(4), 357–371. doi: 10.1080/1606635042000218772

Griffin, R. (2003). From slime mould to rhizome: An introduction to the groupuscular right. *Patterns of Prejudice, 37*(1), 27–50. https:doi.org/10.1080/0031322022000054321

Hern, A. (2019, Apr 18). Facebook bans far-right groups including BNP, EDL and Britain first. *The Guardian*. Retrieved from www.theguardian.com/technology/2019/apr/18/facebook-bans-far-right-groups-including-bnp-edl-and-britain-first

Home Office. (2019). *Revised prevent duty guidance: For England and Wales.* Retrieved from www.gov.uk/government/publications/prevent-duty-guidance/revised-prevent-duty-guidance-for-england-and-wales

Hope not Hate. (2019). *Exposed: For Britain and "white genocide" conspiracy theory.* Retrieved from www.hopenothate.org.uk/2019/04/18/exposed-for-britain-and-white-genocide-conspiracy-theory/

Koehler, D. (2014). The radical online: Individual radicalization processes and the role of the Internet. *Journal for Deradicalization*, (1), Winter 2014/15, 116–134.

Lawrie, J. P. (2020). *Violence on the streets of London.* Retrieved from www.hopenothate.org.uk/2020/06/16/violence-on-the-streets-of-london/

Lee, B. (2016, Feb 5). *Who are Pegida UK?* [Blog post]. Retrieved from www.radicalisationresearch.org/guides/pegida-uk/

Lott-Lavigna, R. (2020, July 13). Far-right demonstrators got drunk and attacked police while 'defending' a statue in London. *Vice News.* Retrieved from www.vice.com/en/article/ep4zmp/far-right-demonstration-london-churchill-statue

Macklin, G. (2018). 'Only bullets will stop us!'–The banning of national action in Britain. *Perspectives on Terrorism, 12*(6), 104–122. www.jstor.org/stable/26544646

Mayer, N., & Tiberj, V. (2015). Ou est passée la gauche? De la victoire de 2012 à la déroute de 2014. In O. Duhamel & E. Lecerf (Eds.) *L'état de l'opinion* (pp. 17–36). Paris: Seuil.

McGlashan, M. (2020). Collective identity and discourse practice in the followership of the Football Lads Alliance on Twitter. *Discourse & Society, 31*(3), 307–328.

Mohorita, V. (2017). Afričania a Aziati sa hrnú na Ukrajinu, aby sa odtiaľ vďaka zrušeným vízam dostali do EÚ. Na rane sú Slovensko, Poľsko, Maďarsko. *Hlavné správy.*. Retrieved from www.hlavnespravy.sk/africania-aziati-sa-hrnu-na-ukrajinu-aby-sa-odtialvdaka-zrusenym-vizam-dostali-eu-na-rane-su-slovensko-polskomadarsko/1095058 [Accessed 8 August 2017].

Muis, J., Klein, O., & Dijksta, G. (2020). Challenges and opportunities of social media research: Using Twitter and Facebook to investigate far right discourses. In S. D. Ashe, J. Busher, G. Macklin, & A. Winter (Eds.), *Researching the Far Right: Theory, Methods and Practice* (pp. 147–163). London: Routledge.

Office of National Statistics. (2020). *Sexual orientation, UK: 2018.* Retrieved from www.ons.gov.uk/peoplepopulationandcommunity/culturalidentity/sexuality/bulletins/sexualidentityuk/2018

Perrineau, P. (2014). *La France au front.* Paris, France: Librairie Arthéme Fayard.

Pilkington, H. (2016). *Loud and Proud: Passion and Politics in the English Defence League.* Manchester: Manchester University Press

Poole, E. (2018). Anti-Muslim propaganda on Twitter and the role for the far-right. *Medya ve Din Araştırmaları Dergisi, 1*(1), 135–137.

Prentice, C. (2018). *Meet the For Britain Movement.* Retrieved from www.hopenothate.org.uk/2018/04/26/meet-britain-movement/

Puschmann, C., Ausserhofer, J., Maan, N., & Hametner, M. (2016, April). Information laundering and counter-publics: The news sources of Islamophobic groups on Twitter. In *Proceedings of the International AAAI Conference on Web and Social Media*. 10(2), 143–150. Retrieved from: https://ojs.aaai.org/index.php/ICWSM/article/view/14847.

Ralph-Morrow, E. (2020). The right men: How masculinity explains the radical right gender gap. *Political Studies, 70*(1), 26–44. https://doi.org/10.1177/0032321720936049

Ravndal, J. A., & Bjørgo, T. (2018). Investigating terrorism from the extreme right: A review of past and present research. *Perspectives on Terrorism, 12*(6), 5–22. Retrieved from www.jstor.org/stable/26544640

Russia Today. (2018, June 7). Ex-member of neo-Nazi group was Leeds election candidate, claims anti-racism organization. *Russia Today.* Retrieved from www.rt.com/uk/429014-neo-nazi-national-action/

Shekhovtsov, A. (2017). *Russia and the Western Far Right: Tango Noir.* New York: Routledge.

Spaaij, R. (2008). Men like us, boys like them: Violence, masculinity, and collective identity in football hooliganism. *Journal of Sport and Social Issues*, *32*(4), 369–392. https://doi.org/10.1177/0193723350 8324082

Sprinzak, E. (1995). Right-wing terrorism in a comparative perspective: The case of split delegitimization. *Terrorism and Political Violence*, 7(1), 17–43. https://doi.org/10.1080/09546559508427284

Stier, S., Posch, L., Bleier, A., & Strohmaier, M. (2017). When populists become popular: comparing Facebook use by the right-wing movement Pegida and German political parties. *Information, Communication & Society*, *20*(9), 1365–1388. https://doi.org/10.1080/1369118X.2017.1328519

Taguieff, P. A. (1993). From race to culture: the new right's view of European identity. *Telos*, *1993*(98–99), 99–125. doi:10.3817/0393099099

Taylor, M., Holbrook, D., & Currie, P. M. (Eds.). (2013). *Extreme Right Wing Political Violence and Terrorism*. London: Bloomsbury.

Traverso, E. (2019). *The New Faces of Fascism: Populism and the Far Right*. London: Verso Books.

UCAS. (2018, August 16). Students in England, Wales, Northern Ireland receiving their exam results will find out today if they are going to university. *UCAS*. Retrieved from www.ucas.com/corporate/news-and-key-documents/news/record-percentage-young-people-are-university

van Prooijen, J. W. (2017). Why education predicts decreased belief in conspiracy theories. *Applied Cognitive Psychology*, *31*(1), 50–58. https://doi.org/10.1002/acp.3301

Vernalls, R. (2018, March 15). National action: Alleged neo-nazi group member had 'get banged' image of murdered MP Jo Cox. *The Independent*. Retrieved from www.independent.co.uk/news/uk/crime/national-action-soldiers-neo-nazi-terrorism-jo-cox-white-vehvilainen-barrett-court-a8256646.html

Warriner, K., Nagoshi, C. T., & Nagoshi, J. L. (2013). Correlates of homophobia, transphobia, and internalized homophobia in gay or lesbian and heterosexual samples. *Journal of Homosexuality*, *60*(9), 1297–1314. https://doi.org/10.1080/00918369.2013.806177

Waters, A. M. (2018). *Beyond Terror: Islam's Slow Erosion of Western Democracy*. USA: Something or Other Publishing.

Wilson, R. E., Gosling, S. D., & Graham, L. T. (2012). A review of Facebook research in the social sciences. *Perspectives on Psychological Science*, 7(3), 203–220. https://doi.org/10.1177/1745691612442904

Wood, V. (2020, June 14). "Multiculturalism was forced on us': After Black Lives Matter protest, the far right march on Westminster'. *The Independent*. Retrieved from www.independent.co.uk/news/uk/home-news/far-right-protest-london-black-lives-matter-churchill-statue-cenotaph-edl-a9564 986.html

17

WEAPONISING THE ALLIANCE FOR THE UNITY OF ROMANIANS (AUR)

Novelties and Continuums in Romania's Far-Right Political Extremism

Alexandra Coțofană

Introduction

In December 2020, the conservative nationalist party *Alianța pentru Unirea Românilor* (the Alliance for the Unity of Romanians), or AUR[1], led by 34-year-old George Simion, became the fourth most powerful party in Romania, only one year after it was founded (2019). AUR obtained over 500,000 votes in the December 6, 2020 legislative elections, by relying almost exclusively on Simion's social media presence for the party's electoral campaign (Code for Romania, 2020). Simion's Facebook page had a remarkable impact amongst traditional voters of the country's largest parties, PSD (The Social Democratic Party) and the centre-right PNL (the National Liberal Party). The voter demographics surprised political analysts as AUR received the vote of the Romanian diaspora, which would traditionally go to the centre-right PNL, and the vote of young people. The latter demographic of voters led historians to evoke the tremendous support amongst university students that the far-right Iron Guard[2] had in the 1930s (Ziare, 2020). This parallel has elicited calls to get a better understanding on how AUR operates, as the fascist Iron Guard founded in 1929 was a paramilitary, antisemitic, ultranationalist group, which started as non-violent, but eventually orchestrated one of the goriest pogroms in Europe, targeting Jewish civilians in Bucharest (Ioanid, 1993).

The alarmed Romanian press called AUR "bizarre" (Eremia, 2021), "extremist" (Radio Europa Liberă Moldova, 2021), "neo-fascist and antisemitic" (Kiss, 2021), "mind-boggling and Putinist" (Iancu, 2020), and "the useful idiots of the far-right" (Furtună, 2020), while Romanian academics have organized a series of talks (True Story Project. n.d.) to understand the similarities between AUR and the country's interwar far right. This chapter explores narratives of AUR leaders and draws historical connections to sketch the party's logic and world view. I argue that sensationalizing AUR as the new far right creates a historical false dualism, in which there are only two moments of extreme far-right political discourse and practice: AUR in 2020 and the Iron Guard of the 1930s. This study argues that the themes adopted by AUR are part of a continuum of ideas and practices that started long before the

DOI: 10.4324/9781003032793-21

1930s and have been endorsed by several ideological projects across the political spectrum. By de-sensationalizing and historically locating AUR within a continuum, the Romanian case could offer an understanding with broader applications in the rethinking of the logics of societal reaction towards non-violent extremist groups.

Introducing AUR: Origins, Ideology & Modus Operandi

Simion's Facebook page experienced an organic growth that resulted in 530,350 likes and 800,322 followers[3] in 2021 (Simion, n.d.). The young leader won the hearts of his new voters with social-media messaging alone, aimed at an electorate confined in front of their electronic devices by state-mandated Covid-19 lockdown measures. AUR's successful political narrative relied on historically recurring civic disenchantment with the political class and on the fact that the electorate had been primed by political and social media discourse in the last few years to receive anti-globalist, conspiracist, and protochronist[4] (a belief that Romanians and their ancestors developed a civilization before all other countries) ways of thinking. The themes in the discourse of its three main leaders, George Simion, Claudiu Târziu, and Sorin Lavric differ slightly from each other but rely on familiar tropes from both Romania's interwar far-right regime (loss of national "suzerainty"[5] to globalizing occult forces, loss of ethnic purity, and loss of religious identity), as well as concepts popularized by Romania's Communist Party, which governed in the latter half of the 20th century (focus on the agrarian and working sectors, as well as on the people). While AUR leadership did not create these narratives, this chapter follows the sources of these forms of non-violent discourse to understand why voters embraced a logic of a war of ideas against the system, as well as the role that history and geography played in this process.

As a non-violent extremist group, AUR has grown its audience through vocal extremism on social media, and most recently in the Romanian Parliament, with ideologue Sorin Lavric speaking of the party's willingness to commit martyrdom for their ideology – yet its leadership has not engaged in or supported any physical violence. AUR promoted their identity as the opposite to a corrupt political class, which it wants to dismantle. The context in which AUR operates is fertile, as it is represented by a population increasingly disenchanted with, and critical of, career politicians in the country, as well as primed to subscribe to global conspiracy theories that they erroneously accept as home-grown. Concerns from state and non-state actors regarding AUR have been related to the latter's expressed desire for totalitarian rule through the elimination of all other parties, and to the extremist, far-right ideas that the party can now express on two vital platforms: social media and mainstream politics, through the seats they have gained in the Parliament.

Methodologically, discourse analysis has been the most useful tool in the collection and interpretation of textual and visual data, both in archival text and in AUR's narratives. Based on the party's reliance on social media, it seemed suitable to explore AUR's discourse through its Facebook platforms. AUR has had a remarkable amount of access to their electorate through social media, as Romania's lockdown has often prevented people from engaging in many of their regular rituals. Indoor activities became the norm, and Romanians engaged with their electronic devices, using social media platforms for news and important decisions, such as choosing political candidates. Furthermore, Covid-19-lockdown and safety measures have limited scholars' ability to directly interview and engage with members of non-violent and violent extremist groups, forcing a reliance on secondary sources (Rrustemi, 2020, p. 3).

Exploring AUR through the conceptual lens of non-violent extremism necessitates a problematization of the term. In current Western European literature, the concept has been used predominantly to make sense of the Muslim other, and to further understand the nuances of perceived threats that loom over Europe (see discourse prevalent in Baran, 2005; Hamid, 2016; Cordesman, 2017, Gillian, 2019). In the British context, for example, non-violent extremism has been feared as a fertile breeding ground for radicalization (Hamid, 2016, p. 9). In Germany on the other hand, Basic Law articles 1–5 indicate compatibility between the German constitution and non-violent extremism, as long as an organization's purpose is not to commit crimes (Herzog Zu Mecklenburg & Anthony, 2020, p. 8), thus differentiating between extremism (or what we might call violent extremism) and radicalism (or what we might call non-violent extremism).

The fact that non-violent extremism has been politicized by state and non-state actors at national and international levels has impacted the way that the academic community uses the term (Rrustemi, 2020, p. 15). The relationship between researchers and members of non-violent extremist groups can be impacted by factors such as mutual distrust owing to a perception of difference in political values. This only adds to the already strained relationship between non-violent extremist groups and governing majorities. Taking a step further, Alex P. Schmid (2014) argues that the distinction between violent and non-violent extremism is altogether problematic, as states have both collaborated with and distanced themselves from non-violent extremists groups, and the labels applied to the latter have changed based on the preferences and interests of governing majorities.

The chapter traces the complexities of ethno-centrism, populism, and ethno-nationalism, to set the analytical tone for the next sections. Next, the investigation traces the seemingly benign concept of protochronism through its national and regional engagements with political extremism in the last century. The concept's associations with ethnic nationalism, antisemitism, and the Holocaust reveal its very real potential for violence. Later, the chapter examines Simion's political trajectory, the importance of social media in his ascension, his ideological predecessors, and his closest collaborators in AUR and adjacent to the party, whose ideological values reveal AUR's vast potential to trigger violence in followers.

Categorizing AUR: Recognizing Conceptual Crossroads

The European practice of creating hierarchies and shades of whiteness are never-ending. Non-Christians have historically suffered the most from racial othering (Kakel, 2011), the practice of using concepts of racial "difference" and "otherness" to organize society. Yet the recent Brexit referendum showed that those who find themselves at the physical margins of Europe are also perceived as being on the darker end of the racial spectrum, which came with a plethora of orientalisms, stereotypes, and conspiracies (Keinz and Lewicki, 2019). Achille Mbembe blames these forms of ideological excess on late Eurocentrism, "a Eurocentrism that is still more rancid and aggressive, even more deaf, blind, and vindictive than in the past" (2021). Despite being the targets of orientalism and marginalization, Romanians have used cultural forms and meanings as battlegrounds in the formation of a state whose logic is ethnocidal and purist (Beck, 1989). In order to discuss the imaginaries and narratives that primed the electorate for AUR's 2020 success, it is important to trace the ideological continuities of past Romanian political regimes.

Critics have assigned many labels to AUR, including that of a populist party (Recorder, 2021). Globally, the concept of populism has recently been used to signal a right-leaning political tendency, which in turn has banalized the notion and associated it with a particular way of enacting populism, rather than allowing it to function as a theoretical category meant to aid us in the analysis of political logic. In political theory, populism is understood as a political logic defining a separation between institutions and the people (Anastasiou, 2019). In other words, the people in populism should contain everyone and anyone, allowing a discussion of a populist possibility (although even at its purest, the term evokes unquestioned, hegemonic narratives and ways of being in the world). As both ruling institutions and the people can manifest heterogeneous character, a plethora of political imaginaries and discourses can emerge, which are highly dependent on their context and sometimes contradict each other. For example, if populism is imagined as a category that can be associated with democracy, then it cannot be imagined as populated by a particular demographic functioning through an ethnocentric logic.

The question then remains: Is populism central to the democratic process or is it the opposite? The concept of people is governed by ambiguous political potential, as it has historically signified both an inclusive democracy and an exclusivist nation. At the same time, the term is authoritative through its discursive role in nation-building projects, often saying more about the interests of ruling institutions than about the everyday realities of the people.

In ethno-centric narratives, the concept of national identity has been imbued with a logic that uses ancestors and folklore to imagine an ethnic unity, which in turn identifies and excludes religious and ethnic others. George Mosse's *Völkisch* movement (a German ethno-nationalist movement that created the concept of *blood and soil*) has played an important role in this process, imagining it as an idealization of the essence of the people (Mosse, 1966, p. 9). Historically, the movement did not emulate its model, as it benefited the elites who created the concept more than the peasants and workers the ideology imagined as the stock of this identity. Furthermore, ethno-centric national identity has not been a trait of right-wing regimes only – the ethno-historical uniformity imagined by the regimes in the search of renewed nationalism continues to have a hegemonic effect, as it did under Romanian socialism, and further, after the 1989 revolutions that swept Eastern Europe. During these regime changes, people around the world and Europe in particular have continued to experience state violence, yet the post- WWII era is sometimes treated as a post-racial era.

AUR's Historical Revisionism: Assembling Romanian Extremism from the Past

Ethno-centrism can sometimes look more benign than we would think. During the 19th and early 20th century, Romanian political regimes have directed their attention at archaeology and the creation of national collective identities (Henţ, 2018). This effort focused heavily on connecting the ancient Dacian civilization that inhabited parts of the Balkanic peninsula to Romanian stock, and on imagining a narrative of protochronism, in which the Dacians preceded all other civilizations (Pârvan 1926). Yet this ideological work is not unique to Romania. The protochronic nature of Albania suggests the nation is home to an older culture than the ancient Greeks (Aref, 2003), Estonia is argued to be the well-spring of all civilizations (Saks, 1966), former Georgian president Zviad Gamsahurdia was an avid promoter of Georgian protochronism (Nodia,1996), while Chechen writer S.H. Nunuev claimed in his 1998 book, *Haxu h CBamcHHaa McTopua* that both the Bible and the Quran have Chechen roots (Alexe, 2015).

Protochronism can be traced historically and can have effects on policy and ways of governing, as it did in Romania. The Romanian occupation of Transylvania at the end of WWI did not result in kind and equal treatment of the Hungarians who inhabited the territory. Most Romanians were peasants, and while there were Hungarian peasants, urban and land-owning Hungarians, like their Saxon and Jewish neighbours, enjoyed significantly greater political and economic privileges in Transylvania's cities. After Transylvania was allocated to Romania, Hungarian Jews who for generations had enjoyed relative freedom under Habsburg rule and had advanced to the upper strata, were now saddled with the double burden of both Hungarian and Jewish identities (Ioanid, 1998).

The Romanian Holocaust, in which pogroms and military operations took the lives of almost 400,000 Jews, is partly attributable to historical factors. In the 17th and 18th centuries, Jews migrated en masse from Galitia to Romania, in part to escape anti-Semitism, but also to take advantage of offers made by rulers of the Romanian Principates who wanted to develop commerce (Petrovsky-Shtem, 2014). Thus, a new social stratum was born, which quickly triggered dissent amongst the established population, based on nationalistic, religious, and economic hatred.

As a result of the treaties that created Greater Romania in 1918, the country doubled in size, and much of its new population was made up of ethnic minorities. The new country might have avoided a crisis if its ethnic nationalism had been transformed into civic nationalism. Instead, the state encouraged Romanian peasants, the majority of the population, to facilitate the new nation-state's development by becoming urbanized and educated, and forming a new middle-class, which they did, displacing an already urbanized middle-class, the majority of whom were Jewish. It is vital to mention that anti-Semitism was rife not just among right-wing intellectuals and politicians, but among liberals as well (Oncioiu, 2016).

Political antisemitic discourse overlapped with student movements, as some politicians were also teaching in universities, and soon, the far-right nationalist Iron Guard was formed. In the interwar period, the intellectual elite grew considerably in number as a consequence of democratization. The number of young people in the population also grew, and they were more daring, more idealist, more inclined towards extremes, more experimental, and generally less tolerant (Boia, 2012, p.27). They did not wish to follow in the footsteps of previous generations and find a place ideologically within Western Europe, nor were they looking to the East for solutions. The Iron Guard borrowed nationalistic French anti-Semitism and imbued it with Christian Orthodoxism (Cârstocea, 2014, p.6).

The Romanian obsession with inventing mystical origins begins with Nicolae Densuşianu's *Dacia Preistorică* (1913), which suggested that the Latin language from which Romanian evolved has its roots in the Dacian language and imagines that the organization and ethos of 20th century states is based on Dacian administrative forms. This discourse is maintained on social media pages linked to AUR in 2021. In reality, a Dacian language probably did not exist, and the colonial Latin language coexisted with a number of languages and dialects. To imagine a common Dacian language is to project upon the past the demographic density of today's Romania, with its urban centres, infrastructure, deforested areas, etc., when in fact the same space 2,000 years before was sparsely populated, and we have no way to know what language geographically disparate peoples used to communicate when they met each other (Alexe, 2015).

When the communist Ceauşescu regime slipped into its nationalist phase in the 1980s, the focus on the Dacians was renewed once more. Though nationalism and communism are ideologically incompatible, discourse played a central role in reimagining the nation. The July Theses[6] in 1971, a discourse by Romanian leader Nicolae Ceauşescu, positioned protochronism at the core of national propaganda. This was done in an environment where nationalism was not difficult to embrace. Despite the dedication of the early communist regime to Marxist principles, the last two centuries had cemented in national discourse the idea of a unique Romanian legacy (Verdery, 1994).

AUR's Campaign Tactics: From Soccer to Politics via Populism

During his campaign, George Simion centred his political narrative around opposing foreign business monopoly in Romania and making inquiries into political corruption and the deforestation of national parks. The campaign further focused on Romanian traditions, including the Dacian nationalist myth. The young politician posted an image on his website on April 15th, 2019, with the headline, *George Simion: alăturaţi-vă bătăliei pentru recâştigarea demnităţii naţionale* ("George Simion: join the battle to regain national dignity"). In the image, Simion is pictured in a special handshake with a bearded man. The man wears a traditional hemp shirt, tied around the waist with a ribbon in the colours of the Romanian flag, while a Phrygian cap[7] covers the top of his head.

In the short post accompanying the photo, Simion writes:

> From here, from where our origins stem, from the Dacian capital of Sarmisegetuza, we would like to send an important message to all Romanians: we must again be what we once were and be more, we must regain our national dignity, we must reclaim the history of our nation, and make a GREAT Romania in Europe and a GREAT Romania in the world. We can do it! Join the campaign, join our battle to regain national dignity![8]

> *(Simion, 2019)*

The message of this narrative calls for the imagined core of the ethno-nation to make the nation great once more, and is not new in Romania. In the early 1990s, Corneliu Vadim Tudor's Partidul România Mare (the Great Romania Party) used a newspaper by the same name to spread his ideas. He was often criticized for ultra-nationalist, anti-Semitic (Andreescu, 2012), anti-Roma (ERRC, 2006), anti-Hungarian, and homophobic (Tudor, 2018) slander. Similarly, the People's Party, led by television presenter Dan Diaconescu, gained its electoral success through Diaconescu's television channel OTV. OTV was eventually shut down by the National Audio-Visual Council due to its racist and antisemitic content (Voinea, 2015). Far-right movements have been most visible and active in neoliberal democracies in Europe and the US. Like Simion's AUR and its electoral base, which grow increasingly aggressive on social media, many have used social media (Web 2.0) to propagandize and spread fear of the unknown and the occult discursively moulded in a wide variety of ways, from imagining George Soros at the ultimate evil, to liberal politicians leading pizza shop child sex trafficking rings (Albrecht et al, 2019).

Simion's devotion to the ethno-state goes further. His name has long been associated with his commitment to the cause of uniting Romania and the Republic of Moldova, also known as Bessarabia. From Bucharest squares to concrete railroad partitions, the country is covered in unionist stencils reading "Basarabia e România" (Bessarabia is Romania). The message has been heavily promoted by Simion and his supporters, so much so that his activism got him banned from entering the Republic of Moldova, the sovereign state also known as Bessarabia. The ban was interpreted as a form of martyrdom in the name of the national creed, as his half-Bessarabian colleague Sorin Lavric declared (Lavric, 2021). Simion's arrival into mainstream Romanian politics took place symbolically on Romania's national day (December 1, 2019) when he announced the establishment of AUR in the city of Alba Iulia, where the union of the Romanian provinces took place in 1918.

Simion's early supporters supported the idea of a union between Romania and Bessarabia. As an ultras (devout football fan) himself (Digi Sport, 2020), George Simion won over football fans when he gathered factions of ultras on the Facebook page Uniti sub Tricolor (n.d.). Here, Simion asked that they forget about their inter-team rivalries, and instead refocus their attention on their shared national identity. Despite the success of his initiative, these groups were not a broad enough demographic to get AUR seats in the parliament during the December 2020 legislative elections. Simion directed the messaging on his Facebook page towards attacking tenured politicians and their alleged corruption. He became more radical in his criticism of national and global politics, a criticism that many citizens were primed to accept by years of imported right-wing social media narratives. He also adopted the idea of Dacian–Romanian continuity, as shown in the photo above. Simion also enlisted the help of a team, naming Claudiu Târziu as his second in command. Târziu is one of the founding members of the Romanian anti-abortion group Coalition for the Family[9] with experience in organizing the 2018 nation-wide referendum for a "normal" (meaning heterosexual) family (Târziu, 2021).

Târziu radicalized AUR further by co-opting his online Christian publication Rost (Rost Online [n.d.],), where he frequently publishes flattering articles about the interbelic Romanian far-right leader Corneliu Zelea Codreanu. Other AUR members include right-wing intellectuals, doctors, and former military personnel who use their social media presence to spread conspiracy theories about Covid-19 and the so-called globalist New World Order, as well as to create moral panics about the imminent danger of individual freedoms being taken away. Ironically, while most of these narratives emulate the concerns of the current American far-right, AUR and its supporters blend global discourses with autochthonous imaginaries of Romanian protochronism and exceptionalism, through the generic national myth of continuity between an ancient people called Dacians[10] and their noble heirs, the 21st century Romanian people.

Târziu recruited his long-time acquaintance, Sorin Lavric, an eloquent intellectual who left the medical field to become a philosopher, gained a seat in the 2020 parliament, and is now the AUR president of the Senate. Both Târziu and Lavric have recently been more vocal as they have taken on more public roles. Lavric's engagements with the media deserve particular attention, as he regularly appears on TV shows funded by the Romanian Orthodox Church, or on traditionally right-wing, conspiracist channels. In these appearances, he has expressed racist views, claiming that the Roma are a social plague, speaking of the recent waves of refugees to Europe as a premeditated colonization from a neo-Marxist European Union set on destroying the white race (Păduraru, 2021), and likening refugees to weeds that violently take over a rose garden (Conte, 2018). Lavric considers the political to be inherent to the masculine spirit, but sees homosexuality as unnatural (Nicolae, 2018) and women as genetically lacking a sense of purpose (Dumitru, 2020). He references his medical degree to legitimize his conspiracy theories against Covid-19, vaccinations, and his refusal to wear a mask (Păduraru, 2021).

Just as important, Lavric evokes parallels with the interwar far-right more than the other AUR leaders, as referenced by many of his recent speeches in the Senate, that commemorate former legionnaires imprisoned by the Communist regime. In a speech immediately following the 2020 elections, he declared:

> For us (n.a. AUR), it is the dawn of an ideological war, the end of which will be symbolised by the elimination of the present political class. Four years from now, we will have extricated the parties from the Parliament. We will change the faces, we will purify the language, we will welcome the joy of being Romanian. We will relive the mystical taste of being Christian near every church in the country. We will regain the warmth we get at the thought of being one in the virtue of belonging to a nation. We will welcome the ecstasy of being part of a whole called Romania. We will venerate the memory of political prisoners.[11]

Lavric's totalitarian narrative here, mixed with Orthodoxism and purism, points to similar words used by Corneliu Zelea Codreanu, the leader of the Iron Guard, who envisioned a country in which existing parties, all corrupt, would be eliminated and replaced by one movement, one captain. These logics are also central to Benito Mussolini's speeches, where totalitarianism was presented as the only solution, imagining a political movement that became synonymous with the state, and its leader became all-powerful (Falasca-Zamponi, 2000).

In this same vein, another parallel can be drawn. Corneliu Zelea Codreanu was discursively sanctified as the party leader, and was referred to as "The captain, golden mouth[12], Great Prophet and Evangelist of the ways of God" (Schmitt 2017, p.9). Lavric edges towards this sanctification when he calls Simion "the charismatic[13] leader of this party, who has pushed the Party forward through an incredible amount of devotion and work, George Simion (…) this beautifully crazy man"[14] (Lavric, 2021).

Towards an AUR "Winning Strategy"? From Dacian Gold to Political Gold

George Simion's photo with the modern-day Dacian is a perfect metaphor for how AUR won over its electorate. Simion and his party have relied on years of work by people on social media creating the discourse that became their foundation in 2020. Their electorate resonated with AUR's ideas because they had seen them before on Facebook pages that count tens, sometimes hundreds of thousands of followers. I arrived at these pages around 2016 while doing fieldwork in Romania on politics and the occult, when a number of family and friends invited me to join these Facebook groups.

I watched the discourse change to anti-globalist, conspirationist, and far-right extremist in ways strongly reflected in AUR and George Simion's discourses of Romanian exceptionalism and the idea that Romania has always been desired by powerful outside empires because of its sacred land and resources, including gold (often called Dacian gold), silver and other precious metals. People following these social media accounts, and later AUR and Simion's accounts, were indoctrinated with the idea that the Dacian–Romanian continuity makes Romania the longest ever inhabited and the most filled with mystery, wonder, and the esoteric, and that it is the site of amazing feats of science and technology that continue to go unrecognized, hidden even, by Western empires attempting to maintain their supremacy. These narratives are fertile ground for conspiracy theories to take root within the logic of protochronism.

One of Simion's most trusted party members, a retired general and marathon runner named Ilie Roșu, received 13.4% of the votes in the county of Vrancea and ran for the Senate. In photos posted to his public Facebook account, he is waving the Romanian flag in his right hand. The flag in his left hand has been accepted, through film and literature, to be the Dacian flag – the image on it represents a hollow metal wolf said to have terrified the Dacian's enemies on the battlefield. In Roșu's imaginary, and in the minds of many others, the Dacian–Romanian continuity and the protochronism of the Romanian people are undeniable truths.

Such flags can be purchased online and in the Bucharest store *Lupul Dacic* (the Dacian Wolf). I have visited the store on multiple occasions during my fieldwork, and many of the products evoke a Dacian past, from Phrygian caps to leather bracelets, bags, and T-shirts with Dacian symbols and messages printed on them. The store also offers a plethora of antisemitic books and books on conspiracy theories, and one can often overhear deliberations between shopkeepers and clients on issues concerning anti-globalist conspiracy theories and Romania's exceptionalism, as well as theories on banal numerology and semantics that interpret everything as being initiated by the Dacians.

The store's owner, Daniel Roxin, is a quasi-notorious personality. He uses his significant presence on Facebook[15] to promote George Simion and other AUR candidates. In one post on December 2, 2020, days before the elections, Roxin wrote:

> The only real, PATRIOTIC manifestation this December 1 took place in Alba Iulia, and was organized by AUR and George Simion. They discussed DACIA, king Burebista, and the union between Romania and Bessarabia. Over 500 Romanians with Romanian flags broke the blockade in the city of the Great Union.[16]
>
> *(Roxin, 2020a)*

In another Facebook post on December 5, 2020, he noted:

> How would it be if the GETO-DACIAN Mihai Vinereanu, the linguist who demonstrated that the Romanian language has first and foremost Thraco-Geto-Dacian roots, would get a place in the Romanian Parliament after the December 6 elections? Mihai Vinereanu is a candidate on the first position on the AUR electoral lists, in the county of Vâlcea.[17]
>
> *(Roxin, 2020b)*

Roxin's personal Facebook page promotes objects from the Lupul Dacic store, and he reposts many articles from his blog (Roxin, 2021), ranging from pro-Trump opinion pieces both before and after President Biden took office, where he accused the latter of being part of a global neo-Marxist dictatorship and pursuing an LGBT agenda; to denying the existence of and the political agenda against the Covid-19 virus; to promoting astonishing Romanian inventions – and cautioning the reader about global elites who are hiding Romanian greatness from the world. He uses concepts such as "neo-Marxism", "The Great Reset", and "medical apartheid". Despite arguing for anti-globalism, Roxin borrows these terms from far-right groups in the West, spewing anti-Hungarian, anti-Putin, anti-Soros propaganda, and blends them with articles on Dacian origin stories, Dacian hidden treasures (mainly gold or archaeological wonders) and uses terminology from Romanian folklorist Nicolae Densușianu. A roguish polymath, Roxin also produces a film series about antisemitic poet Mihai Eminescu, focusing on his life as a martyr for his political ideas and conspiracies on how and why he was killed, and another film series on the Dacians. The Dacians, an archaeological extension of the Romanian people, are presented in his documentary as the first and best at everything, inventors of everything from Christmas to the Yin Yang symbol.

Roxin is almost exclusively re-shared in posts on many other pages focused on non-violent far-right extremism in Romania, such as *Comunitatea Hyperboreea* (1,253 likes/1,340 followers) and *Mistere la Granitele Cunoasterii* (39,672 likes/40,112 followers). His content is also shared by pages representing parts of the Romanian far right focused on Dacian content, such as *Asociatia Geto-Dacii* (54,544 likes/53,334 followers), *Adevarul despre Daci* (113,608 likes/110,792 followers), and *Cunoaste Lumea* (66,114 likes/66,600 followers). *Lupul Dacic Blog*[18] (13,539 likes/13,220 followers) shares anti-Covid conspiracies, framing Bill Gates and Soros as master puppeteers, claiming the vaccine is the product of Satan, and the World Health Organisation as a terrorist organization. Like Roxin, this website expresses pro-Trump positions and cites Fox News for evidence that we are no longer allowed to decide how our children are raised, because of the far-left occult global governance. They promote the Great Reset conspiracy as well as Roxin's merchandize. On July 28, 2020, the administrator of *Lupul Dacic Blog* wrote:

> The entire world is participating in an occult ritual of corona-initiation, even though only few will understand this. The unprecedented measures and policies that the world governments have been undertaking since the start of Operation Coronavirus – like the quarantine, the isolation, the hand washing, wearing the masks, social distancing and others – all these are in reality just aspects of a ritual of occult initiation.[19]

On the same day, the administrator of the blog noted:

> the preparations for the planetary genocide are in their last steps. In a few months, they will start the Great Decimation (probably in September-October). The operation has been going on for a long time, but silently. It is the most daring blow to mankind at the hands of the puppeteers who managed to take over the world. They were set from the beginning to start this mega-extermination, even some thirty, forty years ago.[20]

Conclusion

The main purpose of this chapter has been to analyse the narratives of AUR leaders, in order to understand how the party fits into the local and regional political landscape. Most state and non-state actors treat AUR as an exception to the ideological climate – the importance of the study resides in the fact that it follows the ideological continuities from the interwar Romanian right, as well as the country's socialist regime in the second half of the 20th century, and current imported conspiracy theories, to understand the party as what it is – a product of its environment.

The chapter started by looking at the December 2020 electoral results as the moment when mainstream attention turns towards AUR, then introduces the party's winning strategies, markedly the role that social media platforms have played in the small party's surprising win. As the chapter progresses, it reveals the three leaders of the party, Simion, Târziu, and Lavric, and introduces some of the political continuities that bridge AUR with the Iron Guard and the Romanian Communist Party. AUR's extremism is then analysed, particularly their affinity for totalitarian discourse, and the chapter explains why the electorate was ready to support a political formation like AUR, noting their long-term disenchantment with Romania's corrupt politicians, but equally drawing attention to recent years, when social media and the press have been inundated with imported conspiracy theories.

The chapter then moves to shed light on some of the theoretical complexities included in studying this topic: the fact that Romanians are both the victims and perpetrators of ethno-centric violence; that there is a need to relocate the theoretical dimension of populism; and that ethno-centric national identity is a feature that tends to persist long after a far-right regime falls. Further, the work looks at manifestations of protochronism Romania and the area, and links this seemingly benign logic with ethnic nationalism, racism, and antisemitism. In the next section, the chapter delves into the evolution and narratives of George Simion, his ideological predecessors, and his partners, Târziu and Lavric. The latter two are becoming central to AUR and are leaving a mark in mainstream media. Last but not least, the chapter ends with a section of other partners and supporters of AUR, as their ideas reveal a great potential for violent extremism.

AUR's non-violent extremism is a complex phenomenon. While it is treated by Romanian state and non-state actors (scholars, political analysts, commentators) as a unique moment, paralleled only by the violent rise of the Iron Guard in Romania's 1930s, its continuities delve deeper. Observing similarities between AUR and the Iron Guard can prove helpful to making sense of the former's logics but should be accompanied by an investigation into the discourses of political actors across the spectrum to draw clearer pictures of the elements present in AUR's discourse. From Dacian–Romanian continuities, to populism, Orthodoxism, borrowed right-wing beliefs and the imaginary of having created them autochthonously, these themes span more than a century and, pieced together, can give us a better idea of how AUR came to be successful. Non-violent extremist movement is expanding to neighbouring Moldova, as, at the time of the author writing this conclusion, George Simion is touring Western Europe to garner the support of the Romanian diaspora there. AUR cannot be treated as a passing moment, but as the result of many decades of ideological continuities.

Notes

1 The acronym means "gold" in Romanian.
2 Throughout the chapter, Iron Guard and Legionnaire will be used interchangeably.
3 Figures referring to June 30, 2021.
4 From Greek, "before time", the term started being instrumentalized in Romania in the 1860s, as a theme used to explore Romania's role in Europe. After WWI, the term started to gain traction in Romanian political circles, where the far-right Legionnaire movement and the Iron Guard organization adopted it as a way to legitimate their martyrdom. The term was further given importance under the Ceausescu regime, with Edgar Papu's 1974 essay "Romanian protochronism", where he argued for a Dacian-Romanian ancient culture having existed a priori to the other European cultures (Papu, 1974, p.199).
5 According to the Merriam-Webster dictionary (n.d.), suzerainty is the dominion of a suzerain, an overlord.
6 The July Theses were inspired by Ceauşescu's visits to Mongolia, Vietnam, North Korea, and the People's Republic of China, where he observed the extensive focus on national transformation.
7 The Phrygian cap is believed to have been worn by the Dacians and therefore is an attempt by AUR to connect with the Dacian nationalist myth.
8 Original:

> De aici, de unde ne sunt originile, de la Sarmizegetusa, din capitala dacilor, vrem să transmitem un mesaj important pentru toţi românii: trebuie să fim iarăşi ce am fost şi mai mult decât atâta, trebuie să ne recâştigăm demnitatea noastră naţională trebuie să ne recucerim istoria neamului nostru şi să facem o Românie care să fie MARE în Europa şi MARE în lume. Putem! Alăturaţi-vă campaniei, alăturaţi-vă în anii aceştia bătăliei pentru recâştigarea demnităţii naţionale.

9 An attempt to modify the Romanian constitution that stipulates marriage is the "non-coercive agreement between spouses" to "non-coercive agreement between a man and a woman". The legislative attempt failed.
10 In the materials I analyse, people use Dacian interchangeably with Geto-Dacian, sometimes Thraco-Geto-Dacian. I use such terms interchangeably as well in my analysis.
11 Original:

> Pentru noi începe un război ideologic al cărui deznodămînt va sta in înlăturarea actualei clase politice. În patru ani vom disloca partidele din Parlament. Vom schimba figurile, vom primeni limba, vom aduce bucuria de a fi români. Vom regăsi gustul mistic de a fi creştini în umbra oricărei catapetesme din bisericile din ţară. Vom recăpăta căldura pe care ne-o dă gîndul de a fi una în virtutea apartenenţei la un neam. Vom aduce exaltarea de a fi parte dintr-un întreg numit România. Vom întreţine cu veneraţie memoria deţinuţilor politici.

(Gorgan, 2020)

12 Reference to John Chrysostom, Early Church Father in the Byzantine Church, celebrated for his prophetic, God-given eloquence.

13 Lavric uses the term "harismatic", meaning, in the religious context of Romanian Orthodoxy, a gift received from the Holy Ghost.

14 Original: "liderul harismatic al acestui partid, care a impins Partidul printr-un devotement si o munca incredibila, este George Simion (…) acest nebun frumos."

15 Followed by 43,820 people on June 30, 2021.

16 Original:

> Singura manifestaţie reală, PATRIOTICĂ, de 1 Decembrie a avut loc la Alba Iulia şi a fost organizată de AUR şi George Simion. S-a vorbit despre DACIA, Burebista şi Unirea cu Basarabia. Peste 500 de români cu steaguri tricolore au spart blocada din oraşul MARII UNIRI...

17 Original:

> Cum ar fi dacă GETO-DACUL Mihai Vinereanu, lingvistul care a demonstrat că limba română are în primul rând rădăcini traco-geto-dacice, ar intra în Parlamentul României, după alegerile din 6 Decembrie? Mihai Vinereanu candidează de pe prima poziţie pe listele AUR, în Vâlcea...

18 Figures referring to January 2021, the page was deleted in June 2021.

19 Original:

> Întreaga lume participă la un ritual ocult al corona-iniţierii, deşi puţini vor fi cei care vor înţelege asta. Măsurile şi politicile fără precedent, pe care le desfăşoară guvernele din întreaga lume din momentul declanşării Operaţiunii Coronavirus – cum ar fi carantina, izolarea, spălarea pe mâini, purtarea de măşti, distanţa socială şi altele – de fapt sunt aspecte ale unui ritual al iniţierii oculte.

20 Original:

> Pregătirile Genocidului planetar sunt pe ultima sută de metri. În câteva luni va începe Marea Decimare (probabil în septembrie – octombrie). Acţiunea se desfăşoară de multă vreme, dar cu multă timiditate. Este cea mai îndrăzneaţă lovitură aplicată omenirii de către păpuşarii ce au reuşit să preia controlul planetei. Ei erau hotărâţi să înceapă această megaexterminare chiar şi cu treizeci, patruzeci de ani în urmă.

Bibliography

Albrecht, S., Fielitz, M., & Thurston, N. (2019). Introduction. In M. Fielitz & N. Thurston (Eds.), *Post-Digital Cultures of the Far Right: Online Actions and Offline Consequences in Europe and the US* (pp. 7–24). Bielefeld: Transcript.

Alexe, D. (2015). *Dacopatia şi alte rătăciri româneşti*. Bucharest: Humanitas.

Anastasiou, M. (2019, July). Popular or Hegemonic Subject? On the Limits of Democratic Populism. *POPULISMUS Working Papers*, 9, 1–21.

Andreescu, C. (2012, October 19). Corneliu Vadim Tudor: "În România n-a existat Holocaust." *DCNews*. Retrieved August 23, 2021, from https://web.archive.org/web/20121026012412/http://www.dcn ews.ro/2012/10/corneliu-vadim-tudor-in-romania-n-a-existat-holocaust/

Aref, M. (2003). *Albanie ou l'incroyable odyssée d'un peuple pré-hellénique*. Paris: Mnemosyne.

Baran, Z. (2005). Fighting the War of Ideas. *Foreign Affairs*, 84(6), 68–78. doi:10.2307/20031777

Beck, S. (1989). Ethnic Identity as Contested Terrain Introduction. *Dialectical Anthropology*, 14(1), 1–6.

Boia, L. (2012). *Capcanele istoriei. Elita intelectuală românească între 1930 şi 1950*. Bucuresti: Humanitas.

Cârstocea, R. (2014, October). Anti-Semitism in Romania: Historical Legacies, Contemporary Challenges. *ECMI Working Papers*, 81, 1–39.

Code for Romania. (2020, December 8). *Rezultate Vot*. Retrieved August 23, 2021, from https://rezul tatevot.ro/elections/112/results

Conte, C. (2018, March 14). Vasile Bănescu în dialog cu Sorin Lavric. O distrugere a etosului european? *Contemporanul*. Retrieved August 23, 2021, from www.contemporanul.ro/clubul-ideea-europeana/vas ile-banescu-in-dialog-cu-sorin-lavric-o-distrugere-a-etosului-european.html

Cordesman, A. (2017, October 17). Islam and the Patterns in Terrorism and Violent Extremism. *Center for Strategic and International Studies*. Retrieved from www.csis.org/analysis/islam-and-patterns-terror ism-and-violent-extremism

Densuşianu, N. (1913). *Dacia Preistorică*. Bucuresti: Carol Göbl.

Digi Sport. (2020, December 7). *Cine este George Simion, ultrasul care conduce partidul AUR, marea surpriză a alegerilor parlamentare.* Retrieved August 23, 2021, from www.digisport.ro/special/cine-este-george-simion-ultrasul-care-conduce-partidului-aur-marea-surpriza-a-alegerilor-parlamentare-963655

Dumitru, S. (2020, December 8). Sorin Lavric, liderul AUR care șochează în declarații: romii sunt „o plagă socială" și femeia e „văduvită de simțul destinului". *AlephNews.* Retrieved August 21, 2021, from https://alephnews.ro/guvern/sorin-lavric-liderul-aur-care-socheaza-in-declaratii-romii-sunt-o-plaga-sociala-si-femeia-e-vaduvita-de-simtul-destinului/

Eremia, R. (2021, April 4). Bizareriile partidului AUR: decizii și personaje ciudate. *Adevărul.* Retrieved August 4, 2021, from https://adevarul.ro/news/politica/bizareriilepartidului-aur-decizii-personaje-ciudate-1_6069d6015163ec42719b9b8f/index.html

ERRC. (2006, February 14). *Romanian Equality Watchdog Rules Anti-Romani Speech by Romanian Politician Is Discriminatory.* Retrieved August 21, 2021, from www.errc.org/cikk.php?cikk=2513

Falasca-Zamponi, S. (2000). *Fascist Spectacle. The Aesthetics of Power in Mussolini's Italy.* Berkeley: UC Press.

Furtună, M. (2020, December 14). Idioții utili ai extremei drepte. *Spectrul.* Retrieved August 4, 2021, from https://spectrul.ro/2020/12/14/idiotii-utili-ai-extremei-drepte/

Gilligan, A. (2019, 21 February). The Baroness, Islamic Extremists and a Question of Free Speech. *The Telegraph.* Retrieved August 23, 2021, from www.telegraph.co.uk/news/uknews/11488175/The-baroness-Islamic-extremists-and-a-question-of-free-speech.html

Gorgan, C. (2020, December 8). Sorin Lavric, lider AUR: "Pentru noi începe un război ideologic al cărui deznodământ va sta in înlăturarea actualei clase politice". *Gazeta de Cluj.* Retrieved August 23, 2021, from https://gazetadecluj.ro/sorin-lavric-lider-aur-pentru-noi-incepe-un-razboi-ideologic-al-carui-deznodamant-va-sta-in-inlaturarea-actualei-clase-politice/

Hamid, S. (2016). *Sufis, Salafis and Islamists. The Contested Ground of British Islamic Activism.* London: I.B. Tauris.

Henț, A. (2018). Arheologie în Național-Comunism. Dacii și „Istoria De Parastas". *SARGETIA,* IX (XLV) Deva, 87–105.

Herzog Zu Mecklenburg, M., & Anthony, I. (2020). Preventing Violent Extremism in Germany: Coherence and Cooperation in a Decentralized System. *Stockholm International Peace Research Institute.* Retrieved June 30, 2020 from www.sipri.org/publications/2020/working-paper/preventing-violent-extremism-germany-coherence-and-cooperation-decentralized-system

Iancu, P.M. (2020, December 7). Europa și aiuritorul AUR, acest faur al putinismului românesc. *DW.* Retrieved August 23, 2021, from www.dw.com/ro/europa-%C8%99i-aiuritorul-aur-acest-faur-al-putinismului-rom%C3%A2nesc/a-55848669

Ioanid, R. (1993). The Holocaust in Romania: The Iasi Pogrom of June 1941. *Contemporary European History,* 2(2), 119–148. https://doi.org/10.1017/s0960777300000394

Ioanid, R. (1998). *The Holocaust in Romania: The Fate of Jews and Gypsies in Fascist Romania, 1940–1944.* Chicago, IL: Ivan R. Dee.

Kakel, C.P. (2011). Racial 'Othering': 'Manufacturing Difference'. In C. P. Kakel (Ed.), *The American West and the Nazi East* (pp. 46–76). Palgrave Macmillan, London. https://doi.org/10.1057/97802303 07063_3

Keinz, A., & Lewicki, P. (2019) Who Embodies Europe? Explorations into the Construction of European Bodies. *Anthropological Journal of European Cultures,* 28(1), 7–24. doi:10.3167/ajec.2019.280104

Kiss, R. (2021, March 29). Senatorul Târziu: AUR, acuzat nefondat că este un partid neo-fascist și antisemit. Orice calomnie împotriva AUR e și împotriva României. *Digi24.* Retrieved August 23, 2021, from www.digi24.ro/stiri/actualitate/politica/senatorul-tarziu-aur-acuzat-nefondat-ca-este-un-partid-neo-fascist-si-antisemit-orice-calomnie-impotriva-aur-e-si-impotriva-romaniei-1477323

Lavric, S. [Sorin]. (2021, March 27). De ziua Unirii cu Basarabia, 27 martie, cuvintele unui semi-basarabean la statuia lui Vasile Lupu, în centrul orașului Orhei. [Facebook video]. Retrieved August 4, 2021 from www.facebook.com/watch/?v=810326299693917

Mbembe, A. (2021, July 1). Notes on Late Eurocentrism. *Critical Inquiry.* Retrieved from https://critinq.wordpress.com/2021/07/01/notes-on-late-eurocentrism/

Merriam-Webster. (n.d.). Suzerainty. *Merriam-Webster.com Dictionary.* Retrieved August 22, 2021, from www.merriam-webster.com/dictionary/suzerainty

Mosse, G.L. (1966) *The Crisis of German Ideology: Intellectual Origins of the Third Reich,* London: Weidenfeld & Nicolson.

Nicolae, A. (2018, January 3). Dialog INCITANT și CURAJOS la Televiziunea Patriarhiei Române: Polonia și Ungaria sunt cele două fortărețe care se opun curentului federalist venit de la Bruxelles/ Toleranța NU este o valoare în sine. Din punct de vedere creștin este o slăbiciune. *ActiveNews*. Retrieved from www.activenews.ro/stiri-social/Dialog-INCITANT-si-CURAJOS-la-Televiziunea-Patriarhiei-Romane-Polonia-si-Ungaria-sunt-cele-doua-fortarete-care-se-opun-cur entului-federalist-venit-de-la-Bruxelles-Toleranta-NU-este-o-valoare-in-sine.-Din-punct-de-vedere-crestin-este-o-slabiciune-150647

Nodia, G. (1996). Political Turmoil in Georgia and the Ethnic Policies of Zviad Gamsakhurdia. In B. Coppieters (Ed.), *Contested Borders in the Caucasus* (pp. 73–89). Bruxelles: VUBPRESS.

Oncioiu, D. (2016). Ethnic Nationalism and Genocide: Constructing "the Other" in Romania and Serbia. In Ü.U. Ümit (Ed.) *Genocide* (pp. 27–48). Amsterdam: Amsterdam University Press.

Păduraru, P. (2021, June 18). Interviu cu Sorin Lavric (AUR) „Românii au fost îndopați cu minciuni și nu mai au o busolă, dar se vor trezi". *Timpul*. Retrieved August 23, 2021, from www.timpul.md/articol/interviu-cu-sorin-lavric-(aur)-sa-fiu-i-eu-o-momaie-cum-au-fost-30-de-ani-toi-politicienii-notri-nu-pot--164794.html

Papu, E. (1974). Protocronismul românesc. *Secolul XX* (5–6): 8–11.

Papu, E. (1977). *Din clasicii noștri. Contribuții la ideea unui protocronism românesc*, Bucuresti: Editura Eminescu.

Pârvan, V. (1926). *Getica. O protoistorie a Daciei*. Bucuresti: Cultura Națională.

Petrovsky-Shtem, Y. (2014). *The Golden Age Shtetl: A New History of Jewish Life in East Europe*, Princeton, NJ: Princeton University Press.

Radio Europa Liberă Moldova. (2021, April 15). *România: Partidul extremist AUR crește în popularitate*. Retrieved August 23, 2021, from https://moldova.europalibera.org/a/rom%C3%A2nia-partidul-extremist-aur-cre%C8%99te-%C3%AEn-popularitate/31204729.html

Recorder. (2021, January 13). *Cum a ajuns AUR a patra forță politică din România*. Retrieved August 23, 2021, from https://recorder.ro/cum-a-ajuns-aur-a-patra-forta-politica-din-romania/

Rost Online. (n.d.). *Rezultate căutare pentru: Zelea*. Retrieved from www.rostonline.ro/?s=zelea

Roșu, I. [Ilie]. (2019, June 16). Tibles Maraton cu drapelul Romaniei si steagul dacilor [Facebook update]. Retrieved August 23, 2021, from www.facebook.com/photo/?fbid=2949970381710763&set=a.2949969748377493

Roxin, D. [Daniel]. (2020a, December 2). Singura manifestație reală, PATRIOTICĂ, de 1 Decembrie a avut loca la Alba Iulia și a fost organizată de AUR și George Simion. S-a vorbit despre DACIA, Burebista și Unirea cu Basarabia [Facebook status update]. Retrieved from www.facebook.com/daniel.roxin/posts/2273577356122364

Roxin, D. [Daniel]. (2020b, December 5). Cum ar fi dacă GETO-DACUL Mihai Vinereanu, lingvistul care a demonstrat că limba română are în primul rând rădăcini traco-geto-dacice, ar intra în Parlamentul României, după alegerile din 6 Decembrie? Mihai Vinereanu candidează de pe prima poziție pe listele AUR, în Vâlcea... [Facebook status update]. Retrieved from www.facebook.com/permalink.php?story_fbid=3548708741911234&id=263216097127198

Roxin, D. [Daniel]. (2021, June 30). *Blog Categoria Articole*. Retrieved August 23, 2021, from https://daniel-roxin.ro/category/articole/

Rrustemi, A. (2020). Countering and Preventing (Non) Violent Extremism. Research and Fieldwork Challenges. *Hague Centre for Strategic Studies*. Retrieved from https://hcss.nl/report/countering-and-preventing-non-violent-extremism-research-and-fieldwork-challenges/

Saks, E.V. (1966). *Esto-Europa: A Treatise on the Finno-Ugric Primary Civilization in Europe*. Montreal: Boreas Publishing House.

Schmid, A.P. (2014). Violent and Non-Violent Extremism: Two Sides of the Same Coin?" The International Centre for Counter-Terrorism. *The Hague*, 5(5). Retrieved June 30, 2021, from https://icct.nl/publication/violent-and-non-violent-extremism-two-sides-of-the-same-coin/

Schmitt, O.J. (2017). *Corneliu Zelea Codreanu. Ascensiunea și căderea "Căpitanului"*. Bucuresti: Humanitas.

Simion, G. (n.d.). Timeline [Facebook page]. Retrieved August 4, 2021, from www.facebook.com/george.simion.unire/

Simion, G. (2019, April 15). *VIDEO // George Simion: alăturați-vă bătăliei pentru recâștigarea demnității naționale*. Retrieved from https://georgesimion.ro/stiri/1467/video-george-simion-alaturati-va-batal iei-pentru-recastigarea-demnitatii-nationale/

Târziu, C. (2021, August 18). *Curriculum Vitae*. Retrieved from https://claudiutarziu.ro/despre-mine/curriculum-vitae/

True Story Project. (n.d.). Events [Facebook page]. Retrieved from www.facebook.com/truestoryproject1/events/?ref=page_internal

Tudor, C.V. [Corneliu Vadim Tudor]. (2018, October 3). Vadim Tudor: Nu vrem căsătorii între homosexuali! [Facebook video]. Retrieved August 4, 2021, from www.facebook.com/watch/?v= 920132554838205

Uniți sub Tricolor, (n.d.) Timeline [Facebook page]. Retrieved from www.facebook.com/unitisubtrico lor2013

Verdery, K. (1994) *Compromis şi rezistenţă: cultura română sub Ceauşescu.* Bucuresti: Humanitas.

Voinea, M. (2015, March 4). Mizeriile din istoria OTV, televiziunea care l-a îngropat pe Dan Diaconescu. De la serialul Elodia la „teribilul Puleaşcă". *Adevărul.* Retrieved from https://adevarul.ro/news/societ ate/mizeriile-istoria-otv-televiziunea-l-a-ingropat-dan-diaconescu-serialul-elodia-teribilul-puleasca-1_54f7031e448e03c0fd37fa59/index.html

Ziare.com (2020, Decembre 7). *De ce au votat romanii un partid extremist. Profesor de istorie: "Programul de guvernare al AUR e o imbinare de fascism cu comunism".* Retrieved from https://ziare.com/george-simion/ stiri-george-simion/de-ce-voteaza-romanii-partide-extremiste-1648978

18

FAR-RIGHT NATIONALIST POLITICS IN TURKEY

Division of the Nationalist Camp Between the MHP and the Good Party

Giray Gerim

Introduction

The far right is not a homogeneous entity, and for this reason, defining its attributes on a general plane is not sufficient to understand far-right parties and movements that have different ideological grounds in each case (Golder, 2016; Mudde, 2019). However, if we were to isolate the ideological core, the common or "animating force" of far-right movements, it could be a principal emphasis on ethnonationalism, which also accommodates an aspiration to return to what proponents articulate as the traditional values of a nation (Bar-On, 2018, p. 43; Rydgren, 2018, p. 23). The point in common with the political parties and groups under this umbrella term is that they envisage the solution to almost all socio-economic issues through an in-group/out-group distinction shaped by nationalism (Halikiopoulou and Vlandas, 2019, p. 416). Far-right actors are highly concerned about the homogeneity of their nations, and they usually share xenophobia and anti-establishment populism as common features (Camus and Lebourg, 2017; Rydgren, 2018). However, the Turkish case displays a very different picture mainly due to three reasons: the historical roots of its main far-right party, the high political polarisation in the country, and the recent division within the country's far-right politics which is also linked to this polarisation.

In Turkey, ultra-nationalism and far right have become synonymous with the *Milliyetçi Hareket Partisi* (MHP) since the party's establishment in 1969, and according to Öniş (2003, p. 31), this party is the closest one in the Turkish political spectrum to where the far right coincides in Western politics, considering its ideological premises.[1] The party has been associated with many violent incidents, particularly those of the party's youth organisation, the Idealist Hearths (*Ülkü Ocakları* – ÜO) (Gümrükçü, 2021). The party's place in democratic politics has been often questioned due to this organisation, which is considered to be a projection of paramilitary power of the right-wing especially during the tumultuous years preceding the 1980 military coup which saw violent clashes between various political factions (Heper and İnce, 2006; Öniş, 2003). It is argued by some scholars that the ÜO used violence as a tool against rival political groups and organisations after this period as well, and this violence was tolerated and legitimised, especially when coalitions of which the MHP was a partner were

DOI: 10.4324/9781003032793-22

ruling the country (Gourisse, 2021; Gümrükçü, 2021; Kumral, 2017).[2] Considering this, it can be expected that the above-mentioned polarisation in Turkish politics and the recent division that resulted in the founding of a new party, the Good Party (*İYİ Parti*), may have implications for the relationship of the Turkish far right with violence.

The entire political situation requires a fresh analysis of the far right especially regarding the emergence and existence of this new actor. This is necessary both to understand the place of the far right in the recent polarisation that has shaped Turkish politics and to re-interpret the relationship of the Turkish far right with violence/non-violence. Despite these, it is still difficult to find studies in the literature that analyse the Turkish far right through this division and by including this new actor. This study examines the Turkish far right, taking these new developments into account. It hypothesises that the ideological structure of the MHP, along with its secular-conservative cleavage in Turkish politics, played an important role in the split of the Turkish far right and the emergence of the Good Party, and this split increased the radical-isation potential of the MHP. Thus, the chapter has two central research questions: (1) What are the main factors that led to the division in the Turkish far right and the emergence of the Good Party? (2) What is the effect of this division on the violence potential of the Turkish far right? To answer these questions, this chapter will first address the ideological background of far-right nationalism together with the relevant historical and political cleavages to shed light on the social and political basis of far-right nationalism in the country. After that, it will investigate the recent political alliances, election results, and political discourses of the leaders (and notable figures) of the two parties in question. The theoretical insights obtained from the social cleavage theory will be utilised to constitute a basis for the research. By this means, the research attempts to elucidate the interrelations between the political actors of Turkish far-right nationalism and their social ground within a theoretical framework by paying attention to divisions, alignments, factions, and also their relationship to violence. All in all, this chapter aims to contribute to the literature on nationalist extremism by addressing the previous questions and shedding light on far-right politics in Turkey.

Cleavage Theory

One of the key components taken into account when examining party politics is how social cleavages in a country shape voter support (Norris, 2005). In their seminal work, Lipset and Rokkan (1967, pp. 14–15) identify four salient lines of cleavage as the consequences of the two revolutionary processes, known as the national and industrial revolutions.[3] According to their approach, European party politics in particular were structured by social conflicts dating back to the 1920s and earlier. Thus, they argue that the party systems in Europe are frozen within the cleavages caused by these conflicts to a great extent (Veugelers, 1997).

The cleavage theory has been criticised in various ways so far (Hooghe and Mark, 2018). According to some studies, various factors (such as economic prosperity, increasing educa-tional opportunities, and increased communication among countries) have changed social structures, and these, in turn, invalidated or at least weakened the theory. In addition, some scholars have claimed that this freezing is an exaggerated inference and that this hypothesis has no validity before the 1960s either (Özbudun, 2013). According to Elff (2009), although the new conventional wisdom suggests that the impact of social divisions on political behaviours has been declining, the relation between political choices and social divisions can be under-stood through changing political positions of parties, and when such changes are taken into consideration, social divisions again gain their explanatory power on political behaviours and cleavages.

It should be remarked that, as well as social stratification and group consciousness, the existence of a certain organisation or party that attributes a particular set of values and designates an identity to the group is essential for a cleavage (Bartolini and Mair, 1990; Bértoa, 2012; Mair, 2006). Since cleavages are not simply translated into political systems, Sartori (1969, p. 209) draws attention to the translation process and argues that it calls for translators. As he argues, the assumption that cleavages are just reflected in political systems but not reproduced by these systems is problematic as such an assumption ignores that cleavages can be activated, channelled, reinforced, distorted, reshaped, or repressed by the actors and operators of a political system. Therefore, the agency is quite important when we think about the reflection of cleavages in political systems (Norris, 2005). In other words, whereas party systems are widely considered as consequences of the cleavages in their societies, they are also active constructors of those cleavages (Bornschier, 2010; Sartori; 1969). When the agency of political movements and parties also has to be seriously reckoned with, it can be asserted that the relevance of cleavages has not vanished in contemporary politics but transformed, and new parties have the opportunity to bring about changes in party systems (Bornschier, 2010; Hooghe and Mark, 2018). Such an approach to political cleavages is critical to be able to comprehend and explain the division in the far-right nationalism in Turkey.

Socio-Political Cleavages and Right-Wing Nationalism in Turkey

Özbudun (2013, pp. 6–7) argues that the cleavage theory is also significantly revealing for the Turkish case. As a result of the late industrialisation of Turkey, the cleavages that emerged with the Industrial Revolution are not so prominent in this country. However, centre-periphery and church-state cleavages, which have emerged as a result of the country's national revolution, are the dominant cleavages in politics. Even though Turkey does not have an institutional and autonomous church, a similar partition can be observed between devout Muslims and enthusiastic secularisers. Moreover, this cleavage is largely overlapped and combined with the centre-periphery cleavage.

The new Turkish state highlighted a territorial, voluntaristic, and political understanding of the nation to a large extent (Cagaptay, 2006, p. 157) although racist terminology was occasionally, vaguely, and incoherently used in the Kemalist[4] discourse early in the Turkish state's foundation (Aytürk, 2011, p. 334).

On the other hand, there was an intensive assimilation campaign in order to bring all Muslim people under the umbrella of official Turkish identity especially through the expansion of Turkish language education. In this definition of Turkishness, the nominal Islamic identity and cultural heritage of former Muslim millet became significant despite the strict secularisation process. Islam was accepted in terms of identity, but the same could not be said for its religious dimensions. To put it differently, Islam was pushed out of the public and political spheres, and limited to the individual sphere as a religion. Moreover, the political actors trying to bring Islam back to the political sphere faced harsh resistance from state institutions.

The foundational reforms aimed at modernising Turkey in the 1920s, therefore, created a deep secularist–Islamist cleavage in Turkish society. While secularist elites were taking over key institutions, conservative groups were repressed by the state; thus, the conflict was ignored and subsumed to a greater extent (Aydın-Düzgit, 2019; Cagaptay, 2006). In 2002, the electoral success of the Justice and Development Party (*Adalet ve Kalkınma Partisi* – AK Party) changed this situation, however, and the covert conflict in society that had been brewing for 80 years consequently became the main axis of polarisation in Turkish politics. Although the Turkish party system was highly fragmented before 2002, with the beginning of the AK Party dominance, we can observe three main actors in this political scene other than this party (Musil, 2018, p. 84).

While the *Cumhuriyet Halk Partisi* (CHP), which is identified as putting forth a centre-left, social democratic, and secularist platform, has taken second place in the consecutive elections, the MHP, of which the salient feature is Turkish nationalism, occupied third place. The other actor can be considered as a chain of pro-Kurdish parties, which were represented by independent candidates until taking place in the parliament under a party banner by crossing the 10% threshold in the 2015 elections.

The AK Party's ideological discourse has become more nationalistic after the failure in the process of the Kurdish Opening[5] process in 2015 and the July 15 coup attempt in 2016 due to increasing security concerns. Moreover, the right-wing political parties represented in the parliament had removed themselves from the party political scene one by one with the rise of the AK Party, and parallel to that, the CHP had strengthened its place on the left. Both of the developments made the MHP's range of action extremely limited (Bacık, 2011, p. 172). It would be apt to state that the MHP's ideological origins and the tensions among the factions within the party were compelling it to take a clear position in this new conjuncture while the polarisation in the public sphere was increasing.

Moreover, the undisputed position of the leader and the inoperative nature of the inter-party channels prevented a democratic leadership race in practice although they are open in theory. One can point to the eventful party congresses and to the fact that the candidates who have attempted to challenge the incumbent leader Devlet Bahçeli have been prevented in various ways including expulsion from the party. As a result of such a situation, in October 2016, the expulsion of Meral Akşener, who was standing out as an alternative name for leadership within the party, accelerated the quest for a new nationalist party. Eventually, in October 2017, a group led by those dismissed from the MHP founded the Good Party together with some noteworthy names who had served in other right-wing parties.

What has rendered this division and the establishment of the new party more important for Turkish politics are the developments after the failed coup attempt in the country. After this attempt, Bahçeli, who claimed that the state's survival was in danger, totally put aside his severe oppositional rhetoric, offered unconditional support for the ruling AK Party, and position the MHP side by side with this party by taking part in the People's Alliance (*Cumhur İttifakı*). In contrast to this, the Good Party formed the Nation Alliance (*Millet İttifakı*) with the Republican People's Party (CHP), the country's main opposition party which is located on the centre-left of the political spectrum.[6] This picture highlighted Turkish nationalists on both the ruling and opposition fronts and brought the gravity of nationalism in the politics of Turkey into a different dimension, making the influence of the far right in the government and opposition more tangible.

Taking into account the possible costs, the MHP clearly changed its side on the Turkish political scene with this manoeuvre, and it paved the way for the split that gave birth to a new party. But why exactly did this happen? Why did Bahçeli and the party find this sharp turn necessary? In my opinion, an analysis of the ideological roots of this far-right actor is what we need to apprehend this split that has reshaped Turkish politics.

An Overview and Ideological Background of the MHP as the Main Actor of Far Right

In order to understand the internal conflict of the MHP that resulted in the emergence of a new party, it is essential to read the ideological background of the party together with the religious conservative–secular Kemalist rift, which is a dominant political cleavage in Turkish politics. In this part, I argue that the party was founded on this cleavage and tried to maintain this position for a long time until the process that spawned the Good Party.

The military coup of 1960 is one of the most important events in the fault line between religious conservative and secular sides in Turkey. While the secular segment accepts this military intervention as a revolution restoring the secular structure of the state, the conservative segment sees it as an immoral and cruel intervention because it usurps the will of the nation. The long-time leader of the nationalist movement, Türkeş, was one of the most prominent names of the junta that carried out this intervention; yet, he tried to keep himself and his party away from this secular–religious conflict as much as possible. His famous "Nine Lights Doctrine" claimed to define a third way outside of communism and capitalism (Başkan, 2006, p. 91). Moreover, it was an effort to reconcile the Muslim people with the Kemalist state in accordance with the obscurantist approach of the MHP (Bacık, 2011, 175–176).

The Republican Villagers Nation Party (RVNP), one of the two important parties that continued its existence with the CHP after the military coup in 1960, experienced a significant change with the joining of retired soldiers who took part in the military coup in 1965. This group, led by Alparslan Türkeş, took over the leadership of the party in the same year, and the new leadership advocated a secular nationalist and republican Kemalist line (Erken, 2014, p. 204). This situation gradually changed in the congresses of 1967 and 1969, when the name of the party was changed to the MHP. The principal actors such as Türkeş and Dündar Taşer aimed to carry the discourse and ideology of the party to a nationalist conservative line. Therefore, especially after the 1969 congress, the MHP became a party that synthesised Turkish nationalism with Islam. This synthesis featured by the MHP in the 1970s was also a political strategy to attract the religious voters and to mobilise them against the leftist/socialist groups since they were viewed as enemies of the religion (Çınar and Arıkan, 2002, p. 27). Actually, adopting this strategy is not surprising in the MHP's case since nationalism in Turkey after the single-party period is a conservative ideology to a large extent, and at the popular level, it has always embodied Islam (Armstrong, 2012; Uzer, 2016). In other words, the democratisation of Turkish party politics brought Turkish nationalism from its secular line to a more conservative and religious line since it had to take into account the values and sensitivities of the population in Anatolian provinces. As a result, religion became more and more intertwined with politics (Uzer, 2016, pp. 163–164), and the MHP was formed as a "predominantly Sunni, provincial, and conservative" party (pp. 125–126).

The conservative ideology and rhetoric of the party disturbed both the retired soldiers who joined the RVNP alongside Türkeş and the secular Turkists who gathered around Hüseyin Nihâl Atsız. This clash caused the latter group to break away from the party. Moreover, the ÜO's overemphasis on Islam and religious discourses could at times be disturbing even for leadership that embraced the nationalist conservative line. One of the examples of this was that Türkeş suspended the publication of *Nizam-ı Alem* magazine, which belonged to the ÜO, in line with the complaints received from the party board expressing discomfort with the magazine's excessive emphasis on Islamic rhetoric (Erken, 2014, p. 214). This shows the leader's attention not to position the party directly against the secular foundational ideology and somehow keep the balance while mobilising the voter through religious discourse.

The expansion of the ÜO in high schools and universities was also a noteworthy factor in the party's religious conservatism. As the movement expanded among the people, Islamic influence dramatically increased. The atmosphere of violence in the country before the 1980 military coup had an important contribution to this situation. Conflicts between left and right militant groups were evaluated through an atheist socialist-religious nationalist confrontation; this paved the way for nationalist conservative youth to call their losses "martyrs" in religious jargon and, in this way, to have a more intense relationship with religion (Erken, 2014, p. 212). Besides the religious emphasis, the ÜO accommodates a statist connotation in addition to nationalism. While nationalism refers to people's devotion to the well-being and interests of their nation, this movement has embraced a particular kind of statism that equates the nation with the state and precedes state's well-being and interests as the utmost embodiment of the nation (Başkan, 2006; Çınar and Arıkan, 2002).[7] From 1965 to 1997, although Turkish far-right nationalism was seen under the leadership of Türkeş alone, the autonomous structure of the ÜO brought with it the influence of different nationalist thinkers and ideologues in different branches. For this reason, the ideology and discourses of the MHP were far from being fed by a single source or reflecting a single line (Erken, 2014, p. 215) and the party's conservative religious standing was balanced by its statism since the state had a rigid secular stance. Consequently, during this period it would be difficult to summarise the party's approach as anti-secular when it comes to the relevant political cleavage.

After Türkeş's death, Bahçeli took the leadership in 1997 after a very eventful and violent party congress in which he competed against Tuğrul Türkeş, Alparslan Türkeş's son. Under Bahçeli's leadership, the autonomy of the party organisation and local branches of the ÜO came to an end. Branches that did not fully comply with the party's directives were abolished. Members were trained through publications and party schools; Bahçeli built a discipline based on autocracy within the party (Çınar and Arıkan, 2002, p.30). The MHP took important steps to improve its public image under Bahçeli's tenure, who also had an academic background (Heper and İnce, 2006, p. 875). The ultra-nationalist MHP and ÜO of the 1970s, which in the eyes of a significant part of the public, were associated with murders and other mafiatic crimes and were being replaced by a more restrained MHP moving towards the centre (Öniş, 2003, p. 35). When he became the second party with 17.98% in 1999 and came to power with the coalition, Devlet Bahçeli's statesman image started to stand out even more (Heper and İnce, 2006). In many serious problems faced by the government, Bahçeli's attitude was to act in harmony without causing a crisis, even if it would disturb the electoral base. As an example, although the party complained about the state's ban on the headscarf and asked its voters to vote for the solution to this problem, when Nesrin Ünal, a headscarved candidate, was selected as a deputy, she took off her headscarf to the enter the parliament for the parliamentary oath.

Similarly, he did not see the decision not to execute the death penalty imposed on Abdullah Öcalan as a problem that could disrupt the coalition, and this drew serious criticism from the electorate. Moreover, his attitude towards the party members who criticised the party and its coalition partners was extremely harsh. With this attitude, Bahçeli was giving the message that he prioritised his state and its interests, not himself or his party (Çınar and Arıkan, 2002, pp. 32–38).

With the beginning of the AK Party era in November 2002, the MHP took a new stance in the opposition side. The party was strongly opposed to the AK Party's liberal reforms since it was considered a deviation from the state's foundational roots. In the electoral campaigns, the MHP accused the AK Party of abetting separatism. According to Bahçeli, the AK Party was tolerant of the Kurdish separatism; hence, the party was harmful to the national structure of the country. As another significant issue, Bahçeli had a clear stance in favour of the Turkish army officers on trial in the Ergenekon and Balyoz cases. He stated that the Turkish Armed Forces and the Turkish nation was targeted and the unity of the Turkish nation was put in danger with this case ("Bahçeli: Evet Ergenekon," 2013). These lawsuits brought by prosecutors known to be close to the Gülen movement was openly supported by the AK Party since it was evaluated as a showdown with the old Turkey and its secular nationalist forces; yet, the MHP saw the cases as plots designed to weaken the Turkish army. Bahçeli opposed the Gülen movement, which would later be recognised by the state as a terrorist organisation although the movement had good relations with the government in those years; he even nominated a general who was tried in court cases, Engin Alan, as a candidate of the MHP for parliament (Bacık, 2011, pp. 178–181).

Despite his strong opposition, Bahçeli seemed to struggle to stay within the limits of democratic politics and to steer the ÜO away from streets (Heper and İnce, 2006). He also supported the government in some situations of crisis such as Abdullah Gül's ascent to the presidency and legal acts to abolish the headscarf ban, which could be deemed as appropriate political policies regarding the party's conservative electoral base. Since its establishment, the MHP has embraced many different and at times contradictory ideological elements such as secularism, Islam, popular nationalism, militarism, statism, and Ottomanism, and displayed an ambiguous party identity that was based on traditionalist form of obscurantism according to Bacık (2011, p. 171). However, as argued earlier in this study, the severe political polarisation in Turkey in the 2010s made it impossible for the MHP to maintain its position on this cleavage in the long run and compelled the party to clearly take a side.

Rethinking Far-Right Nationalism in Turkey: Cleavages, Alliances, and Emergence of the Good Party as a New Actor

In his study addressing the far right's reaction to the Kurdish Opening in Turkey, Celep (2010) discusses that the MHP and the AK Party resemble each other in terms of ideology and discourses relying on conservatism and nationalism; yet, there are historical and ideological distinctions between these parties considering their ways of conceiving the ethnic and linguistic differences in society. The political tradition that created the AK Party is relatively tolerant towards such differences within the limits of its religious approach (Aktürk, 2018; Gerim, 2020), whereas the MHP is predicated on a mono-culturalist ideology. It is possible to assert that the previously discussed statist disposition of the MHP is also a critical factor making a serious difference between them. This statism has accommodated some nationalist symbols identified with the foundations of the Turkish state.

It caused the MHP to stand side by side with the Kemalist and secular CHP on the common ground of nationalism in some important policy agenda items of Turkish politics. One of the prominent examples of this situation was the nationalist reaction of both parties against the AK Party's abolition of the nationalistic student oath, which had been practised in schools since the 1930s (Uzer, 2016, p. 222). On the other hand, the MHP's statist nationalism, relying on the equivalence between the state and nation, led the party to a predicament in the face of an immense power shift in the state. The AK Party opposed the established understanding of centre-right governments to negotiate the country with the state and rule with Kemalist forces embedded in the state. Erdoğan struggled to eliminate them in order to be the sole decision-making power in the state and this struggle was successful to a great extent (Bacık, 2011, p. 173). In addition, the polarisation of society around the AK Party and the CHP over the secular–conservative religious cleavage also narrowed the MHP's scope of action.

The failed *coup d'etat* in July 2016 marked the beginning of an entirely new era. Erdoğan declared a state of emergency to cleanse the state from members of the Gülen movement[8], whom he held responsible for the coup attempt. According to him, this movement was a network of betrayal that infiltrated and polluted every institution of the state; for this reason, it was necessary to unite around the government for the survival of the state and the nation. Bahçeli responded positively to this call, and afterwards, the MHP started to provide unlimited and unconditional support to the ruling party.

On the other hand, the intra-party opposition in the MHP was rising after the elections in November 2015. Especially the fact that the party fell behind the HDP in its number of parliamentary deputies was harshly criticised by dissidents in the party. They enforced legal means to convene the party congress in May 2016. Nevertheless, at the end of this process, the prominent figures of the opposition and those who announced their candidacy against Bahçeli were expelled from the party. In the end, the prominent figures of the opposition founded the Good Party under Meral Akşener's leadership in October 2017.

The AK Party turned the parliamentary system into a presidential system in April 2018 with the full support of the MHP under the state of emergency and after that, these parties decided to hold an early election in June 2018. This decision was largely evaluated as an action to prevent the Good Party's participation in this election since this newly founded party had not yet assembled the whole of its organisational structure in all provinces of Turkey ("Erken Seçim," 2018). Yet, there was a way to overcome this obstacle. A party that had a group in the parliament could obtain the right to participate in elections, regardless of the condition of being organised in all provinces of the country. The CHP offered "to lend" 15 deputies to the Good Party so that this party would be able to form a group in the parliament and the Good Party accepted this offer.

The Good Party obtained 9.96% of the votes and became the fifth party in the June 2018 elections, whereas the MHP took fourth place with 11.9%. However, the Good Party's place in the Nation Alliance meant more than this percentage with regard to the power balance in Turkish politics.[9] As a right-wing nationalist party, the Good Party avoided the perception that the major confrontation in the political arena is between nationalist and anti-nationalist fronts. Moreover, it prevented this competition between the alliances from being portrayed as a polarisation between the left and right wings.

In order to comprehend the ideological framework of this party, it is critical to notice the emphasis on Atatürk and republican symbols in its discourse. The opening of the headquarters building of the Good Party, a few weeks after the party's establishment, on 11 November 2017 gave important clues about this. The selection of music played at the ceremony had a symbolic meaning. Besides the songs such as "*Ölürüm Türkiyem*," which are identified with the MHP, "*İzmir Marşı*," the popular music of the country's secular republican contingent, was also played. In her speech, Akşener implicitly referred to the cancelled celebration ceremonies of the republican national days during the AK Party rule due to various excuses such as the leaders' health conditions. She stated that Republic Day (October 29) was celebrated by the government that year because the fact that the Good Party was established put pressure on the government ("İYİ Parti genel merkezi," 2017). Parallel to this, the silhouette and signature of Atatürk, along with Akşener's photograph, appeared on the cover of the election declaration prepared by the party before the June 2018 general elections.

In July 2020, the conversion of Hagia Sophia from a museum to a mosque, which had been a sensitive issue for Turkish conservative voters, was also a remarkable event in terms of showing the political stance of the Good Party. The party conveyed its message to its conservative voters, stating that it supports this decision. Nevertheless, after Atatürk was indirectly targeted in a speech given by the President of Religious Affairs, Ali Erbaş, at the re-opening of Hagia Sophia as a mosque,[10] the Good Party did not remain silent. Akşener reprimanded Erbaş, stating that "in history, no one has come out who is an enemy of Atatürk but a friend of the Turks. Shame on you"[11] ("Akşener'den Diyanet İşleri," 2020).

Another indicator of the party's ideological line is that it has undertaken the role of channelling the reaction against Syrian refugees in Turkish society. After the MHP began to act in alliance with the AK Party, it stopped criticising this party's policy on Syrian refugees and its rhetoric based on religious fellowship. Thus, the Good Party appeared as the party that criticised this policy most vocally. The party organised a workshop on the return of refugees to Syria and presented a roadmap to the public ("İYİ Parti, üç aşamalı," 2019). The prominent names of the party such as Ümit Özdağ (who was later expelled from the Good Party and established the Victory Party (Zafer Partisi – ZP) in August 2021) and mayoral candidates of the party such as İlay Aksoy stated that Syrians pose the danger of changing the ethnic structure of the country against Turks. Thus, the party has stood closer to the stance represented by the far right in Europe on the refugee issue. Despite this, unlike the ÜO, the party's youth organisations avoided violence altogether and avoided street protests that could potentially turn into violence. Thus, even if it is possible to claim that the party accommodates some extremist attitudes such as in the refugee issue, it has a decisive non-violent stance.

It has been a short time since its establishment for the party to establish a stable electoral base; that is why it is still early to have a clear picture of the party's voter profile. However, the few studies and polls that have already been conducted show that the party's secular nationalist stance examined above is representative of the electorate to a large extent. According to a survey conducted after the general elections in June 2018, the Good Party's vote percentage was 16% among voters with higher education degrees while its general percentage was 9.96%, and the MHP seems to have 11% among voters with this educational level while it recorded 11.9% in the general elections (IPSOS, 2018). Another research on the Good Party electorate concluded that compared to the AK Party and MHP voters, they are more urbanised and more educated; they show socio-economic characteristics close to the CHP voters and they see the CHP as a more appropriate second option than the AK Party and the MHP (TEAM, 2019). The section of another comprehensive voter survey that focuses on religious beliefs and practices also makes an important point in this regard. While the rate of those who say "I fulfil all my religious requirements" is 36.8% in the MHP voters, it is 14.6% in the Good Party voters. While the rate of voters who said "I have no religious belief" was 9.5% among the Good Party voters, none of the MHP voters gave this answer (Metropoll, 2020).

Of course, it would be a mistake to view the Good Party voters directly as the former MHP voters; because all the studies mentioned previously show that around half of the Good Party voters are former centre-left and centre-right voters and time will reveal if the party can hold them as steady supporters. However, considering the nationalist far right, it is still possible to evaluate the opposition's separation from the MHP and the subsequent establishment of the Good Party as a dealignment and realignment, respectively. In other words, the Good Party transferred a significant social cleavage that was also apparent within the MHP to a political plane. Yet, it was predictable that a new party to represent Turkish nationalism would not be easily acceptable for all dedicated MHP supporters and the ÜO since the new party is in an alliance with the left and takes part in the "other" front in the highly polarised Turkish political sphere. Therefore, after the foundation of the Good Party, the tension between these political actors, both of which aim to represent Turkish nationalism, was quite high. Furthermore, it is difficult to state that it has always stayed in the non-violent stage.

Struggle to Represent the "Cause" of Turkish Nationalism: Shifts between Non-violence and Violence

On 11 January 2019, in Trabzon, where he came for the propaganda of the People's Alliance for the local elections, Erdoğan called the MHP member mayor candidate, who would also be supported by the AK Party. The candidate asked for Erdoğan's permission to make the grey wolf (*bozkurt*) sign which was largely been associated with the MHP, and Erdoğan let him do it ("MHP'nin adayı," 2019). Akşener criticised this behaviour by referring to this issue in her group speech the following week. Referring to Erdoğan and Bahçeli, who called the Nation's Alliance as an alliance of shame (*zillet ittifakı*) Akşener touched on this event for a long time in his speech:

> Do you know what the real shame is? It is to get permission from those who trampled Turkish nationalism in order to make the grey wolf sign, which is the value of the Turkish nation for thousands of years. The grey wolf is not a symbol of a political party. It is the symbol of the great Turkish nation with its right and left, east and west. From the money minted by Atatürk to the first statues of the Republic, there are traces of it everywhere... The grey wolf does not get permission from anyone. This is why foreigners called Mustafa Kemal "the grey wolf".
>
> *(Akşener, 2019)*

Thus, in a way, she declared that they were the flag bearers of Turkish nationalism because another political tradition dominated the MHP. Also, referring to Atatürk and his era, she pointed out that the secular republican stance in their understanding of nationalism was different from the MHP and People's Alliance.

Similarly, in the same month, a young man requested permission to take a photo with her while making the grey wolf sign during her visit to İzmir; she addressed him and stated that he should not get permission from anyone to make this sign since it is the symbol of Turkishness. In October 2020, this time Akşener visited Kayseri and the traditional marquee, which was used by Türkeş, the previous leader of the MHP. She gave a photo with the Good Party members doing the same sign. The MHP party representatives reacted harshly to this situation and made a statement which claimed that "those who are in the alliance of shame and cooperating with the enemies of the Turks" did not have the right to make a grey wolf sign ("Meral Akşener'in bozkurtlu," 2020).

On the other hand, this tension between rival sides of nationalist politics did not stay at the level of word fight and evolved into violence against those who criticised Bahçeli and stood close to the Good Party. The fact that Ahmet Çelik, the concessionaire of *Yeniçağ* Newspaper, is also the Istanbul Deputy of the Good Party, and that *Yeniçağ* has taken a critical attitude towards the MHP, made this newspaper the target of the ÜO. On 11 May 2019, a group of seven to eight people brutally attacked Yavuz Selim Demirağ, a journalist who works for *Yeniçağ*, with baseball bats on his way to home after a TV program he attended ("Yeniçağ yazarı," 2019). The Good Party put forth a motion to establish a commission to investigate the attack on Demirağ on 14 May 2019, but it was declined by the votes of the deputies of the MHP and AK Party ("Gazeteci Demirağ'a saldırının araştırılması," 2019). Similar attacks targeted the journalists and well-known nationalist figures taking an opposing stance against the MHP and Bahçeli, such as Sabahattin Önkibar, Ahmet Takan, Yaşar Karadağ, and Murat İde, who was also Akşener's press advisor.

At least as striking as these attacks, however, were the MHP's attitude towards the attacks and the statements of the MHP members. On 20 June 2019, a founding member of the Good Party, Metin Bozkurt, was attacked by a group of eight people in the parking lot of his workplace. Akşener and the Istanbul Provincial President of the Good Party, Buğra Kavuncu, condemned the attack and called for restraint. They declared that the party members would void the provocation attempts and would not respond in the same way to those who resort to violence. On the other hand, a central board member of the MHP, Ahmet Yiğit Yıldırım,[12] made a statement of support to the attackers via Twitter and saluted them. He was claiming that Ekrem İmamoğlu, the presidential candidate of the Nation Alliance for Istanbul Metropolitan Municipality, was a PKK (Partiya Karkerên Kurdistan – Kurdistan Workers' Party) sympathiser, and those who introduced themselves as "Idealist" (Ülkücü) and supported İmamoğlu would sooner or later meet the "Idealist justice" (İYİ Parti'nin kurucu üyesi, 2019). Similarly, after İsrafil Kumbasar, a lawyer and a former columnist of Yeniçağ, was attacked by a group of young people from the ÜO due to his severe criticism of the MHP leader, the group deputy chairman of the party heaped ridicule on Kumbasar's photo right after the attack, and the chairman of the ÜO shared a post praising the attack and making fun of Kumbasar ("Öldüresiye dövüldü," 2020).

So, why did the MHP openly undertake these attacks? It is difficult to fully understand the reasons behind this within the limit of the party's relations with the Good Party. However, beyond these relations being associated with violence is not new for the MHP and the ÜO. According to Kumral (2017), the MHP continued to utilise violence as a complementary component in its politics in a way directed to the socialists, communists, and leftist youth in the 1990s, and to the Kurdish migrant population in the Western cities of Turkey in the 2000s. Furthermore, she argues that the MHP has made use of violence by incorporating it into the party's electoral strategies and she asserts that there was no negative relationship between electoral popularisation and violence in the case of this party. However, what is new is that the public sphere in Turkey has been highly polarised in recent years around the alliances and a new nationalist party takes part in the other side with the centre-left main opposition party of the country. More precisely, when the main far-right actor, the MHP, changed its position from the opposition to a strong supporter of the ruling AK Party, its dealigned supporters were realigned by a new nationalist actor that takes a side in the rival alliance. Given this political atmosphere of the country, crossing the borders of non-violence may increase the risk for adverse encounters between alliances.

Concluding Remarks

The Turkish far right, which has been examined in this study, provides an intriguing example of non-violent far-right extremism although the limits of non-violence have in recent times been violated. As an example, the MHP has shown fierce reactions, which included or at least approved of violence, to opposition and criticism that may target its leadership and/or its claim to be the sole representative of the nationalist wing as previously examined in this study. But, contrary to that, this party's response to the Syrian refugee crisis has not been harsh compared to the cases of far right in many other countries and has so far not led to any anti-immigrant violence despite the fact that Turkey has been the country hosting the largest number of these refugees.[13] Moreover, linked to the AK Party's deep identification with the state as a result of its long-term rule, the conventional statist stance embedded in Turkish nationalism has recently prevented the MHP from adopting anti-establishment populism, which is a feature observed in many far-right movements.

In recent years, the existential danger to the survival of the state and nation has been cited by the MHP as the reason for its new position in Turkish politics and offering full support to the AK Party. However, the party could not persuade a significant portion of its voters due to the existing cleavages and polarisation in the Turkish sphere as well as the party's long-lasting harsh opposition to the ruling party. As a noteworthy result, this study shows that a nationalist far-right movement may also bear some serious consequences when it makes political manoeuvres by ignoring cleavages in a country, and in this way, it points out that cleavages are relevant in radical party politics as well.

The formation of the Good Party by the intra-party opposition[14] in the MHP as a political actor that primarily aims to attract the dealigned nationalist voters has changed the balances in Turkish politics regarding the subsequent alliances. It is still early to categorise the Good Party as a radical or far-right party considering its voter profile and party figures coming from non-nationalist politics. Among the party electorate, the nationalist but leftist voters who previously voted for the CHP should also be reckoned with. However, it is clear that the party is a new home for the urban, secular, and educated nationalist voters, and has so far kept an absolute distance from violence, contrary to the discussed profile of the MHP/ÜO. Therefore, the Good Party appears as the non-violent agent or translator that is essential to transform a cleavage or a sub-cleavage into a political party system, which is discussed before in this study (Bartolini and Mair, 1990; Bértoa, 2012; Bornschier, 2010; Mair, 2006; Sartori, 1969).

This study aimed to answer two key questions: (1) What are the main factors of the split in the Turkish far right that gave birth to the Good Party? (2) How might this divide affect the potential for violence in the flank in question? We can summarise the answers obtained by this study to these questions as follows: (1) The MHP, as the party representing the Turkish far right, was ideologically just above the partially veiled cleavage in the country. When this cleavage became the centre of the political system with the recent polarisation in Turkish politics, this party had to take sides and it finally sided with the AK Party. This led to a serious fracture in the party. (2) The Good Party's stance from violence and the different social status of its voters with the MHP base showed that those who broke off from the MHP and the ÜO were relatively moderate far-right elements. This brought the danger of further radicalisation of the remaining segment. The cases of violence examined in the study also point to this.

As argued by Mudde (2019), although the policy power of far-right parties is limited due to their position in opposition in most of the cases, they largely affect the discourses of mainstream parties and exert immense influence on setting political agenda in their countries. The right-wing nationalist actors examined in this study constitute appropriate examples supporting this argument with their roles in the rival alliances. It is obvious that the struggle between them will not only remain within the boundaries of the far-right or nationalist politics but will also be decisive for the entire Turkish political scene and the place of violence/nonviolence in this scene.

Notes

1 However, as Heper and İnce (2006, p. 880) discussed, it is difficult to define the MHP with features such as ethnonationalism, racism, and xenophobia, which are prominent in many of the far-right parties in Western Europe. According to them, the party emphasises commitment to a common culture rather than ethnicity and promotes a kind of cultural nationalism. Although this nationalism has occasional ethnic references and is unlikely to be classified as civic nationalism, it would be equally wrong to classify it as ethnic nationalism.

2 Although the ÜO continues its activities in Turkey on a legal basis, its relations with violence cause serious reactions in the international arena. As an example, France banned the activities of the "Grey Wolves" in the country in November 2020, and the European Parliament called on the European Council to review the possibility of adding the ÜO to the EU terrorist list in its 2020 report on Turkey (Ertan, 2021).

3 Since Lipset and Rokkan did not provide a clear definition of the concept of cleavage and sometimes used it in an ambiguous way, the studies dealing with this concept have presented their own definitions usually depending on their analytical approaches (Bértoa, 2012, p. 17). In this study, it is used as a "durable pattern of political behaviour of structurally defined groups" (Bornschier, 2010, p. 5).

4 Kemalism (also called Ataturkism or *Atatürkçülük*) is the founding ideology of the Republic of Turkey, formed by six principles known as Republicanism, Nationalism, Populism, Statism, Secularism, and Revolutionism/Reformism (Ahmad, 1993, p. 63). This ideology outlines the construction of a new nation in Turkey through a secular and modernising nationalism.

5 The Kurdish opening was the process initiated by the AK Party government in 2009, aiming to solve the long-term ethnic problem in the country, the Kurdish problem, and to end terrorism by expanding the scope of democratic rights and freedoms. Although the initiative, which followed a fluctuating course, turned into a "peace process" between 2013 and 2015, this process collapsed in July 2015, and the armed conflicts between the PKK and Turkish Armed Forces resumed (Gunter, 2016).

6 The Felicity Party (*Saadet Partisi* – SP) and the Democrat Party (*Demokrat Parti* – DP) are the junior partners of this alliance.

7 This is one of the reasons why the crimes committed by the people from this movement were usually viewed as linked to or encouraged by some factions or mechanisms in the Turkish state.

8 Also called *Hizmet* (service) or *Cemaat* (community), it is a movement based on the teachings of its leader Fethullah Gülen, who is a Sunni cleric residing in America since 1999. Although it has the appearance of a Muslim fraternal organisation with an international network in many sectors, especially in education, it is recognised as a terrorist organisation by countries such as Turkey and Pakistan and international organisations such as the Gulf Cooperation Council. The movement, which was positioned as an ally of the AK Party governments until 2013, fell out with this party after this year. Turkey holds this movement responsible for the failed *coup d'etat* attempt on 15 July 2016.

9 Although the FP and the DP are also the right-wing partners of this alliance, the first one's vote percentage was 1.34% and the second did not even participate in the elections as an independent party.

10 Erbaş stated that in the Turkish-Islamic tradition, anyone who touches pious foundation property is cursed. This statement was evaluated as an attack on Atatürk who had turned this historical monument from a mosque into a museum in 1935 although Erbaş later remarked that he did not target any specific person.

11 All Turkish to English translations in this chapter are made by the author.

12 Later, he was appointed as the chairman of the ÜO in July 2020.

13 Considering the fact that almost all of the refugees are Muslims may render this situation more understandable. The party's traditional conservative nationalism with religious emphasis and recent partnership with the ruling AK Party, which attaches remarkable value and importance to Muslim fellowship in its ideology and politics, can be seen as key factors to curb anti-immigrant reactions in this case.

14 Although it is possible to see people who were previously in the centre-right and centre-left parties, such as the previous party spokesperson Aytun Çıray who was a deputy of the CHP before, among the founders of the party, the core of the Good Party was formed by opposition figures who broke with the MHP.

References

Ahmad, F. (1993). *The Making of Modern Turkey*. London and New York: Routledge.

Akşener, M. (2019). *Akşener: "Bozkurt kimseden İzin almaz"*. Retrieved from www.youtube.com/watch?v=Zy2vf5oqHs8

Akşener'den Diyanet İşleri Başkanı Erbaş'a: Yazıklar olsun size. (2020, July 28). *Cumhuriyet*. Retrieved from www.cumhuriyet.com.tr

Aktürk, Ş. (2018). One nation under Allah? Islamic multiculturalism, Muslim nationalism and Turkey's reforms for Kurds, Alevis, and non-Muslims. *Turkish Studies*, *19*(4), 523–551. https://doi.org/10.1080/14683849.2018.1434775

Armstrong, W. (2012). Turkish nationalism and Turkish Islam: A new balance. *Turkish Policy Quarterly*, *10*(4), 133–138. http://turkishpolicy.com/Files/ArticlePDF/turkish-nationalism-and-turkish-islam-a-new-balance-winter-2012-en.pdf

Aydın-Düzgit, S. (2019). The Islamist-Secularist divide and Turkey's descent into severe polarization. In T. Carothers & A. O'Donohue (Eds.), *Democracies Divided: The Global Challenge of Political Polarization* (pp. 17–37). Washington, D.C.: Brookings Institution Press.

Aytürk, I. (2011). The racist critics of Atatürk and Kemalism, from the 1930s to the 1960s. *Journal of Contemporary History*, *46*(2), 308–335. https://doi.org/10.1177%2F0022009410392411

Bacik, G. (2011). The Nationalist Action Party in the 2011 elections: The limits of oscillating between state and society. *Insight Turkey*, *13*(4), 171. Retrieved from www.insightturkey.com/articles/the-nationalist-action-party-in-the-2011-elections-the-limits-of-oscillating-between-state-and-society

Bahçeli: Evet Ergenekon cumhuriyet tarihinin en büyük hesaplaşması. (2013, August 7). *Hürriyet*. Retrieved from www.hurriyet.com.tr

Bar-On, T. (2018). The radical right and nationalism. In J. Rydgren (Ed.), *The Oxford Handbook of the Radical Right* (pp. 17–41). New York: Oxford University Press.

Bartolini, S., & Mair, P. (1990). *Identity, Competition, and Electoral Availability: The Stabilization of European Electorates 1885–1985*. Cambridge: Cambridge University Press.

Başkan, F. (2006). Globalization and nationalism: The Nationalist Action Party of Turkey. *Nationalism and Ethnic Politics, 12*(1), 83–105. https://doi.org/10.1080/13537110500503877

Bértoa, F. C. (2014). Party systems and cleavage structures revisited: A sociological explanation of party system institutionalization in East Central Europe. *Party Politics, 20*(1), 16–36. https://doi.org/10.1177%2F1354068811436042

Bornschier, S. (2010). *Cleavage Politics and the Populist Right: The New Cultural Conflict in Western Europe.* Philadelphia, PA: Temple University Press.

Cagaptay, S. (2006). *Islam, Secularism and Nationalism in Modern Turkey: Who Is a Turk?* London and New York: Routledge.

Camus, J. Y., & Lebourg, N. (2017). *Far-Right Politics in Europe* (J. M. Todd, Trans.). Cambridge, MA: Harvard University Press.

Celep, Ö. (2010). Turkey's radical right and the Kurdish issue: The MHP's reaction to the "democratic opening". *Insight Turkey, 12*(2), 125–142. Retrieved from www.jstor.org/stable/26331446

Çınar, A., & Arıkan, B. (2002). The nationalist action party: Representing the state, the nation or the nationalists? *Turkish Studies, 3*(1), 25–40. https://doi.org/10.1080/714005706

Elff, M. (2009). Social divisions, party positions, and electoral behaviour. *Electoral Studies, 28*(2), 297–308. https://doi.org/10.1016/j.electstud.2009.02.002

Erken, A. (2014). Ideological construction of the politics of nationalism in Turkey: The Milliyetci Hareket Partisi (MHP), 1965–1980. *Nationalism and Ethnic Politics, 20*(2), 200–220. https://doi.org/10.1080/13537113.2014.909159

Erken Seçim. (2018). İYİ Parti geçime girebilecek mi? (April 20). *BBC News Türkçe.* Retrieved from www.bbc.com/turkce/haberler-turkiye-43832878

Ertan, N. (2021, May 20). Will Turkey's Grey Wolves land on EU terror list. *Al-Monitor.* Retrieved from www.al-monitor.com/originals/2021/05/will-turkeys-grey-wolves-land-eu-terror-list

Gazeteci Demirağ'a saldırının araştırılması Meclis'te reddedildi. (2019, May 14). *Cumhuriyet.* Retrieved from www.cumhuriyet.com.tr

Gerim, G. (2020). The Kobani events and contesting political discourses on the Kurdish question in Turkey. *Acta Politologica, 12*(1), 1–19. https://doi.org/10.14712/1803-8220/41_2019

Golder, M. (2016). Far right parties in Europe. *Annual Review of Political Science, 19,* 477–497. https://doi.org/10.1146/annurev-polisci-042814-012441

Gourisse, B. (2021). In the name of the state. The Nationalist Action Party (MHP) and the genesis of political violence during the 1970s. *Turkish Studies,* 1–21. https://doi.org/10.1080/14683849.2021.1885295

Gümrükçü, S. B. (2021). Ideology, discourse, and alliance structures: Explaining far-right political violence in Turkey in the 1970s. *Terrorism and Political Violence,* 1–15. https://doi.org/10.1080/09546553.2021.1895121

Gunter, M. M. (2016). The Kurdish issue in Turkey: back to square one? *Turkish Policy Quarterly, 14*(4), 77–86. http://turkishpolicy.com/article/786/the-kurdish-issue-in-turkey-back-to-square-one

Halikiopoulou, D., & Vlandas, T. (2019). What is new and what is nationalist about Europe's new nationalism? Explaining the rise of the far right in Europe. *Nations and Nationalism, 25*(2), 409–434. https://doi.org/10.1111/nana.12515

Heper, M., & İnce, B. (2006). Devlet Bahçeli and 'far right' politics in Turkey, 1999–2002. *Middle Eastern Studies, 42*(6), 873–888. https://doi.org/10.1080/00263200600922981

Hooghe, L., & Marks, G. (2018). Cleavage theory meets Europe's crises: Lipset, Rokkan, and the transnational cleavage. *Journal of European Public Policy, 25*(1), 109–135. https://doi.org/10.1080/13501763.2017.1310279

IPSOS (2018). *24 Haziran 2018 Cumhurbaşkanı Seçimi ve Milletvekili Genel Seçimi Sandık Sonrası Araştırması – 2 Temmuz 2018.* Retrieved from www.ipsos.com/tr-tr

İYİ Parti genel merkezi açıldı. (2017, November 11). *Gazete Duvar.* Retrieved from www.gazeteduvar.com.tr

İYİ Parti'nin kurucu üyesi Metin Bozkurt saldırıya uğradı, MHP saldırganlara "Selam olsun" dedi. (2019, June 20). *Independent Türkçe.* Retrieved from www.indyturk.com/

İYİ Parti, üç aşamalı Suriyeli planı açıkladı. (2019, December 17). *Milliyet.* Retrieved from www.milli yet.com.tr

Kumral, Ş. (2017). Ballots with bullets: Elections, violence, and the rise of the extreme right in Turkey. *Journal of Labor and Society, 20*(2), 231–261. https://doi.org/10.1111/wusa.12287

Lipset, S. M. & Rokkan, S. (1967). Cleavage structures, party systems, and voter alignments: An introduction. In S. M. Lipset & S. Rokkan (Eds.), *Party Systems, and Voter Alignments: Cross National Perspective* (pp. 1–61). New York: The Free Press.

Mair, P. (2006). Party system change. In Katz R. S. and Crotty W. (Eds.), *Handbook of Political Parties* (pp. 63–73). London: Sage.

Meral Akşener'in bozkurtlu pozuna tepki. (2020, October 22). *Sözcü.* Retrieved from www.sozcu.com.tr/2020/gundem/meral-aksenerin-bozkurtlu-pozuna-tepki-6093374/

Metropoll. (2020). *Türkiye'nin Nabzı – Ağustos 2020.* Retrieved from www.metropoll.com.tr/arastirma lar/turkiyenin-nabzi-17/1865

MHP'nin adayı Erdoğan'dan izin istedi: Bozkurt işareti yapabilir miyim? (2019, January 12). *Sputnik News.* Retrieved from https://tr.sputniknews.com

Mudde, C. (2019). *The Far Right Today.* Cambridge: Polity Press.

Musil, P. A. (2018). Assessing the level of party cartelisation in contemporary Turkey. In S. Sayarı, P. Ayan Musil & Ö. Demirkol (Eds.), *Party Politics in Turkey* (pp. 80–97). London: Routledge.

Norris, P. (2005). The 'New Cleavage' thesis and the social basis of radical right support. Paper presented at Panel 36–10 'Modeling Support for Extreme Right-Wing Parties' 2nd September 2005 at the American Political Science Association Annual Meeting, Washington, D.C.

Öldüresiye dövüldü MHP'li Grup Başkanvekili de paylaştı. (2020, March 24). *Odatv.* Retrieved from https://odatv4.com/

Öniş, Z. (2003). Globalization, democratization and the far right: Turkey's Nationalist Action Party in critical perspective. *Democratization, 10*(1), 27–52. https://doi.org/10.1080/13510340312331294017

Özbudun, E. (2013). *Party Politics and Social Cleavages in Turkey.* Boulder, CO: Lynne Rienner Publishers.

Rydgren, J. (2018). The radical right. In J. Rydgren (Ed.), *The Oxford Handbook of the Radical Right* (pp. 23–39). New York: Oxford University Press.

Sartori, G. (1969). From the sociology of politics to political sociology. *Government and Opposition, 4*(2), 195–214. https://doi.org/10.1111/j.1477-7053.1969.tb00173.x

TEAM. (2019). *Seçmen Blokları Zayıflıyor: İYİ Parti Seçmen Analizi – Ekim 2019.* Retrieved from www.teamarastirma.com/

Uzer, U. (2016). *An Intellectual History of Turkish Nationalism: Between Turkish Ethnicity and Islamic Identity.* Salt Lake City, UT: The University of Utah Press.

Veugelers, J. (1997). Social cleavage and the revival of far right parties: The case of France's National Front. *Acta Sociologica, 40*(1), 31–49. https://doi.org/10.1177%2F000169939704000103

Yeniçağ yazarı Yavuz Selim Demirağ evinin önünde saldırıya uğradı. (2019, May 11). *Habertürk.* Retrieved from www.haberturk.com/

19

THE GREEK WHITE POWER MUSIC SCENE

Feeding Extremism with Lyrics

George Kordas

Introduction

Whilst defining the radical-right party family, Mudde (2007, p.49) highlighted how "this study draws a clear line between populist radical right parties and various forms of the extreme right" specifically, as he mentioned (2007, p.49), "extreme right parties are undemocratic, and often elitist, whereas populist radical right parties are nominally democratic and populist." According to Mudde's definition, the radical-right party family consists of the populist radical-right (in a wider sense) and the extreme-right families. Whilst Mudde acknowledges the broader view and electoral success of the populist radical-right during the last two decades, the situation is different with the extreme right. The third wave of the radical-right transformation gave us the most contemporary version of the family, as it abandoned its fascist roots in favour of xenophobia and turned to the working classes, seeking more electoral gains in the process (von Beyme, 1988, p.11). In parallel, the gap between the extreme right and the radical sides of those parties became much more apparent, as those belonging to the extreme right continued to undermine democracy (Backes, 2010, p.166).

However, such an anti-democratic position by the extreme right has often been followed by illegal actions against the organisation's target groups, mainly the LGBTQ community, immigrants and refugee populations. To overcome the legal barricades erected to prevent such violence, extreme-right organisations have also adopted non-violent actions over the past 50 years, such as producing their music and following a specific type of lifestyle, thus defining their subculture.[1] This chapter will focus on the music, particularly within the Greek extreme right and its white power music scene. By following the storyline of the white power music scene growth in Greece, I tracked the violent narratives of the white power songs and how they fomented violence in Greek society. Lastly, the actual threat posed by the extreme-right groups in Greece will be highlighted by presenting how non-violent extremism worked in favour of extremist actions.

This chapter has the following structure: a review of existing research will shed light on crucial concepts, that is, the extreme right and white power music by approaching music as a subculture. The following section will focus on the Greek case, offering a historical review of Greece's national white power music scene and its links with extreme-right parties and

DOI: 10.4324/9781003032793-23

organisations. Then, continuing with the methodology, the author will present a grounded theory approach to these phenomena that will apply to the current study. The chapter's following section consists of the coding and analysis of white power music songs. Lastly, the study will explain how the songs' violent content has driven supporters to undertake hate crimes. Before concluding, the chapter will offer an extensive explanation of Greece's extreme-right groups, their current situation and the perceived threat to Greek democracy.

Defining the Extreme Right

Researchers have long highlighted the different definitions extremism could have. Lipset (1959, p.347) attempted "to show that extremist ideologies and groups can be classified and analysed in the same terms as democratic groups, i.e., right, left, and centre." Therefore, Lipset (1959, p.348) argued "the right extremists are conservative, not revolutionary." Later, in the mid-1960s, Rush (1963, p.64) argued that "Extreme Right is consistent with the notion of political extremism." Therefore, Rush supported his choice of the term extreme right as "the use of the adjective 'extreme' seems more appropriate than that of 'radical'" (1963, p.64). Rush focused on the extreme right's individualistic nature, comparing it to the collectivist nature of governments and societies (1963, p.73). *Authoritarian Personality* – Adorno *et al.*'s (1950) seminal work – paved the way for most of the studies of the extreme right. Following Adorno, Falter and Schumann created a ten-point scheme to define right-wing extremism, with the following features: "hyper-nationalism, ethnocentrism, anti-communism, anti-parliamentarism, anti-pluralism, militarism, law and order thinking, a demand for a strong political leader, anti-Americanism and cultural pessimism" (1988, p.101).

Notwithstanding the importance of those works, the definition of the extreme right became part of the chaotic – and challenging to define – field of far-right studies. In the mid-1990s Mudde (1996) attempted to clarify the differences between radicalism and extremism and end this terminological chaos. Characterising the latter as anti-constitutional and anti-democratic compared to right-wing radicalism, Mudde made a significant contribution to the field (Mudde, 1996, p.231). A decade later, in their research about extreme-right activism, Klandermans and Mayer (2006, p.6) argued that "if one combines these different models, which indistinctly apply to extremist voting and extremist activism, four basic features – authoritarianism, lack of education, economic insecurity and social isolation – supposedly help turn someone into an RWE (right-wing extremist)." Nevertheless, Mudde's approach – and subsequent definitions (1996, 2007) – remains the most commonly accepted definition in the field of far-right studies. Mudde (1996, p.206) carried out a study to investigate the frequency of the term "right-wing extremism" in the bibliographies of far-right studies' literature. He found five features as the most frequently mentioned: nationalism, racism, xenophobia, anti-democracy and the strong state (Mudde, 1996, p.206). In 2007, Mudde specified his theory, arguing in favour of a minimal and a maximal definition. More specifically, Mudde (2007, pp.16–20) based his minimal definition on the features of nationalism and nativism, whilst the maximal one includes nativism, authoritarianism and populism (Mudde, 2007, pp.22–23).

Backes (Backes, 2010, pp. 163–167) also highlighted the importance of Mudde's definition. He used it to emphasise the differentiation between radicalism and extremism, rejecting the findings of the German researchers at the Cologne Institute for Comparative Research who proposed that radicalism had been replaced by extremism. Instead, as Backes (2010, p.166) explains, the acceptance (or not) of democratic methods differentiates radicalism from extremism. Thus, whilst radicalism accepts democratic methods but not democratic values, extremism dismisses anything related to democracy as a whole.

Defining Extreme-Right Subcultures

As their name suggests, subcultures are a subset of parent cultures. Clarke *et al.* (2006, pp.6–7) drew from the social classes' theory to clarify the content of such a relationship. As they argue, each social class is connected to its "class cultures." Those cultures are divided into the dominant and sub-set cultures, better known as the "parent" (dominant) culture and subculture. Their relationship becomes competitive, whereas they coexist in a hegemonic structure (Clarke, 2006). In particular, subcultures are a part of the "parent" culture with which they share similarities and are approached comparatively to the "parent" culture. With this comparison, the subcultures' unique content can be highlighted.

Although not all subcultures create a clear and coherent structure and identity (Clarke *et al.*, 2006, p.7), their main aim is to express an authentic lifestyle against media-constructed products (Hebdige, 2002, p.85; Thornton, 2003, p.181). Furthermore, as subcultures mostly rise during periods of crisis, they are linked with social movements, constructing specific worldviews whilst adopting a specific lifestyle (Kolovos, 2015, p.85). Moreover, as the core of subcultures consists of social clashes, they are more attractive to youth, creating what are known as "youth subcultures" (Clarke *et al.*, 2006, p.7).

Such subcultural milieus are readily demonstrated in music, especially since the 1980s and the rise of punk music. Bennet (2018, p.6) has been sketching challenges for British youth since the mid-1970s and how punk represented the best solution for youths to express themselves. Whilst punk was quickly politicised, it was connected with the extreme left, opening a new political music field. Shaffer (2017, pp.63–67) showed how the transformation of the British far right demonstrated to the extreme left new methods it could adopt to expand its membership base. Music was one such solution, pushing the British far right to challenge its possibilities in the field.

White Power Music

White power music was created by Ian Stuart Donaldson, a British musician who combined "hatecore" music with rock against communism (RAC), and the punk-like "oi!" music in the late 1970s (Shaffer, 2017, pp.86–89). RAC – a music style created by the British far right (Shaffer, 2017, pp.73–75) – politicised white power music, therefore referring both to the extreme left anti-capitalism and extreme-right nationalism (Symvoulidis, 2008, pp.61–65; Shaffer, 2017, pp.89, 184). The National Front (NF), and later the British National Party (BNP), initially patronised the music scene, offering the first example of an official link between a political party and an extremist section of the electoral body (Shaffer, 2017, pp.84–90). Donaldson gained worldwide popularity and created the Blood & Honour network, which promoted the global connection and interaction among the neo-Nazis (Love, 2016, pp.40–44). Following Ian Stuart Donaldson's death in 1993 (Shaffer, 2017, p.172), Blood & Honour was already an established authority for the white power music scene by promoting bands, publishing journals, recording music and highlighting its links with extreme-right parties. Later on, the network came under the control of Combat-18 – a publicly racist and neo-Nazi group formed out of the BNP – which radicalised its actions and openly targeted people of minority backgrounds (Shaffer, 2017, pp.172–179). Both networks were banned in many countries due to their antisemitic and neo-Nazi discourses and violent forms of activism.

Historical Review of the Greek White Power Music

The history of white power music in Greece goes back to the early 1980s (N.A., 2007, p.19). Ian Stuart Donaldson was a prominent figure in the British far-right scene in relation to the diffusion and strengthening of white power music. More specifically, in 1987, Donaldson founded the white power music organisation Blood & Honour, referring directly to the Nazi slogan "Blut und Ehre" ("Blood and Honour") (Dyck, 2017, p.19). The organisation's main target was to promote white nationalist music (Love, 2016, p.43). Whilst Blood & Honour expanded its network globally, its Greek branch was founded in 1999 (Symvoulidis, 2008). Nevertheless, it was in 1987 that the Greek white power music's first politicised song, "Voreia Ipeiros" ("North Epirus"), was released by the band Lost Patriots (Tipaldou, 2012). The relationship between Greek white power music and the neo-Nazi party Golden Dawn has been visible since the first days of Greece's white power music. Explicitly, "the first nationalist concert in Greece was held on 24 December 1994, in the club Aquarius, with the band Cause of Honour, whilst a pre-concert gathering had taken place in the offices of the neo-Nazi party 'Golden Dawn'"(Kordas, 2013, p.79). Nevertheless, it was not until 25 October 2003 that the second biggest white power concert in Greece, "Youth Celebrations," was organised (again) by "Golden Dawn" (N.A., 2010).

Pavlos Fyssas'[2] murder on 14 September 2013 brought about massive changes. It showed how the party and the white power music scene were connected politically and through activism. Whilst the peak of the white power music scene in Greece was linked with the rise of Golden Dawn's popularity – working as a communication vessel for the party's membership and aimed at recruiting new members – back in 2005, the first "Skinhouse" music venue in Greece was created in the northwestern city of Trikala. Remaining, until it closed, the only official place for white power music concerts in Greece, it was linked with some members of the local football team's hooligan scene. At the same time, some of its concerts had a more practical purpose – offering financial help to comrades who were prosecuted for illegal actions. Therefore, Golden Dawn's electoral rise was clear to those involved with the white power music scene, as both journalists and scientists attempted to research and understand the links between the party of Golden Dawn and those at the margins of the extreme right. The new situation compelled members to suspend their musical production and use the internet to become anonymous.

Methodology

This study answers the following main research question: *How have the violent narratives within Greek white power songs affected the broader nationalistic milieu in the country?* To answer this question, the author will apply constructivist grounded theory to analyse the content of the sample of collected songs. This research argues that white power music has converted non-violence as a critical facet of the Greek extreme-right activism to violence. Nevertheless, before entering the discussion section, it is important to sketch out the methodology applied to the current research, that is, constructivist grounded theory, a part of qualitative methodology. Therefore, I will briefly analyse its most essential characteristics and how they are connected with my research. As Bryman (2012, p.36) highlights:

> Qualitative research … has rejected the practices and norms of the natural scientific model and of positivism in particular in preference for an emphasis on how individuals interpret their social world; and embodies a view of social reality as a constantly shifting emergent property of individuals' creation.

Therefore, Flick *et al.* (2004, p.8) explain that "data collection in qualitative research is characterised, above all, by the principle of openness," which offers questions on "an open formulation." Beausoleil (2014, p.21) refers to openness as receptivity which is "by definition, an affective state, and the decision to open oneself to alternative views is thus both a precognitive and embodied one." Furthermore, Giwrgos Tsiwlis (2014, p.32) argues that openness directs researchers to avoid shaping hypotheses during their first level of research. To achieve that, he highlights the importance of subjectivity for qualitative research and recognition of the researcher's ontology (Mills *et al.*, 2006, p.26; Robson and McCartan, 2016, p.20).

Grounded theory appeared during the 1960s due to the dominance of quantitative methodology in social sciences and the absence of quality rules for qualitative studies (Dunne, 2011, p.112). As the theory's name describes, "it refers to data grounded in fact and generating theory from that [those] data" (Stern, 1985, p.150). Its data-driven nature directs the theory's creation, which resulted during the theory's first years in restricting the importing of other theoretical approaches to the researcher's data. Stern (1985, p.150) argued that the "theory comes from data," as "hypotheses are linked together" from the "investigator" who presents "an integrated theory to explain the problem under study." Talking about a data-driven theory (Stern 1985, p.150), it was forbidden among grounded theorists to import other theoretical approaches to the researcher's data during the theory's first years. Whilst it remains a long debate for the various schools of grounded theory, the existing literature is accepted, as Strauss and Corbin first highlighted back in 1990 (p.56).

Theoretical sampling, theoretical sensitivity and coding processes represent the essential characteristics of grounded theory. Since the beginning, theoretical sampling has been described as simultaneous data collection, coding and analysis (Glaser and Strauss, 1967, p.45; Glaser, 1978, p.37). Theoretical sensitivity focuses on the researcher's ability to filter his/her data according to his/her experience, therefore being an active part of the research process (Strauss and Corbin, 1990, p.42). Theoretical sampling can contribute to the researcher's coding by clarifying how the collected data connect to the research (Morse and Clark, 2019, pp.145–166). Through the coding process, data identification proceeds are categorised and, finally, generated the definitions that will ensure the analysis of the studied subjects (Charmaz, 1995, p.37; Bryant, 2017, pp.118–119).

From the different theoretical approaches that have appeared since the advent of grounded theory, this current chapter follows Cathy Charmaz's constructivist version. According to Charmaz (2014, p.12), there is a multi-level and structured social reality of which the researcher remains an inextricable part. Thus, although the action is at the core of the theory, grounded theory's coding process aims at staying in active communication with the participants' experiences by constructing the researchers' reality without explaining it (Mills *et al.*, 2006, p.12; Charmaz, 2007, p.398). Charmaz acknowledged three coding levels during the coding process: open coding, axial coding and selective coding. Each drives the researcher more profoundly into his/her data until the theory is finally generated. Therefore, during the coding process, I will compare the data relating to differences and similarities in what is known as the "constant comparative method" (Glaser and Strauss, 1967, p.105; Niedbalski and Slezak, 2019, pp.96–97). Such an innovative approach to analyse the qualitative data is split in four stages. Glaser and Strauss (1967, p.106) specified them as follows: (1) comparing incidents applicable to each category, (2) integrating categories and each properties, (3) delimiting the theory and (4) writing the theory. There is a strong interaction between those stages, as the researcher "is forced to consider much diversity in the data" (Glaser and Strauss, 1967, p.114). By importing the term of *diversity* in grounded theory, Glaser and Strauss (1967, p.114) highlighted how "each incident is compared with other incidents, in terms of as many similarities and differences as possible." Consequently, the researcher stays a lot in each stage, comparing and analysing the data, then moves to the next stage, and if there is such need, he may return to the first stage and replay his steps, in a cyclical, dynamic process.

By analysing the data and the categories created, the present research attempts to create a theory that will explain former concerns (abduction). In this research, the author used MAXQDA software to support data analysis. MAXQDA belongs to a rising number of similar software programs that have been used during the last decades in qualitative research, known as computer-assisted qualitative data analysis systems (CAQDAS). Such software handles and manages data more creatively, creating time efficiencies for exploring data (Corbin and Strauss, 2015; Costa *et al.*, 2017:). Apart from the above, MAXQDA can design a hierarchical coding system suitable for grounded theory analyses. Following the philosophy of grounded theory, codes and memos are essential to the MAXQDA process since they sketch the researcher's profile as the decision-maker for their content (Kuckartz and Radiker, 2019; Woolf and Silver, 2018). Adding MAXQDA helped the author to delve deeper into the data and understand how white power music helped to shape extreme-right members' behaviours by functioning as a non-violent subculture that triggers violent reactions.

Some difficulties arose whilst collecting data for this research. Due to prosecution for illegal actions, the Greek extreme right returned to anonymity in the guise of their preferred foreign forums and online activism through blogs. Such a behaviour draws its historical roots from the NF's first concerts in Great Britain during the 1980s (Shaffer, 2017). Whilst anonymity offers the extreme-right actors and the white power scene the opportunity to remain undercover in Greece, abroad members continue to interact and strengthen their networks by using online bulletin board forums (like rac-forum.org and Stormfront). Consequently, anonymity contributes to the sample's diversity, dividing it into two different periods: the former from the early 1990s until Pavlos Fyssas' murder in September 2013, whereas the latter covers the post-murder period and its aftermath for the Greek extreme right.

Exploring the Data

Although white power music is diffused throughout white power networks, accessing that content has become increasingly challenging in Greece during the last decade. Once, the scene functioned under specific security measures, but the visibility it gained forced it to return underground. During the years of visibility of such groups, I had the opportunity to download their material, as they offered it for free to enlist more supporters. Since 2018, the blog "rac88hellas"[3] has reappeared, offering a rich database of Greek and global white power music, consisting of 471 songs. In this chapter, the author will code and analyse the collected data, categorise the findings and, finally, answer the main research question.

Following Charmaz's three-level coding system, the first coding level consists of open coding. For this analysis, the author collected everything that could match this research in a general framework. Consequently, the author could input all the white power songs – 95 songs – available from different pages online into the first level. Subsequently the author was able to add a further 95 songs to the first coding level. Then, by acknowledging the vast extent of the collected data, the author proceeded to do the axial coding. In that analysis, the author filtered the collected data and deleted duplicates and similar entries. The final sample, after recoding, consisted of 42 songs, covering 9 bands, between 1988 and 2013, sketching a historical moment for Greek white power music.

The search for the Greek white power music's violent narratives gave me 56 cases. To boost the categories' cohesion, the author moved to Charmaz's (2014, p.138) second coding

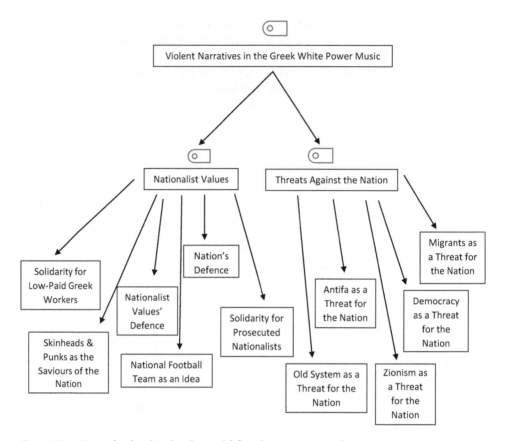

Figure 19.1 Hierarchical code-subcodes model for white power music lyrics.

level, focused coding. Through the MAXQDA software, the author constructed a hierarchical coding system. More specifically, the author chose the hierarchical code-subcodes' model from the MAXMAPS' menu to optimise the relationships between the codes. Therefore, the author constructed the model in Figure 19.1.

As shown in Figure 19.1, the coding process provided two core categories that describe the violent narratives in Greek white power music: the nationalist values and the threats against the nation. Both can be divided into subcategories, meaning, in the case of the nationalist values: defence of nationalist values, solidarity for low-paid Greek workers, the national football team as an idea (representative of the whole nation), solidarity for prosecuted nationalists, defence of the nation and the skinheads and punks as the saviours of the nation. At the same time, threats against the nation have been highlighted from the old system, being Antifa, Zionism, democracy and immigrants, as potential subcategories of real threats.

Discussion: How Non-violent Rhetoric Can Foster Violent Action

White power music aims at approaching current and traditional topics by presenting the core of the extreme-right ideology to a broader audience whilst interacting with the political situation. As its name suggests, white power music first appeared as music for white people, especially after being adopted by the British far right. "Oi!" music was its ancestor, as Ian Stuart

Donaldson created it after combining British punk with West Indian reggae (Love, 2016). Whilst it never abandoned its roots in "oi!" music, white power music integrated new topics into its songs successfully. Shaffer (2017, p.89) describes how Margaret Thatcher's neoliberal politics and attacks against the working classes simultaneously with the Labour Party's decline during the 1980s created a political opportunity for the British far right. Consequently, white power music's political identity was already visible, becoming a core characteristic of its identity.

As the sample shows, "oi!" music is used as an *imprimatur* for white power music bands. "Oi!" music was known for its political content, offering musicians the opportunity to criticise politics according to their beliefs. In my research, I found that "oi!" music is linked with political content, drawing from the first years of white power music. Nevertheless, I have to mention that there are references to that kind of music in the subtext of the songs. The references to white power music's roots continue with RAC. During the first days of the white power music scene, Europe was divided due to the Cold War, and the extreme right was defined as anti-communist. Even though 1989 marked the end of communism, the extreme right had to find a new enemy and turned its attention to capitalism. Their targets included businesses, the state and all those who promoted capitalism, undermining the nation-state's power.

The white power music scene never hid its members' activities, even at the peak of extreme-right activity in Greece between May 2012 and April 2015 (when Golden Dawn's trial began). Such an example is sport, with a particular focus on football. As their songs explain, the stadium stand is an honourable place to express their love for their team. Nevertheless, this did not prevent them from combining their belief in their team with a very firm belief in their ideology. As described earlier, after coding the sample, the author found many references concerning anti-semitism and racism against minorities. These two subjects are part of the core of white power music, providing a conspiracy world view in which the nation and the race are attacked by "the Zionists" that control the world. Their discourse against minorities found fertile ground among the working classes in Greece, even before the economic crisis, because it had become cheaper to employ foreigners.

Greece's relationships with its neighbouring countries have also provided material for new songs, contributing to the extreme-right members' non-violent subculture. It seems that Golden Dawn's electoral success in 2012 was the turning point for such a violent radicalisation. Before 2012, what was reported were some instances where violence was directed against immigrants or left-wing supporters. Those were occasional events attempting to boost the extreme right's underground image whilst fighting to control the streets.

The first recorded attack was in 1998 against the student Dimitris Kousouris near the courts in the centre of Athens. Even though a prominent member of Golden Dawn, Periandros Androutsopoulos, was involved, there were no links between the young Greek white power music scene and these attacks. A group of journalists under the name "Ios" ("Virus"), who investigated Golden Dawn's violent actions, argued that such attacks drew key similarities with Mussolini's *Squadristi* (Ios Press, 1998). In 2001, the "*Galazia Stratia*" ("Blue Army") was founded to support the Greek national football team. They were involved in pogroms against Albanians, and they displayed Nazi symbols in the stadium, but there is no specific connection with white power music (Kleon, 2014). Until 2012, the only recorded attack to involve a member of the white power music scene had occurred in 2005. In Monastiraki, at the centre of Athens, Panagiotis 'Porky' Roumeliotis, singer of the band War Criminals, attacked and stabbed two young men because one of them wore a jacket that displayed an anti-Nazi logo (Symvoulidis, 2008).

After Golden Dawn entered the Greek and the European Parliament, connections were made between white power songs and specific attacks from the extreme-right political spectrum. Following the coding results, the following values were exported from the white power music: solidarity for the prosecuted nationalists, solidarity for the low-paid Greek workers, defence of the nation and defence of nationalist values. Solidarity in both cases is present in white power songs.

Solidarity in both cases is present in white power songs. In particular, following the decision by Nikos Dendias, the Minister for Public Order and Citizen Protection at the time, Golden Dawn's leader Nikos Michaloliakos and 22 other prominent members of the organisation (among whom were its more active parliamentary members) were arrested and imprisoned on charges of creating and managing a terrorist organisation (Vythoulkas, 2013). Nationalists were often under police investigation due to the attacks they were involved in, although after the Pavlos Fyssas' murder in September 2013, Golden Dawn's core activists were imprisoned. The white power band "Pride & Pain" has expressed its solidarity since 2010 with its song "*Lefteria stous Ethnikistes*" ("Freedom to Nationalists"). Even though in 2010 Golden Dawn was still politically weak, the song referred to a rotten system that attacks and imprisons nationalists instead of irresponsible politicians.

Antisemitism, as was previously presented, is expressed in the form of a global Zionist conspiracy against the nations. Such a belief triggered the most extremist part of the Greek neo-Nazis called "*Anentachtoi Maiandrioi Ethnikistes*" ("Uncommitted Meander Nationalists") to attack Jewish synagogues across the countries and paint Nazi symbols in cemeteries and other public places (Chondrogiannos, 2017). However, after the group's arrest, a significant decline in such attacks was observed. Tension between Greece and Turkey and other neighbouring countries on foreign policy have been imprinted in white power songs. Former disagreements with Albania regarding Northern Epirus (a Western Balkans' region) inspired songs like "Northern Epirus" by "Cause of Honour." Northern Macedonia is also of great significance for the extreme right because of Alexander the Great's history. Therefore, they were against any similar name being given to the former Democratic Republic of Macedonia, an issue that the White Pride Rockers approached in their song "*Skopje.*"

Notwithstanding the importance of the above categories, the most violent actions have occurred against immigrants and anti-fascist activists (as part of Antifa type former organisations). Having already highlighted the intensely competitive nature of their coexistence with other nationalities, the threat expressed against those groups cannot be omitted. These songs came to fulfil their purpose after 2012 when Golden Dawn members attacked Egyptian fishers in Keratsini (N.A., 2014). Golden Dawn members were also behind the murder of the young Pakistani, Sahzat Luckman (N.A., 2013). In the early 1990s, Golden Dawn members were often involved in clashes with left-wing supporters in an attempt to clarify who ruled the streets. Similarly – and in parallel with Golden Dawn's parliamentary presence – there were many attacks against worker-owned places which supported immigrants and leftist actions. Pavlos Fyssas' murder in September 2013 was the first attack by Golden Dawn after entering the Greek Parliament against someone having a Greek identity. Fyssas, a left-wing rapper, was known for his anti-fascist songs and lived in Keratsini, a stronghold of Golden Dawn in Piraeus. Even though his murder resulted from a planned attack by Golden Dawn members, it seems that they were triggered by his activism and his songs and not by some white power verses. This fact created an adverse situation as, until now, white power music had provoked violent actions and not the victimisation of the creators of anti-fascist songs. Having said that, Fyssas' murder happened due to his hostile attitude against the extreme right (JailGoldenDawn, N.A., n.d.). Until then, the Greek extreme right had been categorising its enemies in specific minorities, such as immigrants (i.e. Luckman, the Egyptian fishers), as well as in places that represented the centre of the conspiracy theories that the extreme right disseminated, such as the Jewish cemeteries (vandalised by the Anentachtoi Maiandrioi Ethnikistes–Uncommitted Meanders Nationalists, AME).

Targeting an anti-fascist movement persona can be seen as a radicalisation of the extreme right's activities, a part of their broader mobilisation after entering the Greek Parliament: for example, attacks against market stalls owned by immigrants (N.A., 2012), and, against mainly left-wing squats in Athens (Maragkidou, 2018). These attacks did not stop during the party's parliamentary representation, but it seems that they began being directed against specific persons instead of places.

Conclusion

Music was transformed from a simple subculture of the Greek extreme right into a weapon that often triggered violent extremism following the rise and decline of Greece's extreme right between 2010 and 2019. Nowadays, extreme-right groups are only active online and are connected with the neo-Nazi blog, Mavros Krinos. Their new material mainly contains texts and not music, proposing the redirection of their activities as a more theoretical framework instead. During Golden Dawn's electoral rise, there had been some debate as to whether democracy in Greece was threatened or not. Even though Golden Dawn's members were jailed, the impact only hit the party and not the broader extreme-right Greek milieu. Following extreme-right blogging activity since 2012, I observed how often they changed their identities or stopped their activities whilst new manifestations of their activism appeared – especially in the online sphere. Although I cannot link all these online activities, members seem to become active under specific conditions in the real world (e.g. attacking immigrant camps).

This chapter discussed how music could be used for specific purposes by extremist groups after constructing their subculture. Grounded theory has offered the possibility of approaching white power music from the point of view of the subjects studied. This research discussed how the Greek white power music scene constructed its worldview and was gradually transformed into a vector for Greek extreme-right violence. Future studies on the topic could expand on the supply-side of party politics. Grounded theory can be combined with parties' manifestos to study the political opportunities that boosted the extreme-right subculture between 2009 and 2019, a crucial period for Greek society.

Notes

1 Hebdige (2002, p.90) contributed significantly to the subcultures' field by defining that "subcultures represent 'noise' (as opposed to sound): interference in the orderly sequence which leads from real events and phenomena to their representation in the media." Sarah Thornton (2003, p.8) distances herself from the University of Birmingham's Centre for Contemporary Cultural Studies seminal works. Instead, she understands subcultures as "those taste cultures which are labelled by media as subcultures and the word subcultural as a synonym for those practices that clubbers call 'underground.'" Clarke *et al.* (2006, pp.6–7) viewed subcultures "in terms of their relation[ship] to the wider class-cultural networks of which they form a distinctive part." Therefore, they argued that "sub-cultures are sub-sets – smaller, more localised and differentiated structures, within one or other of the larger cultural networks ... Subcultures, then, must first be related to the 'parent cultures' of which they are a sub-set." Searching for more recent examples of subculture for the research, I found two articles regarding skinheads. In the first one, Johansson *et al.* (2017, pp.2–3) explicitly explained how subculture is an open interaction with its societal and sociopolitical environment. The latter (Madfis & Vysotsky, 2020, pp.224–226) just reviews the subculture's bibliography. For a thorough reading, see also: Bennet and Guerra (2020); Gildart *et al.* (2021).

2 Pavlos Fyssas' murder, on 17 September 2013, marked, as Liz Fekete (2020, p.8) mentions the end of state tolerance against Golden Dawn. After the neo-Nazi party entered the Greek Parliament in the 2012 double elections, it radicalised its activism (Georgiadou, 2019, p.200), attacking minorities and extreme-left supporters. Until September 2013, Golden Dawn's most notorious actions were the murder of the Paqistani national Shehzad Luqman, attacks in Egyptian fishermen in Keratsini and attacks in extreme-left squats. Nevertheless, Pavlos Fyssas' murder triggered a shockwave in the Greek political and social life, as it marked the first time the neo-Nazi party murdered a Greek due to his political beliefs. Pavlos Fyssas was an anti-fascist raper, known for his anti-Nazi songs and his personality in Keratsini and Nikaia. Whilst watching a football game in a local café in Keratsini, on 17 September 2013, members of the Golden Daw arrived in the café, in what later revealed to be a well-organised raid. After some verbal attacks between Pavlos Fyssas and Golden Dawn members, Giwrgos Roupakias – deputy financial manager of Nikaia's Local Organisation – attacked Pavlos Fyssas with a knive, murdering him (N.A., n.d.). During the Golden Dawn trial that followed – the party was blamed for being a criminal organisation – it was revealed that some of the most prominent party's parliamentary members were aware of Pavlos Fyssas' murder.

3 http://rac88hellas.blogspot.com

References

Adorno, T. W., Frenkel-Brunswik, E., Levinson, D. J. and Sanford, R. N. (1950) *The Authoritarian Personality*, New York, USA: Harpers.

Backes, U. (2010) *Political Extremes: A Conceptual History from Antiquity to the Present,* Abingdon: Routledge. https://doi.org/10.4324/9780203867259

Beausoleil, E. (2014) 'The Politics, Science, and Art of Receptivity,' *Ethics & Global Politics*, 7 (1), pp.19–40. https://doi.org/10.3402/egp.v7.23231

Bennet, A. (2018) 'Conceptualising the Relationship between Youth, Music and DIY Careers: A Critical Overview,' *Cultural Sociology*, 12 (2), pp.140–155. https://doi:10.1177/1749975517750760

Bennet, A. and Guerra, P. (eds.) (2020) *DIY Cultures and Underground Music Scenes,* New York, USA: Routledge. https://doi.org/10.4324/9781315226507

Bryant, A. (2017) *Grounded Theory and Grounded Theorizing: Pragmatism in Research Practice,* Oxford, UK: Oxford University Press.

Bryman, A. (2012) *Social Research Methods,* New York, USA: Oxford University Press. https://doi:10.1093/acprof:oso/9780199922604.001.0001

Charmaz, K. (1995) 'Grounded Theory,' in J. Smith, R. Harre and L. van Langenhove (eds.), *Rethinking Methods in Psychology,* London, UK: Sage, pp.27–49. http://dx.doi.org/10.4135/9781446221792.n3

Charmaz, K. (2007) 'Constructionism and the Grounded Theory Method,' in J.A. Holstein and J.F. Gubrium (eds.), *Handbook of Constructionist Research,* New York, USA: The Guilford Press, pp.397–412.

Charmaz, K. (2014) (2nd ed.) *Constructing Grounded Theory: A Practical Guide through Qualitative Analysis,* London, UK: Sage.

Chondrogiannos, T. (2017) *I nea Chrysi Avgi ekkolaptetai sto Menidi (The New Golden Dawn Is Breeding in Menidi).* Retrieved from: www.vice.com/el/article/pay73y/h-nea-xrysh-aygh-ekkolaptetai-sto-menidi

Clarke, J. (2006) 'The Skinheads and the Magical Recovery of Community,' in S. Hall and T. Jefferson (eds.), *Resistance through Rituals: Youth Subcultures in Post-war Britain,* Oxon, UK: Routledge, pp.80–83. https://doi.org/10.4324/9780203357057

Clarke, J., Hall, S., Jefferson, T. and Roberts, B. (2006) 'Subcultures, Cultures and Class,' in S. Hall and T. Jefferson (eds.), *Resistance through Rituals: Youth Subcultures in Post-war Britain,* Oxon, UK: Routledge, pp.3–59. https://doi.org/10.4324/9780203357057

Corbin, J. and Strauss, A. (2015) (4th ed.) *Basics of Qualitative Research: Techniques and Procedures for Developing Grounded Theory,* Thousand Oaks, USA: Sage.

Costa, A.P., de Sousa, F.N., Moreira A. and de Souza, D.N. (2017) 'Research through Design: Qualitative Analysis to Evaluate the Usability,' in A.P. Costa, L.P. Reis, F.N. de Sousa and A. Moreira (eds.), *Computer Supported Qualitative Research,* Cham: Switzerland: Springer, pp.1–12. https://10.1007/978-3-319-43271-7.

Dunne, C. (2011) 'The Place of the Literature Review in Grounded Theory Research,' *International Journal of Social Research Methodology*, 14 (2), pp.111–124. https://dx.doi.org/10.1080/13645579.2010.494930

Dyck, K. (2017) *Reichsrock: The International Web of White-Power and Neo-Nazi Hate Music*, New Jersey, USA: Rutgers University Press.

Falter, J. W., Schumann, S. (1988) 'Affinity towards Right-Wing Extremism in Western Europe,' *West European Politics*, 11 (2), pp.96–110. https://doi:10.1080/01402388808424684

Fekete, L. (2020) 'Lessons from the Fight against Golden Dawn,' *Race & Class*, 61 (4), pp.50–67. https://doi.org/10.1177/0306396820906074

Flick, U., von Kardoff, E. and Steinke, I. (2004) 'What is Qualitative Research? An Introduction to the Field,' in U. Flick, E. von Kardoff and I. Steinke (eds.), *A Companion to Qualitative Research*, London, UK: Sage. pp.3–11.

Georgiadou, V. (2019) *I Akra Dexia stin Ellada: 1965-2018 (The Far-Right in Greece: 1965-2018)*, Athens, Greece: Kastaniotis.

Gildart, K., Gough-Yates, A., Lincoln, S., Osgerby, B., Robinson, L., Street, J., Webb, P. and Worley, M. (eds.) (2021) *Hebdige and Subculture in the Twenty-First Century: Through the Subcultural Lens*, Cham, Switzerland: Palgrave Macmillan. https://doi:10.1007/978-3-030-28475-6

Glaser, B. (1978) *Theoretical Sensitivity: Advances in the Methodology of Grounded Theory*, Mill Valley, USA: Sociology Press.

Glaser, B.G. and Strauss, A. (1967) *The Discovery of Grounded Theory: Strategies for Qualitative Research*, New Brunswick, USA: Aldine Transaction.

Hebdige, D. (2002) *Subculture: The Meaning of Style*, London, UK: Routledge. https://doi.org/10.4324/9780203139943

Ios Press, (1998) *Allaxte miala giati tha sas liwsoume san ta skoulikia (Change Your Minds; Otherwise, We Will Crush You like Worms)*. Retrieved from: www.iospress.gr/extra/xrisavgi-1.htm

Johansson, T., Andreasson, J. and Mattsson, C. (2017) 'From Subcultures to Common Culture: Bodybuilders, Skinheads, and the Normalization of the Marginal,' *SAGE Open*. https://doi.org/10.1177/2158244017706596

Klandermans, B. and Mayer, N. (2006) 'Right-Wing Extremism as a Social Movement,' in B. Klandermans and N. Mayer (eds.), *Extreme Right Activists in Europe: Through the Magnifying Glass*, Oxon, UK: Routledge, pp.3–16. https://doi.org/10.4324/9780203004395

Kleon, I. (2014) *Skini Prwti: Fevrouarios 2005, Gipedo Panathinaikou, GADA, Patriarcheio Ierosolymwn (First Scene: February 2005, Panathinaikos Football Stadium, GADA, Patriarchate of Ierosolyma)*. Retrieved from: https://xyzcontagion.wordpress.com/2014/10/11/kryfa-04-parakratos-nazistiko-zombi/#more-4273

Kolovos, I. (2015) *'Koinwnika Apovlita'; I istoria tis punk skinis stin Athina, 1979-2015 ('Social Wastes'; History of the Punk Scene in Athens, 1979-2015)*, Athens, Greece: Aprovleptes Ekdoseis.

Kordas, G. (2013) 'I mousiki skini tis Chrisis Avgis (The Music Scene of Golden Dawn),' *Yearbook 2010-2012*, Athens, Greece: Asini, pp.77–86.

Kuckartz, U. and Radiker, S. (2019) *Analysing Qualitative Data with MAXQDA: Text, Audio, and Video*, Cham, Switzerland: Springer. https://doi.org/10.1007/978-3-030-15671-8

Lipset, S.M. (1959) 'Social Stratification and Right-Wing Extremism,' *The British Journal of Sociology*, 10 (4), pp.346–382. https://doi.org/10.2307/587800

Love, N. S. (2016) *Trendy Fascism: White Power Music and the Future of Democracy*, Albany, USA: State University of New York Press.

Madfis, E. and Vysotsky, S. (2020) 'Exploring Subcultural Trajectories: Racist Skinhead Disengagement, Desistance, and Countercultural Value Persistence,' *Sociological Focus*, 53 (3), pp.221–235. https://doi.org/10.1080/00380237.2020.1782791

Maragkidou, M. (2018) *"Tous allaxate ta ladia;" – I Epithesi tis Chrisis Avgis sto "Synergeio" Epitelous Dikazetai ("Did You Have Them Hell?" – Golden Dawn's Attack to the Left-Wing Squad of "Synergeio" finally Is Put on Trial)*. Retrieved from: www.vice.com/el/article/pax8gz/toys-alla3ate-ta-ladia-h-epi8esh-ths-xryshs-ayghs-sto-synergeio-epiteloys-dikazetai

Mills, J., Bonner, A. and Francis, K. (2006) 'The Development of Constructivist Grounded Theory,' *International Journal of Qualitative Methods*, 5 (1). pp.25–35. https://doi.org/10.1177%2F160940690600500103

Morse, J.M. and Clark, L. (2019) 'The Nuances of Grounded Theory Sampling and the Pivotal Role of Theoretical Sampling,' in A. Bryant and K. Charmaz (eds.) *The Sage Handbook of Current Developments in Grounded Theory*, London, UK: Sage, pp.145–166. https://dx.doi.org/10.4135/9781526485656.n9

Mudde, C. (1996) 'The War of Words Defining the Extreme Right Party Family,' *West European Politics,* 19 (2), pp.225–248. https://doi:10.1080/01402389608425132

Mudde, C. (2007) *Populist Radical Right Parties in Europe,* New York, USA: Cambridge University Press. https://doi.org/10.1017/CBO9780511492037

N.A. (n.d.). *Dolofonia Pavlou Fyssa (Pavlos Fyssa's Murder).* Retrieved from: https://jailgoldendawn. com/%CF%85%CF%80%CE%BF%CE%B8%CE%AD%CF%83%CE%B5%CE%B9%CF%82/ %CE%B4%CE%BF%CE%BB%CE%BF%CF%86%CE%BF%CE%BD%CE%AF%CE%B1- %CF%80%CE%B1%CF%8D%CE%BB%CE%BF%CF%85-%CF%86%CF%8D%CF%83%CF%83 %CE%B1/

N.A. (2007) 'I Elliniki Skini (The Greek Scene),' *Blood & Honour Hellas,* 18, p. 19.

N.A. (2010) *Psila sto Metwpo Live – 4th Giorti Ellinikis Neolaias (To the Battlefront Live – 4th Greek Youth Celebration).* Retrieved from: https://web.archive.org/web/20101019041549/http://resistance-hellas. blogspot.com/search/label/%CE%93%CE%B9%CE%BF%CF%81%CF%84%CE%AE%20%CE%9D %CE%B5%CE%BF%CE%BB%CE%B1%CE%AF%CE%B1%CF%82

N.A. (2012) *Nea epithesi tis Chrysis aygis se laiki agora sto Mesologgi (Golden Dawn's New Attack on Market Stalls in Mesologgi).* Retrieved from: www.news247.gr/koinonia/nea-epithesi-tis-chrysis-aygis- se-laiki-agora-sto-mesologgi.6168490.html

N.A. (2013) *Dolofonia Sahzat Luckman (Murder of Sahzat Luckman).* Retrieved from: https://jailgoldend awn.com/%CF%85%CF%80%CE%BF%CE%B8%CE%AD%CF%83%CE%B5%CE%B9%CF%82/ %CE%B4%CE%BF%CE%BB%CE%BF%CF%86%CE%BF%CE%BD%CE%AF%CE%B1-%CF% 83%CE%B1%CF%87%CE%B6%CE%AC%CF%84-%CE%BB%CE%BF%CF%85%CE%BA%CE %BC%CE%AC%CE%BD/

N.A. (2014) *I epithesi stous Aigyptious psarades sto Perama ton Iounio tou 2012 (The Attack against Egyptian Fishers in Perama, June 2012).* Retrieved from: https://jailgoldendawn.com/%CF%85%CF%80%CE %BF%CE%B8%CE%AD%CF%83%CE%B5%CE%B9%CF%82/%CE%B1%CE%B9%CE%B3% CF%8D%CF%80%CF%84%CE%B9%CE%BF%CE%B9-%CE%B1%CE%BB%CE%B9%CE%B5 %CF%81%CE%B3%CE%AC%CF%84%CE%B5%CF%82/

Niedbalski, J. and Slezak, I. (2019) 'The Main Features of NVivo Software and the Procedures of the Grounded Theory Methodology: How to Implement Studies Based on GT Using CAQDAS,' in P.A. Costa, L.P. Reis and A. Moreira (eds.), *Computer Supported Qualitative Research: New Trends on Qualitative Research,* Cham, Switzerland: Springer, pp.90–101. https://doi.org/10.1007/978-3-030- 01406-3_8

Robson, C. and McCartan, K. (2016) *Real World Research: A Resource for Users of Social Research Methods in Applied Settings,* Chichester, UK: John Wiley & Sons.

Rush, G.B. (1963) 'Toward a Definition of the Extreme Right,' *The Pacific Sociological Review,* 6 (2), pp.64–73. https://doi.org/10.2307%2F1388686

Shaffer, R. (2017) *Music, Youth and International Links in Post-War British Fascism: The Transformation of Extremism,* Cham, Switzerland: Palgrave Macmillan. https://doi.10.1007/978-3-319-59668-6

Stern, P.N. (1985) 'Using Grounded Theory Method in Nursing Research,' in M.M. Leininger (ed.), *Qualitative Research Methods,* Toronto, Canada: Grune & Stratton Inc, pp.148–160.

Strauss, A. and J. Corbin (1990) *Basics of Qualitative Research: Grounded Theory Procedures and Techniques,* Newbury Park, USA: Sage.

Symvoulidis, C. (2008) *Oi! I Mousiki twn Skinheads (Oi! The Music of Skinheads),* Ioannina, Greece: Isnafi.

Thornton, S. (2003) *Club Cultures: Music, Media and Subcultural Capital,* Cambridge, UK: Polity Press.

Tipaldou, S. (2012) 'Rock for the Motherland: The White Power Music Scene in Greece,' in A. Shekhovtsov and P. Jackson (eds.), *White Power Music: Scenes of Extreme Right Cultural Resistance,* Northampton, UK: Searchlight Magazine and the Radicalism and New Media Research Group, The University of Northampton, pp.47–55.

Tsiwlis, G. (2014) *Methodoi kai Technikes Analysis stin Poiotiki Koinwniki Erevna (Methods and Techniques of Analysis in Qualitative Social Research),* Athens, Greece: Kritiki.

von Beyme, K. I. (1988) 'Right-wing Extremism in Post-War Europe,' in K. I. von Beyme (ed.), *Right-Wing Extremism in Western Europe,* London, UK: Frank Cass and Company Limited, pp.1–18. https:// doi.org/10.4324/9781315035338

Vythoulkas, D. (2013) *Egklimatiki organwsi I Chrysi Avgi – Synelifthi kai o 22os katazitoumenos (video) (The Golden Dawn Is a Criminal Organisation – its 22nd Wanted Member Has Been Arrested (Video))*. Retrieved from: www.tovima.gr/2013/09/28/politics/egklimatiki-organwsi-i-xrysi-aygi-synelifthi-kai-o-22os-katazitoymenos-binteo/

Woolf, N.H. and Silver, C. (2018) *Qualitative Analysis using MAXQDA: The Five-Level QDA Method*, Oxon, UK: Routledge. https://doi.org/10.4324/9781315268569

20

THE IDENTITARIAN MOVEMENT AND ITS CONTEMPORARY MANIFESTATIONS

Tamir Bar-On

Introduction

The anthropologist Benjamin R. Teitelbaum created a tripartite typology to parse out the different violent and non-violent aspects of the organized far right. In his monograph, titled Lions of the North: Sounds of the New Radical Nordic Nationalism, Teitelbaum differentiates between "race revolutionaries," "cultural nationalists," and "Identitarians" (Teitelbaum, 2017, p. 5). Race revolutionaries include the Swedish Nordic Resistance movement and see themselves as "white nationalists" or "National Socialists."[1] They believe in a national or transnational community based on blood ties and tend to be marginalized from mainstream politics. Cultural nationalists are represented by the Sweden Democrats, participate in electoral politics, and are open about assimilating various groups within the dominant culture. The dividing line between these three categories is not always clear when it comes to the empirical reality of far-right extremism, but these ideological strains are linked by "their resistance to immigration and multiculturalism, all of which they believe threaten the imagined purity of a national people" (Thorleifsson, 2018, para. 3).

Yet, *Identitarians*, in contrast to race revolutionaries and cultural nationalists, who prioritize one major criterion in defining the nation, believe that nations are defined both by their ethnicity and by their culture. Hence, they insist that each nation should preserve its distinctive ethnic and cultural characteristics, which means that citizens should act to prevent any major demographic or cultural changes, including those due to large-scale population displacement, mass migration, or foreign invasion.

In recent years, an anti-globalist, metapolitical, and socially conservative yet culturally innovative and provocative Identitarian movement (IM) has emerged in many European countries, beginning in France. Metapolitics here refers to the long-term struggle in civil society to influence dominant attitudes, beliefs, or worldviews. The IM is a collection of movements that has now also spread outside of Europe, to the Americas and as far as Australia and New Zealand in the anglophone-speaking world (Vardon, 2011; Willinger, 2013, 2014; Les Identitires, 2017; Müller, 2017; Zúquete, 2018; Sellner, 2019; Schwochert, 2020). Teitelbaum (2017) insists that Identitarians are less interested in mainstream politics than defeating liberalism, Marxism, and

DOI: 10.4324/9781003032793-24

Christianity, as well as spreading white nationalist ideology. The IM engages in what Zuqueté calls "metapolitics with a punch" (Zúquete, 2018, p. 37). In short, this connotes a commitment to a long-term attempt to change mentalities in civil society using the model of the French New Right (*nouvelle droite*), but with a modification that leaves the purely cerebral world of metapolitics to engage ordinary white Europeans through street demonstrations, openly challenging state authorities, and shocking events and advertisement campaigns.

Interestingly, both cultural nationalists and the Identitarians have been accused by the left of being "xenophobic," "racist," "far right," or even "fascist" (Rodat, 2017; Speit, 2018). Many academics equate cultural nationalism with "cultural racism," but this is not a view accepted by all scholars. For debates on claims of the IM as racist or fascist, Speit (2018) is useful. After all, as Speit notes, the motto of the Identitarians is "100% identity – 0% racism," *not* "blood and soil" (Speit, 2018, p. 11). It is also true, however, that some white nationalists or neo-Nazis have called themselves Identitarians, perhaps to disguise their more radical views, thereby further confusing matters. Such was the case with Identity Europa in the US.

In reality, *Identitarianism* is distinctive from fascism (or neo-fascism), Nazism (or neo-Nazism), traditional racism, white supremacism, and imperialism, but is beyond the boundaries of mainstream conservatism. Moreover, the IM differs from French *Nouvelle Droite* (New Right) thinkers such as Alain De Benoist precisely because the latter is resigned to the metapolitical realm in contrast to the youthful activism and guerrilla tactics of the IM; the IM is more anti-Muslim and anti-immigrant compared to De Benoist; and the IM rejects the *Nouvelle Droite* leader's "right to difference" formula based on an ethnopluralist framework (Bar-On, 2007, pp. 17–18). This connotes a communitarian approach where both immigrants and host cultures can maintain their distinctive ethnic and cultural differences (including regional and national cultures) in the face of homogenizing forces such as capitalism, Americanization, state bureaucratization, the European Union (EU), state assimilationist policies, or liberal pro-immigration and multiculturalism regimes.

As Identitarian thinker Faye (2011, p.3) notes, Identitarianism is only interested in fighting "for our own people's destiny" and he argues that De Benoist unwittingly supports immigration and thus the replacement of white Europeans by non-whites and non-Europeans (Camus, 2019; De Benoist, n.d; Faye, 2011). In fairness to De Benoist, he has always criticized immigration (which he argues is caused by capitalism) and leads to a cultural loss for "home" and "host" societies.

This chapter will proceed in four steps. First, it examines the French and European origins of the IM and shows how it has spread beyond Europe. Second, the IM's philosophical origins and ideology will be examined, including a brief exploration of the inter-war Conservative Revolution, the seminal impact of the *Nouvelle Droite*, and the key influences of the French ethnonationalist right (e.g., Renaud Camus, Pierre Vial, and Guillaume Faye). Third, the political trajectories, ideas, and selected texts of the IM's main thinkers, including Markus Willinger, Martin Sellner, and Richard B. Spencer will be explored. Fourth, the conclusion discusses the strategies, impact, and future of the IM.

Are the IM's strategies based on metapolitics and entryism (or, the way a state, party, organization, or movement uses a political strategy to join one or more organizations in order to expand its influence and ideas. Entryism might operate clandestinely or openly) successful? This chapter argues that the IM engages in "metapolitics with a punch" and longs for a peaceful revolution against liberal multiculturalism and globalism. This chapter also sheds light on how IM sees violence and a possible civil war in Euro-American societies as a "legitimate reaction against ominous trends" (Zúquete, 2018, p. 332) and believes that its sacred mission is to end the "racial degradation" of Europe and to stop the end of white Europeans (Zúquete, 2018, pp. 277–279). In order to define key terms more clearly from the start, it is essential to shed light on political ideologies relevant to this analysis.

The Origins of *Identitarianism* and Spread to Europe and Beyond

France has produced numerous ideological innovations, including the French Revolution, the birth of fascist ideology (Sternhell et al., 1995), the creation of the *Nouvelle Droite*, and the birth of the IM. While the IM has French origins, it later spread throughout Europe, and then made its way to North America (outside Mexico), Australia, and New Zealand, and even South America (Johnson, 2013, p. xv). It is interesting how even white nationalists in the US, who view identity in racial terms, show affinity for peoples of white European descent in South America, including Argentina and Uruguay.

They argue that whites worldwide must unite because they are threatened by liberal multi-culturalism and anti-racism policies. Due to the "blending of distinct European immigrant stocks," white nationalists insist that there is "an ever more blended, generic white identity" today (Johnson, 2013, p. xv). In short, the primary identity of whites must not be nationalism per se but their white European racial identity. The earliest manifestations of the IM were *Jeunesses Identitaires* founded in 2002 and *Bloc Identitaire* (BI) created in 2003, originally a youth wing of *Génération Identitaire* (Generation Identity – GI). It was only after 2012 that the IM spawned the creation of GI chapters (Génération Identitaire, n.d), offshoots, and like-minded movements throughout Europe (e.g., in various regions of France, Italy, Belgium, Germany, Austria, Switzerland, Italy, Spain, the United Kingdom, Sweden, and Central and Eastern European countries such as Czech Republic and Hungary), the United States, Canada (especially Quebec), Australia, and New Zealand, and even Chile.

Zúquete (2018) argues that the neo-fascist movement CasaPound used occupied houses, various associations, and food drives for the "indigenous" poor, concerts, and sporting events to push its Identitarian message and thus played a decisive role in the origins of the IM (Zúquete, 2018, pp. 60–61). Although they privilege a daring type of movement politics of a theatrical variety, the IM has supported political parties with "a like-minded disposition" (Zúquete, 2018, p. 5), especially nationalist and national-populist political parties.

The Australian scholar Richards (2019) noted that the Syrian civil war in 2011 and the ensuing "migration crisis" in Europe, the viscissitudes of economic globalization, and growing instability in the Middle East and North Africa (and by extension in Europe, including Islamist terrorist attacks on European soil) allowed various radical-right outfits, including the IM, to campaign "on the basis of culturally prevalent anti-immigration and anti-Islam sentiments" (p. 2). The IM shocked with its daring mosque raid in Poitiers, pork, and wine lunches in order to taunt Muslims and "reconquer" lost territories. As part of its modus operandi, IM also used controversial pro-European identity banners (e.g. "Emigration kills Africa, immigration kills Europe," "Against Islamists, Defend Europe") and attempted to protect European borders by disrupting the work of search and rescue ships of illegal migrants in the Mediterranean (Génération Identitaire, n.d; Hope Not Hate, n.d; Les Identitaires, n.d.a).

The IM sought to create networks and communities of like-minded activists imbued with fidelity to an "Identitarian" way of life. By using the "Identitarian" label, the IM was able to portray its movement as anti-racist and anti-fascist and in favour of defending white European cultural and ethnic identities (Metapedia, 2020). To this end, Swedish Identitarians also created a "New Right" and "Identitarian" antidote to Wikipedia called Metapedia. It is billed as "The alternative encyclopedia." It uses language, vocabulary, and a metapolitical approach in order to win hearts and minds.

Yet, anti-racist groups such as the Southern Poverty Law Center (2015) view the IM as racist, exclusionary, and in favour of ethnic separatism for whites. In 2019, the German Federal Office for the Protection of the Constitution labelled the IM as "right-wing extremist" ("Germany: Identitarian Movement Classified as Right-wing Extremist," 2019). Although it is largely a non-violent metapolitical movement, in a controversial decision *Génération Identitaire* was banned by the French state in 2021 for racial incitement, violence, and paramilitary ties (Willsher, 2021). The French Interior Minister Gerald Darmanin posted the decree to ban GI on Twitter, suggesting it lamented the group's "structure and military organization," adding that GI can be regarded "as having the character of a private militia" ("France Bans Far-Right Group Generation Identity", 2021, para. 2).

It noted that it had supposed links to far-right groups and received donations from the Christchurch mosque shooter, the Australian terrorist Brenton Tarrant. The decree also claimed that GI advanced "an ideology inciting hatred, violence and discrimination of individuals, based on their origin, their race or their religion." Little concrete evidence was provided for these charges. Thus, dissident rightists complain that such bans are attempts by liberal European states to silence discussions about multiculturalism, immigration, Islam and Islamism, "white survival," and the complicity of political and corporate elites in the denigration and demise of peoples of white European ancestry (Taylor, 2011).

Identitarians see their struggle on behalf of European identities as "invested with a quasi-religious sacredness" (Zúquete, 2018, p. 370). Identitarians are obsessed with the maintenance and preservation of the distinctive ethnic and cultural identities of white Europeans. As French Identitarian thinker, Philippe Vardon (2012), noted: "We cannot repeat it enough. If one of the major questions of the 20th century was the right to self-determination, the central question of our century is the right of peoples to self-preservation." Or, another French Identitarian, Fabrice Robert (2014), suggested that the key issue of our times is "the disappearance of our people!".

The IM argues that cultures and peoples around the world, as well as immigrants in white-dominated societies in Europe, the US, Canada, Australia, or New Zealand, are able to maintain and celebrate their cultural and ethnic identities, but whites are denied that right and their cultures are denigrated and even face extinction. For the IM, white European ethnicities from Russia and France to the US and Argentina face the greatest threat to their existence as people because of the following trends: liberal and socialist multiculturalism policies, unrestrained legal and illegal immigration, demographic (birth rate) trends that favour non-whites and Muslims in relation to whites, a conquering and imperialistic Islam, Islamist terrorism, crimes committed by immigrants, the immigrant takeover of city neighbourhoods, and even the replacement of whites by non-whites throughout Europe (Faye, 2016; Camus, 2019). This replacement of whites should be stopped by a policy called "the Great Return" of non-Europeans to their countries of origins, whether they are citizens or non-citizens of European states (Zúquete, 2018, p. 157).

The website and publishing house Arktos Media (based in Budapest) it is perhaps the largest distributor of radical-right literature in the world. It was founded in India in 2009 by the Swedish businessman and Alt-Right thinker Daniel Friberg and John B. Morgan, an American editor. It was launched in 2010, relocated to Sweden in 2014, and later Hungary in 2015.

Even the Christchurch mosque terrorist Brenton Harrison Tarrant seemed to have strong identitarian views, although the Identitarian thinker and key mobiliser Martin Sellner had openly distanced himself from Tarrant (Wilson, 2019). The 2019 terror attacks against two mosques in Christchurch, New Zealand, killed 51 people. Tarrant's manifesto railed against "the great replacement" (or genocide) of whites through mass immigration in Europe, North

America, Australia, and New Zealand. He donated 1,500 euros to *Identitäre Bewegung Österreich* (IBÖ), the Austrian branch of GI in Europe, as well as 2,200 euros to *Génération Identitaire*, the French branch of the group. He even had e-mail communication with IBÖ leader Martin Sellner.

Like the IM, the Alt-Right leader Richard B. Spencer identifies as an "Identitarian." Like other IM leaders, he has also a metapolitical path and thus distanced itself from neo-Nazis and white supremacists and increasingly used the Internet to attract new followers (Bar-On, 2021, p.2). Identitarians have been particularly conspicuous in German-speaking countries such as Germany and Austria, especially the numerous public rallies of PEGIDA – Patriotic Europeans against the Islamization of the Occident (*Patriotische Europäer gegen die Islamisierung des Abendlandes*). Its demonstrations in Dresden from 2014 to 2015, or at the height of a massive wave of Syrian migrants to Germany, numbered from 350 to 25,000 people (Khan, 2015).

Pegida has spread to various countries, even beyond the German-speaking world. In 2016, representatives of 14 like-minded allies, including Pegida Austria, Pegida Bulgaria, and Pegida Netherlands, met with Lutz Bachmann and Tatjana Festerling in the Czech Republic to sign the Prague Declaration. It argues that the "history of Western civilisation could soon come to an end through Islam conquering Europe" ("Pegida Meets with European Allies in the Czech Republic", 2016, para. 8). Other signatories included the Czech organizations *Blok proti islámu* (Bloc against Islam), *Odvaha and Dawn* – National Coalition (Czech: *Úsvit – Národní koalice*) in conjunction with the Polish National movement, the Conservative People's Party of Estonia and Italy's Lega Nord. IMs are a small yet vocal standout feature in societies that pride themselves on cultural openness or multiculturalism, such as Canada, Australia, and New Zealand.

Identitarians are united by an ethos of youthful optimism, activism, daring, adventure, and rebellion; a desire to promote the primordial place of white ethnic identities in political life; and a cutting-edge type of "metapolitics with a punch" (Zúquete, 2018, pp. 37–39). Or, as Matthew Rose explains, "Identitarianism is a youth movement" and it "claims Europe as the rightful and exclusive possession of its historic peoples" (Rose, 2021, p. 109). It is thus no accident that Identitarians valorize revolutionaries across the political spectrum from Che Guevara to the martyrs of the Paris Commune in 1871 (Zúquete, 2018, pp. 40–41). Identitarianism is today global, particularly through the spread of Identitarian literature through Arktos (a Budapest-based publishing house that promotes IM and other radical-right tracts globally), communication and exchanges between Identitarians across national borders, and the translation of Identitarian tracts (Zúquete, 2018, p. 98–104).

Identitarianism is ultimately also a lifestyle based on the importance of the desire to change the mentalities of all peoples of white European heritage. By white European heritage, Identitarians mean all peoples and ethnicities of white racial extraction from Portugal and the United Kingdom to Russia in Europe and North America to South America. The IM has thus created Identitarian houses, clubs, bars, sporting associations, and websites. These include organizations such as Nissa Rebela (created in 2007 and based in Nice) and Paris Project Apache (launched in 2009), the French Identitarian band Fraction; CasaPound Italia (which became famous in 2009 for occupying houses in Rome and promoting lectures, sports clubs, and musical activities); *Terre et Peuple*, a magazine and organization that promotes an Identitarian vision based on the "brotherhood" of all European peoples. This group has chapters in France, Belgium, Italy, and Portugal (Zúquete, 2018, p. 70). Identitarian houses have flourished throughout Austria; Arktos was also able to promote IM authors worldwide. Greg Johnson has peddled Identitarian ideas through Counter-Currents publishing house and a Chilean group Identitas propagates Identitarian writers.

While Identitarians have undertaken bold guerrilla tactics and have a significant social media following even in officially multicultural Canada (Southern, 2017; Wilson, 2020). The Canadian activist Lauren Southern, who has evolved her positions in recent years, has promoted a theme dear to Identitarians, namely, "The Great Replacement" theory. The number of followers is indeed small. French scholar, Stéphane François, insisted that the size of the original IM in France was merely 1,500–2,000 in 2017 (Rousset, 2017). It was estimated that in Germany the IM had 600 members in 2019 (Croucher, 2019). Unite Against Fascism insisted that the IM in the United Kingdom merely had 200 activists in June 2019 (Raw, 2019). Yet, if we think of CasaPound in Italy, IM movements in Germanic-speaking countries and Central and Eastern Europe, the US Alt-Right, and other IMs in Australia, New Zealand, Canada, and South American countries, the numbers certainly rise.

Moreover, the rejection of the liberal and Marxist agendas of the 1968 generation (Vardon as cited in Willinger, 2013, pp.9, 13); a radical critique of globalization, immigration, multi-culturalism, and Islam; the notion of a cultural and ethnic "great replacement" of whites by non-whites; and the desire to create more ethnically homogeneous white European societies are Identitarian concerns that reach far more supporters than the existing membership. See, the Identitarian tract by Markus Willinger where he writes: "The ideology of the '68ers has infected Europe. It is a sickness that will kill us if we don't find a cure" (Willinger, 2013, p. 13). Or the Identitarian thinker Philippe Vardon notes that his movement *Génération Identitaire* was founded "against the generation of the '68ers, who hold prominent posts of responsibility in almost all sectors of society and who are largely responsible for the chaos we must currently face" (as cited in Willinger, 2013, p. 9).

The symbol of the IM (a yellow lambda on a black background), which is used pri-marily in Europe by GI and sometimes other like-minded movements in various countries, commemorates the Battle of Thermopylae in which Ancient Greek city-states fought during the second Persian invasion of Greece (Weiß, 2013). For the IM, it thus represents the pan-European struggle against foreigners, Persians, Muslims, and non-Europeans in general.

Origins and Precursors of the IM

While we have already talked about the IM worldview, the origins of the IM go far deeper and include the inter-war Conservative Revolutionary movement, the major impact of the *Nouvelle Droite*, and especially the works of French ethnonationalist right thinkers such as Renaud Camus, Guillaume Faye, and Pierre Vial. Here we might add what Camus (2019), in his *Le Grand Replacement*, calls a dedication to his "two prophets" who predicted "racial war" in Europe: Enoch Powell and Jean Raspail. Prominent scholar on the IM Zúquete cites the Italian Marxist Antonio Gramsci (1891–1937), Conservative Revolutionary thinkers, the *Nouvelle Droite*, and Faye, Vial, and Dominique Venner as the key philosophical inspirations for the IM (Zúquete, 2018, pp. 7–26). Some pro-Fascist and conservatively traditional authors such as Julius Evola have also influenced elements of the IM, including Danniel Friberg (Teitelbaum, 2017, p. 163). Zúquete (2018) also notes that French and Italian groups as diverse as *BI* and CasaPound took these aforementioned thinkers and promoted a new generation of activism that sought to go beyond *Nouvelle Droite's* (ND) metapolitics.

In the next section of this chapter I briefly highlight the worldviews of each of these thinkers, which Zúquete argues influenced the IM's ideology. I stress that the ND and French ethnonational right in particular are the seminal influences on the IM. These movements have influenced numerous IM ideas and themes, including metapolitics and the desire for a peaceful revolution against liberal multiculturalism and globalism, the sacred character of the struggle of European whites, and the belief that violence and civil war are normal reactions to an "extremist," "globalist," and "multiculturalist" liberal system.

Metapolitics and Traditionalism

Gramsci argued that the key to revolutionary change (or conversely the maintenance of an existing system) was the control of culture, dominant attitudes, and worldviews in civil society (Adamson, 2014; Gramsci, 1982). *Nouvelle Droite* thinkers like De Benoist (1979) pioneered a right-wing form of Gramscianism in the 1970s: "The French right is Leninist without having read Lenin. It hasn't realized the *importance of Gramsci*. It hasn't seen that cultural power threatens the apparatus of the state" (De Benoist, 1979, p. 19). The IM followed the ND's right-wing form of Gramscianism. For example, GI (n.d) notes on its website that it is devoted to "education" and "metapolitics" for European youth from non-immigrant backgrounds. Like Gramsci, the IM in theory believes that a peaceful revolution is possible if European societies promote counter-hegemonic narratives against the dominant liberal multicultural and "globalist" system.

Owing to social media and guerrilla tactics, the IM expanded its popularity and helped spread radical-right-wing ideas from an elite intellectual to a larger mass audience. The largely non-violent tactics of the IM were based on Gramscian lessons. That is, when issues of ethnic identity, immigration, multiculturalism, globalization, and Islam are more openly discussed, the "silent majority" would embrace the solutions of the IM. In short, the IM was fundamentally concerned with winning the "war of ideas" in relation to the majority of "original Europeans" (i.e. white Europeans). Its identity was wedded to what political scientist Jean-Yves Camus (2018) called the creation of a transnational "white nation." This idea was already advanced by De Benoist and Venner as early as 1963 through the magazine *Europe-Action*.

Another ideological inspiration to IM is Julius Evola (1898–1974), an Italian philosopher who penned Mussolini's manifesto of "spiritual racism." He was also a key inspiration for neo-fascists and radical-right terrorists after World War Two, an anti-Semitic conspiracy theorist, and a "radical Traditionalist" (Teitelbaum, 2020). Traditionalists insist that all major religions share a perennial wisdom, or primordial and universal truths. The IM, however, differs from Evola and those neo-fascists because it does not openly espouse the use of violence to advance its anti-globalist theses.

The Swiss-born author Armin Mohler (1920–2003) called Conservative Revolutionary thinkers such as Ernst Jünger, Oswald Spengler, Carl Schmitt, Ernst Niekisch, and Hans Blüher the "Trotskyites of the German Revolution" and saw them as a "healthy" alternative to the Hitlerian "travesty" (1994, pp. 351–354). Mohler was a former secretary for Ernst Jünger and sympathetic to the *Nouvelle Droite* and German New Right. De Benoist cites CR thinkers as one of his key influences and CR thinkers embodied a non-Nazi German variant of fascism, which sought to unite ultra-nationalist, soldierly, and worker values (Griffin, 1994, pp. 104–115).

The Key Role of the Nouvelle Droite

A few extra words about the *Nouvelle Droite* are necessary because they clearly impacted the non-violent metapolitical orientation of the IM. As one scholar notes, "Benoist has maintained a critical distance from Identitarian activists, but they are unquestionably his ideological children" (Rose, 2021, p. 109). After World War II and the horrors of the Holocaust, the world entered an epoch of de-colonization from the 1950s to 1970s and thus an "anti-imperial" and "anti-colonial" age (Brzezinski, 2008, pp. 205–208). Therefore, it should come as no surprise that totalitarianism, war, the use of violence, open defence of racism, imperialism, and colonialism were increasingly discredited worldwide.

In particular, this was especially the case for liberal democracies where parliaments, the peaceful resolution of conflicts, respect for state sovereignty, free trade, and the use of regional and international institutions were viewed as antidotes to exaggerated expressions of nationalism and ultimately wars (Doyle, 1983a; 1983b; 1986). While violent extremists of the right, left, Islamist, or environmental varieties still exist around the world, non-violent extremists have become more prominent, "normal," and mainstream in Euro-American societies (Bar-On, 2007; Miller-Idris, 2017; Mudde, 2019). As a result, many sectors of the radical right in Euro-American societies abandoned violence and migrated to the parliamentary and metapolitical realms (Bale, 2018).

There were some exceptions such as the neo-fascists' "strategy of tension" and terrorism in the Italy of the 1970s. That is, capturing seats in parliament and winning the "war of ideas" in civil society became key tactics of the post-war radical right. The metapolitical approach was best represented by the *Nouvelle Droite* (or "European New Right"), a group of French intellectuals led by De Benoist, created in 1968 in order to re-evaluate the outdated tactics of the Old Right, fascism, Vichy regime, and the legacy of French colonialism (Bar-On, 2013; Telos Press, 1993).

Borrowing from the New Left and the experiences of the May 1968 protests, the *Nouvelle Droite* pioneered what we earlier called a "Gramscianism of the right," which sought to win the "laboratories of thought" from the liberal-left elites throughout Europe as a precondition for destroying egalitarianism, liberal democracy, capitalism, and multiculturalism, as well as creating a heterogenous world of homogeneous communities (Bar-On, 2001; McCulloch, 2006; Copsey, 2013). While Identitarian thinkers and the *Nouvelle Droite* lament the liberal-left legacy of 1968, the ND sees the 1968 generation as an example to emulate precisely because they "conquered" the media, academia, and other "laboratories of thought" (GRECE, 1998).

While the *Nouvelle Droite* had its heyday in the France of the late 1970s and early 1980s, its ideas would influence the discourse changes of radical-right parties throughout Europe (e.g. a focus on metapolitics, the "anti-racist" mantra, the "right to difference" of ethnic and cultural communities, and worldwide ethnopluralism), government officials, and various civil society organizations (Duranton-Crabol, 1988; Spektorowski, 2003, 2012; McCulloch, 2006; Bar-On, 2014). If violence was largely jettisoned by most of the post-war radical right by the 1980s, there were elements within the *Nouvelle Droite* and outside that criticized the French intellectuals for being too metapolitical (including Faye and the Belgian thinker Robert Steuckers) and failing to change the lives of "original Europeans" (i.e. titular ethnic or national majorities and neither immigrants, nor minorities) through concrete political action (François, 2019, p. 99).

The French Ethnonationalist Right

Finally, the ethnonationalist right is linked to but distinctive from the *Nouvelle Droite*. It is probably the most fundamental influence on the IM. Following Faye, Vial, Venner, and Camus, the IM focused on creating and promoting homogeneous regional, national, pan-European, and white ethnic identities. It sought to create a primordial white European identity that would be an extended "white nation" in Euro-American societies and beyond. It railed against the onslaught of so-called "homogenization": capitalist globalization, Muslim immigration (and refugees), the EU, and state-imposed liberal multiculturalism. It urged white Europeans to stick together politically; to challenge the alleged Islamization of Europe; to avoid "the great replacement" of "original Europeans" (white Europeans); to end "anti-white racism"; to reverse multiculturalism; called for "re-migration" (i.e. the return of European immigrants and refugees to their countries of origins, including citizens); and longed for the "re-conquest" of European lands from Muslims because the latter allegedly "control" Europe due to high birth rates, immigrant criminality, "no-go zones," abuse of the generosity of the welfare system, Islamist terrorist acts on European soil, and the denigration of original white Europeans (or, the peaceful ethnic cleansing of Muslim immigrants from Europe) (Camus, 2019; Faye, 2007, 2011, 2019; Les Identitaires, n.d.b).

Another key IM thinker Dominique Venner (1935–2013) was a French historian and journalist. He was a former member of the *Organisation armée secrète* (OAS – Secret Army Organization) that sought to assassinate French President Charles de Gaulle for his support for Algerian independence. A founder of the magazine *Europe-Action* in conjunction with De Benoist in 1963, Venner, pioneered a pan-European white nationalism. He became a hero for the Identitarian cause because of his suicide on 21 May 2013, inside the cathedral of Notre Dame de Paris (Camus, 2019, pp. 241–247). Although he was a pagan, Venner appreciated Christian civilization (Mamère, 2017). He argued that Christian civilization was being undermined by the threat of "Afro-Maghreb immigration" (Venner, 2013). Echoing Faye and Camus, he insisted that unrestricted immigration would lead to the "total replacement of the population of France, and of Europe" (Venner, 2013). In a letter sent to Radio Courtoisie, he views his suicide as a protest "against pervasive individual desires that destroy the anchors of our identity, particularly the family, the intimate base of our multi-millennial society" ("Un homme se suicide dans la cathédrale Notre-Dame de Paris", 2013). The suicide was a call to action for all Identitarians throughout Europe. Metapolitics was not enough. The IM needed more Venners with unyielding fidelity to the cause of white Europeans. In an age when ethnic identities of non-Europeans have been praised since the anti-colonial struggles of the 1950s and 1960s, Venner saw his struggle in sacred terms as one that championed the cause of the "silent majority" of white Europeans.

Like Venner, Faye was impatient and called Identitarians to action. He warned white Europeans that if they do not reverse the current demographic, immigration, and pro-multiculturalism regime in Europe, there would be an imminent and cruel civil war between white Europeans and non-white and especially Muslim immigrants (Faye, 2019). Major Islamist terrorist attacks, whether in Paris in 2015 or Brussels in 2016, reinforced for Identitarians Faye's dark, apocalyptic warning of a European civil war.

Faye was not the only Identitarian to warn of a "clash of civilizations," ceaseless ethnic conflicts, or a coming civil war. This civil war could in theory be avoided if white Europeans opted for a metapolitical revolution again multiculturalism, Islam, and globalism in Euro-American societies. Yet, this was unlikely because Euro-American elites were largely liberal and worked against the racial interests of their own – white Europeans. Pierre Vial (b. 1942), an academic medievalist, an *Nouvelle Droite* leader, and founder of the Identitarian association *Terre et Peuple* (Land and People), delivered a lecture in 2000, suggesting that the "ethnic coloniza-tion" of France was taking place and exacerbated because non-European immigrant communi-ties were of a different "biological" constitution (Shields, 2007). Following the *Nouvelle Droite*, Vial longed for a "true cultural revolution," which was "the ethnic revolution, the revolution of identity" (Shields, 2007, p. 148). This revolution based on identity would require that white Europeans show solidarity with each other; return to the land; and show pride in maintaining their ethnic and racial identities by getting rid of non-European Muslim immigrants from European lands.

The final key and important ideological driving force behind the IM is Renaud Camus, the architect of "The Great Replacement" theory that has become so notorious in recent radical right terrorist attacks and is central to the IM's worldview. It has influenced IM thinkers as diverse as Vardon, Willinger, and Spencer, but also the worldview of Christchurch terrorist Tarrant. Indeed, the French state cited Tarrant's alleged links. It argues that both national and global elites are working to harm the white population of Europe and to replace them with non-European peoples, especially non-whites and especially Muslims. As we saw earlier, this theme was also advanced by Guillaume Faye.

For Camus (2019), whites are being replaced by non-whites due to demographic trends (low white European birth rates and excessively high Muslim birth rates), criminality and no-go zones controlled by immigrants, Islamist terrorism, pro-immigration and pro-multiculturalism policies, and the denigration and deculturation of white European cultures. Contrary to the views of the liberal-left, this was no conspiracy theory for Camus, but a haunting reality for whites and a threat to their very existence. In order to further support "The Great Replacement" theory, Camus quotes former Algerian President Houari Boumédiène, who argued that one day millions of people would leave the Global South for the Global North in order to "conquer" it through high birth rates (2019, p.114). Camus (2019) calls these immigration and demographic trends "counter-colonization" or even "colonization" (p. 115). Following Brecht, he argues that the ultimate aim of this project is "to change the people"; "The Great Replacement"; "The Great Deculturation," and the total replacement of whites by non-whites (Camus, 2019, p. 116).

Key Contemporary IM Thinkers

At this point, the IM's key thinkers and ideas will be explored, including Fabrice Robert, Martin Sellner, Markus Willinger, and Richard B. Spencer, who have all headed IM movements in the past couple of decades. Those thinkers are united by a commitment to metapolitics and the desire for a peaceful revolution again liberal multiculturalism and globalism, the sacred character of the struggle of European whites, and the belief that violence and civil war are normal reactions to an "extremist," "globalist," and "multiculturalist" liberal system.

Fabrice Robert (b. 1971) is a French Identitarian who created BI, which later became *Les Identitaires* (Bouchet, 2001, pp. 243–275). A radical rightist with Holocaust negationist tendencies in his youth, Robert, later condemned the anti-Semitism and anti-Zionism of the radical right – a position in line with Faye's who sees it as a distraction from the defence of white European ethnic identities and the fact that Islam and Islamism rather than Jews are the primary "enemies" for Europeans (Faye, 2007). In 2014, under the BI banner, he campaigned for the re-migration of immigrants to their non-European countries of origin. In 2018, he took part in an anti-Islamization campaign with a pork meal in the heart of Goutte-d'Or, a neighbourhood with a large concentration of Muslims, but the police intervened and banned the gathering. Ultimately, Robert was convinced in a quasi-religious manner that action was needed to maintain the survival of white Europeans.

Moving to the German case, and law school dropout and former philosophy student in Vienna, Martin Sellner (b. 1989), is an Austrian Identitarian and leader of the *Identitäre Bewegung Österreichs* (IBÖ, IM of Austria). Like some other Identitarians, he has a past linked to neo-fascist or neo-Nazi activity. When he was 17, Sellner placed a swastika on a synagogue and was sentenced to 100 hours of community service in a Jewish cemetery. By 2016, Sellner stated that he had completely broken with neo-Nazism (Reuter, 2016). In April 2016, he disrupted a theatre performance of Elfriede Jelinek's *Die Schutzbefohlen* with 30 other activists because of the play's engagement with migrants seeking asylum. Like *Nouvelle Droite* thinkers, Sellner is indebted to the theories of the German philosophers Martin Heidegger and the Carl Schmitt.

He – as many other European and non-European sections of the IM – endorses "The Great Replacement" theory. As noted earlier, the Australian terrorist Brendon Tarrant communicated with Sellner and donated money to his organization before his terrorist attack in New Zealand but does not necessarily support his use of violence.

Recall that the French state banned GI. It is noted that it had supposed links to far-right groups and received donations from the Christchurch mosque shooter Brenton Tarrant. The IM's metapolitical framework tries to avoid the image of an Old Right wedded to the open utilization of terrorist violence. Similarly, Alt-Right thinker Spencer condemned the use of violence (i.e. the killing of a left-wing counter-protestor) in Charlottesville, Virginia, during the "United the Right" rally. Sellner's girlfriend is Brittany Pettibone, another Alt-Right activist, and they were both denied entry to the United Kingdom in 2017.

Finally, another important IM theoretician is Markus Willinger... "We don't want Mehmed and Mustapha to become Europeans" (Willinger, 2013, p. 38); he stated in order to show his disdain for Islam, Muslims, and non-Europeans on European soil. Like Sellner and Faye, he believes in "The Great Replacement," as well as longing for the end of multiculturalism and remigration in his writings. He is the author of two key Identitarian tracts: *Generation Identity – A Declaration of War Against the '68ers* (2013) and *A Europe of Nations* (2014). In the former work, Willinger (2013) notes that his generation faces a foreign invasion without bullets and faces "no resistance from its indigenous residents" (p. 14) (white Europeans); that (in a nod to ethnopluralism) foreigners can "hold on to their own identities, and let us have ours" (p. 38); that "European belongs to the Europeans alone" (p. 38); and that "is rising up to dethrone the '68ers" (p. 15). In the latter work, Willinger (2014) celebrates the Brexit decision; sees the EU as "the enemies of European peoples"; and favours a "Europe of our ancestors and children" and a "Europe of nations" rather than a liberal, imperial Europe backed by the US (pp. 8–9).

As noted earlier, the IM exists on both sides of the Atlantic. Born in Boston in 1978, Spencer is the president of the National Policy Institute, a white nationalist think tank. White nationalism, writes Alt-Right thinker Greg Johnson, is "a political philosophy that seeks to define national identity in racial rather than religious, cultural, or creedal terms" (2013, p. xiv). Spencer, the leading spokesman of the Alt-Right in the US, is self-described as an "Identitarian" (Hegeman & Ortiz, 2018), and his primary identity looks for inspiration in the history of white European societies. His role has been central in spreading the Alt-Right message to the broader American public through both mainstream and online media platforms. He has cultivated a respectable and intellectual image, as well as stressed that, even in the face of violence, the movement will stick to its message and metapolitical orientation.

He gave a breath of fresh air to the extremist elements of the radical right, which from the 1970s to the 1990s were dominated by neo-Nazi and Christian identity groups like the Aryan Nations, National Alliance, and World Church of the Creator. These groups were openly racist and anti-Semitic, imperialistic, genocidal, and even violent practitioners of terrorism (Stern, 2019, p. 26). Spencer gained greatest fame for the "Charlottesville Statement" (or "Alt-Right Manifesto") penned on 11 August 2017, as well as organizing the "Unite the Right" rally in Charlottesville, Virginia (11–12 August 2017). One of the key chants in the protest was "Jews Will Not Replace Us," thus echoing "The Great Replacement" theory. As pointed out earlier, not all Identitarian thinkers and supporters are anti-Semitic, but certainly Spencer is as highlighted by point 2 of his manifesto:

> Jews are an ethno-religious people distinct from Europeans. At various times, they have existed within European societies, without being of them. The preservation of their identity as Jews was and is contingent on resistance to assimilation, sometimes

expressed as hostility towards their hosts. "Judeo-Christian values" might be a quaint political slogan, but it is a distortion of the historical and metaphysical reality of both Jews and Europeans.

(Spencer, 11 August 2017)

Point 1 of the manifesto is just as revealing and highlights the Identitarian concern for maintaining and advancing the interests of the white race in its various permutations:

Race is real. Race matters. Race is the foundation of identity. White is shorthand for a world-wide constellation of peoples, each of which is derived from the Indo-European race, often called Aryan. "European" refers to a core stock – Celtic, Germanic, Hellenic, Latin, Nordic, and Slavic – from which related cultures and a shared civilization sprang.

(Spencer, 11 August 2017)

As the previous quote demonstrates, Spencer's primary commitment is to "save" white Europeans worldwide from the "madness" of liberal multiculturalism; this commitment to his peoples is quasi-religious and white European racial consciousness can be promoted through changing mentalities in civil society. Manifestos, websites, publishing houses, music, the press, and universities are all sites of contestation where white European racial identities can rise and flourish. Spencer has also been a champion of creating transnational links with people of white European ancestry, especially nationalists and ultra-nationalists, from Hungary and Russia to the United Kingdom and Canada and even South America.

Besides the "Alt-Right Manifesto," Spencer's major work is an edited volume entitled *The Uprooting of European Identity* (2016). The book's promotion jacket states the following and echoes both Faye and Camus: "The White man lives in a world his race once dominated and in which Black and Brown are now colonizers, in which European heritage is being taken away piece by piece: cultural heroes, literature, popular icons, identity ultimately, everything" (Spencer, 2016). In addition, the work sees whites as "victims" of multiculturalism and cultural dispossession, and insists that "non-whites are vengeful and intent on destroying white identity." Like Wilmot Robertson, the US author of *The Dispossessed Majority*, he lamented liberal multiculturalism, changing (Northern European) white demographics, and perceived anti-white racism in the West generally (Robertson, 1981).

A Summary of Key IM Ideas

Recall that it has been argued that the IM shares a number of dominant themes, including a commitment to "metapolitics with a punch," the hope for a peaceful revolution against liberal multiculturalism and globalism, the quasi-religious desire to save white Europeans from multiculturalism and even extinction, and the belief that a civil war will be a natural response to the complicity and failure of European elites in advancing a pro-globalist and pro-Islam agenda. While IM thinkers come from various countries on both sides of the Atlantic, they share numerous ideas that lead to an Identitarian consciousness and worldview:

(1) An anti-universalist and anti-globalist philosophy that rejects liberal and left-wing worldviews that seek to homogenize diverse peoples into a universal framework that is applicable to all peoples, cultures, or races.
(2) Ethnic, cultural, and racial identities are real; they matter in a globalized world where white identities are threatened, and those identities should be the primordial concerns of whites.

(3) The struggle to maintain white European cultures from extinction is a pan-European and even global struggle.

(4) White Europeans must maintain their identities and allow them to flourish at regional, national, European, and global levels.

(5) White Europeans are threatened with the spectre of cultural extinction due to low birth rates of whites and high birth rates of non-white Europeans (especially Muslims), anti-racism and pro-multiculturalism policies (which promote race-mixing and threaten whites) the "colonization" of European neighbourhoods by non-whites and Muslims, and Islam and Islamist terrorism (Islam is viewed as an imperialistic religion and a threat to Western civilization).

(6) Ethno-masochism and xenophilia, or the hatred of one's own ethnicity and the love of foreigners, exacerbate white cultural extinction.

(7) "The Great Replacement" of whites is taking place rapidly; it is a reality, and it is not a conspiracy theory.

(8) In order to end "The Great Replacement," the substitution of white Europeans by non-white, non-Europeans, Euro-American political elites must end pro-multiculturalism, pro-immigration, and pro-anti-racism policies that discriminate against white Europeans and lead to their extinction.

(9) Yet, even in the eyes of IM activists and ideologues, political elites on the liberal-left and even right-wing nationalists must go further in order to avoid "The Great Replacement." They must reconquer territories that are largely controlled by non-white immigrants, criminals, and terrorists. They must also promote a policy of remigration in which non-white immigrants and refugees leave Europe. They must advance a policy of national preference that favours white European ethnicities and people in government jobs, welfare benefits, and corporate support (Front National, 1993). In this respect, first the *Front National* (FN – National Front) and later its successor *Rassemblement National* (National Rally) both support national preference.

(10) If "The Great Replacement" is prevented, a civil war could be avoided, but this is not likely because white European masses and elites fail to see these aforementioned dangers.

(11) A valorization of white European identities will mean an attack on the liberal capitalist ideal and greater social solidarity amongst white Europeans.

(12) If the creation of a white European identity is increasingly necessary to guarantee white survival, then a pan-European army is needed to curtail US and Muslim power and challenge their desire to impose liberal, multicultural, or Islamist models worldwide.

(13) While the IM disagrees on the degree of "Jewish collusion" in "The Great Replacement," Faye and Jared Taylor accept that Jews can be whites and are allies in the struggle against multiculturalism and Islam. While Spencer sees Jews as enemies promoting multiculturalism and "The Great Replacement" (Taylor, 2011), they agree that whites should focus on reviving their own identities; fight liberal multiculturalism; and promote white ethnic solidarity at a time when many ethnic groups and cultures worldwide are defending themselves from homogenizing and globalizing forces.

(14) The route to success for the IM is not merely the metapolitical framework inherited from the ND, but a metapolitical approach that is combined with action, or "metapolitics with a punch" (i.e. the creation of movements, shock and guerrilla campaigns against immigration and refugees, advertisements of the rapes of white women by Muslim immigrants, or the "re-conquering" of white European territories in immigrant neighbourhood. That is, concrete political action in order to arrest "The Great Replacement" of whites.

(15) History matters. The ancient battles against Muslims, the achievements of Christian and Western civilizations, and the cultural memories of the ancestors all help to promote white European identity and pride.

(16) All white Europeans now face the decisive hour of choice: Submission to race-mixing and multiculturalism (i.e. the "true" racism) and "The Great Replacement," or strategies for survival, rebellion, and even war to maintain white European identities.

(17) In order to "make Europe great again," Identitarians call for more nationalists, more exits from the EU, and more world leaders like Putin and Orbán that put national interests above liberal multiculturalism or pro-corporate lobbies. Yet, above all a transnational white European identity must act to reverse the liberal notion that political allegiance must be based on shared political ideals, like the American and French Revolution. Instead, Identitarians insist that our primordial identities must be a common cultural, ethnic, or racial background.

(18) This struggle on behalf of people of white European ancestry is worldwide; is imbued with a sacred aura; and is linked to the fight of all peoples and nations against globalism and multiculturalism.

If we think of these aforementioned 18 points related to the IM, they might be better summarized in Table 20.1 that highlights the IM's "anti-'s" (what the IM is against), assessment of societal trends, fears, tactics and strategies, and policy solutions.

Let us break down the concepts in Table 20.1. In relation to these four checklists, of particular interest here is the notion of non-violent extremism and the IM's relationship to metapolitics and violence. The IM's long list of "anti-'s" connotes a vehement rejection of liberal society and its permutations, especially globalism and multiculturalism. For outsiders, this rejection of liberalism appears "extreme" or even "violent," but for the IM it is "common sense" to radically reject a society that seeks to purportedly destroy white European identities and all identities through the twin logics of capitalism and globalization.

If we examine the IM's assessment of societal trends, hatred of white European cultures and nations, the Great Replacement, and European civil war are existing realities in a multicultural, globalized, and homogenized world. These trends are pushed by the US superpower as the liberal society par excellence and Muslim countries because they engage in a supposed common front in order to destroy white European societies and their cultural and racial identities. Above all, the struggle for white European identities is seen as primal and "sacred" and hence the tactical sophistication (i.e. "metapolitics with a punch," guerrilla tactics, and rejection of the use of violence). If white European identities are "sacred," multiculturalism is viewed as traitorous to one's people, nation, and the white "race" worldwide. While violence should be avoided because one does not want to give liberals an opportunity to crush white racial and political solidarity, it is probably inevitable because multiculturalism, globalism, and the forces of Islam are in the ascendancy and "violently" challenge the very existence of whites.

A global brotherhood of white Europeans, perhaps creating white ethnostates as Identitarian Richard Spencer suggests, is a political necessity and a question of survival for the "white race." The IM's policy solutions will reverse the negative societal trends that favour globalists, multiculturalists, and Islam, as well as lead to a new post-liberal, post-multicultural epoch where white European cultures, nations, and ethnicities are once again "free" and "sovereign" peoples in their own lands.

Table 20.1 The key ideological concepts of the Identitarian movement

IM anti-'s
anti-universalist
anti-globalist
anti-liberalism
anti-multiculturalism
anti-capitalism
anti-Islam
anti-Islamism

IM's assessment of societal trends
The Great Replacement
ethnomasochism
xenophilia
loss of cultural and historical memories
disdain of patriotism and nationalism

IM's fears
The Great Replacement
cultural and racial extinction
end of nations and nationalism
"one-world civilization"
European civil war
Muslim political control
US hegemony

IM's tactics and strategies
sacralize struggle for white European identities
"metapolitics with a punch"
rejection of use of violence
guerrilla tactics/campaigns
violence inevitable in multicultural societies
white racial consciousness and political solidarity
global brotherhood of white Europeans

IM's policy solutions
abolish multiculturalism
abolish non-European immigration/refugees
re-conquer "lost territories
re-migration
nationalism and national preference
pull out of EU
pan-European army

Source: Author.

Conclusion

As noted earlier in this chapter, the IM is weeded to four key themes: "metapolitics with a punch," the hope for a peaceful revolution against liberal multiculturalism and globalism, the quasi-religious desire to "save" white Europeans from multiculturalism and even extinction, and the belief that a civil war will be a natural response to the complicity and failure of European elites in a pro-globalist and pro-Islam agenda. For Identitarians, there is a "spiritual basis of human identities" (Rose, 2021, p. 109) and thus the promotion of white European identities is viewed as "primeval" rather than partisan (i.e. based on "right" and "left" divisions).

If fascism was famously viewed as an ultra-nationalist and revolutionary "third way" beyond liberalism and socialism (Payne, 1980; Sternhell, 1983; Gentile, 2005; Eatwell, 2006), the IM is a "fourth way"; it neither belongs to the Old Right ghettos of fascism and terrorist violence nor does it have a home in the radical-right political parties. Breaking from the Old Right penchant for violence, the narrow intellectual metapolitical universe of the *Nouvelle Droite*, and the desire for immediate parliamentary power, the IM forges – and continues to forge – a "fourth way" for Europe's radical right. In short, the IM is a youthful, invigorating, and energizing activist force that links former Old Rightists, parliamentary forces, and the ND's metapolitical innovation in new wineskins. Three scholars noted that the IM straddles the French National Front (*Front National* – FN – now *Rassemblement National* – RN), the *Nouvelle Droite*, and the Old Right universe of neo-Nazism (Hentges et al., 2014). Yet, it appears that most IM thinkers have jettisoned any links to Nazism (or neo-Nazism) or fascism (or neo-fascism). Their concerns are not those of the inter-war years. Rather their concerns are contemporary and related to immigration, multiculturalism, anti-racism education, a perceived decaying and disappearing white European identity, and rejection of globalism and Islam.

The IM has a number of disagreements, especially about the Jewish question, or the role of Aleksandr Dugin's Traditionalist Eurasian philosophy (which longs for an alliance between all Traditionalist forces worldwide against Western liberalism, including Muslims). Recall that the IM is anti-Islam and anti-Islamism. Yet, the IM has charted a metapolitical path that is mixed with youthful activism. It remains an open question how it will transform European identities wedded to liberal multiculturalism and the EU. There is no easy path to create white European ethnic solidarity across national borders, arrest immigration, multiculturalism, the Great Replacement, and implement IM proposals such as remigration. The IM's positions are revolutionary for the liberal-left and establishment right, but they show that ethnocentrism and ethnic resentment are "not exclusive to the non-Western world" (Zúquete, 2018, p. 365). Moreover, they demonstrate that for some white European identity is a "sacred" cause that – in their eyes – must never be abandoned.

In order for the IM to grow and gain success it will have to achieve more policy victories: more Brexits, the rise of nationalist movements, and European public opinion that increasingly turns away from multiculturalism. While the IM has crafted transnational links and movements throughout Euro-American societies and beyond, its proposals might be far too revolutionary for the majority of white Europeans. Unlike the *Nouvelle Droite*, the IM will not simply wait for long-term changes of mentalities to take place amongst white Europeans. It will continue to shock with spectacular and theatrical gestures, which it hopes will awaken a new generation of white Europeans to save its people from a supposed and silent "genocide." Violence is rejected by the IM in favour of a long-term conquest of mentalities in civil society. Yet, IM thinkers from Faye to Camus always hint at the possibility of violence in European societies and often put the blame squarely on the backs of Europe elites, which are viewed as "traitors" to the "sacred" cause of maintaining and promoting white European identities. Zuqueté's notion of "metapolitics with a punch" is seen as an alternative to that use of violence – guerrilla tactics, shocking advertisement campaigns, and the shaming of political, legal, military (and police) authorities that promote a proimmigration, multiculturalist, or pro-globalist agenda. Yet, established authorities on the centre, centre-right, and liberal-left have often tried to promote the idea that the IM is violent, racist, and even fascist.

Note

1 National Socialists are indebted to the ideals of the German National Social movement and the Nazi regime from 1933-1945. White nationalism is a more recent term and connotes a philosophy wedded to thinkers such as Richard B. Spencer, Greg Johnson, and Jared Taylor, whom define themselves as whites or peoples of white European descent. For white nationalists, whites worldwide from the Americas and Europe and beyond must unite to defeat multiculturalism and globalization – twin menaces for the survival of the white race. Some white nationalists long for the creation of white ethno-states as an antidote to liberal multiculturalism. White nationalists are not white supremacists because they believe that all peoples are entitled to a homeland and they are against imperialism and colonialism. See, for example, Geary et al. (2020).

Bibliography

Adamson, W. L. (2014). *Hegemony and Revolution: Antonio Gramsci's Political and Cultural Theory*. Brattleboro, VT: Echo Point Books and Media.

Bale, J. M. (2018). *The Darkest Sides of Politics, I Postwar Fascism, Covert Operations, and Terrorism*. New York: Routledge.

Bar-On, T. (2001). The Ambiguities of the Nouvelle Droite, 1968-1999. *The European Legacy, 6*(3), 333–351. http://dx.doi.org/10.1080/10848770120051349

Bar-On, T. (2007). *Where Have All the Fascists Gone?* Aldershot: Ashgate.

Bar-On, T. (2013). *Rethinking the French New Right: Alternatives to Modernity*. New York: Routledge.

Bar-On, T. (2014). The French New Right: Neither Right, Nor Left? *Journal for the Study of Radicalism, 8*(1), 1–44. DOI: 10.14321/jstudradi.8.1.0001

Bar-On, T. (2021). The Alt-Right's Continuation of the 'Cultural War' in Euro-American Societies. *Thesis Eleven, 163*(1), 43–70. https://doi.org/10.1177/07255136211005988

Bouchet, C. (2001). *Les Nouveaux Nationalistes* [*The New Nationalists*]. Paris: Déterna

Brzezinski, Z. (2008). *Second Chance: Three Presidents and the Crisis of American Superpower*. New York: Basic Books.

Camus, J. Y. (2018). Le mouvement identitaire ou la construction d'un mythe des origines européennes. *Fondation Jean-Jaurès*. Retrieved from www.jean-jaures.org/publication/le-mouvement-identitaire-ou-la-construction-dun-mythe-des-origines-europeennes/

Camus, R. (2019). *Le Grand Remplacement* (5th ed.). Plieux: Chez l'auteur.

Copsey, N. (2013). *Au Revoir* to "Sacred Cows"? Assessing the Impact of the *Nouvelle Droite* in Britain. *Democracy and Security, 9*(3), 287–303, DOI: 10.1080/17419166.2013.792249

Croucher, S. (2019, July 11). Identitarian Movement, Linked to Christchurch Mosque Shooter, Classified as Extremist Right-Wing Group by German Intelligence Agency. *Newsweek*. Retrieved from www.newsweek.com/identitarian-movement-extremist-far-right-germany-1448710

Darby, L. (2019, August 5). How the 'Great Replacement' conspiracy theory has inspired white supremacist killers. *The Telegraph*. Retrieved from www.telegraph.co.uk/news/2019/08/05/analysis-great-replacement-conspiracy-theory-has-inspired-white/

De Benoist, A. (n.d). *Manifesto of the French New Right in the Year 2000*. Retrieved from www.4pt.su/en/content/manifesto-french-new-right

De Benoist, A. (1979). *Vu de droite: anthologie critique des idées contemporaines* [*Seen from the Right: Critical Anthology of Contemporary Ideas*]. Paris: Copernic.

Doyle, M. W. (1983a). Kant, Liberal Legacies, and Foreign Affairs. *Philosophy & Public Affairs, 12* (3), 205–235. Retrieved from www.jstor.org/stable/2265298

Doyle, M. W. (1983b). Kant, Liberal Legacies, and Foreign Affairs, Part 2. *Philosophy & Public Affairs, 12*(4), 323–353. Retrieved from www.jstor.org/stable/2265377

Doyle, M. W. (1986). Liberalism and World Politics. *The American Political Science Review, 80*(4), 1151–1169. https://doi.org/10.2307/1960861

Duranton-Crabol, A.M. (1988). *Visages de la Nouvelle droite: le GRECE et son histoire* [*Faces of the New Right: GRECE and Its History*]. Paris: Presses de Sciences Po.

Eatwell, R. (2006, June). Introduction: New Styles of Dictatorship and Leadership in Interwar Europe. *Totalitarian Movements and Political Religions, 7*(2), 127–137. https://doi.org/10.1080/14690760600642149

Faye, G. (2007). *La Nouvelle Question juive* [*The New Jewish Question*]. Paris: Broché.

Faye, G. (2011). *Why We Fight: European Visions of the Post-Catastrophic Age*. London: Arktos Media.

Faye, G. (2016). *The Colonisation of Europe (trans. Roger Adwan)*. London: Arktos Media Ltd.

Faye, G. (2019). *Ethnic Apocalypse: The Coming European Civil War* [Ebook Arktos Media].

France bans far-right group Generation Identity. (2021, March 3). *Deutsche Welle*. Retrieved from www.dw.com/en/france-bans-far-right-group-generation-identity/a-56760300

François, S. (2019). Guillaume Faye and Archeofuturism. In M. Sedgwick (Ed.), *Key Thinkers of the Radical Right: Behind the New Threat to Liberal Democracy* (pp. 91–101). New York: Oxford University Press.

Front National. (1993). *300 mesures pour la renaissance de la France* [*300 Measures for the Rebirth of France*]. Paris: Broché.

Geary, D., Schofield, C., & Sutton, J. (Eds.) (2020). *Global White Nationalism: From Apartheid to Trump*. Manchester: Manchester University Press.

Génération Identitaire. (n.d). *Pillars of our political work*. Retrieved March 24, 2020, from www.generation-identity.co/

Gentile, E. (2005). *The Origins of Fascist Ideology 1918–1925*. New York: Enigma Books.

Germany: Identitarian movement classified as right-wing extremist. (2019, July 11). *Deutsche Welle*. Retrieved from www.dw.com/en/germany-identitarian-movement-classified-as-right-wing-extremist/a-49550414

Gramsci, A. (1982). *Selections from the Prison Books*. New York: Lawrence and Wishart.

GRECE. (1998). *Le Mai 1968 de la nouvelle droite* [*May 68 of the New Right*]. Paris: GRECE, 1998).

Griffin R (Ed.). (1994). *Fascism*. Oxford: Oxford University Press.

Hegeman, S. & Ortiz, P. (2018). Nazis on Campus: A Union and Community Responds. *Thought & Action, 34*(1), 7–22. www.nea.org/assets/docs/2018_TA_Hegeman.pdf

Hentges, G., Kökgiran, G., & Nottbohm, K. (2014). Die Identitäre Bewegung Deutschland (IBD) – Bewegung oder virtuelles Phänomen? [The Identitarian Movement Germany (IBD) – Movement or Virtual Phenomenon?]. *Forschungsjournal Soziale Bewegungen – PLUS*, Heft 3 (2014), 1–26. http://ibwatchout.blogsport.de/images/IBD1.pdf

Hope Not Hate. (n.d). France – Hope Not Hate. Retrieved March 24, 2020, from www.hopenothate.org.uk/research/islamophobia-hub/profiles/wider-scene/france/

Johnson, G. (2013). *New Right vs. Old Right & Other Essays*. San Francisco, CA: Counter-Currents Publishing.

Khan, M. (2015, January 13). Germany: Anti-Islam Pegida protest rally draws record 25,000 in Dresden. *International Business Times*. Retrieved from www.ibtimes.co.uk/germany-anti-islam-pegida-protest-rally-draws-record-25000-dresden-1483097

Les Identitaires. (n.d.a). *En mots* [*In words*]. Retrieved March 24, 2020, from www.les-identitaires.com/les-identitaires-lexique-mots-politique/

Les Identitaires. (n.d.b). *Laboratoire d'idées pour la défense de notre civilisation* [*Laboratory of ideas for the defense of our civilization*]. Retrieved March 24, 2020, from www.les-identitaires.com/

Les Identitaires. (2017). *30 mesures pour une politique d'identité et de remigration* [*30 Measures for an Identity and Remigration Policy*]. Nice: IDées.

Mamère, N. (2017, January 25). Dominique Venner, martyr d'un contre-mai 68 [Dominique Venner, martyr of a counter-May 68]. *Nouvelles de France*. Retrieved from www.ndf.fr/poing-de-vue/21-05-2013/exclusif-les-raisons-dune-mort-volontaire-par-dominique-venner/?fb_source=pubv1

McCulloch, T. (2006). The Nouvelle Droite in the 1980s and 1990s: Ideology and Entryism, the Relationship with the Front National. *French Politics, 4*(2), 158–178. https://doi.org/10.1057/palgrave.fp.8200099

Metapedia. (2020). *Identitarianism*. Retrieved March 24, 2020, from https://en.metapedia.org/wiki/Identitarianism

Miller-Idriss, C. (2017). *The Extreme Gone Mainstream: Commercialization and Far Right Youth Culture in Germany*. Princeton, NJ: Princeton University Press.

Mohler, A. (1994). German Nihilism. In R. Griffin (Ed.), *Fascism* (pp. 351–354). Oxford: Oxford University Press.

Mudde, C. (2019). *The Far Right Today*. Cambridge: Polity.

Müller, M. (2017). *Kontra Kultur* [Counterculture]. Schnellroda: Antaios.

Payne, S.G. (1980). *Fascism: Comparison and Definition*. Madison, WI: The University of Wisconsin Press.

Pegida meets with European allies in the Czech Republic. (2016, January 23). *Deutsche Welle*. Retrieved from www.dw.com/en/pegida-meets-with-european-allies-in-the-czech-republic/a-19000895

Raw, L. (2019, June 4). Generation identity and the global threat of right wing extremism. *Byline Times*. Retrieved from https://bylinetimes.com/2019/06/04/generation-identity-and-the-global-threat-of-right-wing-extremism/

Reuter, B. (2016, May 20). 'Right-wing hipsters' increasingly powerful in Austria. *Huffington Post*. Retrieved from https://libguides.library.usyd.edu.au/c.php?g=508212&p=3476096

Richards, I. (2019, September). A Philosophical and Historical Analysis of 'Generation Identity': Fascism, Online Media, and the European New Right. *Terrorism and Political Violence*, 1–20. https://doi.org/10.1080/09546553.2019.1662403

Robert, F. (2014, October). Victoires patriotiques, victoires identitaires: Envisager l'avenir [Patriotic Victories, Identity Victories: Looking to the Future]. *Identitaires*, No. 20, 7.

Robertson, W. (1981). *The Dispossessed Majority* (4th ed.). London: Howard Allen Inc. Publications.

Rodat, S. (2017). Cultural Racism: A Conceptual Framework. *Revue des Sciences Politiques*, *54*(2017), 129–140. https://link.gale.com/apps/doc/A494585403/AONE?u=anon~e6a0a866&sid=googleScholar&xid=6ae7477b

Rose, M. (2021). *A World After Liberalism: Philosophers of the Radical Right*. New Haven, CT: Yale University Press.

Rousset, J. (2017, February 23). Mouvance identitaire et Front National: la porosité est réelle [Identitarian Movement and the National Front: The porosity is real]. *Sud Ouest*. Retrieved from www.sudouest.fr/politique/mouvance-identitaire-et-front-national-la-porosite-est-reelle-3406952.php

Schwochert, C. (2020). *Angeklagt: Die Identitäre Bewegung* [*Accused: The Identitarian Movement*]. Riesa: Nation & Wissen.

Sellner, M. (2019). *Identität: Geschichte eines Aufbruchs* [*Identity: History of a New Departure*]. Schnellroda: Antaios.

Shields, J. G. (2007). *The Extreme Right in France: From Pétain to Le Pen*. London: Routledge.

Southern, L. (2017). *The Great Replacement* [Video]. Retrieved from www.youtube.com/watch?v=OTDmsmN43NA

Southern Poverty Law Center. (2015). *American racists work to spread 'identitarian' ideology*. Retrieved March 24, 2020, from www.splcenter.org/hatewatch/2015/10/12/american-racists-work-spread-'identitarian'-ideology

Speit, A (Ed.). (2018). *Das Netwerk der Identitären: Ideologie und Aktionen der Neuen Rechten* [*The Network of the Identitarians: Ideology and Actions of the New Right*]. Berlin: Ch. Links.

Spektorowski, A. (2003). The New Right: Ethno-Regionalism, Ethnopluralism and the Emergence of a Neo-fascist 'Third Way'. *Journal of Political Ideologies*, *8*(1), 111–130. https://doi.org/10.1080/13569310306084

Spektorowski, A. (2012). The French New Right: Multiculturalism of the Right and the Recognition/Exclusionism Syndrome. *Journal of Global Ethics*, *8*(1), 41–61. https://doi.org/10.1080/17449626.2011.635688

Spencer, R. B. (2016). *The Uprooting of European Identity*. Arlington, VA: Washington Summit Publishers.

Spencer, R. B. (2017, August 11). What it means to be Alt-Right. *Alt.Right.com* (The manifesto is no longer online and a scanned PDF version was last accessed on April 24, 2021).

Stern, A. M. (2019). *Proud Boys and the White Ethnostate: How the Alt-Right Is Warping the American Imagination*. Boston: Beacon Press.

Sternhell, Z. (1983). *Ni droite ni gauche: L'idéologie fasciste en France* [*Neither Right Nor Left: Fascist Ideology in France*]. Paris: Editions du Seuil.

Sternhell, Z., Sznajder, M., & Asheri, M. (1995). *The Birth of Fascist Ideology: From Cultural Rebellion to Political Revolution*. Princeton, NJ: Princeton University Press.

Taylor, J. (2011). *White Identity: Racial Consciousness in the 21st Century*. Oakton, VA: New Century Foundation.

Teitelbaum, B. R. (2017). *Lions of the North: Sounds of the New Nordic Radical Nationalism*. New York: Oxford University.

Teitelbaum, B. R. (2020). *War for Eternity: Inside Bannon's Far-Right Circle of Global Power Brokers*. New York: HarperCollins Publishers.

Telos Press. (1993). Origins and Metamorphoses of the New Right an Interview with Pierre-André Taguieff. *Telos*, *1993*(98–99), 159–172. doi: 10.3817/0393099159

Thorleifsson, C. (2018, February 1). Lions of the north: Sounds of the new nordic radical nationalism by Benjamin R. Teitelbaum. *EuropeNow*. Retrieved from www.europenowjournal.org/2018/01/31/lions-of-the-north-sounds-of-the-new-nordic-radical-nationalism-by-benjamin-r-teitelbaum/

Un homme se suicide dans la cathédrale Notre-Dame de Paris [A man commits suicide in Notre-Dame cathedral in Paris]. (2013, May 21). *France Info.* Retrieved from www.francetvinfo.fr/faits-divers/un-homme-se-suicide-dans-la-cathedrale-notre-dame-de-paris_1655545.html

Vardon, P. (2011). *Eléments pour une contre-culture identitaire* [*Elements for an Indentity Counter-Culture*]. Nice: IDées – SDIN.

Vardon, P. (2012, December). Direction: Reconquete! *Identitaires*, No. 12, 7.

Venner, D. (2013, May 21). La manif du 26 mai et Heidegger [The May 26 strike and Heidegger]. *Dominique Venner.* Retrieved from www.dominiquevenner.fr/2013/05/la-manif-du-26-mai-et-heidegger/

Weiß, V. (2013, March 21). Nicht links, nicht rechts – nur national [Not left, not right – only national]. *Die Zeit.* Retrieved from www.zeit.de/2013/13/Die-Identitaeren?utm_referrer=https%3A%2F%2Fwww.google.com%2F

Willinger, M. (2013). *Generation Identity – A Declaration of War Against the '68ers.* London: Arktos Media.

Willinger, M. (2014). *A Europe of Nations.* London: Arktos Media.

Willsher, K. (2021, March 3). France bans far-right 'paramilitary' group Génération Identitaire. *The Guardian.* Retrieved from www.theguardian.com/world/2021/mar/03/france-bans-far-right-param ilitary-group-generation-identitaire

Wilson, J. (2019, May 16). Christchurch shooter's links to Austrian far right 'more extensive than thought'. *The Guardian.* Retrieved from www.theguardian.com/world/2019/may/16/christchurch-shooters-links-to-austrian-far-right-more-extensive-than-thought

Wilson, J. (2020, August 9). Lauren Southern is on the comeback trail, and Australian conservatives are all too happy to help. *The Guardian.* Retrieved from www.theguardian.com/commentisfree/2020/aug/10/lauren-southern-is-on-the-comeback-trail-and-australian-conservatives-are-all-too-happy-to-help

Zúquete, J. P. (2018). *The Identitarians: The Movement Against Globalism and Islam in Europe.* Notre Dame, IN: University of Notre Dame Press.

21

FAR-RIGHT PEGIDA

Non-violent Protest and the Blurred Lines Between the Radical and Extreme Right

Sabine Volk and Manès Weisskircher

Introduction

Extremist actors on the right end of the political spectrum are often associated with physical violence such as riots or hate crimes (Koopmans & Olzak, 2004; Ravndal, 2018; Witte & Bjørgo, 1993) and a rejection of democracy (Mudde, 2007; see also Carter, 2018). This contribution, however, focuses on the seeming paradox of a far-right actor that not only refrains from using violent forms of action, but actively promotes the ideal of non-violence, while claiming support for democracy. It draws on the Dresden-based organization PEGIDA (*Patriotische Europäer gegen die Islamisierung des Abendlandes*; Patriotic Europeans against the Islamization of the Occident), one of the largest and most durable instances of far-right street mobilization in recent European politics. Leading activists portray PEGIDA as "peaceful protest", not only pursuing non-violent forms of action, but even propagating an ideal of "non-violent resistance" (Volk, 2022c). At demonstrations, speakers usually express their support for the idea of democracy, even calling for the need to defend democracy. Scholarship long regarded PEGIDA as an example of the European "populist radical right" (Druxes & Simpson, 2016; Volk, 2020b; Vorländer, Herold, & Schäller, 2018). Germany's intelligence services have recently come to a different conclusion: in March 2020, the Federal Office for the Protection of the Constitution referred to Lutz Bachmann, PEGIDA's leading activist and public face, as a "right-wing extremist" (Bundesamt für Verfassungsschutz, 2020). In May 2021, the Saxon branch of Germany's intelligence service classified PEGIDA as a whole as an "extremist" and "anti-constitutional movement" due to its increasing radicalization over time (Landesamt für Verfassungsschutz, 2021). PEGIDA therefore offers a critical case (Snow, 2004) to discuss the blurred lines between the radical and the extreme right in 21st century far-right politics (Pirro, 2022) which underlines the need to refine these categories.

This contribution focuses on two key dimensions to explore the tensions between radicalism and extremism in the case of PEGIDA, namely its forms of action as well as its ideology. In line with the distinction between the "extremism of method" and the "extremism of thought" (Richards, 2015, p. 371), radicalism and extremism may refer to both forms of action chosen by activists and their underlying ideology and ideas. Scholars focusing on methods define radical actors as those refraining from using physical violence, while extremist actors "tend – circumstances permitting – to engage in aggressive militancy, including criminal acts and mass

DOI: 10.4324/9781003032793-25

violence in their fanatical will for gaining and holding political power" (Bötticher, 2017, p. 74 emphasis in original). Crucially, extremist actors might temporarily refrain from using phys- ical violence for pragmatic rather than ideological reasons, and thus be characterized as not- (yet-)violent (Schmid, 2014). More frequently, political science scholars focusing on far-right ideology distinguish between radicalism and extremism based on attitudes toward democracy (Mudde, 2007; see also Carter, 2018): "Populist radical right" forces, usually characterized by the thick ideology of xenophobic nationalism ("nativism") and authoritarianism as well as the thin ideology of "populism", may question minority rights as well as liberal checks and balances, but they approve of (unrestricted) majority rule. Extremist forces, on the other hand, reject the idea of majority rule per se.[1]

In this chapter, we argue that we need to refine these distinctions in a political context where non-violent forms of action and the support for the idea of democracy have become dominant features across the political spectrum. We maintain that two other features mark contemporary extreme-right politics in Germany: the dehumanization of immigrants and political opponents, including representatives of the political establishment, leftist counter demonstrators, and the mainstream media, as well as the delegitimization of institutions and actors of real-existing democracy as "dictatorial" or "totalitarian". Our analysis of PEGIDA underlines the import- ance of these two extremist ideological elements. Such a perspective acknowledges research that has underlined the complex relationship of the concept of "extremism" with attitudes toward violence and especially, democracy and constitutionality (Backes, 2009, pp. 175–192). It also adds to recent debates in German politics: During the COVID-19 pandemic, targeting parts of the so-called anti-Corona protestors, the Federal Office for the Protection of the Constitution introduced the, less specific, concept of the "delegitimization of the state releant for the protec- tion of the constitution" (Bundesamt für Verfassungsschutz, n.d.). Our contribution draws from previously published and ongoing empirical research, including both conventional and virtual ethnographic fieldwork, as well as a comprehensive review of the numerous existing studies on PEGIDA, both in German and English.

In the following, we first discuss some of the key facts about and explanations of PEGIDA's rise and persistence. Second, we examine PEGIDA's non-violent forms of action and high- light the ideal of non-violence in its ideology, sustained by references to the so-called Peaceful Revolution toward the end of the German Democratic Republic (GDR) in 1989/1990. Third, we emphasize that despite PEGIDA's claim of support for democracy, activists dehumanize pol- itical opponents and delegitimize real-existing democracy, pointing to the extremist features of its ideology.

The "Patriotic Europeans": PEGIDA's Emergence and Persistence

PEGIDA emerged in Dresden, the capital of the eastern German federal state of Saxony. Initially established as a Facebook group, the "Patriotic Europeans" mobilized a few hundred participants during their first protests in October 2014, a year before the peak of the so- called refugee crisis[2] in Germany (Vorländer et al., 2018). Only a few weeks later, the social movement organization managed to attract large-scale support: in the winter of 2014/2015, PEGIDA mobilized about 20,000 followers on several occasions. These massive numbers created a media hype in Germany and beyond, rapidly making PEGIDA more than just an issue of local or regional politics. While the organization's popularity declined over the course of the first half of 2015, it experienced a revival during the intensification of the "refugee crisis" in the second half of the year. Even though PEGIDA was unable to hold the momentum, it has now persisted for eight years (Volk, 2022a). After 2015, PEGIDA has consistently mobilized support, even though sometimes only as a "small-scale" phenomenon typical for many extra-parliamentary far-right groups in Europe (Caiani, della Porta, & Wagemann, 2012, p. 212). For special occasions such as protest anniversaries, however, it has still managed to attract a few thousand followers.

PEGIDA is part of the broader contemporary far-right social movement in Europe, with the opposition to (especially Muslim) immigration as its main goal (Berntzen, 2019; Castelli Gattinara & Pirro, 2019). PEGIDA strongly criticizes political, cultural, and media elites and is at least partially in favour of handing over more political power to "the people" (i.e. direct democracy). In this context, PEGIDA forms also part of a large far-right network in Germany, marked by increasing activism in the country's protest arena (Hutter and Weisskircher, 2022). Most importantly, the rise of PEGIDA went along with the electoral breakthrough and radic-alization of AfD, the first-ever established far-right party in the German *Bundestag* (Arzheimer, 2015, 2019).

PEGIDA's main form of action is a standardized street demonstration which the group organizes in a weekly to fortnightly rhythm in the center of Dresden. Protest events take around two hours and typically include speeches by PEGIDA leaders and guests, followed by a march ("evening walk") in the city center until participants gather again to sing the German national anthem. The group even continued to mobilize for online and offline protest events during the lockdown in the context of the COVID-19 pandemic when street demonstrations were for-bidden or highly restricted (Volk, 2021). PEGIDA does not engage in other direct-action forms of protest such as violent riots, vigilantism, or occupations.

While the organizers have been notoriously unwilling to talk to mainstream media or scientists, four different scientific teams conducted protest surveys soon after PEGIDA emerged (Geiges, Marg, & Walter, 2015; Patzelt & Klose, 2016; Rucht et al., 2015; Vorländer, Herold, & Schäller, 2016b). Common findings were that (1) expectedly, much more men than women joined the protests; (2) unexpectedly for some, that their level of income was average, and not below-average; (3) unexpectedly for some, their level of formal education was slightly higher than the German average, and (4) expectedly, almost all of them showed support for the new far-right party AfD (*Alternative für Deutschland*, Alternative for Germany), back then not in the German national parliament yet. All surveys however suffered from the problem of low response rates, which may have biased the sample: The more "moderate" followers were more likely to respond to the survey (for a detailed discussion see Reuband, 2015; Teune & Ullrich, 2015). While some participants were members of far-right organizations such as fraternities or the Identitarian movement (also known as Generation Identity, *Identitäre Bewegung*), many demonstrators appeared to be non-organized.

Since the emergence of PEGIDA, the group's ties to AfD have been important, but not always friendly. Instead, a combination of support, competition, and rejection marked their relationship (Weisskircher & Berntzen, 2019). Both PEGIDA and parts of AfD have imagined PEGIDA to be the street version and AfD to be the parliamentary arm of Germany's far right (Weisskircher et al. 2022). Thus, PEGIDA leaders have cooperated with local and regional AfD politicians, while a few key AfD figures have attended and spoken at PEGIDA events. The recent radicalization of AfD has increased the forms of open cooperation. In 2018, their *rapprochement* culminated in the joint organization of a so-called march of grief in the eastern German city of Chemnitz, following a murder involving two Middle Eastern asylum seekers. Similarly, Björn Höcke, one of the leading figures of the far-right wing of the party, spoke at an anniversary event in February 2020, and returned to Dresden in September 2021. PEGIDA leader Lutz Bachmann even announced in 2020 that he had filed an application for AfD mem-bership, even though it is difficult to assess whether this statement should be taken at face value.

Beyond the leadership, some PEGIDA followers regularly carry AfD flags – or even chant the party's name.

Despite intense efforts to copy PEGIDA protests in other German cities, often pushed by established far-right actors, many spin-offs remained unsuccessful. Even the few relatively large mobilization attempts outside of Dresden eventually remained marginal, such as LEGIDA in the eastern German city of Leipzig, or PEGIDA Munich, involving the well-connected local far-right activist Michael Stürzenberger. While PEGIDA initially had only weak ties to the organized far-right scene, Dresden-based PEGIDA has successfully networked with other far-right grassroots initiatives from across Germany, notably the protest groups Future Homeland (*Zukunft Heimat*) from the eastern German region of Brandenburg, as well as New Right initiatives such as the far-right think tank Institute for State Politics (*Institut für Staatspolitik*), the initiative One Percent (*Ein Prozent*), and the German branch of the Identitarian movement.

Finally, PEGIDA's mobilization beyond Germany was also moderately successful. Despite serious attempts to use the PEGIDA label in countries such as Austria, Norway, Sweden, Switzerland, or the United Kingdom, activists in these countries largely failed to gather large-scale support (Berntzen & Weisskircher, 2016; Dafnos & Allchorn, 2021). Moreover, and in line with efforts by other contemporary far-right groups, PEGIDA tried to construct a pan-European far-right movement (Nissen, 2020; Volk, 2019). However, its "Fortress Europe" alliance of far-right organizations, mostly from Central and Eastern Europe, was only short-lived. Nevertheless, PEGIDA has made itself a name in the far-right scene way beyond Dresden and even Germany. International politicians and prominent activists such as Geert Wilders (Party for Freedom, Netherlands), Martin Sellner (Identitarian movement, Austria), Tommy Robinson (PEGIDA UK and formerly English Defence League, United Kingdom), Filip Dewinter (Vlaams Belang, Belgium), and Heinz-Christian Strache (formerly Freedom Party of Austria, Austria) have been guests at PEGIDA events. Likewise, PEGIDA activists have traveled to take part in far-right marches outside of Germany, for instance the Polish Independence Day march in Warsaw in 2018.

Reasons for why PEGIDA emerged and only persisted in Dresden relate both to agency and structure. The original team of organizers around public face Lutz Bachmann were 12 individuals without ties to the established far-right scene, but with specific organizational skills and links to the local sports and party scene that allowed them to initiate and sustain the protests (Vorländer et al., 2018, pp. 7–8). For instance, while Bachmann had not been active in politics prior to PEGIDA, he had contributed to Dresden's public life as a volunteer in the course of a destructive flood in 2013 (Vorländer et al., 2018, p. 3). Beyond agency, the former territory of the GDR has already been a stronghold of Germany's far right since the 1990s (Weisskircher, 2020). Within the eastern German context, the city of Dresden and the region of Saxony are well-known for their conservative political culture (Dostal, 2015) and strong local and regional patriotism (Vorländer, 2016) as well as, similar to eastern Germany in general, a strong far-right scene (Backes & Kailitz, 2020). Moreover, local and regional politics have been shaped by the transition from real-existing socialism to capitalism in the 1990s and the persistent subjective and objective inequalities between the east and the west of Germany (Mau, 2019; Ther, 2019; Weisskircher, 2020).

PEGIDA as "Non-violent Resistance": Memories of the "Peaceful Revolution"

Physical violence by the far right, mainly against immigrants, has been a regular occurrence in German politics (König & Jäckle, 2017, 2018). It is again the eastern states where far-right violence is more prevalent than in the rest of the country (Backes, 2020). The critical event of the 2015/2016 New Year's Eve sexual assaults by Arab and North-African immigrants in the western German city of Cologne led to a surge of far-right violence across Germany, especially in little populated areas and in the east (Frey, 2020). PEGIDA, however, seems to qualify as a non-violent social movement organization both in terms of methods and ideology: Generally, the groups' forms of action do not include physical violence. Moreover, the ideal of non-violence is a key element of PEGIDA's discourse, also manifested in frequent historical references to the East German "Peaceful Revolution" of 1989/1990 (Volk, 2022b; Weisskircher, 2022).

Based on our ethnographic observations, PEGIDA's key form of protest, the street demonstration, has an orderly, calm, and overall non-violent character. In Dresden, violent confrontations with counter demonstrators and journalists have only rarely been recorded. Similarly, there is little evidence of physical violence against asylum seekers, immigrants, or people of color in the immediate context of protest events in Dresden. The overall orderliness of the events conveys a feeling of personal physical safety amongst the crowd – at least for participant observers who appear to be ethnic central or northern Europeans, do not interact much with the other participants, or challenge what is being said on stage. Nevertheless, it is crucial to highlight that protest events served as a meeting and networking point for violent individuals and groups such as the Group Freital (*Gruppe Freital*), which was responsible for a series of attacks against asylum seekers homes in the region (Schneider, 2020). Yet, these acts of violent extremism took place outside of PEGIDA's organizational and symbolic structures.

Ideologically, PEGIDA even highlights the ideal of non-violence. The notion of peacefulness counts among the core features of PEGIDA's discourse since the beginning of its street mobilization. Importantly, the group's founding myth builds on the rejection of religious and ethnic violence. At the outset of their activism in 2014, PEGIDA activists portrayed the foundation of the group as a response to cases of violent conflict between supporters of the Kurdish Workers' Party (PKK) and Islamists in Germany in the fall of 2014 (Vorländer et al. 2016, p. 5). Accordingly, the group's official slogan, "Non-violent ('*gewaltfrei*') and united against religious wars on German soil", underlines its peaceful self-understanding. In a similar vein, the logo attempts to carry a non-violent message. It is a pictogram that shows a human figure throwing the symbols of (allegedly) violent organizations and ideologies into a trash can, including the logos of the so-called Islamic State (IS), the PKK, and the Antifa, as well as the swastika. Similarly, PEGIDA organizers typically emphasize that the organization is a "civilian" or "civic" movement (*Bürgerbewegung*) at the "center of society" (*Mitte der Gesellschaft*).

Regular references to the memory of the East German "Peaceful Revolution" sustain PEGIDA's discursive frame of peacefulness and non-violence (Volk, 2022c). The term "Peaceful Revolution" refers to the mass protests which contributed to the demise of the GDR. Specifically, the notion refers to the absence of large-scale public, police, or military violence in the context of the mass protests. This dimension was of particular importance in the local context of Dresden: In October 1989, a large demonstration had triggered violent confrontations between protestors and GDR police. Afterwards, both sides took up negotiations and thus created a blueprint of cooperation between citizens and state for the following demonstrations in Dresden and across the entire GDR, which then remained largely non-violent (Widera, 2020, p. 11).

PEGIDA activists draw from the memory of the "Peaceful Revolution" as a cultural resource to flesh out the ideal of non-violence. PEGIDA strategically adopted some of the most important symbols associated with the 1989 protests as well as with the East German peace movement of the 1980s more broadly (Richardson-Little & Merrill, 2020). Most importantly, PEGIDA copies the model of the 1989 "Monday Demonstrations" by taking to the streets on Mondays, and by chanting the slogan of the 1989 protests, namely "We are the people" ("*Wir sind das Volk*"). Also, demonstrations typically take place in front of the historically reconstructed *Frauenkirche*, a church in the center of Dresden whose ruin became a symbol of reference of the East German peace movement in the 1980s. Demonstrators make both direct symbolic references to the movement and the Peaceful Revolution, for instance by carrying flags featuring the peace dove and placards displaying one of the German peace movement's logos, namely "swords into plowshares" ("*Schwerter zu Pflugscharen*"). PEGIDA speakers also regularly close the demonstrations with proud references to the event's peaceful character. It is no surprise then that the initial title of PEGIDA's Facebook group and the organization writ-large referred to "Peaceful Europeans" instead of "Patriotic Europeans".

The analysis of PEGIDA as a non-violent protest group also shows how memory matters to understand social movement organizations in general, and the forms of actions that they select. When studying the tactical repertoire of protestors, social movement scholars have long highlighted the importance of cultural understandings instead of merely instrumental reasoning (Jasper, 1997). Approaching culture as a "toolkit" providing movements with symbols, narratives, and rituals (Swidler, 1986), memory can be understood as one of various cultural resources available to movements to generate meaning in their activism (Daphi & Zamponi, 2019; Kubal & Becerra, 2014). Empirical research has shown that memories of democratic transitions have the potential to sustain particularly powerful movement frames – especially in political communities which remember democratic transition as citizen-led rather than elite-negotiated (della Porta, Andretta, Fernandes, Romanos, & Vogiatzoglou, 2018). The case of PEGIDA illustrates how political protest draws from memories of an allegedly citizen-led and largely peaceful democratic transition as a powerful discursive resource beyond political and ideological boundaries (Volk, 2022c).

Extremist Features in PEGIDA Discourse Despite Its Support for Democracy

Apart from its commitment to non-violence, PEGIDA also claims to support democracy and constitutionality, even portraying itself as the safeguard of democratic values. For instance, PEGIDA's movement manifesto, the so-called Theses of Dresden from early 2015, respects basic democratic principles, the rule of law, and calls for an expansion of direct democracy. At demonstrations, speakers usually express their support for the idea of democracy. In 2020, PEGIDA emphasized its claim to protect German democracy by advertising its demonstrations as "marches for our constitution", "for our democracy", and "for our civil rights" in the context of the COVID-19 pandemic. If extremism requires engagement in violent forms of action (Bötticher, 2017; Schmid, 2014) as well as opposition to democracy (Carter, 2018; Mudde, 2007), PEGIDA should be qualified as radical rather than extremist. This corresponds to the dominant scholarly perspective which is that PEGIDA's forms of action as well as ideology, at least in its early years of activism, can hardly be categorized as extremist (Kocyba, 2020; Vorländer, Herold, & Schäller, 2016a), but rather fall into the category of what is commonly described as "populist radical right", and hence a variant of radical right ideology (Volk, 2020b; Vorländer et al., 2018).

In addition, to many observers PEGIDA does not appear as extremist because it is neither a clearly nationalist nor revisionist movement, which would have long been typical for extremist actors in the German context. The "E" in the acronym stands for "Europeans", and PEGIDA constructs Germany as part of the European community. Central and Eastern Europe is portrayed as the last bastion of "true Europeanness" where European culture, heritage, and tradition are still cherished (Caiani & Weisskircher, 2020; Volk, 2019, 2022a). PEGIDA also does not have a clearly revisionist position on Germany's National Socialist past. As mentioned earlier, the swastika in a trash can is part of its logo, and activists have attempted to distance themselves from far-right extremism such as the neo-Nazi marches on the anniversary of the destruction of Dresden during World War II on 13 February, organized by the National Democratic Party since the 2000s (Volk, 2020a). Similarly, while early PEGIDA supporters held stronger xenophobic and nationalist attitudes than the German population in general, only a small minority of demonstrators had a comprehensive extreme-right worldview, including chauvinism, anti-Semitism, and the trivialization or even negation of the Holocaust (Geiges et al., 2015; Kocyba, 2020; see also Rucht et al., 2015; Vorländer et al., 2016b).

Yet, we maintain that there are important extremist elements in PEGIDA's ideology. We argue that the activists' focus on the dehumanization of immigrants and political opponents as well as the delegitimization of actors and institutions of real-existing democracy as "dictatorial" or "totalitarian" reflects important and often neglected ideological features of contemporary extremism. Hence, non-violent extremism may be characterized not only by the opposition to democracy as such, but also the rhetorical undermining of real-existing democratic systems as dictatorship or totalitarianism.

First, PEGIDA leaders and followers engage in dehumanizing discourse on immigrants and political opponents, including representatives of the "establishment", counter demonstrators, and the mainstream media. Indeed, already in the early days of PEGIDA, its Facebook fan pages have publicly displayed "a completely deteriorated culture of discussion" (Vorländer et al., 2018, p. 23). Ethnographic observations of PEGIDA demonstrations reveal that speeches and chants at public events bear similarly degrading content. Specifically, the group denies basic rights and dignity to immigrants and political opponents. Speakers engage in hate speech against non-European immigrants, leftist counter demonstrators, and political elites.

They regularly attack immigrants as "lazy" and "dangerous law-breakers", and call for the immediate deportation of large numbers of refugees and asylum-seekers. Verbal abuse of Muslim immigrants tends to be particularly ruthless, including their harassment as "murderer Muslims", "rapist Muslims", and "barbarians", while the religion of Islam is degraded as the "most important, existential threat to Germany ... responsible for terror, war, killing, oppression of women, hatred of Jews, hatred of homosexuals ..." (Stürzenberger, 2019). Similarly, PEGIDA organizers degrade the leftist counter demonstrators as both lazy and dirty "social parasites" who "have never worked" and "never wash" (Bachmann, 2019). Especially harsh attacks are typically directed against the environmentalist Fridays for Future movement which PEGIDA portrays as a decadent aberration of 21st-century politics. Speakers dub the youth movement as "Fridays for truancy", and abuse Greta Thunberg, leader and public face of the movement, as "mentally disabled" and "suffering from fetal alcohol spectrum disorder" (Bachmann, 2019).

At times, PEGIDA's verbal abuse of political opponents is followed by public accusations of rabble-rousing as well as legal proceedings. Among recent examples are Bachmann's address from 7 October 2019, in which he referred to the members of Germany's Green Party as "terrorists", "vermin of the people", "asocial maggots", and "parasites" that "we" (PEGIDA supporters) should "throw into a ditch" and then "fill up the ditch" (Bachmann, 2019). Similarly, some of PEGIDA's attacks against the mainstream media, construed as "lying press" and part of the "leftist establishment", have been brought to court, for instance Bachmann's abuse of a media representative as "a self-declared journalist who loiters around attempting to formulate halfway meaningful sentences" (Springer, 2020). Apart from the PEGIDA organizers, also some of the guest speakers have been accused of rabble-rousing, including anti-Islam activist Irfan Peci as well Tommy Robinson, former leader of the English Defence League, who were invited to PEGIDA's seven-year anniversary event on 17 October 2021 (Vollmer et al., 2021).

Second, PEGIDA's ideology carries extremist traits due to the group's attacks on the institutions and actors associated with real-existing democracy in reunited Germany as "dictatorial". In fact, activists do not only criticize elected political representatives, but reject them as totalitarian. It is again memory, not only of the GDR and Peaceful Revolution, but also of the Nazi dictatorship, which serves as a discursive resource to sustain PEGIDA's argument (Volk, 2022c). Specifically, memory serves as a key rhetorical shortcut to denounce institutions and actors associated with the Federal Republic of Germany as undemocratic and totalitarian based on the comparison of contemporary Germany with both the GDR and Nazi dictatorships. For instance, speakers regularly state that reunited Germany is "as bad as" or "worse" than the past communist system, and followers carry placards demanding "no third dictatorship in Germany!".

Similarly, the group used to harshly attack long-term chancellor Angela Merkel, denying her political legitimacy and calling for her immediate dismissal ("*Merkel muss weg*"). Placards carried by demonstrators portray her as Hitler or designate her as the "biggest disrupter in German history". Also, PEGIDA denounces the established political parties as a hidden one-party system, blaming the conservative CDU (*Christlich-Demokratische Union*, Christian Democratic Union) to build a new GDR-style "unity party" together with the leftist SPD (*Sozialdemokratische Partei Deutschlands*, Social Democratic Party of Germany), Greens (*Bündnis 90/Die Grünen*) and the Left (*Die Linke*). In this context, the Office for the Protection of the Constitution is framed as the secret service of a dictatorial regime, using methods of oppression comparable to those of the GDR's "*Stasi*".

Historical comparisons of contemporary German politics with past dictatorships have gained importance in the group's rhetoric over the course of the COVID-19 pandemic, tying in with German and international far-right discourses on an emerging "Corona-dictatorship" (Volk, 2021). In this context, speakers at protest events even contemplate violence against political representatives, thus contradicting their alleged ideal of non-violent resistance. Bachmann hinted at the benefits of violence against the allegedly totalitarian political elites on several occasions. In a YouTube broadcast of 18 March 2020, he claimed that "we exchanged the rascals against full-grown criminals in 1989 and 1990", and pondered that "one should have chosen the Romanian model back then in 89", referring to the violent overthrow and killing of the Romanian communist state leader Nicolae Ceaușescu (Bachmann, 2020).

Conclusion

This chapter has underlined the blurred lines between radicalism and extremism with regard to both forms of action and ideology in contemporary far-right politics, analyzing the example of Dresden-based PEGIDA. We find that even though PEGIDA relies on non-violent forms of action, propagates the ideal of non-violence, and expresses support for democracy, the group's ideology still contains extremist features, which are the dehumanization of immigrants and political opponents as well as the delegitimization of actors and institutions linked to real-existing democracy as "dictatorial" or "totalitarian". The case of PEGIDA thus shows that the established categories of radicalism and extremism in international political science scholarship on the far right need to be further refined, especially in a political context where non-violent forms of action and the support for the idea of democracy have become dominant features across the political spectrum. More specifically, it is mainly ideological elements manifesting the rejection of human dignity and pluralism that reflect extremist ideology in contemporary politics, and that clash with more complex understandings of democracy beyond majority rule (Carter, 2018).

Difficulties in pinpointing radicalism or extremism on the far right are not restricted to the study of PEGIDA, but reveal a more general ambivalence in contemporary European far-right politics, not limited to social movements. Also actors inside established far-right parties such as AfD, the Freedom Party of Austria or the Italian Lega pursue discourses of dehumanization and delegitimization, while acting non-violently, adhering to the ideal of non-violence and supporting the idea of democracy. Clear-cut distinctions between radical or extreme organizations are therefore often more difficult to make than commonly assumed (Pirro, 2022).

Indeed, the blurred lines between radicalism and extremism in the case of PEGIDA are particularly strongly pronounced due to its organizational form as a social movement group, where a large variety of actors – leaders, speakers, supporters, social media followers, among others – is involved in the public construction of ideology. In this context, an ethnographic perspective has been key in shedding more nuanced light on PEGIDA as an instance of far-right extremism as it yields novel insights into the ambiguous protest events between positively associated historic symbolism and extremism of thought. Such a perspective reveals that contemporary far-right actors tend to have hybrid ideologies, drawing from both radical and extremist ideas.

Acknowledgments

This research has received funding from the European Union's Horizon 2020 research and innovation programme under grant agreement No. 765224, and from the Research Council of Norway under grant agreement no. 303219.

Notes

1 Accordingly, the German intelligence service refers to extremists as those who reject "liberal democracy", which Germany's official parlance labels *"freiheitliche demokratische Grundordnung"*.
2 The term "refugee crisis" commonly refers to the political and social implications of the stark increase in the number of asylum seekers in the richest economies of the European Union in 2015/16.

References

Arzheimer, K. (2015). The AfD: finally a successful right-wing populist Eurosceptic party for Germany? *West European Politics, 38*(3), 535–556.
Arzheimer, K. (2019). "Don't mention the war!" How populist right-wing radicalism became (almost) normal in Germany. *JCMS: Journal of Common Market Studies, 57*(S1), 90–102.
Bachmann, L. (2019). Speech at PEGIDA demonstration. Retrieved from www.youtube.com/watch?v=t0D9mDGlstI
Bachmann, L. (2020). 18.03.2020 Extra-Lutziges zur Merkelansprache. Retrieved from www.youtube.com/watch?v=2IedIznYiEY
Backes, U. (2009). *Political extremes: A conceptual history from antiquity to the present.* London: Routledge.
Backes, U. (2020). Sachsen: Eine Hochburg rechtsmotivierter Gewalt? In U. Backes & S. Kailitz (Eds.), *Sachsen – Eine Hochburg des Rechtsextremismus?* (pp. 217–232). Göttingen: Vandenhoeck & Ruprecht.
Backes, U., & Kailitz, S. (Eds.). (2020). *Sachsen – Eine Hochburg des Rechtsextremismus?* Göttingen: Vandenhoeck & Ruprecht.
Berntzen, L. E. (2019). *Liberal roots of far right activism: The anti-Islamic movement in the 21st century.* London: Routledge.
Berntzen, L. E., & Weisskircher, M. (2016). Anti-Islamic PEGIDA beyond Germany: Explaining differences in mobilisation. *Journal of Intercultural Studies, 37*(6), 556–573.

Bötticher, A. (2017). Towards academic consensus definitions of radicalism and extremism. *Perspectives on Terrorism, 11*(4), 73–77.

Bundesamt für Verfassungsschutz. (2020, December 3). BfV-Pressekonferenz vom 12. März 2020 zum Stand der Bekämpfung des Rechtsextremismus: Eingangsstatement von BfV-Präsident Thomas Haldenwang. Retrieved from www.verfassungsschutz.de/SharedDocs/reden/DE/2020/statement-hal denwang-presekonferenz-stand-der-bekaempfung-des-rechtsextremismus.html

Bundesamt für Verfassungsschutz. (n.d.). Verfassungsschutzrelevante Delegitimierung des Staates. Retrieved from www.verfassungsschutz.de/DE/themen/verfassungsschutzrelevante-delegitimierung-des-staates/verfassungsschutzrelevante-delegitimierung-des-staates_node.html

Caiani, M., della Porta, D., & Wagemann, C. (2012). *Mobilizing on the extreme right: Germany, Italy, and the United States*. Oxford: Oxford University Press.

Carter, E. (2018). Right-wing extremism/radicalism: Reconstructing the concept. *Journal of Political Ideologies, 23*(2), 157–182.

Castelli Gattinara, P., & Pirro, A. L. P. (2019). The far right as social movement. *European Societies, 21*(4), 447–462.

Dafnos, A., & Allchorn, W. (2021). *Far-right protest Britain*. Retrieved from www.linct-aa.org/app/downl oad/32126571/Far-Right+Mobilisations+in+Great+Britain+2009-2019FRGB-Research-Rep ort-1.pdf

Daphi, P., & Zamponi, L. (2019). Exploring the movement-memory nexus: Insights and ways forward. *Mobilization: An International Quarterly, 24*(4), 399–417.

della Porta, D., Andretta, M., Fernandes, T., Romanos, E., & Vogiatzoglou, M. (Eds.). (2018). *Legacies and memories in movements: Justice and democracy in southern Europe*. Oxford: Oxford University Press.

Dostal, J. M. (2015). The Pegida movement and German political culture: Is right-wing populism here to stay? *The Political Quarterly, 86*(4), 523–531.

Druxes, H., & Simpson, P. A. (2016). Introduction: Pegida as a European far-right populist movement. *German Politics and Society, 34*(4), 1–16.

Frey, A. (2020). 'Cologne changed everything'—The effect of threatening events on the frequency and distribution of intergroup conflict in Germany. *European Sociological Review, 36*(5), 684–699.

Geiges, L., Marg, S., & Walter, F. (2015). *Pegida: Die schmutzige Seite der Zivilgesellschaft?* Bielefeld: Transcript.

Hutter, S., & Weisskircher, M. (2022). *New contentious politics. Civil society, social movements, and the polarization of German politics*. German Politics, online first.

Jasper, J. M. (1997). *The art of moral protest: Culture, biography, and creativity in social movements*. Chicago: Chicago University Press.

Jäckle, S., & König, P. (2017). The dark side of the German 'welcome culture': investigating the causes behind attacks on refugees in 2015. *West European Politics, 40*(2), 223–251.

Jäckle, S., & König, P. (2018). Threatening events and anti-refugee violence: an empirical analysis in the wake of the refugee crisis during the years 2015 and 2016 in Germany: *European Sociological Review, 34*(6), 728–743.

Kocyba, P. (2020). Pegida: Ausdruck rechtsextremen Protests? In U. Backes & S. Kailitz (Eds.), *Sachsen – Eine Hochburg des Rechtsextremismus?* (pp. 81–100). Göttingen: Vandenhoeck & Ruprecht.

Koopmans, R., & Olzak, S. (2004). Discursive opportunities and the evolution of right-wing violence in Germany. *American Journal of Sociology, 110*(1), 198–230.

Kubal, T., & Becerra, R. (2014). Social movements and collective memory. *Sociology Compass, 8*(6), 865–875.

Landesamt für Verfassungsschutz. (2021, May 7). *Landesamt für Verfassungsschutz stuft Pegida zur erwiesenen extremistischen Bestrebung ein*. Retrieved from www.verfassungsschutz.sachsen.de/download/2021_05_ 07_PEGIDA_BO_korr.pdf

Mau, S. (2019). *Lütten Klein*. Berlin: Suhrkamp.

Mudde, C. (2007). *Populist radical right parties in Europe*. Cambridge: Cambridge University Press.

Nissen, A. (2020). The trans-European mobilization of "Generation Identity." In O. C. Norocel, A. Hellström, & M. B. Jørgensen (Eds.), *Nostalgia and hope: Intersections between politics of culture, welfare, and migration in Europe* (pp. 85–100). Cham: Springer.

Patzelt, W. J., & Klose, J. (2016). *Pegida: Warnsignale aus Dresden*. Dresden: Thelem Verlag.

Pirro, A. (2022). *Far right: The significance of an umbrella concept*. Nations and Nationalism, online first.

Ravndal, J. A. (2018). Explaining right-wing terrorism and violence in Western Europe: Grievances, opportunities and polarisation. *European Journal of Political Research, 57*(4), 845–866.

Reuband, K.-H. (2015). Wer demonstriert in Dresden für Pegida? Ergebnisse empirischer Studien, methodische Grundlagen und offene Fragen. *Mitteilungen des Instituts für Deutsches und Internationales Parteienrecht und Parteienforschung, 21*(1), 133–144.

Richards, A. (2015). From terrorism to 'radicalization' to 'extremism': Counterterrorism imperative or loss of focus? *International Affairs, 91*(2), 371–380.

Richardson-Little, N., & Merrill, S. (2020). Who is the Volk? PEGIDA and the contested memory of 1989 on social media. In S. Merrill, E. Keightley, & P. Daphi (Eds.), *Social movements, cultural memory and digital media: Mobilising mediated remembrance* (pp. 59–84). Cham: Springer International Publishing.

Rucht, D., Daphi, P., Kocyba, P., Neuber, M., Roose, J., Scholl, F., & Zajak, S. (2015). *Protestforschung am Limit. Eine Soziologische Annäherung an Pegida* [Ipb working paper]. Berlin: Verein für Protest- und Bewegungsforschung. Retrieved from Verein für Protest- und Bewegungsforschung website: https://protestinstitut.eu/wp-content/uploads/2015/03/protestforschung-am-limit_ipb-working-paper_web.pdf

Schmid, A. (2014). *Violent and non-violent extremism: Two sides of the same coin?* The Hague: International Centre for Counter-Terrorism.

Schneider, A. (2020, January 17). Pegida ist der gemeinsame Nenner. *Sächsische Zeitung.* Retrieved from www.saechsische.de/plus/pegida-ist-der-gemeinsame-nenner-5160218.html

Snow, D. A. (2004). Case studies and social movements. In D. A. Snow, D. della Porta, B. Klandermans, & D. McAdam (Eds.), *The Wiley-Blackwell encyclopedia of social and political movements.* Hoboken, NJ: Wiley.

Springer, C. (2020, December 14). Dresdner Gericht verurteilt Lutz Bachmann. *Sächsische Zeitung.* Retrieved from www.saechsische.de/dresden-gericht-verurteilt-lutz-bachmann-5338970.html

Stürzenberger, M. (2019). Speech at PEGIDA-demonstration. Retrieved from www.youtube.com/watch?v=-5cUTvx0JI8

Swidler, A. (1986). Culture in action: Symbols and strategies. *American Sociological Review, 51*(2), 273–286.

Teune, S., & Ullrich, P. (2015). *Demonstrationsbefragungen. Grenzen und Potenziale einer Forschungsmethode.* Berlin, Germany: Institut für Bewegungsforschung.

Ther, P. (2019). *Das andere Ende der Geschichte. Über die Große Transformation.* Berlin: Suhrkamp.

Volk, S. (2019). Speaking for "the European people"? How the transnational alliance Fortress Europe constructs a populist counter-narrative to European integration. *Politique Européenne, 66,* 120–149.

Volk, S. (2020a). Commemoration at the extremes: A field report from Dresden 2020. *Cultures of History Forum,* online first.

Volk, S. (2020b). 'Wir sind das Volk!' Representative claim-making and populist style in the PEGIDA movement's discourse. *German Politics, 29*(4), 599–616.

Volk, S. (2021a). Die rechtspopulistische PEGIDA in der COVID-19 Pandemie: Virtueller Protest "für unsere Bürgerrechte." *Forschungsjournal Soziale Bewegungen, 34*(2), 235–248. doi:10.1515/fjsb-2021-0020.

Volk, S. (2022a). Conceptualising Europe from the far right: The mobilisation of intellectual heritage in Germany. Journal of European Studies. Online first: https://doi.org/10.1177/00472441221115564.

Volk, S. (2022b). Explaining PEGIDA's 'strange survival': An ethnographic approach to far-right protest rituals. Political Research Exchange. Online first: https://doi.org/10.1080/2474736X.2022.2136036.

Volk, S. (2022c). Resisting leftist dictatorship? Memory politics and collective action framing in the far-right populist PEGIDA movement. *European Politics and Society,* 1–17.

Vollmer, J., Schneider, A., Springer, C. & Weller, A. (2021, October 17). Festnahme bei Demo in Dresden. *Sächsische Zeitung.* Retrieved from www.saechsische.de/dresden/dresden-pegida-demos-legen-dresdner-innenstadt-lahm-5546770-plus.html

Vorländer, H. (2016). Zerrissene Stadt: Kulturkampf in Dresden. *Aus Politik Und Zeitgeschichte, 66*(5–7), 22–28.

Vorländer, H., Herold, M., & Schäller, S. (2016a). PEGIDA – eine rechtsextremistische Bewegung? In G. Pickel & O. Decker (Eds.), *Extremismus in Sachsen: Eine kritische Bestandsaufnahme* (pp. 109–118). Leipzig: Edition Leipzig.

Vorländer, H., Herold, M., & Schäller, S. (2016b). *PEGIDA Entwicklung, Zusammensetzung und Deutung einer Empörungsbewegung.* Wiesbaden: Springer.

Vorländer, H., Herold, M., & Schäller, S. (2018). *PEGIDA and new right-wing populism in Germany.* Basingstoke: Palgrave Macmillan.

Weisskircher, M. (2020). The strength of far-right AfD in eastern Germany: The east-west divide and the multiple causes behind "populism." *The Political Quarterly, 91*(3), 614–622. DOI:10.1111/1467-923X.12859.

Weisskircher, M. (2022). The importance of being eastern German: the multiple heartlands of Germany's far right. In Centre for Baltic and East European Studies (Ed.), *State of the Region Report 2021: Identity and the Far Right in the Baltic Sea Region and Eastern Europe Today* (pp. 91–99). Stockholm, Sweden: Centre for Baltic and East European Studies (CBEES), Södertörn University.

Weisskircher, M., & Berntzen, L. E. (2019). Remaining on the streets. Anti-Islamic PEGIDA mobilization and its relationship to far-right party politics. In M. Caiani & O. Císař (Eds.), *Radical right "movement parties" in Europe* (pp. 114–130). London: Routledge.Widera, T. (2020). Angespannte Herbsttage: Revolution in Dresden 1989—Bedingt friedlich. *Dresdner Hefte: Beiträge zur Kulturgeschichte*, (140), 6–12.

Weisskircher, M., Hutter, S. & Borbáth, E. (2022). *Protest and Electoral Breakthrough. Challenger Party-Movement Interactions in Germany*. German Politics, online first.

Witte, R., & Bjørgo, T. (Eds.). (1993). *Racist violence in Europe*. Basingstoke: Palgrave Macmillan.

22

METAPOLITICS AND THE US FAR RIGHT

On the "Non-violent" Approach to Alt-Right Social Transformation

Dustin J. Byrd

Introduction

Amidst the recent upsurge of Western and white nationalism, an outburst of extremist political violence exposed a severe fissure between two competing factions within the newly emerging far-right movement in the West. On the one hand, some factions within the American "Alt-Right" look favourably on political violence as an effective means of bringing about the desired white ethno-state. On the other hand, there are those that argue for a non-violent transformation of the West, particularly in North America and Western Europe. This group looks askance at their violent counterparts, including the neo-Nazis, seeing their accelerationist public demonstrations, street brawls, and terrorist attacks as being counter-productive to their white nationalist cause. They point to the fact that after violent attacks, such as the 2015 massacre of parishioners at Emanuel African Methodist Episcopal Church, in Charleston, South Carolina by the white supremacist Dylann Roof, a movement began to remove all confederate flags, statues, and memorials from the American public sphere. The August 2017 "United the Right" rally in Charlottesville, Virginia, led to numerous lawsuits that has subsequently crippled the American leadership of the movement. This rally was attended by various far-right groups, including neo-Nazis, neo-Confederates, the Ku Klux Klan, Identity Evropa, the Proud Boys, and followers of the Alt-Right leader Richard Spencer. In Europe, after the 2011 bombing of the government district in Oslo, Norway, killing eight, and the massacre of 69 members of the Workers' Youth League on Utøya Island, all done in a single morning by the ethno-nationalist Anders Behring Breivik, Norway's Prime Minister, Jens Stoltenberg, reemphasised Norway's commitment to freedom, multiculturalism, and tolerance (AP, 2011). Soon after, Scandinavia became one of the prime destinations for Arab refugees fleeing from the civil war in Syria. Likewise, in New Zealand, after the right-wing identitarian Brenton Tarrant massacred 51 Muslims in two mosques in Christchurch, the New Zealand government doubled down on its commitment to a "diverse" population, denouncing white nationalism and other forms of white identity politics. These, and many other instances of right-wing extremist political violence, done in the name of *rassenpolitik* (racial politics), demonstrated to many within

DOI: 10.4324/9781003032793-26

the far right that violent tactics only impeded the advancement of their white nationalist goals. As such, violence was counterproductive; it did not accelerate the desired race war, but rather turned the population off from what they saw as their central message: the need to renew Western society.

Numerous influential leaders in the American Alt-Right subsequently argued that the intimidating rallies, street brawls, and acts of terrorism, were ultimately ineffective, not because they violated their ethical commitment to non-violence, but rather because of the intellectual and ethical context within which such violent actions occurred, i.e., the liberal consensus, with its apotheosis of multiculturalism, inclusivity, and diversity. If such violent measures were to be effective, they had to first find legitimacy within the society that they occurred. In other words, the cultural-ethical context, which at the present moment condemns such political violence, had to be transformed. For influential white nationalists, such as Greg Johnson and Jared Taylor, such a social transformation could only come through a non-violent remoulding of the norms and values of their societies.[1] Non-violent "metapolitics," not political violence, could serve as a vehicle for a radical renewal of American society along racial lines. In order to understand the processes by which non-violent means of social transformation are effectively deployed, the American Alt-Right turned to the tactics of their older predecessor in Europe, the New Right (*Nouvelle Droite*), who had already appropriated the work of the Italian Marxist-Leninist, Antonio Gramsci, in their own metapolitical struggle.

In this chapter, I will investigate the Alt-Right's adoption of "metapolitics" as a non-violent means to achieve what Gramsci called "cultural hegemony," the social precondition for "political hegemony." Starting from Gramsci's *Prison Notebooks,* I will argue that Gramsci developed the notion of metapolitics as a means of overcoming the deficiencies in Marxism's purely economic interpretation of class struggle. In Gramsci's thought, Marx's class struggle would no longer be fought on a battlefield or in the streets, nor would it take place within politics. Rather, it would migrate to the realm of culture, i.e., the *kulturkampf* (culture war). From there, I will move to my primary focus: The Alt-Right's adoption of the Marxist idea of metapolitics as a means of countering their two most prominent enemies: "Cultural Marxism" and traditional conservatism. I will show that the Alt-Right's and other American identitarian groups' appropriation of metapolitics is not new, but rather has been learned from their European predecessors, the New Right, especially from the work of Alain de Benoist and Guillaume Faye.

Lastly, I will argue that the non-violent nature of the Alt-Right's metapolitical strategy, geared towards a peaceful transformation of society, contributed to the violence that marked the presidency of Donald J. Trump. Although the "intellectuals" of the Alt-Right did not participate in the insurrection against American democracy on 6 January, 2021, they did however contribute to the overall conditions that led to such a violent attack.

Antonio Gramsci's Concept of Metapolitics

The Marxist Antonio Gramsci wrote his *Prison Notebooks* while incarcerated in Mussolini's fascist Italy. Like the Frankfurt School, Gramsci was bewildered by the fact that nationalist sentiments trumped the masses' class considerations during World War I, causing millions of working-class men to side with their nations as opposed to their classes.[2] This was a major setback for Marxist theory, which failed to provide an adequate reasoning for such a phenomenon. In light of this, Gramsci theorised that Marx over-emphasised the economic factor in human relations and deemphasised the role of culture in the formation of class consciousness. The "superstructure," or culture, was not fully determined by the economic base, as Marx theorised, but rather the norms, values, and principles that are dominant within the superstructure often determine how individuals and societies relate to matters of the base as well as organise their political-economic institutions (Fernia, 1987, p. 27).[3] In other words, the class considerations of the subaltern working masses can be overridden by the superstructure and the ideology it inculcates in the masses. As such, the answer to understanding the problem of national loyalty above class consciousness lay not in economics, but in mass psychology, and it is to the psychological realm that Gramsci turned to formulate his most important political concept: hegemony.

For Gramsci, hegemony is a social-political order in which a singular worldview dominates a given group, wherein a singular conception of reality is monolithic, and thus informs and determines the totality of the individual's and collective's lifeworld. In other words, hegemony is achieved when the subaltern comes to accept, adhere to, and advocate for a singular interpretation of reality and orientation of action that is identical to the interests of the ruling class (Gramsci, 2000, pp. 422–424).[4] There are a couple essential principles that are very important to understand about Gramsci's concept of hegemony: first, akin to Marx's notion of "ideology," the worldview that the masses accept, adhere to, and advocate for, is contrary to their own class interests. As such, they suffer from "false consciousness," which leads them to actively support policies, practices, and beliefs that harm their own well-being. Second, Gramsci constructs his concept of hegemony within a traditional political dichotomy – between force and consent. Governments, ruling classes, and other forms of oppressive rule, often dominate (*dominio*) their subject population through direct physical means or through coercion, whereupon the threat of violence, whether that is physical, systemic, or symbolic, instils obedience in the subaltern class to the rule of the hegemon. Nevertheless, this form of domination is mercurial, and thus often fails to establish any form of permanence.

A constant state of war exists between ruler and ruled, and thus such governance is precarious at best. On the other hand, a ruling class can dominate through consent, via what Gramsci calls "intellectual and moral leadership" (*direzione intellettuale e morale*) (Fernia, 1987, p. 24). In this form of domination, traditional intellectuals of the ruling class disseminate their self-interested ideology to the subaltern classes in such a way that is forms their collective consciousness, wherein they internalise the prevailing ideology as their own, thus coming to identify with it (Gramsci, 2000, pp. 189–190).

As such, their personal convictions become identical with the convictions of the prevalent norms, which, in the last analysis, are norms that serve a stable reproduction of the prevailing hegemony, i.e., the dominant social-political status quo. In this form of domination, consent of the dominated for their own domination is achieved by the dominators. Through the skilful labour of the intellectuals, the subaltern class is enlisted into the infrastructure that exists to maintain social statics. This is a self-perpetuating and physically non-violent form of domination, as the identity, sense of self, and sense of worth of the co-opted subaltern becomes synonymous with the well-being of the dominant conditions. Attacks on the prevailing order are thus experienced psychologically by the system-integrated subaltern masses as attacks on themselves, and they will risk their own lives and property to preserve the social order they identify with.

It is one thing for Gramsci to say that the ruling class has a certain psychological power over those they prevail over, but Gramsci has to identify the means through which the legitimacy of the prevailing order is inculcated into the subaltern. In other words, in what ways do the subaltern come to accept and/or reproduce their own domination? In order to answer that, Gramsci turns momentarily from Marx and Lenin to Hegel.

The Struggle for Hegemony Within Civil Society

In his *Philosophy of Right*, Hegel conceptualises society as having a tripartite nature: family, which serves as the foundation of society; civil society, the realm wherein the individual pursues their own self-interest; and the state, wherein the interests of the whole take shape in a universal advocate (Hegel, 2010, pp. 187–380). Although these three realms are conceptually separated, they all can influence the other in profound ways. Family dynamics accompany the individual into civil society; the influence of civil society determines the policies pursued in the state by individual legislators, and the prevailing ideology of the state moulds the worldview that parents bequeath to their children in the family. This being the case, Gramsci realised that Marxist revolutionary politics, outside of the non-hegemonic realm of Czarist Russia, failed miserably to enlist enough social force by which they could overthrow the dominance of capitalism and the ruling elites.

Marxist politics, being determined primarily through economic concerns, took place almost exclusively within the realm of the political, the realm of the bourgeois state, as they tried to gain direct control of state institutions via violent revolution. However, the ruling classes of Western and Central Europe not only had control of the state, but also benefited from their hegemonic cultural influence over their own population, which enforced the status quo of their rule. Even if a vanguard of revolutionary Marxists were able to seize control of the state, they would be surrounded by a population discontent with Marxist rule, since such a rule would not have secured the ideological consent of the subaltern masses, who still would share the consciousness of their bourgeois masters. In other words, the Marxists, ruling as a minority, would not possess the power of *consent* via the ideological hegemony over the population if the state was taken by force. Seeing the disconnect, Gramsci advocated for the retreat of Marxism from the realm of the state to the realm of civil society, as means of non-violently creating a cleavage between the ruling class (and their handmaiden in the state) and the legitimacy for their rule that is created via mass psychology through the institutions of civil society. Civil society was to become the arena of war between Marxists and the bourgeois ruling class, not the state, and such a war within civil society would predominantly be non-violent in nature. This would be a war of ideas, not a war of arms.

For Gramsci, the institutional arenas of civil society are predominately the church, education systems, the arts, and media, including entertainment and news organisations (Fernia, 1987, pp. 26–29).[5] Through these mediums, a collective consciousness that is loyal to, and identical with, the status quo is formed. The ideological legitimation needed to establish and maintain a sense of permanence for the given social hierarchy is disseminated, for example, through a church that preaches obedience to God's authority and the authority that God has established; an education system that indoctrinates the youth into believing the national myths that glorify the founding of the nation and its future destiny; the arts that convey a sense of an already-established ideal society, as opposed to arts that serve as grand inquisitors for the status quo; cultural institutions that fund and disseminate projects that hypnotise the masses into lethargy; and the media, which entertains the subaltern masses with bread and circus, as well as mould the way they see the world, themselves, and their ruling class via news. For Gramsci, as long as the state can disseminate its ruling ideology through the various segments of civil society, the apparatuses wherein a social consciousness is formed remain entirely at the disposal of the hegemon. War on the people is not needed to gain their submission; social indoctrination achieved that goal peacefully and it did so with the consent of the governed (Adamson, 2014, pp. 170–179).

Unlike Marx, who dismissed the "superstructure" of culture (religion, education, the arts, etc.) as being mere epiphenomena of base economic realities, Gramsci saw clearly that it was within the domain of civil society that the true struggle for social dominance must first occur. In this sense, politics is downstream from culture. What was needed, Gramsci thought, was best articulated decades later by the revolutionary German student of the prominent critical theorist Herbert Marcuse, Rudi Dutschke, who said that in order to fundamentally transform society, the revolutionary Left needed a peaceful but thorough *long march through the institutions* (Dutschke, 2006). In other words, the struggle to liberate society from the shackles of capitalism and the bourgeois ruling class was not via direct participation in politics or political violence, both of which further cement the norms of the status quo, but rather to gain influence in those institutions of civil society by "organic intellectuals," that could form the collective consciousness of the subaltern masses (Gramsci, 2000, p. 425).[6]

The "war of maneuver [sic]," (i.e., a direct and often violent frontal attack against the status quo) had to be replaced by a "war of position," a non-violent war of ideals, values, and principles, fought on the battlefields of civil society, in which the winning of "hearts and minds" is the primary goal, not the violent destruction or overthrow of the ruling class and/or the state (Gramsci, 2000, pp. 430–431). Gramsci theorised that once the counter-hegemonic thought of the organic intellectuals crossed a certain threshold within society, a legitimation crisis would occur for the already existing state. Having thus prevailed intellectually and culturally over the hegemony of the bourgeois ruling class, the seizure of the political apparatus could then legitimately occur. This would happen within the context of a society already primed for revolutionary change, since the consciousness of the subaltern masses had already accepted the basic worldview and moral perspectives of revolutionary Marxism.[7]

New Right Metapolitics

What Antonio Gramsci referred to as the "war of position," New Right thinkers refer to a "metapolitics," i.e., the struggle to advance an alternative worldview through various forms of non-violent cultural contestations in civil society.[8] Metapolitics, as such, is not the talk about politics, nor politics itself, but rather the exercise of Nietzschean "great politics" (*grosse Politik*): the cultural struggles that served to overcome the present condition and advance *civilisational* goals, as opposed to the localised petty politics of politicians (Nietzsche, 2014, p. 111; Drochon, 2016, pp. 153–179). As such, Alt-Right's great politics is meant to project Western civilisation's destiny in the future through a radical transformation of society by reclaiming the long-forgotten roots of the Greco-Roman and Germanic civilisation while attempting to translate those roots into a contemporary worldview and way-of-being. As such, it is an attempt to fundamentally change the values, principles, and ideals that form the foundation of present liberal society. Such an alternative worldview would serve as a counter-hegemonic narrative that seeks to first, undermine the on-going "Cultural Marxism" of the Left, as well as the liberal consensus that is championed by mainstream centrist political parties, including the conservative parties (Johnson, 2013, pp. 18–19; O'Meara, 2013, p. 27).

In the American context, the metapolitics of the Alt-Right is an attempt to decouple whites from the cultural and political liberalism that has dominated the West at least since the "1968 generation," and win them over to white identity politics of white nationalism, anti-globalism, and anti-immigration, as a way of purifying American society.[9] The goal is to make the European/White ethno-sphere free of foreign influence and racial minorities. Such a metapolitical goal crystallises in what Greg Johnson, an American White nationalist author, calls "Whitopia," i.e., "White Utopia" (Johnson, 2018, pp. 95–103).

The appropriation of Gramsci's notion of metapolitics first occurred in Europe with the establishment of the "New Right." Having broken away from mainstream conservative politics, the "Old Right" as they're called pejoratively, thinkers like Alain de Benoist, Guillaume Faye, and Dominique Venner, attempted to form a loose body of thought that, like the Frankfurt School on the Left, engaged in a robust critique of modern society, albeit from a rightward perspective (Andersen, 2018, 73–87). Having lost the culture wars against the liberals and Marxists in the 1960s, these reactionary thinkers chose to continue their struggle against what they called "Cultural Marxism" by using the same tools and methods of the Gramsci inspired cultural Marxists: they focused on the transformation of Western culture as opposed to the seizing of the state (O'Meara, 2013, pp. 61–76).

Nevertheless, unlike the Frankfurt School, the work of the New Right was not immediately influential upon the societies it was meant to rescue. When the New Right was formed, the liberalisation of Western culture was in full advance. The context of such a time kept the New Right relatively marginalised, contained within a few journals, voiced by a few academics, and kept out of the mainstream public sphere. Although thinkers within the New Right looked at the Frankfurt School with both admiration and disgust, having learned much from their critique of society while simultaneously rejecting their ultimate goals, those within the Frankfurt School often disagreed with the New Right concerning the influence the Frankfurt School had on Western society.

Thinkers within the New Right believe that the Frankfurt School's and other forms of Western Marxism's metapolitics have been incredibly successful at breaking down the traditional norms of Western society, thus preparing it for multiculturalism and the acceptance of "diversity" as a social benefit. It is claimed by the New Right that the Frankfurt School has won the 20th century in the West and continues to enjoy a hegemonic status through their capture of the means of metapolitical dissemination, especially the education system and media, which stealthily forms the consciousness of the subaltern masses, thus preparing it for the reification of cultural liberalism and liberal political hegemony. As such, the successes of Cultural Marxism emanating from the Frankfurt School and its successors have become the metapolitical model for the New Right: culture wars before politics. If the mainly Jewish Frankfurt School undermined and dissolved the traditional Greco-Roman, Germanic, and Christian identity of the West, the New Right would be the countervailing force that would resurrect such a traditional identity and restore it to its rightful place, thus creating an ironclad Western identity that clearly distinguishes between the West and its rightful people, and the others, who do not belong in the West.[10]

Much like the Frankfurt School, who it is claimed seized upon a state of crisis within the West to introduce its non-conformist philosophy, the initial thinkers within the New Right believed that the historical situation, most likely another crisis within Western civilisation, specifically within the prevailing liberal hegemony, would provide the opportunity by which the decades long metapolitical work could find its realisation. In other words, when the cultural, political, economic, and civilisational norms established by the liberal consensus began to lose legitimacy, this crisis context would result in the need for, and normalisation of, a countervailing worldview, one that specifically addressed the dysgenic nature of liberalism, i.e., the New Right.

As such, the labour of the New Right, beginning with the 1968 founding of *Groupement de Recherche et d'Études pour la Civilisation Européenne* (GRECE), was to prepare for such moment by engaging the disaffected and aggrieved population in a robust dialogue, discourse, and debate, wherein their alternative worldview, their cultural critique, their political philosophy, would become increasingly acceptable in light of the dysgenic tendencies of the collapsing liberal societies (Andersen, 2018, pp. 73–87). Nevertheless, GRECE, especially the core intellectuals that comprised it, particularly Alain de Benoist, Guillaume Faye, and Dominique Venner, did not take a passive role as mere spectators of liberalism's demise; their metapolitics was designed to be "accelerationist": to bring about the collapse of liberal hegemony by creating a million different fractures within the core ideals of liberalism.

Like the Frankfurt School, the New Right seized upon the contradictions within liberal society, its failures to realise its essential promises, and its inner-antagonisms that prejudiced certain values, ideals, and principles over others, such as cultural diversity over cultural homogeneity; the willed community (*Willensgemeinschaft*) over the ethnic community (*Volksgemeinschaft*); globalism over localism; and cosmopolitanism over the "fundamental right to difference" (ethnopluralism/ethno-differentialism; Faye, 2016). Again, following the model of the Frankfurt School, the New Right's critique entered into the realm of the arts, science, social sciences, philosophy, literature, psychology, history, and all other domains where unwritten liberal values (and sometimes Marxist values) determine the parameters of what is valid and was invalid, what is morally acceptable and what is unacceptable, and what is politically orthodox and what is politically heterodox.

According to the ethno-nationalist, Michael O'Meara, GRECE's own intellectuals attempted to inspire and organise the New Right's alternative worldview first through its various publications, conferences, and public engagements (O'Meara, 2013, p. 65). Through such mediums, they would "seek to undermine the liberal order by discrediting its underlying tenets and affirming those traditional European ideas supportive of the identities and communities it champions," all in an attempt to attain "cultural hegemony" (O'Meara, 2013, p. 65).

New Right Metapolitics Migrates to America

Much of the same angst with traditional conservativism and Cultural Marxism that was prevalent in Europe in the late 20th century could also be found in the United States in the beginning of the 21st century. Echoing their European counterparts, there were some American thinkers, such as the paleoconservatives Paul Gottfried and Patrick Buchanan, as well as the white supremacist Jared Taylor, who viewed both the Democratic and Republican parties in the United States as being two differing parties adhering to the same liberal hegemony (Sedgwick, 2019, pp. 102–154).[11] Bourgeois liberalism, whether in a Roosevelt form, i.e., the Democrats, or in an older more libertarian form, as in the Republican Party, enjoyed a hegemonic status, as both of the dominating parties shared the same philosophical bases: economics over culture, social dynamics over social statics, secularity over religiosity, and an "Enlightened" America that is uniquely destined to lead the European civilisation away from its historical roots towards a more "progressive" and globalised tomorrow.

As such, there was only a façade of political choice in America; in all matters essential, the two parties were the same. As such, those influenced by the European New Right questioned the conservatism of those who championed the free market, immigration, and the celebration of multiculturalism, as did Ronald Reagan and other mainstream conservatives. Simultaneously, they questioned the continual degeneration of Western culture, as pop-culture, the product of unholy alliance of capitalist corporations and Cultural Marxism, gained influence over American culture, especially the youth.

From this context grew a youth-oriented alternative to the prevailing liberal status quo: the alternative right or Alt-Right, a term coined by the white nationalist Richard Bertrand Spencer and his older counterpart, Paul Gottfried (Hawley, 2017, p. 32). Following much of the thought of the European New Right, the American Alt-Right called for a renewal of the European ethno-sphere through white separatism, the end of non-European immigration, the removal of unwanted ethnicities (regardless of their citizen status), the expulsion of Muslims, and the end of Jewish control of the country, media, and cultural institutions. Through *explicit* white identity politics, the Alt-Right attempted to first, separate itself from mainstream conservatives, who they thought only were engaged in *implicit* white identity politics, and second, to fabricate an academic veneer of respectability for racism, antisemitism, Islamophobia, xenophobia, white supremacy, the myth of white genocide, and the quest for their ultimate goal: a white ethno-state.[12]

In an attempt to follow the more respectable strategies of the New Right, the Alt-Right leader Richard Spencer, who degrees from the University of Virginia and the University of Chicago, edited numerous publications, including the paleoconservative *Taki's Magazine*, and the pseudo-academic journals *American Conservative and Radix Journal* .[13] However, these older forms of metapolitical thought dissemination were supplemented by a much more effective form of mass communication: social media. The use of Facebook, Twitter, 4Chan, 8Chan, and other social media platforms, translated Alt-Right academic ideology into memes, slogans, and troll language, for young, disaffected Americans who were not attracted to academia or academic-like events and publications. Alongside of the social media, Spencer became the American editor of the website AltRight.com, and in 2010 founded *AlternativeRight,* a webzine dedicated to an intellectual approach to white nationalism, while disseminating such a worldview to aspirational "organic intellectuals" on the far right (Sedgwick, 2019, p. 228). In fulfilling the dual role of intellectual vanguard as well as presenting himself as the champion of whites who feel disenfranchised in "their" country, Spencer himself imitates the role of the organic intellectual that was conceived by Antonio Gramsci.

Due to his growing prominence, Spencer would eventually take the helm of the National Policy Institute (NPI), a far-right think tank that he led during the 2016 election of Donald J. Trump. It was at an NPI conference that he first became visible in the broader American public sphere, when he famously praised Trump's electoral victory by raising his glass of bourbon and proclaimed, "hail Trump, hail our people, hail victory," which elicited Nazi salutes from his most young audience (Sedgwick, 2019, pp. 224–241). Although other Alternative Right groups and publications existed, such as Matthew Heimbach's Traditionalist Worker Party, as well as Andrew Anglin's Daily Stormer and Brad Griffin's Occidental Dissent, it was Spencer who became the public face of the Alt-Right, due to his charisma, good looks, and intellectual arrogance.

The Alt-Right's non-violent metapolitical strategy did not attempt to fundamentally change the social consciousness of the whole within the realm of civil society, but, like pop culture, targeted the youth, as they would be the most impressionable of the subaltern class and least committed to the liberal hegemony. Through the deliberate shaping of the social consciousness of the American youth, a younger generation of disgruntled Americans could serve as the medium through which an Alt-Right long march through the institutions could occur. This approach to metapolitics did not mirror the work of the New Right per se, whose targeted audience was much broader and much more academic, but rather it mirrored the work of the New Left in the 1960s, whose non-conformist philosophy appealed mainly to the university-bound sons and daughters of the working class who saw the residue of fascism in their societies as having the potential to rise again, especially amidst the Cold War (Wellmer, 1987).

The non-violent metapolitical strategy of the Alt-Right was to divide and conquer younger Americans, especially millennials and Generation X, taking advantage of the fact that the world those two generations inhabited was less prosperous and less hopeful than their parents' generation. By making the claim that a dysgenic liberal hegemony caused a decline in the living standards, a degeneration in Western culture, and the *Völkerchaos* (racial chaos) of multiculturalism, the Alt-Right attempted to form a collective anti-liberal social conscious that could serve as the medium for their eventual non-violent transformation of American culture.

Anti-white culture had to be replaced by pro-white culture if such hegemony would be achieved. Like the New Right in Europe, the American Alt-Right attempted to undermine political liberalism as a whole, both in its conservative articulation as well as its culturally liberal articulation. In Spencer's Alt-Right manifesto, he writes that the Alt-Right "wages a situational and ideological war on those deconstructing European history and identity. The decrepit values of Woodstock and Wall Street mean nothing to us" (Sedgwick, 2019, p. 234). As such, it attempted to non-violently convert traditional conservatives to its alternative form of white nationalist conservativism, including its overt racism, misogyny, Islamophobia, and antisemitism, while simultaneously destroying the Cultural Marxists, which included the influence of the Jews and their new weapon of choice: Muslims.[14]

Trump and the Alt-Right: Dialectical Metapolitics

The election of Donald J. Trump was widely seen as a triumph for the Alt-Right and their metapolitical endeavours. Although Trump's foray into the political realm was a significant deviation from Gramsci's theory about culture before politics, it was one that initially served the Alt-Right's metapolitical struggle for hegemony within American civil society. Although Donald Trump was never a reader of Alt-Right political theory, many of his personal views on cultural issues overlapped those of the Alt-Right.

By winning the presidential election in 2016, Trump's brand of a more vulgar right-wing nationalism prepared the conditions within traditional conservative circles for the normalisation of Alt-Right ideas, including: the limitation or end of immigration from non-European countries; the restriction of refugees entering the country; the mass deportation of illegal immigrants; the ban on Muslim immigration; the praise of outdated notions of manliness; the identification and demonisation of cultural liberalism and/or socialism as an existential threat to the nation, and the end of cosmopolitanism, globalism, and allegiances to international institutions. Trump's own close relationship with the Russian President, Vladimir Putin, who is often hailed by the ethno-nationalists as their champion, was seen by many in the Alt-Right as Trump's own move toward "Authoritarian Traditionalism," a vision of an advanced technological world animated by retrotopian values and culture (Shekhovtsov, 2018).[15] As developed by the Russian political and cultural theorist Alexander Dugin, there is a deep strain of authoritarian traditionalism within the broader Alt-Right coalition (Dugin, 2012; Sedgwick, 2019, pp. 155–169). This normalisation of far-right ideas not only within civil society, but to some extent within the state via Trump's administration, had the effect of expanding the Overton window in civil society; that which was unthinkable to say in the public sphere had been given license and legitimacy by an American President, who used his populist appeal to voice the discontent of the aggrieved white subaltern masses.

As such, the head-of-state became the most effective means of Alt-Right metapolitics, post-2016.

Trump, as a self-avowed counter-hegemonic political force, embodied the dialectical nature of metapolitics: he further accelerated the dialectical antagonisms between the politics of *status quo maintenance* and the politics of *radical transformation*. Unlike other conservatives, or even "fascist revolutionaries," Trump attempted to reconcile corporate-friendly conservative economics and white identity politics, which often made uncomfortable bedfellows within the Republican

Party. While advancing certain cultural critiques that were shared by the Alt-Right, i.e., the transformative aspect of his presidency, he also maintained the orthodoxy of Republican economics, such as the deregulation of corporations and banks, as well as tax cuts for upper-income earners, i.e., the maintenance component of his presidency.

This half revolution was denounced by many of those who were his early Alt-Right followers, as it appeared to them that Trump functionalised the economic discontent of the nation only to further the very economic powers that diminish the white ethno-sphere. Because Trump's Make America Great Again (MAGA) movement failed to *radically* transform the culture of the United States, he lost much support from the organic intellectuals of the Alt-Right, including Richard Spencer, who later saw Trump's functionalisation of white nationalism as a means to further his own interests, not transform the country.[16] While the prominence of the organic intellectuals of the Alt-Right had already began to wane after Charlottesville's Unite the Right rally in 2017, the energy behind the MAGA movement among the white subaltern masses grew in strength behind Trump, as he continued his populist rhetoric against the so-called establishment on their behalf. By the end of his presidency,

Alt-Right ideology and the hatred of the "establishment" that it contributed to, so saturated Trump's supporters that even those who were mildly critical of Trump were subject to death threats. The non-violent dissemination of Alt-Right cultural critique, via Trump, which was aimed at transforming the social consciousness of the subaltern masses, contributed to the violent attack on Congress, on 6 January, 2021, wherein a loosely knit alliance of far-right citizens, fuelled by conspiracy theories about a stolen election, attempted to seize the US capitol building, take US Senators and Congress members as hostages, and stop the official certification of the electoral votes. As such, the non-violent metapolitics strategy of the Alt-Right contributed to the production of a social-political powder keg that merely needed a match for it to explode into political violence.

What we can say for certain is that even though the non-violent "form" of Alt-Right metapolitics can be correctly described as a peaceful method of social transformation, the content of such metapolitics prepares the way for violent insurrections, for it alienates and detaches the subaltern masses not only from the prevailing hegemonic worldview, but also from the idea that society can be transformed by peaceful democratic means. As such, the non-violent strategies of Alt-Right metapolitics have become gateways to restorative and/or transformative violence as we have also seen in Christchurch and other locations across the globe.

Conclusion

As we have seen, the Alt-Right's inability to transform the United States along the lines of their racial worldview through violent means lead to an abiding frustration. This frustration with the liberal cultural hegemony, and the impotence of violence against that hegemony, led to the development of a more intellectual strand of the Alt-Right, one that looked to the New Right in Europe for a non-violent method by which they could influence American society. In doing so, they appropriated the method of metapolitics, or the "war of position," as developed by the Marxist Antonio Gramsci, which had been deployed by the New Right in Europe for decades. This shift to the culture wars allowed them to move the struggle against Cultural Marxism, as well as traditional conservatism, from the streets and the state to civil society. A metapolitical struggle, they believed, would eventually create a legitimation crisis between aggrieved white Americans from the liberal status quo, a result that the violent tactics of their neo-Nazi and other fascist predecessors failed to achieve. Having abandoned violent extremism, their non-violent culture war tactics would allow them to enter into the public sphere as "organic intellectuals," to use Gramsci's term, determined to halt the degeneration of the nation. However, even though Alt-Right leaders like Greg Johnson and Jared Taylor rejected violence against their perceived enemies, the influence of their metapolitical critique of liberalism, multiculturalism, and diversity, etc., laid the groundwork for the violence that accompanied Donald Trump's presidency, including the attack on Congress on 6 January, 2021. Those who shared their critique of the liberal hegemony did not share the same commitment to non-violence as a political tactic. In the end, it is clear is that even though the metapolitical method of social transformation is itself peaceful, a mere contestation of ideas, it throws a dark shadow: it conditions the possibility for violent extremism, as it inculcates a desperate feeling among the already aggrieved that cultural hegemony can only be maintained or brought to fruition through violent action.

Notes

1 Greg Johnson is one of the most prominent white nationalist voices in the United States. He is a prolific author of blogs and books, which he publishes through his own publishing house, Counter-Currents Publishing Ltd. His literary advocacy for white Americans has been highly influential upon the metapolitics of the Far-Right "intellectuals" in the United States. Additionally, Jared Taylor is a highly educated (Yale and the Paris Institute of Political Studies) American white nationalist who established the New Century Foundation and its magazine, *American Renaissance,* both dedicated to the advancement of "white interests" and "white identity politics" in the United States. On the older side, Jared Taylor is often looked at as a grandfather-like figure in the white nationalist movement.

2 The Institute for Social Research, better known as the "Frankfurt School," formed after the catastrophe of World War I in Frankfurt, Germany. It was comprised of mainly Jewish sociologists, philosophers, and psychoanalysts, drawing upon the works of Marx, Freud, Nietzsche, as well as German Idealists such as Kant and Hegel, in an attempt to diagnose the ills of society that caused World War I. Its most important figures included Theodor W. Adorno, Max Horkheimer, Herbert Marcuse, and Erich Fromm. Although not official members of the institute, individuals such as Walter Benjamin and Ernst Bloch play important roles in defining the overall philosophical trajectory of the Frankfurt School. Today, Jürgen Habermas remains the most prominent of Frankfurt School scholars.

3 The immediate theoretical background to Gramsci's work is classical Marxism, wherein Marx thought culture was epiphenomenal: it was the result of economic realities. As such, economics, or the "economic base," determines culture, i.e., the "superstructure" of society. Therefore, changes in the economic base results in changes in the realm of culture. Gramsci will reverse this analysis, seeing culture as the primary arena of class contestation as opposed to political-economy.

4 The term "subaltern" is deployed by Gramsci to designate any class of people subject to the hegemony of a more powerful class.

5 Although Gramsci identifies Hegel as the source for his understanding of civil society, it is clear that Gramsci's Marxism led him to formulate it differently than Hegel.

6 By "organic intellectuals," Gramsci intended men whose political economic philosophy was informed by their workaday existence, as they would uniquely be in possession of the practical wisdom, plain speech, and working-class sensibilities needed to effectively convey the revolutionary ideology to the working class. As such, they would not be disconnected from the masses as the "traditional intellectuals" often were, but would exist among the people, and serve as the primary voice of counter-hegemonic philosophy and moral formation, upon which new institutions would be created.

7 This struggle to undermine the prevailing culture that legitimates and reifies the status quo is what is commonly called culture wars (*kulturkampf*), and the Marxists that fight it have been dubbed "cultural Marxists."

8 The term metapolitics was first formulated by the German liberals in the 18th and early 19th century, including Karl von Rotteck (1775–1840), a German political activist, theorist, and historian, but was made accessible to the Right through the French reactionary and monarchist, Joseph de Maistre (1753–1821), who advocated for social hierarchy. For Maistre, metapolitics referred to the essential values, principles, and ideals that serve as the basis of politics, i.e., to capture those metapolitical values was to capture political power.

9 The "68ers," as they're often called by the New Right and the Alt-Right, are members of the "baby boom" generation who rebelled against the perceived conservatism of their societies, especially in the youth revolts of 1968. According to the Swedish identitarian, Joakim Andersen, these non-conformists wanted "endless freedom, freedom from family bonds, from collectives, from traditions, and from ideals" (Anderson, 2018, 124–125). They are often accused of being the cause of the West's modern dysgenic condition.

10 Much of the New Right's underlying thought about identity politics, especially the identification of the enemy, is rooted in their appropriation of Carl Schmitt's political philosophy, especially its "us versus them" dichotomy as the essence of politics (Schmitt, 1996, p. 35).

11 Paleoconservatism is a conservative political philosophy that blends American nationalism with "traditional" Christian values; it generally supports isolationism and minimal migration; stricter government oversight of the free market economy, and rollbacks on programs that advance multiculturalism and ethnic diversity. It often opposes neoconservatism and its attempts to project American power abroad via the military.

12 The Alt-Right believes that traditional American conservativism is implicit white identity politics. That means, in fact, traditional conservatives engage in a mild form of white identity politics, but due to political correctness and other social factors, they will deny it in public. The Alt-Right doesn't deny the nature of their politics; they are explicit white identity politics, openly advocating for "white interests" as opposed to doing it from behind political camouflage.

13 The white nationalist Jared Taylor's academic credentials are also used to bolster legitimacy for his racist positions. Taylor has an undergrad degree from Yale University and an MA from the Paris Institute of Political Studies (Science Po). Additionally, he speaks fluent French and Japanese, having lived in France, West Africa, and Japan. He is also the editor of the journal *American Renaissance,* which sponsors annual academic-like conferences wherein white nationalist speakers from all over the world present their work.

14 One of the Alt-Right's most insidious claims is that Jews are helping Muslims immigrate to the West, wherein the process of Islamisation of will "replace" the white Christians, who had persecuted the Jews ever since the Roman Empire embraced Christianity. This "replacement theory," at least in its American articulation, which combines antisemitism and Islamophobia, is the origins of the white nationalist phrase "Jews will not replace us," which was chanted through the streets of Charlottesville, Virginia, in August of 2017. It was also repeated by Robert Gregory Bowers, who murdered eleven Jewish worshipers in the Tree of Life synagogue in October 2018, in Pittsburgh, Pennsylvania.

15 This form of authoritarian traditionalism is similar to Guillaume Faye's concept of Archeofuturism (Faye, 2010).

16 In an interview with CNN, on 16 July, 2019, Spencer said of Trump, "He gives us nothing outside of racists tweets. And by racist tweets, I mean tweets that are meaningless and cheap and express the kind of sentiments you might hear from your drunk uncle while he's watching [Sean] Hannity" (Daughtery, 2019).

Bibliography

Adamson, W. (2014). *Hegemony and Revolution: A Study of Antonio Gramsci's Political and Cultural Theory.* Brattleboro, VT: Echo Point Books & Media.

Andersen, J. (2018). *Rising from the Ruins: The Right of the 21st Century.* London: Arktos.

Associated Press. (AP). (2011, July 16). "Norway's prime minister tells Country to 'guard freedom' at memorial service." The Guardian. Retrieved May 21, 2021, from www.theguardian.com/world/2011/aug/21/norway-memorial-oslo-victims

Daughtery, Owen. (2019, July 16). "CNN slammed for having white nationalist Richard Spencer on to talk about Trump's tweets." Retrieved December 12, 2020, from https://thehill.com/homenews/media/453419-cnn-slammed-for-having-white-nationalist-richard-spencer-on-to-talk-about

Drochon, H. (2018). *Nietzsche's Great Politics.* Princeton, NJ: Princeton University Press.

Dugin, A. (2012). *The Fourth Political Theory.* London: Arktos.

Dutschke, G. (2006). *Rudi Dutschke: Wir hatten ein barbarisches, schönes Legen.* Cologne: Kiepenheuer & Witsch GmbH.

Faye, G. (2010). *Archeofuturism: European Visions of the Post-Catastrophic Age.* London: Arktos.

Femia, J. V. (1987). *Gramsci's Political Thought: Hegemony, Consciousness, and the Revolutionary Process.* New York: Oxford University Press.

Gramsci, A. (2000). *The Antonio Gramsci Reader: Selected Writings 1916–1935.* In D. Forgacs (Ed.), *Hegemony, Relations of Force, Historical Bloc* (pp. 189–221). New York: New York University Press.

Guillaume F. (2016). *The Colonisation of Europe.* London: Arktos Media.

Hawley, G. (2017). *Making Sense of the Alt-Right.* New York: Columbia University Press.

Hegel, G.W.F. (2010). *Elements of the Philosophy of Right.* In A. W. Wood (Ed.), *Ethical Life* (pp. 187–380). Cambridge: Cambridge University Press.

Johnson, G. (2013). *New Right versus Old Right.* San Francisco, CA: Counter-Currents Publishing Ltd.

Johnson, G. (2018). *The White Nationalist Manifesto.* San Francisco, CA: Counter-Currents Publishing Ltd.

Nietzsche, F. (2014). *Beyond Good and Evil/On the Genealogy of Morality.* Stanford, CA: Stanford University Press.

O'Meara, M. (2013). *New Culture, New Right: Anti-Liberalism in Postmodern Europe.* London: Arktos.

Schmitt, C. (1996). *The Concept of the Political.* (Trans.) George Schwab. Chicago: University of Chicago Press.

Sedgwick, M. (Ed.). (2019). *Key Thinkers of the Radical Right: Behind the New Threat to Liberal Democracy.* New York: Oxford University Press.

Shekhovtsov, A. (2018). *Russia and the Western Far Right: Tango Noir.* New York: Routledge.

Wellmer, A. (1987). "Terrorism and the Critique of Society." In Jürgen Habermas (Ed.), *Observations on the Spiritual Situation of the Age* (pp. 283–307). Cambridge, MA: MIT Press.

23

ANTI-GENDER CAMPAIGNS AS A THREAT TO LIBERAL DEMOCRACY

Elżbieta Korolczuk

Introduction

When the Berlin Wall came down in 1989 we all had this hope of freedom and entering an era beyond ideology. But while we were delighting in that hope, powerful forces prepared for the next step of the global sexual revolution. Don't ask me who these forces are, but I see this revolution taking place at a global scale, with a clear intent to destroy the basis of the family. The destruction of the family uproots every single human being. We become atomized human beings who can be manipulated to do anything.

(Gabriele Kuby in: Vail, 2014, p. 2)

These words by the German sociologist Gabriele Kuby, author of several books and an intellectual leader of European ultra-conservative circles, aptly sum up the narrative put forward by the anti-gender movement (Kuhar & Paternotte, 2017). Along with other activists and intellectuals engaged in campaigns opposing gender equality and sexual democracy, Kuby warns against an approaching collapse of Christian civilisation, a collapse which is allegedly being precipitated by sexual revolution, feminism and the gay liberation movement. She claims that a war has been waged against the "natural family" and traditional forms of sexuality by "genderists," feminists and political institutions, which spread moral corruption under the guise of gender mainstreaming and anti-discrimination policies (Kuby, 2015). Kuby's views encapsulate much of the ideological stance of the ultra-conservative movement, which groups together organisations, groups and individuals opposing gender equality, sexual democracy, new reproductive technologies and the very idea that gender is socially constructed. The representatives of this transnational network – the *anti-gender movement* – readily employ the term "culture war" and often use combat-related words such as "battle," "fight," "weapons" and "threat" (Graff & Korolczuk, 2021) to imply the urgency and seriousness of the conflicts around sexuality and gender identity. They depict opponents of "gender" as virtuous and non-violent people, who are under ruthless attack by morally corrupt global elites (Kuhar & Paternotte 2017; Kalm & Meeuwisse 2020; Korolczuk & Graff 2021).

DOI: 10.4324/9781003032793-27

The vision of ultra-conservative civil society organisations (CSOs) and religious institutions as protectors of ordinary people against unnamed but powerful forces violently attacking families and children is emotionally alluring, but is it true? Existing research shows that the key organisations and networks behind the global anti-gender campaigns can be seen as elite themselves: they are powerful, well-funded and well-connected, and they often forge alliances with politicians, business elites and members of European aristocracy (Datta 2018, 2019; Kuhar & Paternotte, 2017; Provost & Archer, 2020; Rivera, 2019). In many countries, including Brazil, Italy, Poland and the United States, anti-gender actors have begun cooperating closely with right-wing populist and extremist parties, trading political support for access to decision-making processes and financial assistance from the state (Rivera, 2019).

This chapter aims to provide an up-to-date picture of the activities of the anti-gender movement, and analyse its ideological agenda, and political goals. The movement comprises of transnational and national civil society organisations, representatives of religious institutions and intellectual authorities who promote socially conservative discourse and fight for legal changes such as a ban on abortion and reproductive technologies, limiting the rights of LGBT+ communities and prohibiting gender studies at universities (Kuhar & Paternotte, 2017; Roggeband & Krizsán, 2018; Verloo, 2018). The question is whether such organisations and networks should be seen simply as a sign of ideological diversification of civil society or rather as a threat to liberal democracy. The focus of this chapter is on transnational actors and the activities of key organisations linking European, American and Latin American contexts. Two organisations are discussed in detail: the influential transnational network called the World Congress of Families (WCF) and the Polish organisation named the Ordo Iuris Institute, which has been connected to another transnational network –Tradition, Family and Property (TFP) (Datta 2019; Gilloz et al 2017).

By analysing these two organisations I will examine how the goals of the anti-gender movement are related to specific political initiatives within a complex web of national and transnational actors. These actors are all connected personally, organisationally and financially. In-depth analysis of public statements, key documents and speeches delivered by anti-gender actors helps us to identify the key discursive strategies employed by this movement. These strategies include the vilification of opponents, victim–perpetrator reversal, constructing moral panics and normalising extreme ideas such as homophobia.

This chapter is based on data gathered during eight years of studying the anti-gender movement in Poland and abroad.[1] The dataset includes hundreds of texts such as books and interviews with intellectual authorities within European anti-gender circles, such as Gabriele Kuby and Pope Francis; statements and articles published on the websites of anti-gender groups and organisations (e.g. Agenda Europe, CitizenGo, Ordo Iuris Institute, TFP, the WCF); media reports; published interviews with representatives of the anti-gender movement; and official statements by religious institutions (such as the Vatican) and state representatives. Textual analysis of this data was supplemented by qualitative analysis of 26 interviews conducted between 2019 and 2021 with representatives of Polish, Italian and European organisations, most of which are working to ensure gender equality and sexual democracy (e.g. *Non Una di Meno*, ILGA Europe and International Planned Parenthood Federation Europe) and some which oppose "gender" and reproductive rights (e.g. *Pro Vita e Famiglia* in Italy and Ordo Iuris Institute in Poland).

The author also attended over 20 demonstrations and rallies organised by both gender conservative and gender progressive organisations in Poland, Italy and Sweden between 2012 and 2021. In March 2019, the author took part in the WCF in Verona (Italy) as well as in the feminist counter-event named Cita Trans Feminista, which was organised by feminist, LGBT+ and left-oriented actors. Reports published by organisations and media outlets such as the European

Parliamentary Forum on Population and Development and Open Democracy were also helpful in contextualising the analysis, along with results of opinion polls conducted on the national and European level.

The chapter starts with a discussion on civil society as a heterogeneous phenomenon, which includes organisations and actors that oppose liberal values and democratic norms such as pluralism, human rights and inclusion of minorities. The following sections discuss the structure, ideology and goals of the anti-gender movement, as well as the discursive strategies of ultraconservative actors operating in Poland and transnationally. The conclusion section sums up the outcomes of the study showing that the political agenda of the anti-gender movement is not only contradictory to democratic values, but the discursive strategies employed by such actors should be further analysed as a conveyor belt to engagement in violent extremism.

The Anti-gender Movement: Ultra-conservative Ideology and Transnational Cooperation

This analysis focuses on ultra-conservative organisations which oppose the idea that gender is a social construct, promote homophobic and misogynistic views, and spread moral panic around the downfall of Christian civilisation due to low fertility rates, the alleged demise of the traditional family and "sexualisation of children" by gays and feminists. Together with the representatives of religious institutions such as the Vatican, some Protestant churches and Russian Orthodox Patriarchate, these organisations form the *global anti-gender movement* (Case, 2016). This well-connected network of NGOs, public intellectuals and religious institutions cooperates closely with right-wing political parties, business elites and European aristocracy to counter gender equality and sexual democracy (Datta, 2018; Kuhar & Paternotte, 2017; Graff & Korolczuk, 2021). This chapter analyses the anti-gender movement as part of a broader wave of political extremism which represents a major challenge for democracy.

The anti-gender movement is perhaps most visible on the local level. Mass protests against marriage equality held under the banner of *La Manif Pour Tous* in France, the anti-LGBT+ and antifeminist backlash in Putin's Russia, as well as continuous attempts to limit access to abortion on Poland hit the headlines both at home and abroad (Datta, 2018; Graff & Korolczuk, 2021; Kuhar & Paternotte, 2017; Scrinzi, 2017). However, local campaigns are frequently initiated and coordinated by ultra-conservative organisations and groups active globally such as Agenda Europe, a clandestine transnational network established by 20 US-based and European ultra-conservative organisations in 2013, which today includes over 100 organisations from 30 European countries (Datta, 2018). Other important anti-gender CSOs include the Political Network for Values funded in 2014 as a transnational platform integrating legislators and political representatives interested in transatlantic dialogue and CitizenGo, an online platform founded in Spain in 2013 with the aim to mobilise people to sign petitions to defend "life, family, and liberty"; as of 2021, petitions are available in 12 languages and the group holds campaigns in 50 countries all over the globe.

The contemporary global anti-gender movement employs a variety of strategies to challenge what it sees as a hegemony of liberal and left forces. In the words of Antonio Arsuaga, founder and director of CitizenGo, the enemies of the movement include "Gramscians, leftists, cultural Marxists, radical feminists [and] LGBT totalitarians … who want to shut us up" (author's notes from the WCF conference in Verona, 2019). Civil society actors, religious fundamentalists and ultraconservative intellectuals supporting the movement combine various strategies to achieve their goals. They advocate for legal changes (e.g. aiming to prevent the ratification and implementation of the Istanbul Convention and limit access to abortion via the One of Us European citizens' initiative) and intervene at the level of transnational organisations and meetings (e.g. they held an alternative summit in 2019 in Nairobi, where an official UN meeting was held to celebrate the 25th anniversary of the International Conference on Population and Development in Cairo). Simultaneously, ultra-conservative actors attempt to change the language used in debates on sexuality and women's rights. They employ terms such as human rights and women's rights to oppose abortion rights and marriage equality legislation, and to mobilise people at the grassroots level against a wide range of issues from the decriminalisation of homosexuality in Uganda to depicting transsexual characters on Netflix (e.g. via online platforms such as CitizenGo). Such organisations seek legitimacy and public support by carefully calibrating their discourse to different contexts, frequently concealing their origins, political connections and sources of funding (Graff & Korolczuk, 2021; Kuhar & Paternotte, 2017). While their self-presentation usually highlights their pro-democratic character, respect for human rights and the fact that they want to promote love and peace (Kalm & Meeuwisse 2020), the campaigns supported by the anti-gender movements often result in deepening polarisation and hatred against minority groups.

The present analysis focuses on two cases. The first is the WCF, founded in 1997 in the United States and renamed the International Organisation for the Family in 2016; it has over 40 official partner organisations around the world, including countries such as Russia, and links various right-wing political parties and religious authorities. WCF regularly holds international congresses which bring together representatives of ultra-conservative organisations from all over the globe, fundamentalist religious actors (representing various denominations, including Catholic, Orthodox and Evangelical), right-wing politicians and other elite actors representing business and aristocratic families. Since 1997 conventions have been held in different capitals around the world, including Prague, Geneva, Mexico City, Hungary and most recently in 2019 in Verona.

The current leader of the WCF, Brian Brown, stated during his opening speech at Verona that the main aim of the organisation is "to defend, promote, protect and lift up something so true, something so basic, something so beautiful – the family" (author's notes from the WCF conference in Verona, 2019). However, a close analysis of the discourses promoted by the WCF and its policy goals paint a very different picture. In its daily operations it does not promote social policies supporting families or protecting children from marginalised communities, but rather focuses on challenging women's reproductive rights and the rights of sexual minorities. WCF representatives have been engaged in opposing marriage equality legislation in the United States and supported anti-LGBT+ legislation in countries such as Russia and Uganda. In 2013 Larry Jacobs, WCF's managing director, said in an interview with *End Times* radio host Rick Wiles

> … the law [on anti-gay propaganda] in the Russian Duma passed on first reading, it would ban propaganda to minors, preventing them [LGBT+ people] from corrupting children. What a great idea and the rest of Europe is going the other way, legalizing LGBT propaganda
>
> *(quoted in: Southern Poverty Law Center).*

The ban against conveying "propaganda of non-traditional relations" (i.e. information about homosexuality) to minors adopted by the Russian parliament (*Duma*) in 2013 and the Uganda Anti-Homosexuality Act passed in December of the same year significantly contributed to an increase in harassment of LGBT+ people in both countries, including public "outings" via newspapers and social media sites, death threats, beatings of activists and people stigmatised as gay, as well as physical attacks and killings (Yudina, 2021; Human Rights Watch, 2019). Available data also shows that in both contexts the legal changes have further entrenched hatred against LGBT+ people and stigma attached to non-normative behaviours and identities (Pew Research Center, 2019). WCF's support of political homophobia has led to it being added to a list of hate groups by the Southern Poverty Law Center, an American non-profit advocacy organisation specialising in civil rights.

The second network is TFP, established in Brazil by Plinio Corrêa de Oliveira in 1960. In recent decades the group has spread to Europe and today connected organisations can be found in many countries, including France and Poland. TFP combines anti-communism and gender-conservative views with a neoliberal economic stance, and according to Margaret Power it has a long history of cooperating with far-right and extremist movements "ranging from the New Right in the United States, to military dictatorships in South America, to the World Anti-Communist League" (Power, 2010, p. 86). In some countries, such as France, local branches of TFP have been labelled as a sect, based on accusations of indoctrinating school children at institutions run by the organisation; however, globally TFP remains strong, partly due to its strategy of setting up independent but closely collaborating organisations in various countries.

In the early 2000s, Poland became one of the centres of the network through the activities of the Father Piotr Skarga Association, connected to the TFP branch in France (Datta, 2019; Dauksza et al., 2020). In 2013, the Association co-funded another organisation which became one of the key anti-gender actors in Poland: the Ordo Iuris Institute for Legal Culture (OI). The official website (ordoiuris.pl) states that OI is a think-tank gathering "academics and legal practitioners with the aim of promoting a legal culture based on respect for human dignity and rights." In practice the foundation mainly focuses on opposing women's reproductive rights and anti-discriminatory measures concerning the LGBT+ community. In 2016, Ordo Iuris became involved in the Stop Abortion campaign which aimed to introduce a blanket ban on abortions in Poland, including in cases of serious foetal malformations or rape which were legal at the time. The bill also included prison sentences of up to five years for women who had terminated their pregnancy.

The mass protests of Polish women led to the proposal being buried in parliamentary commissions, but in 2019 the foundation launched another highly controversial campaign. Ordo Iuris drafted the Local Government Charter of the Rights of the Family (LGCRF) and encouraged local authorities (municipalities or *voivodships*) to sign the charter to ensure the "healthy and safe education of children and respect for parental rights" (author's translation of www.kartarodzin.pl). The charter was a response to the Mayor of Warsaw Rafał Trzaskowski signing of the LGBT+ Declaration aimed at counteracting discrimination against the LGBT+ community. Ordo Iuris harshly criticised the declaration and launched a petition to pressure Trzaskowski to withdraw his signature, which was signed by over 22,000 people. Close to 100 municipalities and regions of Poland signed the charter promoted by Ordo Iuris and another 90 declared themselves free from the alleged "LGBT+ ideology," determined to ban equality marches and anti-discriminatory education in schools. Both campaigns evoked immediate associations with zoning practices of the Nazi era which led to the segregation of Jews in European cities, hence the municipalities which joined them were dubbed "LGBT+-free zones" (Ciobanu, 2020).

Homophobic discourse promoted by ultra-conservative civil society actors, the Catholic Church and the ruling Law and Justice party led to increased violence against LGBT+ people in the country. As in other countries where homophobic campaigns are also held, in Poland opinion polls show that anti-LGBT propaganda influences people's attitudes. The 2019 CBOS report revealed that after several years of positive changes, when the percentage of people declaring that same-sex partnerships should be legalised was rising, this trend was halted in 2019 (CBOS, 2019). In July 2019, Poland witnessed attacks on the participants of the Białystok Equality March. According to the media, over 4,000 football fans and neo-Nazis verbally and physically assaulted several people, and the police resorted to using tear gas and rocket grenades to tame the attackers (Dehnel, 2019). Similar events took place in many other cities where such marches were held; for example, the author has witnessed events in the town of Radomsko where several people were attacked at the end of the 2019 Equality March. In the city of Lublin two opponents of equal rights brought a homemade explosive device to the Equality March held on 28 September. Fortunately, the couple was apprehended by the police before the bomb was deployed, but two reporters were seriously injured during the event (Wilk, 2019). Similar attacks followed: in February an individual with a knife attacked a gay couple walking hand-in-hand down the street in Warsaw, and in March 2021 a group of right-wing attackers beat up a group of LGBT+ activists exercising outdoors in the city of Gdańsk. Following a logic all too familiar from history, discursive dehumanisation invites physical violence, and the lack of condemnation of such attacks from the authorities encourages the perpetrators.

Discursive Strategies of the Anti-gender Movement

There are three key mechanisms through which anti-gender actors encourage and bolster social polarisation and extremist attitudes. These include spreading moral panics on moral degeneration; vilifying already marginalised groups such as LGBT+ individuals by portraying them as members of powerful and evil global elites; and normalising extreme ideas such as homophobia and misogyny in public discourse by presenting them as a "defence of the traditional family" and children.

Analyses of the discursive strategies of the extreme right show that such actors frequently employ scapegoating and blame shifting. As Ruth Wodak (2015) has described, vilification of specific groups, frequently those that are already marginalised and oppressed, helps to present social and economic problems as the result of elitist conspiracies, and to claim victimhood by the right-wing actors, even when they hold the power. This tactic is part of a broader discursive strategy of polarisation, aimed at justifying the discrimination of minorities. When the "other" is seen as powerful and a danger to our wellbeing or even survival, resistance, including physical violence, can be conceived of as an act of self-defence.

Wodak (2015) also states that right-wing actors usually deny explicit racism or exclusion and aim to accentuate positive self-presentation. "Speakers, in denying prejudice, will claim that their criticisms of minority group members are 'factual,' 'objective' and 'reasonable,' rather than based upon irrational feelings, and will accordingly employ a range of discursive strategies of legitimisation" (Wodak, 2015, p. 82). To this end, representatives of the anti-gender movement claim that disadvantaged groups, such as LGBT+ individuals or women (especially feminist activists), are in fact members of powerful and wealthy elite, which is generously funded by wealthy individuals such as George Soros or Bill Gates. According to such conspiracy theories, these actors control transnational institutions such as the UN, and operate behind the scenes to "sexualise" children and bring destruction to the traditional family. In the words of Kuby

> The idea of changing our sex upsets the notion of what it means to be human. It is the deepest rebellion against the conditions of our human existence that you can possibly imagine. It makes people sick and rootless … What will this make of us? A whole mass of sexualized consumers who can be manipulated to do anything. At the same time, the division between rich and poor is growing globally, so we have a concentration of

wealth and power in a minority and masses of people who have no roots. That is what the gender mainstreaming agenda is apparently aiming at

(Kuby in: Vail, 2014)

The victim–perpetrator reversal and the claim that opposition to gender equality and sexual democracy is an act of resistance against "ideological colonisation" have become a key discursive tactic of the anti-gender movement (Korolczuk & Graff, 2018). Opposition to women's reproductive rights, sex education and anti-discriminatory measures – dubbed by these actors as an onslaught of "gender ideology" – have thus been presented as a brave defence of common people's basic rights and children's safety.

This discursive strategy was reflected in numerous speeches and debates at the 2019 WCF in Verona. Antonio Arsuaga, president of CitizenGo and one of European leaders of the anti-gender movement, claimed that conservative forces need to consolidate and work together because "this cultural war is a global war. They control the mainstream media, the parties, they run NGOs funded by Soros, the enemies of the family have multiple faces" (author's note from WCF in Verona). A similar vision was presented during the meeting by the Italian politician Georgia Melloni, leader of the far-right party Brothers of Italy, who suggested that it were the liberal and left forces that have launched a smear campaign against the WCF:

> They accused us of so many things [in the media], they say we are reactionists, unlucky, unpresentable, obscurantist, that it is a scandal that there is someone who wants to defend the natural family founded on marriage, which wants to stimulate the birth rate, who values human life, wants to support educational freedom, which means no to gender ideology.
>
> *(recording from WCF in Verona, 2019, original in Italian)*[2]

"They" are usually not named but defined by their actions and ideological views. It is clear however, that "they" are influential and dangerous, ruthlessly attacking "the natural family" and individuals who value human life. Frequently, ultra-conservative actors "express thinly veiled antisemitic views, e.g. when attacking George Soros as the embodiment of both global capital and a Jewish conspiracy against Christianity" (Graff & Korolczuk, 2021, p. 98). Anti-gender intellectuals portray liberals and leftists as those who use economic power to spread moral degeneration, with the aim of controlling the population's minds and lives.

The anti-gender movement elaborates the danger to children that the cultural war allegedly brings. As observed by Roman Kuhar and David Paternotte (2017), similarly to the opponents of the sexual revolution in the United States in the 1970s, one of the key arguments of contemporary ultra-conservative actors is that "gender ideology" endangers the healthy development of children, and goes against parents' rights to decide on their offspring's education. Sex and anti-discriminatory education are presented as a road towards early "sexualisation" of youth and promotion of sex change. According to anti-gender activists, acquiring knowledge regarding sexuality results in the "hypersexualisation of children," making them ideal prey for paedophiles (Kuhar & Paternotte, 2017, p. 18). Such arguments have been raised by the Ordo Iuris foundation against the LGBT+ Declaration signed by Warsaw's mayor in 2019.[3] According to representatives of the organisations, the declaration:

> contains a range of ideological postulates, which violate standards of ideological impartiality of public authorities, and the announcement of introduction of permissive sexual education in accordance with WHO standards to schools, [...] raises

reasonable doubts in terms of the constitutional principle of children's protection against demoralization.

(Local government Charter of the Rights of the Family)

Protection of children served as the main justification behind the campaign targeting local authorities to sign the Local Government Charters of the Rights of the Family. The ultimate goal was presented as saving children from abuse and freeing local communities from "LGBT ideology," which, according to Ordo Iuris chairman Jerzy Kwaśniewski, "involves the deconstruction of the natural concept of gender, sexuality and family" (author's translation of Kwaśniewski's tweet, 20 September 2019).

Representatives of OI publicly stressed that this project had nothing to do with harassment or discrimination of LGBT+ individuals but it was aimed to protect school children from "sexualisation" and "indoctrination." In practice, however, the campaign is based on the assumption that sex education or any information regarding the existence and experiences of LGBT+ people are a form of intolerable indoctrination and violence. As stated on the IO website

It is unacceptable to earmark public property or public means for projects whose nature assumes undermining constitutional identity and autonomy of marriage and the family, including, in particular, projects implemented within the scope of education.

(Local government Charter of the Rights of the Family)

This carefully drafted position does not even include words such as homosexuality or LGBT (besides the paragraph where the LGBT+ Declaration is mentioned), which is why Ordo Iuris threatened to sue anyone who publicly claims that they aim to discriminate against sexual minorities. The LGBT+ community, however, interpreted these campaigns and public statements as highly discriminatory, responding with the message "We are people, not ideology" (Pacewicz, 2019). Moreover, after the Polish Commissioner for Human Rights appealed against declarations about "LGBT-free zones" to the administrative court, Ordo Iuris backed local politicians supporting such zones and represented them in court. The foundation continues to promote the view that "LGBT ideology" exists and poses a threat to Polish families and children, e.g. by holding public debates under the banner "Let's stop gender politics and LGBT+ ideology," such as the meeting organised in May 2019 in Białystok.

As in the case of the WCF, open homophobia is carefully avoided in the language of OI. It is coded as a "defence of the family," which indicates that the introduction of the Family Charters is not a discriminatory measure but a noble and worthy cause. The same rhetoric has been employed in another campaign, which aims to replace the Istanbul Convention – the Council of Europe's treaty to prevent violence against women – with the so-called Family Rights Convention. The slogan of the campaign reads "Stop gender. Stand for family!" (https://stopg enderconvention.org/), and the main claim is that the very use of the concept of "gender" in the convention threatens the existence of heterosexual marriage and family. The role of gender stereotypes in causing violence against women is downplayed by OI representatives as allegedly unfunded and ideological, as they promote the view that the best strategy to counteract gender-based violence is to promote heterosexual marriage.

By presenting extreme ideas such as homophobia and misogyny as the defence of the "traditional family" and children, the anti-gender movement not only normalises such views in public debates but also mobilises people to act on them. In contrast to the immoral and cunning "genderists," people involved with the anti-gender movement and politicians who support them position themselves as benevolent and besieged defenders of life, freedom and common sense. In the words of Jacopo Coghe, Vice-President of the 13th Congress of Families:

> The world needs heroes, today more than ever we need heroes. And you're the heroes, you here in this room. I also say this to the politicians present here: you're heroes today, you're an example of freedom […] because there are those who didn't want you to be here, those who didn't want to conform with us freely, democratically, with their own ideas.
>
> *(13th Congress of Families, Verona, author's recording,*
> *original in Italian)*

This Manichean division is imbued with a sense of threat and moral urgency: all means become justified if one is fighting for the future of human civilisation, and since the end is nigh all decent people should engage in the struggle. However, the documentary showing debates concerning LGBT+ rights at provincial assemblies and city councils in Poland exposes some of the consequences of such rhetorical strategies. The politicians compare "LGBT+ ideology" to cancer, equate homosexuality with paedophilia and zoophilia, talk about LGBT+ people as sick and depraved, and claim that they are "carriers of LGBT+ ideology" (Nodzyńska, 2020). Although Ordo Iuris refutes the allegations of promoting homophobia, its campaigns clearly strengthened the process of dehumanisation through language, which has been identified as one of key mechanism facilitating discrimination of specific groups and leading to political violence (Wodak, 2015).

Can Civil Society Be Dangerous to Democracy?

In debates on extremism and radicalisation, civil society is frequently portrayed as an antidote to these trends, rather than a potential source of the problem. This view is shared by many academics and practitioners alike. Civil society is frequently understood as a space of collective engagement on behalf of what people see as the common good, including activities ranging from mass social movements and protests to grassroots initiatives (Jacobsson & Korolczuk, 2017). This space is imagined as being separate from the state and the sphere of formal party politics, but in reality it is usually interconnected with it: sometimes, grassroots movements develop and become institutionalised as political parties and sometimes political actors encourage CSOs to cooperate more closely and pursue specific goals together. While such cooperation can indeed strengthen democratic practices and values such as equality, solidarity and pluralism, in some cases it may be detrimental to democracy.

Robert Putnam's (1994) vision of civil society as a crucial element of stable and functioning political regimes is reflected in policy reports such as the 2019 OSCE Guidebook "The Role of Civil Society in Preventing and Countering Violent Extremism and Radicalization that Lead to Terrorism." Over time, however, researchers have started to look at CSOs with a critical eye (Foley & Edwards, 1996; Roggeband & Glasius 2020). They challenge the "notion of the inherent virtuousness of civil society, its unquestionably beneficial role in strengthening democracy and assumed liberal preferences of civil society actors need to be reassessed" (Ekiert, 2021, p. 3). In the post-communist context Petr Kopecky and Cas Mudde (2003) observed that civil society also has a dark side – "uncivil society" – comprising organisations and groups which do not embrace liberal values, such as Hungarian skinheads, and who employ contentious politics as the main organisational strategy, such as the Polish Self-Defence farmers' organisation. While their analysis focused on the post-communist region, the trend itself is global (Mudde, 2016).

In a similar vein, scholars analysing the roots of the electoral successes of right-wing popu-list parties in Hungary and Poland in the last decade have shown that these victories should be, at least partly, attributed to the active engagement of CSOs in promoting the political agenda of Fidesz and Law and Justice (e.g. Greskovits, 2017; Ślarzyński, 2018). In both countries, the right-wing populist regimes, which stifle freedom of speech, curtail the rights of minorities (including Roma people and LGBT+ communities) and seize control over independent polit-ical institutions, the judiciary and the media, ascended to power with the help of CSOs. Today, CSOs working closely with Hungarian and Polish governments include government-organised non-governmental organisations as well as existing associations and foundations which claim to be devoted to strengthening democracy. As shown by Marcin Ślarzyński,a dense network of local clubs focused around *Gazeta Polska* (a right-wing weekly magazine) supported the Law and Justice party during electoral campaigns, provided new cadres on the local level and functioned as a "transmission belt" between local communities and the party (Ślarzyński 2018, p. 154). In Hungary, the right accumulated substantial social capital due to the activities of the Civic Circles movement, a network of conservative organisations founded by Viktor Orbán in 2002 (Greskovits, 2017).

Throughout the 2000s and 2010s, the international community of scholars concerned with extremism and security experts mainly focused on Islamist groups; however, there has been growing recognition that in most countries right-wing extremism should be considered to be a much bigger threat (della Porta et al., 2012; Mudde, 2016; Youngblood, 2020). Right-wing organisations and networks which espouse nativism and ethno-nationalism, in many cases alongside racism, anti-Semitism and Islamophobia, frequently embrace strategies of violence and disavowal for democratic processes (Wodak, 2015).

"Over the last decade, the far-right movement was responsible for 73.3% of all extremist murders in the United States. In 2018, this statistic rose to 98%" (Youngblood, 2020, p. 2). At the same time, the landscape of far-right and extremist movements is changing: activism is more diffused and less centred around specific organisations, it mainly takes place online and frequently on a transnational level (Mulhall & Khan-Ruf, 2021; Youngblood, 2020). Scholars also observe that contemporary extremist groups such as Identitarians and other proponents of white supremacy, as well as right-wing populist and far-right parties, readily employ misogynistic and ultra-conservative rhetoric on gender and sexuality to attract members and normalise their radical message among the wider audience (Mulhall & Khan-Ruf, 2021; Roth, 2020). Thus, it is of crucial importance to examine how ultra-conservative views are produced, employed and promoted on the national level, how homophobic and anti-feminist discourses are disseminated transnationally to the benefit of right-wing populism and extremism, and what are the consequences of these processes, especially for minority groups.

Conclusions

While anti-gender organisations claim to promote traditional family values, defend heterosexual marriage and religious freedom, analysis of the narratives and political initiatives promoted by ultra-conservative NGOs shows that the movement mainly focuses on promoting anti-choice and anti-LGBT+ views and policies, on opposing sex education, and on challenging anti-discriminatory measures such as the Istanbul Convention. Examining the discourses and activities of WCF and Ordo Iuris reveals that these organisations promote the view that anti-discriminatory laws and education present a major threat to the family and children, and spread such opinions in the media and public debates.

There are three main discursive strategies employed by the anti-gender movement: spreading moral panics by presenting "gender" and "LGBT ideology" as a threat to children; scapegoating minorities which justifies hostility towards marginalised groups; and normalising extreme views in public debates by presenting them as a defence of the "traditional family." These strategies have been identified by scholars of right-wing extremism as facilitating radicalisation and potentially leading to politically motivated aggression. The anti-gender political agenda is contradictory to democratic values such as pluralism, equality and individual freedoms, and in some cases the campaigns and discourses promoted by organisations opposing "gender" have contributed to violence. Consequently, while the activities of the anti-gender movement can be interpreted as a form of non-violent political extremism, its discursive strategies and campaigns should be further analysed as a conveyor belt to engagement in violent extremism.

These findings reveal the need to rethink normative concepts of civil society and recognise its deeply heterogeneous nature. While some CSOs aim to promote both democratic practices and values such as plurality, individual and minority rights, others claim to support illiberal versions of democracy, contributing to the deepening of polarisation and acceleration of social conflicts. The cases examined in this chapter suggest that researchers studying the roots of contemporary extremisms and the crisis of democracy should look not only at groups which openly embrace racism, antisemitism and xenophobia, but also those which promote anti-feminist and anti-LGBT+ political agendas under the guise of "fasmily values." The growing alliances between civil society actors opposing equality and right-wing populists also indicate that scholars need to pay more attention to the ways in which issues concerning gender and sexuality have become key political fault lines in the contemporary world.

Notes

1 The author wishes to acknowledge that work on this chapter has been assisted by the program "Civil Society Elites? Comparing elite composition, reproduction, integration and contestation in European civil societies" sponsored by the Riksbanken Jubileumsfond (grant number M17 0188:1).
2 This and other speeches given in Italian were translated by Cecilia Santilli.
3 In recent years, Ordo Iuris has started to cooperate closely with the Law and Justice government, which supports its various initiatives financially and organisationally. One example of such close collaboration is Collegium Intermarium, a higher education institution opened by Ordo Iuris in 2021 in Warsaw, which is financially supported by the Polish Ministry of Education and Science, and by state-owned enterprises such as PZU.

References

Case, M. A. (2016). The Role of the Popes in the Invention of Complementarity and the Vatican's Anathematization of Gender. *Religion and Gender, 6*(2), 155–72..

CBOS. (2019). *CBOS News.* CBOS. Retrieved from: www.cbos.pl/PL/publikacje/news/2019/20/newsletter.php.

Ciobanu, C. (2020, February 25). A Third of Poland Declared 'LGBT-Free Zone.' *Balkan Insight.* Retrieved from: https://balkaninsight.com/2020/02/25/a-third-of-poland-declared-lgbt-free-zone/.

Datta, N. (2018). *"Restoring the Natural Order": The Religious Extremists' Vision to Mobilize European Societies against Human Rights on Sexuality and Reproduction.* Brussels: The European Parliamentary Forum on Population & Development.

Datta, N. (2019). Modern-Day Crusaders in Europe. Tradition, Family and Property: Analysis of a Transnational, Ultra-Conservative, Catholic-Inspired Influence Network. *Političke Perspektive, 8*(3), 69–105. https://doi.org/10.20901/pp.8.3.03

Dauksza, J., Gielewska, A., Szczygieł, K., Lebel, A., & Dal Piva, J. (2020, December 28). Założyciele Ordo Iuris finansują milionami konserwatywną krucjatę na świecie. *Onet Wiadomości.* Retrieved from: https://wiadomosci.onet.pl/swiat/zalozyciele-ordo-iuris-finansuja-milionami-konserwatywna-krucjate-na-swiecie/fhh4rqw.

Dehnel, J. (2019, July 28). The Struggle for LGBT Equality: Pride Meets Prejudice in Poland. *The Guardian*, sec. World news. Retrieved from https://www.theguardian.com/world/2019/jul/28/lgbt-gay-rights-poland-first-pride-march-bialystok-rage-violence

della Porta, D., Caiani, M., & Wagemann, C. (2012). *Mobilizing on the Extreme Right: Germany, Italy, and the United States*. Oxford: Oxford University Press.

Ekiert, G. (2021). *Civil Society as a Threat to Democracy: Organizational Bases of the Populist Counterrevolution in Poland*. CES Open Forum Series. Harvard: Harvard University.

Foley, M., & Edwards, M. B. (1996). The Paradox of Civil Society. *Journal of Democracy*, 7(3), 38–52. http://dx.doi.org/10.1353/jod.1996.0048

Gilloz, O., Hairy, N., & Fleming, M. (2017). Getting to Know You: Mapping the Anti-feminist Face of Right-Wing Populism in Europe. *OpenDemocracy*. Retrieved from: www.opendemocracy.net/en/can-europe-make-it/mapping-anti-feminist-face-of-right-wing-populism-in-europe/.

Graff, A. & Korolczuk, E. (2021). *Anti-Gender Politics in the Populist Moment*. New York: Routledge. https://doi.org/10.4324/9781003133520

Greskovits, B. (2017). *Rebuilding the Hungarian right through civil organization and contention: The civic circles movement* [Working Paper]. Retrieved from: https://cadmus.eui.eu//handle/1814/47245.

Human Rights Watch. (2019, November 17). Uganda: Stop Police Harassment of LGBT People. *Human Rights Watch*. Retrieved from: www.hrw.org/news/2019/11/17/uganda-stop-police-harassment-lgbt-people

Jacobsson, K., and Korolczuk, E, eds. (2017). *Civil Society Revisited: Lessons from Poland*. New York and Oxford: Berghahn Books.

Kalm, S. & Meeuwisse, A. (2020). For Love and for Life: Emotional Dynamics at the World Congress of Families. *Global Discourse*, 10(2): 303–320. https://doi.org.10.1332/204378920X15784019972237.

Kopecky, P., & Mudde, C. (Eds.). (2003). *Uncivil Society?: Contentious Politics in Post-Communist Europe*. New York: Routledge.

Korolczuk, E. & Graff, A. (2018). Gender as 'Ebola from Brussels': The Anti-colonial Frame and the Rise of Illiberal Populism, *Signs: Journal of Women in Culture and Society, 43*(4): 797–821. https://doi.org/10.1086/696691

Kuby, G. (2015). *The Global Sexual Revolution: Destruction of Freedom in the Name of Freedom*. Translated by James Patrick Kirchner. Kettering, OH: LifeSite/Angelico Press.

Kuhar, R., and Paternotte, D. eds. (2017). *Anti-Gender Campaigns in Europe: Mobilizing against Equality*. London and New York: Rowman & Littlefield Publishers.

Local Government Charter of the Rights of the Family. (2019). Retrieved from Ordo https://en.ordoiu ris.pl/family-and-marriage/local-government-charter-rights-family

Mudde, C. (Ed.). (2016). *The Populist Radical Right*. New York: Routledge.

Mulhall, J., & Khan-Ruf, S. (2021). *Far-Right Extremism in Europe*. London: HOPE not hate Charitable Trust.

Nodzyńska, P. (2020). 12 mln Polaków mieszka w "strefach wolnych od LGBT." Zobacz dokument "Tu nie chodzi o ludzi." *Gazeta Wyborcza*. Retrieved from: https://wyborcza.pl/7,82983,26088548,12-mln-polakow-mieszka-w-strefach-wolnych-od-lgbt-zobacz.html.

OSCE. (2018). *The Role of Civil Society in Preventing and Countering Violent Extremism and Radicalization that Lead to Terrorism: A Guidebook for South-Eastern Europe*. Organisation for Security and Co-operation in Europe. Retrieved from:www.osce.org/secretariat/400241.

Pacewicz, K. (2019, February 8). Homofobiczneszczuciedziała. *wyborcza.pl*. Retrieved from: https://wyborcza.pl/7,75398,25035564,homofobiczne-szczucie-dziala.html.

Paternotte, D., & Kuhar, R. (2018). Disentangling and Locating the "Global Right": Anti-gender Campaigns in Europe. *Politics and Governance, 6*(3), 6–19. DOI: https://doi.org/10.17645/pag.v6i3.1557

Pew Research Center. (2019). *Pew Global Attitudes & Trends Question Database*. Pew Research Center. Retrieved from: www.pewresearch.org/global/question-search/

Power, M. (2010). Transnational, Conservative, Catholic, and Anti-Communist: Tradition, Family, and Property (TFP). In: M. Durham & M. Power (Eds.), *New Perspectives on the Transnational Right* (pp. 85–105). New York: Palgrave Macmillan US.

Provost, C., & Archer, N. (2020). Revealed: $280m 'Dark Money' Spent by US Christian Right Groups Globally. *OpenDemocracy*. Retrieved from: www.opendemocracy.net/en/5050/trump-us-christian-spending-global-revealed/.

Putnam, R. D. (1994). *Making Democracy Work: Civic Traditions in Modern Italy* (1st edition). Princeton: Princeton University Press.

Rivera, E. (2019). *Unraveling the Anti-Choice Supergroup Agenda Europe in Spain*. IERES Occasional Papers.

Roggeband, C, & Glasius, M. (2020). "Uncivil Society." In R. A. List, H. K. Anheier & S. Toepler (Eds.) *International Encyclopedia of Civil Society* (pp. 1–7). Cham: Springer International Publishing.

Roggeband, C., & Krizsán, A. (2018). Reversing Gender Policy Progress: Patterns of Backsliding in Central and Eastern European New Democracies. *European Journal of Politics and Gender, 1*(3), 367–385. https://doi.org/10.1332/251510818X15311219732356

Roth, J. (2020). "Intersectionality Strikes Back: Feminist Struggles Against Right-Wing Populism in the Americas." In J. Roth & G. Dietze (Eds.), *Right-Wing Populism and Gender. European Perspectives and Beyond* (pp. 285–308). Bielefeld: Transcript.

Scrinzi, F. (2017). A 'New' National Front? Gender, Religion, Secularism and the French Populist Radical Right. In M. Köttig, R. Bitzan, & A. Petö (Eds.), *Gender and Far Right Politics in Europe* (pp. 127–140). New York: Palgrave Macmillan.

Ślarzyński, M. (2018). Rola Klubów 'GazetyPolskiej' w Sukcesie Politycznym Prawa i Sprawiedliwości w 2015 Roku. Aktorzy Lokalni Czy Aktor Ogólnokrajowej Sfery Publicznej III RP? *Przegląd Socjologiczny, 67*(2), 139–158. https://doi.org/10.26485/PS/2018/67.2/6

Southern Poverty Law Center. (nd). *World Congress of Families*. Retrieved from: www.splcenter.org/fighting-hate/extremist-files/group/world-congress-families.

Vail, B. J. (2014, September 8). *The Global Sexual Revolution and the Assault on Freedom and Family: Interview with Gabriele Kuby*. [Catholic World Report]. Retrieved from: www.catholicworldreport.com/2014/09/08/the-global-sexual-revolution-and-the-assault-on-freedom-and-family/.

Verloo, M. (Ed.). (2018). *Varieties of Opposition to Gender Equality in Europe* (1 edition). New York: Routledge.

Wilk, S. (2019, October 2). 200AD. "Skąd ładunki wybuchowe na Marszu Równości w Lublinie?" *Polityka*, Retrieved from: https://www.polityka.pl/tygodnikpolityka/spoleczenstwo/1926920,1,skad-ladunki-wybuchowe-na-marszu-rownosci-w-lublinie.read.

Wodak, R. (2015). *The Politics of Fear: What Right-Wing Populist Discourses Mean*. London: Sage.

Youngblood, M. (2020). Extremist Ideology as a Complex Contagion: The Spread of Far-Right Radicalization in the United States Between 2005 and 2017. *Humanities and Social Sciences Communications, 7*(1), 1–10. https://doi.org/10.1057/s41599-020-00546-3

Yudina, N. (2021). *'Potiussero, quamnunquam'*: Hate Crimes and Counteraction to Them in Russia in 2020. the SOVA Center. Retrieved from: www.sova-center.ru/en/xenophobia/reports-analyses/2021/02/d43611

PART 4

Post-modern Extremisms?

Non-violent Left-Wing, Feminist and Environmental Movements Since the 1970s

24

THE CASE OF DiEM25

A Unique Transnational Political Movement in 21st-Century European Politics

James F. Downes, Valerio Alfonso Bruno and Edward Chan

Introduction

This chapter examines Democracy in Europe Movement 2025 (DiEM25) as a unique case study as it stands as a transnational, radical-left movement operating at the pan-European level by mobilising activists across European Union (EU) member-states and taking part in elections. Despite the limelight and heightened public expectations during its founding, DiEM25 experienced a relatively dismal electoral result in its first main electoral contest, i.e., the 2019 May European Parliament Elections. This chapter introduces DiEM25 as an ambitious pan-European/transnational political movement and at the same time explain its disappointing electoral performances through a comparative European lens.[1] DiEM25 was launched in Berlin by former Greek Finance Minister Yanis Varoufakis on the 9th February 2016 as a "pan-European" platform to "democratise Europe" (DiEM25, 2016). DiEM25 was founded in order to continue the failed attempt of the Greek radical left party, Syriza, to snub the neo-liberal status quo and salvaging the disintegrating EU with a renewed, social democratic outlook. Currently, there are more than 128,000 party members. DiEM25's organisational structure comprises the coordinating collective for centralised control and the spontaneous collective that work on the local level by organising grassroots activities and assemblies. More importantly, the electoral wing of DiEM25 allows its members to form political parties or electoral alliances with other existing parties in order to compete more effectively in national or European elections (DiEM25, 2016).

DiEM25 can be viewed as a unique grassroots transnational political movement, with a revolutionary ideology opposed to the neo-liberal vision embraced by the elites in the EU. Though DiEM25 belongs to the far-left of the political spectrum, its core ideology is relatively moderate by seeking to reform the existing democratic systems across Europe and inside the EU (internally). Unlike some of the other extremist groups in the *Routledge Handbook of Non-Violent Extremism* (e.g., see Manès Weisskircher and Sabine Volk's chapter on the far-right PEGIDA street protest-based movement in Germany), DiEM25 is a radical left group that is primarily committed to peaceful political change, through democratic elections and international cooperation (Varoufakis, 2018).

DiEM25's peaceful means of enacting change is likely to have fostered divisions amongst some European radical left groups across Europe, who tend to advocate more revolutionary and

DOI: 10.4324/9781003032793-29

extreme forms of political change. Some of the more extreme leftist anarchist groups in Greece have previously sought to adopt violent means to achieve their political outcomes. Anarchist groups in Greece such as The Conspiracy of Fire Nuclei (SPF) carried out a series of attacks in late 2016 that effectively targeted institutions which were blamed in Greece for the worsening economic situation. Other anarchist groups, such as Rubicon (Rouvikonas) in Greece have also sought to adopt violent methods to enact political change. These ideological differences between more moderate radical left movements such as DiEM25 and extreme left anarchist groups demonstrate significant divisions amongst the far-left over the specific methods to enact political change in society.

Our choice of DiEM25 as a case study for this analysis has two main reasons. First, we view DiEM25 as a unique radical left political/social movement that transcends European national boundaries and the confines of the nation-state. At the transnational level in Europe, there is no such radical left organisation that bears an ideological resemblance to DiEM25. DiEM25 also does not only rely on social movements to influence political transformation. Instead, it is a political movement with electoral ambitions at the transnational level (particularly at the European Parliament level). It is important to differentiate DiEM25 from the United European Left-Nordic Green Left, which is an EU parliamentary group among various political parties on the left-wing of the political spectrum. Such a unique blend of social movements, populist radical left and political parties require serious academic attention.

Second (and relatedly), according to Varoufakis (2018), DiEM25 is seen to be a sequel of the once successful radical left Syriza Party in Greece, in combating a neo-liberal conception of Europe – devoted to de-regulation, the erosion of workers' rights and market-focused economic aims. It helps shedding light on the development of radical left politics in Europe, especially on the recent sub-par electoral performance of the radical left in elections during the last decade. Arguably, the case of DiEM25 speaks to both transnational movement and radical left politics.

Our chapter draws on a wide variety of existing literature on DiEM25 and electoral results from the 2019 European Parliament Election. Key theoretical frameworks from the diverse scholarly fields of comparative politics, social movements and populism will be applied to further investigate DiEM25 and situate this within the broader context of competing political parties and transnational social movements in contemporary European politics. Drawing on recent elections data at the supranational level (i.e., the EU level) enables us to provide a clearer picture about the main patterns and trends encompassing the electoral fortunes of DiEM25 as a transnational radical left political movement.

The originality of our chapter lies in the fact that we build on existing theoretical debates on DiEM25 in demonstrating the electoral limitations, ideological weaknesses and most importantly the structural constraints due to the sui generis EU context, of this unique radical left transnational political/social European movement. Therefore, our chapter's main original contribution to the existing literature (see Fanoulis & Guerra, 2020; De Cleen et al., 2020; Moffitt, 2017) on DiEM25 is in illustrating how a number of ideological shortcomings (within DiEM25) have negatively impacted DiEM25's electoral fortunes (particularly at the recent 2019 European Parliament elections). We conclude the chapter by outlining the overall limitations and viability of the radical left transnational political movement in contemporary Europe.

Exploring the DIEM25 Through the Existing Literature

This section of the chapter explores the existing literature on the topic of transnational populist social movements alongside DiEM25. We first start with a brief conceptual definition of populism. In reviewing the literature on DiEM25, we provide a thematic-based approach, in identifying two core themes (the construction of a transnational people of Europe and radical left ideology in Europe) that have underpinned current academic scholarship on DiEM25. We then identify a key gap in the literature that relates to the lack of research connecting DiEM25's recent electoral fortunes, to the movement's ideology and organisation.

Defining DiEM25 as a "Populist Radical Left" Transnational Movement

There is extensive scholarly literature on defining the concept of populism. The populism literature tends to distinguish between three main approaches or strands of academic literature to the study of populism (Mudde & Rovira Kaltwasser, 2014): the *"strategic"* approach (viewing populism as a strategy for electoral success), the *"discursive"* approach (viewing populism as a discourse or a political style) and the *"ideational"* approach (viewing populism as an ideology/or coherent set of ideas). In this chapter, we draw on the ideational approach, which has increasingly become the dominant approach in the field of populism over the last decade.

According to the ideational approach, populism's key feature (Mudde & Rovira Kaltwasser, 2014; Rooduijn et al., 2019) is its focus on the Manichean antagonism between the "pure" people and the so-called corrupt elites. This anti-establishment notion of politics tends to unite different types of populist parties and movements, on both the left and right of the political spectrum. We draw on this widely accepted definition of populism in our chapter and we classify DiEM25 as a populist radical left transnational movement. We view DiEM25 as (a) "populist", in the sense that the political/social movement claims to represent the people (citizens across Europe) against the corrupt elite (The EU) showing harsh Euroscepticism (general opposition to the current project of the EU; Cisar & Weisskircher, 2022).

Furthermore, we view DiEM25 as (b) a transnational political movement, in the sense that the movement operates beyond the nation-state level, at the broader pan-European level, through mobilising activists and supporters across Europe, alongside participating in European Parliament elections. DiEM25's ideological features also bear ideological similarities to a number of recent populist radical left parties in Europe (i.e., such as Syriza in Greece and Podemos in Spain) through emphasising anti-capitalist (particularly in seeking to redress grievances of economic inequality), alongside internationalist and radical policies (March, 2017).

The Construction of a Transnational People of Europe

Scholars such as De Cleen et al. (2020) alongside Moffitt (2017) have argued that constructing a transnational people at the nation-state level poses numerous problems. Cisar and Weisskircher (2022) have noted that language barriers remain a substantial barrier to success for transnational movements such as DiEM25, with English comprising the main language for the party's organisation. Cisar and Weisskircher (2022) have demonstrated that this has been a large barrier for DiEM25's success at the transnational level, particularly with the language barrier impeding DiEM25's ability to convey clear messaging on policies at the transnational level, amongst the rank-and-file party members/activists.

Transnational political movements are a complex phenomenon that has been thoroughly analysed in the literature over the last two decades (Bennett, 2005; Chabot et al., 2002; Della Porta & Mattoni, 2014; Della Porta et al., 2015; Smith, 2013; Smith et al., 2017). The sociologist Jackie Smith (2017), an expert on transnational organisations and movements has argued that the defining features of transnational movements are in how they mobilise beyond the nation-state to create a shared aim. At the same time, Smith has also written about how transnational movements have the capacity to define people's interests and identities beyond the confines of the nation-state. Recent literature on transnational movements (FitzGibbon et al., 2016; Guerra & FitzGibbon, 2019; Leruth et al., 2017) have analysed how transnational political movements at the EU level have focused on issues such as Euroscepticism to mobilise support.

Nonetheless, the role that populism plays in developing transnational mobilisation remains an under-researched area in the academic literature. In this regard, scholars such as Moffitt (2017), De Cleen et al., (2020) alongside Fanoulis and Guerra (2020) have focused on the limitations and difficulties of transnational populism, through focusing on DiEM25 as a case study. Moffitt (2017) has highlighted the limits of transnational populist movements, alongside the conceptual tensions that derive from the construction of a transnational people. Moffitt (2017) has also written extensively about the people of transnational populism, referring to the people that populists appeal to and claim to speak for and how movements such as DiEM25 transcend the borders of the nation-state. The people under transnational populism are also spread out over several different national contexts, or indeed may be spoken of at a level above the nation-state. Regarding the nature of the elite, Moffitt (2017) adds that

> While "the people" of transnational populism are necessarily spread beyond the borders of the nation-state, the same condition is not necessary for the enemy of the transnational people— "the elite". While the transnational people spoken for under transnational populism might be opposed to a transnational, supra-national or international elite— all familiar targets of populists of both national and transnational character—they could equally be opposed to a specific national elite. […] The difference between national and transnational populism thus lies in the construction of "the people", rather than hinging on the character or construction of the "elite".
>
> *(Moffitt, 2017, p.2)*

The construction of a transnational people is not an exclusive feature of the populist radical left, as is often observed in Eurosceptic movements and parties (FitzGibbon et al., 2016), nor is it an exclusive domain of European politics (Van Gelder, 2011). If it is true that internationalism, even when latent, remains an important feature of left-wing populism in Europe, together with the socio-economic focus and inclusiveness (March, 2017; March & Mudde, 2005), it is important to distinguish between both transnationalism and internationalist populism (Moffitt 2017; De Cleen et al., 2020)[2]. De Cleen (2017) argues that the distinction between international and transnational populism is a matter of degree. International populism tends to portray the people as underdogs. Transnational populism also seeks to bring together nationally organised political actors and nationally defined people as underdogs.

Radical Left Ideology in Europe

A second and broader theme that underpins the existing literature is research that has focused on the nature and role of contemporary radical left ideology in Europe. Similar to the first theme explored above, this literature has tended to explore the challenges that left-wing transnational populist movements have faced, primarily due to ideological shortcomings and tensions. European transnational populist movements leaning towards the left-wing of the political spectrum have also tended to inherit political tensions already existing within the camp of the left (Berman, 2019).

There exists a complex relationship between populism and left-wing radicalism. There has also been increased debate on the topic of left-wing populism in Europe, particularly since the 2008–2013 economic crisis amongst the wider academic scholarship. During a momentous period of change in European politics over the past decade, there has arguably been a shift within intellectual debates about left-wing populism and amongst radical left political movements (Damiani, 2019, 2020; Fassin, 2020; Mouffe, 2020; Charalambous & Ioannou, 2019). The populist radical left movements in Europe, with their "inclusionary populism" (Mudde & Rovira Kaltwasser, 2013), aimed at migrants and gender minorities, alongside the willingness to democratising democracy, based on social inclusion (alongside issues such as pacifism, feminism, sensitivity to civil rights and environmentalism) have attempted to socially and politically aggregate different categories into a new historical bloc, developing new community-organising processes (Damiani, 2019) at the grassroots level of politics.

However, the re-construction of the people on the principle of what Laclau (2005) has defined as a "logic of equivalence" is a project not immune to difficulties and contradictions in practical terms (Berman 2019). For example, to mobilise people around criticism of governments in times of crises is easy, but to frame those interests into a collective project of the communal government in democratic institutions is extremely complex (Damiani, 2019, p. 304) with several barriers emerging. Moreover, the relationship between populism and left-wing radicalism represents a "double-edge sword' (Charalambous & Ioannou, 2019, p. 264). Providing solutions to mobilise and construct a people may come at the potential cost of offering deceptive politics, i.e., a deceptive invocations of the popular (Seferiades, 2019; Parsi, 2021). A wider set of literature (Laclau, 2005; 2006; Laclau & Mouffe, 2014; Damiani, 2019; 2020) has examined how transnational political/social movements can be an empowering force, in leading to class struggles and at the same time helping to construct a clearer notion of identity.

Whilst the literature relating to DiEM25 has focused on two key themes relating to transnationalism and radical left ideology in Europe, this chapter stresses an important gap in the literature on DiEM25: there is considerably little academic research in the literature on the electoral fortunes of the movement. This chapter therefore explores this area further, by providing a theoretical account of how DiEM25's recent electoral fortunes at the transnational level (the 2019 European Parliament) can be explained by the inherent difficulty of being "transnational" and "populist" simultaneously as well as the lack of distinctiveness suffered by the block of radical left. This approach allows us to build on recent theoretical debates surrounding DiEM25 (Fanoulis and Guerra, 2020; De Cleen et al., 2020; Moffitt, 2017) and enables us to understand DiEM25's future as a viable transnational political/social movement in contemporary European politics. This section of the chapter highlights DiEM25's recent poor electoral fortunes (particularly at the 2019 European Parliament Election). This chapter argues that DiEM25's recent underwhelming electoral performances are primarily due to its transnational nature and ideological structure. These ideological and structural shortcomings make it incredibly difficult for DiEM25 to create a clear policy agenda for voters across Europe, particularly at the complex transnational level of politics.

DiEM25 participated in the 2019 European Parliament Election via forging an electoral alliance called the "European Spring' with other ideologically similar parties and stood for European Parliamentary (EP) elections in several countries, such as Germany and Greece. Drawing on the 2019 European Parliament Election Data of the overall vote and seat shares enables us to illustrate the poor electoral performance of DiEM25. Table 24.1 provides a breakdown of the overall electoral results for DiEM25 and their affiliated transnational groups at the 2019 EU Parliament Election, across seven European countries in Denmark, France, Germany, Greece, Poland, Portugal and Spain.

Table 24.1 Electoral results of DiEM25 at the 2019 European Parliament Elections

Country	Party Name	Percentage Vote Share (%)	Seats Won
Denmark	Alternativet (The Alternative)	3.4%	0/13
France	Génération.s (Generation.s)	3.3%	0/74
Germany	Demokratie in Bewegung (Democracy in Motion)	<1% (0.3%)	0/96
Greece	MeRA25 (The European Realistic Disobedience Front)	3%	0/21
Poland	Lewica Razem (Left Together)	1.2%	0/51
Portugal	LIVRE (FREE/Time to Move Forward)	1.8%	0/21
Spain	Actúa (Act)	<1%	0/54
	Izquierda Positivo	(Left in Positive)	0/54

Source: The Electoral Data in this table was derived from two main sources. Primarily the Electoral Data was obtained from The Official Website of the European Parliament (EuroParl) and supplemented with information about the electoral results of affiliated DiEM25 individual candidates across different countries from the DiEM25 Official Website. EuroParl: www.europarl.europa.eu/election-results-2019/en/european-results/2019-2024/ DiEM25: https://diem25.org/the-results-are-in-heres-who-was-elected-to-lead-our-movement-3/

Despite a stellar international line-up with Yanis Varoufakis himself standing in Germany, DiEM25 suffered a disappointing electoral setback in the 2019 European Parliament election. As shown in Table 24.1, DiEM25 did not win any seats at the 2019 EU Parliament Election. The highest vote share they received across all countries was a mere figure of 3.4% in Denmark. Such an electoral disappointment has served as a wake-up call for DiEM25, in showing that so far, the movement has been far from becoming an influential force in the European political arena. This has arguably led to both serious and fundamental doubts about the influence of their overall ideology at the transnational level of politics. Furthermore, DiEM25's barren electoral run typifies the overall disappointing performance amongst the radical left in recent years across Europe. The electoral support for the radical left did improve compared to that in the early 1990s. Other than the oft-discussed examples such as Syriza in Greece and Podemos in Spain, there is a lack of clear examples across Europe, whereby radical left parties enjoyed any notable electoral breakthrough (Bruno & Downes, 2018). More than often, we can observe radical left parties delivering sub-par electoral performances, despite often high expectations (see Keith, 2016). We argue that DiEM25 alongside other radical left party families in Europe have tended to suffer from ideological difficulties that have arguably hampered their electoral viability.

However, despite the electoral failure of DiEM25 at the transnational level, offshoot national groups (affiliated with DiEM25 at the transnational level) have managed to achieve parliamentary representation. For example, MeRA25 in Greece was only founded in 2018 (also by Yanis Varoufakis) and achieved parliamentary representation at the 2019 Greek national parliamentary (legislative) elections, achieving 3.4% of the vote and nine seats overall. MeRA25's party ideology focuses on anti-austerity socialist (democratic socialist) policies, alongside pro-Europeanism. MeRA25 has also sought to introduce a European "Green New Deal" (Varoufakis, 2018). Aside from the electoral success experienced by MeRA25 in Greece, electoral success for DiEM25 and its affiliated political parties has been underwhelming at the transnational level of politics, particularly across EU countries. The next section of the chapter provides a theoretical account for why DiEM25 has been unable to translate its ideology and policies effectively at the "transnational" level.

The Complexity of Being Both "Transnational" and "Populist" at the Same Time

It is conceptually challenging for transnational populists to make a case for themselves as being both "transnational" and "populist". Populists in Europe have long been no stranger to "transnational" practices or networks. There has been a palpable trend of informal transnational collaboration amongst major populist radical right parties (i.e., the Identity and Democracy Group in the European Parliament) alongside affiliation with ultra-conservatives in Russia, with a view to further legitimating the far-right in the mainstream political discourses (Futak-Campbell & Schwieter, 2020). However, the transnational element did not go beyond key ideological differences and pushed their agenda by way of forming a far-right network. As outlined previously in this chapter, the concept of "people" is usually nationally bound (at the level of the nation-state) which has given rise to common terms such as *das Volk* (the people). Political representation is still often assumed to operate within the structure of a nation-state (De Cleen & Stavrakakis, 2019). By transcending and operating beyond the nation-state level, populists have much more work to be done for explicitly defining who exactly are the precise "people" that they are seeking to represent with reference to their ethnic or national characteristics (Moffitt, 2017). Instead of taking the easier route by claiming to represent the people from a particular nation or geographical boundary, all these conceptual complexities pile up the populists' burden in pushing for their own transnational discourse.

The example of the pan-European far-right Patriotic Europeans against the Islamisation of the Occident (PEGIDA) can illustrate the difficulties faced by a typical transnational populist movement, albeit coming from the right-wing side of the political spectrum. The PEGIDA movement claimed to represent European citizens as a whole and espoused pan-Europeanism. PEGIDA's core ideology opposes Islam and can also be seen as Eurosceptic. However, PEGIDA has struggled to draw a clear distinction between the so-called Saxon or German and European peoples. PEGIDA has also largely failed to create international collaboration (Berntzen & Weisskircher, 2016). Arguably, PEGIDA's ideology was confusing as they failed to completely get rid of their inherent sense of German chauvinism, (Volk, 2020) which was reflected in the origin of the movement and their nativist ideology. This further underlines the difficulties in constructing a consistent and articulate transnational populist ideological discourse.

Despite the challenges in constructing a transnational populist discourse, DiEM25 has further complicated their discourse by not completely replacing their nationalist narrative. Upon qualitative content analysis on DiEM25's core party manifesto and strategies, De Cleen et al (2020) found that DiEM25 did not just make an unwavering case for purely representing the transnational "people" as a whole. Instead, they made an even more ambitious attempt to speak for both the "people" in Europe and the national "peoples" at the same time. DiEM25 attempted to reconcile two vastly different constructions by arguing that achieving transnational democracy would be a precondition for recovering democracy at the local level. Engaging in this transnational entanglement arguably took a toll on DiEM25 as they struggled to offer a coherent and articulate ideology in their run-up to the 2019 EU Parliament Election. Therefore, our main argument here concerns whether a transnational populist narrative can be readily promoted and perceived easily by ordinary citizens across Europe, particularly beyond the level of the nation-state.

The Radical Left Being Closer to the Mainstream Parties in Europe

Populist parties can often have the advantage of adopting ideological positions that are distant from mainstream parties to compete for voters' support. In general, both the radical left and the radical right are found to be much further away from mainstream parties' position on key issues such as the EU and in adopting anti-establishment positions (Halikiopoulou et al., 2012; Immerzeel et al., 2015). In turn, populist parties often ride on anti-neoliberal sentiments shared among the people. In general, radical right parties often differentiate themselves from mainstream parties by placing strategic emphasis on key issues like immigration (Downes & Loveless, 2018). In addition, mainstream parties' ideological preferences have tended to increasingly converge and to present themselves as genuine alternatives to mainstream politics (Katz & Mair, 2018). Comparatively speaking, the radical left has tended to be much closer to the mainstream than the radical right and become less appealing to the voters that are disenchanted by the establishment. On the issue of the EU, both the left and right are often Eurosceptics and often express discontent about the wider process of European integration. However, the form of Euroscepticism they espouse contains nuanced differences. The radical left does not reject the idea of European integration per se. What they are against is a neo-liberal version of the EU. Their form of reformist or "soft Euroscepticism", which often stems from civic nationalism, is substantively different from "hard Euroscepticism" espoused by the radical right (Halikiopoulou et al. 2012; Della Porta et al., 2017).

The latter form of Euroscepticism often entails a fundamental rejection of the EU as an institution and displays a blanket objection to European integration. Alongside their national counterparts, such as Syriza in Greece, DiEM25 was never hostile to the original intention of the EU as an institution but its antipathy towards the EU was primarily aimed against the elites, such as in the executive branch of the European Commission (Varoufakis, 2016). Radical left parties have tended to adopt a much less pronounced (and therefore distinctive) anti-EU (i.e., "soft" Eurosceptic) position, compared to the right. This may in part explain why the radical left in general has failed to capitalise on the rise of populism sentiment over the last decade of crises across European politics. In turn, this same line of argumentation may also be applied to the case of DiEM25.

The Inability to Offer a Clearly Distinctive Narrative that Can Compete with the Radical Right

The relative shortcoming of radical left ideology compared to the radical right goes beyond its lack of a clear distance from mainstream positions. We would venture to argue that it goes as far as the lack of an appealing narrative. A line of literature argues that the radical left as a whole has suffered from a depletion of ideas in the post-communist era, with some of these parties simply recycling the interventionist policies offered by social democratic parties that are also facing decline (see March & Mudde, 2005; March, 2012; Keith, 2016). The radical left is often accused of embracing ideas that are too abstract, which is likely to be unable to be translated into clear and easily accessible language for ordinary voters. Their key positions on immigration issues have been weakened by their internationalist outlook and often loses out to the simple message offered by the radical right that plays out in the message of fear or threats posed by the overall influx of immigrants (McGowan & Keith, 2016). The xenophobic/nativist platform of the radical right also allows them to manipulate and translate identity-based politics into political capital (i.e., votes).

Being the epitome of the radical left, what DiEM25 offers is a much more complex and abstract policy platform. The roadmap and details of democratising the EU and having a transnational European project is likely to come across too many voters as too complex, if not obscure and ambiguous to ordinary voters. The technical backgrounds of DiEM25 key members, such as Slavoj Zizek and Yanis Varoufakis may also play a role in this overall explanation. Despite their fame in the intellectual community, their communication strategies may come across as too abstract and ambiguous, in terms of translating complex policy ideas into clear messages for ordinary voters across Europe.

The Future of Populist Radical Left: Transnational Political Movements in Europe

This chapter examined DiEM25 as a peculiar case study. The transnational nature of DiEM25 makes this chapter a valuable contribution in the study of contemporary European politics. This chapter defined DiEM25 as a distinctive "populist, radical transnational left" social movement in Europe. This chapter found that whilst DiEM25 constitutes a unique political organisation in European politics, DiEM25 has struggled to effectively convey its message amongst many voters, particularly in disseminating its overall ideology at the often-complex transnational level of politics across the EU. Despite the prominent influence of former Greek Finance Minister Yanis Varoufakis at the helm of the movement, the underwhelming and poor electoral performance of DiEM25 at the 2019 European Parliament Election further illustrated the movement's distinct lack of electoral potential in future electoral contests across the EU. Various explanations were put forward for the lack of electoral success in this chapter, ranging from the complex nature of the transnational organisation that criss-crosses national boundaries, to ideological shortcomings and complexities, that made it difficult for DiEM25 to articulate their socio-economic ideological platforms into a coherent policy package for voters. Our chapter has made several original contributions to academic scholarship about the populist radical left and transnational movements, particularly regarding connecting the often complex and contradictory ideology of DiEM25 with its recent electoral failure at the 2019 European Parliament Election.

Most importantly, the findings of our chapter aim to offer three crucial directions for future research, relating to the fields of populism, social movements and party politics literature in European politics. First, the support for the contemporary populist radical left at the individual level (i.e., "voters") should be explored further, in examining the types of voters that vote for this party family alongside how the radical left mobilises voters at the grassroots level.

Second, more academic work needs to be conducted regarding the effectiveness of the populist radical left as an (a) pan-European political party (i.e., the use of non-violent political participation) and (b) social movement organisations alongside contemporary "transnational social movements" in Europe across different regions (i.e., West v. East). Finally, it is important to generalise the findings from this single case study of DiEM25 to multiple competing political parties and transnational social movements in Europe, such as the ideologically pro-EU federalist political party Volt Europa (Volt). This generalisation could allow further insights into what works and doesn't work when it comes to transnational parties and social movements – filling out the empirical research on this fascinating area of political mobilisation.

Notes

1 We define a pan-European/transnational political movement throughout this chapter as a movement that transcends the nation state and seeks transformative change at the EU level.

2 Following Moffitt and De Cleen, we consider internationalism as (a) international cooperation and coordination between parties and movements and (b) transnationalism, as the construction of a movement or a party around people from different countries, while the former would be a platform for several different forms of populism.

References

Bennett, W. L. (2005). Social movements beyond borders: Understanding two eras of transnational activism. In D. Della Porta and S. Tarrow (Eds.), *Transnational Protest and Global Activism* (pp. 203–226). Washington DC: Rowman & Littlefield publishers.

Berman, S. (2019). *Democracy and Dictatorship in Europe: From the Ancien Régime to the Present Day.* Oxford: Oxford University Press.

Berntzen, L. E., & Weisskircher, M. (2016). Anti-Islamic PEGIDA beyond Germany: Explaining differences in mobilisation. *Journal of Intercultural Studies, 37*(6), 556–573.

Bruno, V. A. & Downes, J. F. (2018, 8 August). Why has the populist radical right outperformed the populist radical left in Europe? *London School of Economics e-prints.* Retrieved from: https://blogs.lse.ac.uk/europpblog/2018/08/08/why-has-the-populist-radical-right-outperformed-the-populist-radical-left-in-europe/.

Chabot, S., Ayres, J. M., Caniglia, B. S., Giugni, M. G., Hanagan, M., & Tarrow, S. (2002). *Globalization and Resistance: Transnational Dimensions of Social Movements.* London: Rowman & Littlefield.

Charalambous, G. & Ioannou, G. (Eds.). (2019). *Left Radicalism and Populism in Europe.* Abingdon: Routledge.

Cisar, O. & Weisskircher, M. (2022). *Left-wing social movements between strong European identities and the challenges of transnational activism: The case of DiEM25.* In P. Blokker (Ed) *Imagining Europe: Transnational Contestation and Civic Populism* (pp. 33–57). London: Palgrave.

Damiani, M. (2019). Radical left-wing populism and democracy in Europe. In C. de La Torre (Ed.), *The Routledge Handbook of Global Populism* (pp. 295–306). Abingdon: Routledge.

Damiani, M. (2020). *Populist Radical Left Parties in Western Europe: Equality and Sovereignty.* Abingdon: Routledge.

De Cleen, B. (2017). Populism and nationalism. In C. Rovira Kaltwasser, P. Taggart, P. Ochoa Espejo &, P. Ostiguy (Eds.). *The Oxford Handbook of Populism* (pp. 342–362). Oxford: Oxford University Press.

De Cleen, B., Moffitt, B., Panayotu, P., & Stavrakakis, Y. (2020). The potentials and difficulties of transnational populism: The case of the democracy in Europe Movement 2025 (DiEM25). *Political Studies, 68*(1), 146–166.

Della Porta, D., & Mattoni, A. (2014). Patterns of diffusion and the transnational dimension of protest in the movements of the crisis: An introduction. *Spreading protest: Social movements in times of crisis.* Colchester: ECPR Press, Studies in European Political Science Series. Retrieved from Cadmus, European University Institute Research Repository, at: http://hdl.handle.net/1814/32471

Della Porta, D., A., M., Calle, A., Combes, H., Eggert, N., Giugni, M. G., & Marchetti, R. (2015). *Global Justice Movement: Cross-National and Transnational Perspectives.* Abingdon: Routledge.

DiEM25. (2016). A Manifesto for Democratising Europe. Retrieved from: www.diem25.org

Downes, J. F., & Loveless, M. (2018). Centre right and radical right party competition in Europe: Strategic emphasis on immigration, anti-incumbency, and economic crisis. *Electoral Studies, 54*(1), 148–158.

Fanoulis, E., & Guerra, S. (2020). Veridiction and leadership in transnational populism: The case of DiEM25. *Politics and Governance, 8*(1), 217–225.

Fassin, D. (2020, 18 December). The blind spots of left populism. *openDemocracy.* Retrived from: www.opendemocracy.net/en/rethinking-populism/blind-spots-left-populism/

FitzGibbon, J., Leruth, B., & Startin, N. (Eds.). (2016). *Euroscepticism as a Transnational and Pan-European Phenomenon: The Emergence of a New Sphere of Opposition.* Abingdon: Routledge.

Futak-Campbell, B., & Schwieter, C. (2020). Practising populism: How right-wing populists negotiate political competence. *JCMS: Journal of Common Market Studies, 58* (4), 890–908.

Guerra, S., & FitzGibbon, J. (2019). *Transnational Euroscepticism vs Transnational Euroalternativism.* Colchester: ECPR.

Halikiopoulou, D., Nanou, K., & Vasilopoulou, S. (2012). The paradox of nationalism: The common denominator of radical right and radical left Euroscepticism. *European Journal of Political Research, 51*(4), 504–539.

Immerzeel, T., Lubbers, M., & Coffé, H. (2016). Competing with the radical right: Distances between the European radical right and other parties on typical radical right issues. *Party Politics, 22*(6), 823–834.

Keith, D. (2016). Failing to capitalise on the crisis: The Dutch Socialist Party. In L. March, & D. Keith (Eds.), *Europe's Radical Left: From Marginality to the Mainstream?* (pp. 155–171). London and New York: Rowman & Littlefield.

Laclau, E. (2005). *On Populist Reason*. London: Verso.

Laclau, E. (2006). Why constructing a people is the main task of radical politics. *Critical Inquiry*, *32*(4), 646–680.

Laclau, E., & Mouffe, C. (2014). *Hegemony and Socialist Strategy: Towards a Radical Democratic Politics*. (1st ed. 1985). London: Verso Trade.

Leruth, B., Startin, N., & Usherwood, S. (Eds.). (2017). *The Routledge Handbook of Euroscepticism*. Abingdon: Routledge.

March, L. (2012). Problems and perspectives of contemporary European radical left parties: Chasing a lost world or still a world to win? *International Critical Thought*, *2*(3), 314–339.

March, L. (2017, 24 July). Interview #17: Luke March on Left Populism. *Political Observatory on Populism*. Retrieved from: https://populismobserver.com/2017/07/24/interview-17-luke-march-on-left-populism

March, L. & Mudde, C. (2005). What's left of the radical left? The European radical left after 1989: Decline and mutation. *Comparative European Politics*. *3*(1), 23–49.

Marsili, L., & Varoufakis, Y. (2017). *Il terzo spazio. Oltre establishment e populismo*. Roma-Bari: Laterza.

McGowan, F., & Keith, D. (2016). The radical left and immigration: Resilient or acquiescent in the face of the radical right. In D. Keith, & L. March (Eds.), *Europe's Radical Left: From Marginality to the Mainstream?* (pp. 89 –111). London: Rowman & Littlefield.

Moffitt, B. (2016). *The Global Rise of Populism: Performance, Political Style, and Representation*. Stanford: Stanford University Press.

Moffitt, B. (2017). Transnational populism? Representative claims, media and the difficulty of constructing a transnational 'people'. Javnost-The *Public*, *24*(4), 409–425.

Mouffe, C. (2020, 15 September). Why a populist Left should rally around a green democratic transformation. *openDemocracy*. Retrieved from: www.opendemocracy.net/en/rethinking-populism/left-populist-strategy-post-covid-19/.

Mudde, C. (2004). The populist zeitgeist. *Government and Opposition*, *39*(4), 541–563.

Mudde, C. & C. Rovira Kaltwasser. (2013). Exclusionary vs. inclusionary populism: Comparing the contemporary Europe and Latin America. *Government and Opposition*, *48*(2), 147–174. doi: https://doi.org/10.1017/gov.2012.11

Parsi, V. E. (2021). *The Wrecking of the Liberal World Order*. Cham: Palgrave Macmillan.

Rooduijn, M., Van Kessel, S., Froio, C., Pirro, A., De Lange, S., Halikiopoulou, D., & Taggart, P. (2019). *The PopuList: An overview of populist, far right, far left and Eurosceptic parties in Europe*. Retrieved from: https://popu-list.org/.

Seferiades, S. (2019). Populism as 'deceptive invocations of the popular': A political approach. In G. Charalambous, & G. Ioannou (Eds.). *Left radicalism and populism in Europe* (pp. 223–256). Abingdon: Routledge.

Smith, J. (2013). Transnational social movements. *The Wiley-Blackwell Encyclopedia of Social and Political Movements*. Doi: https://doi.org/10.1002/9780470674871.wbespm454. Retrieved: https://onlinelibrary.wiley.com/doi/full/10.1002/9780470674871.wbespm454

Smith, J., Plummer, S., & Hughes, M. M. (2017). Transnational social movements and changing organizational fields in the late twentieth and early twenty-first centuries. *Global Networks*, *17*(1), 3–22.

Van Gelder, S. (Ed.). (2011). *This Changes Everything: Occupy Wall Street and the 99% Movement*. Oakland, CA: Berrett-Koehler Publishers.

Varoufakis, Y. (2016, 7 September), *Europe's Left After Brexit*. Retrieved from: https://diem25.org/europes-left-after-brexit/

Varoufakis, Y. (2017). *Adults in the Room: My Battle with Europe's Deep Establishment*. London: Vintage.

Varoufakis, Y. (2018, 13 March). MeRA25: A New Greek Political Party. In *openDemocracy*. Retrieved from: www.opendemocracy.net/en/can-europe-make-it/mera25-new-greek-political-party/

Volk, S. (2020). 'Wir sind das Volk!' Representative claim-making and populist style in the PEGIDA movement's discourse. *German Politics*, *29*(4), 599–616.

25

LEFT-WING RADICALISM IN AUSTRALIA

The Complexities of the Radical Left's (Non)Violent Struggle Against Fascism

Mario Peucker, Julian Droogan and Sarah Holmes

Introduction

Throughout its long history the far-left has never existed as a coherent movement or ideology with a singular political vision, or agreement on the aims or strategies to be used for its attainment. This unbounded and diverse character is as true today as it was in the past. Indeed, there remains a lack of clarity around the key characteristics of the far-left, as well as the precise point at which leftist movements can rightly be termed either "radical" or "extremist". Scholars have been unable to reach consensus on how to define far-left political movements or left-wing extremism and radicalism, with the very attempt being described as a "potential terminological minefield" (March & Mudde, 2005, p. 24).

The wide array of terminology used reflects this conceptual confusion. An incomplete list of terms adopted over the past 70 years or so includes the "far-left", the "radical left", the "extreme left", the "sectarian left", the "authoritarian left", and "left-wing authoritarianism" (Peucker, 2020). This is not to mention descriptions such as Marxist, communist, anarchist or Maoist, referring to the political philosophies of far-left movements, groups and individuals. Terms such as "antifascism" have gained currency to describe notable and highly visible militant and activist movements, themselves sometimes identifying with broad international collectives or brands such as Antifa[1] or the Black Bloc (Dupuis-Déri, 2010; Copsey, 2018). Opposition to fascism has been a central ideological marker of most, if not all, far-left groups since the 1920s. Recently, however, militant antifascism has become a conceptual lens through which a significant portion of the far-left self-identifies.

With a history spanning the globe and reaching back to at least the late 19th century, it is hardly surprising that the core values of the radical left have been diverse, shifting and unsuitable as a platform upon which to build any robust or inclusive definition. As this chapter illustrates, to attempt to define the far-left today in any monolithic or static manner is to do injustice to its ideological diversity, as well as the flexibility and situational contingency of its expressions. For the purpose of this chapter, however, we propose the following heuristic definition: the common denominator of the far-left is their pursuit of a radical version of anti-capitalist and anti-imperialist egalitarianism (March & Mudde 2005; Visser et al., 2014; McCoy, Jones & Hastings, 2019).[2]

DOI: 10.4324/9781003032793-30

This chapter presents empirical findings from two Australian studies on far-left mobilisation. Both studies focus in particular on radical left opposition to fascism and racism, which has been a central area of activity for radical left groups around the world for almost a century. The first study draws on interviews and ethnographic fieldwork conducted in Victoria to examine radical left offline mobilisation against the rise of the far-right through the second half of the 2010s. The second study analyses content from nine Australian Antifa Facebook accounts between 2019 and 2020 to map their online messaging, use of iconography and narratives.

Public, and to some extent academic, debates around antifascism within far-left movements have been dominated by two interconnected claims, which we discuss in order to contextualise the presentation of our research findings in the second part of this chapter. The first is the portrayal of the antifascist struggle as a fundamentally *reactive* form of political activism. The second is the allegation that this form of antifascism is inherently *violent* and physically confrontational, which has led some policymakers to label antifascist groups as street gangs (allegedly void of any ideological agendas) or domestic terrorist (allegedly driven by an extreme ideology; United States White House, 2021).

Reactive Antifascism?

While much research on the radical left in Australia and elsewhere is historically focused, revealing a complex interplay between leftist radical and extremist movements and left-wing politics through the 20th century and beyond, contemporary debates have often been dominated by a concern with militant and at times violent antifascist movements. These became increasingly active and visible in the 2000s (Dupuis-Déri, 2010), and more so after 2015. Such a narrow focus on contemporary and highly visible forms of antifascism has resulted in framing the radical left as a fundamentally reactive phenomenon emerging purely in response to the growth of far-right politics and extremism. In effect, this preoccupation with confrontational antifascism as a reactive outgrowth from right-wing extremism not only suggests an artificial equivalence between the two, it also obscures the wider ideological diversity and aims of radical left antifascism. More broadly, it ignores the diversity of the contemporary radical leftist *milieu* and cuts it off from the deep historical continuum of leftist activism from which it draws its sense of history, identity and mission.

It is difficult to appreciate the diversity of the contemporary radical left without first situating it within its historical context. Members usually consider themselves to represent a direct continuation of international revolutionary leftist political movements spanning the past century or longer (Vysotsky, 2020; Guerin 2020, p. 23). The 20th century provides a kaleidoscope of differing, and at times antagonistic, strands of leftist political thought, activism, and revolutionary fervour that provide the ideological and cultural foundation and inspiration for the contemporary radical left milieu. These include various strands of Marxism and socialism, the most influential being the Leninist, Trotskyist, and communist doctrines, as well as Chinese Maoist thought (Thompson, 1996). In some contradiction to these is the tradition of anarchism and its offshoots, deriving from late 19th century Europe and the works of Russian thinker Mikhail Bakunin (Anderson & O'Gorman, 2005).

Although socialist and anarchist activists are capable of collaborating on unifying causes such as antifascism, the ideological differences between them, specifically their differing visions of political philosophy and its implementation, makes it impossible to reduce the radical left to a single unifying ideology. What (revolutionary) socialist or anarchist radical-left and antifascist movements do often have in common, is their dedication to framing the source of contemporary social injustice and fascism as the international capitalist political economy and a commitment to its removal, possibly through direct action and (eventual) revolution.

Recent research on Antifa and the wider far-left antifascism movement have revealed it to be more than simply a "quintessential reactive phenomenon" (Copsey, 2016, p. 158), focused only on confronting and eradicating fascism (Arlow, 2020; Vysotsky, 2015; Bray, 2017). Antifascism encompasses a broader and more ambitious series of goals drawn from a deeper set of ideological currents. At times, these ideological perspectives can be contradictory. Vysotsky (2020) argued that in the United States, Antifa, while anarchist in orientation, attracts individuals from across the radical left, including socialists, communists and Marxists, as well as those advocating a range of environmental, pro-working class, and social justice causes. The fluid nature of Antifa's organisation and the need to build broad coalitions across the ideological spectrum of leftist politics to meet the immediate challenge of the far-right makes it an ideologically diverse movement.

Rather than reducing anti-fascism to a purely reactive movement, it may be more appropriate to understand it as a platform that has come to bridge a range of sectarian divisions from across the radical left in response to a looming single-issue crisis, similar to the way in which the Vietnam War and conscription temporarily unified the Australian radical left 50 years earlier (Marks, 2019). In this case, however, the crisis is the perceived global rise of far-right extremism and fascist-like authoritarian government (Vystosky, 2020), which is regarded as being inherently linked to the capitalist system.

As noted by Arlow (2020) in his study of Antifa in Ireland, where the far-right threat is less significant compared to other countries, Antifa nonetheless provides a space for the broad convergence and unity of radical factions that transcends the notoriously fragmented ideological landscape of leftist activism. This convergence is more than simply a pragmatic alliance of convenience but reflects a common culture and history of left-wing struggle. This situation of antifascist movements within a deep tradition and shared cultural history is emphasised by Vysotsky (2020) and Bray (2017). Vysotsky (2020) is at pains to emphasise Antifa as simultaneously a social movement, a subculture, and a militant antifascist organisation. Bray (2017, p. xiv) argues that antifascism as a counter-movement is best understood as "a method of politics, a locus of individual and group self-identification, and a transnational movement that adapted pre-existing socialist, anarchist and communist currents to a sudden need to react to the fascist menace".

The Role of Violence

One central aspect of the divergent operational strategies adopted by the multifaceted radical and extreme left revolves around the use of violence by segments such as Antifa or the Black Bloc (Dupuis-Déri, 2010). The notions of "direct action" (Vysotsky, 2015, p. 238) and "diversity of tactics" (Dupuis-Déri, 2010, p. 63; Vysotsky, 2020, pp. 92–96), which includes the option of violence, are central to this question. The use of violence is one tactical option available to radical leftist antifascist movements, but one that is rarely used, certainly in contemporary Australia.

This has not prevented public commentary, as well as some academic analyses, from focusing on the radical left's use of violence. Indeed, since the mid-20th century conservative elements in the Australian press have emphasised the anarchy, chaos and violence of leftist movements and protests (Marks, 2019). More recently, media commentary on antifascist movements (such as Antifa) has regularly reduced the complexity of the radical left to violent "thugs", "gangs" and even "terrorists" (Pyrooz & Densley, 2018), often suggesting an equivalence between them and the militant far-right.

This stands in contrast to much more nuanced findings of emerging empirical work undertaken within far-left *milieus*. Although the scholarship on contemporary left-wing extremism or radicalism is still underdeveloped, there is evidence that suggests a reductionist analysis through the lens of violence ignores the multifaceted nature of these movements' *modus operandi*, their ideological rationales (Copsey, 2018), and personal and systemic motivational drivers (Dupuis-Déri, 2010; Juris, 2005; Vysotsky, 2015; Bray, 2017).

Such diversity of opinion on the appropriateness of using violence has long been expressed among Australia's radical left. In the 1960s and 1970s, for example, Australia did not experience episodes of mass state violence against protesters as occurred in the United States or Western Europe (Marks, 2019), and violence from the radical left was also minimal (Campion, 2020). By the late 1980s and 1990s violence was adopted as part of a tactic by antiracism groups in Victoria. Fox (2019) recounts how seminal experiences of the successful confrontation of fascist groups in Melbourne solidified a commitment to direct action among the activist left. Violence crystallised a theoretical commitment to the historical struggle against fascism into a direct and empowering praxis. Yet, even as groups such as the Melbourne-based Campaign Against Nazis (CAN) developed a militant strategy to confront fascism, any commitment to violent action was complex, ambiguous and debated. Over time, CAN rejected violent confrontation and shifted its strategy to non-violent tactics such as deplatforming (the attempt to boycott a person and their views through blocking their access to public spaces). According to one of its 1997 broadsheet articles, "CAN does not believe in the use of terrorist style tactics against [neo-Nazi group] National Action. NA are a political problem that requires a political solution" (Fox, 2019, p. 237).

Overall, Australian antifascist groups have used militant tactics such as direct confrontation during protests and "squadding" (the patrolling of streets and targeted attacking of those deemed "fascists"). However, they have done so in a limited, often situational manner, and not without reservations. As shown in the case studies below, violence is not considered to be effective in the long term, being counter to the need to build a broader community-based movement that can attract and unite disparate left-leaning groups willing to stand up against racism and injustice. Violent tactics are generally neither categorically condemned nor advocated but wielded strategically and situationally. The result is that violent tactics may be used in different ways and at differing times, depending on specific local circumstances.

One of the limitations of much public discourse and academic analysis of the radical and extreme left has been its approach through the lens of terrorism or violent extremism studies (Geifman, 2013; Allington et al., 2019; for a critical perspective Conway et al., 2018; LaFree, 2018). Survey-based research in Europe has revealed a connection between those who identify as "very left-wing" and a support for violent protest and violence against anti-democratic groups (Allington et al., 2019). However, a reductive focus on abstract support for violence obscures a wider agenda and relatively limited and situational use of violence. Certainly, a historical perspective on the extreme left through the late 19th and 20th centuries provides numerous examples of anarchist and Marxist inspired terror groups (Malkki, 2018). According to David Rapoport's influential wave theory of the evolution of terrorism, the first three waves, "anarchist", "anti-colonialist" and "new-left", were all fundamentally left-wing in orientation; this only changing with the introduction of a proposed "religious" wave in 1979 (Rapoport, 1999). Today, however, radical and extreme left-wing movements in the West do not seem to engage in terrorist activity, despite the rhetoric of political leaders such as former US President

Donald Trump (United States White House, 2021), and their use of violence is, as we have seen, contested.

Case Studies

Below we discuss initial findings from two current research projects. The first examines radical left offline mobilisation against the rise of Australia's far-right and their attempt to dominate public spaces in the second half of the 2010s. The second study focuses on the online messaging of nine Australian Antifa groups on Facebook and their strategic use of international iconography and narratives to fit local contexts.

Study 1: The Offline Struggle of the Radical Left Against the Far Right

The findings discussed here are part of a larger research project examining the dynamic interplay between radical left and far-right groups and movements in Australia. It was conducted between 2019 and 2021 by Victoria University in partnership with the Institute for Strategic Dialogue as part of their involvement with the international think tank consortium Centre for Resilient and Inclusive Societies. The following section draws on extensive ethnographic fieldwork within radical left *milieus* in Australia and a series of informal and three formal in-depth interviews with activists who consider themselves Socialists and/or Marxists. It discusses radical left antifascist offline activism between 2015 and 2019 in the state of Victoria.

Over the past century, the radical left in Australia has encompassed a range of diverse grassroots movements, mobilisation agendas, groups and political parties. Next to indigenous rights, anti-nuclear power, women's and queer emancipation, to name a few (Piccini, Smith & Worley, 2018), antifascism has remained a continuous sphere of action for the radical left since the 1920s (Cresciani, 1980). The first two decades of the 2000s, especially since the mid-2010s, saw the re-emergence of overt far-right movements in Australia, initially through anti-Islam movements such as Reclaim Australia, but quickly spreading to White supremacist and neo-Nazi groups such as Antipodean Resistance (Peucker & Smith, 2019). With it came a corresponding growth in antifascist action (Fox, 2019).

In the following we provide an overview of how the radical left responded to this rise of the far-right between 2015 and 2019, a time when physical confrontations occurred frequently, especially in the context of street protests. There is consensus among academics (Dean et al., 2016; Peucker & Smith, 2019), most public commentators, and intelligence agencies (ASIO, 2020) about the rise of Australia's far-right since the mid-2010s. These groups have sought public visibility on and offline, holding street protests across the country. The state of Victoria alone saw almost two dozen such events between April 2015 and January 2019, organised by far-right groups agitating against Islam, refugees, alleged "African crimes", "men's rights" or simply their exclusivist version of an (ethno)nationalist Australia (Peucker et al., 2020).

With organisational structures already well established, the radical left responded in 2015 by organising counter-protests and opposing the far-right more broadly. A central feature of this left-wing countermovement was the emergence of new local antiracism and antifascism networks, such as #No Room for Racism and the Campaign against Racism and Fascism (CARF). These newly established networks and coalitions have strong ideological and personal links with socialist and other radical left groups, differentiating them from other antiracist organisations.

CARF, which soon became the main actor within this counter-movement in Victoria, claimed they held 20 counter-protests against the far-right between 2015 and 2019 (*CARF event August 2020).* In most cases, civil society or community groups not linked to radical left ideologies were less involved or at least less visible during these counter-protests. Thus, the public image of these reactive antifascist mobilisations, which mostly outnumbered their far-right opponents, were dominated by antifascist, socialist placards, slogans and, as one socialist activist proudly stated, "rowdy, confrontational tactics" (*activist #3, August 2020).*

The rise of the far-right and their street rallies mobilised the radical left and provided them with a sense of urgency. One activist maintained that the different groups involved in the first counter-protest in April 2015 "came together and said we really need a serious and ongoing opposition to this kind of [fascist] ideology and the political environment" (*activist #3, participant observation, online, 11 August 2020).* This marked the beginning of a new phase in the evolution of Australia's radical left, with countering fascism moving into the centre of their agenda for years to come.

According to our interviews and ethnographic fieldwork, there have been ongoing internal debates about the form this opposition should take, with answers shifting over time. One basic tenet everyone in the antifascist radical left seems to agree with was: Do not *debate* the far right or try to win over individuals who subscribe to far-right ideologies. "The project of the left, and of antifascism more generally, is not to engage with the ideas of them [on the far-right] as though they are logical [...] Sitting down with them and discussing ideas is a really bad approach" (*activist #6, participant observation, online, 20 September 2020).* During a CARF meeting, one activist emphasised the approach of publicly confronting, disrupting and exposing the far-right as fascists: "We want to isolate fascists and not convince them to be non-fascist. Challenging their access to public space, demoralising them psychologically" (*activist #1; participant observation, Melbourne 11 August 2019).* This echoes the aim of CARF, as outlined in their *Welcome to CARF* brochure, "to directly confront [the far-right] in the street and prevent them from controlling public spaces" (CARF, n.d.). It also resonates with international research on antifascist movements that describe their direct actions as a response to the political, physical and spatial threat presented by the far-right (Vysotsky, 2020, pp. 134–141).

While there seemed little disagreement about the physically confrontational nature of their antifascist actions, activists highlighted ongoing internal debates about the use of explicitly violent tactics. As one female activist (*activist #6, participant observation, online, 20 September 2020*) stated: "some think we just have to find fascists out there and beat them up. Violence is the only language they understand – the brutal fist of the antifascist fighter [...] I see the appeal of that, but that is only part of the answer". What is more important than situational confrontation, she argued, is to "broaden out the movement" by "finding allies in different movements including trade unions and among everyday working-class people" (#6). She, like others, pointed to the successful tactics of the Anti-Nazi League in the late 1970s and early 80s in Britain. In their view, this antifascist and socialist group was "not afraid to be confrontational". More importantly, however, the group allegedly managed to establish a broad left-wing working-class mass movement, "exposing the radical right", whilst "trying to implement *being antifascist* as part of a left-wing consciousness" (activist #7, *participant observation, online, 20* September 2020).

The key element of the radical left strategy against the far-right is not violent confrontation but to "build the forces of antifascism of the left, of progressive movements, of antiracist movements, of anti-capitalist movements, which give some indication about how society can fundamentally be transformed for the better" (#7). This resonates with Copsey and Merrill (2020, pp. 129–130) who found in their research on militant Antifa in the United States, where a representative of Portland's Rose City Antifa highlighted the importance of having "community support" and building and maintaining positive relationships with other groups beyond militant antifascism.

According to another long-standing antifascist activist (*activist #8, participant observation, online, 20 August 2020*), there had been internal debates early on within the antifascist movement in Melbourne about the role of squadism, often associated with militant Black Bloc tactics (Dupuis-Déri, 2010). He described "squadism" as the action of small antifascist activist groups who "organise secretly, wear masks and go and punch a fash [fascist] [...] find them in pubs and bash them". He, like others in the group, was critical of these tactics, and he extended his criticism to the initiation of violence by individual antifascists during standoffs with the far-right or police in the streets. He mentioned two reasons for this.

The first resonates with the prefigurative politics of socialist movements, which, in the case of the radical left, pursue a radically democratic political system (Vysotsky, 2015). "It's very un-democratic, you know, out of a large group of [antifascist protesters] one throws a brick at a cop and everyone gets pepper-sprayed [...] they had no say and were used as a cover for the little adventure [of that one person]" (#8). Similarly, Copsey and Merrill (2020, p. 129) in their study on Antifa in Portland, United States, argue that their "internal culture of horizontal consensus gives space for the expression of a variety of concerns, but it also means that no single individual can dictate tactical decisions".

The second reason is that squadism "runs counter to the idea of building a mass movement" (#8). Another activist (#3; *participant observation, online, 20 August 2020*) emphasised that they work towards a grassroots movement with "mass involvement" across "broad layers of society", rejecting "state-based solutions to the threat of the far-right", such as police or government intervention. This criticism towards government and police intervention was expressed frequently during meetings, typically in conjunction with accusations of police violence and government complicity in the allegedly increasing threat of fascism.

According to our fieldwork, violent tactics are generally viewed with scepticism. When they do occur, they tend to be situational and rationalised as a form of self-defence against a fascist threat (Copsey & Merrill, 2020, p. 127; Vysotsky, 2015, p. 249). Militant direct actions are neither categorically rejected nor generally endorsed. They are subject to ongoing internal debates, with shifts depending on context. Pointing to the dynamic interplay between movement-countermovement actions (Busher & Macklin, 2015), our findings demonstrate that during times when far-right groups showed little constraint in their performance of physical violence on the streets, antifascist counter-protesters were prepared to act more physically. One antifascist activist (#1; *participant observation, Melbourne, 11 August 2019*) stated, "we fight when necessary, we are not pacifist".

However, despite this endorsement of *situational* reactive militancy in segments of the radical left, a consensus prevails among those involved in our fieldwork on the problematic optics and lack of long-term effectiveness of violence. This argument has been extended to wearing face masks at protests. "CARF does not condemn, but we also don't promote these tactics", as the CARF *welcome brochure* states: "Not wearing a mask or using bloc tactics is part of having an open, outward-looking orientation that attracts everyone who has anti-racist/-fascist ideas, not just hardened experienced activists" (CARF, n.d.).

While antifascist counter-protests against far-right mobilisation in the streets continued to be dominated by radical left groups, the composition of these counter-protests shifted between 2015 and early 2019, when the far-right held their (at the time of writing) last large public protest. Parallel to these changes, the level of physical escalation diminished.

Initially, especially in 2015 and 2016, there was a significant and visible presence of Antifa and some "Black Bloc type of people" at these counter-events, and public flyers to promote antifascist counter-rallies contained Antifa iconography such as the three arrows or the black-and-red flag next to CARF's logo. Such Antifa symbols did not feature on later counterprotest posters, although this is not to say that Antifa was not in attendance. Several CARF activists confirmed that people who identify as Antifa used to be more present at CARF but their engagement diminished significantly in 2016 *(activist #2, interview, Melbourne, 18 November 2020)* as CARF expressed unease with Antifa actions and optics at protests.

The nature of the counter-rally in St. Kilda in 2019 was different. Physical clashes were less violent, and the group of counter-protesters was more diverse, including a significant proportion of other left-leaning, progressive individuals ("liberal antifascists") and groups (e.g., The Greens). Initially, the counter-protest at a public park resembled a large public picnic. This offered a glimpse of what a broader mobilisation against the far-right might look like. This St. Kilda counter-protest, however, shed light on the inherent tensions within radical left movements in Australia seeking to build a mass movement that is opposed to fascism but also radical in its anti-capitalist stance. What Antifa, CARF and other socialist or anarchist antifascist movements in Australia have in common is their ideological dedication to system change; to "smash" the capitalist system. However, many of the more mainstream protesters against far-right mobilisation may disagree with this explicitly revolutionary agenda.

The struggle against the far-right is linked to this anti-capitalist agenda in two intertwined ways. First, most antifascist activists seem closely affiliated with socialist groups and political parties. "Everyone involved in CARF, as far as I know, is also anti-capitalist", one activist stated during a meeting *(activist #8, participant observation, online, 20 August 2020)*. Hence, the struggle against the far-right is underpinned by individuals' anti-capitalist worldviews. Second, capitalism is seen as a core element of the "political economy" *(antifascist meeting, 10 August 2020)* that allegedly emboldens or produces the far-right and facilitates the rise of fascism (Guerin et al., 2020). While stopping short of equating capitalism with fascism, both are described as "inseparable". As long as we live in a capitalist system, we will have to fight fascism", one activist (#8) asserted, describing capitalism as a system that "brings into existence fascism". As a consequence, there was broad agreement that fighting the far-right is part of "a much more general struggle for a complete overthrow of the capitalist system" *(activist #4, participant observation, online, 20 August 2020)*. This is illustrated by the following assertion of a socialist activist:

> For us today the challenge is to build a socialist movement with people ready to engage in direct confrontation but, more generally, able to build a current for an argument for a different kind of world. We can't just be reactive, but also need to be able to make an argument about how we can have a fundamentally different kind of society.
> *(activist #6, participant observation, online, 20 September 2020)*

For almost half a decade the radical left activists in our fieldwork had been focused on primarily reactive tactics of confrontation to the far-right. Since 2019, however, public far-right mobilisation has significantly diminished, and so have antifascist counter-protests. This allowed many radical left groups to redirect the focus of their anti-fascist commitment seeking to "upskill and grow the movement" *(CARF meeting, August 2020)*, supporting other progressive movements (such as refugee rights and environment action), and confronting the far-right online.

Study 2: Australian Antifa Online

For this study a qualitative thematic analysis of Australian Antifa accounts on Facebook was conducted in 2020. Acknowledging that there is no unanimously agreed conceptualisation of Antifa, we use the term Antifa to refer to what Vysotsky (2020, p. 51) called "formal" antifascist groups, or "affinity groups operating to achieve the goal of opposing fascist mobilisation".

Formal antifascism refers to a political movement similar to what Bray (2017) and Testa (2015) call "militant" antifascism, which they distinguish from liberal antifascism. According to Testa (2015, p. 4), liberal antifascism is a label used for those prepared to work with government and police to oppose fascism and far-right mobilisation, while militant antifascists reject such collaboration. Thus, the term "militant" does not necessarily imply the endorsement or use of violence.

The aim of this study was to identify dominant themes and narratives used on Australian-based Antifa Facebook accounts and to explore what role global and local issues play in their mobilisation in the Australian context. The analysis paid particular attention also to the iconography and symbols used by Australian Antifa groups online. The Australian sample was drawn from Facebook, the most commonly used social media platform for Antifa in the country (in contrast to Antifa groups in the United States and United Kingdom that commonly use Twitter). The content from nine Australian Facebook accounts was manually captured for the period between February and June 2019 and the corresponding period in 2020. The accounts were selected according to their use of traditional icons associated with Antifa such as the two flags (usually black and red: black representing anarchism, red representing socialism) or the inclusion of Antifa and/or antifascist descriptions in their profiles. Accounts were required to be based in Australia, post in English and be publicly accessible without privacy restrictions. The selected accounts relate to groups from five different Australian states: Tasmania, New South Wales, Victoria, Queensland and South Australia. These accounts range in age and activity, with some being recently created within the last two years, while others had been active for over a decade.

The names of the selected accounts included the city, state or region where the group is based, with "Antifa Australia" the only nationwide account. Seven of the accounts adopted either "Anti-fascist Action" or "*Antifaschistische Aktion*" in the profile imagery drawing a direct historical link either to pre-war Germany, where *Antifaschistische Aktion* was launched to unite socialist and communist militants to defend working-class communities (Testa, 2015), or to Anti-Fascist Action, which operated across the United Kingdom throughout the 1990s. This use of labels connected historical struggles with the contemporary actions of groups, situating the accounts as part of a long-standing global antifascist tradition.

In a similar manner to Antifa accounts in the United States (Vysotsky, 2020), Australian Antifa groups adopted Antifa icons and symbols to illustrate their political beliefs and situate them within their specific local context. Seven of the nine accounts used a variation of the two overlapping flags of Antifa in their profile pictures, while the remaining two maintained the consistent visual styling of red-and-black imagery enclosed by a black circle. The choice of symbols placed within these circles was innovative, with flags being replaced with red-and-black computers in one case, and the image of a guillotine in the other.

This choice of logo reflects key themes associated with different Antifa groups. Computers, for example, align with the goals of the local group to "inform the public about fascism" (Antifascism Tasmania), highlighting the important role of online activism and identifying far-right members online in a region where street protests have been extremely rare. The Antifascist Action Albury/Wodonga's adoption of the guillotine symbol, associated with the French Revolution, reflects the group's particular focus on opposing government. Victorian-based "Melbourne Antifascist Info" adopted the traditional two overlapping flags as their profile image but replaced the traditional red-and-black flags with the blue Eureka flag. The Eureka flag has its origin in the 1854 Eureka Rebellion against British colonial authority in the Victorian gold-mining town of Ballarat, and is associated with the Australian union movement, and traditions of resistance, democracy and protest (as well as, ironically, being adopted by some far-right nationalist groups). The use of the Eureka flag in the context of Melbourne Antifascist Info resonates not only with its geographic base in Victoria but also with the group's advocacy for workers' rights, strong unions and a united working class.

In addition to the traditional two flags icon, Antifa Australia adopted a laurel wreath and gears representing both a working-class orientation as well as a subcultural leaning (Vysotsky, 2020, p. 114). Geographic adaptations can be seen with the Queensland-based "Antifascist Gold Coast Crew" which used iconic representations of the Gold Coast, the beach, waves and buildings in combination with the two flags, the Iron Front (three parallel arrows) and laurel. Overall, Australian Antifa iconography is adaptive, drawing on Australian national themes, an international history going back to pre-war foundations, and local visual symbols and popular imagery. In this way it serves to mark diverse ideologies, groups and spaces as antifascist (Vysotsky, 2020, p. 115).

A qualitative thematic analysis of account content, including textual content from posts and comments as well as imagery and videos, was performed to identify key narratives. A total of 1,625 posts were examined, with 1,211 posts from 2019 (February and June) and 414 posts from the corresponding five-month period in 2020. Significant global events occurring during these times impacted the themes present. In March 2019, to name a particularly significant event, an Australian committed a right-wing terrorist attack on two mosques in Christchurch, New Zealand, killing 51 people. In 2020, the coronavirus pandemic impacted the globe, and in late May the popular Black Lives Matter (BLM) protest movement spread from the United States to Australia and beyond.

Three a priori themes were used in the thematic coding, drawing from a review of pertinent literature: the far-right, opposition to government, and opposition to police. These themes were expanded through the adoption of a grounded theory approach which identified themes within the data in an iterative way. This content analysis identified four dominant themes occurring across all accounts as well as secondary themes present on only some accounts.

The dominant themes aligned with topics identified in wider research, but with the one Australia-specific addition of Indigenous rights. The four dominant themes were:

(1) concerns with the far right,
(2) opposition to government
(3) Indigenous rights, and
(4) opposition to police.

Concerns with the far-right emerged as the dominant focus in the posts (20% of all posts), including posts related to specific far-right individuals and groups in Australia and internationally. A focus on the actions of far-right individuals, including posting about their associations and/or arrests, was described as a form of digital activism. Terms such as "coward", "germ", "scum" and "thugs" were used to describe key individuals, while the emerging threat within countries such as the United States, Bulgaria and the Ukraine reinforced the international threat posed by the far-right.

Opposition to the government (11% of posts) and specific Australian political figures was prominent. Many posts referred to politicians such as cabinet minister Peter Dutton or Senator Pauline Hanson and Fraser Anning as representing a political system complicit in wider systemic injustice and oppression. Posts relating to One Nation and Clive Palmer's Australia First Party often highlighted the allegedly racist nature of these parties. Opposition to, and direct action against, the political establishment was demonstrated in posts showing campaign flyers being burnt and signs being vandalised, rather than specific calls for violence or threats.

In the context of Indigenous rights (9% of posts), grievance narratives relating to Australia's history of colonialism and imperialism as well as alleged police oppression were common. Images and memes celebrating the killing of Captain Cook, rather than Valentine's Day, on 14 February were common, as was the sharing of images of graffitied colonialist monuments.

Opposition to police (7% of posts) was expressed frequently and was often raised in the context of the mistreatment of Indigenous individuals and communities. For example, Australian BLM protests focusing on Indigenous deaths in custody and the police removal of traditional custodians from their lands were common. These posts were linked to structural issues of systemic racism and the ongoing effects of colonialism. In 2020, the coronavirus pandemic had a significant influence on the posting activities of Antifa groups. The qualitative analysis demonstrated that posts referring to the pandemic were commonly linked to opposition to the government and police (e.g., power overreach), anti-capitalism, solidarity with working-class people (who were particularly affected by the pandemic) and the existence of structural racism within Australia. In this way, the pandemic was used to emphasise existing ideological narratives rather than prompting the discussion of new issues.

In addition, the content analysis identified several secondary themes that occurred frequently across many but not all accounts and were often connected to the above-mentioned four dominant themes. These included highlighting the power of community organising, support for refugee and immigration rights, and the importance of a strong and united working class. The power of community organising was frequently illustrated through images of peaceful protest, people gathered with banners and signs often expressing solidarity with local and international issues. This was also shown through the concept and practice of mutual care and support of others within the community. Support for refugee and immigration rights was often shown by highlighting the mistreatment of refugees in offshore detention centres or the frequent mental health issues experienced during long periods in detention.

The importance of a strong and united working class to defend worker's rights was emphasised. While images depicted people at protests or pickets with banners and flags, these were often representative of Unions, and individuals within the image were often shown with a raised clenched fist. The frequent mobilisation around these issues demonstrates that Antifa in Australia is driven by a deeper ideological agenda beyond only its opposition to fascism, government, and police.

Of note was the importance placed on community organising and protest to bring about social change towards the creation of more self-reliant communities. This was illustrated by the following 2019 post from Antifa Australia: "Dangerous conservative extremists threaten innocent people. Defend our community from violence-minded conservatives. Defeat the bigoted hate groups through people's protests and organizing". This approach challenges the conceptualisation of Antifa as violent and merely reactive. Indeed, there was a marked lack of explicitly violent narratives found across the data.

Sharing videos and images is an important element of the posting activities of a number of Australian Antifa groups. Many regularly posted visual content related to antifascist actions in public spaces, such as graffitiing. In general, graffiti is used as a form of political communication to convey identity, political messages and allegiances. In public spaces this form of messaging often serves as a territorial marker and a declaration of presence and control by a certain group in the area (Matusitz, 2015, p. 120). Posting images of graffiti online appears to be aimed at promoting these offline activities and extending their reach to a wider audience. It not only visually demonstrates the offline activism and presence of Antifa groups but also underscores the connectedness and solidarity between Antifa movements across the globe. This is particularly the case when images of antifascist graffiti from other countries are shared locally, as illustrated by a post that depicts antifascist graffiti on the side of a building in Germany. Translated into English, the spray-painted message on the side of the building states: "Antifa is not a gang or a youth culture but an abbreviation of antifascism".

Posting images of antifascist icons and phrases in public spaces was also a common way to deliver a political message. In the data set this included anti-police and anti-government narratives, for instance, acronyms and numeric symbols such as "ACAB" and "1312" for coded representations of the phrase "all cops are bastards", and the phrase "no gods no masters no prime ministers" (Finklestein et al., 2020).

Australian Antifa groups also incorporate significant local and global events into visual imagery. Following the Christchurch terrorist attack, for example, murals dedicated to victims of the attack were posted online as expressions of solidarity. Another example is the sharing of images of graffiti and memes celebrating the actions of Will Connolly or "egg boy", who became a local and international symbol of resistance following his "egging" of far-right politician Fraser Anning (Figure 25.1). Similarly, images of milkshakes emerged, and were shared widely following a publicised incident in the United Kingdom where a milkshake was thrown at a prominent far-right figure (Figure 25.2). These events, which illustrate the symbolic nature of physical confrontation, were incorporated into offline tactics and shared through online messaging, becoming symbols of direct action and resistance to the far-right.

Overall, Australian Antifa groups, whilst demonstrating their specific local identity, situate themselves within the global antifascist movement and adopt the common icons, symbols and

Figure 25.1 Online posts of offline Antifa graffiti in reference to an "egg attack" on a far-right politician in Australia.

Source: Adelaide antifascist memes and news.

Figure 25.2 Online posts of offline Antifa graffiti in reference to incident in the UK where a milkshake was thrown at a prominent far-right figure.

Source: Antifascist Gold Coast Crew.

themes of antifascist mobilisation worldwide. These include an opposition to fascism and the far-right, to the government and police, as well as advocacy for minority groups. Explicit calls for violence were absent in the data set, which resonates with other recent studies on Australia's far-left online (Guerin et al., 2020; Peucker & Davey, 2020), as well as US Antifa's "rhetorical restraint" (Copsey & Merrill, 2020). This assessment contrasts with the widespread association of Antifa and their "direct action" with violence (Pyrooz & Densley, 2018), an association that is academically and empirically contested.

Conclusion

While the scholarship on contemporary anti-globalist, environmentalist, animal rights and other left-leaning, progressive movements has become more extensive (Peucker, 2020), empirical research on the antifascist radical left is still emerging. The two studies presented in this chapter, both part of larger projects, contribute to this scholarly endeavour in the Australian context. Findings are preliminary but point to two central insights. First, the public perception of the radical left, and in particular militant antifascist movements, as inherently violent – either by labelling them criminal gangs (Pyrooz & Densley, 2018) or associating them with terrorism – is misplaced. While antifascist militant direct action remains a behavioural option in Australia, violence plays a very limited role in the contemporary radical left. The use of physical violence against the far-right in public spaces is internally debated and highly context-specific. When it occurs, it is generally regarded as a form of reactive defence against a fascist threat. While security agencies have considered far-right extremism in Australia to be an increasing security problem, its presence in public spaces has diminished since 2019. Accordingly, there is little evidence for militant direct action, defensive or otherwise, by Australia's far-left, although the situation in other countries such as the United States may be different.

Another reason why militancy is discouraged within Australia's contemporary radical left is related to the optics of violent actions, which are considered counterproductive for their larger mission of building a broad community movement against fascism and capitalism. This community building and organising aspect was highlighted in both studies and is often overlooked in public debates.

These findings are linked to the second main conclusion of our studies, challenging the characterisation of far-left (militant) antifascism as being merely reactive. Most of those actively engaged in the far-left's antifascist struggle have a broader vision of how society should look. The convictions of anti-capitalism, anti-imperialism and a working class-led democracy are obvious among those who come from socialist and Marxist backgrounds, but they also apply to anarchist elements and to Antifa in general (Bray, 2017). The socialist revolution may not be the main reason why a militant Antifa group confronts the far-right during a street protest (Copsey & Merrill, 2020), but the struggle against capitalism and related oppression and injustice around the world are central to the agenda of the Australian radical left. This is especially the case at a time when the Australian far-right is no longer seeking to dominate public spaces to the scale that they did in the late 2010s.

Notes

1 Antifa is a constriction of the term "anti-fascism", and refers to an international left-wing, anti-racist, and anti-fascist movement comprised of a decentralised collection of autonomous groups. While diverse, its members share a common commitment to stopping fascism through direct action rather than through a political process.
2 We do not include single-issue movements such as environmentalist or animal protection movement although the people involved in these are predominantly left-leaning and some radical left groups may support these movements.

References

Allington, D., McAndrew, S. & Hirsh, D. (2019). Violent extremist tactics and the ideology of the sectarian far left. Retrieved from www.gov.uk/government/publications/violent-extremist-tacticsand-the-ideology-of-the-sectarian-far-left
Anderson, B. & O'Gorman, R. (2005). *Under three flags: Anarchism and the anti-colonial imagination.* London: Verso.
Arlow, J. (2020). Antifa without fascism: The reasons behind the antifascist movement in Ireland. *Irish Political Studies, 35*(1): 115–137. doi.org/10.1080/07907184.2019.1570139
ASIO. (2020). Director-General's annual threat assessment. Retrieved from www.asio.gov.au/publications/speeches-and-statements/director-general-annual-threat-assessment-0.html
Bray, M. (2017). *Antifa: The anti-fascist handbook.* Melbourne: Melbourne University Press.
Busher, J. & Macklin, G. (2015). Interpreting "cumulative extremism": Six proposals for enhancing conceptual clarity. *Terrorism and Political Violence, 27*(5): 884–905. doi.org/10.1080/09546553.2013.870556
Campaign Against Racism and Fascism (CARF). (n.d.). *Welcome to CARF! Build the Left to Fight the Right!* Melbourne: CARF.
Campion, C. (2020). "Unstructured terrorism"? Assessing left wing extremism in Australia. *Critical Studies on Terrorism, 13*(4): 545–567. doi.org/10.1080/17539153.2020.1810992

Conway, L., Houck, S., Gornick, J. & Repke, M. A. (2018). Finding the Loch Ness Monster: Left-wing authoritarianism in the United States. *Political Psychology, 39*(5): 1049–1067. doi.org/10.1111/pops.12470

Copsey, N. (2016). *Anti-fascism in Britain (second revised and updated edition).* London: Routledge.

Copsey, N. (2018). Militant antifascism: An alternative (historical) reading. *Society, 55*(3): 243–247. doi.org/10.1007/s12115-018-0245-y

Copsey, N. & Merrill, S. (2020). Violence and restraint within Antifa: A view from the United States. *Perspectives on Terrorism, 14*(6): 122–138.

Cresciani, G. (1980). *Fascism, anti-Fascism and Italians in Australia: 1922–1945.* Canberra: ANU Press.

Dean, G., Bell, P. & Vakhitova, Z. (2016). Right-wing extremism in Australia: The rise of the new radical right. *Journal of Policing, Intelligence and Counter Terrorism, 11*(2): 121–142. doi.org/10.1080/18335330.2016.1231414

Dupuis-Déri, F. (2010). The Black Blocs ten years after Seattle: Anarchism, direct action, and deliberative practice. *Journal for the Study of Radicalism, 4*(2): 45–82. DOI:10.2307/41887658

Finklestein, J., Goldenberg, A., Stevens, S., Jussim, L., Farmer, J., Donohue, J. & Paresky, P, (2020). Network enabled anarchy: How militant anarcho socialists networks use social media to instigate widespread violence against political opponents and law enforcement. Retrieved from http://ncri.io/wp-content/uploads/NCRI-White-Paper-Network-Enabled-Anarchy.pdf

Fox, V. (2019). "Never again": Fascism and anti-fascism in Melbourne in the 1990s. *Labour History, 116*: 215– 240. doi.org/10.3828/jlh.2019.10

Geifman, A. (2013). The liberal left opts for terror. *Terrorism and Political Violence, 25*(4): 550–560. doi.org/10.1080/09546553.2013.814494

Guerin, C., Davey, J., Peucker, M. & Fisher, T. J. (2020). The Interplay between Australia's political fringes on the right and left online: Messaging on Facebook. *CRIS.* Melbourne. Retrieved from https://static1.squarespace.com/static/5d48cb4d61091100011eded9/t/5fbd6e90b80a0221e87dabe2/1606250196323/The+Interplay+Between+Australia_Political_Fringes_final.pdfJuris, J. S. (2005). Violence performed and imagined militant action, the Black Bloc and the mass media in Genoa. *Critique of Anthropology, 25*(4): 413–432. doi.org/10.1177/0308275X05058657

LaFree, G. (2018). Is Antifa a terrorist group? *Society, 55*(3):248–252. DOI:10.1007/s12115-018-0246-x

Malkki, L. (2018). Left-wing terrorism. In A. Silk (Ed.), *Routledge handbook of terrorism and counter terrorism* (pp. 87–97). London: Routledge.March, L. & Mudde, C. (2005). What's left of the radical left? The European radical left after 1989: Decline and Mutation. *Comparative European Politics, 3*(1): 23–49. doi.org/10.1057/palgrave.cep.6110052

Marks, R. (2019). "1968" in Australia: The student movement and the new left. In J. Piccini, E. Smith, & M. Worley (Eds.), *The far left in Australia since 1945* (pp. 134–150). Routledge: New York.

Matusitz, J. (2015). *Symbolism in terrorism: Motivation, communication and behaviour.* London: Rowan & Littlefield.

McCoy, J., Jones, D. & Hastings, Z. (2019). Building awareness, seeking solutions: Extremism & hate motivated violence in Alberta. Retrieved from https://preventviolence.ca/publication/building-awareness-seeking-solutions-2019-report/

Peucker, M. (2020). Symbiotic radicalisation: The interplay between far-right and far-left activism in Victoria: Literature review. *Centre for Resilient and Inclusive Societies.* Victoria University. Retrieved from https://static1.squarespace.com/static/5d48cb4d61091100011eded9/t/5f8910b2d349c741382fce8a/1602818237394/Literature+review_symbiotic+radicalisation.pdf

Peucker, M. & Davey, J. (2020, 15 December). Does Australia's radical left pose a security threat? What the empirical evidence tells us. *ABC Religion & Ethics.* Retrieved from: https://www.abc.net.au/religion/does-the-radical-left-pose-a-security-threat-to-australia/12987240

Peucker, M. & Smith D. (Eds.), (2019). *The far-right in contemporary Australia.* Singapore: Palgrave Macmillan.

Peucker, M., Spaaij, R., Smith, D. & Patton, S. (2020). Dissenting citizenship? Understanding vulnerabilities to right-wing extremism on the local level. Melbourne: Victoria University. Retrieved from http://vuir.vu.edu.au/41501/

Piccini, J., Smith, E. & Worley, M. (Eds.), (2018). *The far left in Australia since 1945.* London: Routledge.

Pyrooz, D. & Densley, J. (2018). On public protest, Violence, and street gangs. *Society, 55*(3): 229–236. DOI:10.1007/s12115-018-0242-1

Rapoport, D. (1999). The fourth wave: September 11 and the history of terrorism. *Current History, 100*(650): 419–424. doi.org/10.1525/curh.2001.100.650.419

Testa, M. (2015). *Militant anti-fascism: A hundred years of resistance.* London: AK Press.

Thompson, W. (1996). *The left in history: Revolution and reform in twentieth-century politics*. London: Pluto Press.

United States White House. (2021). Statement from the Press Secretary, January 5th. Retrieved from www.whitehouse.gov/briefings-statements/statement-press-secretary-010521/

Visser, M., Lubbers, M., Kraaykamp, G. & Jaspers, E. (2014). Support for radical left ideologies in Europe. *European Journal of Political Research, 53*(3): 541–558. doi.org/10.1111/1475-6765.12048

Vysotsky, S. (2015). The anarchy police: Militant anti-fascism as alternative policing practice. *Critical Criminology, 23*(3): 235–253. doi.org/10.1007/s10612-015-9267-6

Vysotsky, S. (2020). *American Antifa. The tactics, culture, and practice of militant antifascism*. London: Routledge.

26

OVERTHROWING THE CAPITALIST SOCIAL ORDER

The Forgotten Extremism of the British Women's Movement

George Stevenson

Introduction

The women's liberation movement (WLM), and the New Left milieu[1] it was a part of, was formed in what James Vernon has described as the "brief life" of Britain's social democracy (Vernon, 2010, pp. 408–409). The use of liberation – in common with the Gay Liberation Front (GLF) of the same time – was a nod to both the need and potential for a radical, or *extreme* overhaul of all societal structures of oppression, whether they were sex and gender norms, hierarchical organisational forms, or the capitalist system. The "personal" was "political" and that meant all systems of thought and social relations were open for transformation. This is what Nancy Fraser (2013, p. 1) has subsequently called an "explosion" in the social democratic "imaginary".

None could deny, therefore, that the WLM was a radical movement but was it "extremist"? Answering this question is complicated by the nebulousness of a concept like extremism. As Schmid has pointed out, extremism is an inherently relational concept and is consequently open to a myriad of definitions dependent on the observer (Schmid, 2014). At its simplest, "extremism" could be reduced to political violence, which, at least when committed by non-state actors, is always considered extreme (Baran, 2005; Mider, 2013; Schmid, 2014; Lowe, 2017).

However, there is a consensus – from governmental definitions (HM Government, 2011; European Commission, 2020) to academic scholarship (Baran, 2005; Backes, 2010; Eatwell and Goodwin, 2010; Schmid, 2014; Lowe, 2017) – that non-violence can also be "extreme" if it meets certain criteria. Namely, "extremism" requires an explicit ideological rejection of the rule of law and/or a direct challenge to existing state authorities (Backes, 2010; Eatwell and Goodwin, 2010; Midlarsky, 2011; Schmid, 2014; Lowe, 2017). In practice then, it is usually the state that acts as the arbiter of extremism whereby its own violence, social structures and institutions are deemed acceptable while the violence of non-state actors and political challenges to the state's social structures are "extreme". In this chapter, I will use this definition

DOI: 10.4324/9781003032793-31

to demonstrate that the British WLM's rejection of, and intent to overthrow, the capitalist social order met these criteria. The movement should therefore be understood as form of feminist extremism, albeit one that saw itself as challenging the extremism of a patriarchal capitalist political economy.

I will begin by examining the relationship between the WLM and issues of extremism and political violence, as well as exploring how this is situated within broader narratives around the supposed non-violence of women's activism. I will then demonstrate how one of the WLM's most extreme challenges to British social institutions came from struggles in the field of social reproduction. However, I will note that the extremism of their demands has been both forgotten and neutered in their contemporary expression, particularly the demand for universal basic income (UBI). I will explain how the WLM premised this demand on an extremist ideological position that sought to overthrow the capitalist social order, not simply to reform it. Based on the analysis of these struggles, I will conclude that the British feminist movement in this period fits well within discussions of political extremism as the movement's ideas and activism presented an explicit threat to the dominant power structures of capital and the British state.

The WLM, Feminism and Non-violence

In the last decade there has been a similar explosion of interest in the British WLM's role in these attempted transformations. At the time of writing, the digitised archive of one of the movement's key publications, *Spare Rib*, remains available while a recent oral history research project, "Sisterhood and After", has deposited 60 interviews – predominantly with women's liberationists – in the British Library (British Library, 2012). The WLM has also resurfaced in popular culture through films like "Made in Dagenham" (Cole, 2010), which dramatised a famous equal pay strike from 1968, and "Misbehaviour" (Lowthorpe, 2020), which centred on the 1970 "Miss World" protest.

The surge of attention has also been reflected in the academic literature with a diverse range of approaches to the movement. At a broad level, the WLM has been situated as part of the New Social Movements of the late-1960s and 1970s, sharing activism, ideologies and social networks with socialist and black political mobilisations, as well as the GLF and disability movements (Hughes, 2015; Robinson, 2013). Focusing on the WLM itself, Natalie Thomlinson (2012) has explored the difficult relationship between feminism and race, specifically through attempted collaborations and tensions between black and white feminists in the feminist second-wave up to the 1990s.

Similarly, George Stevenson (2019) examined the interaction between the WLM and class politics in the 1970s, noting how a predominantly middle-class movement nevertheless engaged deeply – but also critically – with socialism and the labour movement. Nicholas Owen (2013) investigated the consequences of men's exclusion from the WLM for the movement's politics and the persistent challenges that the "problem of men" created regardless. Utilising her work on the "Sisterhood and After" project, Margaretta Jolly (2017; 2019) has studied the significance of the oral history method for the study of British feminism as well as analysing the themes that emerge in second-wave feminists' life histories. The WLM's theorising of sex and gender has been shown to be significant to contemporary battles over trans rights, with the British movement in particular articulating that whilst gender is a social construct, sex is rooted in biological reality with damaging consequences transwomen in Britain (Hines et al., 2020).

However, the issue of political violence within and around the WLM has escaped attention. In most accounts, the WLM and the wider New Left milieu it was part of, has been defined in opposition to violence, which was associated with patriarchal power relations within the family and society (Walkowitz, 2019). This understanding of women's activism is not specific to the WLM: "peace" is seen to be at the core of Western feminism (Eschle, 2017; Cortright, 2008; Titcombe, 2013). Women are coded as being victims of violence, rather than perpetrators at both the macro level of military conflict and the micro level within the home (Cortright, 2008).

There is, according to Catherine Eschle a "special relationship between women and peace" (Eschle, 2017, p. 471). Feminist activism became intimately connected with peace movements at various moments, none more so than the Greenham Peace Camp in the 1980s. The camp, over-whelmingly led and populated by women, aimed to force the removal of US cruise missiles from a British military base. Niamh Moore asserts that interpretations of Greenham played a potent role in the construction of the "maternalist peace activist" as a myth of essentialist feminisms (Moore, 2008, p. 283). The "construction" of this narrative is supported by Titcombe's (2013) work, in which she demonstrated that some sections of the WLM, fragmenting by the early 1980s, were critical of how the protestors' messaging and action diverted attention away from challenging patriarchy directly, thereby problematising any simple confluence between "feminism" and "peace". Indeed, her re-evaluation of the historiography of Greenham dovetails with Moore (2008) as she points out that it was only later that the protests were classified as a specifically radical *feminist* movement (Titcombe, 2013).

The revision of Greenham as an avowedly feminist project highlights that the relationship between second-wave feminism and political violence was more complex than outright rejection. As J. D. Taylor (2015) has argued, although political violence is usually written out of histories of the New Left, this is complicated by the existence of the "Angry Brigade", which committed 26 terrorist attacks against property between 1970 and 1971 (Taylor, 2015). Hilary Creek, a participant in the "Brigade", who was later prosecuted was also active in the women's movement and Christiansen's (2011) study of the "Angry Brigade" suggests that this was reflective of wider engagement with political violence amongst the New Left, at least on an intellectual level.

As Taylor (2015, p. 894) notes, some women's liberationists, such as Lynne Segal, saw the Angry Brigade as an example of "more macho, warlike paranoid and desperate politics" but this was a matter of debate in feminist circles. WLM groups and other parts of the New Left offered solidarity when Creek and other Brigade members were put on trial (Christiansen, 2011; Taylor, 2015). Moreover, one of the early WLM protests at the Miss World contest in London in 1970 included flour-bombing Bob Hope, which whilst not overtly violent was not easy to suggest as peaceful either (Taylor, 2015). It was a similar story outside of Britain. The Weather Underground group in the United States, and violent Red cells in Europe, as examples, included women participants and took on some feminist ideas in their rhetoric and political analysis (Varon, 2004).

Women's liberationists like Elizabeth Wilson personified this complex relationship. Wilson (1986) was part of the Angry Brigade defence group and found that their treatment by the authorities was "a crash course in political reality" (p. 42). She reflected:

> It permanently altered my understanding of the world; henceforth I knew that "repressive arm of the state" is no mere piece of academic Marxist jargon – there really is an iron fist inside the velvet glove of consumer capitalism.
>
> *(Wilson, 1986, p. 42)*

For Wilson, adjacency to the Angry Brigade's political violence revealed where violence really lay – in the heart of the capitalist state. Rather than encouraging her to see political violence as a necessary tool of social change, the failure of the Angry Brigade pushed her towards larger mainstream organisations of the working class, especially the labour movement (Wilson, 1986). Her rejection of violence was a pragmatic decision rather than an absolutist rejection of violence in any circumstances. Schmid argues that this strategic perspective on violence is therefore better understood as "not-violent" rather than "non-violent" because it is not an absolutist commitment to non-violent methods but rather a strategic decision based on effectiveness (Schmid, 2014, pp. 13–14). In short, a non-violent approach would be prepared to switch to violence if it was perceived as more useful whereas a non-violent approach would be maintained regardless of the circumstances. Thus, while she ended up in the same place as more critical feminists, Wilson problematised the simplistic association between women's activism and peace and demonstrated that the women's movement did not always stand in total opposition to political violence.

The WLM's most prominent media output, *Spare Rib*, underlined the nuances of feminist perspectives on political violence in its platforming of women's voices during the Troubles in Northern Ireland, such as in 1972 when the magazine interviewed members of women's groups on both sides of the conflict. Interviewees openly expressed support for violent action if a peaceful resolution was impossible, with one interviewee about to stand trial for a bank robbery (Fell, 1972). For women in Northern Ireland at this time, peace was not necessarily the most important political principle (Wahidin, 2016). Indeed, this was a position taken up by British women in the Women's Social and Political Union decades earlier, which engaged in a terror campaign including arson, bombing and widespread property damage in their efforts to win the vote (Jorgensen-Earp, 1997). They placed an absolute restriction on harm against others but their actions show that the Angry Brigade's tactics sat comfortably within at least one feminist political tradition.

Thus, as Eschle (2017, p. 471) has argued, the "special relationship between women and peace" should be problematised but not discarded. Second-wave feminists and the wider New Left seldom engaged in political violence but they were often adjacent to it. Some rejected it as inherently patriarchal but many were willing to analyse its utility; though they did reject it as an overt political strategy. Nevertheless, the women's movement's primary extremism lay elsewhere.

Methodology

This chapter focuses on the revolutionary intent of the WLM's mostly neglected attempts to restructure the processes of social reproduction through demands for what would now be thought as a UBI. This analysis will be based on a critical literature review of current histories of UBI, archival material and oral histories relating to the WLM's demand for financial and legal independence. Specifically, I will examine the dominant historiographical narratives of UBI to show how feminist activism and intellectual contributions to the development of contemporary UBI demands are often absent. I will then compare this absence with a case study of the feminist demand for legal and financial independence, wages for housework (WFH) and a guaranteed income in the period from approximately 1972 to 1979. These sources illustrate the *extreme* nature of the challenge to the dominant socio-economic order of the time that sections of the WLM and adjacent women-led movements, such as Claimants' Unions (Cus) presented through claims for "independence" or "wages for housework". I will explain how the mainstream demands of the British WLM elided this extremism and examine how feminists constructed other demands around basic income that were more radical than some of their "postcapitalist" successors. Through this discussion, I will argue that the British WLM contained an extremist ideological position that was put into practice by some of its groups and activists.

Histories of UBI and the Left

The increasing global significance of the demand for a UBI was demonstrated in 2020 when the World Bank published a guide to "Exploring Basic Income" (Gentillini et al., 2020). UBI has become such a reasonable demand that it has been recognised by one of the central institutions of global capitalism as worthy of detailed consideration. However, this is not the first time UBI has entered elite political discourses. As Peter Sloman has shown, basic income is an "old idea" (Sloman, 2016, p. 205). It was expressed by Thomas Paine in 1797, by Bertrand Russell and parts of the British Quaker movement after the First World War and by some socialist economists in the 1930s and, through Juliet Rhys-Williams, formed a counter proposal to the Beveridge Report in 1940s and 1950s Britain (Sloman, 2016). Srnicek and Williams (2016) extended this history to include small experiments in the United States and Canada in the 1960s and 1970s, something also focused on by Bregman (2018) in his support for the policy, as well as noting that its current prominence is an echo of how close a version of basic income came to being implemented by both Richard Nixon and Jimmy Carter. However, after this brush with political realisation, the UBI was pushed aside by the neoliberal revolution and mostly forgotten until a recent resurgence with new experiments and proponents (Srnicek and Williams, 2016; Mason, 2015; Bregman, 2018).

This story is closely paralleled by the Left's fortunes over the same periods. Just as the potential implementation of UBI was discarded in the 1970s, the United Kingdom, alongside many developed capitalist nations, took a neoliberal turn (Beck, 1992; Fisher, 2009), pushing the WLM into what Sheila Rowbotham described as a more "defensive" mode, thus seeking to preserve gains made rather than having the capacity to pursue its more totalising project of social change (Rowbotham, 1990, p. 170). Within neoliberalism, there is space for cultural and individualistic forms of feminism, anti-racism, and the LGBTQ movement, and even the potential to carve out popular niches in mainstream culture (Beck, 1992; Inglehart, 2008). However, this required a neutering of the revolutionary aspects of the New Left's political formations. Neoliberal feminism can call for women to be equally paid and educated consumers but never for a fundamental reconstruction of economic production or social reproduction.

Culture can pivot only to the extent that it does not inconvenience capital. This narrative of "no alternative", a political universalism of the Right fatally inhibited more extreme feminist political formations. Indeed, more than inhibited, the 1980s was a period of crushing defeat for the radical Left in general. In the space of three years in Britain between 1983 and 1986, the Labour Left was defeated by defections and Thatcherism in a landslide general election, the National Union of Mineworkers, the most powerful trade union in the country, was beaten in a long and bitter struggle in 1984–1985, the print unions crushed by Rupert Murdoch, and the Greater London Council, an experiment in New Left municipalism, was disbanded by the Thatcher government (Wainwright, 2020). Neoliberal capitalism eviscerated its opponents and discarded almost all forms of Left extremism imagined or otherwise (Hall & Jacques, 1991; Beck, 1992; Fisher, 2009; Gilbert, 2017, 2020).

The histories of UBI, the New Left and the WLM are therefore intertwined. However, basic income is linked to the WLM not only through a shared retreat in the face of neoliberal ascendance but also directly through feminist contributions to its intellectual development and political salience. This relationship is not always clear from the existing literature or prominent proponents of the policy. In *Postcapitalism*, Paul Mason writes that basic income is not an especially radical policy and is primarily focused on responding to the mass automation of work that will result in there being "too few work hours to go around" (Mason, 2015, p. 285). Its more radical edge is in providing an "antidote" to David Graeber's (2018) "bullshit jobs" thesis, which suggests that huge numbers of jobs in contemporary capitalist economies are socially worthless. For Mason, UBI will liberate these workers from this unnecessary labour. Liberation therefore plays a role in Mason's support for UBI as a key component of a "postcapitalist" future but there is no recognition of its ties to 1970s feminist radicalism, nor how an extreme an upheaval UBI would be to the social order. Rutger Bregman (2018) offers similar justifications for the policy in *Utopia for Realists*.

He emphasises that UBI is a more practical solution to both poverty and the automation of work than technocratic means-testing common to Western welfare systems, and places a similar emphasis on the reduction of the working week and liberation from paid labour. However, like Mason, he does not situate the idea within its political or intellectual history, particularly its fundamental links to second-wave feminism. In this they join the World Bank's publication in noting UBI's potential to challenge our understanding of work but neglect any consideration of feminist intellectual history on this topic (Gentillini et al., 2020).

Although neglected in their history of basic income, Alex Williams and Nick Srnicek's "Inventing the Future" does much better on recognising the theoretical links with feminism, noting that it is "a feminist proposal" and politicises the "generalised way in which we are all responsible for reproducing society: from informal to formal work, from domestic to public work, from individual to collective work" (Srnicek & Williams, 2016, p. 122). It is the focus on UBI's impact on "informal" and "domestic" work that distinguishes Williams and Srnicek's position from Mason's and Bregman's and allows them to make important points about the potential to create a political demand that bridges the divide between the employed and unemployed (p. 121). Nonetheless, they too imply that their position goes further than second-wave feminist demands for independence or even the coterminous "wages for housework" (WFH) bloc of the women's movement.

They suggest WFH effectively politicised domestic labour – entirely ignored in Mason and Bregman's accounts of automation – but that UBI enhances this approach by politicising the "generalised way in which we are all responsible for reproducing society" (Srnicek & Williams, 2016, p. 122). Moreover, they argue that whereas "wages for housework" reinforced the relationship between wages and work, UBI breaks it (p. 122). Kathi Weeks (2011) also recognizes that the development of UBI is connected to women's movements of this period to the extent that, as the latter notes, a national WLM conference passed a motion for a UBI demand in 1977. However, this was quickly dismissed and forgotten, seemingly by the WLM itself and in subsequent histories (Yamamori, 2010; Miller et al., 2019).

Thus, much of the existing work on UBI either ignores the contributions of the second-wave feminist movement altogether or denotes them as being an inherently less radical challenge to the capitalist social order. However, this conceals how the intellectual foundations and conclusions for both the demand for financial and legal independence and "wages for housework" were almost identical to contemporary calls for UBI. As Weeks (2011, p. 115) has argued, the dismissal of older feminist ideas can be a result of the "iterative" style of feminist historiography in which each "wave" improves on the last rather than the "nonlinear, multidirectional, and simultaneous" ways in which political demands emerge (Weigman, 2000, p. 824). I will examine next how, far from being practical or limited in scope, parts of the British women's movement presented an extreme and total challenge to capitalism that sought to reconstruct wage labour and social reproduction in ways that parallel radical contemporary approaches and go beyond others.

George Stevenson

The Women's Movement and Demands for Economic Liberation

The "wages for housework" demand was set out originally in a short book by Mariarosa Dalla Costa and Selma James, *The Power of Women and the Subversion of Community*, but the demand was explicated in a series of pamphlets and debates between 1971 and 1975 (James, 2012). They argued that capitalist production is built on a hidden form of exploitation, that of the wage-less housewife, hidden precisely because this labour was unwaged (Dalla Costa & James, 1971). The result was that, "*Where women are concerned, their labor [sic] appears to be a personal service outside of capital*" [italics in original] (Dalla Costa and James, 1971, p. 10). Thus, informal or domestic labour should be recognised with a wage to reveal the invisible labour contained in social reproduction. They were concerned with conceptualising the role of the family as an essential part of the "social factory" of capitalism (Weeks, 2011, p. 119). In so doing, they sought to understand capital as a "social relation which we struggle to destroy (James, 2012, p. 132)".

When the demand was presented in full by James (1972, pp. 67–68) later that year, the semantics shifted to focus on "wages for housework" but the principle of collapsing the distinction between the productive and reproductive spheres remained: "We demand a guaranteed income for women and for men, working or not working, married or not… we demand wages for housework". However, the conceptualisation of this demand as wages *for* housework robbed the idea of its radical potential in the eyes of many feminists (see Malos, 1980). Moreover, according to Weeks (2011, p. 119), the presentation of WFH as a contribution to Marxist formulations of capital exacerbated the tendency for these debates to "degenerate[sic] into a contest to locate the definitive passage from Marx that would resolve the dispute once for all", while Stevenson (2019) notes that discussions around whether housework was "productive" in a Marxist sense also detracted from the radical content of the demand itself.

Nonetheless, WFH's proponents' wider arguments made their intent to challenge capitalism clear. James and Dalla Costa were explicit that WFH was designed to reveal the "other area of hidden capitalist exploitation" (James, 2012, p. 145) so that once it was identified as work, it could consequently be refused: "your production is vital for capitalism… refusing to *work*, is a fundamental level of social power (p. 142)". Silvia Federici described this as a "revolutionary perspective" because "*It is the demand by which our nature ends and our struggle begins because just to want wages for housework means to refuse that work as the expression of our nature*, and therefore to refuse precisely the role that capital has invented for us" (Federici, 1975, p. 4). The intent was not to take wages for *housework* but through that demand to reject the entire structure of capitalist wage labour. Any payment was not to be exchanged for labour but as a form of independence and liberation, a refusal of the ethics of work (Weeks, 2011). This was an explicit rejection of the existing state structures and the political economy on which they were based, thereby meeting the criteria for an "extremist" ideological position (Backes, 2010; Eatwell & Goodwin, 2010; Midlarsky, 2011; Schmid, 2014; Lowe, 2017).

Although the WFH framing was not accepted by large sections of the WLM, this extreme ideological perspective was widely shared. Many feminists saw social reproduction as the revolutionary bridge between struggles in the home and the workplace, a way of threatening and reconstructing the capitalist social order in all of its forms (Freeman & Tate, 1974; O'Malley, 1974; Coulson et al., 1975; Malos, 1980; Rowbotham, 1980). This was exemplified by Elizabeth Wilson, a critic of the WFH demand, who nonetheless agreed that struggles over the politics of social reproduction were built on rebellion against the capitalist work ethic, and further to that, were a "public demonstration and a way of saying things are not the way we want them – *this* is how they should be (Wilson, 1986, pp. 37, 39)."

Thus, despite many disagreements about the exact demand that was required, the women's movement in this period shared an understanding that attacking the institution of domestic labour was a way of attacking the capitalist social order at its roots. The "wages for housework" position was simply the one that was most explicit that the role of a basic income was to disrupt the wage relation, not to reinforce it.

Two Paths: Reform or Revolution

Although there was consensus within socialist and Marxist sections of the women's movement that reproductive labour was at the centre of capitalism's exploitation of women, the routes to challenging this diverged. Within the "mainstream" of the women's movement, exemplified by the agreed demands of the WLM, this feminist analysis resulted in the adoption of a fifth demand at the national conference in 1974 – the demand for financial and legal independence (McIntosh, 2011). However, the emphasis shifted from challenging the role of *capital* to the role of the *state* in institutionalising women's role as domestic labourers dependent on a male partner (The Women's Liberation Campaign for Legal and Financial Independence; TWCLFI, 1975.)

Nevertheless, the document carried a radical intent, arguing that politico-legal structures of the state made "any experimentation in social and sexual relations virtually impossible" (TWCLFI, 1975, p. 1). The analysis was predicated on the same liberatory ideals as forms of reproductive struggle, such as WFH, but addressing problems with the state led to remedies having a more technocratic and reformist focus. The pamphlet critiqued a series of laws and state actions, such as cohabitation, child benefits and family income support, that limited women's freedom (TWCLFI, 1975). It culminated in a series of further demands for reforms to each specific area of the law but chose not to make any UBI demand for either women, all reproductive labourers, or all citizens (TWCLFI, 1975). The demands concluded with a summary of their limited nature: "These demands are only minimal and not comprehensive. They can perhaps best be used as a basis for further discussion and campaigns" (TWCLFI, 1975, p. 10).

However, within the wider women's movement, particularly women activists in other political formations, the extremism was preserved. Women in Claimants' Unions (CUs) – collectives organised around those receiving benefits of some kind from the state – also analysed the range of discriminations women experienced within the benefits system but took a far more combative tone. They produced a handbook, "Women in Social Security" in 1976, which consistently emphasised the power relations inherent in the capitalist state. The cohabitation section, for example, asserted that "Humiliation, harassment and intimidation are the tools of the trade of the SS (social security) snoopers", deliberately drawing parallels with fascism and showing an illustration of a CU knife severing the heads of inspectors, the police and the judiciary, represented as the many-headed hydra of the state apparatus (CU Women, 1976, p. 8). They did not call for political violence in their action but it was an acceptable part of their discourse, once more highlighting how the women's movement in this period is better understood as taking a pragmatic non-violent approach to social change than an ideologically non-violent one.

Unlike the formal demand of the WLM, the CU women's aim was not technocratic reform but to situate the state as the enemy of the working class and women in particular. The handbook advised that claimants must "never meet the S.S. alone" and to "tell them nothing beyond what you have to", while in the event of a snooper watching you, you should "let the tyres down, take a photo, turn a hose pipe on him etc" (CU Women, 1976, pp. 11, 17 & 19). The welfare state itself is dismissed as "a con, state control over the working class... supporting the notion of the nuclear family", a notion the CU women wished to abolish in pursuit of "liberation for millions of women" (CU Women, 1976, pp. 29 & 27). For the CU women, the state structures and the rule of law were not simply in need of reform, they were fundamentally illegitimate.

Moreover, the handbook emphasised that the disciplinary processes of the patriarchal state were intimately linked to the political economy of capitalism. In this they shared their analysis with WFH, arguing that capitalism is only concerned with work that produces profit, thereby naturalising reproductive labour as women's role (CU Women, 1976, pp. 26–27; James, 2012, p. 145; Federici, 1975, p. 4; Miller et al., 2019). Nevertheless, they were sceptical of the implication of wages *for* housework, but their own demand, "a GUARANTEED INCOME FOR EACH INDIVIDUAL AS OF RIGHT without a means test, and with no strings attached [sic]", was framed in the same language of destroying capitalist wage slavery as WFH proponents (CU Women, 1976, p. 26).

Thus, like many in the women's movement, whether connected to WFH or other theoretical approaches, the CU women understood that reproductive labour was at the heart of capitalist exploitation and state oppression, a nexus of power that feminists needed to abolish. The disputes and tensions between these groups obfuscated the level of cross-fertilisation in ideas and the crossover in activist bases with many CU women also participants in WFH or the WLM (Stevenson, 2019). When understood more broadly, the women's movement in this period, especially at its radical edges presented an extreme challenge to capitalism that prefigured the work of contemporary UBI supporters.

When Srnicek and Williams (2016) framed a UBI as an increase in class power enabling time to reflect on social forces, both WFH and the CU women had developed the same perspective four decades earlier. The absence of these feminist stories from historical overviews of the UBI demand indicate that the women's movement's struggles in this field are an often-forgotten form of political extremism (Gentillini et al., 2020; Mason, 2015; Bregman, 2018).

Conclusion

Women's movements in the West have been primarily associated with peaceful forms of activism and resistance. However, through an analysis of the British second-wave women's movement's activism and ideology, I have shown that feminism's relationship to political violence and extremism was more complex than is often assumed. The movement rarely engaged in political violence – the flour-bombing of Bob Hope at the Miss World Protest was a mild exception to the rule – but its activists existed within a milieu that included violent groups. Prominent women's liberationists were involved in defending the Angry Brigade and were prepared to stand in solidarity with other violent struggles, such as in Northern Ireland, both of which showed violence was not anathema to all feminists. Similarly, women in Claimants' Unions were comfortable using violent imagery towards the state and its representatives. Overall though, adjacency to political violence resulted in rejection of it as a political strategy, either because violence was seen to express patriarchal norms or simply as a recognition of its limitations against the repressive state apparatuses.

Nevertheless, the WLM's actions and ideology complicate the concept of non-violent extremism. They illustrate, alongside other extremisms discussed in this handbook, that there is not always a clear distinction between violence and non-violence in political activism. Indeed, the Women's movement in this period may be better thought of as an example of a "not-violent" extremism rather than as a "non-violent" one. In its solidarity with some forms of political violence and its willingness to make use of violent imagery, the Women's movement at times sat within what Baran (2005) has described as a "gray zone of militancy" (p. 70). Thus, the Women's movement at that time demonstrated that absolutist forms of non-violent extremism are rare and that the motivations for non-violence activism are complex and contextual.

However, there is no ambiguity about the women's movement's extremism in this period. Although its official demands were primarily reformist, this belied the radicalism that exploded in the movement around social reproduction. Across its many political expressions, from the WFH, through the WLM and women's activism in CUs, the movement presented a direct challenge to capitalist political economy and the patriarchal state. Women activists sought to smash the system of wage slavery and the disciplinary powers of the state through demands for "wages for housework" and a guaranteed income for all. For them, this was not a response to a more automated economy, as some contemporary theorists have understood similar demands (Bregman, 2018; Mason, 2015), but a necessary assault on an illegitimate and extreme social order. Recovering this framing can help us to understand extremism in two important ways.

First, certain reformist policies in our contemporary societies are often a result of more extremist histories. Whilst policies like UBI may be seen intermittently as feasible reform measures, considered even by capitalist states, these histories have often ignored feminist constructions of these demands. As a result, the far more extreme and revolutionary feminist potential of these policies to reconstruct the entire political-economic order has been neglected. Second, it was this economic extremism, in the form of a thorough critique of the capitalist mode of social reproduction and activism in opposition to it, that constituted the Women's movement's most serious threats to both capital and patriarchy. Thus, as a case study of non-violent extremism, British feminism in this period shows that it is essential that studies of both feminism and extremism take account of the economic fields of conflict, not only the political and cultural.

Note

1 The British "New Left milieu" refers to the interconnected and overlapping ideological commitments and activism of the non-parliamentary political left in the 1960s and 1970s, which was organised around principles of collective liberation from capitalism whilst also rejecting the "Actually Existing Communism" of the Soviet Union. See Hughes (2015) and Davis (2008) for a more detailed discussion.

Bibliography

Backes, U. (2010). *Political Extremes: A Conceptual History from Antiquity*. London: Routledge.

Baran, Z. (2005). Fighting the War of Ideas. *Foreign Affairs*, *84*(6), 68–78. DOI:10.2307/20031777.

Beck, U. (1992). *Risk Society: Towards a New Modernity*. London: Sage.

Bregman, R. (2018). Utopia for Realists: And How We Can Get There. London: Bloomsbury.

Christiansen, S. M. R. (2011). "The Brigade Is Everywhere": Violence and Spectacle in the British Counterculture. In T. Brown and L. Anton (Eds.), *Between the Avant-Garde and the Everyday: Subversive Politics in Europe from 1957 to the Present*. (pp. 47–57), Oxford: Berghahn Books.

Claimants' Union Women. (1976). *Women and Social Security: A Handbook from the Claimant's Union Movement*. Politics/Policy 27, Feminist Archive South.

Cole, N. (2010). *Made in Dagenham* [Film]. Paramount Pictures.

Cortright, D. (2008). *Peace: A History of Movements and Ideas*. Cambridge: Cambridge University Press.

Coulson, M., Magas, B. and Wainwright, H. (1975). 'The Housewife and Her Labour under Capitalism' – A Critique. *New Left Review*, *89*(1). Retrieved from: https://newleftreview.org/issues/i89/articles/margaret-coulson-branka-magas-hilary-wainwright-the-housewife-and-her-labour-under-capitalism-a-critique.

Dalla Costa, M. and James, S. (1971). The Power of Women and the Subversion of Community, 1–36. Retrieved from: www.e-flux.com/wp-content/uploads/2013/05/2.-Dalla-Costa-and-James-Women-and-the-Subversion-of-the-Community.pdf?b8c429.

Eatwell, R. and Goodwin, M. J. (2010). Introduction: The 'New' Extremism in Twenty-First Century Britain. In R. Eatwell and M. J. Goodwin (Eds.), *The New Extremism in 21st Century Britain*. London: Routledge.

Eschle, C. (2017). Beyond Greenham Woman? Gender Identities and Anti-nuclear Activism in Peace Camps. *International Feminist Journal of Politics, 19*(4), 471–490. DOI: 10.1080/14616742.2017.1354716.

European Commission. (2020). A Counter-Terrorism Agenda for the EU: Anticipate, Prevent, Protect, Respond. Retrieved from: https://ec.europa.eu/home-affairs/sites/default/files/pdf/09122020_communication_commission_european_parliament_the_council_eu_agenda_counter_terrorism_po-2020-9031_com-2020_795_en.pdf.

Federici, S. (1975). *Wages against Housework*. Bristol: Falling Wall Press. Retrieved from: https://caringlabor.files.wordpress.com/2010/11/federici-wages-against-housework.pdf.

Fell, A. (1972). And There's Another Side… Six Interviews with Women in Ireland. *Spare Rib, 3*, 11–26. Retrieved from: General Reading Room, National Library of Scotland, Edinburgh.

Fisher, M. (2009). *Capitalist Realism: Is There No Alternative?* Washington, DC: Zero Books.

Fraser, N. (2013). *Fortunes of Feminism: From State-Managed Capitalism to Neoliberal Crisis*. London: Verso Books.

Freeman, C. and Tate, J. (1974). *Class Struggle*. [Birmingham Women and Socialism Conference 1974]. Feminist Library (Bishopsgate Institute) Pamphlet Collection.

Gentillini, U., Grosh, M., Rigilini, J. and Yemtsov, R. (2020). *Exploring Universal Basic Income: A Guide to Navigating Concepts, Evidence, and Practices*. Washington DC: World Bank.

Gilbert, J. (2017, April 24). Forty Years of Failure: How to Challenge the Narrative of Hard Brexit. *OpenDemocracy*. Retrieved from www.opendemocracy.net/en/opendemocracyuk/forty-years-of-failure-how-to-challenge-narrative-of-hard-brexit/.

Gilbert, J. (2020). *Twenty First Century Socialism*. Cambridge: Polity.

Hall, S. and Jacques, M. (1989). Introduction. In S. Hall and M. Jacques (Eds.). *New Times: The Changing Face of Politics in the 1990s*. (pp. 11–22). London: Lawrence and Wishart.

HM Government. (2011). *Prevent Strategy*. Westminster: The Stationary Office. Retrieved from: https://assets.publishing.service.gov.uk/government/uploads/system/uploads/attachment_data/file/97976/prevent-strategy-review.pdf.

Hines, S. (2020). Sex Wars and (Trans) Gender Panics: Identity and Body Politics in Contemporary UK Feminism. *The Sociological Review, 68*(4), 699–717.

James, S. (2012). *Sex, Race and Class – The Perspective of Winning. A Selection of Writings 1952–2011*. London: PM Press.

Jolly, M. (2017). After the Protest: Biographical Consequences of Movement Activism in an Oral History of Women's Liberation in Britain. In K. Schulz (Ed.), *The Women's Liberation Movement: Impacts and Outcomes*. (pp. 298–320). Oxford: Berghahn Books.

Jolly, M. (2019). *Sisterhood and after: An Oral History of the UK Women's Liberation Movement, 1968–Present*. Oxford: Oxford University Press.

Jorgensen-Earp, C. R. (1997). *"The Transfiguring Sword": The Just War of the Women's Social and Political Union*. London: University of Alabama Press.

Lohman, K. and Worley, M. (2018). Bloody Revolutions, Fascist Dreams, Anarchy and Peace: Crass, Rondes and the Politics of Punk, 1977–84. *Britain and the World*, 11(1), 51–74. DOI: 10.3366/brw.2018.0287.

Lowe, D. (2017). Prevent Strategies: The Problems Associated in Defining Extremism: The Case of the United Kingdom. *Studies in Conflict and Terrorism, 40*(11), 917–933. DOI: 10.1080/1057610X.2016.1253941.

Lowthorpe, P. (2020). *Misbehaviour* [Film]. 20th Century Fox.

Malos, E. (1980). Introduction. In E. Malos (Ed.), *The Politics of Housework*. London: Allison and Busby.

Mason, P. (2015). *Postcapitalism: A Guide to Our Future*. London: Allen Lane.

Mayo, M. (1977). Introduction. In M. Mayo (Ed.), *Women in the Community*. London: Routledge and Kegan Paul.

McIntosh, M. (2011). *Mary McIntosh Discusses Financial and Legal Independence*. British Library, Sisterhood and After Collection. Retrieved from: www.bl.uk/collection-items/mary-mcintosh-financial-and-legal-independence.

Mider, D. (2013). The Anatomy of Violence: A Study of the Literature. *Aggression and Violent Behaviour*, 18, 702–708. https://doi.org/10.1016/j.avb.2013.07.021.

Midlarsky, M. I. (2011). *Origins of Political Extremism: Mass Violence in the Twentieth Century and Beyond*. Cambridge: Cambridge University Press.

Miller, A., Yamamori, T. and Zelleke, A. (2019). The Gender Effects of a Basic Income. In M. Torry (Ed.), *The Palgrave International Handbook of Basic Income*. (pp. 133–153). Cham: Springer International Publishing.

Moore, N. (2008). Eco/Feminism, Non-violence and the Future of Feminism. *International Feminist Journal of Politics*, *10*(3), 282–298. DOI: 10.1080/14616740802185486.

Owen, N. (2013). Men and the 1970s British Women's Liberation Movement. *The Historical Journal*, *56*(3), 801–826.

Robinson, L. (2013). *Gay Men and the Left in Post-War Britain: How the Personal Got Political*. Manchester: Manchester University Press.

Rowbotham, S. (1980). The Carrot, the Stick and the Movement. In E. Malos (Ed.). *The Politics of Housework*. London: Allison and Busby.

Schmid, A. P. (2014). Violent and Non-violent Extremism: Two Sides of the Same Coin? *International Centre for Counter-Terrorism Paper*. Retrieved from: opev.org/wp-content/uploads/2019/10/Violent-and-Non-Violent-Extremism-Alex-P.-Schmid.pdf.

Sloman, P. (2016). Beveridge's Rival: Juliet Rhys-Williams and the Campaign for Basic Income, 1942–55. *Contemporary British History*, *30*(2), 203–223. DOI: 10.1080/13619462.2015.1077443.

Srnicek, N. and Williams, A. (2016). *Inventing the Future: Postcapitalism and a World without Work*. London and New York: Verso.

Stevenson, G. (2019). *The Women's Liberation Movement and Class Politics*. London: Bloomsbury.

Taylor, J. D. (2015). The Party's Over? The Angry Brigade, the Counterculture, and the British New Left, 1967–72. *Historical Journal*, *58*(3), 877–900. DOI:10.1017/S0018246X14000612.

The Women's Liberation Campaign for Legal and Financial Independence. (1975). *The Demand for Independence*. Women's Collections 2, HQ1297, TUC Library Collections, London Metropolitan University.

Titcombe, E. (2013). Women Activists: Rewriting Greenham's History. *Women's History Review*, *22*(2), 310–329. DOI: 10.1080/09612025.2012.726118.

Varon, J. (2004). *Bringing the War Home: The Weather Underground, The Red Army Faction, and Revolutionary Violence in the Sixties and Seventies*. London: University of California Press.

Vernon, J. (2010). The Local, the Imperial and the Global: Repositioning Twentieth-century Britain and the Brief Life of Its Social Democracy. *Twentieth Century British History*, *21*(3), 404–418. DOI:10.1093/tcbh/hwq026.

Wahidin, A. (2016). *Ex-combatants, Gender and Peace in Northern Ireland: Women, Political Protest and the Prison Experience*. New York: Palgrave Macmillan.

Wainwright, H. and Littler, J. (2020). Municipalism and Feminism: Then and Now. *Soundings*, *74*, 10–25. DOI: 10.3898/soun.74.01.2020.

Walkowitz, J. R. (2019). Feminism and the Politics of Prostitution in King's Cross in the 1980s. *Twentieth Century British History*, *30*(2), 231–263. DOI:10.1093/tcbh/hwz011.

Weeks, K. (2011). *The Problem with Work: Feminism, Marxism, Antiwork Politics, and Postwork Imaginaries*. Durham and New York: Duke University Press.

Weigman, R. (2000). Feminism's Apocalyptic Futures. *New Literary History*, *31*(4), 805–825. DOI:10.1353/nlh.2000.0053.

Wilson, E. (with Weir, A.) (1986). *Hidden Agendas: Theory, Politics, and Experience in the Women's Movement*. London and New York: Tavistock Publications.

Yamamori, T. (2014). A Feminist Way to Unconditional Basic Income: Claimants Union and Women's Liberation Movements in 1970s Britain. *Basic Income Studies*, *9*(1–2), 1–24. DOI:10.1515/bis-2014-0019.

27

BECOMING THROUGH NON-VIOLENT RESISTANCE

The Rise of Feminist Consciousness in Chile

Melany Cruz

Introduction

Feminism has historically engaged with the questions of violence and non-violence. Whether engaging with practices of non-violence, such as anti-war or civil rights movements, or with theoretical questions of the meaning and implications of violence for women, feminist thinkers and activists have largely contributed to the rethinking of the role of non-violent resistance. This chapter focuses on the rise of the feminist movement in Chile over the last few years, focusing particularly on the role played by feminists during the social uprising of 2019. This chapter argues that there is a connection between the rise of feminist consciousness and the practices of non-violence. It is here proposed that an understanding of non-violence should be neither "strategic" nor "principled", but one that is instead reflected on as a form of *necessity* within the Chilean feminist movement in the context of the expansion of an anti-neoliberal movement. Thus, this study aims to contribute to both an empirical understanding of the contemporary feminist movement in Chile, and provide a novel conceptualisation of the uses of non-violence.

The chapter focuses on the feminist theoretical discussion around consciousness and non-violence, providing a few illustrations from the experiences of resistance which emerged during the uprising in Chile in 2019. The first section presents a brief discussion of the meaning of, and differences between, "consciousness-raising" and "becoming" a feminist in the feminist theories of Sara Ahmed and Sandra Lee Bartky. The following section discusses different approaches to the idea of non-violence, drawing a distinction between pacifist and non-pacifist approaches to non-violent resistance from a feminist perspective. The third section describes the emergence of the current feminist movement in Chile, followed by a theoretical and empirical analysis of the political ideas and positions of the *Coordinadora 8 de Marzo* (C8M) and the *Asamblea Feminista Plurinacional* (AFP), both central organisations of the feminist movement in the country. This section discusses the radical anti-neoliberal dimension of the movement and its non-pacifist approach in resisting state violence during the social uprising. The chapter concludes by reflecting on how this case is not unique, but belongs to an expansion of feminist activism in Latin America.

DOI: 10.4324/9781003032793-32

Theories of Consciousness-Raising and Becoming a Feminist

Feminist thinkers have long theorised the questions of *how one* becomes or comes to *see them-selves* as a feminist. Feminism, as both an ideological and political movement, has encountered traditional conceptions, mainly from Marxism, of consciousness-raising to explain the experience and meanings of *being* a feminist. Several accounts and debates have emerged from this in the development of feminist political thought (Sowards & Renegar, 2004). For the purpose of this chapter, I want to refer to the distinction between the idea of "consciousness-raising" and the notion of "becoming" a feminist as the cognitive and affective dimensions of an ongoing process.

To be a feminist involves an active process of self-consciousness of what it means to be a woman in society. As Marx conceptualised the necessity of "class-consciousness" for the recognition of capitalist exploitation and the movement towards a revolutionary transformation, feminists have theorised the need of feminist consciousness to achieve the end of patriarchy. Feminist Kathie Sarachild claimed that during the 1970s the process of feminist consciousness-raising was a "radical" one, which was "interested in getting to the roots of problems in society" (Sarachild, 1978, p. 144). The process of consciousness-raising for radical feminists was rooted in the realisation and recognition of women's conditions through lived experiences of discrimination and abuse in everyday social relations. For Sarachild, this program of actual activism was far from an individualistic issue. The raising of feminist consciousness could only occur in concordance with other feminists and women through collective organisation and action. "Actions brought to the public for the specific purpose of challenging old ideas and raising new ones" (Sarachild, 1978, p. 145), which at the time of her writing, meant establishing educational spaces for women that would enable them to collectively identify their oppression.

Similarly, Sheila Rowbotham argues that consciousness-raising seems at first to be "fragmented and particular", however, "in order to discover its own [feminist] identity as distinct from that of the oppressor it has to become visible to itself" (Rowbotham, 2015, p. 27). This radical account of feminism, which was committed to revolutionary purposes in the 1960s and 1970s, claims that consciousness does not simply take part "within itself but when it knows itself in relation to what it has created apart from itself" (Rowbotham, 2015, p. 28), meaning that consciousness emerges when related to the condition of oppression and exploitation that women face under capitalism. For Rowbotham, the political nature of women's revolutionary consciousness relates to the problems of presence and absence of women within revolutionary movements and what they can contribute to movements for political transformation.

Alternately, from a more phenomenological perspective, Sara Ahmed describes becoming a feminist as a sensation. The process of gaining "a sense of things", especially those things that tend not to make sense in our society (Ahmed, 2017, p. 21). It is the sense of wrongdoing, the sense of injustice that triggers the feelings and thoughts which lead to becoming a feminist. Such a process, she indicates, is sometimes mediated by our bodies, especially when they have been violated. "The violence does things. You begin to expect it. You learn to inhabit your body differently through this expectation" (Ahmed, 2017, p. 24). Through this experiential process, the feminist consciousness is formed in the ways "we re-describe the world we are in" by identifying personal experience with the experiences of others, building a view of the "patterns and regularities" (Ahmed, 2017, p. 27) of those experiences. According to Ahmed, the process of becoming a feminist involves not only the gathering together and discussing of lived experiences; it is not even necessarily about clearly identifying the structures that oppress women. Rather, it is the formational process of disarming and rebuilding the world that is forced upon women, that for the most part (re)produces the violence we collectively experience.

These two similar yet differing accounts of what it means to become a feminist are relevant for an understanding of feminist accounts of violence and non-violence. Although Sandra Lee Bartky is not directly referring to violence, she presents an important synthesis of feminist consciousness that permits the introduction of questions pertinent to this chapter. She argues that feminists live in a contradiction between victimisation and the joyfulness of consciousness (Bartky, 1975, p. 429). To become a feminist involves the dialectic of recognising oneself as a victim who has sustained injury and who "live exposed to injury" (Bartky, 1975, p. 431), whilst also seeing oneself as the source of power to revoke such a sense of victimisation, the evocation of joy in fighting against oppression. This dialectical moment presented by Bartky touches upon some of the elements I will analyse for the case of feminist non-violence in Chile. However, I will also take distance from the idea of victim consciousness by presenting contrasts with what has been developed in theories of violence and non-violence.

Feminism and the Issue of Non-violence

Feminism and gender studies have made important contributions to the debate on political violence, especially in the field of international relations, influencing discussions about war, terrorism and security. By expanding the frontiers of what is "political" about violence, feminist scholars have attempted to disrupt the dichotomies between public/private and aggressive/passive violence (Sjoberg, 2012). Similarly, feminist scholars have contributed to an understanding of the notion of non-violence in peace studies (Gay, 2019). Discursive and affective dimensions of both violence and non-violence studies have also been the result of feminist interventions, providing the experience of violence as a lens and as an analytical tool to help conceptualise and understand these phenomena. For this chapter, I want to focus on the debate presented within (feminist) political theory by arguing along the lines of Judith Butler's notion of non-violence as an ethical practice of resistance and as empowerment; a form of self-defence. This is not understood as the individual capacity to defend oneself, but rather the expansion of the self as interdependency with others. This interdependence also relates to the entanglement between the practice of violence and non-violence (Butler, 2020). I will turn to this debate further in this chapter, but firstly I want to briefly present the different theoretical elements that constitute a feminist approach to non-violence.

The question of non-violence can be addressed from a tactical/strategic and ethical point of view. A pragmatic approach to non-violent action focuses on *the most effective means* to achieve the mobilisation of "popular power" (Atack, 2012, p. 7). This tactical approach to non-violence has also been identified as "civil disobedience" (see Rawls, 2000) with focus on forms of collective action that are characterised by the absence of (physical) violence. Examples in the literature are vast, such as the anti-war movement, anti-apartheid and the civil rights movement in the United States (Vinthagen, 2015; Zunes, 1999). On the other hand, ethical or principled approaches to non-violence aim to promote the ideas and values of "avoiding or replacing violence in political action and social relationships" (Atack, 2012, p. 9). Scholars have paid particular attention to Gandhi and Luther King as examples of ethical non-violence.

Anti-war and pacifist feminist movements had an important presence in the United Kingdom and the United States during the 1970s and 1980s. According to Frazer and Hutchings, this era of connection between feminism and pacifism was justified on several grounds: (a) "an interconnection between patriarchy, violence and war; (b) the mutual dependency between public (war) and private (interpersonal) violence; (c) the importance of structural violence; and (d) a rejection of instrumental justifications for violence" (Frazer & Hutchings, 2020, p. 157). The use of violence was seen as to be complicit with the oppressor and to actively aid in the (re) production of violence embedded in society. Radical feminists, on the other hand, criticised pacifism for its narrow focus on *actual* war, describing it as a "distraction" from the *other* war that was waged "against women" (Frazer & Hutchings, 2020, p. 159). Radicals argued that "to renounce the possibility of using violence is to affirm women's lack of agency and to play into the existing sex-gender order", whereby women were determined by the feminine/peaceful and masculine/violent dichotomy (Frazer & Hutchings, 2020, p. 160). This debate took place in the context of the anti-war movement and the development of the idea of "just war theory" (Peach, 1994). Despite differences, feminists managed to break the traditional contradiction between "ethical" and "strategic" dimensions of non-violence because of the epistemological commitment to interlinking theory and practice.

Regarding the theoretical dimensions of violence in Latin American feminism, the Argentinian anthropologist, Rita Segato, is also concerned with the debate concerning the war against women. Though not referring to the radical European tradition, Segato places her analysis in the reality of feminicide and rape in Latin America, using the killing of women in *Cuidad de Juarez* as an illustration of what *war* entails in this context.[1] *War* is neither declared nor always visible, she states, but *war* is expressive (Segato, 2016, p. 39). Expressive violence does not have an instrumental purpose – as means to an end – but is used as a form of controlling, dominating and colonising the feminised body. Violence when expressed against women is the expansion of state sovereignty and a form of dramatisation of domination that exists in societal gender relations (Segato, 2016, p. 39). To some extent, Segato, as a pacifist feminist, identifies violence with masculinity. This is defined as a mandate that permits the order of domination and the reproduction of violence which, as said before, is not always visible or physical. She also indicates that the expressive dimension of violence against women is possible because of the existence of a "pedagogy of cruelty" formed by the repetition and normalisation of violence by the limitation and restriction of empathy in our society (Segato, 2016, p. 21). This means that "cruelty is a message" (Segato, 2016, p. 24) that transforms bodies into objects through processes of reification (Universidad de Chile, 2019). Although Segato does not provide an account of non-violence, she explains expressive violence as giving way to the possibility of resistance.

Similarly, Argentinian thinker Veronica Gago argues that the war against women needs to be understood as the mapping of simultaneous and interrelated forms of violence that intersect in women's bodies. "To trace the modes of connection is to trace meaning, because it renders visible the machinery of exploitation and extraction of value that involves increasing thresholds of violence" (Gago, 2020, p. 57). This is relevant because by producing such meanings "allows [one] to produce a language that goes beyond categorizing ourselves [women] as victims" (Gago, 2020, p. 59). This is the primary form of resistance which emerges from both Segato and Gago's theory, to break with dichotomies existent in some of the literature on gender-based violence regarding victimisation. The resistance of non-violence is both "ethical" and "strategic", as I will explain with the case of feminism in Chile.

Becoming a Feminist Through Non-violent Resistance

A Brief History of the Recent Feminist Movement in Chile

In the last months of 2019, Chile experienced a popular revolt (Tijoux, 2020) triggered by a 30 pesos (£0.03) rise of metro fares in the capital Santiago. The first protestors were predominantly female secondary schoolers who rushed metro stations by jumping the barriers and disrupting the regular functioning of commuters. Videos quickly emerged on social media of what looked like a *joyous* stampede. The students erupted from the normal traffic, chanting protest songs which echoed throughout entire stations and, eventually, the entire country. In the late hours of 18th October 2019, people began to spontaneously gather at different locations in the city, provoking a snowballing of protest which continued to gather momentum over several months across most cities in the country (Cruz, 2020; Vargas Muñoz, 2020). People came together under the banner: "it is not 30 pesos, it is 30 years", to convey a message of discontent which covered the entire history of the emergence and consolidation of neoliberalism in the country (Ferretti & Dragnic, 2020b). In this process, feminist organisations were central in galvanising the movement and participating in protests.

The key participation of, particularly female, students is not just an anecdote in this context.[2] The feminist student movement played a leading role in street protests in 2018. This period was called by the media and activists *El Mayo Feminista* [The Feminist May], evoking parallels with May 1968. That May in 2018, feminists from Higher Education Institutions (HEI), both public and private, demanded the end of "sexist education" and an end to the secrecy around sexual harassment and abuse within educational institutions (Castillo, 2018; Grau, 2018, p. 95). The protests of *Mayo Feminista* created a distinctive aesthetic of the non-violent form of resistance that has continued to define the feminist movement until now. The feminist movement has disrupted public space using traditional and non-traditional practices of protest, which has been seen throughout the last three *Huelgas Feminista* [Women's Strikes] on 8 March 2018, 2019, and 2020, and during the social uprising and Constitutional Referendum of October 2020. These moments have fundamentally shaped the recent history of non-violent resistance in the Chilean feminist movement.

Broadly speaking, feminist movements in Chile are characterised mainly by urban, university-educated women (Grau, 2018). This group represents the public face of activism. However, feminists within the movement claim that their political and social base is broader than what the media and the traditional political system tends to present. Feminist thinkers and activists consistently refer to "feminisms" as a way of recognising the diverse composition of the movement, which also includes sexual dissidents (*disidencias*), non-binary people, indigenous women and transwomen (Grau, 2018, p. 94). The class composition is also diverse, from middle-class professionals to working-class union organisers. For these reasons, it is difficult to profile the feminist movement as a homogenous organisation. Perhaps the main feature is its *horizontalidad*. This means that there is not a hierarchical organisation, whether in decision-making or in the actions taken. Instead of formal leaders of the movement, there exists a system of *vocerias* – spokespersons – who are recognisable to different groups within the movement.[3]

For this chapter, I focus my analysis on two of the main organisations within the movement: the C8M and the AFP. The former works as a network of feminist groupings across the country following the international call for the Women's Strike on International Women's Day (Arruzza, Bhattacharya, & Fraser, 2019). The C8M advocates for a social and political recognition of social reproduction as labour, making visible the role that women play in the (re) production of society. They define themselves and their goals thusly:

> We want to make feminism a perspective and transversal political action of social movements, to promote the encounter, dialogue and collective action between different organisations and build a common agenda of mobilization as a majority feminism against the precariousness of life.
>
> *(Coordinadora Feminista 8M · Quiénes Somos, n.d.)*

The AFM, on the other hand, originates from the social uprising of October 2019. This is an assembly born of the convergence of several feminist organisations and groups, including feminist factions of unions and political parties. They emerged as the feminist response to the national demand to write a new constitution. The assembly writes

> Although they have tried to erase us from the history books and keep us out of decision-making, today we recognise ourselves as promoters of social transformation (…). This October 25th we will take history into our own hands again, when we approve to overturn what was imposed on us during the dictatorship and build a new Constitution through a Parietal Constitutional Convention. "Together we make history" [the assembly slogan] was born from the feminist Constituent Power, based on our experiences and political memories, our comradery, and, above all, on our dreams for a country where life is worth living, where diversity, inclusion and freedom become custom
>
> *(JuntasHacemosHistoria, n.d.)*

Both organisations have particularities and complexities beyond the scope of this chapter, though they do serve as illustration of the importance of looking at non-violent resistance as a radical political project, which in this case opposes the advance and maintenance of neoliberalism in Chile. Discourses such as "self-recognition" and "collectiveness", as in the above quotes, are part of the project of looking to entwine consciousness-raising and radical resistance. In what follows, I will focus on *what* is radical about the feminist movement and *why* non-violence is relevant in the formation of feminist consciousness and the expansion of the movement.

Anti-neoliberalism at the Heart of the Movement

Both the C8M and the AFP share principles that identify feminism as an essential dimension for the political transformation of the country, especially within the conditions of structural violence produced by neoliberalism. As Zerán indicates, the resistance against all *violences* is shared across most feminist groups (Arruzza, Bhattacharya, & Fraser, 2019). Violence is presented in a plural way to identify the multiplicity of sources of violence perpetuated and multiplied by the conditions of neoliberalism imposed on the country during the authoritarian regime of Augusto Pinochet[4] (Ferretti & Dragnic, 2020a). Therefore, the anti-neoliberal agenda is at the heart of feminism in Chile. Privatisation of education, health, pensions and housing lay bare the material conditions of gender inequalities (Millán, 2018; Schild & Follegati, 2018), which deeply affect indigenous women and non-binary people. The policing of female bodies due to the lack of reproductive rights, such as abortion, sexual education and anti-sexual harassment laws, are linked to the conservative domination inherited from the dictatorship. Drawing from Segato and Gago's account, activists identified these elements as *violences*, which operate structurally, symbolically, physically and emotionally in the experience of women and non-binary people. In this sense, there is a "war of ideas" against neoliberalism, which aims to reshape the ways in which society thinks and reflects about the impact of neoliberal reforms on their lives. To reshape those societal ideas, feminists argue for the necessity of returning to expressions of non-violence that allow everyone to reveal *violences*. Here, I want to particularly focus on the role played by the non-violent resistance of "*la toma*" and the feminist assemblies.

As Castillo (2018) indicates, the rise of feminism in Chile "not only took place but has been taking the place. The feminist protest (…) has opted for the political strategy of *la toma*"

(Castillo, 2018, p. 35). *"La toma"* is a colloquial term for an occupation. It is rooted in the word *tomar*, to take, which implies not only to occupy a space illegally – as occupations are traditionally understood – but also taking space as one's own. The notion of recuperation of the loss of political, cultural and social spaces due to the imposition of neoliberalism is embedded in the uses of *la toma*, which not only serves as a tactical form of non-violent resistance, but also an ethical form, as it centres the need of taking back what has been denied, especially to women and non-binary people. These occupations were particularly popular during the *Mayo Feminista* (Zerán, 2018, p. 10). From taking the physical spaces of universities to taking the universities as a place for feminism,[5] these demands were added to historical calls to achieve a public education, free from neoliberal market and sexist logics (Richard, 2018, p. 116; Zerán, 2018, p. 10).

La toma is normally accompanied by assemblies, which have been essential for feminist organisation since the uprising. This form of non-violent resistance is less accounted for by the theory of non-violence, though assemblies are an important space for the feminist movement. In simple terms, assemblies are physical or online spaces in which feminists gather to organise, share and learn. There is nothing new in its format compared to historical forms of social assemblies, but feminists have used them as an intellectual front and a space of becoming. Gago defines them as a "situated apparatuses of collective intelligence. They are spaces for taking root and projecting, where we experience the *potencia* of thinking together" (Gago, 2020, p. 155). Similar to Sarachild's idea of educational spaces for women as places of consciousness-raising, Gago gives the assembly a political meaning of being "simultaneously situation *and* process" (Gago, 2020, p. 156). Looking at both the C8M and AFP, they define themselves through the assembly, by situating the role of women within the country through demands such as "never again without us", which implies the historical isolation from political spaces and decision-making which women and non-binary people have long suffered. Importantly, the assembly is a space of process, indicating ideas of encounter and memory as organising tools in themselves. The assembly permits feminists to build towards transformational politics without losing sight of the path of historical oppression, especially related to memories evoked from the dictatorship.

These forms of resistance are key for the formation and expansion of anti-neoliberal narratives, not only because they permit growth in collective knowledge, but because through these spaces such narratives are transformed by way of a (re)connection to the historical origins of suffering. It is in suffering that an important part of *becoming* a feminist emerges. In Ahmed's terms, repetition of experiences allows us to "re-describe the world we are in" (Ahmed, 2017, p. 27). By identifying forms of collective connection and to learn that individual experiences of suffering are in fact widely shared with others permits a movement beyond individual identification to collective transformation. This is similar to Butler's idea of vulnerability and dependency that is at the foundation of the idea of non-violence (Butler, 2020; Zembylas, 2020). Agreeing with Claudia Leeb, "suffering is conceptualised as the bodily moment of physical agony that tells us that things should be different" (Leeb, 2017, p. 2). For Leeb, suffering is both a profound subjective experience and "the most objective moment" (Leeb, 2017, p. 18) because it operates in a dialectic between body and mind. In other words, suffering permits political transformation built from the point of victimisation, as Lee Bartky understood. Suffering, as a body/mind experience, is based upon a dialectical movement in which political subjects, in this case feminists, identify their physical moment of pain with historic and systemic capitalist relations (Leeb, 2017, pp. 21–24). But *how* is this dialectical thinking possible?

I argue that the rise of feminist consciousness emerges when a collective suffering surpasses the identity of individual victimisation. This can happen when collective suffering is recognised in spaces of resistance. These spaces massify the necessity of overcoming the forms of suffering which issue from, in this case, neoliberalism. Assemblies and occupations are spaces of non-violence that allow the resurgence of feminist consciousness by way of recognition that all *violences* are also sources of resistance. In Butler's terms, these spaces are expressions of political action that permit the interruption and suspension of systematic violence, which for her is the ethos of the politics of non-violence (Butler, 2020).

An important example is the international campaign of *Ni una Menos*[6] [Not one (woman) less] that is largely promoted by the C8M in Chile. This campaign organised against feminicide and *machista* violence across several countries in Latin America. The campaign largely focuses on connecting physical violence to the character of state power. Although the (neoliberal) state does not physically enact such violence, feminists argue that the state facilitates feminicide by maintaining sexist juridical processes, giving excessive power to police and dismantling networks of social care and support. Similar examples of this narrative relate to the campaign to legalise abortion, which has seen few gains in recent years but has yet to be completed due to the limitations imposed by the political and religious class, who were highly connected to those who supported the dictatorship and implemented neoliberalism in the country.

The interweaving of experiences of suffering, created mainly by the *violences* of neo-liberalism, allows the projection of a radical critique that has been transformed into a political force within the country, gaining both increasing support and opposition. Feminists in Chile have developed their political practice and thinking by taking neoliberalism at its roots, interlinking this politico-economic project with the growing and continuous violence against women and non-binary people. Non-violence therefore converts into a mechanism of *self-defence*, in Butler's terms, as a possibility of surviving, which largely is self-guarded in collective spaces, such as assemblies.

Resisting Sate's Violence

Groups opposed to feminism have grown alongside the massification of the movement. No different from other places (Marshall, 2013), online bullying, simplification of feminist ideas and resistance from conservative groups, such as far-right political parties and religious and evangelical organisations, are common. Nevertheless, I want to focus here on one of the main adversaries of feminism in Chile: the state and its police force, which have been particularly active in the targeting of women during the uprising of 2019. As mentioned earlier, this has been an important milestone for social transformation in Chile, significantly advancing an anti-neoliberal agenda in the country (Cruz, 2020).

According to the National Institute of Human Rights (INDH) between 18 October 2019 and 18 March 2020, 2,349 victims of human rights abuses were identified, 455 of which were women (Instituto Nacional de Derechos Humanos, n.d.). The violation of human rights was particularly related to "the abuse of the riot gun and the inhuman, cruel and degrading treatments with sexual connotation" (Instituto Nacional de Derechos Humanos, n.d.) including the undressing and sexual abuse of women being the third most reported action used by the police against civilians.[7] In addition, more than 101 cases of ocular injuries were reported, in which people were shot directly in their eyes, resulting in loss of vision (Instituto Nacional de Derechos Humanos, n.d.). During these months, multiple reports were made to feminist organisations about sexual assault, inappropriate touching and sexualised insults against hundreds of women committed by the police.

The collective trauma of rape used as a form of torture by state officers revives the memory of those women abused during the dictatorship, creating historical connections of suffering and the subsequent reviving of an anti-state political narrative within the feminist movement. For activists, this is a form of politico-sexual violence, which relates to Segato's idea of "expressive violence" in which the state enacts control over women's bodies in order to extend its sovereign power, especially in the context of a social revolt which aims to overturn the status quo.

As a response to these *violences*, one of the most significant moments of feminist resistance was performed by the artistic collective *Las Tesis*. The performance, which consisted of dancing to a song written by the collective, importantly impacted the consciousness of gender-based violence perpetrated by state forces. The protest song entitled *A rapist in your path*, makes reference to the national police slogan "a friend in your path" in order to ironically parallel how the police approach women with violence and abuse, not only during the uprising but throughout modern Chilean history. The song includes references to the police anthem, changing parts of it to reflect on the patriarchal structure of the police,[8] as well as highlighting the responsibility of the juridical system and the government in the continuation of sexist *violences.*

The dance was first performed in the centre of Santiago by around 200 women, from which it gained national recognition. Later the dance was performed by over 2000 women outside the Supreme Court of Chile, the Court of Appeals of Santiago, and the Court-martial Court of the Chilean Army, Chilean Air Force and Carabineros de Chile.[9] The reaction to the performances from state figures was astounding. The Police Institution (*Carabineros de Chile*) prosecuted a complaint against the collective *Las Tesis* in the courts, claiming that the performance was instigating violence against the institution of the police and promoting civil disorder, referring to one of the videos produced by the collective in which they claimed, "all police officers are rapists" (*Carabineros Se Querelló Contra Colectivo Las Tesis*, n.d.). After several months in dispute, international organisations – such as the United Nations – asked the police to withdraw the accusation against the collective, indicating that the group are defenders of human rights and that they and their performance should be protected as an expression of freedom of speech (Mostrador, 2020). This reaction from the police, whilst not unusual, neatly symbolises the effect non-violent resistance can have when it comes to the organisation promotion and impact of feminist ideas.

The performance of *Las Tesis* also encapsulates a second aspect of what *becoming* a feminist means, namely the emergence of consciousness through collective processes of joy. As Lee Bartky indicates, the dialectics of feminist consciousness interlink victimisation and joy as a form of empowerment towards liberation. The feelings of suffering and joy do not work in opposition, on the contrary, it is the experience of feeling them simultaneously that allows the process of *becoming* to transform into something material and actionable. The performance of *Las Tesis* can be considered an act of non-violent resistance, but not in the sense of pursuing peace. The non-violence of such an act permits the opening of a societal fissure, one that renders visible the ways in which political violence is perpetrated against women.

The body plays an important role in the analysis of non-violent resistance. It is the bodies that encounter violence that also embrace acts of non-violence, such as the performance of *Las Tesis*. Against notions of non-violent resistance as a principled political decision, within the feminist movement non-violence becomes a necessity, one in which the body – through performance – moves forcefully and in a determined way to stop the violence directed at them. Also, the collective gathering of bodies permits what Segal calls "moments of radical happiness" (Segal, 2018, p. 69). Joy, as with suffering, is an important affective dimension of resistance as it permits the expansion of the necessity of action, the possibility to re-signify the political space for feminists, as well as what it means to resist in a non-violent way (Souza, 2019). As Serafini indicates, *A rapist in your path* demarks the use of bodies for feminist space through collective expression. "Through their song and their movements, they are protesting, but they are also enacting a series of values such as sorority and (transnational) solidarity, horizontality, collectivity and the accessibility of both political and artistic participation" (Serafini, 2020, p. 294). These elements are manifestations of both strategic and ethical non-violence.

Another relevant example that arose during the uprising, and which serves to reveal the importance of the body in non-violent resistance, comes from the role played by the so-called *primera linea*, or frontline. Although, for the most part, protests were peaceful, including participation of elderly people, families and children, clashes with the police were also common, as well as the eruption of fires and destruction of property. In this context, groups of young people would organise themselves as a frontline to protect the public from police brutality, literally putting their bodies at the front of clashes with police. Their role was varied, from catching tear gas grenades, to building shields designed to prevent the police from breaking-up the marches. In essence, the *frontline* worked as a shield which aimed to ensure that protests and marches were a secure place for all citizens. The action of the *primera linea* permitted the massification of protests, allowing the protests to be more inclusive and alleviating the fear of state repression. Their aesthetic was characterised mainly by masked faces, protecting themselves with colourful homemade shields. Their use of violence was always in response to state violence, and primarily consisted in the throwing of stones at the police and building barricades to resist sustained skirmishes.

Feminists were also part of the frontline. Although women were a minority, they participated in different roles within the frontline, confronting both the presumptions about women not engaging in political violence, as well as sexist behaviours within the frontline. The double resistance from feminists prompted a reaction from the state regarding the frontline. Soon after the beginning of the protests, the Chilean government ordered an *anti-capucha* (anti-masks) law which would make the use of face coverings during protests illegal. This was a clear attempt at stopping the action of people in the frontline, but also one that sought to criminalise an aesthetic that feminists had adopted since the *Mayo Feminista*. During this time, feminists not only interrupted the country's normality for two months with traditional manifestations, but the movement also explored a disruption of the patriarchal forms of communication that were broadly accepted by social movements. The use of bodies was key to this disorder. Feminists covered their faces with *capuchas* (masks) whilst uncovering their breasts to the public. Hundreds of naked bodies danced and moved across the streets of Santiago, revealing, through use of the female body, historical feminist questions such as the women's ownership of their own bodies as a form of resistance. As Grau articulates, "the individualised faces disappeared behind those purple *capuchas,* the colour of feminism, in an aesthetic collective rebellion that will leave a mark in the social memory" (Grau, 2018, p. 93). It would seem that, as far as the state was concerned, the non-violence of wearing a mask became more of a concern for the police than the fires started in the streets. The symbolism of masks as an aesthetic of resistance not only served a strategic purpose, but a symbolic one of signifying the importance of a political unity beyond individualism, something that was used to represent the essence of the feminist movement against neoliberalism.

The feminist movement does not typify any of the main categories used in the theory of non-violence. They do not approach these practices of resistance as either a strategy or as a principle. They do not oppose the use of violence per se as a form of resisting oppression, as seen in their support of the frontline, nor do they think pacifism and non-violence must be the core focus of the feminist movement. On the contrary, non-violence for feminists represents a necessity for political radicalness and reflexivity to build a political project that makes visible all the *violences* that neoliberalism (re)produces upon those who are unseen as subjects; to those, in Butler's terms, who live a "less grievable life" (Butler, 2006, 2020).

Conclusion

This chapter has presented a discussion of the rise of feminist consciousness in Chile drawing from their practices and notions of non-violence. This study has argued that the dialectics of the collective emotions of suffering and joy permits a (re)definition of the *self* that forms a radical anti-neoliberal feminist consciousness. This means that the feminist movement not only creates a feminist identity but permits defiance of the neoliberal subject in attempt to demolish a socioeconomic system that has inflicted numerous *violences* against women and non-binary people. In this sense, the dimension of non-violence in the feminist movement is not limited to traditional concepts of "strategic" and "principled" non-violent resistance but is rooted in a necessity of making visible a system of injustice which is predominantly (re)produced by the state throughout a history of oppression inherited from a dictatorial past.

The rise of feminist consciousness in Chile is not an isolated case. We are seeing a growing non-violent resistance that places anti-neoliberal and anti-capitalist sentiments at the core of their movements across Latin America (see Natalucci & Rey, 2018; Torres Falcón, 2020; Parilla, 2020; Rojas Buitrago, 2020). Similar expressions of consciousness-raising and radical resistance have also been visible in, for example, the wake Sarah Everard's murder in the United Kingdom (Cruz, 2020; Aljazeera, 2021; The Guardian, 2021). This chapter has aimed to demonstrate the importance of looking at and questioning radical resistance beyond traditional scopes and to explore the ways in which contemporary feminist activism is changing the ways in which we understand, see, and experience state violence, not just in the context of authoritarianism but also in democratic societies.

Notes

1 Segato's definition of "war" contains several dimensions that are not limited to traditional conceptions produced mainly in European theory. For the Argentinean thinker, war represents the broad violent social relations that characterise Latin America, including the expropriation of land from indigenous people, the forced migration due to paramilitary forces, and the rise in feminicides in the region. She argues for an intersectional understanding of war that permits the interconnection of these phenomena.

2 Chile has a long history of politicised student movements that have had important influence on the political landscape of the country. The contemporary expression of this has been highly influenced by the 2006 *Revolucion Pinguina* and the 2011 "Free Education Movement" (Silva, Kronmüller, Cruz, & Riffo, 2016).

3 This system arose as a form of communication between the movement and wider society, without a clear connection to political parties and institutions. Spokespersons are democratically elected by small committees that might represent different branches or working groups of the movement, for example, feminism and unions, feminism and environmental issues, feminism and communities, and so on.

4 Chile endured 17 years of far-right dictatorship between 1973 and 1990. The regime was led by the military under command of General Augusto Pinochet.

5 This is the reason why the movement in 2018 was demanding institutional changes in HEI, such as parity policies in the selection of academic and non-academic staff and parity in the election lists for management positions at all levels of universities (Castillo, 2018, p. 36).

6 This movement, which originates in Argentina, cuts across the organisations mentioned earlier, since all feminist groups are in some way related to the mobilisation of the demands of *Ni Una Menos*.

7 "Undressing" was reported by 302 people, after beating (1615 cases) and shooting (1334 cases) (Instituto Nacional de Derechos Humanos, n.d.).

8 Author's translation of the song: "Patriarchy is our judge/That imprisons us at birth/And our punishment/Is the violence you DON'T see. Patriarchy is our judge/That imprisons us at birth/And our punishment/Is the violence you CAN see. It's the femicide/Impunity for my killer/It's our disappearances/It's rape! And it's not my fault, not where I was, not how I dressed (x4). The rapist WAS you/the rapist IS you/It's the cops/It's the judges/It's the system/It's the President. This

oppressive state is a macho rapist (x2). The rapist IS you (x2). Sleep calmly, innocent girl/Without worrying about the bandit/Over your dreams smiling and sweet/Watches your 'loving' cop [in reference to the Police's anthem]".

9 The performance has been replicated several times in Chile, as well as in over 40 countries across the world. These videos are some of the presentations made in Chile: www.youtube.com/watch?v=yJGE 9zqgna8.

References

Ahmed, S. (2017). *Living a feminist life*. Durham: Duke University Press.

Aljazeera (2021). Sarah Everard's murder sparks moment of reckoning in UK. Retrieved from www.aljaze era.com/podcasts/2021/3/19/sarah-everards-murder-sparks-moment-of-reckoning-in-uk

Arruzza, C., Bhattacharya, T., & Fraser, N. (2019). *Feminism for the 99 percent: A manifesto*. London; Brooklyn, NY: Verso.

Atack, I. (2012). *Nonviolence in political theory*. Edinburgh: Edinburgh University Press.

Bartky, S. L. (1975). Toward a phenomenology of feminist consciousness: *Social Theory and Practice*, *3*(4), 425–439. https://doi.org/10.5840/soctheorpract1975349

Butler, J. (2006). *Precarious life: The powers of mourning and violence*. London; New York: Verso.

Butler, J. (2020). *The force of nonviolence: An ethico-political bind*. Brooklyn: Verso Books.

Carabineros se querelló contra colectivo Las Tesis. (n.d.). Retrieved from www.24horas.cl/regiones/valparaiso/ carabineros-se-querello-contra-colectivo-las-tesis-4262568

Castillo, A. (2018). De la revuelta feminista, la history y Julieta Kirkwood. In F. Zerán (Ed.), *Mayo Feminista: La rebelión contra el patriarcado* (Primera edición, pp. 35–48). Santiago, Chile: LOM Ediciones.

Coordinadora Feminista 8M · Quiénes Somos. (n.d.). Retrieved 11 January 2021, from https://cf8m.cl/ quienes-somos/

Cruz, M. (2020, October 20). Today is Chile's chance to Bury Pinochet's Legacy. *Tribune Magazine*. Retrieved from https://tribunemag.co.uk/2020/10/today-is-chiles-chance-to-bury-pinochets-legacy

Cruz, M. (2021, March 15). It was feminicide: Naming Sara Everard's murder. *Social Sciences Birmingham*. Retrieved from https://blog.bham.ac.uk/socialsciencesbirmingham/2021/03/15/it-was-feminicide- naming-sarah-everards-murder/

Ferretti, P., & Dragnic, M. (2020a). Chile: La revuelta en el laboratorio neoliberal. In O. Grau, L. Follegati, & S. Aguilera (Eds.), *Escrituras feministas en la revuelta* (1st ed.). Santiago, Chile: LOM Ediciones.

Ferretti, P., & Dragnic, M. (2020b, February 14). Revolt in Chile: Life against Capital. *Viewpoint Magazine*. Retrieved from www.viewpointmag.com/2020/02/13/revolt-in-chile-life-against-capital/

Frazer, E., & Hutchings, K. (2020). *Violence and political theory*. Cambridge, UK; Medford, MA: Polity.

Gago, V. (2020). *Feminist international: How to change everything* (L. Mason-Deese, Trans.). London; New York: Verso.

Gay, C.W. (2019). Pacifism, feminism, and nonkilling philosophy: A new approach to connecting peace studies and gender studies. In J. Kling (Ed.), *Pacifism, politics, and feminism: Intersections and innovations*, pp. 137–154. Leiden; London: Brill Rodopi. https://doi.org/10.1163/9789004396722

Grau, O. (2018). Un cardo en la mano. In F. Zerán (Ed.), *Mayo Feminista: La rebelión contra el patriarcado* (Primera edición). Santiago, Chile: LOM Ediciones.

Instituto Nacional de Derechos Humanos, Mapa de violaciones a los derechos humanos. (n.d.). Retrieved 11 January 2021, from https://mapaviolacionesddhh.indh.cl/public/estadisticas.

Juntas Hacemos Historia. (n.d.). Retrieved 11 January 2021, from www.juntashacemoshistoria.cl/?fbclid= IwAR0BF6GM8TaYM6oOkBhUZGoTh9OaN6XKRb_C2AFuowu83_1jlm2GHGc87Ds

Leeb, C. (2017). *Power and feminist agency in capitalism: Toward a new theory of the political subject*. New York: Oxford University Press. https://doi.org/10.1093/acprof:oso/9780190639891.003.0005M arshall, S. E. (2013). Antifeminist movements (United States). In D. E. Snow, D. della Porta, B. Klandermans, & D. McAdam (Eds.), *The Wiley-Blackwell encyclopedia of social and political movements*. Oxford: Blackwell Publishing Ltd.

Millán, M. (2018). La eclosión del sujeto del feminismo y la crítica de la modernidad capitalista. *Pléyade (Santiago)*, (22), 131–156. https://doi.org/10.4067/S0719-36962018000200131

Mostrador, E. (2020, August 24). ONU pide a Carabineros y autoridades que retiren denuncia contra Las Tesis. Retrieved 11 January 2021, from El Mostrador website: www.elmostrador.cl/braga/2020/08/ 24/onu-pide-a-carabineros-y-autoridades-que-retiren-denuncia-contra-las-tesis/

Natalucci, A. L., Rey, J. (2018). Una nueva oleada feminista? Agenda de género, repertorios de acción y colectivos de mujeres. *Estudios Políticos y Estratégicos, 6*(2), 14–34.

Parrilla, B. (2020). ¡Nosotras podemos!: performance, cuerpo y espacio público en el marco de las movilizaciones feministas en Argentina. *Conexión,* (13), 83–102.

Peach, L. J. (1994). An alternative to pacifism? Feminism and just-war theory. *Hypatia, 9*(2), 152–172.Rawls, J. (2000). *A theory of justice.* Oxford: Oxford University Press.

Richard, N. (2018). La insurgencia feminista de mayo 2018. In F. Zerán (Ed.), *Mayo Feminista: La rebelión contra el patriarcado* (Primera edición). Santiago, Chile: LOM Ediciones.

Rojas Buitrago, M. (2021). Resistiendo y re-existiendo frente a la colonialidad: las mujeres a través del movimiento Ni Una Menos en América Latina, *Repositorio Institucional – Pontificia Universidad Javeriana.* Retrieved from https://repository.javeriana.edu.co/handle/10554/51883?show=full

Rowbotham, S. (2015). *Woman's consciousness, man's world.* Brooklyn, NY: Verso.

Sarachild, K. (1978). Consciousness-raising: A radical weapon. In *Feminist revolution: An abridged edition with additional writings.* New York: Random House. Retrieved from www.rapereliefshelter.bc.ca/learn/resources/consciousness-raising-radical-weapon-kathie-sarachild

Schild, V., & Follegati, L. (2018). Contingencia, democracia y neoliberalismo: Reflexiones y tensiones a partir del movimiento feminista en la actualidad. Entrevista a Verónica Schild. *Pléyade (Santiago),* (22), 157–179. https://doi.org/10.4067/S0719-36962018000200157

Segal, L. (2018). *Radical happiness: Moments of collective joy.* Brooklyn: Verso Books.

Segato, R. L. (2016). *La guerra contra las mujeres* (Primera edición). Madrid: Traficantes de Sueños.

Serafini, P. (2020). "A rapist in your path": Transnational feminist protest and why (and how) performance matters. *European Journal of Cultural Studies, 23*(2), 290–295. https://doi.org/10.1177/1367549420912748

Silva, C., Kronmüller, C., Cruz, M., & Riffo, I. (2016). Empoderamiento en el Movimiento Estudiantil, Años 2011–2012 en Chile. *Universitas Psychologica, 14*(4), 1299. https://doi.org/10.11144/Javeriana.up14-4.eeme

Sjoberg, L. (2012). Feminist reflections on political violence. In M. Breen-Smyth (Ed.), *The Ashgate research companion to political violence* (p. 19). London: Routledge.

Souza, N. M. F. de. (2019). When the body speaks (to) the political: Feminist activism in Latin America and the quest for alternative democratic futures. *Contexto Internacional, 41*(1), 89–112. https://doi.org/10.1590/s0102-8529.2019410100005

Sowards, S. K., & Renegar, V. R. (2004). The rhetorical functions of consciousness-raising in third wave feminism. *Communication Studies, 55*(4), 535–552. https://doi.org/10.1080/10510970409388637The Guardian. (2021). Police clash with mourners at Sarah Everard vigil in London. Retrieved from www.theguardian.com/uk-news/2021/mar/13/as-the-sun-set-they-came-in-solidarity-and-to-pay-tribute-to-sarah-everard.

Tijoux, M. E. (2020). Octubre 2019: Rebelión popular en Chile? *Pléyade: Revista de Humanidades y Ciencias Sociales, Especial: Revueltas en Chile,* 31–34.

Torres Falcon, M. (2020). La interlocución del movimiento feminista con el gobierno mexicano: El caso de la alerta por violencia de género. *Revista Mexicana De Estudios De Los Movimientos Sociales, 4*(2), 57–78.

Universidad de Chile. (2019). *Violencias Políticas y Resistencias con Rita Segato.* Retrieved from www.youtube.com/watch?v=qohZvMNEJoA

Vargas Muñoz, R. (2020). La implosión de la ciudad neoliberal. *Pléyade: Revista de Humanidades y Ciencias Sociales, Especial: Revueltas en Chile,* 65–71.

Vinthagen, S. (2015). *A theory of nonviolent action: How civil resistance works.* London: ZED Books.

Zembylas, M. (2020). Butler on (Non)violence, affect and ethics: Renewing pedagogies for nonviolence in social justice education. *Educational Studies, 56*(6), 636–651. https://doi.org/10.1080/00131946.2020.1837835

Zerán, F. (Ed.). (2018). *Mayo Feminista: La rebelión contra el patriarcado* (Primera edición). Santiago, Chile: LOM Ediciones.

Zunes, S. (1999). The role of non-violent action in the downfall of apartheid. *The Journal of Modern African Studies, 37*(1), 137–169.

28

THE DEGROWTH MOVEMENT IN FRANCE

From the Edges to the Centre of the Ecological Debate

Tahir Karakaş

Introduction

As contemporary societies face the frightening reality of global warming, the idea of Degrowth, as a real alternative to this crisis, has now reached maturity. The idea started in the early 1970s in a world where consumer society had declared complete and utter victory. Today, "Degrowth" stands out as a significant intellectual and political movement, promising a radical shift that would allow humanity to overcome one of the greatest challenges in its history, the ecological crisis. As recent research (Goar, 2019) shows, 52% of French people say that environmental protection is their first concern. Ariès (2007) describes Degrowth as "the child of a generation orphan of utopia, one that had to learn, in pain, to mourn the illusions of previous generations" (Ariès, 2007, p. 59). Since then, Degrowth has sought to create its own path; it debates, experiments, organises and makes itself heard. It has ceased to be a "UFO in the political microcosm" (p. 18), as Latouche (2004) called it nearly two decades ago.

Between a blind and pessimistic catastrophism, which does not propose a way out, and a timid ecology lacking radicalism in both its diagnosis and proposals, the Degrowth movement has become, for many, a credible alternative enabling the transition towards a new society. According to a recent survey (Odoxa, 2019), French citizens are increasingly sensitive to ecological issues, 54% of the French population considering Degrowth as the most effective way to solve ecological problems. A society built on Degrowth's principles would be built on new values, which fundamentally constitute a harsh criticism of modern Western societies. In the words of Duverger (2011), "degrowth could well become the new socio-economic paradigm of our world in crisis" (p. 227).

This chapter draws on three sets of resources covering the period from the early 1970s to the present day: texts by the precursors and theorists of Degrowth; academic and non-academic research carried out in the field; and writings of activists, particularly those published in periodicals close to the movement. To gain a clear view of the birth and development of the movement, we need to understand its ideology and the practices implemented to achieve its objectives. But it is also important to note that this study does not claim to treat the Degrowth movement in France exhaustively, treating all its aspects in a detailed and in-depth manner.

DOI: 10.4324/9781003032793-33

Such an endeavour would require much more extensive research. Instead, this chapter provides an overview of the Degrowth movement in France, its ideology and its objectives by examining its historical development and then moving through the emblematic figures who define the movement. This study also discusses the transition desired by the supporters of Degrowth and seeks to understand the internal debates about strategy and policy. Finally, this chapter analyses the position of "Degrowth" as a radical movement in relation to violence.

Intellectual Sources and Development of the Degrowth Movement

The sources of inspiration for the Degrowth movement are many and varied. Degrowth theorists, both academic and non-academic, rely on the philosophers of ancient Greece such as Diogenes and Epicurus as well as on contemporary figures like George Orwell, Jacques Ellul, Gandhi, Cornelius Castoriadis, Charles Fourier and Leo Tolstoy (Biagini, Burray, & Thisset, 2017; Duverger, 2011; Latouche, 2016; Muraca, 2013). The precursors of the movement make a longer list, with people belonging to different historical and philosophical backgrounds who yet share a common or similar vision of some of the essentials dear to the movement.

First, there is an axiological reading of Western history in terms of the ideas that constitute the philosophico-political heart of Degrowth. Even if this reading is able, in certain cases, to broaden its field of analysis to other cultural traditions, it remains primarily European in focus. It's approach therefore entails a historical assessment of Western values. Degrowth theorists – in essence then – identify a tension, even a conflict, between two antagonistic sets of values that govern European civilisation from ancient Greece to the present day. According to Degrowth theorists, this conflict takes place between two irreconcilable approaches: the first advocates the path of moderation and the awareness of limits as a virtue; and the second, on the contrary, values man's capacity to overcome himself, to get rid of the conditions that determine him, without thinking finely about the consequences that this transgressive search of conquest may generate. In this axiological confrontation, Degrowth seeks – above all – to re-establish a sense of limits and autolimitation in the face of the excess (*hubris*) that Degrowth theorists believe is inherent – especially in modern Western societies.

Consequently, from the point of view of Degrowth theorists, moderation as an essential trait of ancient wisdom is the remedy against the storms that characterise modern man. An appeal to frugality and a distrust of instrumental and economic reason are the distinctive elements of Degrowth's position. But the critical force of Degrowth is deployed when it comes to the ideas of progress, development and technology. This is because these concepts constitute the ideological foundation on which modern societies are built. In addition, the refusal of cultural uniformisation and the Westernisation of the world; the promotion of conviviality against individualism and competition; and, of course, a critique of productivism and limitless economic growth mark the terrain on which the critical activity of Degrowth exists.

Having outlined the key contours of Degrowth ideology and researching the origins of Degrowth thought in a more specific and profound sense, we need to first look at the period that French economist Jean Fourastié (1970), referring to the years that succeeded the second world war, calls the "the glorious thirty years". In European history, this period indicates the birth and then the rise of consumerist society on the old continent, following the example set in North America. However, the economic prosperity that industrialised countries, especially European ones, recorded during these years thanks to robust growth, was called into question towards the end of the glorious 30 years, and, as a result, an awareness of the ecological limits and costs of this economic growth gradually developed. This consciousness played a decisive role in the birth of the Degrowth movement as it raised questions about our planet's physical capacity to support such economic growth in the long term. The foundational question therefore arose: Is it possible to have infinite economic growth in a world with finite natural resources?

The classic study, *The Entropy Law and the Economic Process* (1971) by Nicholas Georgescu-Roegen, the Romanian-born American economist who coined the word "Degrowth",[1] and the famous "The Meadows Report" prepared and published by the Club of Rome under the title *The Limits to Growth* (1972). Georgescu-Roegen answers the above question negatively by claiming that economic growth will one day necessarily come up against a natural barrier, namely the biophysical limits of the Earth. Once this threshold is crossed, our planet would no longer be able to meet the material needs of economic growth. To put it very briefly, the originality of Georgescu-Roegen's contribution is that he was the first, in the history of economic thought, to analyse in-depth the economic process, that is to say, the production and consumption of goods, from the point of view of the laws of thermodynamics and evolutionary biology (Georgescu-Roegen, 1971). The results of his analyses made him the founder of a new scientific discipline, now called "bioeconomics", and revolutionised economics by showing that an economy aiming for infinite growth is not possible for the simple fact that the economic process is subject to the limited biological and physical capacities of the Earth. According to the law of entropy, to which Georgescu-Roegen refers, since the planet's resources which, in the form of energy or matter such as fossil fuels and minerals form the basis of economic activity, are not all renewable, the sustainability of a society of growth based on a classical model of economic development is quite simply impossible. This critique would not only prove very rich in ideas that would inspire Degrowth theorists, but would also serve as "the liaison point of the different traditions of growth critique" (Muraca & Schmelzer, 2017).

Besides Georgescu-Roegen's original contribution, a second source of inspiration for the thought of "Degrowth" is a fruitful tradition, very critical of modernity and its fundamental concepts and ambitions. Therefore, the main characteristic of this heterogeneous "school of thought" is the problematisation of Western modernity and capitalism on the institutional, technological, economic, philosophical and societal levels. One of the important figures of this tradition, Ivan Illich, occupies an essential place in the pantheon of Degrowth theorists. It is in his works that the "Degrowth" finds a vibrant, in-depth analysis of modern society's contradictions (educational and medical systems, transport). In his works, the "Degrowthers" found indispensable arguments for their ideological struggle against the growth economy and its productivism. As a theoretical reference for the movement, Illich's thought fits into the culturalist critique of growth and development (Petridis, Muraca, & Kallis, 2015) and operates as a "democratic source" (Flipo, 2007).

Indeed, Illich goes beyond the bioeconomic critique, which demonstrates the inconceivability of infinite economic growth on a planet with limited resources, to explain that such growth is not only unsustainable but also undesirable (Latouche, 2013a). Illich (2003) focuses mainly on the counter-productivity of development and points out its harmful effects on culture, highlighting instead conviviality, which means the control of tools by man as opposed to the hegemony of tools controlled by a "body of specialists". Northern economic imperialism, in the form of the hegemony of growth in the South, is not only a source of inequality and injustice but also a gateway to this heteronomy that breaks the social fabric by destroying conviviality. In short, man is becoming, according to Illich (2004), an accessory of the megamachine, "a cog of the bureaucracy", which corresponds to a new form of "the human enslavement" (p. 456).

As a source of inspiration for the Degrowth movement, Illich's thought is certainly decisive. Yet, reducing Degrowth to the critique of modernity as seen in Illich, or to the principles of bioeconomy, would be reductive. It needs also to be noted that the appearance of "Degrowth" is intimately linked to the birth of political-ecological thinking in France after May 1968. André Gorz is one of the pioneers of political ecology in France and a good reader and friend of Illich. He belongs to a post-war generation of French Marxist intellectuals influenced by existentialism and disillusioned with the Soviet experience of socialism. Long under the shadow of his friend, the philosophical star of the time, Sartre and Althusser, Gorz was gradually rediscovered starting in the 2000s – becoming an inescapable source of influence on "Degrowth" and, more generally, of political ecology.[2]

One of the focal points of his thought that growth objectors find valuable is Gorz's attention to the excesses of capitalism and the devastating effects of the endless pursuit of growth, whether in a capitalist or socialist form. Reading and admiring his contemporary Georgescu-Roegen (Gorz, 1978), Gorz became aware of the underlying incompatibility between productivist capitalism's ambitions and limited natural resources. In a visionary moment, Gorz (1978) foresaw the possible recuperation of the ecological cause by capitalism, that is, the birth of green capitalism, which "accommodates ecological constraints" (p. 9). Furthermore, Gorz (1993) inspired the Degrowth movement by criticising the centrality of the economy in Western societies and advocating an exit from the economy to create an anti-capitalist and anti-productivist society, which he calls "the civilisation of liberated time" (p. 13).

Degrowth's distrust of technological society is one of the essential traits that characterise its thought. This distrust can be viewed as an extension of the critique of modernity in which Degrowth engages from its beginnings as a movement. Jacques Ellul, known for his criticism of technicality, is a major intellectual reference for Degrowth in this particular area. One of the central figures of the movement, Serge Latouche (2011), called "the Pope of Degrowth", recognises his debt to the author of *The Technological Society* (1954) and explains that Ellul is, along with Georgescu-Roegen and Illich, one of those who have indicated the limits of growth (p. 145). Nevertheless, the real value of Ellul to the movement comes from his revelation of the totalitarian character of the technical phenomenon (Ellul, 1954). According to Ellul, what defines societies today is neither the spectacle, as Guy Debord argues in the same years, nor the simulation or consumption analysed by Jean Baudrillard, but technically that has become autonomous. He tirelessly insists that technical processes no longer serve us to dominate nature or escape its constraints, but, on the contrary, it is we who serve it. What is lacking in ecological thought, from Ellul's point of view (Chastenet, 1994), is indeed a "global analysis of the technical phenomenon and technical society" (p. 183). Latouche (2013b) recognises the importance of Ellul's thought for the evolution of the Degrowth movement: "The critique of technical excessiveness and the analysis of *technical totalitarianism* constitutes a centrepiece of the degrowth project" (p. 10).

One of the aspects that makes the Degrowth movement original in the world of environmental movements is the multidimensional nature of its analysis of capitalism. Like most ecological movements, "Degrowth" benefits from Marxist or culturalist critiques of the capitalist system. Still, its strength comes from the fact that it problematizes capitalism on the level of the collective imagination. In the eyes of Degrowth, capitalism does not simply correspond to a system with its own dialectic, apparatus, institutions and techniques that allow it to survive.

Capitalism also corresponds to a world of imaginary meanings. In this domain, Cornelius Castoriadis is one of the thinkers often cited and commented on by Degrowth theorists. Beyond his emphasis on individual and collective autonomy against institutional heteronomy, his critical analyses targeting economic growth, consumerism, industrial development and its ecological consequences – themes that are recurrently encountered in Castoriadis' universe of thought,

418

the originality of his contribution to Degrowth is found in his questioning of the colonisation of the imaginary by the economy. "We do not want an unlimited and thoughtless expansion of production; we want an economy that is a means and not the end of human life" (Castoriadis, 2005, p. 301). Breaking the hegemony of the economy and putting an end to the primacy of economic reason is, according to Castoriadis (1996), "the immense difficulty we have to face" (p. 96). What Latouche (2011) would later call the "decolonisation of the imaginary", drawing inspiration from "the colonisation of the imaginary" formulated by Castoriadis, would become one of the strategic pillars of the "Degrowth" movement.

This first period corresponds to the intellectual maturation of the seeds of Degrowth in the confluence of various intellectual attractions. This period is followed, by a second period (starting in the early 2000s) giving birth to the popularisation of Degrowth's society project and activism for its achievement. However, as Muraca and Schmelzer (2017) point out, the debates on economic growth and development that lie at the origin of the Degrowth movement were overshadowed for more than two decades (1980–2000) by the introduction of the idea of sustainable development. The debates on this concept were decisive in the "rebirth of Degrowth", this time as a political movement (Duverger, 2011). By acknowledging this, Latouche (2011) makes clear that the "need to denounce the imposture of sustainable development" is "historically at the origin of the movement" (p. 30). Sustainable development, from the point of view of growth objectors, amounts to saying "pollute less to pollute longer" (Ariès, 2011, p. 17), merely a belated invention of capitalism undermined by the scientific evidence that points to its responsibility in the current ecological crisis.

After this interim period, the UNESCO international colloquium organised in 2002 under the title "Undoing development, remaking the world" marks the beginning of the new phase of the Degrowth movement in France. Since this colloquium, many similar conferences on themes directly or indirectly linked to Degrowth have been organised in France and elsewhere, with the participation of many theorists, academics, researchers, activists and citizens (Abraham, Lewy, & Marion, 2015). Also in 2002, the Institute of Economic and Social Studies for Sustainable Degrowth was created in Lyon, and would become the centre of the movement in France. The journal *Entropia*, subtitled *Revue d'étude théorique et politique de la décroissance* (*A Journal for the Theoretical and Political Study of Degrowth*), was created in 2006 and would publish 16 issues on various themes related to Degrowth before ceasing publication in 2014. Also in 2006, some growth objectors met under the banner of the *Parti pour la décroissance* (Party for Degrowth) created by Vincent Cheynet, founder of the Casseurs de pub (Adbusters) association in 1999, which is today the heart of the movement in France, and editor-in-chief of the newspaper *La décroissance*, which has been in place since 2004.[3] *Silence* has also significantly contributed to revive and disseminate debates on Degrowth, by publishing its first article on Degrowth in 1989, its first dossier in 1993 (Gamblin, 2019, p. 4) and a special issue on the same theme in 2002. The Research and Degrowth collective, founded in 2007 by François Schneider, Denis Bayon and Fabrice Flipo, organised, in cooperation with their partners, the first international conference on Degrowth in Paris in 2008, which played a key role in the internationalisation of Degrowth, particularly at the academic level. Today the movement remains active in France, and various actors are conducting various actions to disseminate its ideas. On the theoretical level, Serge Latouche, Paul Ariès, Agnès Sinaï, Cheynet, Flipo, Schneider, among others, have contributed for many years to nourishing the movement. It is clear that despite its heterogeneity and the internal differences on various subjects, the movement is gaining more and more visibility in France and has already established itself as a permanent fixture in the country's intellectual and political landscape.

The Ideology of the Degrowth Movement

Talking about the ideology of "Degrowth" is difficult for at least three reasons. First, Degrowth does not present anything suggested by the classic sense of the term "ideology". An ideology undoubtedly refers to a set of ideas, beliefs and (at first sight) coherent discourses which underlies a movement, indicating the path to follow for the realisation of its project of societal transformation. Therefore, it can be legitimately inferred that every ideology claims to contain an absolute truth, which means that ideologies are closed and dogmatic systems of thought. Degrowth is in the process of being formed, that it is continuously questioning itself; it is a matter of thought in the process of becoming, and of a movement in "gestation" and "incomplete", still "under construction" (Ariès, 2007), and flexible in terms of ideas (Duverger, 2011).

They also argue that ideology should be used in the critical sense and that Degrowth is essentially an emancipatory and liberating movement in this regard (Bayon, Flipo, & Schneider, 2010; Flipo, 2017; Latouche, 2019a), emphasising that Degrowth does not tend to lead to the dogmatism experienced in the twentieth century's bipolar ideological rivalry. Degrowth theorists are suspicious of the word "ideology" and use it, where appropriate, in a rather negative and non-constructive sense: "ideology of growth", "ideology of progress", "ideology of sustainable development", "liberal ideology" or "ideology of productivism". These terms describe the thinking of Degrowth's opponents and are used above all to denounce their ideological base, which has become immune to all criticism.

It is for this reason that the central figures of Degrowth, when they refer to growthism as an ideology, occasionally do not hesitate to replace the concept "ideology" with the word "religion" (Latouche, 2019a, p. 5; Ariès, 2007, p. 16; Cheynet, 2008, p. 11) or to use the phrase "secular and materialist religion" (Latouche, 2019b, p. 1) to underline the blinding and hegemonic nature of the growth paradigm.

The second difficulty is that Degrowth as a movement is heterogeneous; there is no single Degrowth movement in France but several Degrowth movements (Duverger, 2011; Ariès, 2018). In the face of the mainstream Degrowth conception which considers itself more to the left, there is also a Degrowth of the right, even of the extreme right, the classic example being the French writer Alain de Benoist of the "Nouvelle Droite" (New Right) whom Ariès (2007) considers to be one of the "elements not to frequent" (pp. 290–291). Also, as shown by the appearance, starting in 2015, a new generation of journals and magazines, such as *Limite*, *Le Comptoir*, *Philitt*, *Accattone* and *Rascar Kapac*, the right is starting to be more and more interested in ideas put forward by the Degrowth movement (Cazenave, 2018).

And the third difficulty is that, even if we leave aside this right-wing versions of the Degrowth movement, Degrowth would still be difficult to classify according to the classic left-right ideological divide. As Cheynet (2014) points out, Degrowth "opposes the left by its rejection of progressive ideology and the right by its anti-capitalism" (p. 12). This difficulty derives from the diversity of its sources of inspiration, which sometimes seem difficult to reconcile, or even contradictory. According to Latouche (2018), even if its primary source of inspiration is the great thinkers of the left, Degrowth cannot be reduced to an ordinary left-wing movement since it aims above all to go beyond the idea of productivism and growth, values commonly shared by both the left and the right (Latouche, 2009).

As it presents itself as a revolutionary anti-capitalist and non-violent project aiming at a definitive exit from economic reason, neither the left nor the right, in the classical sense, can meet the requirements put forward by the proponents of Degrowth. This peculiar ideological position is debated within the Degrowth movement itself. It attracts, in particular, socialist ecologist critics (Löwy, 2020), who accuse them of not seeing the heart of the problem, which, according to them, is to be found in the class struggle rather than in an *Aufhebung* of the economy in the Hegelian sense aimed at by the Degrowth project (Latouche, 2011, p. 114).

The Degrowth movement is iconoclastic insofar as it develops a thoroughgoing critique of the values and grand dominant myths of the modern epoch. It seeks to radically transform our axiological imaginary by rehabilitating a new system of values which preaches, among other things, self-restraint, measure, frugality, simplicity and conviviality. Therefore, we must take the term "Degrowth" essentially as a critical apparatus deployed to expose the hegemony of productivist ideologies. In this precise sense, we can speak of Degrowth as being an anti-ideological thought and movement, one that positions itself at the antipodes of what is currently understood by the concept of ideology. It is here that we join Ariès (2007) when he presents Degrowth on the critical level, as a "missile word" (*mot-obus*) intended to undermine the collective imaginary dominant in contemporary societies (p. 39). Latouche (2010) maintains that "non-growth" would provide a more effective tool to express this criticism, since it is, in truth, a question of abandoning the faith or leaving behind the religion of growth, similar to the function the concept of "atheism" executes in the face of "theism" (p. 17).

As the term "Degrowth" suggests, the ideological struggle of Degrowth focuses above all on a critique of the "idolatry" formed around growth and the fundamental concepts of its productivist world. "Degrowth is to say no" (Cheynet, 2014, p. 36). In a broader sense, it is the overcoming of a certain kind of modernity, and the idea of progress reduced to a quantitative logic, that Degrowth seeks in order to make possible a new societal project. Indeed, what Degrowth targets is the metaphysical and ideological background of growth. In other words, the target is "the congenital excessiveness of modernity" (Latouche, 2019a, p. 36). We saw above that the Degrowth movement's roots lie partly in the critique of the productivism of the 1970s. But after this first period of the intellectual movement of Degrowth, we located the real birth of the movement in the early 2000s.

Leaving behind the current capitalist model is a common desire shared by growth objectors. On the other hand, this necessary exit would not move in a direction towards productivist socialism. For degrowthers, the centre of gravity of the debate is no longer the class struggle between the two antagonistic classes, the bourgeoisie and the proletariat, as described by Marx and Engels in the 19th century. Henceforth, the new ideological cleavage consists of knowing whether we are on the side of productivism, of "always more", or on the side of this new "horizon of meaning" which proposes a model of society which, depending on the author, is called "a convivial society" (Illich, 1973), a "society of frugal abundance" (Latouche, 2011) or "voluntary simplicity" (Ariès, 2011), one in which well-being is no longer reduced to material goods, and in which having no longer replaces being.

Strategies for a Degrowth Society

The Degrowth community still debates which strategies would enable a transition from current growth societies to a Degrowth society. Thus, it is difficult to speak of a consensus among the representatives of Degrowth on the stages, actors and policies of the transition (D'Alisa et al., 2015, p. 15). Indeed, the subject requires more research (Petridis et al., 2015). "Degrowth" is not uniform or one-dimensional, which means that there are many ideas and proposals for getting out of today's consumer society. On this point, Latouche argues:

> The degrowth project reopens the human adventure to the plurality of destinies. Degrowth is not a *path* but a matrix of alternative possibilities. We cannot therefore

propose a "turnkey" model of a degrowth society, but only outline the fundamentals of any sustainable non-productivist society.

(Latouche, 2019a, p. 50)

We know that the objects and themes on which internal debates focus include: relocation of production, direct democracy, a system of alternative and local currencies, reduction of working hours, the introduction of unconditional basic income and a maximum authorised income, exit from fossil fuels, reorganisation of urban space, redefinition and reframing of economic activity in a post-growth society, and the engagement of the Degrowth movement in electoral politics. The 2000s onwards saw, alongside the theoretical discussions on the strategies and stages of the realisation of a post-growth society, an accumulation of concrete experience and the writing of a history of pro-degrowth mobilisations.

The Degrowth movement's members have engaged in different modes of activity to propagate their ideas and make their project credible in the eyes of the French public. Periodicals such as *La décroissance* and *Silence*, many websites, associations and collectives, academic and non-academic meetings have contributed to disseminating the theses of "Degrowth" at a local and national level. The same actors have, on multiple occasions, undertaken militant actions to promote their cause. For example, the *journée sans achat*, the French version of Buy Nothing Day, has since 1999 been called for in France by *Casseurs de pub* to denounce consumerism and waste.

Growth objectors support and participate, as a militant movement, since their birth in Lyon in the early 2000s, in similar mobilisations such as collective meals, boycott actions and anti-advertising campaigns (D'Alisa et al., 2015, p. 23; Blanc-Noel, 2010; Duverger, 2011). There are also attempts in France to go beyond theoretical debates and mobilisation actions and put the principles of Degrowth into real-life practice. Can Decreix[4] is one of the best-known examples of these attempts to materialise Degrowth. It is a place of Degrowth experimentation, initiated gradually from 2012 by Schneider and his friends. Moreover, in recent years, new associations and collectives have emerged in different French cities to give more visibility to Degrowth and to try to provide concrete experiences of the ideas of Degrowth (Gamblin, 2019b). On this point, it is interesting to note that supporters of Degrowth tend to bring about change first on a small local scale or directly in their personal lives without waiting for the large systemic transformation they advocate (Schmelzer & Eversberg, 2017). Finally, at the electoral political level, the *Parti pour la Décroissance*, which offers a platform to make the voice of Degrowth heard, has participated in several elections even if it remains in the minority within the movement itself. Today, it is struggling to broaden its scope of influence.

Despite two decades of theoretical and militant evolution, Latouche (2018) admits for his part that the transition desired by growth objectors seems to have difficulties to fall into place. These difficulties are at least partly linked to the hegemony of a lifestyle dictated by a consumer society that he describes using the metaphor of drug dependence (Latouche, 2005, p. 10). The remedy is found, according to Latouche (2007), in reopening "the space of inventiveness and creativity of the imaginary blocked by economist and progressivist totalitarianism" (p. 23). Thereafter structural changes should be implemented while acknowledging that a "soft transition" is not possible (Latouche, 2018). Taking a similar approach, Muraca (2013) emphasises the need to achieve change culturally and at the level of the collective imaginary for a radical transformation of society towards Degrowth: "The anti-systemic potential of Degrowth does not only address structural changes but also involves the transformation of social and cultural patterns of recognition and the social imaginary" (Muraca, 2013).

The idea of the decolonisation of the imaginary, inspired by Castoriadis and the anthropological critique of imperialism, starts from the observation that societies are the translations of a specific conceptual imaginary, one basically composed of articles of faith. In other words, societies are based on "imaginary significations" or "truths" (Flipo (2017, p. 151). To succeed in bringing about a change towards Degrowth, it is, therefore, essential to confront those elements which we hold to be unshakeable truths, such as growth, development and progress, in order to overcome them. Latouche (2015) also insists that "[w]ith growth and development, we are dealing with a process of conversion of mentalities, a process of an ideological and quasi-religious nature, aiming at establishing the imaginary of progress and economy" (p. 119). Getting ourselves out of the ideology of growth, out of this "mental invasion", would mean "a change of software or paradigm" (Latouche, 2019a, p. 97). According to this approach, the decolonisation of the imaginary would ultimately lead to a de-Westernisation of minds, meaning a definitive exit from the economy.

Awareness-raising activities, concrete individual and collective experiences undertaken by various Degrowth actors, certainly have an essential role in deconstructing the dominant imaginary. If the Degrowth movement attacks advertising in particular, as is the case in the example of the *Casseurs de pub*, it is because advertising constitutes a very useful tool for manipulating the population and spreading the consumerist lifestyle.

Planned obsolescence, another pillar of consumer society, is also a favourite target of critical Degrowth activity. However, these kinds of struggles, against the economisation of minds, do not appear sufficient to accomplish the real transition. "The aspiration for a better world, the concrete utopia of Degrowth, is therefore unfortunately not enough to trigger a passage to action" (Latouche, 2019a, p. 107). Even if education, the habit of questioning established truths and the construction of "autonomous knowledge" through a "benevolent association with alterity and strangeness" (Flipo, 2017, p. 160), can contribute to the decolonisation of the imaginary, a collective renunciation of consumerism must go through a real collective detoxification, one which cannot be carried out voluntarily.

The pedagogy of catastrophes, first formulated by D. D. Rougemont and developed by François Partant and then by Jean-Pierre Dupuy can, from Latouche's point of view, contribute to awareness of the need to move towards new horizons and, thus, to provoke a radical break in the imaginary (Latouche, 2004, p. 117). On the other hand, Ariès (2009) remains sceptical about the benefits of catastrophes, stating that such moments of crisis can lead to both the best and the worst: "In fact, crises more often give birth to Hitler and Stalin than to Gandhi". For Ariès, a political project for Degrowth would trigger ruptures through participatory voluntarism, rather than by waiting for the aid of real conditions to come in the form of disasters to guide us towards change. Therefore, what matters from his point of view is the decolonisation of the imaginary, and this constitutes the "negativity" of Degrowth. In addition to this, Ariès maintains, Degrowth must arm itself with a "positivity", that is to say, with a new political project that would complement the scientific theories on which it is built (Ariès, 2007, pp. 322–323; Ariès, 2011, p. 173).

Degrowth as a Non-violent Radical Movement

The Degrowth movement claims to be radical (Cheynet, 2005, p. 146; Latouche, 2011, p. 183). It is radical insofar as we use the term in a sense faithful to the etymological origins of the word "radical" derived from the Latin "*radix*", meaning "root". Degrowth is radical because it develops a vertical discourse, one which stipulates that understanding and resolving contemporary societies' problems requires transcending superficial analyses such as those adopted by proponents of green capitalism, sustainable development or even productivist socialism. What is necessary is an in-depth analysis of the facts capable of shedding light on the nature of the impasse in which contemporary societies find themselves. Therefore, it is in this desire to go beyond what is merely given, and to descend into the depths to discover the true nature of what appears as a problem, that we find the radicality of the discourse employed by the objectors to growth. In other words, it is in the search for the very roots of the elements under study that Degrowth intends to be radical. Its analysis shows that the root of the problem lies in productivism and in its metaphysics of progress, which is shared by both left and right as products of Western modernity.

This methodical radicalism puts into practice a definitive break with consumer society to create a different society around a new set of values. In this sense, Degrowth is both a radical and a revolutionary project. It aims to reestablish a sense of limits against a Promethean spirit which recognises none. On this point, it is important to note that this radical and revolutionary posture of Degrowth does not refer to the establishment of a new balance of power or to a will to power. In fact, its mistrust of politics as the conquest and exercise of power is the expression of its anti-authoritarian stance and its non-violent philosophy (Latouche, 2019a, p. 66). To explain how Degrowth remains faithful to a non-violent and anti-authoritarian philosophy, Cheynet (2014) argues that "Degrowth's wager of 'non-power' – which is not powerlessness but non-violence – is the only peaceful exit" (p. 175). On the question of violence, then, the defenders of degrowth seem to be in perfect agreement, categorically excluding it as a means to the change envisaged by their project (Cheynet, 2005, p. 142; Latouche, 2007, pp. 102–103; Liegey, 2014). Even though there are ambiguities and internal discords in the Degrowth universe on several major ideological and political points, there is no doubt that the movement remains resolutely non-violent. In this regard, Liegey and Nelson (2020) tell us: "The degrowth movement is clear about rejecting any kind of violence, just as it is clear about rejecting any kind of authoritarianism" (p. 178). The Degrowth movement rejects any recourse to violence and proposes itself as a democratic and pluralist alternative, one that will help to prevent the violence that the worsening effects of the ecological and social crisis may generate in the future, a crisis that may provide fertile ground for authoritarian drifts claiming to offer an effective exit from the disaster. As Latouche (2008) observes

> The need to prevent a global ecological catastrophe could lead to new forms of Neo-Fascist ideology. Our main objective is to prevent this by influencing the principal actors in the current political debate and stimulating the virtuous behaviour required to eventually achieve ecological democracy
>
> *(Latouche, 2008, p. 226)*

For Cheynet (2005), a "Degrowth" movement that is imposed instead of chosen would pose significant problems in terms of democracy, by creating a favourable ground for the development of authoritarian and violent drifts claiming to act in response to the urgency of ecological problems (p. 141). The Degrowth proponents agree that their approach is motivated by the desire to combat the *undemocratic* development at work in contemporary societies (Bayon et al., 2010, pp. 210–211).

So, against such drifts, according to the degrowthers, democracy is one of its essential values. This pacifist and democratic discourse adopted by Degrowth is further confirmed by field research results (Eversberg & Schmelzer, 2018) conducted during the Fourth International Conference on Degrowth for Ecological Sustainability and Social Equity, which took place in September 2014 in Leipzig. Even though most of the more than 3000 participants of this international meeting were German, this research still gives us an idea about objectors to growth in general. Regarding the question of violence, an overwhelming majority of the participants, composed of researchers, academics, activists and sympathisers, refused to consider violence as a legitimate means of conducting the struggle for realising a society of Degrowth, and believed that change must come from below and not through a revolutionary break (Eversberg & Schmelzer, 2018).

On the other hand, despite the semantic clarity that the concept of violence seems to have at first sight, its meaning is a matter of controversy in current research on non-violence among radical movements (Schmid, 2011). Nonetheless, the non-violence advocated by Degrowth is, to put it in Schmid's (2014) terms, "principaled and absolute, not pragmatic and opportunistic-ally context-specific" (p. 13). Thus, we can conclude that despite the radicality of its discourse and its project of societal transformation, the Degrowth movement is strictly non-violent and seeks a democratic solution to the civilisational crisis of humanity to prevent the appearance of the violence and authoritarianism that would take advantage of the urgency of the situation. In this way, Degrowth presents itself as a pacifist path towards moderation, reasonableness and self-restraint against the extremism of societies of excess unable to perceive the long-term consequences of their lifestyle.

Conclusion

As an intellectual and political movement, Degrowth emerges from an evolution that has been in process for the last several decades. This evolution has taken place under very diverse influences that are sometimes difficult to reconcile. This difficulty can be observed – especially when considering its intellectual sources and its ideological position. As far as significant segments of the French population are concerned, the Degrowth movement has succeeded in eliminating the negative connotations, such as the deconstruction or destruction of growth, to which the word "Degrowth" gives rise at first glance (Odoxa, 2019). Indeed, in a country like France, where pessimism is part of the dominant collective psychological heritage, proposing Degrowth as a new model of society constitutes a real challenge. What distinguishes Degrowth from other anti-systemic environmental movements, which owe their origins more or less to the same historical and cultural conditions, is the radicality of its analysis, locating the heart of the problem in the search for exponential economic growth. Therefore, the question posed by Degrowth is directed at the eschatology of growth so as to reveal the perceived nonsense of infinite growth. As long as we cling to the latter trajectory, degrowthers suggest that we risk colliding with the very physical realities of the biosphere and finding ourselves deprived of meaning.

Today, in the world of radical ecological movements, Degrowth has made its own way and seems to be convincing more and more people. This interest in Degrowth – and, more generally, in all environmental movements – is closely linked to the development of an ecological awareness arising from the countless scientific studies coming from different fields, all exposing the unsustainability of the current model and revealing a planet in crisis (IPCC, 2021). Thus, in the Anthropocene, the anthropocentrism of modern man, which was built on nature–culture antagonism and visceral instrumentalism, is more and more shaken in his relation to the Earth. This slow but steady paradigm shift leads to the restructuring of political ideas and to action around the question of ecology. It constitutes a favourable ground for the radical questioning of the current organisation of society.

The gradual rise of European environmental movements and parties promises more visibility for "Degrowth". In France, the word is now spoken in the precincts of government itself, from the President Macron (Macron, 2020) to the Minister of Economy and Finance Bruno

Le Maire (Le Maire, 2021), despite the negative meaning that is often attributed to it. In the dominant thinking of the current liberal right, Degrowth is viewed as roughly equivalent to misery, the return to candlelight, a new form of romantic *passéisme* or even an anti-democratic and patriarchal form of thought. On the other hand, leftist movements, Degrowth is gaining ground. From the radical left to the socialist left, the question of Degrowth arises more and more often. Part of this political family has already distanced itself from growthism. They no longer seek to reconcile growth with ecological constraints and recognise Degrowth as a plausible and legitimate alternative to capitalist society.

Notes

1 Georgescu-Roegen himself did not use the word "degrowth" in his *magnum opus*. However, in 1979, he approved the publication of the French translation of a collection of his articles by Jacques Grienwald and Ivo Rens under the title *Demain la décroissance. Entropie, écologie, économie* (*Tomorrow Degrowth: Entropy, Ecology, Economy*). This is the first book to have the word "degrowth" in its title (Duverger, 2011, p. 48).
2 However, Gorz's interest in ecology dates back to the early 1970s, and he seems to be the first to have used the term "degrowth" in French in a positive sense, during a debate on ecology (D'Alisa, Demaria, & Kallis, 2015, p. 1).
3 *La décroissance* is the main newspaper of the degrowth movement in France, first published quarterly and then monthly, and sold more than 30,000 copies per issue in 2015 (D'Alisa et al., 2015, p. 28).
4 For more information see https://candecreix.degrowth.net/ and also *Silence* n° 441, 2016.

References

Abraham, Y.-M., Lewy, A., & Marion, L. (2015). Comment faire croître la décroissance? *Nouveaux Cahiers du socialisme, 14*, pp. 25–31.
Ariès, P. (2007). *La décroissance: Un nouveau projet politique*. Villeurbanne: Golias.
Ariès, P. (2009, May 2). Décoloniser notre imaginaire de consommateur. *Libération*. Retrieved from www.liberation.fr/france/2009/05/02/decoloniser-notre-imaginaire-de-consommateur_555779
Ariès, P. (2011). *La simplicité volontaire contre le mythe de l'abondance*. Paris: La découverte.
Ariès, P. (2018, December 13). Décroissance: "Nous voulons seulement passer d'une jouissance d'avoir, à une jouissance d'être". *Le monde*. Retrieved from www.lemonde.fr/planete/article/2018/12/13/decroissance-nous-voulons-seulement-passer-d-une-jouissance-d-avoir-a-une-jouissance-d-etre_5397014_3244.html
Bayon, D., Flipo F., & Schneider F. (2010). *La décroissance: 10 questions pour comprendre en débattre*. Paris: La découverte.
Biagini, C., Murray, D., & Thiesset, P. (2017). *Aux origines de la décroissance:* Cinquante penseurs. Paris: L'échappée.
Blanc-Noel, N. (2010). Décroissance ou "décroissantisme": les filiations intellectuelles d'une idéologie politique. *Annuaire français des relations internationales, 11*, 93–122.
Castoriadis, C. (1996). *La monté de l'insignifiance. Les carrefours du labyrinthe*. Paris: Seuil.
Castoriadis, C. (2005). *Une société à la dérive:* Entretiens et débats 1974–1997. Paris: Seuil.
Cazenave, F. (2018, Decembre 2). Derrière la décroissance, de la gauche à la droite identitaire, une multitude de chapelles. *Le monde*. Retrieved from www.lemonde.fr/economie/article/2018/12/02/derriere-la-decroissance-une-multitude-de-chapelles_5391604_3234.html
Chastenet, P. (1994). *Entretiens avec Jacques Ellul*. Paris: La table ronde.
Cheynet, V. (2005). Décroissance et démocratie. In M. Bernard, V. Cheynet, & B. Clémentin, (Eds.), *Objectif décroissance* (141–148). Paris: Parangon.
Cheynet, V. (2008). *Le choc de la décroissance*. Paris: Seuil.
Cheynet, V. (2014). *Décroissance ou décadence*. Vierzon: Le pas de côté.
D'Alisa, G., Demaria, F., & Kallis, G. (2015). *Degrowth: A vocabulary for a new era*. New York; London: Routledge.
Duverger, T. (2011). *La décroissance, une pour demain*. Paris: Sang de la Terre.Ellul, J. (1954). *La technique ou l'enjeu du siècle*. Paris: Armand Colin.

Eversberg, D., & Schmelzer, M. (2018). The degrowth spectrum: Convergence and divergence within a diverse and conflictual alliance. *Environmental values, 27,* 245–267. doi: 10.3197/096327118X15217309300822

Flipo, F. (2007). Voyage dans la galaxie décroissante. *Mouvements: des idées et des luttes, 50,* 143–151. doi: 10.3917/mouv.050.0143

Flipo, F. (2017). *Décroissance, ici et maintenant.* Neuvy-en-Champagne: Le passager clandestin.

Fourastié, J. (1970). *Les trente glorieuses ou la révolution invisible de 1946 à 1975.* Paris: Fayard.

Gamblin, G. (2019a). Le mouvement décroissant en France a bientôt 20 ans. *Silence, 476,* 4–5.

Gamblin, G. (2019b). A Lyon, les nouveaux réseaux de la décroissance. *Silence, 476,* 16–18.

Georgescu-Roegen, N. (1971). *The entropy law and the economic process.* Cambridge: Harvard University Press.

Goar, M. (2019, February 28). L'écologie, ce nouvel horizon politique. *Le monde.* Retrieved from www.lemonde.fr/politique/article/2020/02/28/l-ecologie-ce-nouvel-horizon-politique_6031116_823448.html

Gorz, A. (1978). *Écologie et politique.* Paris: Seuil.

Gorz, A. (1993, mars). Bâtir la civilisation du temps libéré. *Le monde diplomatique,* p.13.

Illich, I. (2003). Le développement ou la corruption de l'harmonie en valeur. In *Défaire le développement: Refaire le monde* (9–14). Paris: Parangon.

Illich, I. (2004). *Œuvres – volume I.* Paris: Fayard.

IPCC. (2021). *Summary for policymakers. In: Climate change 2021: The physical science basis. Contribution of working group I to the sixth assessment report of the Intergovernmental panel on climate change.* Retrieved from www.ipcc.ch/report/ar6/wg1/downloads/report/IPCC_AR6_WGI_SPM_final.pdf

Latouche, S. (2004). *Survivre au développement: De la décolonisation de l'imaginaire économique à la construction d'une société alternative.* Paris: Mille et une nuits.

Latouche, S. (2005). *Décoloniser l'imaginaire: La pensée créative contre l'économie de l'absurde.* Paris: Parangon.

Latouche, S. (2007). *Petit traité de la décroissance sereine.* Paris: Mille et une nuits.

Latouche, S., & Paolini, F. (2008). Degrowth: A slogan new ecological democracy: Interview with Serge Latouche. *Global environment, 2,* 222–227.

Latouche, S. (2009). La décroissance comme projet politique de gauche. *Revue du MAUSS, 34*(2), 38–45.

Latouche, S. (2010). *Le pari de la décroissance.* Paris: Fayard/Pluriel.

Latouche, S. (2011). *Vers une société d'abondance frugale: Contresens et controverses de la décroissance.* Paris: Mille et une nuits.

Latouche, S. (2013a). *La décroissance permet de s'affranchir de l'impérialisme économique / Interviewer: Anthony Laurent.* Retrieved from https://reporterre.net/La-decroissance-permet-de-s

Latouche, S. (2013b). *Jacques Ellul contre le totalitarisme technicien.* Neuvy-en-Champagne: Le passager clandestin.

Latouche, S. (2015). Decolonisation of imaginary. In G. D'Alisa, F. Demaria, & G. Kallis, (Eds.), *Degrowth: A vocabulary for a new era* (117–120). New York; London: Routledge.

Latouche, S. (2016). *Les précurseurs de la décroissance. Une anthologie.* Neuvy-en-Champagne: Le passager clandestin.

Latouche, S. (2018, December 13). Serge Latouche: "La décroissance vise le travailler moins pour travailler mieux". *Le monde.* Retrieved from www.lemonde.fr/climat/article/2018/12/13/serge-latouche-la-decroissance-vise-le travailler-moins-pour-travailler-mieux_5397115_1652612.html

Latouche, S. (2019a). *La décroissance.* Paris: Que sais-je?

Latouche, S. (2019b). *Comment réenchanter le monde: La décroissance et le sacré.* Paris: Payot & Rivages.

Le Maire, B. (2021). *Interview de M. Bruno Le Maire, ministre de l'économie et des finances, à CNews le 28 septembre 2021, sur l'augmentation des prix de l'énergie, la défiscalisation des pourboires payés en carte bancaire, le Livret A, la réforme des retraites et l'élection présidentielle de 2022 / Interviewer: Laurence Ferrari.* Retrieved from www.vie-publique.fr/discours/281734-bruno-le-maire-28092021-politique-economique

Liegey, V. (2014). La décroissance s'inscrit dans une tradition politique de gauche. Retrieved from https://comptoir.org/2014/12/08/vincent-liegey-la-decroissance-sinscrit-dans-une-tradition-politique-de-gauche/

Liegey, V., & Nelson, A. (2020). *Exploring degrowth: A critical guide* [Kindle version]. London: Pluto Press.

Löwy, M. (2020). Eco-socialism and/or De-growth. Retrieved from www.letusrise.ie/rupture-articles/2wl71srdonxrbgxal9v6bv78njr2fb

Macron, E. (2020, June 29). Déclaration de M. Emmanuel Macron, président de la République, sur la Convention citoyenne pour le climat et ses propositions, à Paris le 29 juin 2020. Retrieved from www.vie-publique.fr/discours/275505-emmanuel-macron-29062020-convention-citoyenne-pour-le-climat

Meadows, D. H., Meadows, D. L., Randers, J., & Behrens W. W. (1972). *The limits to growth: A report for the Club of Rome's project on the predicament of mankind*. New York: Universe Books.

Muraca, B. (2013). Décroissance: A project for a radical transformation of society. *Environmental values*, *22*(2), 147–169. doi: 10.3197/096327113X13581561725112

Muraca, B., & Schmelzer, M. (2017). Sustainable degrowth: Historical roots of the search for alternatives to growth in three regions. In I. Borowy & M. Schmelzer (Eds.), *History of the future of economic growth: Historical roots of current debates on sustainable* degrowth (174–197). London: Routledge.

Odoxa. (2019). "Baromètre de l'économie. Octobre 2019.", September 26 [Survey report] Retrieved from www.odoxa.fr/sondage/barometre-economique-doctobre-francais-plus-ecolos-jamais/

Petridis, P., Muraca, B., & Kallis, G. (2015). Degrowth: Between a scientific concept and a slogan for a social movement. In J. Martinez-Alier & R. Muradian (Eds.), *Handbook of ecological economics* (176–200). Cheltenham: Edward Elgar Publishing.

Schmelzer, M., & Eversberg, D. (2017). Beyond growth, capitalism, and industrialism? Consensus, divisions and currents within the emerging movement for sustainable degrowth. *A journal for and about social movements*, *9 (1)*, 327–356.

Schmid, A. P. (2011). Glossary and abbreviations of terms and concepts relating to terrorism and counter-terrorism. In A. P. Schmid (Ed.), *The Routledge handbook of terrorism research* (598–707). London: Routledge.

Schmid, A. P. (2014). Violent and non-violent extremism: Two sides of the same coin? ICCT Research paper. Retrieved from www.icct.nl/download/file/ICCT-Schmid- Violent-Non-Violent-Extremism-May-2014.pdf

29

A SPATIAL ACCOUNT OF NON-VIOLENT ENVIRONMENTAL EXTREMISM IN AUSTRALIA

Kate Galloway

Introduction

The global dimensions of the climate crisis have spawned a world-wide movement agitating for governmental action. Decentralised, networked activism through groups such as Extinction Rebellion (XR) and School Strike 4 Climate (SS4C) have attracted localised participation. In Australia, these movements' aims overlap with local concerns expressed by groups such as #StopAdani and Lock-the-Gate Alliance (LGA)—advocating for a habitable planet reflecting intergenerational equity through a shift from an extractive carbon economy. Their diverse membership is collectively considered to be "activist", branded by media, government, and in general discourse, as "extremist" (Ricketts, 2017), "radical activism …apocalyptic in tone, [that] brooks no compromise, all or nothing" (Morrison, 2019)—and even as "terrorist" (Burke, 2014; Christensen, 2016; James, 2019; Burdon, 2020).

In Australia, climate action builds on a well-established environmental movement opposed to governments' pro-development stance and longstanding prioritisation of mining and clearing agricultural land. Since at least the 1970s, tensions between the State and environmentalists highlight competing attitudes to land management in Australia: "land is either a resource to be extracted for profit or an ecosystem that must sustain us all" (Burdon, 2015, p. 7). Environmental groups have now coalesced around opposition to extractive industry and its effect on land and climate. The question, though, is whether in the current politically charged climate, contemporary environmental movements in Australia constitute an extremist, or even terrorist, threat, as some have claimed.

The four environmental groups analysed here adopt the tactic of non-violent direct action through street marches, sit-ins on private property and in public places, and blockades of private lands. Such methods contest the assertion of private ownership and the use of public space, claiming these places as a site of protest. They challenge the "desocialised and depoliticised" (Keenan, 2015, p. 29) spatial order, imposed by the "network of lines on a map that make the physical space understandable and manageable" (Keenan, 2015, p. 28).

This chapter analyses non-violent environmentalism through a spatial lens, seeking to counter assertions in public discourse that it is an "extremist threat". This study first provides an

DOI: 10.4324/9781003032793-34

overview of the genesis, ideologies, and methods of four groups. It then analyses their charac-terisation by the State as extremists. This chapter suggests that environmental activism becomes extremist—in the eyes of the State—when activists are involved in physical occupation of spaces that is different from the State's spatial ordering. It contends, however, that such a categorisation is misplaced. Its method draws from legal geography whose aim is to "trac[e] the manifestations of law upon space" (Bennett & Layard, 2015, p. 414). Characterising protest in terms of its location and analysing the responses of law-makers establishes a "lawscape" (Graham, 2011) representing the co-constitution of the legal, the spatial and the social (Bennett & Layard, 2015, p. 409). Thus, the challenge to State authority over spatial ordering generates the categorisation of extremism, rather than any genuine pipeline to or connection with terrorism. This error warrants a more nuanced understanding of the movement.

Non-violent Environmental Extremism

In the face of a global climate catastrophe, government and corporate inaction around the world has generated a groundswell of grassroots action seeking urgent change in law, policy, and practice to mitigate environmental collapse. From this vantage point, it is the business-as-usual approach of government and industry that might be considered extremist, rather than a movement aimed at preserving life on this planet (Hasler, 2020). Paradoxically, self-professed political conservatives promote the expansion of coal mining and new gas exploration (Gas Fired Recovery, 2020), while rejecting emissions targets and climate mitigation generally (Crowley, 2017; Ali et al., 2020). Yet in public discourse, law and policy, it is environmental activists who are labelled "extremists" when performing different activities, including sit-ins, occupation, and peaceful protest in private and public places (Muncie, 2020).

As a social movement, environmentalism eschews hierarchical structures and formal organ-isation. It is truly a "mobilized network of networks" (Neidhardt, as cited in Rucht, 2017, p. 44). Although environmentalism broadly might be concerned with "the environment", it manifests as diverse social movements. While the movement might deal with thematic concerns—all related to the environment—identifying one theme of environmentalism is not easy (Rucht, 2017). Acid rain, climate change, and conservation might all "spur action under the banner of environmentalism" (Uekötter, 2017, p. 420)—yet these themes are not necessarily connected.

Further, environmentalism might be characterised other than by thematic concern. Some environmentalists are motivated by societal concerns, whereby environmental activism is a "movement of crisis" (Rucht, 2017, p. 45). For those objecting to the ravages of capitalism on the planet, the movement might have a "strategic orientation (e.g. [a] reformist and revo-lutionary movement)" (Rucht, 2017, p. 45). Unlike some past localised concerns, activism to promote climate action may combine different categories of social movement. Even then, there are philosophical differences within the movement, such as deep ecology contrasting with anthropocentrism (Brundtland, 1987; Naess, 1989; Nhanenge, 2011). There is also a movement to decolonise environmentalism (Neale & Vincent, 2016; Elvey, 2020) pointing to further fundamental philosophical differences. Environmentalism has for a long time been seen by indigenous peoples around the world as part of the overarching colonial project, amounting to a further dispossession of traditional lands on the grounds of protection of nature. Thus, as Uekötter observes, as a movement, environmentalism has "no common denominator, no common foe, no widely accepted philosophy that holds the movement together" (Uekötter, 2017, p. 443).

Despite the lack of coherence of purpose and philosophy, as a social movement, the core method for achieving its goals tends to be public protest—a form of collective public identity and performance of self-expression (Rucht, 2017, p. 44; Uekötter, 2017, p. 434). Generally, no matter how radical, environmentalism eschews violence against humans (Uekötter, 2017, p. 439). Perhaps for this reason, civil disobedience for environmental purposes is generally socially accepted around the world. Thus, whilst sometimes engaging in notorious and dangerous protests, Greenpeace attracts broad support (Reestorff, 2015; Zelko, 2017). Such activities are generally not considered extremism in the same way as some other forms of protest (Uekötter, 2017, p. 439).

There is, however, a paradox within environmental protest. On the one hand, widespread acceptance of environmental goals is "connected to the growth of the public sphere" (Berger & Nehring, 2017, p. 2). The movement's public performance thus enhances society through engagement and does so on a global scale. On this reading, the notion of a benevolent movement as "extremist" seems incongruous. Yet the emergence of the environmental movement is emblematic also of the "decline and decay" of some basic contours of society in that it "lack[s] territorial place and … cannot be fixed in time or space" (Berger & Nehring, 2017, p. 2). This aspect is perhaps the likely source of the extremist epithet.

The contingency of territory within environmentalism broadly is illustrated by the movement's global networks connecting to local environmental causes (Uekötter, 2017, p. 419). The uptake by grassroots campaigners is "live" community activism. Giving local meaning to the global movement's broader thematic concern expresses social, historical, and political contexts of the relevant locale. Consequently, the branding of environmental activism as "extremist" or not is dependent on the context within which it occurs more than the purpose of the movement or its methods per se.

A Case Study of Australian Environmental Movements

In contrast to Uekötter's observation about the wide acceptance of civil disobedience, environmental activism in Australia is frequently described by the government as "extremist" (Jolley & Rickards, 2020). This attitude can be traced to a decades-long history of environmentalism in Australia and to Australia's engagement with protest more broadly. In the state of Queensland, for example, the right to march in protest was hard fought for over decades of conservative rule. Contemporary movements, part of global mobilisation against climate change, appear to enliven the historical authoritarian political and governmental responses.

Anti-protest

In the decades before conscription for the Vietnam War, Queensland had seen very little political protest by way of public meetings or marches. The legislative framework was already in place, however, under the *Traffic Act 1949* (Qld) requiring a police permit and payment of a fee to gather and to hold a placard in public (Brennan, 1983). At the first anti-conscription protests in 1965, the police were ready to crack down on even peaceful dissidence. For the next two decades, the *Traffic Act* notoriously became a means of shutting down non-violent protest by "students, unionists, environmentalists…liberals, Marxists, communists, [and] anarchists" (Fitzgerald, 1984, p. 573). Despite a "right to march" movement espousing non-violent protest that was especially active during 1977–1979, the Police Commissioner in 1977 pronounced that "[p]ublic behaviour in the streets…has been generally good throughout the State" (Brennan, 1986) thanks in no small part to the operation of what has been described as a police state (Whitton, 1989; Brennan, 1983; Crawford 2009) under premier Joh Bjelke-Petersen.

Blockades and sit-ins have continued to be part of the political landscape in Queensland, notably in relation to environmental protest. Examples include the Daintree Blockade in 1983 (Wilkie, 2017) and the longstanding sit-in protesting the construction of the Kuranda Skyrail in World Heritage listed rainforest (Henry, 1998), and more recently, occupation of areas surrounding proposed coal seam gas and other mining sites (CSG Protester Fined, 2011; Heber, 2013; Ricketts, 2017). The recent political history in Queensland established marching—a form of occupation of public space—as an extremist activity absent any particular underlying protest ideology, or any association with terrorism. However, while a change of government in the late 1980s resulted in greater civil liberties, and despite human rights reform, politically and socially Queensland has retained a tendency towards treating environmental protest as a form of extremism.

Contemporary Environment Movements

More recently, the four environmental movements explored in this chapter—XR, SS4C, #StopAdani, and LGA—have become active in Australia, attracting political and media attention. All four manifest their environmental concern in terms of climate change, and on promoting concrete action to change the trajectory of its effects. They do so, however, through diverse lenses. Not a climate movement as such (Basden, 2019), XR, formed in 2018, distinguishes itself ideologically and practically from longstanding environmental movements such as Greenpeace (Collett, 2019). XR's earliest protest involved occupying the Greenpeace offices in London, urging a narrower focus on the climate crisis and the radical social and economic change required in response.

In contrast to Greenpeace's broader remit of "changing the way humans relate to nature" (Greenpeace International, n.d.) and campaigning for "a greener, healthier world for our oceans, forests, food, climate and democracy" (Greenpeace Australia Pacific, n.d.), XR protests against imminent, global, and catastrophic extinction (Křížkovský, 2019). Despite different focuses, XR shares with the movement more broadly the capacity for global operation, evidenced by its spread from the United Kingdom to 78 countries, with 1178 groups as of May 2021 (Extinction Rebellion, n.d.). Also in 2018, schoolgirl Greta Thunberg started her SS4C protests outside the Swedish Parliament. Thunberg skipped school every Friday to protest against politicians' disrespect for children's education in routinely ignoring climate scientists. Her actions inspired a global but decentralised movement, sometimes referred to as "Fridays For Future" (Borunda, 2019). SS4C activism involves an implicit rejection of capitalism (McKnight, 2020, p. 52), advocating for radical social and political change to address the climate catastrophe. Its singular focus on climate change intersects with that of XR but its success in engaging youth (Boulianne, Lalancette and Ilkiw, 2020) affords a particular (demographic) lens on the same theme, offering a point of difference.

However, in common with XR, as a grassroots movement, protest action taken by any particular SS4C chapter tends to reflect local concerns. For example, Alice Springs protesters in Australia emphasise the impacts of climate change upon Indigenous communities (ABC, 20 September 2019) while still protesting under the SS4C banner. The adaptation of the singular SS4C message to local conditions and concerns reflects the thematic diversity within the environmental movement more broadly. Local to Australia, #StopAdani protests against development of the Carmichael Mine and associated rail projects in Central Queensland (Bravus, 2021) by Indian conglomerate, Adani Group. The company's projects, referred to collectively as the Adani Mine, have become a touchstone for national environmental protest given their effect on the landscape and biosphere, the dispossession of traditional owners (Lyons, 2019), and coal extraction—a key contributor to global greenhouse emissions (Jakob et al., 2020) and thus climate change.

Unlike the other groups, the LGA arose more from localised issues. Its formation addressed the disenfranchisement felt by many farmers in the face of mining approvals on their lands (Jaques & Galloway, 2012). As such, and fitting Rucht's (2017) conceptualisation of environmental activism as an umbrella for different movements, LGA is not an environmental non-government organisation as such. Initially simply a "not in my backyard" action opposed to coal seam gas (CSG), the group evolved to address underlying environmental issues as several existing community groups joined the cause (Hutton, 2012). The group values the preservation of "food bowls, our bushland, our landscapes and our underground water systems" (Hutton, 2012, p. 19). Its united purpose is to generate enhanced legal protection of farmers and rural landholders against the mining sector. Just as the other groups have spread beyond their place of origin, LGA now comprises over 200 member organisations across Australia (Ricketts, 2017). Its activities coincide with those of the other three movements, particularly its protest against the encroachment of CSG onto inhabited areas.

Apart from shared concerns with the environment, intersecting with the theme of climate change, the four movements share other features relevant to analysing their "extremist" categorisation. Those can broadly be described as: all constituting "movements of crisis" (Rucht, 2017, p. 45), sharing a commitment to distributed and participatory engagement (Rucht, 2017, p. 44), and deploying collective (Uekötter, 2017), peaceful, public protest.

"Movements of Crisis"

Each group profiled here is, in its own way, an example of a "movement of crisis" (Rucht, 2017, p. 45) affording them a dimension beyond a concern only with the environment. Kerbo (1982) explains protest occurring on a spectrum from movements of crisis to movements of affluence. The preconditions for a movement of crisis include that they occur in times of "life threatening political or socioeconomic crisis", those who take part are "primarily beneficiary members" and that at their early stage, they are "usually spontaneous and relatively unorganised" (p. 654). Although Kerbo includes the environment movement as a "movement of affluence" and thus a moral or conscience-based project, Rucht's (2017) more recent analysis of the environment movement highlights the possibility of the social context of protest (p. 45). XR, for example, maintains that "[w]e are in the midst of a climate and ecological breakdown" (Extinction Rebellion, n.d.), reflecting Bendell's conclusion that "social collapse is inevitable, catastrophe is probable, and extinction is possible" (Bendell, 2018, p. 20). It seeks expressly to alter society itself, including "shift[ing] the power back to the people to make the bold decisions needed through Participatory Democracy and Citizens' Assemblies" (Extinction Rebellion, n.d.). This is a bold statement of transformative change targeted at the heart of institutions of government that, according to Wilson and Walton, represents "a more subversive agenda" (2019, p. 5).

Thunberg' SS4C frames climate change as an issue affecting children's rights. Members of this movement are those affected by grown-ups' wrong decisions, which are strongly condemned: "you adults are shitting on my future" (Mitra, 2019). In particular, SS4C has looked at governments' adherence to the *UN Convention on the Rights of the Child*, claiming that world leaders have failed young people (Woodward, 2019) who are now facing a crisis due to climate change. The origin of SS4C—Thunberg's solo strike—was spontaneous and without an organised resistance. LGA, too, as a grassroots movement involves what Kerbo (1982) describes as "beneficiary" participation. Its members, like those of SS4C, feel compelled to participate in the movement based on their perception that the movement's concerns are directly relevant to their own lives.

This can be contrasted with an abstract broader threat, or a threat that is seen to apply to others and not oneself. The crisis faced by members of LGA—farmers whose land is under threat, and members of regional communities affected by mining—is that of food insecurity arising from destruction of arable land. Unlike the spontaneity of SS4C and XR, LGA is an organised group arising out of community meetings to address the perceived crisis. However, overall participation is less about morality or conscience (a "movement of affluence") than it is about the crisis faced by those in the pathway of CSG ("beneficiaries" of a protest). In contrast to LGA, #StopAdani has attracted a following well beyond those ("beneficiaries") immediately affected by the mine itself. Participants' core concern is the climate crisis and they focus their protest on the mine's contribution to emissions, both direct and indirect, that fuel it. Such broad and dispersed engagement beyond proximity to the object of protest illustrates the orientation of climate change as a contemporary crisis that directly affects all of us. To use Kerbo's terminology (1982), an issue of global concern such as climate change might position anyone as a "beneficiary" member of a movement protesting against it.

Distributed, Participatory Engagement

The second aspect shared by the four groups is their distributed, participatory engagement, which stands as a feature of environmentalism more broadly. All of the groups feature smaller groups operating at the local level in distributed, networked arrangements emblematic of Neidhardt's "network of networks" (cited in Rucht, 2017, p. 44). XR, for example, is a "participatory, decentralised and inclusive" mass movement of concerned citizens (Gunningham, 2019, p. 199). As important as outcomes alone, it promotes decision-making in assemblies as reflecting a culture of care and compassion that regenerates its activism (Křížkovský, 2019; Westwell and Bunting, 2020).

Similarly, the Australian branch of SS4C describes itself as: "student-led, decentralised, grassroots, non-partisan, non-violent, mission-focused, inclusive, ambitious, creative, and growing" (School Strike for Climate, 2021). The movement adopts a local and bottom-up approach to activism, devoted to participatory democracy and consensus decision-making (Crnogorcevic, 2019). Both LGA and #StopAdani are comprised of individuals and smaller groups working together for a shared outcome. LGA comprises over 200 different member groups across Australia. (Ricketts, 2017). #StopAdani is made up of more than 70 local groups comprising people "from all walks of life … united by a determination to protect people from the disastrous impacts Adani's coal will have on water, land rights, and the world's climate" (Stop Adani, n.d.). Localised organising gives #StopAdani a decentralised mode of operation emblematic of environmental protest (Uekötter, 2017).

All four movements' grassroots and decentralised approach have fuelled their expanding participation. For SS4C and #StopAdani in particular, social media has proven to be a highly effective recruitment tool integral to their engagement strategy (Boulianne, Lalancette, & Ilkiw, 2020; Rupić, 2020). As a globalised or deterritorialised issue the environmental movement faces the challenge of how to motivate action where action necessarily occurs at a particular locale (Boulianne, Lalancette, & Ilkiw, 2020, p. 210). Jost et al. (2018) observe that social media networks provide a vital means of information exchange and motivation that facilitate collective action. As social networks, messages both sent and received via online platforms will draw on existing connections between potential actors (Jost et al., 2018, p. 110) thus amplifying the message and providing the means for localised context.

Even without so-called hashtag activism (Boulianne, Lalancette, & Ilkiw, 2020; Rupić, 2020, p. 210), the XR website (Extinction Rebellion, n.d.) illustrates how social connectedness might also occur, through establishing communities of interest. In addition to location-specific groups throughout the world, there are seven "communities" including XR Disabled Rebels, XR Muslims, and XR Grandparents. The explicit use of communities is a clear illustration of the "network of networks" concept (Neidhardt, as cited in Rucht, 2017, p. 44). For a global movement, the idea of a "tribe" or community endeavour is another way of addressing the challenge of motivating action in the face of the "overwhelming nature of environmental problems" (Boulianne, Lalancette, & Ilkiw, 2020; Rupić, 2020, p. 210).

Collective, Peaceful, Public Protest

Finally, all four groups engage in collective, peaceful, public protest. In contrast to other movements that may engage in civil disobedience from time to time, XR's method involves sustained disruption: persistent and at scale, in full public view. Gluing people to banks in the United States; marching through Pakistan; occupying the Hague in Netherlands; blocking roads in Austria; lying in streets in Chile; blowing whistles in Ghana; shutting down iconic locations in the United Kingdom (Extinction Rebellion, 2019). During 2019 in Brisbane, Australia, XR protests stopped peak hour traffic near the city centre, day after day. "Their main tools have been devices that make the job of clearing them away as slow and painstaking as possible" (Wordsworth, 2019). Globally, including in Australia, SS4C relies heavily on social media to mobilise followers and spread the message—particularly through hashtags (Boulianne, Lalancette and Ilkiw, 2020). While adherents engage in online activism, they also take to the streets. On 20 September 2019, SS4C organised rallies across Australia, to coincide with another planned strike by Thunberg. There were 180,000 participants across Australia bringing multiple cities to a standstill (ABC, 20 September 2019).

#StopAdani is also well known for its principal method of protest via social media, but it has also taken to the streets. On 7 October 2017, it organised a national day of action across Australian cities and towns where "20,000 people formed 60+ enormous human signs literally spelling out #StopAdani with their bodies at iconic locations across Australia" (Stop Adani, n.d.). Despite ostensibly conservative roots, LGA's methods are those of non-violence, non-cooperation and civil disobedience. The initial mode of protest was for landowners to "lock their gates" to CSG companies, refusing to negotiate land access or sale. In addition, it has organised a number of blockades at sites of CSG operations. The largest occurred in Bentley, New South Wales, commencing in 2014, comprising 5000–10,000 protestors and 800 police (Ricketts, 2017). At blockades, tactics include protesters locking themselves onto trees and equipment, and erection of star pickets with steel spikes welded to the end. These tactics have upset farmers who cooperate with CSG companies, citing the disturbance and the lasting impacts of the infrastructure erected (Minerals Council of Australia, 2017).

Although each movement has its own branding and somewhat differentiated aims, they share core characteristics of the environment movement more broadly. In the contemporary context, however, rather than simply a thematic concern for the environment the movements analysed here are driven more by a sense of crisis. Consequently, environmental activism is no longer simply a positive public virtue. It has become instead a political movement that therefore challenges the State. In response the State, supported at least somewhat by public discourse, has labelled the movement as extremist, establishing the groundwork for legal responses to shut it down.

Environmentalism as Extremism

Although emergency measures to combat violent extremism in Australia existed following the two world wars, Australian legislation had not addressed terrorist threats as a long-term policy until 9/11 (Williams, 2011). In the decade following 9/11, however, Australia enacted 54 pieces of "anti-terrorism" legislation (Williams, 2011, p. 1144). The discourse has since shifted to "violent extremism" defined as "a person or group who is willing to use violence; or advocates the use of violence by others, to achieve a political, ideological or religious goal" (Australian Government, 2020). It includes terrorism. Following a 2010 white paper, the government established the Countering Violent Extremism Unit (Barker, 2015). In 2012, reports surfaced that the Australian Security Intelligence Agency was monitoring environmentalists (Dorling, 2012). They were seen to pose a threat to energy infrastructure that was cited to be "greater than terrorists" (Dorling, 2012) and that could have "life-threatening consequences" (Duffy, 2012). Similar attempts to criminalise environmental protest have been reported in the United States, Canada and the United Kingdom (Ahmed, 2014).

Alongside the Commonwealth's promotion of fossil fuels and rejection of climate change mitigation, the Abbott government in 2015 implemented a strategy to counter violent extremism (Commonwealth, 2017). The program included interventions and an evaluation framework. Educational materials to be distributed to schools and parents included a case study of a young person "radicalised" by environmentalists, "cutting off links with her loving family" to engage in tree-spiking and machinery sabotage (Hamilton, 2015). Amidst controversy around the attempt to connect environmental activism with terrorism, the case study was soon removed. However, the materials indicate a persistent characterisation of environmental protest as a form of violent extremism.

In a subsequent analysis of trends in crime, for example, Harris-Hogan (2017) identifies a number of extremist groups and a category of "issue-oriented violence" that includes environmental causes. Somewhat ambiguously, Harris-Hogan observes that environmentally motivated violence has "manifested in a range of organisations, which can be broadly categorised as anti-government or anti-capitalist". However, he goes on to say that "[m]any groups in this category have large support bases and generally do not pose a violent threat to the community" (p. 6). As Harris-Hogan (2017) points out, individual environmentalists have been responsible for violence in Australia. In 2012, for example, a bomb at the Casino office of a CSG operator implicated LGA in a violent act. The LGA affirmed its commitment to non-violent direct action (Lock the Gate calls for calm, 2012), identifying the issue as one of lack of training due to the influx of people with strong feelings against the mining activity. A challenge for distributed groups is to sustain non-violent action. However, given a group's express commitment to peaceful protest, it is also easier for it to disclaim any such activity that operates outside those principles.

With an increasing concern about and responses to a perceived threat of violent extremism, the State has expanded the types of groups it believes constitute a "terrorist" threat. Thus, recently, environmental activism has been identified in political and public discourse as extremist and even as terrorist. This categorisation has been levelled also at the four groups analysed here. Following a report by ex-security operative Wilson and Walton (2019), the United Kingdom officially listed XR as an "extremist ideology" although this categorisation was subsequently withdrawn (Grierson & Dodd, 2020). However, the British Home Secretary said it was important to look at "a range of security risks" and to make assessments "based in terms of risk to the public, security risks, security threats"—evincing remaining caution about XR (Walker, Grierson, & Dodd, 2020). This is apparently reflected also in Australia, where one report alleges that an assistant to the Minister for Home Affairs in a telephone conversation identified XR as an example of a "left wing terror organisation" within the government's revised categorisation of extremist groups (Murphy & Remeikis, 2020).

In Queensland, the Premier denounced XR activism on Brisbane streets. At the behest of the police, her government introduced laws banning "dangerous attachment devices" (*Summary Offences Act 2005* Qld). While politicians and police have described the lock on devices—used both by LGA and XR—as "sinister tactics …[that] are dangerous and designed to harm" there is no evidence of this having occurred (Langford, 2019). Aligned with the rhetoric around XR protests in particular, as a mobile form of protest occurring at multiple sites beyond the mine itself, #StopAdani has been characterised not only as "rent-a-crowd", but also as "terrorism" (Burke, 2014; Christensen, 2016), "economic terrorism" (Walton, 2019) and "ecoterrorism" (Oosting, 2014; Brevini & Woronov, 2017). Government backbencher George Christensen has repeatedly called for #StopAdani protesters and even the leader of the Greens, Adam Bandt, to be jailed as "ecoterrorists" (Dgeiger, 2013; Workman, 2017). In addition, with an impact of the #StopAdani campaign on downstream suppliers to the mine, including major banks who refused to finance, the Commonwealth government flagged creating secondary boycott laws that would allow prosecution of such protests (Morrison, 2019; Burdon, 2020). While it is unlikely that such laws could succeed, couching the problem of protests as "anarchy", "denial of liberties", "a new form of radical activism" and "apocalyptic in tone" (Morrison, 2019) reinforces the categorisation of the protests as a form of extremism and, in the context of the discourse more generally, impliedly also as violent.

By contrast, the response to the SS4C protests focuses on criticising the children participating. Because the movement is youth-led, some argue that children are being manipulated by teachers or parents or are buying into "political correctness" without any theoretical foundation (Sutton, 2019). In the United Kingdom, in the same counter-terrorism context as XR, police warned against young people who neglect to attend school or participate in planned school walkouts. The report also flagged for attention young people who partake in non-violent direct action such as sit-down protests, banner drops or "writing environmentally themed graffiti" (Grierson and Dodd, 2020). The Australian Prime Minister has similarly told school children attending marches in 2018 that they should "be in school" (AAP, 2018).

The discourse of violent extremism manifested also in 2020 during Australia's bushfires, when a government member suggested that the fires had been started by "ecoterrorists" making a point about climate change (Commonwealth, 2020, p. 765). As with security surveillance of fossil fuel protests, the theory of activists lighting wildfires had also taken hold globally, notably in Brazil and the United States (Wilson, 2020; Barnard, 2018). While claims of extremism, anarchism, and terrorism are levelled at environmentalists, neither their ideology nor their methods appear to warrant the labels—raising the question of why they are so categorised. I posit that the reason lies in their challenging the State's spatial order.

Subverting the Spatialised Order

The means of protest of the groups analysed here are avowedly peaceful, despite their goal of civil disruption. Occupying space is their principal method evincing dual spatial dimensions that conflict with State authority over place. The first dimension rests in the relationship between the site of protest and the site of protested activity: the two do not always coalesce. The second is the categorisation of the location of dissent in terms of property—a social and legal concept that suggests a boundedness that determines relationships between people and that place, as well as relationships between people themselves (Nedelsky, 1990). Non-violent environmental protest invokes these dimensions so as to disorient the State's comprehension, through law, of the containment of environmental factors within its imposed "despatialised grid" (Keenan, 2015, p 28): the approved relationship of people to place and what activities people might undertake when there. Within these two dimensions, the methods of protest adopted by the groups described here are "spatialised" in various ways.

In the first dimension, environmental protest might take place at the site of contested mining activity such as the Bentley Blockade in Northern New South Wales and other CSG protests (Kia & Ricketts, 2018; Curran, 2017). LGA blockades tend to occur in situ, interposing the bodies of protesters between the site of the contested activity and those seeking to undertake it. Alternatively, protests might occur in space that is distant from the place of contested activity: #StopAdani activists have protested all over Australia against the mine located in Central Queensland (Colvin, 2020). By contrast, XR and SS4C protests globally attach to activity occurring at no specified place. The spatiality of XR and SS4C protests lies in the material reality of Earth's ecological systems, and the inherent interconnectedness of place and ecological and physical processes. At the same time, however, each protest is emplaced by the location of its own protesters, who connect the global with their local concerns. In this case, the site of protest is not "the inert backdrop to action undertaken by subjects. Rather, space is part of the action" (Keenan, 2015, p. 7).

Protests invoke the second spatial dimension through the property category of the location where they occur. Property might be regarded as public or private—with implications for access and exclusion. As a general proposition, private property at common law operates as a right to exclude all others. Public property, by contrast, is theoretically open to all. Despite its public and thus ostensibly accessible nature, the State jealously guards access in ways that are racialized, gendered, and temporal (Blomley, 2003; Blomley & Pratt, 2001; Blomley, 2016). In the common law tradition, as all land is theoretically held mediately or immediately by the Crown, the State controls all rights to land whether through property or through other means (Galloway, 2012; Lyons, 2019; Ricketts, 2020).

Blockades as a method of protest transgress the legal norms of exclusion that are a core feature of private property. In these instances, the State has already imposed upon landowners' otherwise plenary property rights through the grant of mining rights (Galloway, 2012). The law compartmentalised the land into resources and afforded the State the power to order the space according to differentiated rights over the same physical dimensions. Landowners' desire to re-take possession of "their" place is a subversion of the State's authority, putting LGA's protest activities at odds with the authority of the State to control space. Private property becomes politicised as LGA land-owning farmers invite the public to join them in upholding the property imaginary of their right to exclude. Protest through occupying space belonging to another, inverts assumptions central to property's characteristic spatial ordering and thus, in the eyes of the State, enters the realms of extremism.

By contrast, XR, SS4C and #StopAdani protesters exercise their right to access public space, not private property. Here they come up against State power to impose order upon public spaces. Challenges to State power, outside the State's own conception of its sovereign authority, are thus invested with extremism. Protesters are therefore criminalised for their actions (Paris, 2019), liable to removal by police (Ricketts, 2017). Intermediate spaces such as government offices, private and yet public, are likewise policed through removal, and often charging, of protesters who occupy them.

Conclusions

The groups profiled here provide examples of a movement deemed extremist within Australian political discourse and also, as outlined above, as terrorist, eco-terrorist, or economic terrorist.

There is little to suggest in their ideology or actions, however, that this is a legitimate description of their motive or means. Given the groups' ideologies and methods, it might be asked what prompts the epithets of violent extremism. The suggestion here is that environmentalism is extremist not in terms of ideology. Further, extremism does not necessarily describe the groups' methods per se, given norms that accept public gatherings, free speech, and protest generally (Ricketts, 2020). Instead, what has disrupted the mainstream discourses of capital and power is the groups' subversion of the spatialised order. Such is the importance of space in ordering society that its disruption is perceived as extremism, and even as terrorism (Walton, 2019).

The objectives of the broader environmental movement are sufficiently diffuse to remain of little concern to the State. Indeed, it might suit the State to embrace the message of a cleaner and greener world. In this vein, illustrating the acceptability of environmental concern per se, government backbencher George Christensen excepted "ordinary community groups or individuals who genuinely care about and work to improve the environment, or the locals who have genuine concerns about the impacts of certain projects" (Commonwealth, 2014, p. 10488) from his charge of "eco-terrorism". The dissonance between the discourse of environmental extremism and its reality lies at the intersection of corporate interests, the history of civil liberties in Australia, a fearful electorate (Sengul, 2020), and a post-truth networked mass media context in which assertions might flourish without correction. In this context, the State is free to wield its power, including discursively, and even in the service of the corporate sector.

The means of resolving the impasse between the State and protesters requires reframing the problem. Thus, enhanced civil liberties might assist in legitimising public protest and the occupation of public—and private—spaces to demonstrate shared concerns. Thus far, although environmental activism is included within the State's frame of "violent extremism", it does not meet the threshold for such a categorisation. Nor is there evidence of any pipeline to actual violence. Given that environmental activism has been miscategorised, a more precise policy framework is required. Understanding, or acknowledging, what is generating the protest is a vital first step. Central to an accurate analysis of environmentalism within the broader policy framework is State recognition of the legitimacy of the crisis that is experienced by those protesting. Only then will the State have the analytical tools to think beyond the unhelpful, and incorrect, category of "terrorism" for environmental protest.

So long as the State discounts environmental protestors as engaging in a "movement of affluence" (Kerbo, 1982)—as rent-a-crowd or, pejoratively, as "full-time protesters" (Remeikis, 2019)—it will fail to accurately analyse the protestors' standpoint and consequently will also misconstrue their methods. The analysis required to overcome the government's own shortcomings in its discourse around environmental "extremism" is thus a deeper, more critical, and, ironically, less ideological mapping of the terrain of the movement.

References

AAP. (2018, November 26). Scott Morrison tells students striking over climate change to be "less activist". *The Guardian*. Retrieved from www.theguardian.com/environment/2018/nov/26/scott-morrison-tells-students-striking-over-climate-change-to-be-less-activist.

ABC. (2019, 20 September 2019). "Global climate strike sees 'hundreds of thousands' of Australians rally across the country". *ABC News*. Retrieved from www.abc.net.au/news/2019-09-20/school-strike-for-climate-draws-thousands-to-australian-rallies/11531612.

Ahmed, N. (2014, 22 January 2014). Are you opposed to fracking? Then you might just be a terrorist. *The Guardian*. Retrieved from www.theguardian.com/environment/earth-insight/2014/jan/21/fracking-activism-protest-terrorist-oil-corporate-spies.

Ali, Saleem H., et al. (2020). Climate policy paralysis in Australia: Energy security, energy poverty and jobs. *Energies, 13*(18), pp. 4894–4900. doi:10.3390/en13184894.

Australian Government. (2020). Living safe together. Retrieved from https://www.livingsafetogether.gov.au/get-the-facts.

Barker, C. (2015). *Australian government measures to counter violent extremism: A quick guide*. Retrieved from https://parlinfo.aph.gov.au/parlInfo/download/library/prspub/3650900/upload_binary/3650900.pdf.Barnard, M. (2018, 30 November). Trump and Zinke blame non-existent eco-terrorism for California wildfires. *The Future is Electric*. Retrieved from https://medium.com/the-future-is-electric/trump-and-zinke-blame-non-existent-eco-terrorism-for-california-wildfires-a9e41a5853c6.

Basden, S. (2019, January 10). Extinction rebellion isn't about the climate. *Medium*. Retrieved from https://medium.com/extinction-rebellion/extinction-rebellion-isnt-about-the-climate-42a0a73d9d49.

Bendell, J. (2018). *Deep adaptation: A map for navigating climate tragedy*. Retrieved from www.lifeworth.com/deepadaptation.pdf.

Bennett, L., & Layard, A. (2015). Legal geography: Becoming spatial detectives. *Geograhy Compass, 9*(7), pp. 406–422. doi: 10.1111/gec3.12209.

Berger S., & Nehring H. (2017). Introduction: Towards a global history of social movements. In: Berger S. and Nehring H. (eds) *The history of social movements in global perspective*. London: Palgrave Macmillan (pp. 1–35). https://doi.org/10.1057/978-1-137-30427-8_1.

Blomley, N. (2016). The right to not be excluded. In Amin, A. and Howell, P. (Eds.) *Releasing the commons: Rethinking the futures of the commons* (pp. 89–106), New York, NY, USA: Routledge.

Blomley, N., & Pratt, G. (2001). Canada and the political geographies of rights. *Canadian Geographer/Le Géographe Canadien, 45*(1), pp. 151–166. DOI: 10.1111/j.1541-0064.2001.tb01180.x

Borunda, A. (2019, March 13). These young activists are striking to save their planet from climate change. *National Geographic*. Retrieved from www.nationalgeographic.com/environment/2019/03/youth-climate-strike-kids-save-the-world/.

Boulianne, S., Lalancette, M., & Ilkiw, D. (2020). "School Strike 4 Climate": Social media and the international youth protest on climate change. *Media and Communication, 8*(2), pp. 208–218. doi: http://dx.doi.org/10.17645/mac.v8i2.2768.

Bravus. (2021). Retrieved from www.bravus.com.au/about/.

Brennan, F. (1986). Too much law, not enough order: Reflections on the Queensland experience. Human Rights Commission of Australia. Occasional Paper no 14.

Brennan, F. (1983). *Too much order with too little law*. St Lucia, Australia: University of Queensland Press.

Brevini, B., & Woronov, T. (2017, October 25). Nothing but truthiness: Adani and co's post-truth push for the Carmichael Mine. *The Conversation*. Retrieved from https://theconversation.com/nothing-but-truthiness-adani-and-cos-post-truth-push-for-the-carmichael-mine-85671.2019

Brundtland, G. H. (1987). Our common future—Call for action. *Environmental Conservation, 14*(4), pp. 291–294. doi:10.1017/S0376892900016805

Burdon, P. (2015). *Earth jurisprudence: Private property and the environment*. Oxford, UK: Routledge.

Burdon, P. (2020). Extinction rebellion, knitting nannas and the silencing of dissent. *Australian Environment Review*. March, (pp. 205–209).

Burke, L. (2014, September 25). Nationals MP George Christensen calls Green activists "terrorists". *Sydney Morning Herald*. Retrieved from www.smh.com.au/politics/federal/nationals-mp-george-christensen-calls-green-activists-terrorists-20140925-10lt5a.html.

Christensen, G. (2016, February 8). House of representatives. Private members' Business. *Legal System and the Environment*, pp. 764–766.

Collett, M. (2019, October 9). Who are Extinction Rebellion and why are they blocking your commute to work? *ABC News*. Retrieved from www.abc.net.au/news/2019-10-09/who-are-extinction-rebellion-and-what-do-they-want/11581686.

Colvin, R. M. (2020). Social identity in the energy transition: An analysis of the "Stop Adani Convoy" to explore social-political conflict in Australia. *Energy Research & Social Science, 66*, 101492, pp. 1–12. doi: https://doi.org/10.1016/j.erss.2020.101492. Retrieved from https://www.sciencedirect.com/science/article/abs/pii/S2214629620300694Commonwealth. (2014). *Parliamentary Debates*. House of Representatives. 24 September 2014. 15. Retrieved from https://parlinfo.aph.gov.au/parlInfo/download/chamber/hansardr/7a89c07c-522e-4e24-9643-d3209145b417/toc_pdf/House%20of%20Representatives_2014_09_24_2852_Official.pdf;fileType=application%2Fpdf.

Commonwealth. (2017). *Estimates*. Legal and Constitutional Affairs Legislation Committee, Senate. 24 May 2017. Retrieved from https://parlinfo.aph.gov.au/parlInfo/search/display/display.w3p;query=Id:%22committees/estimate/807f7b9c-c877-4635-9061-8a8a4cff2c82/0003%22

Commonwealth. (2020). *Parliamentary Debates*. Senate. 11 February 2020. Retrieved from https://parli nfo.aph.gov.au/parlInfo/download/chamber/hansards/c220a265-e5aa-42c9-8cd9-19390fabb066/ toc_pdf/Senate_2020_02_11_7493_Official.pdf;fileType=application%2Fpdf.

Crawford, C. (2009). Civil liberties, Bjelke-Petersen and a bill of rights: Lessons for Queensland. *Bond Law Review, 2*(1), pp. 1–23. doi:10.53300/001c.5523

Crnogorcevic, L. (2019, March 8). School Strike 4 Climate: History, challenges and what's next. *Green Left Weekly, 1212* . Retrieved from https://www.greenleft.org.au/content/school-strike-4-climate-history-challenges-and-whats-next.

Crowley, K. (2017). Up and down with climate politics 2013–2016: The repeal of carbon pricing in Australia. *Wiley Interdisciplinary Reviews: Climate Change, 8*(3), p. 458.

CSG protester fined $2000 for blockade. (2011, 8 December). *Brisbane Times*. Retrieved from www.brisba netimes.com.au/national/queensland/csg-protester-fined-2000-for-blockade-20111208-1ol85.html.

Curran, G. (2017). Social licence, corporate social responsibility and coal seam gas: Framing the new political dynamics of contestation. *Energy Policy*, 101, pp. 427–435. doi: 10.1016/j.enpol.2016.10.042

Dgeiger. (2013, 6 March). Greenpeace to protest against Queensland's coal industry. *Daily Mercury*. Retrieved from www.dailymercury.com.au/news/greenpeace-protest-against-queenslands-coal-ind ust/1780855/

Dorling, P. (2012, 12 April). ASIO eyes green groups. *The Sydney Morning Herald*. Retrieved from www. smh.com.au/politics/federal/asio-eyes-green-groups-20120411-1wsba.html#ixzz1rmOVNarN.

Duffy, A. (2012, 12 April). Green groups are worse than terrorists: Government. *Australian Mining*. Retrieved from www.australianmining.com.au/news/green-groups-are-worse-than-terrorists--gov ernment/.

Elvey, A. (2020). Reimagining decolonising praxis for a just and ecologically sustainable peace in an Australian context. In Camilleri, J. & Guess, D. (Eds.) *Towards a just and ecologically sustainable peace* (pp. 275–295). Singapore: Palgrave Macmillan.

Extinction Rebellion. (n.d.). Retrieved from https://rebellion.global.

Extinction Rebellion, various individuals, (2019). *This is not a drill: An Extinction Rebellion handbook*. UK: Penguin.

Fitzgerald, R. (1984). *A history of Queensland from 1915 to the 1980s*. St Lucia: University of Queensland Press.

Galloway, K. (2012). Landowners' vs miners' property interests: The unsustainability of property as dominion. *Alternative Law Journal, 37*(2), pp. 77–81. https://doi.org/10.1177/1037969X1203700202.

Gas Fired Recovery (2020, September 15). Media release. Prime Minister, Minister for Energy and Emissions Reduction, Minister for Resources, Water and Northern Australia. Retrieved from www. minister.industry.gov.au/ministers/taylor/media-releases/gas-fired-recovery.

Graham, N. (2011). *Lawscape: Property, environment, law*. Sydney: Routledge.

Greenpeace Australia Pacific. (n.d.). Retrieved from www.greenpeace.org.au/

Greenpeace International. (n.d.). What We Do. Retrieved from www.greenpeace.org/international/ explore/

Grierson, J., & Dodd, V. (2020, January 12). Extinction Rebellion could sue police over extremist ideology listing. *The Guardian*. Retrieved from www.theguardian.com/environment/2020/jan/11/extinction-rebellion-could-sue-police-listing-extremist-ideology.

Gunningham, N. (2019). Averting climate catastrophe: Environmental activism, Extinction Rebellion and coalitions of influence. *King's Law Journal, 30*(2), pp. 194–202. https://doi.org/10.1080/09615 768.2019.1645424

Hamilton, C. (2015). Tree spiking = Beheading ergo Environmentalism = Terrorism. *The Conversation, 5 October 2015*. Retrieved from https://theconversation.com/tree-spiking-beheading-ergo-environme ntalism-terrorism-48568.

Harris-Hogan, S. (2017). *Violent Extremism in Australia: An Overview*. (Trends and Issues in Crime and Criminal Justice, No 491). Retrieved from https://aic.gov.au/publications/tandi/tandi491.

Hasler O. (2020). Mining as ecocide: The case of Adani and the Carmichael Mine in Australia. In Zabyelina Y. & van Uhm D. (Eds.) *Illegal mining*, Cham: Palgrave Macmillan. doi: https://doi.org/ 10.1007/978-3-030-46327-4_18

Heber, A. (2013, March 23). CSG tensions come to blows. *Australian mining*. Retrieved from www.austr alianmining.com.au/news/csg-tensions-come-to-blows/.

Henry, R. (1998). Performing protest, articulating difference: Environmentalists, Aborigines and the Kuranda Skyrail dispute. *Aboriginal History, 22,* pp. 143–161. doi:10.3316/ielapa.825123272974374

Hutton, D. (2012). Lessons from Lock the Gate Movement. *Social Alternatives, 31*(1), pp. 15–19. doi/10.3316/ielapa.201206396

Jakob, M., Steckel, J. C., Jotzo, F., Sovacool, B. K., Cornelsen, L., Chandra, R., & Urpelainen, J. (2020). The future of coal in a carbon-constrained climate. *Nature Climate Change, 10*(8), pp. 704–707. https://doi.org/10.1038/s41558-020-0866-1

James, E. (2019, November 14). Stoush over Tasmania's anti-protest push. *Canberra Times*. Retrieved from www.canberratimes.com.au/story/6492546/stoush-over-tasmanias-anti-protest-push/?cs=14231.

Jaques, T., & Galloway, C. (2012). Coal seam gas in Australia: Can activists be effective from the margins? *Asia Pacific Public Relations Journal, 13*(2), pp. 35–44. Jolley, C., & Rickards, L. (2020). Contesting coal and climate change using scale: Emergent topologies in the Adani mine controversy. *Geographical Research, 58*(1), pp. 6–23.

Jost, J. T., Barberá, P., Bonneau, R., Langer, M., Metzger, M., Nagler, J & Tucker, J. A. (2018). How social media facilitates political protest: Information, motivation, and social networks. *Advances in Political Psychology, 39*(1), pp. 85–118. doi: 10.1111/pops.12478.

Keenan, S. (2015). *Subversive property: Law and the production of spaces of belonging*. Oxford, UK: Routledge.

Kerbo, H. (1982). Movements of "crisis" and movements of "affluence": A critique of deprivation and resource mobilization theories. *The Journal of Conflict Resolution, 26*(4), pp. 645–663. DOI: 10.1177/0022002782026004004

Kia, A., & Ricketts, A. (2018). Enabling emergence: The Bentley blockade and the struggle for a gasfield free Northern Rivers. *Southern Cross University Law Review, 19*, pp. 49–74. https://ap01.alma.exlibrisgroup.com/discovery/delivery/61SCU_INST:61SCU/1267287000002368.

Křížkovský, M. (2019). Political Ecology as the ground for "new" antisystemic politics? The case of Extinction Rebellion and catastrophic imaginaries. Paper published at Transnational Institute of Social Ecology Conference, Athens, Greece, 25–27 October 2019.

Langford. S. (2019, October 19). The Queensland premier says environmental protesters are using devices "laced with traps". Is there any proof? *SBS The Feed*. Retrieved from www.sbs.com.au/news/the-feed/the-queensland-premier-says-environmental-protesters-are-using-devices-laced-with-traps-is-there-any-proof.

Lock the Gate calls for calm. (2012, December 18). *ABC News*. Retrieved from www.abc.net.au/news/2012-12-18/csg-calm/4433478?date=201212&pfm=ms&pfmredir=sm.

Lyons, K. (2019). Securing territory for mining when Traditional Owners say "No": The exceptional case of Wangan and Jagalingou in Australia. *The Extractive Industries and Society, 6*, pp. 756–766. https://doi.org/10.1016/j.exis.2018.11.007

McKnight, H. (2020). "The oceans are rising and so are we": Exploring utopian discourses in the School Strike for Climate movement. *Brief Encounters, 4*(1), pp. 48–63. DOI: https://doi.org/10.24134/be.v4i1.217

Minerals Council of Australia. (August 2017). Submission on tax deductible gift recipient reform opportunities Discussion Paper. doi: https://minerals.org.au/sites/default/files/MCA_submission_on_Tax_Deductible_Gift_Recipient_Reform_Opportunities_discussion_paper_4_Aug_2017%20(1).pdf.

Mitra, M. N. (2019). Grown-ups have failed us. *Earth Island Journal, Winter 2019*. Retrieved from www.earthisland.org/journal/index.php/magazine/entry/grown-ups-have-failed-us/

Morrison, S. (2019, November 1). Address, 2019 Queensland Resources Council annual lunch. Retrieved from www.pm.gov.au/media/address-2019-queensland-resources-council-annual-lunch.

Muncie, E. (2020). "Peaceful protesters" and "dangerous criminals": The framing and reframing of anti-fracking activists in the UK. *Social Movement Studies, 19*(4), pp. 464–481. doi:10.1080/14742837.2019.1708309.

Murphy, K., & Remeikis, A. (2020, 25 February). Dutton says "Leftwing Lunatics" must be dealt with as ASIO warns of far-right threat. *The Guardian*. Retrieved from www.theguardian.com/australia-news/2020/feb/25/dutton-says-leftwing-lunatics-must-be-dealt-with-as-asio-warns-of-far-right-threat.

Naess, A. (1989). *Ecology, community and lifestyle*. (Trans. Rothenberg, D.). Cambridge, UK: Cambridge University Press.

Neale, T., & Vincent, E. (2016). Instabilities and inequalities: Relations between Indigenous people and environmentalism in Australia today. In Vincent, E., & Neale, T. (Eds.). *Unstable relations: Indigenous people and environmentalism in contemporary Australia*. (pp. 1–24) Perth: Apollo Books.

Nedelsky, J. (1990). Law, boundaries and the bounded self. *Representations, 30* (Spring), pp. 162–189.

Nhanenge, J. (2011). *Ecofeminism: Towards integrating the concerns of women, poor people, and nature into development*. Plymouth UK: University Press of America.

Oosting, P. (2014, 2 April). Barrier Reef protesters are not "eco-terrorists", they're ordinary Australians. *The Guardian*. Retrieved from www.theguardian.com/commentisfree/2014/apr/02/barrier-reef-protesters-are-not-eco-terrorists-theyre-ordinary-australians.

Paris, N. (2019). Suppression of the right to protest. In T. Hollo (Ed.), *Rebalancing rights: Communities, corporations and nature* (pp. 35–48). Canberra, Australia: The Green Institute.

Reestorff, C. M. (2015). 'LEGO: Everything is not awesome!' A conversation about mediatized activism, Greenpeace, Lego, and Shell. *Conjunctions. Transdisciplinary Journal of Cultural Participation, 2*(1), pp. 21–43. https://doi.org/10.7146/tjcp.v2i1.22269

Remeikis, A. (2019, 3 October). Peter Dutton accused of sounding "like a dictator" after urging welfare cuts for protesters. *The Guardian*. Retrieved from www.theguardian.com/australia-news/2019/oct/03/peter-dutton-accused-dictator-urging-welfare-cuts-protesters.

Ricketts, A. (2017). Anti-protest laws: Lock up your nannas. *Alternative Law Journal, 42*(2), pp. 107–111. https://doi-org.libraryproxy.griffith.edu.au/10.1177/1037969X17710624

Ricketts, A. (2020). "We have the right to be arrested and processed according to law": The power of effective police liaison at the Bentley Blockade. *Journal of Australian Studies, 44*(3), pp. 384–400. doi: 10.1080/14443058.2020.1790629.

Rucht, D. (2017). Studying social movements: Some conceptual challenges. In S. Berger & H. Nehring (Eds.), *The history of social movements in global perspective: A survey* (pp. 39–62). London: Palgrave MacMillan. https://doi.org/10.1057/978-1-137-30427-8_2.

Rupić, M.C. (2020). *#StopAdani: The landscape of environmental activism in Australia* (Master's thesis, University of Hawai'i at Manoa, US). Retrieved from www.proquest.com/docview/2429057916?pq-origsite=gscholar&fromopenview=true.

School Strike for Climate. (2021). www.schoolstrike4climate.com/about.

Sengul, K. (2020). "Swamped": The populist construction of fear, crisis and dangerous others in Pauline Hanson's senate speeches. *Communication Research and Practice, 6*(1), pp. 20–37.

Stop Adani. (n.d.). www.stopadani.com/who_we_are.

Sutton, M. (2019, March 14). Climate change student strike inspired by politically correct teaching, academic says. *ABC News*. Retrieved from www.abc.net.au/news/2019-03-14/politically-correct-teaching-to-blame-for-climate-change-strike/10897682.

Uekötter, F. (2017). Myths, big myths and global environmentalism. In S. Berger & H. Nehring (Eds.), *The history of social movements in global perspective: A survey* (pp. 419–447). London: Palgrave MacMillan. https://doi.org/10.1057/978-1-137-30427-8_15.

Walker, P., Grierson, J., & Dodd, V. (2020, January 14). Putting Extinction Rebellion on extremist list "completely wrong", says Keir Starmer. *The Guardian*. Retrieved from www.theguardian.com/environment/2020/jan/13/priti-patel-defends-inclusion-of-extinction-rebellion-on-terror-list.

Walton, K. (2019, December 6). Climate crackdown: Australia throws rule book at activists. *Al Jazeera*. Retrieved from www.aljazeera.com/news/2019/12/16/climate-crackdown-australia-throws-rule-book-at-activists.

Westwell, E. & Bunting, J. (2020). The regenerative culture of Extinction Rebellion: Self-care, people care, planet care. *Environmental Politics, 29*(3), pp. 546–551. doi:10.1080/09644016.2020.1747136

Whitton, E. (1989). *The hillbilly dictator: Australia's police state*. Sydney, Australia: ABC Enterprises.

Wilkie, B. (2017). *The Daintree Blockade: The battle for Australia's tropical rainforests*. Mossman, Queensland: Four Mile Books.

Williams, G. (2011). A decade of Australian anti-terror laws. *Melbourne University Law Review, 35*, pp. 1136–1176.

Wilson, C. (2020, 12 February). An online conspiracy theory about the bushfires was aired in Australia's parliament. *BuzzFeed News*. Retrieved from www.buzzfeed.com/cameronwilson/politician-conspiracy-theory-australia-bushfires-far-right.

Wilson, T., & Walton, R. (2019). *Extremism Rebellion: A review of ideology and tactics*. Retrieved from https://policyexchange.org.uk/wp-content/uploads/2019/07/Extremism-Rebellion.pdf.

Woodward, A. (2019, September 20). Greta Thunberg turns 17 today. Here's how she started a global climate movement in just 18 months. *Business Insider Australia*. Retrieved from www.businessinsider.com.au/greta-thunberg-bio-climate-change-activist-2019-9?r=US&IR=T.

Wordsworth, M. (2019, October 19). Will Queensland's dangerous devices laws stop Extinction Rebellion protests? *ABC News*. Retrieved from www.abc.net.au/news/2019-10-19/queensland-dangerous-devi ces-laws-targeting-protest-movement/11617422.

Workman, A. (2017, 17 October). This politician wants environmental activists to be charged as terrorists. *BuzzFeed News*. Retrieved from www.buzzfeed.com/aliceworkman/eco-terrorists.

Zelko, F. (2017). Scaling Greenpeace: From local activism to global governance. *Historical Social Research/ Historische Sozialforschung, 42*(2), pp. 318–342. doi:10.12759/hsr.42.2017.2.31

30

"ANIMALS AND THE EARTH CAN'T WAIT – GET OFF YOUR ASS AND FIGHT!"

Animal Liberation Front Vigilantism in the Era of Climate Crisis

Genevieve Johnston

Introduction

In the current era of climate crisis, mass extinction, and ecosystem collapse, blame is rightly levied at the fossil fuel industries. Yet the 25–50% of global greenhouse gas emissions produced by animal agriculture (Knight & Tutu, 2013) is largely ignored. We are encouraged to use less water as glaciers melt and aquifers, lakes, and rivers dry up, but most meat-eaters do not know that 15,415 litres of water are used to produce a single kilogram of beef (Hoekstra, 2014). Massive dairy and meat lobbies in North America influence politicians to subsidize the industries to the tune of 38 billion U.S. dollars per year in the United States alone, while the U.S. Department of Agriculture spends 550 million dollars annually on pro-animal food advertising (Simon, 2013).

The Animal Liberation Front (ALF) is recognized across North America as a significant and formidable threat to this "animal industrial complex", which refers to the vast array of corporations and businesses that exploit animals for profit (Noske, 1989). The largely non-violent extremists that comprise the ALF place themselves in the front lines of a battle against these powerful behemoths to protect the earth and animals, not for human enjoyment or use, but for their own intrinsic value. These activists use direct action tactics to pursue the goal of animal liberation. Liberation means that all animals would be free and wild, living in their natural habitats without interference from humans, and all animal industries would eventually cease to exist (Best & Nocella, 2004).

This chapter contributes to the small body of sociological literature on animal liberation extremism in North America, and more broadly to discussions of online radicalization and non-violent extremism, through an analysis of recent activist-written documents from the ALF. Through a qualitative content analysis of online ALF documents, I will explore how North American ALF activists position themselves as vigilantes who mete out justice in societies where animals and ecosystems are considered to be disposable, consumable property by many of the people who profit from, eat and use animal products. The research questions that this chapter seeks to address are (1) How do the activists describe their motivations and the purpose of their actions? And, (2) How do they articulate their role in the broader context of animal liberation? First, I will describe the methods used to gather and analyse research for this work. Next, I will discuss the background, objectives, and tactical choices of the ALF. Then, I briefly discuss vigilantism and the political landscape in which ALF actions take place. Lastly, by analysing recent ALF actions, I will explore how activists position themselves as the hands of justice in the face of animal suffering and ecological destruction.

By revealing the influence of ecological and environmentalist narratives on ALF activist ideology, this research counters depictions of animal liberation extremism as single-issue activism. Specifically, this chapter sheds light on the ways in which ALF activists present themselves, and the direct actions they take on behalf of animals and the earth, as the last hope for ecological and species justice in societies where the majority view nature and animals as existing solely for human use.

Context

History

The ALF originated in England in the early 1970s, evolving from the hunt saboteurs movement – where activists blocked roads and confused hounds by laying false scents – into a broader movement to prevent all forms of animal cruelty (Molland, 2004). Activist Ronnie Lee founded a group of 30 activists after serving three years in prison for his role in a series of attacks against suppliers of animals for experimental research (Monaghan, 2013), and the ALF began a campaign that cost animal industries approximately £250,000 in one year (Combs, 2003). The ALF subsequently spread across the globe, and active cells currently exist in more than 80 countries worldwide.

ALF activity in North America began in the United States in the mid-1970s. Early actions included rescuing 30 cats from the Howard University Medical School in Washington, DC in 1972, the release of two dolphins from a Hawaiian research centre in 1977, and the liberation of a number of laboratory animals from the New York University Medical Centre in 1979 (Recarte, 2016). While early actions primarily targeted laboratories with a view to freeing animals, this has become vastly more difficult in the last few decades because of increased security and the criminalization of such activity, leading activists to change course. The majority of actions in the contemporary era consist of monkey wrenching and other forms of property damage, with the goal of inflicting economic harm to animal enterprises.

Organizational Structure

The ALF is not a group, nor an organization. It has no publicly known members or leaders, no physical office, no organizational structure of any kind. The ALF is, instead, an umbrella term for a non-violent extremist movement composed of clandestine, leaderless, autonomous activist cells. One can only become part of the ALF by taking action in the name of the ALF, and adhering to a set of guidelines (see **Table 30.1**), including one which states that no one, human or animal, may be harmed. Due to the leaderless, clandestine nature of ALF activism, it might seem that the ideological underpinnings of the ALF are less clear than for above-ground social movements. Joose (2007) argues that leaderless resistance movements allow for ideological inclusion in that they may include activists from both ends of the political spectrum because there is no one to decide who may or may not speak for them. These differences

Table 30.1 ALF guidelines

(i)	To liberate animals from places of abuse…and place them in good homes where they may live out their natural lives, free from suffering.
(ii)	To inflict economic damage on those who profit from the misery and exploitation of animals.
(iii)	To reveal the horror and atrocities committed against animals behind locked doors, by performing direct actions and liberations.
(iv)	To take all necessary precautions against harming any animal, human and nonhuman.
(v)	Any group of people who are vegetarians or vegan and who carry out actions according to these guidelines have the right to regard themselves as part of the Animal Liberation Front.

Source: North American Animal Liberation Front Press Office. (n.d.). "Guidelines of the Animal Liberation Front". Retrieved from: https://animalliberationpressoffice.org/NAALPO/background/).

notwithstanding, ALF activist ideology is founded on the belief that animals are sentient wild beings that desire and deserve autonomy, freedom, and empathy (Becker, 2006; Johnston & Johnston, 2020). Further, activists participate based on the belief that direct action alone can save animals and the wild places where they live from harm, and that all other avenues for seeking animal liberation have failed (Cordiero-Rodriegues, 2016).

Goals and Tactics

Unlike mainstream animal rights groups, such as People for the Ethical Treatment of Animals (PETA), the ALF is not concerned with changing consumer habits or petitioning lawmakers for welfare reforms. They seek radical socio-structural changes, and rather than becoming a single-issue movement, they focus on the many intersecting harms caused by human use of animals (Johnston & Johnston, 2017). Some activists reveal atrocious conditions via covert video recording in animal testing laboratories, fur farms, and slaughterhouses, and directly intervene to prevent further suffering and ecological devastation by releasing or rescuing animals in these facilities, and destroying property in order to increase operating costs.

Some argue that activists who engage tactics such as arson cannot be sure that no one is harmed by these actions, and others consider the destruction of property to be a form of violence (Cordiero-Rodriegues, 2016). Actions against animal industries are criminalized, and activists are often vilified as violent terrorists in media portrayals and within academic literature (Braddock, 2015) despite their explicit commitment to non-violence.[1] The use of direct action tactics position animal exploitation and the resultant damage to the earth as a dire and immediate problem that cannot be solved through conventional forms of protest, and one that will not wait for laws to change or animal industries to have a change of heart (Cooke, 2013). ALF activists engage in direct action as an immediate, local, micro-political intervention to prevent animal suffering and ecological harm, or to hinder the activities of animal enterprises that will render them less profitable (Jones, 2004). Perhaps the most measurable impact has been on fur farms and fur retailers in Canada and the United States, where ALF activists taking part in a campaign dubbed "Operation Bite Back" bankrupted many involved in the fur industry through a sustained campaign of mink releases, destruction of breeding records, and attacks on fur stores where expensive coats were destroyed with paint and rancid butter (NAALPO, 2015).

Despite the increased interest in vegan diets over the past decade, and a growing awareness of environmental issues as climate change advances, radical animal liberationists still find themselves at odds with the dominant culture in North America. The domestication, use, and abuse of animals for food, clothing, entertainment, and research are accepted by most people as necessary and desirable. Animal cruelty and ecological harm, even in the most egregious cases, is rarely revealed to the public and is unlikely to have serious, if any repercussions for the perpetrators. Similarly, in North America, even the most ambitious climate change targets and environmental protections set by progressive leadership (such as the current Liberal government's pledge to bring Canada to net-zero emissions by 2050), lack enforceability and action have been significantly derailed by the current COVID-19 crisis. Meanwhile, in the United States, former President Trump pulled the country out of its international commitments to the Paris Climate Accord, funded coal mining, opened oil exploration in the Arctic Wildlife Refuge, and installed a prominent climate change denier as the head of the Environmental Protection Agency. Granted, President Biden has now recommitted the United States to the Paris Accord, but the damage done to the environment will be difficult to repair. In this context, ALF activists feel they must take the law into their own hands. Their words express an understanding that vigilantism is the only moral choice available to respond to what they see as the horrendous injustices of animal confinement, abuse, exploitation, and the poisoning and clearcutting of wild places (Best, 2014). A commonly used phrase that reflects this position and is used in communiqués left behind after a direct action takes place is "there's no justice, there's just us".

Research Method
Collection of Online Data

Determining the perspectives of a clandestine, anonymous network of activists presents a methodological difficulty. For reasons of safety, those in the ALF cannot publicly identify themselves. While it is possible to interview activists who have been imprisoned for their actions (see, e.g., Liddick, 2006), the only other direct source of information about activists is the Communiqués they leave behind when they take direct action. These documents, written by the anonymous activists themselves, offer the most useful data for analysing ideological influences where activists cannot be studied directly (Joosse, 2007). The data analysed for this chapter is comprised of 316 documents collected from the North American Animal Liberation Press Office (NAALPO) website from 2010 to 2020, including 225 Communiqués, 13 essays, 12 interviews, as well as several press releases, mission statements, and pamphlets written by activists in Canada, Mexico, and the United States.

Coding

To code the data, I engaged a qualitative approach to content analysis which is rooted in critical scholarship (Krippendorf, 2004). The focus on interpretations of activists' words allowed me to reveal how they view reality and thus gain a deeper understanding of their motivations (Strega, 2005). To begin the coding process, all the documents were read to get a sense of the whole. This abductive process, where I imposed some predetermined ideas about content that might be of particular relevance to the research questions posed, consisted of highlighting sections that related to ecology, vigilantism, justice, love for animals, and calls to action. Next, I used an open coding method whereby codes freely emerge from the data (Creswell, 2014). To do this, I followed five steps of open coding as outlined by Creswell (2014) and Hsieh and Shannon (2005). A sample of documents was read, and codes were created which were then applied to the entire dataset, amending the codes when necessary. Codes were then organized into broader themes. The quotes which appear in the analysis are those which concretely and eloquently reflect the most common and relevant themes that were observed, or in some cases, serve to highlight counter-narratives that were present in the data. In the following section, I discuss the broad theme of vigilantism, and how ALF action is shaped by existing social and political conditions.

Vigilantism, Political Opportunity Structure and the ALF

Vigilantism as a Response to Structural Injustice

Although some scholars assert that vigilantism is merely a form of political violence (Rosenbaum & Sedberg, 1976), the term as used in this paper follows more closely to the definition provided by Les Johnston. Johnston (1996) asserts that vigilantism involves premeditated action by voluntary, private citizens who act without the support or authority of the state, use force or the threat of force in order to deter real or perceived deviance, and attempt to offer security or protection in response to an inadequate state. According to this definition, vigilantism can be seen not only as a form of extra-state policing of crime (Shih, 2016), but also as a means of social control (although, considering the perspectives of ALF activists on the state-sanctioned "crimes" and "murders" committed against animals by the animal–industrial complex, the former understanding may be emphasized). Sen and Pratton (2008) argue that vigilantism is likely to erupt in societies where there is overwhelming structural injustice, or when individual experiences of victimization are experienced collectively and societies experience a sustained atmosphere of violence.

In order to make sense of these conditions in regards to the ALF's activism, the term is usually not applied to human society, but rather to the lives of animals. Upending our viewpoint in this way provides us with a glimpse into what ALF activists experience as reality: (i) overwhelming structural injustice in societies that devalue and commodify nonhuman animal life; (ii) the constant, everyday violence and death of animals across the dizzying array of animal industries; (iii) collateral damage in the ecosystems destroyed by industries such as oil exploration, manufacturing, mining, forestry, shipping, construction, and so on. ALF activists internalize the individual and collective victimization of the animals they see and know are suffering and dying every second. Like other groups such as the feminist vigilantes in India analysed by White and Rastogi (2009), the ALF seeks to provide justice for those who are excluded from legal forms of justice and are repressed by the state – namely, nonhuman animals.

The ALF differs from many other vigilante movements in a key aspect, since the majority of activists engage in vigilante action either alone or with one or two others, rather than as a larger, more cohesive group. This is necessary not only because of the illegal nature of many of their actions, and their subsequent persecution by industry, governments, and law enforcement, but also because most people in North American societies are unsympathetic to ALF methods and objectives. In the next section, I discuss how, in this context, the suppression of less contentious forms of animal liberation activism may be influencing tactical and ideological shifts within the movement.

Political Opportunity Structure

The political climate in North America, where direct action is often treated as terrorism, would appear, at first glance, to stifle activism, but it is not so simple. The policing of protest, for example through the U.S.'s Animal Enterprise Terrorism Act (AETA), imposes strict sentences for activities which interfere with the operation of an animal enterprise, meaning even relatively peaceful and mainstream actions, such as pamphleting or holding a protest outside an animal enterprise, may be deemed an act of terrorism (McCoy, 2008). Seven activists involved in the Stop Huntingdon Animal Cruelty campaign in the United States received prison sentences for actions as seemingly innocuous as tying up phone and fax lines. In Canada, Bill C–51 makes it a criminal offence to express support for "terrorist" organizations. The Bill also labels many forms of radical activism such as blockades and the destruction of state property as terrorist acts, and allows for the *preventative* detainment of those suspected of intending to break the law (Parliament of Canada, 2015). The policing of previously legitimate forms of protest can, however, have the effect of pushing some activists towards direct action tactics. For example, the persecution of radical earth and animal activists through Operation Backfire in the United States did not deter ALF activists, but resulted in a flurry of actions dedicated to those imprisoned (Potter, 2011). U.S. ALF activists who liberated pheasants from a farm in Oregon in 2016 said that as well as acting in solidarity with their imprisoned comrades, "[t]his liberation was also done as a reminder that when we don't allow fear to prevent us from taking action to directly free animals, we render the AETA obsolete".[2,3]

While legislation and enforcement targeting activism falls into the category of *structural* political opportunity, which as noted has had a mixed impact on ALF activism, the widespread visibility of environmental issues and climate change, both in media coverage and in political rhetoric, constitutes what Meyer and Minkoff (2004) refer to as a *signaling opportunity*, which indicates how receptive the audience may be to the claims made by movements. Whether the ALF is able to reframe themselves as not only a movement for animals, but also for the earth, may lead to increased sympathy for the movement, but it is too soon to make this determination. In the analysis that follows, I share quotes from ALF activists that reveal how, in spite of attempts to persecute and repress their actions, they continue to fight. They do so with the understanding that they are among the few willing to directly defend animals and ecosystems in contemporary North America, despite the risk of punishment and incarceration.

Analysis

The analysis is divided into three thematic sections. The first, "Who is the Real Extremist?" discusses how ALF activists perceive the label of extremist, negotiate the need for extreme action in the face of extreme circumstances, and finally, how some of their more contentious opinions and statements continue to raise tension and set them apart from other less extreme forms of animal activism. The second section, "For the Wild", reveals the ecologically centred viewpoint of activists, and how their love for wild nature and revulsion towards industrialized, technologically advanced society motivates their vigilantism to punish those who refuse to treat animals and nature with respect. The final section "There's No Justice, There's Just Us", emphasizes how activists position themselves as the sole force fighting for animal liberation.

Who is the Real Extremist?

This quote reveals how one activist frames the label of extremist that is imposed on the ALF, while also pointing to the ways in which these labels are more appropriate for the industries they target:

> I would wear the word extremist as a badge if [it] means that I'm actually being disruptive to those industries that I'm trying to stop…It lets you know you're doing something right. So, extremist well, let me tell you what extreme is. Extreme is, as

I said, killing 10 billion animals every year for food. It's taking a knife to the throat of a cow simply to satisfy humans' very selfish taste for flesh. I would consider that to be very extreme.[4]

This activist, incarcerated on charges related to a mink farm release, demonstrates a common perspective on the meaning of extremism as it is applied to the ALF. While most do not perceive themselves to be extremists, they understand that the label is often applied by law enforcement and industry to activists who have a measurable impact on the industry. Some supporters of animal liberation find the label of extremist to be hypocritical, and inappropriate (Sorenson, 2011), but to some it is a badge of honour. Unlike more mainstream activists in the animal rights and welfare sectors, the ALF seeks to directly intervene to protect animals from suffering, and to target animal industry not via legislation or consumer appeals, but by directly affecting profits via sabotage and the release of captive animals (Jones, 2012; Upton, 2012):

> We, the unsilent minority (the 1%, if you will), choose a more direct form of action. we're not delusional enough to believe that this action will shut down the [name] company, let alone have any effect on factory farming as a whole. but we maintain that this type of action still has worth, if not solely for the participant's peace of mind, then to show that despite guards, a constant worker presence, and razorwire fence, the enemy is still vulnerable.[5]
>
> Abusing and torturing animals in horrific conditions of confinement will not continue to be tolerated in Ontario…We call on the fur farmers of Ontario to close your animal prisons and find new and rewarding careers. If you do not close these farms down, we will close them down for you.[6]

Although the second communiqué above calls on governments and farmers to end animal exploitation, it is clear that ALF activists are not idealists that believe that society can be shocked, shamed or persuaded to live peaceably with animals. Indeed, if these sorts of tactics worked, the work of PETA and similar groups to make visible the suffering of captive animals would have swayed society into widespread veganism long ago. The intention of ALF actions is not to steer society towards a more just and ethical treatment of animals. Instead, they are monkeywrenching tactics designed to create difficulties and raise costs for those who choose to profit from the exploitation of animals, with the intention of making these industries too high risk or too unprofitable to continue (Cooke, 2013).

In some cases, these tactics have been effective. The notorious Huntingdon Life Sciences, which operated animal testing laboratories in the United States and United Kingdom, went bankrupt after a sustained campaign by the group Stop Huntingdon Life Sciences (SHAC), who were labelled an extremist group by both the Federal Bureau of Investigation and the Canadian Security Intelligence Service (CSIS) (Walby & Monaghan, 2011). The UK arm of SHAC gained a level of notoriety in 2011 after Brian Cass, the managing director of Huntingdon Life Sciences (HLS), was attacked by activists wielding a baseball bat at a demonstration outside his home.

The question of violence is unquestionably one that is a subject of debate in the animal liberation extremist movement. Although the ALF is non-violent according to their definition of the word, some supporters of the ALF argue that violence is justified in some instances (Flükiger, 2009). For example, some of the past and current Press Officers of NAALPO have called into question the non-violent policy of the ALF. Some ALF activists themselves use threats in order to persuade industry executives to stop harming animals, while stopping short of harming people, as in this communiqué left behind following the liberation of turkeys from a factory farm in Canada: "Exploiters should live in fear, anxiety and torment for the heinous crimes they inflict on our animal comrades. It's about fuckin time they feel exactly what nonhumans feel. We are not playing nice anymore".[7]

It is an overstatement to say that the typical ALF activist is a misanthrope who puts the lives of animals before those of humans. However, there is an element of truth to this. Yet the belief that the lives of animals are more worthy than some human lives does not seem to arise from a misguided hatred of humanity. Rather, it is based on the scientifically backed knowledge that humans are responsible for the current ecological crisis, and are collectively guilty of significantly more violence, destruction and death than any other species. It is undeniable that nearly all ecological and species destruction, pollution, and emissions are a result of the actions of the human species alone – and more specifically, by people living in wealthy, industrialized nations such as Canada and the United States. One imprisoned ALF activist bluntly stated:

> Animals are inherently better than human beings. To clarify, when I say "Animals" this is merely shorthand for "all life upon the planet, minus us". And by "inherently better" I mean collectively, and most of the time individually, more important to the healthy functioning of the Planet than we are. Animals are far more civil, much more intuitive, and far less wicked and worthless than the human race…I am taking the misanthropic position from here on out.[8]

Another anonymously posted essay made a similarly misanthropic point regarding the COVID-19 pandemic, which they viewed as not nearly *enough* of a curb to the destructive habits of human society:

> The majority of the 7.7 billion humans wrecking [sic] havoc on our planet and tor-turing and murdering hundreds of billions of non-human animals annually are con-tinuing to go about their evil business as usual. If one believes, as we do, that humans are the real virus infecting planet earth, we can only bemoan the fact that so many humans will likely remain viable throughout the current pandemic.[9]

These are certainly extreme and contentious views. It is somewhat confusing, and perhaps in some ways hypocritical, to advocate the decimation of the human species while simultaneously being a member of it. It is clear, then, that some activists view themselves as holding a different status among humans as an animal ally – or even by claiming their own animality:

> I reject humanism, its authoritarian roles and traditions and its assigned identity which limits my potential to explore my own animality beyond civilized domestication. There is a war to be waged against society, alongside the non-human animals who refuse domesticated subservience, and who are evicted from their homes due to mass deforestation, human development and technology.[10]

The average omnivorous person in North America is responsible for the deaths of 7000 animals over their lifetime, and for enormous amounts of water, emissions, deforestation, pollution and ecosystem destruction that result from the production, slaughter, packaging, and trans-port of meat. According to the UN Food and Agriculture Organization, the United States produced 46.8 million tons of meat in 2018, Mexico 7 tons, and Canada nearly 5 tons – and these numbers increase every year (Ritchie, 2017). As noted previously, animal agriculture is an extremely ecologically damaging practice, particularly on the large-scale factory farms common in North America (Skolnik, 2017). As revealed in the next section, ALF activists mourn the devastation to wild animals and places which has been brought about by modern capitalist society and human consumption of animals and animal products.

For the Wild

ALF activists are fiercely protective of the natural world and its nonhuman inhabitants, and many hold a principled belief that ecosystems and their inhabitants have an intrinsic value in their own right. ALF activists share with their comrades in the radical earth liberation movement a deep sense of connection and passion for animals and the wild places they inhabit (Becker, 2006; Scarce, 1993). Activists view themselves as inherently wild creatures desiring freedom just as other animals do, countering Enlightenment discourses of human domination over nature (Gaard, 1993). The caging and penning of animals whose natural habitats are great expanses of field, river, and sky are painful for activists, who feel a deep connection with their wild brothers and sisters (Becker, 2006). A communiqué from a release at a mink farm in Guelph, Canada, noted that "[w]e felt we had no choice but to release as many mink as possible from this hell hole. We rejoiced as we watched scores of them escape into the surrounding woods to freedom" (2015). Approximately one quarter of ALF communiqués in this study demonstrate a sense of connection and empathy with wild animals and the earth, or mention a "love of animals" or of "the wild". This is a driving force behind ALF actions. The use of emotional rationales for activism has been dismissed as a stereotypically feminine and weak appeal (Korobov, 2011) by most mainstream animal rights philosophy, which is characterized by masculine preoccupation with rationality (Donovan, 2011; Kheel, 2008). Yet ALF activists, despite their reputation for extreme tactics and intimidating words, feel a deep love for the creatures they fight to free. Below, activists describe a captive lynx freed from a fur farm:

> The sight of a creature so majestic in a state so pathetic cannot be done justice with words. Emaciated and filthy, his beauty was evident even through the matted fur and traumatized stare…to be in such proximity to this creature, staring into his haunting yellow eyes, changed every member of our cell. We could only speculate as to how he had suffered and what he had seen, but we could know with certainty that he deserved a shot at freedom. We opened his cage and left.
>
> There were only two foxes found on the property. They were tall, beautiful and black with glowing eyes…They would only come out if I backed away and watched from afar. As soon as they were out of their cages, they joyously galloped around in circles. It was the most beautiful thing to see. Raiding a fur farm can easily be done by a single person with enough courage and love to do so.[11]

While how a person feels or thinks about animal exploitation may not directly change anything, it seems likely that only those with deep convictions about animal liberation and justice would be willing to put their own freedom on the line to protect and defend animals. In the quote below, which followed an elk farm release, we see how ALF activists view their actions as incremental movements towards the broader goal of total animal liberation:

> With this act we attempted to remove the last barrier between these wild creatures and their new, free lives. Link by link, these barriers will be dismantled in our society,

to create a new ethic of freedom and accountability. Assist us in the struggle for liberation, or stand on the wrong side of history.[12]

As advocates for wild nature, many activists are critical of modern industrialized societies, and what they see as the artificial and human-engineered development of science and technology. They understand many industrial and technological advancements as tools to control and pacify society and separate people from nature (Becker, 2006). After U.S. activists glued locks, smashed windows, and painted green anarchy symbols on a Kentucky Fried Chicken building in Illinois, they left behind a note that signed off "[w]ith hostility towards speciesism and anthropocentric domination and for the destruction of all prisons, cages, and civilized systems of industrial control".[13] Many activists seek a world where humans return to a more natural and harmonious relationship with the earth, and envision a life where socially constructed boundaries and hierarchies between humans, other animals, and ecosystems are dissolved, reflecting an ecocentric, or ecologically centred view that is shared by deep ecologists and ecofeminists (Gaard, 1993; Scarce, 1990; Starhawk, 2004).

> For some of us it was the first liberation of our lives, for many it will not be the last. You feel a great empathy and a gentle tingling in your stomach when the animals look in your eyes…feeling the earth under their feet when only days before they were in tiny cages waiting to be killed. You feel like a part of you is going to be freed with them, and that part of you will be lost in the immensity of the forest.[14]

Activists in upstate New York who dismantled a hunting stand in 2019 stated simply, "[w]e hate this speciesist civilization and want to see the end of the murder and oppression of wildlife".[15] Nearly one-third of Mexican ALF documents critiqued technological and industrial development, with slightly lower percentages among those from the United States and Canada. In Mexico, activists also tend to take action not only against industries that exploit animals but against many beacons of capitalism such as banks and factories. Many view all capitalist enterprises to be exploitative to the earth, animals and people – but rather than seeking a communist or socialist alternative, they envision the total collapse of industrialized, capitalist society. Like some anarchists, Indigenous peoples, ecofeminists, and deep ecologists, many ALF activists "share a desire to recreate the values of a past age when…maternal thinking or the instinctive knowledge of Indigenous peoples enabled human societies to live in harmony with the natural world" (Bretherton, 2001, para. 44). One example is seen below:

> Our proposal is to negate the artificial reality that civilization has constructed, not indirectly, but by seeking a way of life that doesn't involve domination, the most autonomous way of life possible within wild ecosystems and without intermediaries.[16]

By liberating captive wild animals and destroying the very tools which cause harm to animals and ecosystems, activists demonstrate an understanding that people are but one species among many millions, and that they must do everything possible to prevent the human-driven annihilation of our common home: the earth. Activists strike out against industrialized animal enterprise and consumer culture, citing the harm it inflicts on animals and the earth. They act knowing that they may be the animals' only hope.

"There's No Justice, There's Just Us"

Those who engage in ALF action understand themselves to be the sole force directly intervening between the suffering and dying animals and their captors. They view their work as the lone force for justice in a deeply anthropocentric, and sometimes cruel world. In doing so, they refuse the notion that justice can only be brought about through top-down control, and instead seek to dissolve hierarchy and bring about change from the bottom up (Luke, 2007). In this sense they are vigilantes for animals, taking action where no one else will to release and rescue them:

> The souls of the tortured dead cry out for justice. The cry of the living is for freedom. We can create that justice. We can deliver that freedom. The animals have no one but us. We will not fail them.[17]

Activists understand themselves as special, however, not because of any superhuman ability, special skills, or moral superiority, but rather because of their bravery and willingness to do what it takes, despite personal risk. While others stand by and decry animal abuse and protest against the animal industrial complex, only the ALF is doing something in the here and now to prevent suffering; they are a living example of the compassion they envision in a future where animals are free and the earth is protected (Johnston & Johnston, 2020). For these activists, it is the only option their conscience can accept:

> It is a glorious thing that we live in a world where individuals regularly demonstrate the ultimate act of compassion – risking their freedom for the freedom of others.
> They will say that we will not stop short of the complete and total end of the killing of animals for their fur. On this point we are in total agreement. We act with love in our hearts.[18]

While this communiqué gently urges others to join the fight by lauding the bravery and self-lessness of those engaging in direct action, other activists expressed impatience with those who support the cause of animal liberation but do not take an active role in bringing it about. This attitude is visible in the following press release calling for interested activists to take part in "grassroots escalation workshops" in Florida:

> If you understand the animals are in a state of emergency and want to do more, then you are one of us. If you want to continue to write "radical" blogs, use tough words online, and pontificate to a bunch of vegan drones from a Facebook pedestal, then you are one of them. We've drawn our line in the sand…Please join us. Because we are AT WAR.[19]

The justification of radical direct action tactics is often made by calling out the inadequacies of other forms of activism, not only those within the mainstream animal welfare and rights movements, but those who encourage others to engage in direct action without doing so themselves. In the quote above, these people are not just disparaged but constructed as the enemy, or as "one of them". Even those who support the ALF are not spared the ire of the "real" activists who see themselves as freedom fighters and everyone else as passive observers:

We must use our privilege as humans to fight back against the system that keeps animals oppressed. Calling out everyone who talks the animal liberation talk but does not take action. You have temporary freedom to lose, the animals lose their entire lives. They can't wait. The earth can't wait. Get off your ass and FIGHT.[20]

The allusions to battle present in both the quotes above ("war" and "fight") demonstrate the seriousness with which activists view the plight of animals and earth against the existential threat posed to them by human activity. Approximately 20% of ALF documents analysed in this study used warlike terminology. ALF raids on animal breeders and acts of property destruction are often referred to as "attacks", or as retaliation for the attacks on animal life and ecosystems. Animal enterprises are labelled "the enemy", and activists speak of "battles" in which activists sabotage and counter-surveil animal industry owners in response to threats of violence against them. Activists feel that there is no time to lose, no other course of action to take, and that only their own direct actions can address the immediacy of what they see as an all-out war waged by humans against animals and the earth. This uncompromising perspective is necessary, perhaps, for activists to gather the courage to take actions which place their own lives and freedom at such a great risk.

Conclusion

The non-violent extremists that make up the ALF refuse to accept our deeply hierarchical, speciesist societies and their seeming disregard for earth and its animal inhabitants. While governments are beginning to awaken to the dire climate emergency we find ourselves in, their actions remain shamefully inadequate to the danger posed to human and animal life by continuing on our present course. At the time of writing, newly inaugurated U.S. President Biden rejoined the Paris Climate Agreement and canceled the permit for the Keystone XL oil pipeline, two actions which are assumed to indicate a strong commitment to addressing the environmental crisis. Whether it will be enough, with scientists telling us we have less than a decade to prevent irreversible and catastrophic environmental damage, remains to be seen. The world is currently undergoing a rate of species loss that is unprecedented in human existence. Our oceans, the animals that live there, and even our own bodies, are filled with plastic. Forests are disappearing, the old-growth forests which are home to countless species are clear-cut for toilet paper, while rainforests are slashed and burned for cattle ranching (Steinfeld et al., 2006).

In this context, the ALF and other radical activists like them, who seek to directly intervene to liberate animals and destroy exploitative and ecologically harmful industries, find themselves on "the right side of history". While many of us attempt to change the world through changing our lifestyles, consuming differently, or by urging the government to enact stronger environmental or animal protection policy, ALF activists risk prison sentences to strike a blow against exploitation at its source. Motivated by a love of wild nature and the animals who live there, and justifiably angry at human society for destroying nature for our own benefit, ALF activists perceive themselves as a small but irrepressible force fighting for justice.

Yet, although there has been a slow shift in the past decade towards greater societal awareness and interest for animal welfare issues, both in North America and elsewhere, scholarly and public opinion on the legitimacy and moral justifiability of ALF action remains weighted against the movement, often depicting animal liberation extremists as dangerously misanthropic and militant – or, at best, misguided (Francione, 2009; Posluszna, 2015). Like many other non-violent extremists, the ALF exists in the outer fringes of the animal liberation movement, and the ongoing criminalization and persecution of activists by governments and powerful animal industry lobbyists makes it ever more dangerous to take part in ALF actions. Perhaps because of these stresses, it is also possible to understand these activists as compassionate, dedicated and brave individuals who truly hope for, and work towards creating a better world. I close with a quote from an imprisoned ALF activist, which reflects a cautious optimism:

> [H]umanity will stop using the dead bodies of animals for food, research and entertainment, or we will continue to ultimately destroy the environment, which is caused largely by animal agriculture and industrialized civilization. The real question is: will our species become aware and become part of the ecosystem rather than harm it?[21]

Notes

1 Violence, as understood by the ALF, is defined by causing physical harm to a living creature, and does not include damaging property, as do some definitions of violence (Cordiero-Rodriegues, 2016).
2 Communique. Feb 29, 2016. North American Animal Liberation Press Office.
3 In order to protect the confidentiality of activists, the names of posts and associated hyperlinks have not been included for the quotations shared here.
4 Interview (U.S.). (2010, March 31). Retrieved from: North American Animal Liberation Press Office website.
5 Communiqué (U.S.). (2012, January 9). Retrieved from: North American Animal Liberation Press Office website.
6 Communiqué (Canada). (2015, October 2). Retrieved from: North American Animal Liberation Press Office website.
7 Communiqué (Canada). (2020, June 16). Retrieved from: North American Animal Liberation Press Office website.
8 Essay. (U.S.) (2020, January 22). Retrieved from: North American Animal Liberation Press Office website.
9 Essay (U.S.). (2020, April 11). Retrieved from: North American Animal Liberation Press Office website.
10 Essay (Location unknown). (2018, December 1). Retrieved from: North American Animal Liberation Press Office website.
11 Communiqué (U.S.). (2013, August 13). Retrieved from: North American Animal Liberation Press Office website.
12 Communiqué (U.S.). (2011, September 1). Retrieved from: North American Animal Liberation Press Office website.
13 Communiqué (U.S.). (2019, November 21). Retrieved from: North American Animal Liberation Press Office website.
14 Communiqué (U.S.). (2010, May 6). Retrieved from: North American Animal Liberation Press Office website.
15 Communiqué (U.S.). (2019, June 9). Retrieved from: North American Animal Liberation Press Office website.
16 Communiqué (Mexico). (2011, March 3). Retrieved from: North American Animal Liberation Press Office website.
17 Communiqué (U.S.). (2013, September 29). Retrieved from: North American Animal Liberation Press Office website.
18 Communiqué (U.S.). (2013, July 30). Retrieved from: North American Animal Liberation Press Office website.
19 Press Release. (U.S.) (2016, February 15). Retrieved from: North American Animal Liberation Press Office website.
20 Communiqué (U.S.). (2019, July 23). Retrieved from: North American Animal Liberation Press Office website.
21 Interview (U.S.). (2014, June 21). Retrieved from: North American Animal Liberation Press Office website.

Bibliography

Alonso Recarte, C. (2016). Animal liberation, American anti-terrorist culture and Denis Hennelly's Bold Native. *Critical Studies on Terrorism, 9*(2), 247–268. https://doi.org/10.1080/17539153.2016.1163864

Amster, R. (2006). Perspectives on ecoterrorism: Catalysts, conflations and casualties. *Contemporary Justice Review, 9*(3): 287–301. https://doi.org/10.1080/10282580600827991

Becker, M. (2006). Ontological anarchism: The philosophical roots of revolutionary environmentalism. In: Best, S. and Nocella II, A.J. (eds.), *Igniting a Revolution: Voices in Defence of the Earth,* (pp. 71–91) Oakland, CA: AK Press.

Best, S. (2014). *The Politics of Total Liberation: Revolution for the 21st Century.* New York, NY: Palgrave Macmillan.

Best, S. & Nocella II, A. J. (2004). *Terrorists or Freedom Fighters? Reflections on the Liberation of Animals.* New York, NY: Lantern Books.

Braddock, K. (2015). The utility of narratives for promoting radicalization: The case of the Animal Liberation Front. *Dynamics of Asymmetric Conflict, 8*(1), 38–59. https://doi.org/10.1080/17467586.2014.968794

Bretherton, C. (2001). Ecocentric identity and transformative politics. *International Journal of Peace Studies, 6*(2). www.gmu.edu/programs/icar/ijps/vol6_2/Bretherton.htm

Combs, C.C. (2003). *Terrorism in the Twenty-First Century,* (3rd ed). Upper Saddle River, NJ: Prentice Hall.

Cooke, S. (2013). Animal rights and environmental terrorism. *Journal of Terrorism Research, 4*(2), 26–36. https://doi.org/10.15664/jtr.532

Cordeiro-Rodrigues, L. (2016). Is the Animal Liberation Front morally justified in engaging in violent and illegal activism towards animal farms? *Critical Studies on Terrorism, 9*(2), 226–246. https://doi.org/10.1080/17539153.2016.1142797

Creswell, J. W. (2014). *Research Design: Qualitative, Quantitative and Mixed Methods Approaches.* Los Angeles, CA: Sage.

Donovan, J. (1996). Attention to suffering: A feminist caring ethic for the treatment of animals. *Journal of Social Philosophy, 27*(1), 81–102. https://doi.org/10.1111/j.1467-9833.1996.tb00228.x

Flükiger, J.M. (2009). The radical animal liberation movement: Some reflections on its future. *Journal for the Study of Radicalism, 2,* 111–132. https://doi.org/10.1353/jsr.0.0000

Gaard, G. (1993). *Ecofeminism: Women, Animals, Nature.* Philadelphia, PA: Temple University Press.

Hoekstra, A.Y. (2014) Water for animal products: a blind spot in water policy, *Environmental Research Letters, 9*(9): 091003. https://doi.org/10.1088/1748-9326/9/9/091003

Hsieh, H., & Shannon, S. E. (2005). Three approaches to qualitative content analysis. *Qualitative Health Research, 15,* 1277–1288. https://doi.org/10.1177/1049732305276687

Johnston, G., & Johnston, M.S. (2020). "Until every cage is empty": Frames of justice in the radical animal liberation movement. *Contemporary Justice Review, 23*(4), 563–580. https://doi.org/10.1080/10282580.2020.1719361

Johnston, G., & Johnston, M.S. (2017). "We fight for all living things": Countering misconceptions about the radical animal liberation movement. *Social Movement Studies, 16*(6), 735–751. https://doi.org/10.1080/14742837.2017.1319268

Johnston, L. (1996). What is vigilantism? *British Journal of Criminology, 36*(2): 220– 236. https://doi.org/10.1093/oxfordjournals.bjc.a014083

Jones, p. (2004). Mothers with monkeywrenches: Feminist imperatives and the ALF. In: Best, S. and Nocella II, A. J. (eds.), *Terrorists or Freedom Fighters? Reflections on the Liberation of Animals* (pp. 137–156). New York, NY: Lantern Books.

Joosse, P. (2007). Leaderless resistance and ideological inclusion: The case of the Earth Liberation Front. *Terrorism and Political Violence, 19*(3), 351–368. https://doi.org/10.1080/09546550701424042

Kheel, M. (2008). *Nature Ethics: An Ecofeminist Perspective.* Lanham, MD: Rowman & Littlefield.

Knight, A. & Tutu, D. (2013). Animal agriculture and climate change. In A. ç(ed) *The Global Guide to Animal Protection* (p. 254–256). Urbana, IL: University of Illinois Press.

Korobov, N. (2011). Young men's vulnerability in relation to women's resistance to emphasized femininity. *Men and Masculinities, 14*(1), 51–75. Doi: https://doi.org/10.1177/1097184X093569

Krippendorf, K. (2004). *Content Analysis: An Introduction to Its Methodology.* Beverly Hills, CA: Sage.

Luke, B. (2007). *Brutal: Manhood and the Exploitation of Animals.* Urbana, IL: University of Illinois Press.

Meyer, D. S. (2004). Protest and political opportunities. *Annual Review of Sociology, 30,* 125–145. https://doi.org/10.1146/annurev.soc.30.012703.110545

McCoy, K. (2008). Subverting justice: An indictment of the Animal Enterprise Terrorism Act. *Animal Law, 14,* 53–70.

Molland, N. (2004). "Thirty Years of Direct Action". In S. Best & Nocella II, A. J. (eds.), *Terrorists or Freedom Fighters: Reflections on the Liberation of Animals* (pp. 65–81). New York, NY: Lantern Books.

Monaghan, R. (2013). Not quite terrorism: Animal rights extremism in the United Kingdom, *Studies in Conflict & Terrorism, 36*(11), 933–951.https://doi.org/10.1080/1057610X.2013.832117

Morris, M. C., and Thornhill, R. H. (2006). Animal liberationist responses to non-anthropogenic animal suffering. *World Views: Global Religions, Culture, and Ecology, 10*(3): 355–379. https://doi.org/10.1163/156853506778942077

NAALPO (North American Animal Liberation Press Office. (2015). 9 July. "Second Massive Mink Release in Two Months in Ontario (Canada)". Press release. Retrieved from: https://animalliberation pressoffice.org/NAALPO/category/press-releases/

Noeske, B. (1989). *Humans and Other Animals: Beyond the Boundaries of Anthropology.* London, UK: Pluto Press.

Parliament of Canada. (2015). Statuses of Canada 2015: Bill C-51. Retrieved from: www.parl.gc.ca/HousePublications/Publication.aspx?Language=E&Mode=1&DocId=8056977

Posłuszna, E., Scott, S., & Cruz, M. (2015). *Environmental and Animal Rights Extremism, Terrorism, and National Security.* Kidlington, England: Butterworth-Heinemann.

Potter, W. (2011). *Green Is the New Red: An Insider's Account of a Social Movement under Siege.* San Francisco, CA: City Lights.

Regan, T. (1983). *The Case for Animal Rights.* London: Routledge and Kegan Paul.

Ritchie, H. (2017.) Meat and Dairy Production. *OurWorldInData.org.* Retrieved from: https://ourworl dindata.org/meat-production

Rosenbaum, H. J., and Sedberg, P. C., eds. (1976). *Vigilante Politics.* Pennsylvania: University of Pennsylvania Press.

Sagoff, M. (2001). Animal liberation and environmental ethics: Bad marriage, quick divorce. In: Zimmerman, M. E., Callicott J. B., Sessions, G., Warren, K. J., and J. Clark (eds.), *Environmental Philosophy: From Animal Rights to Radical Ecology* (pp. 87–96). Upper Saddle River, NJ: Prentice-Hall.

Scarce, R. (1990). *Eco-Warriors: Understanding the Radical Environmental Movement.* Chicago, IL: Noble Press.

Sen, A., & Pratten, D. (2008). Global Vigilantes: Perspectives on Justice and Violence. In D. Pratten and A. Sen (eds.) *Global Vigilantes* (pp. 1–21). New York: Columbia University.

Shih, E. (2016). Not in my "Backyard Abolitionism": Vigilante rescue against american sex trafficking, *Sociological Perspectives, 59*(1), 66–90. doi: 10.1177/0731121416628551.

Simon, D. R. (2013). *Meatonomic$.* San Francisco, CA: Conari Press.

Skolnik, A. (2017). The CAFO Industry's Impact on the Environment and Public Health. *Sierra: the National Magazine of the Sierra Club,* 17 February. Retrieved from: www.sierraclub.org/sierra/2017-2-march-april/feature/cafo-industrys-impact-environment-and-public-health

Sorenson, J. (2011). Constructing extremists, rejecting compassion: Ideological attacks on animal advocacy from right and left. In: J. Sanbonmatsu (ed.), *Critical Theory and Animal Liberation* (pp. 219–237). Lanham, MD: Rowman and Littlefield.

Starhawk. (2004). *The Earth Path: Grounding Your Spirit in the Rhythms of Nature.* San Francisco, CA: Harper.

Steinfeld, H. et al. (2006). Livestock's Long Shadow: Environmental Issues and Options. Rome, Italy: Food and Agriculture Organization of the United Nations. Retrieved from: www.fao.org/docrep/010/a07 01e/a0701e00.htm.

Strega, S. (2005). The view from the Poststructural margins: Epistemology and methodology reconsidered. In L. Brown and S. Strega (eds.), *Research as Resistance: Critical, Indigenous and Anti-oppressive Approaches* (pp. 199–235).Toronto, ON: Canadian Scholars Press.

Upton, A. (2012). "Go on, get out there, and make it happen": Reflections on the first ten years of Stop Huntingdon Animal Cruelty (SHAC). *Parliamentary Affairs, 65*(1), 238–254. https://doi.org/10.1093/pa/gsr027

Walby, K., & Monaghan, J. (2011). Private eyes and public order: Policing and surveillance in the suppression of animal rights activists in Canada. *Social Movement Studies, 10*(1), 21–37. https://doi.org/10.1080/14742837.2011.545225

31

THE PHONEY WAR?

Radical Environmentalists, Animal Rights Activists and Direct Action

Paul Stott

Introduction

This chapter considers the concept of direct action, and its utilisation by UK political activists in the arenas of animal rights activism and environmentalism across five decades from the 1970s to the 2020s. It focuses on the political tensions within the concept of direct action, an approach characteristically centred on achieving immediate campaign aims, ahead of legal or democratic niceties. A further theme is the changing nature of green activism. Direct action is now proposed and conducted in a political structure where the prominence of environmentalist campaigns, and the representation of green ideals, is greater than ever before. It occurs to a narrative of ecological collapse, a crisis narrative that is accepted by campaigners, and also to an extent, by political elites and government.

This text critically examines the environmental protests led by Extinction Rebellion to argue a conversation develops between protestors and the authorities, and a degree of collaboration appears to be necessary if non-violent direct action is not to be followed by more aggressive tactics. In the specific case of the animal rights movement, it is argued that the success of activists in achieving their political goals, was followed by a reduction in militancy. The war of ideas within organisations occurs against both this historical backdrop, but also unique contemporary circumstances. The growing consensus around a climate emergency, and this being our "darkest hour" (Extinction Rebellion, 2019, p. 1) adds genuine tension to existing debates. If activists believe the world as it is currently operating is doomed, they presumably must win the political struggles they engage in, and win quickly?

The research methodology utilised here is rooted in the use of open-source research methods to identify key themes via activist websites, publications and statements from individuals and groups such as Greta Thunberg, Extinction Rebellion, the Animal Liberation Front (ALF), and Hunt Saboteurs Association. An analysis of primary source material from Extinction Rebellion's theorists is used to establish the organisation's aims and objectives, and activist publications from the green and animal rights milieu dating back to the 1980s are cited. In 2016 two interviews were conducted with Ronnie Lee, one of the key figures in the history of the animal rights movement in this country, and Paul Rogers, the former editor of the *Green Anarchist* newspaper.

DOI: 10.4324/9781003032793-36

The chapter is structured in the following manner. There is first a discussion of the difficulty in locating green political actors on the traditional left/right scale. This leads into a consideration of why deeds have come to be prioritised by both environmentalists and animal rights activists, ahead of ideological positions. This organising principle is demonstrated to be several decades old, but as subsequent sections on Greta Thunberg and Extinction Rebellion demonstrate, direct action is now conducted to the backdrop of a clock seen to be ticking towards environmental destruction. Finally, in an overview of Extinction Rebellion, and its interaction with the authorities, it is argued that the organisation's illiberal tendencies, combined with its core narrative of climate crisis, do not form a barrier against extremism.

Political Classifications: A Challenge

One problem when seeking to analyse animal rights and environmentalist campaigns is a distinct lack of agreement in terms of how we might categorise politically the groups involved. Linear left-right political dichotomies, with extremists readily situated at the far-end of each point of the graph, make less sense here than when applied to groups devoted to fighting the class struggle or opposing immigration. "Green thinkers like to define their political position as 'beyond left and right'" (Dobson, 1994, p. 253). Environmentalists reject the Marxist view that the issue of production is one primarily about ownership and control, instead questioning the volume and nature of production, and the idea that society can remain indefinitely wedded to a cycle of production and consumption (Schumacher, 1974).

This is now applied particularly to the production and consumption of fossil fuels. Green approaches are also inimical to the traditional conservative view that trade is an inherent good, bringing both individual prosperity and differing peoples together in mutually beneficial working relationships. Trade cannot be beneficial if the goods concerned are seen to be harmful. Roger Hallam of Extinction Rebellion perhaps oversimplifies the positions of left and right but makes a recognisably green argument when he complains that the materialist analysts from both traditions "accept the reductive dogma of neoliberalism that money and consumerism dominate our lives. A broad historical analysis shows this is plain wrong" (Hallam, 2019, p. 26).

Similarly, animal rights activists have tended to eschew easy categorisation on the political compass. Whilst the circled A in ALF literature demonstrated an affinity with Anarchism, class struggle anarchist traditions often declined to embrace a movement that was seen as lacking affinity with workers and working-class communities (Class War, 1992, p. 13). Here ALF slogans such as "devastate to liberate" were rejected with the critique of being "devastatingly liberal" (Anonymous, 1994) with the emphasis instead preferred on industrial or community struggles. ALF founder Ronnie Lee was influenced by the Marxist ideas of the Situationists but found greater sympathy with activists from the *Freedom* and *Peace News* newspapers who tended to eschew class struggle (Lee, interview, 2016 August 20, Birmingham, England).

If some anarchists did not want to be animal rights activists, there were also animal rights activists who certainly did not want to be anarchists. Debate between those in the movement who wished to locate animal liberation within broader political campaigning, and those who did not, was at times fierce. For example, *HOWL*, the magazine of the Hunt Saboteurs Association (HSA) ran an "HSA Forum" section, where differing perspectives were presented on political matters. In one issue a writer using the pseudonym ACAB (meaning All Coppers are Bastards) argued the prospects of a hunting ban via legislation was "pie in the sky" and declared "Maybe I am fighting the class war when I'm out sabbing. So what?" (ACAB, 1993).

Internal research conducted by the HSA found that its membership was politically diverse "there are supporters of all parties within the HSA, with Labour and the Green Party coming pretty high. Surprisingly there were Conservative voters, along with supporters of the Liberal Democrats and the Liberal party" (Carter, 1993). The more recent emergence of Extinction Rebellion from 2018 did little to bring a definitive judgement as to where environmental and animal rights activists sit on the political spectrum.

When considering Extinction Rebellion, for example, some categorise the group as figures of the extreme left, seeking to force a radical economic agenda upon society in the name of saving the environment (Spence, 2019). For others however, contemporary green and environmentalist actors are better positioned on the right (Myers, 2020) or as misanthropes, placing the planet above people (Tomlinson, 2020). To add to the confusion, historical overviews of the ecological movement in Britain offer some support for the view that it is one whose initial activists and origins intersected with the far-right (Coupland, 2016) although there is scant evidence of ongoing chronological progression for far-right influence. Indeed, the need for an environmental movement that is ethnically diverse is declared by Extinction Rebellion activists such as Shiva (2019, p. 7) and Hallam (2019, p. 58) although the latter's statement that "people of colour can organise in their own spaces" (Hallam, 2019, p. 58) is not necessarily a ringing endorsement of community integration.

The Mechanics of Environmental Activism: Action Not Words

The tendency of environmental politics to eschew existing political frameworks has facilitated a focus on deeds. The ideals articulated by the Swedish campaigner Greta Thunberg have enjoyed a global impact but centre more on action than any ready location within traditional paradigms. Writing of the 8 September 2018 climate march in Stockholm, Thunberg placed activists in the position of an enlightened minority, explaining her school strike with the words "…if everyone knew how serious the situation is and how little is being done, everyone would come and sit down beside us" (Thunberg, 2019, p. 10). Established political structures and dichotomies are therefore redundant "This is not a political text. Our school strike has nothing to do with party politics. Because the climate and the biosphere don't care about our politics and our empty words for a single second. They only care about what we actually do" (Thunberg, 2019, p. 10).

Here, it is action, not words, which count. Those within Extinction Rebellion also appear comfortable with being an enlightened minority. To quote founding member Roger Hallam: "We should not make the mistake of thinking 'the people have to rise' in the sense of the majority of the population. We need a few to rise up, and most of the rest of the population to be willing to 'give it a go'" (Hallam, 2019, p. 24). For currents, such as Extinction Rebellion, the lack of a standard political trajectory, or distinct ideological roots, has arguably been an advantage in developing a movement rooted, not in political discussion, the workplace or lobbying decision-makers, but action on the streets.

Describing itself as "politically non-partisan" (Extinction Rebellion, About Us, n.d.) in the first month of 2021 its website claims some 1146 local groups internationally and 193 upcoming events (Extinction Rebellion, Rebellion Global, n.d.). The organisation unites around three demands – "tell the truth, act now and beyond politics" – and a list of ten core values, aimed at creating a "regenerative culture" (Extinction Rebellion, About Us, n.d.). Like Thunberg, Extinction Rebellion stress the need for intervention is urgent:

> Traditional strategies like petitioning, lobbying, voting and protest have not worked due to the rooted interests of political and economic forces. Our approach is therefore

one of non-violent, disruptive civil disobedience – a rebellion to bring about change, since all other means have failed.

(Extinction Rebellion, About Us, n.d.)

Less helpfully, this ideological flexibility has seen its supporters and activists clash repeatedly over political direction and the importance, or not, of concepts such as class, race or gender (Kinniburgh, 2020). The organisation's own publications do not help such debates. When prominent activist Sam Knights claims "this is a movement led by indigenous communities and those in the majority world. It is led by women and children and people of colour" (Knights, 2019, 12) specific, named examples of exactly who Knights is talking about, do not follow. Extinction Rebellion entered the era of the George Floyd and Black Lives Matter protests with a political position on whether the police are "good or bad" as "a separate question and one on which we don't need to have any collective position" (Hallam, 2019, p. 32). This would appear to suggest action is likely to remain focused on environmental issues, rather than wider political debates, where, presumably, a unified position would prove difficult to agree.

Direct Action as an Organising Principle

Civil disobedience or direct action[1] requires the personal intervention of activists, for example disrupting a fox hunt or preventing machinery from entering a fracking site. It is considered to be "prefigurative" (Franks, 2006, p. 134) – such actions are regarded as empowering to the participants, and bring an immediate impact which long-term political campaigning may not. It is about "focusing on what needs to be done, rather than what is politically possible" (Thunberg, 2019, p. 28). Its immediacy contrasts significantly with the long-term strategies required to bring about electoral success at the ballot box, or the coalition of assorted interests which may need to be built to enact legislation through parliament. This immediacy is an important factor. Discussing the early days of the hunt saboteur's movement Paul Rogers argues "essentially because legislation seemed so far away, and unachievable, they were taking direct action simply for the very practical reason that it saved lives in the here and now" (Rogers, interview, 2016 August 13, Gravesend, Kent, England.). It was better to act in the field than wait for politicians to ban fox hunting.

Direct action also delivers a message to those who have been campaigning on an issue, without success. Speaking of some of the national animal welfare organisations, the ALF's Ronnie Lee argues "something more hard-hitting needed to be done. These organisations had campaigned for decades and had not actually saved any animals" (Lee, 2016). Participation in direct action also bestows status on the individual and their peers "We are the ones making a difference. We, the people in Extinction Rebellion, and those schoolstriking for the climate, we are making a difference" (Thunberg, 2019, 78). A clear moral distinction can emerge between those who are doing something for the greater good, making a difference, and those who are repeating the failed mistakes of earlier campaigns.

What does "making a difference" mean in practice? How does direct action enable this to happen? In the foreword to a primer on non-violent direct action by Extinction Rebellion's Roger Hallam, an anonymous activist writes on the failure of conventional campaigning to address the dominance of fossil fuel companies. The answer to this is: "No more protests or petitions. Instead non-violent civil disobedience, lots of it and on a large scale. Close down cities until the politicians take action. Or until the people do" (Hallam, 2019, p. 6). Hallam goes on to warn against any holding back by activists, complaining of "an unwillingness to engage with the public directly and organise them to break the law on a large scale" (Hallam, 2019,

p. 31). Epoch shaping change is expected to come from large, sustained protests which then multiply in size in a manner the authorities cannot cope with. Historical examples are given from the US civil rights era, Leipzig in 1989 and Nepal in 2005 (Hallam, 2019, pp. 41–44).

The tactics utilised by campaigners allow considerable space for personal initiative in terms of direct action. In Hallam's proposed structure, activists, formed into small affinity groups of 8–12 people, work together on the day of a demonstration (Hallam, 2019, p. 29) having planned their joint activity. Group members who do not intend to risk arrest are asked to remain in contact with the main protest group. Debate about tactics by adherents of direct action is at times sharp, if to the outsider, a little obscure. Paul Rogers of *Green Anarchist* recalls a debate where activists from *Peace News* objected to the cutting of wire fences at nuclear bases, on the grounds that it was being done clandestinely, and was therefore non-Gandhian! (Rogers, 2016).

Further distinctions exist with the direct action paradigm. The ALF, for example, openly denied it had any members, but recognised those taking direct action, again bestowing status upon those seen to be physically doing something:

> We are not members of the ALF, in fact the ALF has not one single member. We are ALF activists by virtue of the fact that we carry out action, whether on an occasional or frequent basis. Immediately superglue has been squirted into a fur shop lock the person involved becomes an activist
>
> *(ALF, n.d., p. 5)*

Such action may present a significant challenge to the authorities, in that activists may not be centrally coordinated and are potentially less likely to be directed away from more militant tactics by those who emerge as movement spokespeople or theoreticians. It is hard for the authorities to police a free for all. Direct action, it should be recognised, is a tactic that may, or may not, utilise physical force, and/or damage to property. It is not necessarily pacifist. Whilst organisations such as the ALF or HSA have not used deadly violence against their opponents, they have at times been involved in significant public disorder, attacks on buildings and physical violence. One of the core academic articles compiling data on such violence is entitled "Not quite terrorism: Animal rights extremism in the United Kingdom." It lists the use of incendiary devices, damage to personal and public property plus physical attacks where injuries, albeit minor, were recorded (Monaghan, 2013).

A considerable tension also emerges as a result of the strategy of direct action. Even when declared as non-violent, or carried out on inanimate objects such as the fence of a military base, its participants may be breaking the law and accordingly labelled extremists by the media, police and political opponents. Belief in the rule of law, and pressure upon politicians to uphold it, is a component factor in the political structure of liberal democracies. Further, if advocates of non-violent direct action are prevented from demonstrating in a manner that is likely to achieve their aims, some may be tempted to turn towards other methods. This could involve more serious breaches of the law, and even violence. The conundrum in a scenario where non-violent action has not worked, is to carry on with actions in the hope they develop a critical mass (the position outlined by Hallam, above), to pivot towards new methods, or accept defeat. Can climate activists, recruited to Greta Thunberg's and Extinction Rebellion's rhetoric of a climate emergency, accept defeat?

In considering non-violent extremism, it should be noted contemporary direct action possesses considerable tensions and contradictions within it. A characteristic within the ideal is that non-violent direct action comes to exist as a public conversation and a process of negotiation between demonstrators and the authorities. As a tactic, its existence appears highly dependent on the type of society it is being conducted in. Protestors recognise the risk of arrest, and do not use force to resist it. Indeed "Extinction Rebellion has chosen a very particular stance vis-à-vis the police: to actively try to get arrested" (Rafaeli, 2019, p. 41), as part of a "self-sacrificial idea" (Griffiths, 2019, p. 96).

Next comes the police's turn. They must have sufficient officers to make arrests, vehicles to transfer those detained, and cells in which to keep them. They then compete with the protestors in the public relations sphere, with both sides explaining their actions to the media and the public. But what if the police do not play the game? A tacit admission comes from Extinction Rebellion's Sam Knights "The tactics we use in the United Kingdom or the United States are not always effective or safe in other countries, especially those under repressive regimes or dictatorships" (Knights, 2019, p. 12). Presumably no one is going to sit around peacefully waiting for the police to arrest them, if they believe officers will then beat them severely, or take protestors to prisons notorious for ill-treatment of inmates. Jay Griffiths writes in quasi-religious terms about being arrested conducting non-violent direct action during the Extinction Rebellion protests of Easter 2019:

> it gives you strength from within. Ancient values are overly resurrected in this Easter rebellion in London: the values of chivalry and honour, faith in life and being in ser-vice to Our Lady, Notre Dame, Mother Earth, the mother on whom everything else depends
>
> *(Griffiths, 2019, p. 96)*

All this is possible of course, providing the authorities play their part according to the script. This reliance on direct action for political progress also ensures a movement that is likely to be dominated by activists, those willing and able to leave their homes and travel to protests in the big cities. Individuals with family responsibilities or jobs that cannot easily be dropped for periods of protest and arrest, are unlikely to participate in such escapades. The activist minority has a far greater role to play than the silent majority, who, as Hallam alludes above, need not be persuaded to participate, but merely to go along with what campaigners propose.

Direct action brings the potential for a blurring of tactics, where activists combine a series of campaigning tools in the expectation of eventual success. In the case of animal rights activists protesting against vivisection, conventional legal political campaigning could be run against laboratories which conduct experiments on animals (and their suppliers) alongside much more militant actions which utilise threats, vandalism and even physical assaults. This was often the result of detailed research by activists: "They thought a lot about production chains, and where the critical points were and damaging them" (Rogers, 2016). This targeted approach is summed up by ALF activist Keith Mann: "In the case of the animal liberation struggle, it allows small teams to operate independently of each other without any command structure, and to work alongside – not inside – public campaigns" (Mann, 2007, p. 98).

Paul Rogers believes that the increased response of the state to animal rights campaigns in the 1980s and 1990s had a significant effect on the tactic's campaigners used, but that the biggest change leading to a decline in the number of radical activists was ultimately that on a core issue – the abolition of fox hunting – the activists won.

> To a certain extent it was increased repression, but to be honest you have a wasp effect, where you up that and people become more rather than less militant, albeit you have a hardcore doing that. But generally, I think it was due to the sabs being

a stepping-stone into a greater militancy and the majority of those groups dispersed after the criminalisation of hunting.

(Rogers, 2016)

At its high point in the 1980s, the ALF had 30 imprisoned activists (Lee, 2016). Throughout the 1990s *Green Anarchist* regularly published the details of up to dozen imprisoned animal rights activists for readers to support. Without the radicalisation afforded by the world of hunt sabbing, these numbers have dropped significantly. The ALF Supporters Group website's list of prisoners was last updated on 23 October 2015, when it contained just one British activist, plus five overseas ("Current animal rights prisoners of conscience", 2015).

Having been imprisoned twice for animal rights activism, Ronnie Lee became the Press Officer for the ALF largely by accident, as he found that as a known activist, he was being approached by the media for comment. This soon led to appearances on the national news "obviously it was to defend the actions, but also to kind of explain why people took the action" (Lee, 2016). This included the ALF's 1984 claims to have put rat poison in Mars bars (Hansard, 1984) as the company sponsored research into tooth decay, dependent upon experiments on animals. To Ronnie Lee, the aims of the action were simple – "to cause financial loss to the company" (Lee, 2016). The use of a hoax alleging poison is an extreme example of direct action. But the mechanics at its base are simple and recurring across the fields of both historical animal rights protests and contemporary environmental campaigning. The aim is to inflict losses, so a company takes the course of action protestors want it to.

Sometimes the methods used to achieve this, utilise violence and obviously extreme methods such as claims about poison. More commonly they do not. Is there the potential for adherents of direct action to go even further, and kill people? The evidence across the decades suggests not. Another leading ALF activist, Keith Mann, has written of the potential use of deadly violence "It wouldn't be good press and would be arguably less productive than attacking their profits" (Mann, 2007, p. 58).

A New Political Paradigm? The Ticking Clock

There are at least two significant differences between the environmental movement today and that in earlier decades. The first is its prominence. The Green Party enjoys representation in the British parliament and legislatures throughout the West. The global recognition enjoyed by the young Swedish activist Greta Thunberg, has placed green analysis of our societies, centre stage. Significant cuts in CO_2 emissions, and policies such as the advocacy of veganism have a higher profile than ever before. Extinction Rebellion has an appeal beyond the dynamics of a politics rooted in social class or identity.

Consider for example The Climate Emergency Fund – which supports Extinction Rebellion and similar grassroots campaigners. It has received monies from both wealthy donors and corporations (O'Neill, 2019) – suggesting that if this is a movement requesting radical change, it is not one fitting traditional Marxist concepts of the proletariat taking up arms to overthrow the bourgeoisie. Instead, it reflects a desire on the part of many involved in business to mitigate against environmental degradation.

A second significant difference from earlier decades is the air of imminent catastrophe, as increasingly desperate, almost apocalyptic arguments are made to the public. "We now need to change practically everything. We now need a whole new way of thinking" (Thunberg, 2019, p. 99). This call for revolution has not limited the appeal of the overall campaign – Greta Thunberg's declarations moved in a short period of time from protests in Swedish towns, to set piece events at the general assembly of the United Nations, the World Economic Forum, the Houses of Parliament, the French National Assembly, US Congress and European Parliament, to name just six. The message is then echoed by environmental campaigners at the local level. It is therefore worth considering the thrust of Thunberg's advocacy, to consider the accelerated and even desperate tone of many environmental campaigners.

Greta Thunberg's approach is absolutist: "If the emissions have to stop, then we must stop the emissions. To me that is black or white. There are no grey areas when it comes to survival. Either we go on as a civilisation or we don't" (Thunberg, 2019, p. 18). Unless CO_2 emissions end "we are about eleven years away from setting off an irreversible chain reaction, way beyond human control, that will probably be the end of civilisation as we know it" (Thunberg, 2019, p. 63). Her preferred response to this 2030 apocalypse, as set out in a speech at the European Parliament is: "I want you to panic" (Thunberg, 2019, p. 69), i.e. our metaphorical house is on fire. This world view does not preclude Thunberg articulating what may be error or disinformation. For example, her claim the planet is in the midst of its sixth mass extinction "with about 200 species going extinct every single day" (Thunberg, 2019, p. 19) appears grossly exaggerated. The International Union for Conservation of Nature instead declared the extinction of 160 species in the decade 2010–2019 (Brenna, 2020) – a vastly different figure.

As with Extinction Rebellion (below), Thunberg rules out using conventional politics to achieve her aims, and makes the case for a politics rooted in street activism:

> Today we use 100 million barrels of oil every day. There are no politics to change that. There are no rules to keep that oil in the ground. So we can't save the world by playing by the rules. Because the rules have to be changed. Everything needs to change. And it has to start today. So everyone out there: it is now time for civil disobedience
>
> *(Thunberg, 2019, p. 21).*

Thunberg does recognise disparities of wealth, but this is framed in terms of the wealthy global north versus the impoverished global south. At the 2018 UN Climate Change conference in Poland she declared "We are about to sacrifice the biosphere so that rich people in countries like mine can live in luxury" (Thunberg, 2019, p. 28). The Paris Agreement is viewed in terms of "rich countries" versus poor, with direct reference to "we, who already have everything" (Thunberg, 2019, p. 19). This type of rhetoric may not endear environmentalists to the poorer sections of those living in communities in the West, and their representatives, who may not consider themselves to have "everything". As with Hallam's somewhat awkward comments about the participation of ethnic minorities, this is a reminder that the likelihood of environmentalists developing long-term working relationships with those from other traditions, is one fraught with obstacles. The *Gilet Jaunes* protests in France, which began in opposition to President Macron's increased taxation of petrol in order to assist the development of a low-carbon economy, is a further case in point.

Extinction Rebellion: Overview and Analysis

In the introduction to Extinction Rebellion's core text, "This is not a drill", Sam Knights declares a group rooted in science that seeks to build a movement. From the small acorns of just 15 people "on 31 October 2018, we declared ourselves in open rebellion against the UK government" (Knights, 2019, p. 10). This was followed by the series of international protests in April 2019, which in the UK centred on the occupation of five key sites, including Parliament

Square, and the closure of companies involved in fossil fuels. A recurring theme of direct action returned: "We attempted to cause as much economic disruption as we possibly could" (Knights, 2019, p. 10) and he claims the protests cost the UK tens of millions of pounds.

What is perhaps most interesting to this is the response. Whilst over a thousand protestors were arrested, "We were quickly invited to meet senior politicians from all the major parties, including the Secretary of State for Environment, Food, and Rural Affairs, in the very heart of government" (Knights, 2019, p. 10). As with Greta Thunberg, when Extinction Rebellion knocked on the door of the great and the good, it opened. How many other political currents, declaring "open rebellion" against the government, disrupting lawful businesses, and seeing large numbers of its supporters arrested, could expect to be treated in such a manner? It is hard to imagine any group from within the Islamist, far-right or communist traditions receiving such a ready welcome in Whitehall and Westminster. There appears, certainly at this stage, to be something different about the state's response to contemporary environmentalists. If so, it may be difficult in the future for the government to categorise such activists as "extremists" when it has engaged fulsomely with them.

Unlike politicians who seek office, Extinction Rebellion does not aim at gaining maximum support or acceptance for its ideas. Indeed, its media and messaging coordinator, Ronan McNern refers to an approach rooted in past academic research into social movements "which demonstrates that to achieve social change the active and sustained participation of just 3.5 % of the population is needed. It's that 3.5 % that we want to engage" (McNern, 2019, p. 126). How is it doing this? To understand Extinction Rebellion, and to properly locate it in any discussion about political extremism, it is necessary to further consider the thought of one of its founders and key thinkers, Roger Hallam. His 2019 text "Common sense for the 21st century" is subtitled "Only nonviolent rebellion can now stop climate breakdown and social collapse."

Hallam proposes a two-pronged approach to bringing about radical change – mass breaking of the law through non-violent civil disobedience and what is described as "popular democratic mobilisation" (Hallam, 2019, p. 8). Protests are targeted at the government, in the capital city, and should be continuous "one day actions, however big, rarely impose the necessary economic cost to bring the authorities to the table" (Hallam, 2019, p. 9). The strength in depth for those ongoing protests will come – Hallam believes that we are living in an age where the political structure in the western democracies has shifted from reformist to revolutionary. This leaves old environmental organisations such as Greenpeace stuck in the "reformist space which has dominated politics from 1989 until the 2007 financial crisis. Times have changed" (Hallam, 2019, p. 21).

Extinction Rebellion look to put those words into action, seizing the *zeitgeist*. For example, hosting training workshops in what it refers to as non-violent direct action (Extinction Rebellion, 2020a). This training then equips activists for political interventions such as blocking roads, disrupting businesses accused of damaging the planet, and "locking-on" to structures to ensure that the police cannot readily remove them. This approach almost certainly involves disrupting legal activity, bringing protestors into potential conflict with those who disagree with them.

Those affected may range from passers-by to commuters, workers in fossil fuel companies and their suppliers, or simply those who disagree with Extinction Rebellion's analysis. Hallam, however, takes an optimistic view of where large-scale, repeated protest, may lead. "After one or two weeks following this plan, historical records show that a regime is highly likely to collapse or is forced to enact major structural change. This is due to well-established dynamics of non-violent political struggle" (Hallam, 2019, p. 9). However, if the protests fail to deliver the progress Hallam hopes for, what then? This is particularly problematic if the Extinction

Rebellion position of a climate emergency is accepted – a series of difficult questions emerge for the organisation. What will the committed cadre of activists do, if the public and the government does not follow their analysis in how to stop irreversible damage to the planet?

Extinction Rebellion has avoided the type of clashes on demonstrations which characterised earlier adherents of direct action such as the ALF and HSA. Non-violent direct action however, does not eliminate the potential for conflict, or that accusations of violence will not follow contemporary environmentalist actions. For example, one of the Extinction Rebellion's co-founders, Dr Gail Bradbrook was charged with causing criminal damage costing £27,000 after a glass panel was attacked during a protest outside the Department of Transport (Riley, 2019). More seriously, when Extinction Rebellion disrupted commuter traffic at Canning Town station in east London in October 2019, scuffles broke out between commuters and protestors, and a demonstrator was unceremoniously removed, feet first, from the roof of a train he was occupying (Jarvis and Cruse, 2019).

Wider political controversy was to follow when Extinction Rebellion disrupted companies in Hertfordshire, Merseyside and North Lanarkshire responsible for printing a total of ten national newspapers. Several newspapers did not appear the next day, or had significantly reduced print runs. Despite 80 arrests, activists considered this a victory against a media seen as hostile to both the environment and migrants: "The entire institution of the media follows the same toxic rulebook, dehumanising marginalised groups and perpetuating inequality. It has become necessary to block lies in order to free the truth" (Extinction Rebellion, 2020b). A similar protest targeting the media was held in 2019, when Extinction Rebellion picketed YouTube in opposition to its provision of services to those considered to be from "denialist perspectives" on climate change (Boscia, 2019).

The newspaper blockade arguably brought the strongest response to an Extinction Rebellion protest yet, with loud condemnation from senior politicians. Prime Minister Boris Johnson argued that interfering in a free press was unacceptable (BBC News, 2020). The action was also a reminder that environmental protestors such as Extinction Rebellion may be hostile to core values of liberal democracy, such as freedom of the press. Paradoxes also emerge. Roger Hallam has written that "Rebellion is about giving people permission to say what they really think" (Hallam, 2019, p. 25). What if people think differently to Extinction Rebellion when it comes to the environment or on an issue such as immigration? And wish to buy a newspaper which articulates their views?

Extinction Rebellion also rejects parliamentary democracy, promoting the call for decision-making on the climate emergency they have declared, to be led by a "Citizens Assembly on climate and ecological justice" (Extinction Rebellion, 2020,c). Control of what is seen as the most pressing issue of the day, the response to climate change, would be taken away from the democratically elected parliament. Roger Hallam writes of a scenario where: "The plan I outline is for a national Citizens Assembly to take over the sovereign role from a corrupted parliamentary system" (Hallam, 2019, p. 11). This assembly would be selected by quota sampling that would be representative of the country's demographic mix.

Conclusions

The strategy of direct action which sits at the heart of the environmental and animal rights movements considered above, is not a concept which waits for the mechanics of parliamentary democracy to progress. Indeed, it does the very opposite, intervening immediately rather than waiting for legal reforms. Action is all. Problematically it does not wait for or even necessarily seek majority public support. Whilst Extinction Rebellion does not possess the appetite for the more violent and extreme tactics which at times characterised the direct action milieu inhabited by the ALF, *Green Anarchist* or the HSA, there are worryingly illiberal trends within in it – consider, for example, its attitude to views different to its own on issues such as climate change or migration.

What the groups and activists considered in this chapter share is an understanding that past policies, and past politics have failed, and they themselves must act. Direct action and civil disobedience flow from a critique of actual or perceived political failure and the desire to address this via personal intervention on the streets. Such is the scale of this failure, and the resultant crisis, activists need not respect the law. Once the principle of legality is breached, the question for the authorities, and those debating concepts of political extremism, is to ask how far protestors are willing to go? The lessons from the animal rights movement appear to suggest that when campaigns are successful, the militants fade into obscurity.

It is noticeable that at the time of writing, both the UK government and police seem happy to engage with environmental protestors, indeed a rather ritualistic game seems to emerge at the large set piece demonstrations held by Extinction Rebellion. It would be naïve however to expect this phoney war to continue indefinitely. The rejection of parliamentary democracy by environmental activists, and direct action's focus on inflicting financial loss, ultimately place these campaigns outside of the political mainstream. As we get closer to 2030 and the environmental state of no return expected by Greta Thunberg and Extinction Rebellion protestors, what will activists do if their protests are prevented, or lack impact? What happens if the companies they target, ride out any financial loss inflicted? Roger Hallam's concept of demonstrations gaining ever great momentum seems optimistic – Extinction Rebellion appears to lack the inclination, and indeed the politics, to unite more broadly with campaigners outside of the green milieu.

The reliance on enlightened minorities, rather than a desire to convince the majority, does not indicate a firewall against political extremism. Indeed, the potential for conflict as the clock ticks towards 2030, appears likely to increase. The direct action of environmental activists may become far more antagonistic as time progresses – demonstrating the importance of crisis narratives as a call to action for political violence.

Note

1 The terms direct action and civil disobedience are used interchangeably in this text.

Bibliography

ACAB. (1993, Summer 52). Sabbing and the Police (Continued). *HOWL: Magazine of the Hunt Saboteurs Association*, 9.

Animal Liberation Front. (n.d.). *Interviews with Animal Liberation Front Activists*.

Anonymous. (1994). *Animal Liberation: Devastate to Liberate?* Or Devastatingly Liberal? London, England: Pelagian Press.

Anonymous Climate Activist. (2019). Foreword. In Hallam, R. (Ed.), *Common Sense for the 21st Century: Only Nonviolent Rebellion Can Now Stop Climate Breakdown and Social Collapse* (pp. 5–6). Carmarthenshire, Wales: Common Sense for the 21st Century

BBC News, (2020, September 5). Extinction Rebellion Protestors Block Printing Presses. Retrieved from: www.bbc.co.uk.

Boscia, S. (2019, October 17). Extinction Rebels Target YouTube for Cimate Denial, *City AM*, p. 14.

Brenna, L. (2020, February 11). Animal and Plant Species Declared Extinct Between 2010 and 2019, the full list. Retrieved from: www.lifegate.com

Carter, H. (1993, Summer 52). Results of the HSA Market Research Campaign. *HOWL: Magazine of the Hunt Saboteurs Association*, 11.

Class War. (1992). *Unfinished Business: The Politics of Class War*. Edinburgh, Scotland: AK Press.

Colquhoun, Lisa. (1993, Summer 52). Class Issues Are a Distraction. *HOWL: Magazine of the Hunt Saboteurs Association*, 9.

Coupland, Philip M. (2016). *Farming, Fascism and Ecology: A Life of Jorian Jenks*. Abingdon, England: Routledge.

Current Animal Rights Prisoners of Conscience. (2015, October). *ALF-SG newsletter*. Retrieved from www.alfsg.org.uk/current_prisoners.html.

Dobson, A. (Ed.). (1994). *The Green Reader*. London: Andrew Deutsch.

Extinction Rebellion. (n.d). *About Us*. Retrieved from: https://rebellion.global/about-us/.

Extinction Rebellion. (n.d). *Rebellion Global*. Retrieved from: https://rebellion.global/

Extinction Rebellion. (2019). *This Is Not a Drill: An Extinction Rebellion Handbook*. London: Penguin Random House.

Extinction Rebellion. (2020a). *NVDA (Non-violent Direct Action Training)*. Retrieved from: https://extinctionrebellion.uk/event/nvda-non-violent-direct-action-training/

Extinction Rebellion. (2020b, September 5). *Rebel Daily 4: Don't Read the News be the News*. Retrieved from: https://extinctionrebellion.uk/2020/09/05/rebel-daily4-dont-read-the-news-be-the-news

Extinction Rebellion. (2020c). Leaflet: *Join the Rebellion October 7*. Copy in the authors possession.

Franks, B. (2006). *Rebel Alliances: The Means and Ends of Contemporary British Anarchisms*. Edinburgh, Scotland: AK Press.

Griffiths, J. (2019). Courting Arrest, in *Extinction Rebellion, This Is Not a Drill: An Extinction Rebellion Handbook* (pp. 95–98). London: Penguin Random House.

Hallam, R. (2019). *Common Sense for the 21st Century: Only Nonviolent Rebellion Can Now Stop Climate Breakdown and Social Collapse*. Carmarthenshire, Wales: Common Sense for the 21st Century.

Hansard. (1984, November 19). House of Commons Debate Confectionary (Poisoning), 68 cc21–8. Retrieved from: https://api.parliament.uk/historic-hansard

Jarvis, J and Cruse, E. (2019, October 17). Canning Town Attack: Dramatic Moment Extinction Rebellion Protestor Is Pulled Down from Top of London Train in 'Vicious' Clash. *Evening Standard*. Retrieved from: www.standard.co.uk

Kinniburgh, C. (2020, Winter). 'Can Extinction Rebellion Survive?' *Dissent Magazine*. Retrieved from: www.dissentmagazine.org/article/can-extinction-rebellion-survive

Knights, S. (2019). Introduction: The Story so Far. In Farrell, C, Green A, Knights S, Skeaping W (Eds.), *Extinction Rebellion, This Is Not a Drill: An Extinction Rebellion Handbook* (pp. 9–13). London: Penguin Random House.

Mann, K. (2007). *From Dusk 'til Dawn: An Insider's View of the Growth of the Animal Liberation Movement*. London: Puppy Pincher Press.

McNern, R (2019). One by One: A Media Strategy, In Farrell, C, Green A, Knights S, Skeaping W (Eds.), *Extinction Rebellion, 2019. This Is Not a Drill: An Extinction Rebellion Handbook* (pp.126–130). London: Penguin Random House.

Monaghan, R. (2013). Not Quite Terrorism: Animal Rights Extremism in the United Kingdom, *Studies in Conflict & Terrorism*, 36:11, 933–951, DOI:10.1080/1057610X.2013.832117

Myers, F. (2020 January 29). Green Racism. *Spiked*. Retrieved from: www.spiked-online.com/2020/01/29/green-racism/.

O'Neill, K. (2019 September 7). Getty Oil Heiress Pours £500,000 into Extinction Rebellion Fund. *Daily Telegraph*, p. 2.

Rafaeli, JS. (2019). Fighting the Wrong War: JS Rafaeli with Neil Woods. In Farrell, C, Green A, Knights S, Skeaping W (Eds.), *Extinction Rebellion, This Is Not a Drill: An Extinction Rebellion Handbook* (pp. 40–45). London: Penguin Random House.

Riley, E. (2019, November 15). Extinction Rebellion co-founder, 47, 'caused £27,500 of Damage to the Department for Transport When She Smashed a Bullet-Proof Window with a Chisel and Hammer,' *Daily Mail*. Retrieved from: www.dailymail.co.uk

Schumacher, EF. (1974). *Small Is Beautiful*. London, England: Abacus.

Shiva, V. (2019). Foreword. In Farrell, C, Green A, Knights S, Skeaping W (Eds.), *Extinction Rebellion, This Is Not a Drill: An Extinction Rebellion Handbook* (pp. 5–8). London: Penguin Random House.

Spence, B. (2019 October 7). Extinction Rebellion Exposes Left Wing Activism as a Global Elite Sham. *Daily Telegraph*. Retrieved from: www.telegraph.co.uk

Thunberg, G. (2019). *No One Is Too Small to Make a Difference*. London: Allen Lane.

Tomlinson, C. (2020 March 31). Extinction Rebellion: Anti-Human to the Core. *Spiked*, 31 March 2020. Retrieved from: www.spiked-online.com/2020/03/31/extinction-rebellion-anti-human-to-the-core/.

32

"THE GREAT REFUSAL"

Radical Environmental Resistance Against Contemporary Ecological Breakdown

Heather Alberro

Introduction

In the Capitalocene we find ourselves embroiled in a litany of socio-ecological upheavals stemming from a global socio-economic system predicated on endless expansion, commodification and extraction (Moore, 2017). The effects of anthropogenic climate change – more frequent and violent storms and extreme weather events, resource shortages, rising seas and ensuing geopolitical turmoil – are already underway (IPCC, 2021). Perhaps more problematic from an ethical standpoint is the present sixth mass extinction (Ceballos et al, 2020), otherwise poignantly termed "interspecies genocide" (Cafaro, 2015) wherein overexploitation of species and habitat fragmentation has led to the loss of 68% of monitored vertebrate populations per 1970 levels (WWF, 2020).

The aforementioned have infused the present, a time thoroughly pervaded by multifarious forms loss and disintegration, with a heightened sense of urgency starkly exhibited by radical environmental activists (REAs). Since the 1970s, these groups have been engaged in thoroughgoing mobilisations against the mounting ecological contradictions of extractive capitalism. Through their post-anthropocentric worldviews (Ferrando, 2016; Alberro, 2020) and oppositional modes of activism, they express a great "refusal" of the status quo of global capitalism and call for second-order transformations in dominant socio-economic structures and Western modes of human–animal–nature relationality (Breines, 1989; Glasser, 2011).

Drawing on critical theoretical tributaries and empirical data in the form of 26 semi-structured interviews conducted between August 2017 and August 2018 with REAs from Earth First! (EF!), Sea Shepherd Conservation Society (SSCS), Hambacher Forst and Extinction Rebellion, this chapter aims to shed critical light on how their post-anthropocentric worldviews serve to motivate their engagement in emotionally and physically taxing direct-action feats. The latter have been variously labelled as extreme or even terroristic within mainstream discourses (Smith, 2008). The chapter concludes with a discussion of REA's within wider debates around political extremism, and reflections on the role and significance of radical activism as a response to the exigencies of the Capitalocene.

DOI: 10.4324/9781003032793-37

History, Nature and Tactics of REA Movements

Haunted by the spectre of nuclear war, "postwar environmentalism" emerged marked by a burgeoning awareness of the global ecological ramifications of rampant technological change and socio-economic activity within industrial society (Cassegard & Thorn, 2018, p. 565). This awakening proliferated across Western Europe, the United States, and Australia like wildfire, featuring campaigns for clean air and water, the safe disposal of sewage and waste, and improved public health (Rootes, 2014). Modern environmentalism in the Global North[1] was effectively born when over 20 million Americans flocked to attend the first Earth Day on 22 April 1970 (Hernandez, 2007).

Throughout the 1970s, a series of key developments – mounting scientific evidence of environmental degradation, world reports on the limits to growth, the establishment of the United Nations Environment Programme (UNEP), and crucially the "political space" opened up by the New Left, anti-nuclear peace and countercultural movements of the late 1960s and early 1970s – helped entrench reform environmentalism as the new dominant environmental discourse (Meadows et al., 1972; Rootes, 2014). Reformist environmental movement organisations such as Greenpeace and Friends of the Earth gradually became institutionalised. They were accepted by governments as authoritative actors and sources of key environmental expertise, and experienced rapid growths in membership and resources. Moreover, they underwent increasing professionalisation which, crucially, was accompanied by shifts in repertoires from direct-action and protest towards conventional tactics such as lobbying[2] (Van der Heijden, 1997; Berny & Rootes, 2018). Seeking cooperation rather than opposition to government and industry, reformist environmental organisations embraced sustainable development or "ecological modernisation" narratives which maintain that there is no inherent incongruity between boundless economic growth and biospheric integrity (Andersen & Massa, 2000). Rather, the aim is to reconcile economic growth with environmental sustainability through a "greening" of global capitalism, i.e. through technological innovation and individual consumptive changes. For emerging radical movement segments, however, addressing the roots of the climate and ecological crisis required no mere technological or legal alterations but fundamental transformations in our dominant socio-economic systems, values and worldviews.

Radical Environmentalism

From the mid-1970s, profound disillusionment amongst more radical segments of liberal reformist environmentalism spurred a new "fourth wave" of environmentalism known as "political ecologism" or "radical environmentalism" (Rootes, 2014). Groups such as EF!, SSCS, Hambacher Forst, the Climate Camp movement and to an extent even the new civil disobedience movement Extinction Rebellion marked a "step change" within environmental movements (Rootes, 2008, p. 613). As discussed, reformist environmental groups often deploy tactics for curbing ecological decline which are deemed compatible with Western liberal-democratic structures and which cause minimal disruptions to the economic status quo. Pellow's (2014) three-part characterisation scheme sheds light on some of the key political, tactical and ideological distinctions within environmental movements: (1) "radicals" who seek to entirely replace existing political–economic systems, (2) progressives such as SSCS and Extinction Rebelion who exhibit some anti-system identities though generally seek changes from *within* the present system by demanding that governments implement necessary legal and socio-economic changes for mitigating climate and ecological breakdown[3] (Bondaroff, 2020; Milstein et al., 2020), and (3) mainstream groups like Humane society who work towards incremental changes entirely from within the system (p. 57). Of course, in actuality there are no rigid reformist/radical binaries; productive interchanges have always existed between more "radical" and "reformist" ends of the environmental movement spectrum. Moreover, as noted above movement organisations often shift over time from more radical to progressive and even mainstream approaches.

REAs level multidimensional systemic critiques against the socio-ecological depredations of modern capitalism, specifically its need to continuously expand, extract and commodify whole ecosystems in pursuit of profit maximisation. Moreover, they are also often highly critical of Western anthropocentric assumptions of human superiority to and separateness from nonhumans, and the consequent belief that the latter are ours to do with as we wish (Alberro, 2020). For REAs it is oppressive systems like capitalism and Anthropocentrism that must be wholly dismantled; tinkering around the edges through, for instance, funding renewable energy schemes, amounts to too little, too late (Hernandez, 2007, p. 296). Previous research had uncovered an especially strong undercurrent of apocalypticism within REA discourses and mobilisations, wherein widespread ecological collapse is seen as on the horizon. This engenders a host of negative emotions such as fear and a strong temporal sense of urgency, which in turn serve as powerful action motivators (Thorn, 1997; McNeish, 2017; Cassegard & Thorn, 2018; Alberro, 2021). However, more recently some have delineated the emergence of a "postapocalyptic environmentalism" (Cassegard & Thorn, 2018) wherein catastrophic environmental loss is seen as already well underway. The participants featured in this study indeed exhibit a powerful "postapocalyptic" desire to protect what remains amidst contemporary tides of ecological collapse. However, more than this, many seem driven by a concrete utopian conviction that another world more conducive to the flourishing of life is possible and ought to be implemented in the here and now (Alberro, 2021).

Disrupting the Present

REAs engage in a "politics of contention" that manifests via their trenchant criticisms of the structural drivers of ecological exploitation and, notably, through their use of interventionist action repertoires designed to disrupt and stem contemporary tides of ecological breakdown (Tarrow, 2013; Tilly & Tarrow, 2015). Direct Action (DA) was originally coined by anarcho-feminist activist Voltarine de Cleyre (1912). However, this subversive mode of activism received its formal theorisation in the wake of Gandhi's opposition to Apartheid in South Africa and British colonial rule in India, and further evolved from the non-violent direct-action strategies of civil rights and anti-war demonstrations of the 1960s and 1970s (Plows et al., 2004; Tarrow, 2013). DA entails a specific kind of political action associated with anarchist praxis that is "not beholden to the political tactics of the liberal state" (Heynen & Van Sant, 2015, p. 173). Hence why it is often deployed by radical movement forms.

In the case of REA mobilisations, DA takes a number of different forms, e.g. civil disobedience, road blockades, "climate camps" (Saunders, 2012), international environmentalist and indigenous "conflict zones" of resistance against fossil extractivism termed "Blockadia" (Klein, 2015; Estes, 2019), and more controversial acts of economic sabotage or "ecotage" acts such as arson and the dismantling of ecologically destructive machinery. Indeed, it must be stressed that the worldviews and actions of contemporary REAs are far from new. Indigenous peoples the world over continue to engage in fervent resistance against capitalist extractivism (Estes, 2019; McGregor et al., 2020). Nevertheless, of interest for the present research is precisely how REAs, as groups situated largely in the West, come to develop such radical sensibilities which seem to be largely absent amongst the general population (Latour, 1993).

Methodology

Why do REAs risk life and limb for the protection of the Earth and its myriad inhabitants, rather than adopt a "slow snail-like" move towards sustainability, as Latour (1993, p. 5) poignantly enquires? Kopnina (2012, p. 236) further notes that, "Those committed to the struggle of radical environmentalism or animal liberation are among the least understood of all contemporary opposition movements, not only in tactical terms but also ethically and philosophically". As such, I sought to critically investigate some of these key dimensions, namely: What are their motivations? What are the factors underlying their posthumanist orientations towards the human–nature relationship? How do their ecological worldviews inform their purportedly extreme modes of activism? In light of these research questions, qualitative methodologies were selected as they are best suited to revealing the nuances of personal experiences and orientations (Braun & Clarke, 2013).

Because of the interest in uncovering underlying attitudes, worldviews and motivations held by activists, semi-structured interviews were utilised in order to allow more rich elucidation on behalf of the participants (Aberbach & Rockman, 2002, p. 673). Partly due to issues with access, both in terms of geographical location, as well as the nature of the groups under study, face-to-face interviews were largely abandoned in favour of online interviews (McCoyd & Kerson, 2006, p. 390; Deakin & Wakefield, 2014). No notable differences in the quality of interviews obtained were detected. The final sample featured semi-structured interviews with 26 REAs affiliated with groups such as EF!, Sea Shepherd, Hambacher Forst, Hunt Saboteur groups and Extinction Rebellion. Interviews were conducted between August 2017 and August 2018 with activists from the UK and Western Europe, Canada, Australia, North and South America. All data was fully anonymised through the use of pseudonyms for each participant in order to protect their identities. Organisational documents (Bowen, 2009) were also utilised as supplemental data to the semi-structured interviews. Lastly, I utilised thematic analysis (Braun & Clarke, 2013) for developing, contrasting and analysing key themes relevant to the primary research questions and in the search for common threads amongst the varying data sets.

Results

In the following sections I denote two key themes uncovered throughout the research. The first which refers to the activists' post-anthropocentric worldviews and modes of relationality informs the latter (bodies on the line) in complex ways. As discussed below, many of the activists view nonhuman others not as isolated objects or mere resources but as co-terrestrial kin. REAs see themselves as so intimately and inextricably linked with nonhuman kin as to render their defense amidst contemporary ecological decline an urgent ethical imperative. Because of the perceived urgency of climate chaos and rampant biodiversity loss, radical measures that involve physical intervention between protected species and spaces, and forces of destruction are deemed of the essence.

Post-anthropocentric Sensibilities

Traditional Western worldviews tend to feature anthropocentric, or human-centred, concerns with the state of the natural world, i.e. the degree to which it remains a viable material base for the continuity of *human* life. Indeed, this rationale continues to underpin mainstream environmental and sustainable development narratives (Irving & Helin, 2018). In contrast, more eco-centric and bio-centric worldviews perceive nature and nonhuman animals as "valuable for their own sake" (Mrangudakis, 2001, p. 459), or as ends in themselves (Kant & Schneewind, 2002). Previous research on REAs on groups such as EF! and Sea Shepherd suggests that a significant philosophical underpinning of REA groups such as SSCS and EF! is the anti-anthropocentric environmental philosophy of "deep ecology" (Naess, 1973; Taylor, 2008). In direct contrast to the anthropocentrism that has typically characterised Western human–nature–animal relations, deep ecology is a philosophical school and movement that upholds the notion of biospheric egalitarianism and asserts that the whole phenomenal world is imbued with intrinsic value (Naess, 1973); furthermore, all beings' equal rights to flourish and maximise their full potentialities ought to be respected. However, my research suggests that REAs exhibit a complex, shifting and at times contradictory mosaic of ecological sensibilities that can better be categorised as post-anthropocentric (Ferrando, 2016; Alberro, 2020). REAs vehemently reject anthropocentric notions of human separateness and superiority, and often interrogate and reconceptualise humans' ethical responsibilities towards nonhumans (Morton, 2010). However, hierarchical and dualistic constructs of human–animal–nature relations occasionally resurface.[4] Some, for instance, extend special ethical consideration to species perceived as sentient or otherwise possessing human-like characteristics (Sargisson, 2000):

> for me it's about consciousness and the ability to be a sentient being, to like feel joy and pain, suffering, happiness, but also have memory of it and have an ongoing story, and also be able to communicate that in society as well. And, you know, so many other things we could say that make human life valuable, which I think I could definitely see quite a lot of that in, I mean, this is very anthropocentric, but in the "higher" primates. I can see it in some similar creatures like crows and magpies, parrots and dolphins.
>
> *(Atacama, Earth First!, personal communication, 2018)*

> I said to myself, "Here we are killing this incredibly intelligent, beautiful, self-aware, sentient being for the purpose of making a weapon meant for the mass extermination of human beings", and that's when it struck me, as a species we're insane. And from that moment on I said I would do everything I could to protect them against us. So I developed this sort of a biocentric point of view, and I've been fighting against this anthropocentric-dominated culture ever since.
>
> *(Captain, Sea Shepherd, personal communication, 2017)*

Others seem to value species on the basis of their wider ecological significance:

> a whale is far more valuable than a human because whales perform vital ecosystem functions in the seas, which helps maintain phytoplankton populations, and therefore more oxygen. Humans don't produce anything, they destroy.
>
> *(Delfin, Sea Shepherd, personal communication, 2018)*

> I don't view trees as any less valuable than animals. In fact, they're probably even more valuable because they produce the oxygen that we breathe.
>
> *(Squirrel, Earth First!, personal communication, 2018)*

The aforementioned examples denote the persistence of a "logic of extensionism" wherein beings perceived to be ecologically important or posess other desirable characteristics are included within the ethical community; however, boundaries between who matters and who doesn't are still left intact (Celermajer et al., 2020, p. 3). A hierarchy of value still persists. Overall, however, most REAs sought to deconstruct traditional human–animal hierarchies and antagonistic dualisms:

> I went out for a walk with some friends today, and we came across a massive tree that had fallen down, and we were talking about that saying, you know, that, "If a tree falls in a forest does it make a sound if nobody's around to hear it?" And my friend sort of said, "You know, that's just so bloody arrogant to think that things only happen if humans are there to perceive them." And it's like, yeah, that's exactly where I come from on that, you know. Why do we always put ourselves at the center of these things?
>
> *(Horse, Earth First!, personal communication, 2018)*

> we've become very nervous-system-[focused]. Like, a lot of Animal Rights folk won't give credence or any time to any kind of theorizing or philosophizing, or experiential musings on the fact that plants, trees, etc. might have a degree of being, or sentience and intelligence that we can't comprehend as yet because they lack a central nervous system, in the same way that a lot of vegetarians will say, "Oh no, it's alright to eat fish because fish can't feel pain", kind of malarky. And again, it's this grading of superiority.
>
> *(Badger, Earth First!, personal communication, 2018)*

> I don't believe that humans go on top, I also don't believe that animals go on top. I think that we need to find a sustainable middle point in which we exploit each other as little as possible if not at all.
>
> *(Koala, Earth First!/Animal Liberation Front, personal communication, 2017)*

As noted in the excerpts above, many REAs are critical of "gradings of spuperiority" that use arbitrary (and often human-centred) criteria in order to designate certain species as more valuable or important than others. Such examples demonstrate a general striving to deconstruct hierarchies of being and valuation in line with the post-anthropocentric tradition. Activists' motivations for engaging in direct-activism are closely linked with their post-anthropocentric worldviews and apocalyptic (McNeish, 2017) or, increasingly, post-apocalyptic sensibilities. Ecological breakdown and the widespread loss of cherished Earth kin no longer looms on the horizon but is already thoroughly underway. Situated within a crisis-infused present, REA mobilisations increasingly focus on resisting further destruction in the here and now. REAs' deep kinship bonds with the nonhuman world appear crucial in sustaining engagement in emotionally and physically taxing, and often high-risk direct-action feats – i.e. arson of a lignite mine, occupying trees for weeks or months on end, road blockades – even amid widespread feelings of hopelessness (Alberro, 2021). REAs seem to feel so emotionally and socially at stake in the lives of Earth kin that their loss is experienced as no less than the "severing of a social bond" (van Dooren, 2014, p. 136), in turn fuelling their fervent mobilisations:

> I think when you live outside and you live in a place that's going to be destroyed, and I spent about 5 years around protest sites and being on them, you do develop that feeling. You start to really, really identify with the place that you are, and I saw people really identify with individual trees.
>
> *(Horse, Earth First!, personal communication, 2018)*

now I feel when I see whales die, like, my friends are dying, like, it's a person or somebody that I've already seen or connected with.

(Jellyfish, Sea Shepherd, personal communication, 2017)

in the moment of connection, I'm not there...I don't feel anything; I'm lost in connection, you know, I'm completely, just...the sense of self isn't there. The sense of interwoven connectedness with another being doesn't really have space for ego as such, as me having power. It just feels like a longing has been fulfilled.

(Stonehenge, XR, personal communication, 2018)

I could rationalize the concept that we're made of the same atoms and for that reason we're all the same composition, just structured in a different way, and that' a wonderful concept, but that doesn't make me love the trees more than I already do.

(Koala, Earth First!/Animal Liberation Front, personal communication, 2017)

REAs on the whole exhibit a relational ontology that poses fundamental challenges to the central tenets of Western Anthropocentrism – namely that humans are categorically separate from and superior to nonhumans (Plumwood, 2002; Ferrando, 2016). More significantly, many repeatedly refer to other species and the natural world as kin with whom they are inextricably entangled rather than external objects to be protected and preserved. As discussed below, this singular aspect of their sensibilities serves as a powerful motivator for radical action.

Bodies on the Line

REAs' post-anthropocentric sensibilities and deep kinship bonds with Earth others serve as the prime motivational drivers of REA engagement in high-risk and occasionally life-threatening direct-action feats. During many of their former anti-whaling campaigns in the Southern Ocean, SSCS frequently harassed and rammed whaling vessels in order to prevent harpooning and refueling (Nagtazaam, 2013). In 1986, two SSCS engineers destroyed two of Iceland's four whaling ships in Reykjavik Harbour as well as the whale processing station at Hvalfjodur, effectively shutting down Icelandic commercial whaling for 16 years (Coronado, 1986)[5]. EF! Activists, particularly during the group's earlier years, have cut cables powering machinery, engaged in arson of extractive enterprises, and attached themselves to tractors using bicycle D-locks as a largely symbolic tactics intended to generate "manufactured vulnerability" (Doherty, 2005, p. 168). More recently, EF!, Extinction Rebellion and other REA groups have been blockading and occupying various sites along the proposed route for the HS2 high-speed railway in the UK in light of the threats posed to vulnerable ecosystems and species. In December 2020 tensions further rose between REAs and police when a veteran activist occupied a makeshift bamboo structure above the River Colne at the Colne Valley Nature Reserve in order to obstruct HS2 construction (Topham, 2020). For many REAs, desperate times indeed call for desperate measures:

When the law won't fix the problem we put our bodies on the line to stop the destruction. Direct-action draws attention to the crises facing the natural world and it saves lives

(EF!, personal communication, 2017).

what I found was this notion that direct-action is the only real thing that brings real social change. You get slow social change through the ballot box, as regimes change, and you will get slow progress through lobbying and legal approaches. But there's a sense that there has to be a direct-action component to really get quicker change."-
(Squirrel, Earth First!, personal communication, 2018)

we do have a timer going on the environment. This isn't the time to be signing petitions and asking nicely, like, we have to take it into our own hands. So, I think direct-action is instrumental, like, the thing that we need. And with the animals, like, we have a fox hunting ban yet foxes are still dying. I'm not going to ask them to stop killing foxes, I'm not; I'm just going to stop them killing the fox.
(Earth First!/Hunt Saboteurs, personal communication, 2018)

In other words, direct-action brings results when the situation is urgent and conventional tactics are not securing change radially or quickly enough. Often, participants alluded to the inefficacy of parliamentary or traditional modes of political participation – i.e. voting, lobbying – in light of the mounting severity of contemporary climate and ecological breakdown. Many emphasised how decades of attempts at institutional reform through international environmental and climate accords, and national environmental policies have failed to significantly curb climate and ecological degradation (Spash, 2016). Indeed, global biodiversity loss and greenhouse gas emissions (mostly from China, the United States, the EU and India) have only continued to rise. The steep declines in socio-economic activity induced by the COVID-19 pandemic have made no significant impact on longterm warming trends, with the world still on track to reach a catastrophic excess of 3C by 2100 (UNEP, 2020). To add insult to injury, the G7 cohort of the world's wealthiest economies, and those best placed to weather the impacts of climate chaos, are investing billions more into fossil fuel projects than into green sectors in order to spur post-pandemic economic recovery (Laville, 2021). As the latest IPCC report (2021) warns, limiting warming to even 2 degrees by 2100, as espoused by the Paris Agreement, will be virtually impossible without immediate and far-reaching structural transformations across ever sector from transport to food and energy.

However, many participants alluded to the limited transformative potential of relying solely on physically interventionist tactics such as lock-on's and tree sits; rather, the Herculean task of fundamental socio-ecological transformation requires every activist tool in the shed:

We believe in using all of the tools in the toolbox, from grassroots and legal organizing to civil disobedience and monkeywrenching. When the law won't fix the problem, we put our bodies on the line to stop the destruction. Earth First!'s direct-action approach draws attention to the crises facing the natural world, and it saves lives.
(EF! Primer, personal communication, 2011)

You need lots of stuff happening in order for one of the groups to hit across a strategy that will work. So, I do think that it is only from the direct-action scene that something will emerge that can change society fundamentally…
(Meadow, Earth First!, personal communication, 2017)

I have gone and locked myself on in front of the diggers, and it works for a day or for as long as it takes for them to cut you out, and then try again the next day. It's piecemeal. For me, the movement of XR and the other grassroots organizations that are taking direct-action, EF! in disseminating information and gathering activists…we need to mobilize more people in defense of these places, because me, one person with all this passion, I have very little by way of offering to stop this kind of destruction. I need more people to wake up to it.

(Stonehenge, XR, personal communication, 2018)

Although often emphasising the necessity of interventionist DA-style tactics for effectively stemming tides of ecological decline, many REAs like Stonehenge ultimately acknowledge the need for widespread collaboration across movements and segments of the public, and for the deployment of myriad tactics. This alludes to a broader tension within left politics around how fundamental societal transformations ought to be brought about: through oppositional and prefigurative micropolitics or through the seizing of structural (state) power? (Büscher & Fletcher, 2020, p. 178). Nevertheless, REAs often emphasise the need to adopt interventionist direct-action tactics not only in light of their deep kinship bonds with the nonhuman world but also because of its role in foreshadowing more ethical and liveable worlds, as discussed later.

Discussion

"The Great Refusal": Crying "No!" to the Existing Order

An opposition which is directed, not against a particular form of government or against particular conditions within a society, but against a given social system as a whole, cannot remain legal and lawful because it is the established legality and the established law which it opposes

(Marcuse, 1969, p. 66).

Mainstream environmentalism has typically sought to implement first-order changes from within the present system, such as recycling, changes in legislation and "green"za consumption (Plumwood, 2010). In contrast, REAs – so emotionally and ethically embroiled in the lives of nonhumans – seek and engages in second-order changes which entail the transformation of whole oppressive systems (Glasser, 2011). REAs, along with many of today's emergent youth environmental movements such as Fridays for Future, seek to address the *root* causes[6] – ontological, ethical, structural – of socio-ecological decline (Johnson & Burke, 2021; Pickard et al., 2020). Moreover, they desire a wholesale reconstitution of society – namely fundamental changes in how we eat, power our homes, travel, work, and value the nonhuman world – and thus adopt the requisite approaches and strategies. However, in response to REAs' more destructive direct-action tactics, many have drawn on the the pejorative sense of "radical" and referred to them variously as "extremists" and even "eco-terrorists"[7] (Liddick, 2006; Nagtzaam & Lentini, 2007; Eilstrup-Sangiovanni & Bondaroff, 2014; Posluszna, 2015).

In 2001 after their infamous arson attacks against a ski resort in Vail Mountain, Colorado (Dejevsky, 1998), the radical environmental group Earth Liberation Front was labelled the United States' lead domestic terrorist threat (Vanderheiden, 2005). There were no casualties, though the action did result in millions of dollars' worth of damage, which was the intent. Drawing on previous scholarship on political extremism (Safire, 1996; Midlarsky, 2011), Bötticher (2017) offers a consensus definition of political "extremism" as opposed to "radicalism". Herein, extremism is framed as an ideological position embraced by dogmatic anti-establishment movements which: view politics as a struggle for supremacy, are willing to engage in – and at times glorify – criminal acts and mass violence in order to gain political power, eschew diversity in favour of social homogenisation and exhibit a penchant for totalitarian rule over democratic modes of political participation (p. 74). REAs exhibit anti-system or radicalised identities via their engagement in extra-parliamentary modes of political activity for effecting fundamental transformations in mainstream socio-economic and political systems (Dalton & Rohrschneider, 2003). However, REAs venerate diversity and the irreducible singularity of the other – indeed, many are mobilising against the systematic annihilation of life's diverse forms amid the Capitalocene. Moreover, they overwhelmingly favour direct-democratic and non-hierarchical political modalities, and thoroughly reject the use of violence against living entities as a political tool. Radicalism, unlike political extremism, is emancipatory and seeks to enact sweeping socio-economic and political transformations for the betterment of all (Bötticher, 2017) – for REAs, this includes humans as well as nonhumans.

The thoroughly disruptive strategy of DA (Tilly & Tarrow, 2015) is typically justified on moral grounds and adopted when perceived to be the only moral recourse, such as when laws in place are designed to protect corporate and state actors who benefit financially from the exploitation of the natural world (White, 2012; Johnson & Johnson, 2017). From a crimino-logical perspective some have argued that state and corporate inaction on – and in many cases their active thwarting of action against – anthropogenic climate change constitutes among the gravest transnational environmental crimes (Lynch et al., 2010; White, 2012). Today, environmental protectors around the world are being newly threatened by mounting violence and state counter-terrorism measures, from new anti-terrorism legislation in the Philippines targeting climate protestors to the UK Police, Crime, Sentencing and Courts Bill aiming to criminalise non-violent protest (Birss, 2017; Taylor, 2021). Environmental protectors in Latin America at the front lines of resistance against extractive capital's exploitation of resources, land and people continually face not only imprisonment but outright threats to life – approximately 577 were killed between 2010 and 2015 alone (Birs, 2017, p. 316).

Given the general paucity of adequate action on climate and ecological breakdown and urgent need for alternatives modes of being, DA – including ecotage – can be framed as a politically and ethically salient response (White, 2012, p. 128). Ecotage as "violence within circumscribed ethical limits" (Vanderheiden, 2005, p. 436) entails acts of *property* destruction in order to maximise economic damage and thereby hinder extractive enterprises, and is in no way aimed towards harming life or instilling fear. As such, it lacks many of the necessary criteria for a truly terrorist or extremist act. However, DA does have drawbacks, namely concerning its effectiveness at the macro-level, over potentially alienating the public, dangers from repeated transgressions of the law (Moffa, 2012; Berny & Rootes, 2018), and logical inconsistencies with the aims of creating peaceful and non-hierarchical societies (Doherty, 2005). What appears to evoke such vehement opposition to the aims and tactics of REA's is, as Celermajer et al. (2020) poignantly observe, the paradigmatic challenges they represent to the entrenched hierarchy of beings, and their demands for the fundamental transformation of institutions "whose political economy is premised on the exclusion and exploitation of the nonhuman" (p. 16). REAs pose not threats to life or wellbeing but to the interests of capitalist states and corporations.

Conclusion

REA's rise amidst the myriad socio-ecological perturbations of the Capitalocene as New social movement forms presenting fervent "critiques of existing social orders and realities" (Ingalsbee, 1996, p. 266). They challenge the status quo via their direct and oppositional modes of activism, and through their post-anthropocentric worldviews which seek to deconstruct one of the most pervasive Western cultural dominants: human supremacy. REAs' deep kinship bonds with terrestrial kin serve as a particularly powerful action motivator when the latter are perceived to be under threat; such close ties with entitities perceived as kin rather than external objects are what compel many REAs to consequently risk their safety and even their lives for their protection. This sense of urgency and commitment is further heightened amidst extant climate breakdown and the sixth mass extinction, wherein the loss of the earth's diverse life forms continues apace. During such desperate times, REAs deploy every activist tool at their disposal in order to slow and ultimately halt such tides of loss and degradation.

REAs aren't merely mobilising to resist climate chaos and biological annihilation; such prefigurative political groups also seek to enact "utopic alternatives" (Breines, 1989; Yates, 2021) in the present, from a grassroots approach owing to their anarchic aversions to state-authoritative methods of social change (Yates, 2021). At its core prefigurative politics is decidedly utopian (Alberro, 2021), consisting of a "great refusal" of the present. Stemming from the New Left movements of the 1960s, prefigurative political modes are fuelled by an upsurge of radical hopes and sensibilities that anticipate the desired society and sets of relations devoid of exploitation and oppression (Breines, 1989; Franks, 2018). Oppositional and prefigurative movements, "moved by an impious dream of a mythic New Order – ...rise up and cry *No* to the existing order... saying, "You cannot go on assuming you are the true and correct order..." (Cathcart, 1978, p. 243) and further "prophesy the coming of the new" (Griffin, 1969, p. 460). For instance, since its inception in 2006 the radical Climate Camp movement has erected camps around Heathrow's proposed third runway site, Drax power station in Yorkshire, and other extractive sites not only to oppose fossil fuel extraction but, crucially, to live – even if only briefly – more ecologically resilient worlds (Saunders, 2012, p. 829). As the history of societal transformations demonstrates, it's (radical) activism and other forms of grassroots mobilisations – not top-down implementation of legislation – that constitutes "the most fundamental pillar of substantive change" (White, 2012, p. 129; Gunningham, 2019).

REAs offer crucial "parallel universes" (Klein, 2015, p. xxiv) that are fervently opposed to the "Now" of late capitalism, and where ecologically sensitive perceptions, relations and actions are enacted, even if only fleetingly. One may wonder, without their ongoing resistance, how much more we stand to lose.

Notes

1 A fascinating "Global South" precursor to the proliferation of direct-action in the West is India's Chipko movement, founded in 1973 in Uttar Pradesh, wherein rural and indigenous people fought to reclaim control of the forests on which their livelihoods depended. These activists opposed the commercial interests of colluding bureaucrats who sought to exploit the forest's resources by chaining themselves to trees in order to prevent them from being felled (Haynes, 1999).

2 Indeed, recent anti-fracking and fossil fuel divestment campaigns largely adopt reformist emphases on legislative change and other parliamentary modes of political activity (Ogrodnik & Staggenborg, 2016).

3 However, unlike mainstream litigation-based environmental movement organisations (such as Greenpeace and the World Wildlife Fund), SSCS activists generally exhibit more radical identities marked by a rejection of involvement of mainstream society and with it normative methods for bringing about social change (Stuart et al., 2013).

4 Indeed, deep ecology is still predicated on a binary between living entities that exhibit strivings towards flourishing and a deanimated world beyond the five living kingdoms that include plants, animals, fungi, protists and single-celled archaeobacteria. This mode of hyper-separation is problematic for Plumwood (2010) not least because it precludes humans' abilities to empathise with and otherwise relate ethically with the nonhuman world.

5 However, on 29th August 2017, SSCS officially declared the end of their Southern Ocean campaign against Japanese whalers due largely to their inability to match Japan's military-grade surveillance

technology, which tracks SSCS ships' movements in real time via satellite, as well as the passing of new anti-terrorism legislation which specifically targets REA groups such as SSCS.

6 Hence the word radical with respect to REAs in the etymological sense, stemming from the Late Latin *radicalis*, itself from Latin *radic-, radix*, meaning "root" (Merriam-Webster, 2021).

7 The term "eco-terrorism" was coined by former leader of the Center for the Defense of Free Enterprise (CDFE), Ron Arnold, in a 1983 article entitled "Eco-Terrorism" published in Reason magazine (Smith, 2008, p. 545).

References

Aberbach, J., & Rockman, B. (2002). Conducting and coding elite interviews. *PS: Political Science & Politics, 35*(4), 673–676. doi:10.1017/S1049096502001142.

Alberro, H. (2019). Methodological considerations for the special-risk researcher: A research note. *Methodological Innovations, 12*(1), 1–6. doi: 10.1177/2059799119840975

Alberro, H. (2020). 'Valuing life itself': On radical environmental activists' post-anthropocentric worldviews. *Journal of Environmental Values, 29*(6), 669–689. doi: 10.3197/096327120X15752810324093

Alberro, H. (2021). In and against eco-apocalypse: On the terrestrial ecotopianism of radical environmental activists. *Utopian Studies, 32*(1), 36–55. doi:10.5325/utopianstudies.32.1.0036.

Andersen, M. S., & Massa, I. (2000). Ecological modernization—origins, dilemmas and future directions. *Journal of Environmental Policy and Planning, 2*(4), 337–345. doi:10.1080/714852820.

Berny, N., & Rootes, C. (2018). Environmental NGOs at a crossroads? *Environmental Politics, 27*(6), 947–972. doi: 10.1080/09644016.2018.1536293.

Birss, M. (2017). Criminalizing environmental activism: As threats to the environment increase across Latin America, new laws and police practices take aim against the front line activists defending their land and resources. *NACLA Report on the Americas, 49*(3), 315–322. doi: 10.1080/10714839.2017.1373958.

Boggs, C. (1977). Marxism, prefigurative communism, and the problem of workers' control. *Radical America, 11*(6), 99–122.

Bötticher, A. (2017). Towards academic consensus definitions of radicalism and extremism. *Perspectives on Terrorism, 11*(4), 73–77. Retrieved August 20, 2021, from www.jstor.org/stable/26297896.

Bowen, G. A. (2009). Document analysis as a qualitative research method. *Qualitative Research Journal, 9*(2), 27–40. https://doi.org/10.3316/QRJ0902027

Braun, V., & Clarke, V. (2013). *Successful qualitative research: A practical guide for beginners.* London: Sage.

Bradshaw, E. A. (2015). Blockadia rising: Rowdy greens, direct action and the Keystone XL pipeline. *Critical Criminology, 23*(4), 433–448. https://doi.org/10.1007/s10612-015-9289-0

Breines, W. (1989). *Community and organization in the new left, 1962–1968: The great refusal.* Rutgers, the State University: Rutgers University Press.

Buscher, B., & Fletcher, R. (2020). *The conservation revolution: Radical ideas for saving nature beyond the Anthropocene.* London: Verso Trade.

Cafaro, P. (2015). Three ways to think about the sixth mass extinction. *Biological Conservation, 192*, 387–393. https://doi.org/10.1016/j.biocon.2015.10.017.

Cassegård, C., & Thörn, H. (2018). Toward a postapocalyptic environmentalism? Responses to loss and visions of the future in climate activism. *Environment and Planning E: Nature and Space, 1*(4), 561–578. https://doi.org/10.1177/2514848618793331

Cathcart, R. S. (1978). Movements: Confrontation as rhetorical form. *Southernn Speech Communication Journal, 43*(3), 233–247. https://doi.org/10.1080/10417947809372383

Ceballos, G., Ehrlich, P. R., & Raven, P. H. (2020). Vertebrates on the brink as indicators of biological annihilation and the sixth mass extinction. *Proceedings of the National Academy of Sciences, 117*(24), 13596–13602. https://doi.org/10.1073/pnas.1922686117

Celermajer, D., Schlosberg, D., Rickards, L., Stewart-Harawira, M., Thaler, M., Tschakert, P., ... & Winter, C. (2020). Multispecies justice: Theories, challenges, and a research agenda for environmental politics. *Environmental Politics, 30*(1–2), 119–140. https://doi.org/10.1080/09644016.2020.1827608

Cianchi, J. (2015). *Radical environmentalism: Nature, identity and more-than-human agency.* Hampshire: Palgrave Macmillan.

Coronado, R. (1986) Sinking the Icelandic whaling fleet. *No Compromise.* Retrieved from: https://web.archive.org/web/20140307134214/http://www.nocompromise.org/issues/28sinkingwhalers.html

Dalton, R.J., Recchia, S. and Rohrschneider, R. (2003). The environmental movement and the modes of political action. *Comparative Political Studies, 36*(7), pp. 743–771. https://doi.org/10.1177/00104 14003255108

De Cleyre, V. (1912). *Direct action*. Chadwyck-Healey Incorporated. Retrieved from:https://philpapers. org/rec/DECDA

Deakin, H., & Wakefield, K. (2014). Skype interviewing: Reflections of two PhD researchers. *Qualitative Research, 14*(5), 603–616. https://doi.org/10.1177/1468794113488126

Dejevsky, M. 1998. Eco-terrorists burn ski resort. The Independent. Retrieved from: www.independent. co.uk/news/eco-terrorists-burn-ski-resort-1180024.html

Doherty, B. (2005). *Ideas and actions in the green movement*. London: Routledge.

Eilstrup-Sangiovanni, M., & Bondaroff, T. N. P. (2014). From advocacy to confrontation: Direct enforcement by environmental NGOs. *International Studies Quarterly, 58*(2), 348–361.

Estes, N. (2019). *Our history is the future: Standing Rock versus the Dakota Access Pipeline, and the long tradition of indigenous resistance*. London: Verso.

Ferrando, F. (2016). The party of the Anthropocene: Post-humanism, environmentalism and the post-anthropocentric paradigm shift. *Relations: Beyond Anthropocentrism, 4*, 159–173. doi: 10.7358/rela-2016-002-ferr

Franks, B. (2018). Prefiguration. In B. Franks, N. Jun and L. Williams (Eds.), *Anarchism: A conceptual approach* (pp. 28–43). London: Routledge.

Garcia Hernandez, C. C. (2007). Radical environmentalism: The new civil disobedience. *Seattle Journal of Social Justice, 6*, 289–351.

Glasser, H. (2011). Naess's deep ecology: Implications for the human prospect and challenges for the future. *Inquiry, 54*(1), 52–77. https://doi.org/10.1080/0020174X.2011.542943

Griffin, L. M. (1969). A dramatistic theory of the rhetoric social movements. In W. Rueckert (Ed.), *Critical responses to Kenneth Burke* (pp. 456–478). Minneapolis: University of Minnesota Press.

Gunningham, N. (2019). Averting climate catastrophe: Environmental activism, extinction rebellion and coalitions of influence. *King's Law Journal, 30*(2), 194–202. https://doi.org/10.1080/09615 768.2019.1645424

Haynes, J. (1999). Power, politics and environmental movements in the Third World. *Environmental politics, 8*(1), 222–242. https://doi.org/10.1080/09644019908414445

Heynen, N., & Van Sant, L. (2015). Political ecologies of activism and direct action politics. In T. Perreault, G. Bridge, and J. McCarthy (Eds.), *The Routledge handbook of political ecology*. Oxford: Routledge.

Ingalsbee, T. (1996). Earth First! activism: Ecological postmodern praxis in radical environmentalist identities. *Sociological Perspectives, 39*(2), 263–276. https://doi.org/10.2307/1389312

IPCC. (2021). Summary for policymakers. In V. Masson-Delmotte, P. Zhai, A. Pirani, S. L. Connors, C. Péan, S. Berger, N. Caud, Y. Chen, L. Goldfarb, M. I. Gomis, M. Huang, K. Leitzell, E. Lonnoy, J. B. R. Matthews, T. K. Maycock, T. Waterfield, O. Yelekçi, R. Yu & B. Zhou (Eds.), Climate change 2021: The physical science basis. Contribution of working group I to the sixth assessment report of the intergovernmental panel on climate change. Cambridge, UK: Cambridge University Press.

Irving, S., & Helin, J. (2018). A world for sale? An ecofeminist reading of sustainable development discourse. *Gender, Work & Organization, 25*(3), 264–278. https://doi.org/10.1111/gwao.12196

Johnson, E. W., & Burke, J. (2021). Environmental movements in the United States. In B.S. Caniglia et al. (eds.), *Handbook of Environmental Sociology* (pp. 495–515). Springer, Cham.

Kant, I., & Schneewind, J. B. (2002). *Groundwork for the metaphysics of morals*. New Haven: Yale University.

Klein, N. (2015). *This changes everything: Capitalism vs. the climate*. New York: Simon and Schuster.

Kopnina, H. (2012). The Lorax complex: Deep ecology, ecocentrism and exclusion. *Journal of Integrative Environmental Sciences, 9*(4), 235–254. https://doi.org/10.1080/1943815X.2012.742914

Latour, B. (1993). *The pasteurization of France*. Cambridge, MA: Harvard University Press.

Laville, S. (2021). G7 nations committing billions more to fossil fuel than green energy. Retrieved from: G7 nations committing billions more to fossil fuel than green energy | G7 | The Guardian.

Liddick, D. (2006). *Eco-terrorism*. Praeger. Ebook. Retrieved from: http://publisher.abc-clio.com/978031 3042942

Lynch, M. J., Burns, R. G., & Stretesky, P. B. (2010). Global warming and state-corporate crime: The politicalization of global warming under the Bush administration. *Crime, Law and Social Change, 54*(3–4), 213–239. https://doi.org/10.1007/s10611-010-9245-6

Marangudakis, M., 2001. Rationalism and irrationalism in the environmental movement—the case of Earth First!. *Democracy & Nature, 7*(3), 457–467. https://doi.org/10.1080/10855660120092311

Marcuse, H. (1969). *An essay on liberation.* Boston: Beacon Press.

McCoyd, J. L., & Kerson, T. S. (2006). Conducting intensive interviews using email: A serendipitous comparative opportunity. *Qualitative Social Work, 5*(3), 389–406. https://doi.org/10.1177/147332500 6067367

McGregor, D., Whitaker, S., & Sritharan, M. (2020). Indigenous environmental justice and sustainability. *Current Opinion in Environmental Sustainability, 43*, 35–40. https://doi.org/10.1016/j.cos ust.2020.01.007

McNeish, W. (2017). From revelation to revolution: Apocalypticism in green politics. *Environmental Politics, 26*(6), 1035–1054. https://doi.org/10.1080/09644016.2017.1343766

Meadows, D. H., Meadows, D. L., Randers, J., & Behrens, W. W. (1972). *The limits to growth: The 30-year update.* London: Earthscan.

Midlarsky, M. I. (2011). *Origins of political extremism: Mass violence in the twentieth century and beyond.* Cambridge: Cambridge University Press.

Milstein, T., McGaurr, L., & Lester, L. (2020). Make love, not war?: Radical environmental activism's reconfigurative potential and pitfalls. *Environment and Planning E: Nature and Space, 4*(2), 1–20. https://doi.org/10.1177/2514848620901443

Moffa, A. L. (2012). Two competing models of activism, one goal: A case study of anti-whaling campaigns in the South Ocean. *Yale Journal of Internationa Law, 37*, 201–214.

Moore, J. W. (2017). The Capitalocene, Part I: On the nature and origins of our ecological crisis. *The Journal of Peasant Studies, 44*(3), 594–630. https://doi.org/10.1080/03066150.2016.1235036

Morton, T. (2010). Thinking ecology: The mesh, the strange stranger, and the beautiful soul. *Collapse, 6*, 265–293.

Marangudakis, M. (2001). Rationalism and irrationalism in the environmental movement—the case of earth first!. *Democracy & Nature, 7*(3), 457–467. https://doi.org/10.1080/10855660120092311

Murray, J. (2020). HS2 protestors glue themselves to DfT as construction begins. Retrieved from: www. theguardian.com/uk-news/2020/sep/04/hs2-protesters-glue-themselves-to-dft-as-construction-begins

Naess, A. (1973). The shallow and the deep, long-range ecology movement. A summary. *Inquiry, 16*(1–4), 95–100. https://doi.org/10.1080/00201747308601682

Nagtzaam, G. (2013). Gaia's Navy: The Sea Shepherd Conservation Society's battle to stay afloat and international law. *Wm. & Mary Environmental Law & Policy Review, 38*, 613–694.

Nagtzaam, G., & Lentini, P. (2007). Vigilantes on the high seas? The sea shepherds and political violence. *Terrorism and Political Violence, 20*(1), 110–133. doi:10.1080/09546550701723658

Ogrodnik, C., & Staggenborg, S. (2016). The ebb and flow of environmentalism. *Sociology Compass, 10*(3), 218–229. https://doi.org/10.1111/soc4.12353

Pellow, D. N., (2014). *Total liberation: The power and promise of animal rights and the radical earth movement.* Minneapolis: University of Minnesota Press.

Phelps Bondaroff, T. N., (2020). A typology of direct action at sea. In J. Pereira and A. Saramago (Eds.), *Non-human nature in world politics: Frontiers in international relations* (pp. 279–310). Cham: Springer. https://doi.org/10.1007/978-3-030-49496-4_14

Pickard, S., Bowman, B., & Arya, D. (2020). "We are radical in our kindness": The political socialisation, motivations, demands and protest actions of young environmental activists in Britain. *Youth and Globalization, 2*(2), 251–280. https://doi.org/10.1163/25895745-02020007

Plows, A., Wall, D., & Doherty, B. (2004). Covert repertoires: Ecotage in the UK. *Social Movement Studies, 3*(2), 199–219. https://doi.org/10.1080/1474283042000266128

Plumwood, V. (2002). *Feminism and the mastery of nature.* London: Routledge.

Plumwood, V. (2010). Nature in the active voice. In: *Climate change and philosophy: Transformational possibilities,* Irwin, R., *2010*, 32–47.

Posluszna, E. (2015). *Environmental and animal rights extremism, terrorism, and national security.* Oxford: Butterworth-Heinemann Elsevier.

Robé, C. (2015). The convergence of eco-activism, neoliberalism, and reality TV in Whale Wars. *Journal of Film and Video, 67*(3–4), 94–111. https://doi.org/10.5406/jfilmvideo.67.3-4.0094

Rootes, C. (2008). The environmental movement. In M. Klimke and J. Scharloth (Eds.), *1968 in Europe* (pp. 295–305). New York: Palgrave Macmillan.

Rootes, C. (2014). *Environmental movements: Local, national and global.* New York: Routledge.

Stern, N., & Stern, N. H. (2007). *The economics of climate change: The Stern review.* Cambridge: Cambridge University press.

Safire, W. (1996). On language-what's an extremist. *New York Times*, Section 6, p. 14.

Sargisson, L. (2000). Green utopias of self and other. *Critical Review of International Social and Political Philosophy*, *3*(2–3), 140–156.: https://doi.org/10.1080/13698230008403317

Saunders, C. (2012). Reformism and radicalism in the Climate Camp in Britain: Benign coexistence, tensions and prospects for bridging. *Environmental Politics*, *21*(5), 829–846. https://doi.org/10.1080/09644016.2012.692937

Smith, R. K. (2008). Ecoterrorism: A critical analysis of the vilification of radical environmental activists as terrorists. *Environmental Law*, *38*, 495–536.

Spash, C. L. (2016). This changes nothing: The Paris Agreement to ignore reality. *Globalizations*, *13*(6), 928–933. https://doi.org/10.1080/14747731.2016.1161119

Steffen, W., Broadgate, W., Deutsch, L., Gaffney, O., & Ludwig, C. (2015). The trajectory of the Anthropocene: The great acceleration. *The Anthropocene Review*, *2*(1), 81–98. https://doi.org/10.1177/2053019614564785

Stuart, A., Thomas, E. F., Donaghue, N., & Russell, A. (2013). "We may be pirates, but we are not protesters": Identity in the Sea Shepherd Conservation Society. *Political Psychology*, *34*(5), 753–777. https://doi.org/10.1111/pops.12016

Tarrow, S. (2013). *The language of contention: Revolutions in words, 1688–2012*. Cambridge: Cambridge University Press.

Taylor, B. (2008). The tributaries of radical environmentalism. Journal for the Study of *Radicalism*, *2*(1), 27–61. doi: 10.1353/jsr.2008.0028

Taylor, M. (2021). "Environment protestors being criminalised around world, say experts". The Guardian. Retrieved from: Environment protest being criminalised around world, say experts | Environmental activism | The Guardian

Thörn, H. (1997). *Rörelser i det moderna: politik, modernitet och kollektiv identitet i Europa 1789–1989*. Stockholm: Tiden Atena.

Tilly, C., & Tarrow, S. G. (2015). *Contentious politics*. New York: Oxford University Press.

Topham, G. (2020). Veteran activist Swampy among protestors in HS2 site standoff with police. The Guardian. Retrieved from: www.theguardian.com/uk-news/2020/dec/08/veteran-activist-swampy-among-protesters-in-hs2-site-standoff-with-police?CMP=twt_a-environment_b-gdneco&fbclid=IwAR1lGFZi4hUFEWE843cThHoxWpbNzMB2d-WJ0ti-raf-7QFTxlKPkX_1A9o

United Nations Environment Programme (UNEP). (2020) Emissions gap report 2020: Executive summary. Retrieved from: EGR20ESE.pdf (unep.org)

Vanderheiden, S. (2005). Eco-terrorism or justified resistance? Radical environmentalism and the "war on terror". *Politics & Society*, *33*(3), 425–447. doi: 10.1177/0032329205278462

Van Der Heijden, H. A. (1997). Political opportunity structure and the institutionalisation of the environmental movement. *Environmental Politics*, *6*(4), 25–50. https://doi.org/10.1080/09644019708414357

Van Dooren, T. (2014). *Flight ways: Life and loss at the edge of extinction*. New York Chichester, West Sussex: Columbia University Press.

White, R. (2012). Environmental activism and resistance to state–corporate crime. In *State crime and resistance* (pp. 141–153). Routledge. *WWF Living Planet Report 2020*. Retrieved from: www.researchgate.net/publication/344187626_WWF_Living_Planet_Report_2020

World Wildlife Fund (WWF) (2022). Living Planet Report 2022 – Building a naturepositive society. In Almond, R.E.A., Grooten, M., Juffe Bignoli, D. & Petersen, T. (Eds), *WWF, Gland, Switzerland*. Retrieved from: https://www.wwf.org.uk/our-reports/living-planet-report-2022

Yates, L. (2021). Prefigurative politics and social movement strategy: The roles of prefiguration in the reproduction, mobilisation and coordination of movements. *Political Studies*, *69*(4), 1033–1052. https://doi.org/10.1177/0032321720936046

CONCLUSION

Key Findings, Lessons Learnt and Future Avenues of Research

Elisa Orofino and William Allchorn

Introduction

This study started with a dissatisfaction over current discussions on non-violent extremism as a topic relegated to the sidelines of academic literature rather than on the forefront of research as it should. This Handbook has acknowledged the importance of non-violent extremism as a liminal space preceding terror acts but at the same time has argued that non-violent extremism reserves itself as a standing-alone area of study in its own right. The reasons for such an exclusive treatment of non-violent extremism are related to the specificities of the phenomenon itself, which has many different expressions within a variety of ideologies. This volume navigated the reader through religious, far-right and post-modern non-violent extremisms shedding light on the main actors representing each category, their goals in different national contexts.

This volume has taken into consideration the challenges that non-violent extremism might pose as a conveyor belt to violence, refusing at the same time academic assumptions on the unavoidable evolution of extremism into terrorism. Instead, this Handbook acknowledges an imaginary continuum starting with "radicalisation" (as the adoption of a specific set of extreme ideas), moving along with "extremism" (when individuals start acting upon the previously adopted set of ideas, with specific behaviours – not necessarily violent) and finally concludes with "terrorism" as an offending behaviour motivated by a specific set of ideas adopted during the radicalisation stage which eventuates in the choice of individual to use violence to achieve his/her goals.[1]

Although not all radicals become terrorists, it is a fact that all terrorists have moved along the imaginary continuum starting with radicalisation, proceeding with extremism and finally concluding with the terror act. Given the connection between the three stages aforementioned (i.e. radicalisation, extremism and terrorism), this contribution stands as a topical addition to the current academic and political debate on such pressing security issues which stress the need to refocus research on prevention rather than on prosecution. As demonstrated by the analysis of non-violent extremism(s) through a variety of case studies in this volume, the radical ideology and propensity to work with or against the State varies drastically between different groups and geographical contexts.

Evidence of this assumption was provided by the exploration of groups so varied as those encouraging violent action (e.g. Hizb ut-Tahrir), those encouraging intense criticism of the

DOI: 10.4324/9781003032793-38

state (e.g. Pegida) and those with a radically different vision of settled politics (e.g. DiEM25) just to provide some examples. The chapters dedicated to these case studies[2] showed that these groups share the same ideological foundations of the terror-counterparts.[3] However, the methods chosen to achieve their political, social, economic and religious goals do not involve violence. As illustrated throughout the volume and across different ideologies, non-violent extremist groups mostly tend to base their methodology on propaganda and education of their target groups in order to win the hearts and minds of as many followers as they can. They believe that a long-term change requires time to be implemented: people need to accept the ideas sponsored by the specific group, they need to espouse their cause and strongly long for the change-specific groups are advocating for.

Non-violent Extremism(s) at a Glance

After navigating the various sections of this Handbook, the reader would be familiar with a set of specific concepts that all kinds of non-violent extremisms[4] have in common. More precisely, from the case studies illustrated in this volume and the narratives they spread both online and offline, three key elements were identified as common to all non-violent extremisms explored.

As highlighted in Figure I.1, several elements are recurring in all ideological trends of non-violent extremism explored by this Handbook. First, all extremisms would have a clear enemy they intend to fight. This enemy varies according to the specific ideological trend under investigation. It can be the "corrupted West" for the Islamists together with the *kuffar* (unbelievers) and the *Jahili* (non-Muslims, ignorant about Islam) who do not live their life according to Islamic regulations and who usually try to deviate Muslims from their "right path".[5] The enemy could also be the Capitalistic establishment with all its industries, governments and corporate interests obsessed with profits who do not care about the environment, climate change and extinction risks. This is what most eco-radicals groups see as the evil to be challenged.[6] Moreover, the enemy could be a perceived unpurifying force that corrupts a perceived in-group, and therefore corrupts the aims of a religious or ethnic homogenous society. Some crossovers exist and are important to notice. For example, the political *bête noire* of both the non-violent far-left and eco-radicals tends to be big industry.[7] Moreover, the scapegoating of certain religious and ethnic outgroups is an overlapping cause for far-right and Buddhist extremists.

Table 33.1 Comparative components of non-violent extremist ideologies

Ideologies	Enemy to Fight	Group to Protect	Change to Achieve
Islamism	The West, the *kuffar* the *jahili*	The *ummah*	Living abiding *Shari'a* law
Buddhism	Non-Buddhist Minorities	Buddhist Majority	Religious homogeneity
Far Right	Ethnic (Non-White) Outgroup	Native (White) In-Group	Ethnic homogeneity
Incels	Gendered (Female) Outgroup	Gendered (Male) In-Group	Gendered Hierarchy, anti-feminism, sexual redistribution
Far Left	Capitalism, Class System	Working Class	Classless society
Feminism	Men, trans-gender people, patriarchy	Women	Gender-equality, social justice
Eco-radicals	Capitalism, Industries, Governments	Environment and Animals	Green societies, sustainable life-styles

Source: Authors' Own Illustration.

Going back to Figure I.1, non-violent expressions of extremism here explored all have a precise in-group they aim to protect and advocate for. Again, this group varies according to the specific ideology taken into consideration. Taking the Islamists as an example, the group they strongly want to protect are the *ummah,* i.e. the global community of Muslims. However, some groups are quite selective on what they consider as "true Muslims". In the case of Hizb ut-Tahrir, for instance, they publicly present themselves as a pious group of Muslims able to lead the *ummah* towards the correct interpretation of Islam and the correct religious obligations. However, the Hizbies (Hizb ut-Tahrir members) normally have a very bad opinion of other Muslims who do not belong to their in-group.

They tend to see all other competitors (such as the Muslim Brotherhood – see Chapter 8) as misleading individuals, attracting other Muslims towards wrong interpretations of Islam. Nonetheless, the Hizbies, as the great majority of non-violent extremist groups, still tend to sponsor themselves as being able to protect the whole *ummah* if they are willing to accept them as the "blessed leader" able to bring about change (see Orofino & Çobanoğlu's chapter). This is the same within the far-right groups featured within this volume.[8]

The same actors that are regarded as victims in one ideology tend to be regarded as enemies by other groups belonging to different ideologies. This applies to the dichotomy between the Islamists and the far right. If the *ummah* is considered as the group to protect within non-violent Islamist groups, the same *ummah* is considered as the enemy to fight through the lens of far-right groups. In particular, PEGIDA, the Identitarian movement and the Democratic Football Lads Alliance (DFLA) would subscribe to either Eurabia or "Great Replacement" conspiracy theories that suggest a secret cabal of left-wing elites have been facilitating the "invasion" or "over-population" of Europe by the resident and diaspora Muslim populations[9].

Last but not least, Figure I.1 has drawn attention to a third element that is common to all the kinds of non-violent extremism here explored, i.e. the change to achieve. Navigating through the sections of the Handbook makes it evident that all groups (regardless of the ideological trend they belong to) fight for a change. All groups want to change the status quo they live and operate in for several different reasons, mostly related to the fact that it is not adequate for the group they advocate for – it is either too dangerous, too unfair or too unethical. Issues about social justice, security, access to resources all impact the ideal change the groups want to promote and goals they have in mind. These premises are evident when navigating Cruz's chapter for instance. Exploring two feminist groups' protagonists of the social uprising in Chile in 2019 – Coordinadora 8 de Marzo and Asamblea Feminista Plurinacional – this chapter shows how both groups strongly advocated for gender equality and social justice within the uprising.

These groups came together as a form of protest against an extremely penalising national context for specific categories of citizens, in this case women and the working classes. In this respect, Cruz insightfully argues that

the dimension of non-violence in the feminist movement is not limited to traditional concepts of "strategic" and "principled" non-violent resistance but is rooted in a necessity of making visible a system of injustice which is predominantly (re)produced by the state throughout a history of oppression inherited from a dictatorial past.

The idea of a "system of injustice" is also perceived by far-left radicals who seek to combat what they perceive as the mutually combined forces of capitalism and fascism as keeping the working classes in chains. In Bruno, Downes and Chan's chapter, for example, they note how DiEM-25's ideological features bear ideological similarities to other radical left parties in Europe (i.e., such as Syriza in Greece and Podemos in Spain) through emphasising anti-capitalist (particularly in seeking to redress grievances of economic inequality), alongside internationalist and radical policies. Moreover, Peucker, Droogan and Holmes' chapter, they note that anti-fascist movements perceive the global rise of far-right extremism and fascist-like authoritarian government as being inherently linked to the neoliberal global capitalist system. Instead, the far-left seeks to install a classless system devoid of the capitalist system that produces fascist false consciousness of division and oppression.

Similar thoughts about division, oppression and need for re-distribution of resources are shared by the manosphere, especially by the group Incel whose actorship worldwide is increasing (see Hart et al.). Incel calls for the need of a social re-distribution of sex as they believe that men are entitled to have sex by birth regularly. In their opinion, the fact that some of them are not having sex is due to women who are rebelling. As analysed by Hart et al.'s contribution, Incel members see women as dehumanised sex objects who should be forced to have sex to serve men. This group also promotes conversation about the legitimacy of rape as a way to encourage a formal re-distribution of sex. Needless to say that the dissemination of such ideas can foster (and has fostered in the past) violent episodes directed to women around the world.[10]

Lessons Learnt

This Handbook wanted to be the ambitious project of the editors and the outstanding group of authors participating who devote their work to the very controversial theme of non-violent extremism in all its forms. It was not easy to categorise extremisms in different clusters, label them and identify some patterns as all these trends are usually very much more intertwined than we could imagine. However, we made this attempt and we are confident that this Handbook can mark the start of a robust strand of literature devoted to the analysis of "what happens before the bomb goes off" (Neumann, 2008, p.4), entirely devoted to a prevention perspective.

Going back to the initial assumption that all terrorists are radicals, but not all radicals are terrorists, it is essential to take a step back and see what ideological elements can trigger people towards violence, moving along the continuum from radicalisation to terrorism. All ideological elements common to all groups here analysed (i.e. the enemy, the group to protect and the change to achieve) stands as exactly the same in both non-violent and violent expression of Islamism. The non-violent Hizb ut-Tahrir would share the same ideas with Daesh on the need to fight *kuffar* and *Jahili,* but the methodology on how to fight them is what makes the big difference.

This book provided an insightful overview on these ideological similarities between violent and non-violent extremisms and stresses the need to re-focus on non-violent extremism to prevent and better understand violent extremism too. Non-violent extremists are at the forefront of national security agenda across the Western world as they are mostly free to spread inflammatory concepts – mostly anti-government, anti-establishment and openly targeting specific groups in the society – thanks to the human rights framework they operate within (Karagiannis, 2018). They present themselves as mere intellectual groups who are however able to lead people to violence (Orofino, 2015). This Handbook stands as a reminder on the need to go back to prevention to understand what lies below the complexity of the term terrorism and its expressions, and makes the following claims.

Moving Beyond Islamist Extremism: Studying Non-violent Extremism in the Round

Moving on from summary to contributions, one of the key innovations and contributions of this Handbook is its focus on a plurality of non-violent extremisms. For a long-time now terrorism and extremism studies have been overshadowed by violent and jihadi extremism. To some extent, this is understandable in the post-9/11 era. Jihadist perpetrators have come to dominate the threat environment and this has led to prioritising counter measures among policy elites that overwhelmingly focussed on violent and non-violent elements of the Islamist cause and Muslim diaspora. More recently, however, we know that – both in terms of the frequency of attacks and death count – it is the far right that is accounting for a growing number of terror attacks, with a 320% rise in the five years preceding 2019 (Global Terrorism Index, 2019).

New times therefore calls for a new focus and this Handbook has certainly provided fresh perspectives and modalities of extremism that fill scholarly and practitioner needs to get to grips with this new threat environment. Moving beyond Islamist groups, this Handbook has documented the rise of far-right and Buddhist non-violent extremism, new manifestations of feminist, left-wing and environmental radicalism – with groups that simply were not in existence two decades ago and geographies that have been previously overlooked as sites of extremism in the literature. A key aspect of this has been to kick start a scholarly conversation about non-violent extremism as a substantive focus of research in itself as well as unpicking the assumption that non-violent extremism deterministically leads to terrorism in the final instance.

Extremism, Radicalisation and Terrorism as Overlapping Concepts

One of the primary debates raging in the field of terrorism studies at this present time is the extent to which ideological extremism begets radicalisation to violent or non-violent actions. The most influential models (or pathways) explaining the shift from non-violent to violent extremism are Moghadam's (2005) "staircase" to terrorism, McCauley and Moskalenko's (2008) "pyramid" to terrorism, and Baran's (2005) "conveyor belt" to terrorism, that see non-violent extremism as the beginning of a path leading to violence.

As stated in the introduction to this Handbook, however, this is not always the case: there are many who become radicalised and engage in extremism (opposing the system) and yet "do not become foreign fighters, engage in terrorism, or even reach the frontline" (Chassman, 2016, p.213; see also Orofino, 2020). The assumption that all extremists will become terrorists might prevent scholars from studying the challenge against the national governments put forth by those groups whose pressure is not exercised through violence but through the power of ideas. As suggested by Neumann (2008, p.4), extremism is "what happens before the bomb goes off" but what happens in the moment prior to the bomb can last the whole lifetime of a group or individual, and never evolve into terrorism in the final instance.

For many of the groups and movements highlighted in the preceding chapters, many remain radicalised and engage in extremism without resorting to violence.[11] Whether it's left-wing, feminist or environmental forms of extremism, none of the case studies on these forms of progressive (or what is termed here as "post-modern") extremisms rise to the criminal threshold of terrorism. Whilst (mainly in the cases of environmental groups) they might engage in spontaneous acts of political violence, their modus operandi and attack planning cycles are not directed against humans, are based on principled forms of non-violence and tend to be mainly spontaneous rather than premeditated. Indeed, in some cases (particularly when it comes to forms of feminism radicalism), such movements have actively protested against forms of state violence that take place against a persecuted or underrepresented society group.

Moving on to other case studies and thematic areas in this volume, strategic forms of non-violence (and what Alex Schmid (2014) terms "not-violence") have shown to be more prevalent among irredentist or regressive forms of extremism – namely of a religious or far-right extremist nature. Whether it is the Buddhist extremist currents in Myanmar or Sri Lanka or the Identitarian and Far-Right movements in Europe and Turkey, such non-violent movements have seen radicalisation to violence through crisis rhetoric that has enraged action against minority religious and racial groups – either directly or indirectly – in the forms of organised political violence and even terrorism.

This is not to say that all regressive non-violent extremist movements in this volume have seen such a transition. In the case of anti-Islamic protest movements in Europe (e.g. the DFLA and PEGIDA Germany), ascriptions to non-violence have been a key form of "impression management" among movements that seek to maintain legitimacy and political relevance (Goffman, 1969). Moreover, in the religious extremist case, some groups (particularly Tabligh Jama'at, al-Nour Party in Egypt and Kuwait's the Islamic Salafi Alliance in Kuwait) have taken non-violence and participation within mainstream political institutions as a foundational part of their methodology and mode of practice – participating in the electoral process and fielding parliamentary candidates in order to maintain the place of Islam in society and the legal system. In contradistinction, others (like Hizb ut-Tahrir) have chosen to work outside the existing democratic order – not engaging in terrorism and political violence themselves but using so-called inspirational texts in order to embolden others to violent action whilst stopping at the cusp of violent action themselves.

Barriers to Political Violence

Another key lesson learnt that dovetails with the discussion in this new Handbook on non-violent extremism are what are the brakes (or barriers) that turn groups or individuals away from violence. In particular, Busher, Macklin and Holbrook (2019) have recently developed an analytical framework that is useful in this regard. Developed based on case studies of Islamist, far-right and animal rights extremist groups, they developed a fivefold typology to delineate the internal brakes on violent escalation that include: (1) Strategic, (2) Moral, (3) Group-level (self-identification with non-violence), (4) boundary softening (in terms of out-groups or perceived "enemies") and (5) any organisational developments (that aid the above) as being key restraints to this process (Busher, Macklin and Holbrook, 2019, p.9).

Within this volume, we see many non-violent extremist movements applying the brakes to radicalisation towards full-scale terrorism or political violence. In the case of Tabligh Jama'at, for example, it is a more moral form of non-violence associated with a vision of global constructive and wholesome social transformation through religious adherence. In the case of the DFLA, for example, it is a more strategic form of non-violence associated with tactical adherence to peaceful vigils and set-piece protests. In the case of the MHP (Milliyetçi Hareket Partisi) in Turkey, it was organisational developments (i.e. the increase in competition and instability of its core electorate) that led it away from non-violent means to non-violence. This volume there-fore steps beyond the violent-non-violent dichotomy by suggesting there exists blurred lines within groups themselves about whether violence or non-violence exist depending on their individual developmental pathways and organisational trajectories.

Post-organisational Extremist Movements – Antechambers of Violent Extremism?

A final lesson learnt from this Handbook concerns the nature of organisations that ostensibly rely on micro-donations of time, financial aid and online activism in order to sustain such movements. Picked up upon in the cross-sectional Chapters 1 and 2, these sticky or so-called post-organisational non-violent extremist movements stretch out imagination of what constitutes a political organisation and what it means to become a member of one when there are no official structures or codified membership lists or rosters to speak of.

Giving the example of sovereign citizens (SC) movements and QAnon, Baldino and Balnaves find that within the former movement fluid identities and a varied demographic base align within the SC worldview (such as the government is a corrupt and illegitimate corporate entity) in the online space. Moreover, Comerford, Grühl and Davey show how communities of right-wing extremists are coordinating and organising in a looser fashion, often defined by adherence to key tactical, cultural and ideological tropes rather than membership of particular groups. More concretely, they show how categorisations of violence and non-violence get blurred in this post-organisational moment – with the propagation of crisis conspiracy theories and disinformation about population statistics by small right-wing extremist (i.e. the European Identitarian movement) emboldening others across the other side of the world to commit terrorist attacks and atrocities (e.g. the Christchurch Mosque Shootings).

The question therefore arises whether such post-organisational movements – of which there are many not just in the anti-government or far-right extremist space – provide an antechamber to paths of extremist violence or at least provide subcultures in which the dehumanising ideas exist that can in turn lead to political violence. The answer between activism and violence is complicated by this – and whilst no direct correlation occurs – the leaderless and organisationally fragmented nature of such organisations does force one to wonder whether formal, hierarchical structures put a "cap on violence" within extremist social movements.[12]

Future Research

In conclusion, if we were to take up the mantle of a substantive research agenda focused exclusively on non-violent (or vocal extremism itself), there are some really interesting avenues of research and bodies of knowledge that can be furrowed in the coming years and decades. First, a more substantive look at individuals over groups or organisations per se will become even more prescient and important. As we see a shift to non-violent extremist groups largely existing online, formalised structures and memberships will become even more eroded and opaque. To dovetail with this trend, then, ethnographic studies of individuals and their pathways into and out of these groups will become more pressing for researchers – as we get to grips with these new dynamics of activism in the current post-organisational epoch.

Second, a more substantive integration of counter movements, the role of security forces and law enforcement and how this links into the dynamics of non-violent contention will become all the more important in gaining a 360 degree view of what energises and informs the development of non-violent extremist activism at the group level. In this volume, we've rightly emphasised the move away from scholarly reductivism that looks away from the violent–non-violent dichotomy. Going forward, however, we also need to skip disciplinary boundaries within extreme studies and draw on the rich insights of criminology, social movement studies and cultural studies in order to provide a more holistic assessment of how certain non-violent extremist groups coalesce, emerge and subsequently fall into abeyance.

Third, and on a related note, we also need to better integrate micro, meso and macro perspectives when analysing the progression, elaboration and perturbation of non-violent extremist movements. Often analyses of such movements predominantly focus on the groups themselves and the policies enacted against them (i.e. meso-level). More ambitious approaches therefore need to be sought that contextualise the national and international level factors (i.e. the macro-level) that are driving these movements and at the micro-level (as mentioned before the integration of individual level life histories and ethnographic study). This pluralistic and more granular approach will hopefully put (non-violent) extremism studies on a sustainable footing going forward – incorporating new approaches as new movements and threats develop.

Notes

1 See Introduction, Figure I.1 for graphical context.
2 See Chapters 5, 21 and 24.
3 The ideological counterparts that have taken terrorist action that we are referring to are numerous but here are some examples: Daesh for Hizb ut-Tahrir, National Action for PEGIDA and the Red Brigades for DiEM25.
4 This Handbook has explored the following kinds of non-violent extremism: religious extremisms (Part 2), Far-right Extremism (Part 3) and Post-Modern Extremisms, i.e. Left-Wing, Feminist and Environmental (Part 4).
5 See Part 2 on religious extremism.
6 See relevant chapters in Part 4.
7 Chapter 25 together with Chapter 24 have stressed how capitalism is also a matter of concern for non-violent far-left.
8 For example, Greek white power and neo-Nazi movements that are explicitly racist and wish to overthrow the "decadent" system of Western liberal democracy do not sit well with the more coded racism and pro-democratic forces of anti-Islam street movements.
9 See Volk and Weisskircher's chapter.
10 Some well-known examples are Elliot Rodger and Jake Davison's massacres – see introduction for further details. Also see Hart et al.'s chapter.
11 Here, violence is defined as a direct, physical attack on another human being and/or property in the pursuit of a political, religious or ideological aim. There was much debate within the Handbook on this question (i.e. whether more structural, indirect forms of violence should be integrated into our analyses) and both editors encourage readers to delve into these further.
12 An obvious caveat to this are antifascist movements: www.universiteitleiden.nl/binaries/content/assets/customsites/perspectives-on-terrorism/2020/issue-6/copsey-and-merrill.pdf

References

Baran, Z. (2005). Fighting the War of Ideas. *Foreign Affairs*, 84(6), 68–78. doi:10.2307/20031777.

Busher, J., Macklin, G., and Holbrook, D. (2019). The Internal Brakes on Violent Escalation: A Typology. *Behavioral Sciences of Terrorism and Political Aggression*, 11(1): 3–25. DOI: 10.1080/19434472.2018. 1551918.

Chassman, A. (2016). Islamic State, Identity, and the Global Jihadist Movement: How Is Islamic State Successful at Recruiting 'Ordinary' People? *Journal for Deradicalization*, Winter(9), 205–259.

Global Terrorism Index. (2019). Global Terrorism Index 2019 Briefing: Measuring the Impact of Terrorism. Sydney, Australia: Institute for Economics and Peace. Retrieved from: www.visionofhumanity.org/wp-content/uploads/2020/10/GTI-2019-briefingweb.pdf#:~:text=In%20the%202019%20Global%20Terrorism,countries%20improving%2C%20and%2040%20deteriorating.

Goffman, E. (1969). *Strategic Interaction*. Philadelphia, PA: University of Pennsylvania Press.

Karagiannis, E. (2018). *The New Political Islam: Human Rights, Democracy, and Justice*. Philadelphia, PA: University of Pennsylvania Press.

McCauley, C., & Moskalenko, S. (2008). Mechanisms of Political Radicalization: Pathways toward Terrorism. *Terrorism and Political Violence*, 20(3), 415–433. doi:10.1080/09546550802073367.

Moghaddam, F. M. (2005). The Staircase to Terrorism: A Psychological Exploration. *American Psychologist*, 60(2), 161–169 doi:10.1037/0003–066X.60.2.161

Neumann, P. R. (2008). Introduction: In Perspectives on Radicalisation and Political Violence. Paper presented at the First International Conference on Radicalisation and Political Violence, London: International Centre for the Study of Radicalisation and Political Violence. http://icsr.info/wp-content/uploads/2012/10/1234516938ICSRPerspectivesonRadicalisation.pdf.

Orofino, E. (2015). Intellectual Radicals Challenging the State: The Case of Hizb ut-Tahrir in the West, *Contemporary Social Science*, 10(4), 401–412, DOI: 10.1080/21582041.2016.1236212.

Orofino, E. (2020). *Hizb ut-Tahrir and the Caliphate: Why the Group Is Still Appealing to Muslims in the West.* London: Routledge.

Schmid, A. (May 2014). Violent and Non-Violent Extremism: Two Sides of the Same Coin? The Hague: ICCT. Retrieved from: www.icct.nl/app/uploads/download/file/ICCT-Schmid-Violent-Non-Violent-Extremism-May-2014.pdf.

INDEX